T0203066

Lecture Notes in Computer Science 14629

The series Lecture Notes in Computer Science (LNCS), including its subseries Lecture Notes in Artificial Intelligence (LNAI) and Lecture Notes in Bioinformatics (LNBI), has established itself as a medium for the publication of new developments in computer science and information technology research, teaching, and education.

LNCS enjoys close cooperation with the computer science R & D community, the series counts many renowned academics among its volume editors and paper authors, and collaborates with prestigious societies. Its mission is to serve this international community by providing an invaluable service, mainly focused on the publication of conference and workshop proceedings and postproceedings. LNCS commenced publication in 1973.

Kostas Stefanidis · Kari Systä ·
Maristella Matera · Sebastian Heil ·
Haridimos Kondylakis · Elisa Quintarelli
Editors

Web Engineering

24th International Conference, ICWE 2024
Tampere, Finland, June 17–20, 2024
Proceedings

Editors
Kostas Stefanidis
Tampere University
Tampere, Finland

Kari Systä
Tampere University
Tampere, Finland

Maristella Matera
Politecnico di Milano
Milano, Italy

Sebastian Heil
Chemnitz University of Technology
Chemnitz, Germany

Haridimos Kondylakis
University of Crete
Heraklion, Greece

Elisa Quintarelli
University of Verona
Verona, Italy

ISSN 0302-9743 ISSN 1611-3349 (electronic)
Lecture Notes in Computer Science
ISBN 978-3-031-62361-5 ISBN 978-3-031-62362-2 (eBook)
https://doi.org/10.1007/978-3-031-62362-2

This Springer imprint is published by the registered company Springer Nature Switzerland AG
The registered company address is: Gewerbestrasse 11, 6330 Cham, Switzerland

Preface

Welcome to the proceedings of the International Conference on Web Engineering, ICWE 2024.

ICWE is the leading annual event dedicated to the exploration of Web Engineering methods and technologies. Supported by the International Society of Web Engineering (ISWE), ICWE brings together researchers and practitioners from various disciplines to tackle key challenges in Web Engineering. Since its first implementation in 2001 the conference has become a cornerstone event, with this year's 24th edition being hosted by Tampere University in Tampere, Finland. This volume includes all the accepted papers across various conference tracks.

ICWE 2024's theme, "Ethical and Human-Centric Web Engineering: Balancing Innovation and Responsibility," invited discussions on creating Web technologies that are not only innovative but also ethical, transparent, privacy-focused, trustworthy, and inclusive, putting human needs and well-being at the core. This theme recognizes the evolution of the Web Engineering landscape, which in recent years has been profoundly shaped by significant technological advances, particularly with the increasing adoption of artificial intelligence (AI). Web systems have become more robust and multifaceted, enhanced by AI-driven algorithms that personalize user experiences and optimize system performance. Enabled by advances in cloud computing and sophisticated network infrastructures, these developments have facilitated a more interconnected and dynamic online environment. However, as the boundaries of what can be achieved on the Web continue to expand, critical questions emerge: What should we prioritize in our research? And how should these new AI-enhanced technologies be employed within ethical and societal frameworks?

This theme attracted 66 submissions from across the world. The selection process was rigorous, and facilitated by a Program Committee (PC) of distinguished experts. Each submission was single-blind reviewed by at least three PC members, with final decisions made through thorough discussions. We accepted 16 full papers, reflecting an acceptance rate of 24%. The conference also featured competitive sessions for short papers, industrial contributions, demonstrations, and posters, along with a Ph.D. symposium, three cutting-edge tutorials, two workshops, a coaching session for Ph.D. students and young researchers, and one panel. Overall, the final program showcased innovative approaches, novel findings, and thought-provoking ideas. It covered a wide spectrum of topics related to Web infrastructures, human computation, the social and semantic Web, Web services, data analytics, and security and privacy.

We extend our deepest gratitude to everybody who contributed to the organization of the conference, especially the chairs: Niko Mäkitalo and Yongluan Zhou (Posters & Demos), Marco Brambilla and Manos Athanassoulis (Industrial papers), Flavius Frasincar and Evaggelia Pitoura (Tutorials), Georgia Koutrika (Panels), Arianit Kurti and In-Young Ko (Ph.D. Symposium), Cesare Pautasso and Patrick Marcel (Workshops),

Haridimos Kondylakis and Elisa Quintarelli (Proceedings), Alberto Abelló and Aikaterini Tzompanaki (Publicity), Fragkiskos D. Malliaros, Ioannis Katakis, Juho Kanniainen and Mohamed Sharaf (Sponsors), Erjon Skenderi and Maria Stratigi (Web), Zheying Zhang and Antti Sand (Volunteers & Local Organization), and David Hästbacka (Registrations).

We are also grateful to our keynote speakers, Fabio Casati (ServiceNow) and Markku Turunen (Pervasive Interaction Research Group - PERG, Tampere University) for their invaluable insights.

Special thanks go to Martin Gaedke and Tommi Mikkonen, who served as Steering Committee liaisons and provided guidance and support. We appreciate the logistical support from the Tampere University Congress Office, and Springer for publishing this volume. Our heartfelt thanks go to the PC members, the additional reviewers, and the student volunteers, whose dedication ensured the success of ICWE 2024 in both scientific and practical terms.

Lastly, we thank all the authors and members of the ICWE community for their contributions and participation, making ICWE 2024 a landmark event.

April 2024

Sebastian Heil
Maristella Matera
Kostas Stefanidis
Kari Systä

The original version of this book was inadvertently published without this panel paper in the frontmatter "Weaving An Ethical and Human-Centric Web". This has now been added to the FM.

Organization

Conference General Chairs

Kostas Stefanidis	Tampere University, Finland
Kari Systä	Tampere University, Finland

Program Chairs

Sebastian Heil	Chemnitz University of Technology, Germany
Maristella Matera	Politecnico di Milano, Italy

Poster and Demo Chairs

Niko Mäkitalo	University of Jyväskylä, Finland
Yongluan Zhou	University of Copenhagen, Denmark

Industrial Chairs

Marco Brambilla	Politecnico di Milano, Italy
Manos Athanassoulis	Boston University, USA

Tutorials Chairs

Flavius Frasincar	Erasmus University, The Netherlands
Evaggelia Pitoura	University of Ioannina, Greece

Panel Chair

Georgia Koutrika	Athena Research Center, Greece

Workshop Chairs

Cesare Pautasso	University of Lugano, Switzerland
Patrick Marcel	Université de Tours, France

PhD Symposium Chairs

Arianit Kurti	Linnaeus University, Sweden
In-Young Ko	Korea Advanced Institute of Science and Technology, South Korea

Sponsor Chairs

Fragkiskos D. Malliaros	Paris-Saclay University, France
Ioannis Katakis	University of Nicosia, Cyprus
Juho Kanniainen	Tampere University, Finland
Mohamed Sharaf	United Arab Emirates University, United Arab Emirates

Proceedings Chairs

Haridimos Kondylakis	ICS, FORTH, Greece
Elisa Quintarelli	University of Verona, Italy

Publicity Chairs

Alberto Abelló	Universitat Politècnica de Catalunya, Spain
Aikaterini Tzompanaki	CY Cergy Paris University, France

Web Chairs

Erjon Skenderi	University of Helsinki, Finland
Maria Stratigi	Tampere University, Finland

Volunteers and Local Chairs

Zheying Zhang	Tampere University, Finland
Antti Sand	Tampere University, Finland

Registration Chair

David Hästbacka	Tampere University, Finland

Program Committee

Sören Auer	Leibniz University Hannover, Germany
Mohamed-Amine Baazizi	Sorbonne Université, France
Marcos Baez	Bielefeld Univ. of Applied Sciences, Germany
Maxim Bakaev	Novosibirsk State Technical University, Russia
Luciano Baresi	Politecnico di Milano, Italy
Devis Bianchini	University of Brescia, Italy
Gabriela Bosetti	VeryConnect, UK
Andreas Both	DATEV eG, Germany
Alessandro Bozzon	Delft Univ. of Technology, The Netherlands
Marco Brambilla	Politecnico di Milano, Italy
Antonio Brogi	Università di Pisa, Italy
Radek Burget	Brno Univ. of Technology, Czech Republic
Christoph Bussler	Bosch, USA
Carlos Canal	University of Málaga, Spain
Javier Luis Canovas Izquierdo	Universitat Oberta de Catalunya, Spain
Cinzia Cappiello	Politecnico di Milano, Italy
Sven Casteleyn	Universitat Jaume I, Spain
Richard Chbeir	Univ. Pau & Pays de l'Adour, France
Lewis Chuang	Chemnitz University of Technology, Germany
Jürgen Cito	TU Wien and Facebook, Austria
Shridhar Devamane	APS College of Engineering, India
Oscar Diaz	University of the Basque Country, Spain
Schahram Dustdar	Vienna University of Technology, Austria
Jutta Eckstein	IT Communication, Germany
Pablo Fernandez	University of Seville, Spain
Flavius Frasincar	Erasmus University, The Netherlands
Piero Fraternali	Politecnico di Milano, Italy
Martin Gaedke	Chemnitz University of Technology, Germany
Jose García-Alonso	University of Extremadura, Spain

Alejandra Garrido	Universidad Nacional de La Plata, Argentina
Irene Garrigos	University of Alicante, Spain
Cesar González-Mora	University of Alicante, Spain
Julián Grigera	Universidad Nacional de La Plata, Argentina
Hao Han	Konica Minolta, Japan
Dickson K. W. Chiu	University of Hong Kong, China
Epaminondas Kapetanios	University of Hertfordshire, UK
Tomi Kauppinen	Aalto University, Finland
Alexander Knapp	Universität Augsburg, Germany
In-Young Ko	Korea Advanced Institute of Science and Technology, South Korea
Nora Koch	University of Seville, Spain
István Koren	RWTH Aachen University, Germany
Zühal Kurt	Fraunhofer IDMT, Germany
Maurizio Leotta	Università di Genova, Italy
Faiza Loukil	Univ. Savoie Mont Blanc, France
Juan Manuel Murillo Rodríguez	University of Extremadura, Spain
Andrea Mauri	Université Claude Bernard Lyon 1, France
Santiago Melia	Universidad de Alicante, Spain
Kushagra Mishra	Nutanix, Inc., USA
Madhulika Mohanty	Inria and Inst. Polytechnique de Paris, France
Nathalie Moreno	Universidad de Málaga, Spain
Martin Musicante	Univ. Federal do Rio Grande do Norte, Brazil
Tobias Münch	Münch Ges. für IT-Solutions mbH, Germany
Radka Nacheva	University of Economics – Varna, Bulgaria
Elena Navarro	University of Castilla-La Mancha, Spain
Guadalupe Ortiz	Universidad de Cádiz, Spain
Frank Pallas	TU Berlin, Germany
Oscar Pastor	Universidad Politécnica de Valencia, Spain
Cesare Pautasso	University of Lugano, Switzerland
Azzurra Ragone	University of Bari, Italy
I. V. Ramakrishnan	SUNY Stony Brook, USA
Werner Retschitzegger	Johannes Kepler University Linz, Austria
Filippo Ricca	Università di Genova, Italy
Thomas Richter	Rhein-Waal Univ. of Appl. Sciences, Germany
António Rito Silva	Universidade de Lisboa, Portugal
Tarmo Robal	Tallinn University of Technology, Estonia
Gustavo Rossi	Universidad Nacional de La Plata, Argentina
Thomas Springer	TU Dresden, Germany
Abhishek Srivastava	Indian Institute of Technology Indore, India
Diego Torres	Universidad Nacional de La Plata, Argentina
Victoria Torres	Universitat Politècnica de València, Spain

Radu Tudor Ionescu	University of Bucharest, Romania
William Van Woensel	University of Ottawa, Canada
Maria-Esther Vidal	TIB, Germany
Markel Vigo	University of Manchester, UK
Lucas Vogel	TU Dresden, Germany
Erik Wilde	INNOQ, Germany
Manuel Wimmer	Johannes Kepler University Linz, Austria
Marco Winckler	Université Côte d'Azur, France
Yeliz Yesilada	Middle East Tech. Univ. NCC, Cyprus
Nicola Zannone	Eindhoven Univ. of Tech., The Netherlands
Gefei Zhang	HTW Berlin, Germany

External Reviewers

Matteo Bianchi	Politecnico di Milano, Italy
Antonio De Santis	Politecnico di Milano, Italy
Ajay Kumar	University of Missouri-Columbia, USA
Zühal Kurt	Chemnitz University of Technology, Germany
Panagiotis Papadakos	FORTH-ICS, Greece
Shivika Prasanna	University of Missouri-Columbia, USA
Khawar Shehzad	University of Missouri-Columbia, USA
Valentin Siegert	Chemnitz University of Technology, Germany
Jan-David Stütz	Bosch, Germany
Andrea Tocchetti	Politecnico di Milano, Italy
Verena Traubinger	Chemnitz University of Technology, Germany
Chrysostomos Zeginis	FORTH-ICS, Greece

ICWE 2024 Sponsors

Keynotes

Responsible AI in the World of Work

Fabio Casati

ServiceNow, Santa Clara, CA, USA
fabio.casati@servicenow.com

Abstract. When can we say that an AI model or pipeline is "reliable" - literally meaning that we can rely on it? How do we evaluate and choose the most reliable one? How do we take go/no go decisions for our business. These are only some of the questions that AI producers and consumers ask (and ask themselves) every day. Gen AI is now mainstream and the adoption is, for once, living up to the hype at the time of writing. Adoption of Gen AI rests on a few key requirements: first, the identification of high value use cases. Second, the readiness of data. Third, an end-to-end application that implements a use case, from UX to workflows to AI, all working together to deliver the right experience. Finally, quality, risk, and governance considerations.

The process for evaluating gen AI quality and risk and taking adoption decision is different than for "traditional" AI, in part because of the generative nature but mainly because of the nature of the use cases and the way AI is integrated into applications. In some cases, there is no clear cut notion of "correctness" in AI inference, and quality may be influenced by many factors, such as conciseness or appropriateness of the language to the business context. As a consequence, we may fall into the tendency of evaluating systems either anecdotally or using metrics and methods with unclear correlation with AI quality.

Based on dozens of interviews and uncountable interactions with developers, managers, customers, and institutions, in this talk I summarize what I perceive as the key issues in AI quality evaluation and decision making. I will outline the different personas, their perception of who is responsible and accountable for decisions, and the relevant quality and decision factors. I will also discuss risk, and how risk is assessed by different actors at different stages of the production pipeline. I will stress why commonly used practiced are not just insufficient, but outright misleading and how confusion in terminology can and does lead to wrong decision. Finally, I will comment on frequent pitfall in experiment design and reporting, again resulting in leading managers to take the wrong decisions, and how to correct them.

Accessible and Societally Sustainable Web Services

Markku Turunen

Faculty of Information Technology and Communication Sciences, Tampere University, Finland
markku.turunen@tuni.fi

Abstract. Web services play a crucial role in today's digital society. However, ensuring that these services are accessible to all users, regardless of their abilities or disabilities, remains a challenge. Accessible web services are essential for promoting inclusivity and providing equal opportunities for everyone. In addition to accessibility, the sustainability of web services is equally important. Societally sustainable web services consider the long-term impact on society, the environment, and the economy. This talk explores the intersection of accessibility and societal sustainability in the context of web services. It highlights the need for designing and developing services that are both accessible and sustainable. By prioritizing these principles, we can create a more equal and sustainable digital landscape.

The presentation will go over a short history of the accessibility of web services: how a technology that was initially well-defined and easily accessible when used correctly quickly became very challenging in terms of accessibility. We go through the key aspects of accessible web services, such as legislation, technological accessibility, and content accessibility. We look at what kind of challenges different groups of people have and how these can be considered in the planning and implementation of accessible digital services. Although the main focus is on current web services, it is also important to consider the challenges of the future. XR/Metaverse, IoT technologies and games can be very challenging if not enough attention is paid to their accessibility

Accessibility is one key element related to sustainability. We also look at other key issues related to sustainability and especially social accessibility. Examples include e.g. solutions made in developing economies. Finally, we examine the role of other technologies such as artificial intelligence, IoT and social robotics in the development of accessible and sustainable web services of the future.

Weaving an Ethical and Human-Centric Web (Panel)

Abstract. The web has changed how people do business, entertain themselves, exchange ideas, and socialize with one another. In 2000, its inventor, Tim Berners-Lee, called for the active support and participation of programmers, computer manufacturers, and social organizations to manage and maintain this valuable resource so that it can remain a powerful force for social change and an outlet for individual creativity. In 2024, AI is changing the web (as much as our lives) in several ways. Generative AI models are used to generate content, to answer user questions, and to repurpose web content. While the web was conceived as a platform for people to create and share content, fake news, deep fakes, plagiarized AI-generated content flood the web. Is the Web shifting away from Berners-Lee's vision? This panel will discuss the future of the web, opportunities, emerging risks and countermeasures towards weaving an ethical and human-centric web.

Moderator

- Georgia Koutrika, Athena Research Center

Panelists

- Fabio Casati, Servicenow
- Marco Brambilla, Politecnico di Milano
- Flavius Frasincar, Erasmus University
- Eirini Ntoutsi, Bundeswehr University Munich

Contents

Demos and Posters

PhD Symposium

Tutorials

Human-Centric Web Engineering: Trust, Transparency, Inclusivity

Language Models as SPARQL Query Filtering for Improving the Quality of Multilingual Question Answering over Knowledge Graphs

Aleksandr Perevalov[1(✉)], Aleksandr Gashkov[1], Maria Eltsova[3], and Andreas Both[1,2]

[1] Leipzig University of Applied Sciences, Leipzig, Germany
aleksandr.perevalov@htwk-leipzig.de
[2] DATEV eG, Nuremberg, Germany
[3] CBZ München GmbH, Heilbronn, Germany

Abstract. Question Answering systems working over Knowledge Graphs (KGQA) generate a ranked list of SPARQL query candidates for a given natural-language question. In this paper, we follow our long-term research agenda of providing trustworthy KGQA systems – here – by presenting a query filtering approach that utilizes (large) language models (LMs/LLMs), s.t., correct and incorrect queries can be distinguished. In contrast to the previous work, we address here multilingual questions represented in major languages (English, German, French, Spanish, and Russian), and confirm the generalizability of our approach by also evaluating it on low-resource languages (Ukrainian, Armenian, Lithuanian, Belarusian, and Bashkir). For our experiments, we used the following LMs: BERT, DistilBERT, Mistral, Zephyr, GPT-3.5, and GPT-4. The LMs were applied to the KGQA systems – QAnswer and MemQA – as SPARQL query filters. The approach was evaluated on the multilingual Wikidata-based dataset QALD-9-plus. The experimental results suggest that the KGQA systems achieve quality improvements for all languages when using our query-filtering approach.

Keywords: Question Answering over Knowledge Graphs · Query Validation · Query Candidate Filtering · Trustworthiness

1 Introduction

The main objective of Knowledge Graph Question Answering (KGQA) systems is to provide answers $\mathcal{A}$ that fulfill an informational need of a natural language (NL) question q, utilizing a Knowledge Graph (KG) [25]. Recent KGQA developments effort in two development paradigms [20,39,41]: (1) the *information extraction paradigm* – aims at retrieving a set of answers directly based on a particular feature space, and (2) the *semantic parsing paradigm* – aims at converting a NL question into a query or a ranked set of *query candidates* that are

K. Stefanidis et al. (Eds.): ICWE 2024, LNCS 14629, pp. 3–18, 2024.
https://doi.org/10.1007/978-3-031-62362-2_1

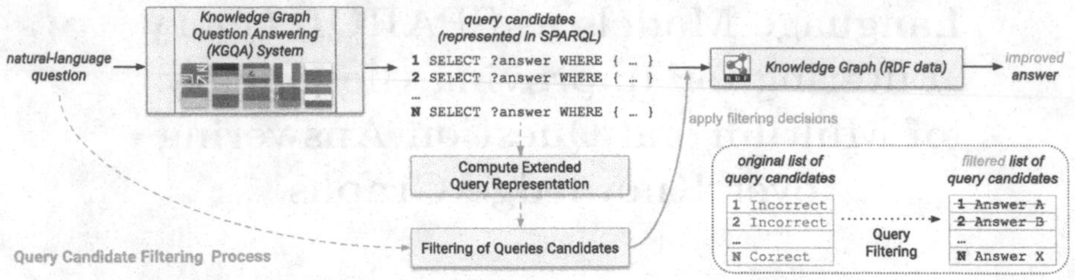

Fig. 1. Big Picture: Query candidate filtering of multilingual KGQA systems.

to be executed on a KG with the sake of retrieving an answer for the question. Let us focus on the semantic parsing paradigm in detail. There, the challenge is that some of the *query candidates might appear incorrect, but still could be prioritized over the correct ones*, leading to a decrease in the quality, and therefore, the trustworthiness of a KGQA system. In this paper, we tackle the previously mentioned challenge by presenting a SPARQL query filtering method that utilizes Language Models (LMs) as filters to differentiate between correct and incorrect SPARQL queries (cf. Fig. 1). In contrast to prior contributions, our work focuses on a diverse set of languages: English, German, Spanish, French, Lithuanian, Russian, Ukrainian, Belarusian, Armenian, and Bashkir. Those languages are provided within the QALD-9-plus [26] – a KGQA benchmark that we use for our experiments. Our main motivation for considering low-resource languages is (1) increasing accessibility of the KGQA systems as only 25.9%[1] of the Web users are English speakers (L1 or L2), and (2) while supporting the low-resource languages, we contribute to the language vitality and the cultural heritage. Therefore, in this work we aim to answer the following *research questions*: RQ1: KGQA system-agnostic – is it possible to establish a quality-improving approach that can be used as an extension to most KGQA systems? RQ2: NL-agnostic – to what degree can the approach be transferred to questions written in different languages (instead of focusing on English input only)?

For our experiments, we use LMs. They are, depending on their type, fine-tuned or instructed as binary classifiers to judge whether a particular SPARQL query can answer a given NL question (*correct*) or cannot (*incorrect*). To ensure high-value insights of the experiments, we use a wide range of LMs. Namely, BERT [15] and DistilBERT [29], open-source instruction-tuned large language models (LLMs) ZEPHYR-7B [35] and Mistral-7B [13], and, finally, proprietary LLMs GPT-3.5 [21] and GPT-4 [22] that represent the current state-of-the-art. In the first experimental stage (S_1), we measure the classification quality on the task of distinguishing between correct and incorrect SPARQL queries provided by the LMs with Precision@1. In the second stage (S_2), we evaluate the effect of applying our query filtering approach on KGQA systems – QAnswer [7] and MemQA (a system introduced in this paper for the sake of providing reference values) – while measuring the QA quality (Precision@1 and Answer

[1] https://www.internetworldstats.com/stats7.htm.

Trustworthiness Score [11]) before and after applying them. Our results show a strong impact on the quality regarding both scores and all languages.

This paper has the following structure. First, we describe the related work regarding KGQA, datasets, and language models (Sect. 2). After that, we present in detail our approach in Sect. 3. Section 4 describes the running of our experiments which data are evaluated and analyzed in Sect. 5 followed by the discussion in Sect. 6. Section 7 concludes the paper and outlines future work.

2 Related Work

Multilingual KGQA Systems. A systematic survey of the research field of multilingual KGQA [25] and an overview of the current state of the field for multilingual and cross-lingual subtasks [18] shows that multilingualism in KGQA is still a major challenge, and recently, there is a trend towards that direction. Among well-known multilingual KGQA systems over Wikidata that are currently available, Platypus [23] has support for three languages, DeepPavlov [3] two languages, and QAnswer eight languages [8]. However, only QAnswer provides an extended list of the internal SPARQL query candidates that we can use for our research. Since QAnswer is a real-world system that offers good answer quality (cf. [1,11,28,32]), the semantics of the query candidates are very similar, often almost identical, although the surface form is different (cf. Fig. 6). A share of multilingual solutions is utilizing machine translation (MT) for translating input questions (e.g., [24,34]), which can be easily integrated into a monolingual system, but this way highly depends on the quality of the used MT methods. According to [18] merely translating texts results in a significant drop in performance in some cases and no improvement in others. Other solutions utilize cross-lingual knowledge transfer (e.g., [10,42]), or implementing multilingual LMs (e.g., [9,27]). The authors of [14] proposed an enhanced NL question to SPARQL conversion methodology for a domain ontology-based QA system in Korean and anticipated that, after appropriate modification, this process can be applied to other languages.

Language Models. BERT [6] is designed to learn representations from unlabeled text by joint conditioning on both left and right contexts in all layers. During pretraining, BERT uses masked language modeling (MLM) and next-sentence prediction (NSP). DistilBERT [29] is a general-purpose pre-trained version of BERT distilled on very large batches, leveraging gradient accumulation (up to 4K examples per batch) using dynamic masking and without the NSP objective.

Mistral-7B [13] is a 7-billion-parameter LM that outperforms the previous best 13B model, LLaMA 2 [12], across all tested benchmarks. ZEPHYR-7B [35] is a LM based on Mistral-7B aligned to user intent. The method avoids the use of sampling-based approaches like rejection sampling or proximal preference optimization and distills conversational capabilities with direct preference optimization from a dataset of AI feedback.

The GPT-3 model [2] is a 175 billion parameter autoregressive LLM applied for all tasks without any gradient updates or fine-tuning, with tasks and few-shot demonstrations specified purely via text interaction with the model. GPT-3 (evolved to GPT-3.5 [40]) showed strong performance on many NLP tasks and benchmarks in the zero-shot, one-shot, and few-shot settings. The GPT-4 model [22] represents a large multimodal model capable of processing image and text inputs and producing text outputs. This is a transformer-based model pre-trained to predict the next token in a document. Both GPT models are multilingual. Despite similar limitations, GPT-4 significantly reduces "hallucinations" relative to the previous GPT-3/GPT-3.5 models [17,19].

KGQA Datasets. Following our research objective, *multilingual KGQA datasets* should meet the following requirements: 1) employing SPARQL over Wikidata as a formal gold-standard query representation; 2) being multilingual (combination of datasets should be multilingual); 3) containing NL representations of questions. However, the recent research [4,5,11,18,25,30,37] indicates the scarcity of the datasets, especially multilingual benchmarks.

To the best of our knowledge, only four existing datasets tackle multiple languages over Wikidata: QALD-9-plus [26], RuBQ 2.0 [28], MCWQ [5], and the recently published Mintaka [31]. However, the latter does not contain a gold standard, i.e., a SPARQL query that would retrieve the correct answer, which is essential for our experiments. MCWQ's languages are Hebrew, Kannada, and Chinese. These languages are rarely employed in research community experiments. The RuBQ 2.0 dataset supports only two languages, MT of questions without any post-editing, and split into very small development (580) and much larger test (2,330) subsets.

The QALD is a well-established benchmark series for multilingual KGQA. QALD-9 [37] contains 558 questions incorporating information of the DBpedia knowledge base. Each question is accompanied by a textual representation in multiple languages, the corresponding SPARQL query (over DBpedia), the answer entity URI, and the answer type. *QALD-9-plus*[2] [26] is an extension of the QALD-9 dataset where extended language support was added, and the translation quality for existing languages was significantly optimized (e.g., for Spanish [33]). The dataset supports English, German, Russian, French, Spanish, Armenian, Belarusian, Lithuanian, Bashkir, and Ukrainian. Additionally, QALD-9-plus added support for the Wikidata knowledge graph. On that account, there is only one dataset matching all our requirements: *QALD-9-plus*.

3 Approach

Our approach revolves around filtering incorrect SPARQL query candidates generated by a KGQA system in response to a NL question. We consider questions in multiple languages, which generalizes our approach more. The core of the approach is to employ fine-tuned or instruction-tuned LMs for binary classification tasks as filters to eliminate incorrect SPARQL queries (see Fig. 1). Let QAS represent a KGQA system, s.t., $QAS^q : NL_q \rightarrow C_q$, where:

[2] https://github.com/KGQA/QALD_9_plus.

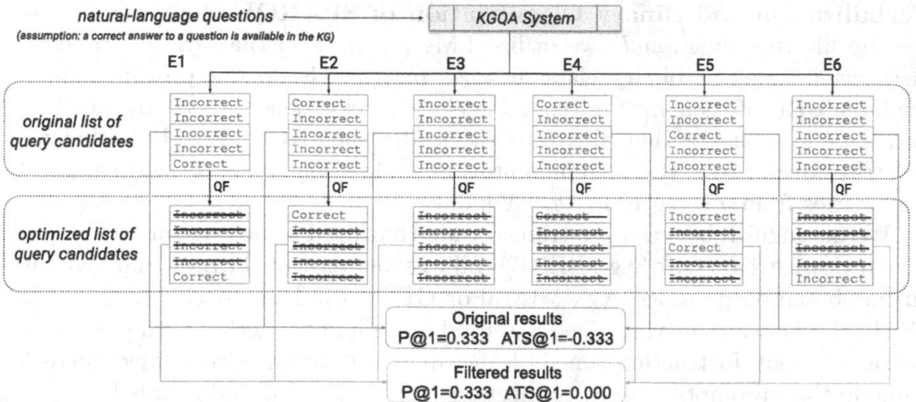

Fig. 2. Impact of Query Filtering on 6 examples (E1 to E6) of lists of 5 candidates evaluated using P@1 and ATS@1. E1 is optimized via the Query Filtering (QF) to a perfect result, in E2 incorrect candidates are removed without changing the result, in E3 and E4 all results are filtered (good for E3 as all incorrect results are eliminated, bad for E4), the optimized results of E5 and E6 have no impact on the quality as an incorrect query candidate is still at the top position. The optimized results have the same P@1 score, however, their trustworthiness is significantly higher.

- Input: NL_q denotes a NL question written in a specific language (e.g., German), where q represents an identifier of the question in a dataset.
- Output: $C_q = \{\text{SPARQL}_1, \text{SPARQL}_2, \ldots, \text{SPARQL}_k\}$ represents the output of the KGQA system for the question q. C_q is an ordered set (i.e., list) of SPARQL query candidates, which may be an empty set, contain one or multiple correct queries, or consist entirely of incorrect queries (6 examples are shown in Fig. 2).

Every question q has a list of *gold standard answers* $\mathcal{A}$ defined by a dataset (can be empty). Following that, a SPARQL query generated by a *QAS* returns another list of answers $\mathcal{A}'$ as *predicted*. Therefore, we evaluate *correctness* of a query with a function *isCorrect* that (1) takes answers produced by a SPARQL$_i$ query $\mathcal{A}'_i$ and gold-standard answers $\mathcal{A}_i$ as input, (2) calculates the F1 score over the provided answer sets, and (3) assigns a *label* = {*correct* , *incorrect*} indicating the correctness of the answer of this query as follows:

$$isCorrect(\mathcal{A}_i, \mathcal{A}'_i) = \begin{cases} correct, & \text{if F1 score}(\mathcal{A}_i, \mathcal{A}'_i) = 1.0 \\ incorrect, & otherwise \end{cases}$$

Therefore, to increase the QA quality by filtering SPARQL query candidates, we need to build a function F that represents a binary classifier, s.t., F : $(NL_i,\ SPARQL_i) \rightarrow label$. Hence, the filtering function F *does not reorder the list but eliminates list items marked as incorrect.* Therefore, the correct query can only be placed at the top of the list if all incorrect ones before it are removed.

Verbalization and Binary Classification of SPARQL Queries . To create the filtering function F we utilize LMs (cf. Sect. 2) that are fine-tuned or instruction-tuned as binary classifiers. As many KGs do not provide human-readable URIs of their entities (e.g., Angela Merkel is denoted as `Q567`[3] in Wikidata), we hypothesize that SPARQL queries for such KGs has to be verbalized, i.e., transformed to a NL-like representation while using labels of the corresponding entities from a given KG (e.g., Wikidata).

We distinguish between pre-trained LMs that need to be fine-tuned to a particular downstream task (e.g., BERT) and instruction-tuned LLMs that generate output based on prompts (e.g., Mistral or GPT-3.5). Task-specific LMs require SPARQL queries to be verbalized and used as an input together with a NL question as an input. Instruction-tuned LLMs can utilize the knowledge injection technique in their prompts to draw connections between a URI and its label.

KGQA Systems. We intend to evaluate the efficiency of our approach to real-world KGQA systems. The following selection criteria were defined for the systems: (a) support of multilingual input; (b) answer questions over the Wikidata KG; (c) response with an ordered SPARQL query candidate list.

In addition, to obtain reference values that will fully demonstrate the potential of our approach, we implemented a KGQA system that holds in memory correct SPARQL queries for questions from KGQA benchmarks defined in Sect. 2. Therefore, we call this system *MemQA*[4]. Given a NL question, MemQA returns a list of SPARQL query candidates, where one is the memorized correct query and all the rest are randomly taken from other questions (i.e., incorrect for the given question). The length of this list can be parametrically changed, and the order of produced SPARQL query candidates is random. Hence, all produced SPARQL query candidates are technically sound and defined by humans, as they originate from human-curated benchmarks.

As a correct query candidate is guaranteed, a perfect query validation with a binary classifier would result in a perfect QA quality – this corresponds to a KGQA system capable of providing reference values for our approach.

Evaluation of QA Quality. To measure the effect of the SPARQL query filtering on QA quality, we use the Precision@1 metric, which is calculated before and after applying the approach. We are using the definition of precision recommended by the DICE group that is intended to resolve typical division by zero error in the case of the sum of true positives and true negatives equals 0.0. For this special case, it was defined that if the true positives, false positives, and false negatives are all 0.0, the precision, recall, and F1 score is 1.0 (calculated according to [36]). We calculate P@1 with respect to the mentioned modification. If every candidate is removed, the confusion matrix is filled with all zeroes, and it is impossible to calculate precision because of division by zero. In this case, we suppose P@1 equals zero if any correct candidate was removed in the filtering process and, otherwise, it equals one. As this metric does not

[3] https://www.wikidata.org/wiki/Q567.

[4] https://github.com/WSE-research/memorized-question-answering-system.

take into account unanswerable questions, i.e., $\mathcal{A} = \emptyset$, we also use the Answer Trustworthiness Score ATS (following the definition in [11]) that is specifically designed to reflect the trustworthiness of QA systems, where for all questions q in a dataset D_i a score per question is computed, summed up, and normalized in range of -1 to $+1$:

$$ATS(D_i) = \frac{\sum_{q \in D_i} f(q)}{|D_i|}, \text{ where } f(q) \begin{cases} +1 & \text{if } isCorrect(\mathcal{A}_q, \mathcal{A}'_q) = correct \\ 0 & \text{if } \mathcal{A}'_q = \emptyset \\ -1 & \text{otherwise} \end{cases}$$

ATS Takes into Account Correct, Incorrect, and Empty Answer Sets. Following the statement "no answer is better than wrong answer", there is no penalty if a KGQA system returns no result (i.e., systems showing fewer incorrect answers to users achieve a higher score). The average Answer Trustworthiness Score score of 0 can be easily achieved by QA system just by responding with no answer to all questions in D. To have positive Answer Trustworthiness Score, a QA system must give more correct than incorrect answers. Thus, the Answer Trustworthiness Score is more strict than other common metrics and an ideal metrics for measuring the quality of KGQA systems.

4 Experimental Setup

Our experiments are divided into major stages. In the *first stage* (S_1), we conduct binary classification experiments to determine whether a verbalized SPARQL query can answer a given NL question (i.e., correct or incorrect). In the *second stage* (S_2), we apply the binary classifiers to an output of two KGQA systems, MemQA and QAnswer, to validate the produced SPARQL query candidates (i.e., filter out incorrect queries). For both stages, we use the QALD-9-plus (QALD) dataset that has train and test splits.

As described in Sect. 3, we use three groups of LMs, namely: MG_1– BERT-like models, MG_2– open-source instruction-tuned LLMs, and MG_3– commercial instruction-tuned LLMs. In particular, the MG_1 contains the multilingual BERT[5] and multilingual DistilBERT[6], the MG_2 contains Mistral 7B[7] and Zephyr 7B[8], the MG_3 contains GPT-3.5[9] and GPT-4[10]. The detailed experimental setup for S_1 and S_2 is described in the following subsections.

4.1 S_1– Classification

We use micro-averaging-based P@1 for the binary classification task evaluation. The train and test data from QALD-9-plus were prepared as follows. As every

[5] https://huggingface.co/bert-base-multilingual-cased.
[6] https://huggingface.co/distilbert-base-multilingual-cased.
[7] https://huggingface.co/mistralai/Mistral-7B-Instruct-v0.1.
[8] https://huggingface.co/HuggingFaceH4/zephyr-7b-beta.
[9] https://platform.openai.com/docs/models/gpt-3-5.
[10] https://platform.openai.com/docs/models/gpt-4-and-gpt-4-turbo.

```
SPARQL candidate: SELECT ?uri WHERE { ?uri wdt:P31 wd:Q131436 . }
Input: List all boardgames by GMT.[SEP]{ ?uri instance of board game }
Label: Correct
```

Fig. 3. The example SPARQL query candidate, input tuple, and the corresponding label, which is used to fine-tune and evaluate MG_1 (BERT-like) models. This example is based on the question with "id=1" from the train split of QALD-9-plus (RDF prefixes are omitted).

```
There is a pair of a question and a SPARQL query:
question: List all boardgames by GMT.
query: SELECT ?uri WHERE { ?uri wdt:P31 wd:Q131436 . }
Label for wdt:P31 is instance of.
Label for wd:Q131436 is board game.
Are the question and the query similar? Answer yes or no.
```

Fig. 4. Example of a prompt in English to MG_2 and MG_3 models based on the question with "id=1" from train split of QALD-9-plus.

question with Id q in a dataset has its own gold standard (i.e., correct) SPARQL query, we randomly assigned SPARQL query for other question with Id r ($q \neq r$) from this dataset to form incorrect candidate (cf. *negative sampling*). Hence, for every question, there are two data examples: $[(NL_q,\ SPARQL_q),\ 1]$ – correct or positive example and $[(NL_q,\ SPARQL_r),\ 0]$ – incorrect or negative example. Therefore, the dataset's classes' distribution is balanced.

The models from MG_1 were fine-tuned on data for a binary classification task. Following our approach (see Sect. 3), we verbalized SPARQL queries using Wikidata labels, i.e., they are represented in an NL-like surface form. Hence, the input tuple for the model NL_i and $SPARQL_i^v$ is connected via `[SEP]` token (see Fig. 3). The target *label* values are encoded as a set over $[1, 0]$ respectively. Both models from MG_1 were loaded and trained using the `transformers` [38] library and Hugging Face[11] model hub. While conducting a grid search procedure for epoch tuning, we empirically determined that both BERT and DistilBERT need 4 epochs to achieve optimal quality on our data. Both models were trained with Adam optimizer [16] and batch size equals 16. The hardware setup has the following characteristics: 64 CPUs AMD EPYC 7502P, 96 GB RAM, and no GPU.

The models from MG_2 and MG_3 were taken "as-is" and were instructed with zero-shot prompts that use the knowledge injection technique. The prompts contain a NL_q, a raw $SPARQL_q$ and a $(URI,\ label)$ tuples, which is a knowledge injection part retrieved from Wikidata (see Fig. 4). Based on the aforementioned information, the models from MG_2 and MG_3 are instructed to produce "yes" or "no" corresponding to a correct or incorrect result. The models from MG_2 were loaded and used via the Hugging Face inference endpoint[12] powered by one

[11] https://huggingface.co/models.
[12] https://huggingface.co/inference-endpoints.

```
Input (German): Liste die Brettspiele von GMT auf.
Query candidates:
1: SELECT ?name WHERE { wd:Q23215 wdt:P1477 ?name.}
2: SELECT ?uri WHERE { ?uri wdt:P31 wd:Q131436 . }
```

Fig. 5. MemQA: SPARQL query candidate list with 2 candidates for the German translation of the question in Fig. 4.

```
Input (German): Liste die Brettspiele von GMT auf.
Query candidates:
1: SELECT DISTINCT ?o1 WHERE { wd:Q131436 wdt:P2354> ?o1 . } LIMIT 1000
2: SELECT ?s0  WHERE { VALUES ?s0 { wd:Q12139612> }}
```

Fig. 6. QAnswer: query candidate list with two candidates for the German translation of the question in Fig. 4 (response is simplified, prefixes are omitted)

NVIDIA A10G GPU. The models from MG_3 were used via the official OpenAI Python library[13]. In particular, we utilized the `gpt-3.5-turbo-1106` and `gpt-4` models respectively. The `temperature` parameter was set to 0 and the other parameters were kept with default values.

4.2 S_2– Question Answering

To evaluate the QA quality and the effect of SPARQL query filtering, we calculate such metrics as Precision@1 (P@1) and Answer Trustworthiness Score (ATS@1) before and after the SPARQL query candidate validation. We obtain the query candidates for each question by asking NL questions from the test data splits of QALD-9-plus to the two systems: MemQA (our system for reference values) and QAnswer (real-world system).

We deploy the MemQA system locally and set it up in a way that it produces a different number of query candidates, which is defined before an experiment, namely: 2, 3, 5, 8, 13, 21, 34, 55 (Fibonacci sequence). This is done for obtaining reference values while having diverse sets of SPARQL query candidates in terms of their length. It is worth underlining that MemQA supports every input language, as it is based on the aforementioned QA datasets. The input and output examples of MemQA are shown in Fig. 5 and 6.

The QAnswer system produces different numbers of query candidates for questions: from 0 to 60 as observed empirically. The system also does not cover all the languages presented in the test datasets, as described in Sect. 2. Therefore, we used four languages both presented in the dataset and supported by QAnswer (English, German, Russian, and Spanish) which have enough data for model training. The QAnswer system was used via its public API[14].

[13] https://github.com/openai/openai-python.

[14] https://backend.app.qanswer.ai/swagger-ui/index.html.

5 Evaluation and Analysis

5.1 S_1– Classification

When working with multilinguality, we determine the best-performing model while aiming at two objectives: the average F1 score and the standard deviation (stdev) of a particular model over all languages [25]. Hence, the joint objective is to achieve the highest average F1 score and lowest standard deviation of the F1 score values. While analyzing the results between the different model groups, the MG_2 has significantly worse quality than MG_1 and MG_3. In turn, MG_1 and MG_3 have comparable quality, however, GPT-4 achieves equally high F1 score on most of the languages despite Bashkir. The BERT, DistilBERT, and GPT-3.5 models achieve the highest quality on high-resource languages (English, German, Russian, French, and Spanish) while the quality of the rest languages has drawdowns. Therefore, BERT-like models and closed-source GPT models significantly outperform open-source LLMs on our binary classification task setting (see online appendix[15]).

5.2 S_2– Question Answering

In this subsection, we present the evaluation results of the two QA systems, MemQA and QAnswer[16]. While applying the SPARQL query filtering approach, we analyze its effect on QA quality. As *MemQA* simulates the behavior of an almost "ideal" KGQA system by having at least one correct SPARQL query in every list of query candidates, we use its results as reference values to show what impact is achievable with SPARQL query filtering for QA in ideal conditions.

In Table 1 we present the results for Answer Trustworthiness Score @1 and Precision@1 calculated when applying our approach on MemQA.

As the *ATS* reflects the idea of "no answer is better than a wrong answer", the results after filtering demonstrate huge improvements, showing that our approach has a very strong impact on the QA trustworthiness given the reference KGQA system MemQA. Just questions in the Bashkir language do not fully benefit from the filtering process. The Precision@1 results in Table 1 indicate a significant improvement in MG_1 and GPT 4 models excluding Armenian for BERT and French for DistilBERT. GPT 3.5 model improves quality for major languages but decreases it for low-resources languages (Belorussian, Bashkir, and Armenian). As these are average values from the experiments, we can conclude that the approach works in general.

The Precision@1 results in Fig. 7 show that the MG_1 and MG_3 models demonstrate an improvement of Precision@1 after applying the filtering approach in half of the experimental cases on the QALD-9-plus dataset.

[15] https://anonymous.4open.science/r/QAfiltering-3C5E/data/resources/classification-pareto.pdf.

[16] The raw data is available in the online appendix at: https://anonymous.4open.science/r/QAfiltering-3C5E/.

Table 1. Results of our filtering method on the MemQA system

Language	No filtering	BERT	DistilBERT	Mistral	Zephyr	GPT 3.5	GPT 4
Answer Trustworthiness Score @ 1							
en	–0.580	0.719	0.720	0.362	–0.264	0.318	**0.904**
de	–0.603	0.524	0.605	–0.640	–0.241	0.330	**0.862**
es	–0.608	0.791	0.736	–0.079	–0.110	0.073	**0.853**
ru	–0.555	0.337	0.338	–0.535	0.018	0.092	**0.783**
fr	–0.574	**0.800**	–0.200	0.113	–0.296	0.427	0.760
be	–0.615	0.137	0.343	–0.025	–0.032	–0.209	**0.883**
uk	–0.654	0.248	0.398	0.156	–0.005	–0.276	**0.922**
ba	–0.597	–0.453	–0.056	–0.015	–0.097	–0.555	**0.000**
lt	–0.579	0.491	0.346	–0.298	–0.181	–0.178	**0.882**
hy	–0.496	0.053	0.305	–0.021	0.095	–0.226	**0.832**
Precision @ 1							
en	0.210	0.854	0.830	0.415	0.209	0.365	**0.904**
de	0.198	0.751	0.747	0.167	0.174	0.520	**0.862**
es	0.196	**0.880**	0.819	0.029	0.006	0.247	0.853
ru	0.223	**0.895**	0.878	0.225	0.458	0.706	**0.895**
fr	0.213	**0.827**	0.393	0.141	0.191	0.453	0.760
be	0.193	0.548	0.559	0.000	0.122	0.106	**0.901**
uk	0.173	0.615	0.648	0.458	0.080	0.226	**0.923**
ba	0.201	0.271	**0.294**	0.002	0.064	0.078	0.000
lt	0.211	0.634	0.542	0.043	0.197	0.410	**0.884**
hy	0.252	0.053	0.505	0.263	0.147	0.137	**0.863**

There are two reasons for the outlier results for Russian, even before filtering, the P@1 is very high. Firstly, QAnswer produces up to 60 candidates for other languages while generating only 3 candidates for Russian in most cases. Secondly, the task of distinguishing correct/incorrect candidates usually becomes trivial for Russian, e.g., for the question "Какой часовой пояс в Солт-Лейк-Сити?" (What is the time zone of Salt Lake City?) the candidates are:

- `SELECT DISTINCT ?o1 WHERE  wd:Q23337 wdt:P421 ?o1 .  LIMIT 1000`
- `SELECT DISTINCT ?o1 WHERE  ?s1 wdt:P31 ?o1 .  LIMIT 1000`
- `SELECT DISTINCT ?s1 ?o1 WHERE  ?s1 wdt:P31 ?o1 .  LIMIT 1000`

The first one is correct, while the two others are just nonsense (the label for `wdt:P31` is "instance of").

In Table 2 we present the average results for Answer Trustworthiness Score achieved on *QAnswer*. The numbers do not appear to be conclusive, but this is because the quality of GPT-4 decreases when the number of query candidates exceeds 6 (see the online appendix. Figure 7 demonstrates the Precision@1 values for datasets and models before and after applying SPARQL query filtering.

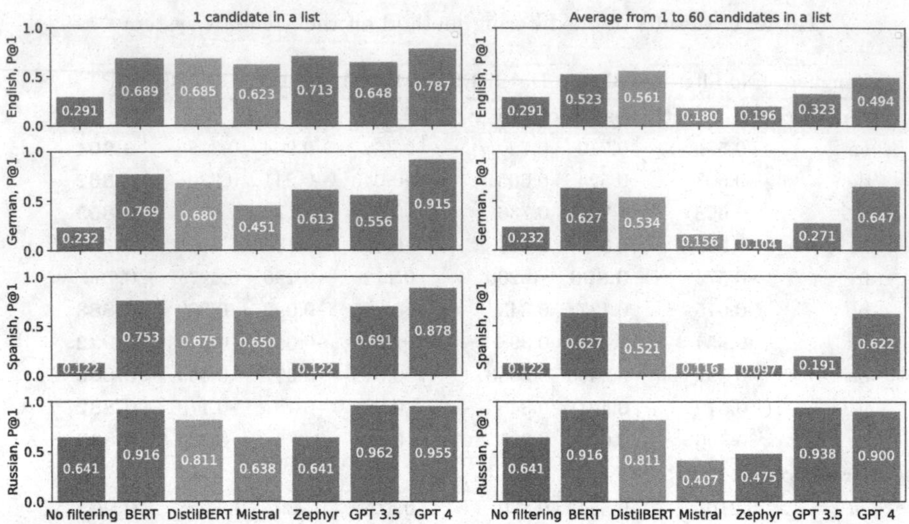

Fig. 7. Precision@1 values for the QAnswer system. The left-hand side of the figure demonstrates the results when the lists of query candidates are cut off to 1 (i.e., there is no second candidate that might move to the top of the list), while the right-hand side shows average values for the candidates' lists from 1 to 60. Each bar demonstrates the value of a particular model. The "No filtering" column shows the metric value without our approach.

Table 2. Results of our filtering method on the QAnswer system aggregated over all different lengths of query candidate lists (from 1 to 60) (see Sect. 4.2).

Language	No filtering	BERT	DistilBERT	Mistral	Zephyr	GPT 3.5	GPT 4
Answer Trustworthiness Score @ 1							
en	–0.418	–0.160	**–0.119**	–0.648	–0.627	–0.375	–0.169
de	–0.535	–0.123	–0.223	–0.694	–0.814	–0.502	**–0.080**
es	–0.756	**–0.206**	–0.339	–0.791	–0.861	–0.684	–0.208
ru	0.282	0.592	0.487	–0.176	–0.057	**0.613**	0.571
Precision @ 1							
en	0.291	0.523	**0.561**	0.180	0.196	0.323	0.494
de	0.232	0.627	0.534	0.156	0.104	0.271	**0.647**
es	0.122	**0.627**	0.521	0.116	0.097	0.191	0.622
ru	0.641	**0.916**	0.811	0.407	0.475	0.938	0.900

6 Discussion

Our results show a strong impact of our approach to the questions in all languages. However, there are some improvement's outliers wrt. languages that are rarely used: Belarusian, Lithuanian, Armenian, and Bashkir as well as to some degree Ukrainian. A post-experiment analysis showed that many questions could not be processed in our approach as labels for the resources were not available, leading to an automatic acceptance of the question (i.e., the filtering method was not applied). This observation highlights a crucial problem while aiming for the accessibility of information from the Web of Data for all humans (cf. [24]). Hence, we can derive here the need for completing the Linked Open Data Cloud at least concerning the resource labels, s.t., a wider information accessibility is supported. Given the poor quality of MG_2 one might argue that the used prompt – although using a straight-forward text – has caused the problems regarding these models. Given additional manual experiments, we tentatively assume that such an LLM-specific prompt optimization would not significantly change the result. A similar point could be made if only English prompts were used. A language-specific prompt might lead to a quality improvement. However, these topics might need additional evaluation beyond the scope of this paper.

7 Conclusions and Future Work

In this paper, we presented an approach for improving the quality of Question Answering over Knowledge graphs. In contrast to other research, we did not present a new KGQA algorithm but a general approach on how to improve the answer quality. In particular, our approach is capable of removing incorrect query candidates, s.t., the number of incorrect results shown to the users is significantly reduced – a fact that strongly increases the trustworthiness of such systems. Additionally, we dedicated our work to developing an approach that also applies to non-English questions. In particular, we evaluated rarely used languages to address the need of people to access information from KGQA systems using their native language (which is not English for most of the worldwide population) without using machine translation. The unique features of our approach are:

(1) The system-agnostic process built on top of the query candidates represented uses the SPARQL format as it is typical in the field of KGQA. Hence, our approach can be applied to existing systems to improve their answer quality (i.e., their trustworthiness). Our experiment provides a rough range of possible improvements to KGQA systems by our approach.
(2) We followed a language-agnostic approach. Hence, it can be transferred to other languages without changing the process. The only requirement is the representation of language-specific labels for the relevant labels in the considered Knowledge Graph. Our results show that our approach can be applied to other languages and will improve the quality of questions represented in other languages as well, with a similar increase of trustworthiness as for English.
(3) Both LLMs and smaller language models can be used for our approach. So that users have the choice of which technology they use. Our experiments show a strong quality improvement for two out of three LM categories used for our experiments. We observed an advantage of closed-source LLMs (which are presumably an order of magnitude larger than the used open-source LLMs), however, they might not apply to all use cases (e.g., because

of privacy issues or as they might imply a significantly higher investment of computing time or cost-per-interaction).

Future work may require experiments with a language-specific prompt, as well as an LLM-specific prompt. Our approach could be extended by using additional KG properties. Additionally, a promising direction for improving the results would be to solve the problem of labels' non-availability of the resources.

References

1. Bisen, K.S., et al.: Evaluation of search methods on community documents. In: Garoufallou, E., Vlachidis, A. (eds.) MTSR 2022, vol. 1789, pp. 39–49. Springer, Heidelberg (2023). https://doi.org/10.1007/978-3-031-39141-5_4
2. Brown, T., et al.: Language models are few-shot learners. Adv. Neural. Inf. Process. Syst. **33**, 1877–1901 (2020)
3. Burtsev, M., et al.: DeepPavlov: open-source library for dialogue systems. In: Proceedings of ACL 2018, System Demonstrations, pp. 122–127. ACL (2018)
4. Cui, R., Aralikatte, R., Lent, H., Hershcovich, D.: Multilingual compositional Wikidata questions. arXiv preprint arXiv:2108.03509 (2021)
5. Cui, R., Aralikatte, R., Lent, H., Hershcovich, D.: Compositional generalization in multilingual semantic parsing over Wikidata. Trans. ACL **10** (2022)
6. Devlin, J., Chang, M.W., Lee, K., Toutanova, K.: Bert: pre-training of deep bidirectional transformers for language understanding. arXiv:1810.04805 (2018)
7. Diefenbach, D., Both, A., Singh, K., Maret, P.: Towards a question answering system over the semantic web. Semant. Web **11**, 421–439 (2020)
8. Diefenbach, D., Giménez-García, J., Both, A., Singh, K., Maret, P.: QAnswer KG: designing a portable question answering system over RDF data. In: Harth, A., et al. (eds.) ESWC 2020. LNCS, vol. 12123, pp. 429–445. Springer, Cham (2020). https://doi.org/10.1007/978-3-030-49461-2_25
9. Efimov, P., Boytsov, L., Arslanova, E., Braslavski, P.: The impact of cross-lingual adjustment of contextual word representations on zero-shot transfer. In: Kamps, J., et al. (eds.) ECIR 2023, vol. 13982, pp. 51–67. Springer, Heidelberg (2023). https://doi.org/10.1007/978-3-031-28241-6_4
10. Evseev, D.: Query generation for answering complex questions in Russian using a syntax parser. Sci. Techn. Inf. Process. **49**(5) (2022)
11. Gashkov, A., Perevalov, A., Eltsova, M., Both, A.: Improving question answering quality through language feature-based SPARQL query candidate validation. In: Groth, P., et al. (eds.) ESWC 2022, vol. 13261, pp. 217–235. Springer, Heidelberg (2022). https://doi.org/10.1007/978-3-031-06981-9_13
12. Jayaseelan, N.: LLaMA 2: the new open source language model (2023). https://www.e2enetworks.com/blog/llama-2-the-new-open-source-language-model
13. Jiang, A.Q., et al.: Mistral 7B. arXiv preprint arXiv:2310.06825 (2023)
14. Jung, H., Kim, W.: Automated conversion from natural language query to SPARQL query. J. Intell. Inf. Syst. **55**(3), 501–520 (2020)
15. Kenton, J.D.M.W.C., Toutanova, L.K.: BERT: pre-training of deep bidirectional transformers for language understanding. In: NAACL-HLT, vol. 1 (2019)
16. Kingma, D.P., Ba, J.: Adam: a method for stochastic optimization. arXiv preprint arXiv:1412.6980 (2014)
17. Koubaa, A.: GPT-4 vs. GPT-3.5: a concise showdown. Preprints (2023)

18. Loginova, E., Varanasi, S., Neumann, G.: Towards end-to-end multilingual question answering. Inf. Syst. Front. **23**, 227–241 (2021)
19. McIntosh, T.R., Liu, T., Susnjak, T., Watters, P., Ng, A., Halgamuge, M.N.: A culturally sensitive test to evaluate nuanced GPT hallucination. IEEE Trans. Artif. Intell. **1**(01), 1–13 (2023)
20. McKenna, N., Sen, P.: KGQA without retraining. In: ACL 2023 Workshop on SustaiNLP (2023)
21. OpenAI: Introducing ChatGPT (2022). https://openai.com/blog/chatGPT
22. OpenAI: GPT-4 technical report. arXiv preprint arXiv:2303.08774 (2023)
23. Pellissier Tanon, T., de Assunção, M.D., Caron, E., Suchanek, F.M.: Demoing platypus – a multilingual question answering platform for Wikidata. In: Gangemi, A., et al. (eds.) ESWC 2018. LNCS, vol. 11155, pp. 111–116. Springer, Cham (2018). https://doi.org/10.1007/978-3-319-98192-5_21
24. Perevalov, A., Both, A., Diefenbach, D., Ngonga Ngomo, A.C.: Can machine translation be a reasonable alternative for multilingual question answering systems over knowledge graphs? In: ACM Web Conference 2022, WWW 2022. ACM (2022)
25. Perevalov, A., Both, A., Ngomo, A.C.N.: Multilingual question answering systems for knowledge graphs-a survey. Semant. Web J. (2023)
26. Perevalov, A., Diefenbach, D., Usbeck, R., Both, A.: QALD-9-plus: a multilingual dataset for question answering over DBpedia and Wikidata translated by native speakers. In: International Conference on Semantic Computing (ICSC) (2022)
27. Razzhigaev, A., Salnikov, M., Malykh, V., Braslavski, P., Panchenko, A.: A system for answering simple questions in multiple languages, pp. 524–537. ACL (2023)
28. Rybin, I., Korablinov, V., Efimov, P., Braslavski, P.: RuBQ 2.0: an innovated Russian question answering dataset. In: Verborgh, R., et al. (eds.) ESWC 2021. LNCS, vol. 12731, pp. 532–547. Springer, Cham (2021). https://doi.org/10.1007/978-3-030-77385-4_32
29. Sanh, V., Debut, L., Chaumond, J., Wolf, T.: DistilBERT, a distilled version of BERT: smaller, faster, cheaper and lighter. arXiv preprint arXiv:1910.01108 (2019)
30. Saxena, A., Chakrabarti, S., Talukdar, P.: Question answering over temporal knowledge graphs. arXiv preprint arXiv:2106.01515 (2021)
31. Sen, P., Aji, A.F., Saffari, A.: Mintaka: a complex, natural, and multilingual dataset for end-to-end question answering. In: 29th International Conference on Computational Linguistics, pp. 1604–1619 (2022)
32. Siciliani, L., Basile, P., Lops, P., Semeraro, G.: MQALD: evaluating the impact of modifiers in question answering over knowledge graphs. Semant. Web **13**(2) (2022)
33. Soruco, J., Collarana, D., Both, A., Usbeck, R.: QALD-9-ES: a Spanish dataset for question answering systems. In: Studies on the Semantic Web, pp. 38–52. IOS Press BV (2023)
34. Srivastava, N., et al.: Lingua franca - entity-aware machine translation approach for question answering over knowledge graphs. In: Knowledge Capture Conference. ACM (2023)
35. Tunstall, L., et al.: Zephyr: direct distillation of LM alignment. arXiv preprint arXiv:2310.16944 (2023)
36. Usbeck, R., et al.: Gerbil: general entity annotator benchmarking framework. In: 24th International Conference on World Wide Web, WWW 2015. (2015)
37. Usbeck, R., Gusmita, R.H., Ngomo, A.C.N., Saleem, M.: 9th challenge on question answering over linked data (QALD-9). In: Semdeep/NLIWoD@ISWC (2018)
38. Wolf, T., et al.: Transformers: state-of-the-art natural language processing. In: Empirical Methods in NLP: System Demonstrations, pp. 38–45. ACL (2020)

39. Xu, S., Culhane, T., Wu, M.H., Semnani, S.J., Lam, M.S.: Complementing GPT-3 with few-shot sequence-to-sequence semantic parsing over Wikidata. arXiv preprint arXiv:2305.14202 (2023)
40. Ye, J., et al.: A comprehensive capability analysis of GPT-3 and GPT-3.5 series models. arXiv preprint arXiv:2303.10420 (2023)
41. Zhang, C., Lai, Y., Feng, Y., Zhao, D.: A review of deep learning in question answering over knowledge bases. AI Open **2**, 205–215 (2021)
42. Zhou, Y., Geng, X., Shen, T., Zhang, W., Jiang, D.: Improving zero-shot cross-lingual transfer for multilingual question answering over knowledge graph. In: NAACL: Human Language Technologies, pp. 5822–5834. ACL (2021)

TraQuLA: Transparent Question Answering Over RDF Through Linguistic Analysis

Elizaveta Zimina[1], Kalervo Järvelin[1], Jaakko Peltonen[1], Aarne Ranta[2], and Jyrki Nummenmaa[1(✉)]

[1] Tampere University, Tampere, Finland
{elizaveta.zimina,kalervo.jarvelin,jaakko.peltonen, jyrki.nummenmaa}@tuni.fi

[2] University of Gothenburg, Gothenburg, Sweden
aarne.ranta@gu.se

Abstract. Answering complex questions over knowledge graphs has gained popularity recently. Systems based on large language models seem to achieve top performance. However, these models may generate content that looks reasonable but is incorrect. They also lack transparency, making it impossible to exactly explain why a particular answer was generated. To tackle these problems we present the TraQuLA (Transparent QUestion-answering through Linguistic Analysis) system – a rule-based system developed through linguistic analysis of datasets of complex questions over DBpedia and Wikidata. TraQuLA defines a question's type and extracts its semantic component candidates (named entities, properties and class names). For the extraction of properties, whose natural language verbalisations are most diverse, we built an extensive database which matches DBpedia/Wikidata properties to natural language expressions, allowing linguistic variation. TraQuLA generates semantic parses for the components and ranks them by each question's structure and morphological features. The ranked parses are then analysed top down according to their patterns, also noting linguistic aspects, until a solution is found and a SPARQL query is produced. TraQuLA outperforms the existing baseline systems on the LC-QuAD 1.0 and competes with ChatGPT-based systems on LC-QuAD 2.0. For the LC-QuAD 1.0 test set, we developed an evaluation approach that accepts multiple ways to answer the questions (some ignored by the dataset) and curated some errors. TraQuLa contains no "black boxes" of neural networks or machine learning and makes its answer construction traceable. Users can therefore better rely on them and assess their correctness.

Keywords: RDF · Question-answering · Rule-based · Linguistic analysis

1 Introduction

The amount of structural data sets on the Web has increased so that e.g. the Linked Open Data Cloud[1] now contains 1,314 datasets in the Linked Data format. For effective

[1] https://lod-cloud.net/

Supported by the Academy of Finland

K. Stefanidis et al. (Eds.): ICWE 2024, LNCS 14629, pp. 19–33, 2024.
https://doi.org/10.1007/978-3-031-62362-2_2

retrieval of information from a knowledge graph (KG), a user should be familiar with its structure and the corresponding query language, e.g., SPARQL. An alternative way is to use a question answering (QA) system converting natural language (NL) questions into the required query language. In the field of question answering over knowledge graphs (KGQA), a lot of effort is devoted to answering questions based on a single KG relation (triple) [2,25,45]. However, new research focuses also on answering complex questions, searching across multiple KG relations [8,33]. Recent approaches often involve neural network techniques [7,21,46], showing increasingly high results, but still "hiding" the logic of their reasoning from the user and making it hard to reveal biases and errors.

We propose TraQuLA a KGQA system for complex questions. TraQuLA is a rule-based system, making the finding of answers to questions transparent and easily explainable. The rules for the system's processing steps were obtained through the analysis of the English language question sets for several popular QA benchmarks: QALD challenges from QALD-1 to QALD-9 [5,34–40] and LC-QuAD 1.0 (training question set, here called training split) [33]. These datasets contain pairs of NL questions and SPARQL queries retrieving the answers in DBpedia. The training split of LC-QuAD 1.0, one of the largest datasets for benchmarking complex KGQA, became our main source of information about the types of complex questions and their parse structures.

Looking for a question's answer, TraQuLA detects its type: the current system can answer *What, Count* and *Ask* (Boolean) questions. Then it extracts the semantic components: named entities, properties and classes. We developed algorithms to build databases of correlations between NL expressions and classes or properties, based on analysis of the training splits, with a view to morphological and lexical variation. The system tolerates spelling mistakes by 1 character for entities, properties or classes. Then, TraQuLA builds parses and ranks them, taking into account the number of coinciding words between the NL questions and NL expressions corresponding to the components in the parse, and some grammatical and structural features. Based on the training splits, we revealed 26 parse structures, falling into 9 parse patterns. TraQuLA analyses the ranked parses top down with respect to their patterns, ambiguous readings of their components and some linguistic aspects, until it finds the answer and produces a SPARQL query.

TraQuLA was first evaluated on the test split of LC-QuAD 1.0 [33]. Our manual curation of the test split showed it does not provide all possible ways to answer the questions correctly and contains errors. We thus carried out a "strict" and a more flexible "revised" evaluation, which tolerated answers that were semantically correct but different from the gold standard given in the strict evaluation. TraQuLA outperformed the state-of-the-art systems even in the strict evaluation. Using property mappings between DBpedia and Wikidata, we showed that the system can be easily adapted to other KGs. TraQuLA was tested on the test split of LC-QuAD 2.0 [8] with competitive performance.

2 Related Work

In KGQA, performance is often evaluated on benchmarks, that until recently were focused on simple questions (e.g. WebQuestions [1], SimpleQuestions [2]). Answering complex questions, referencing to several triples in a KG, has become a target of e.g. the

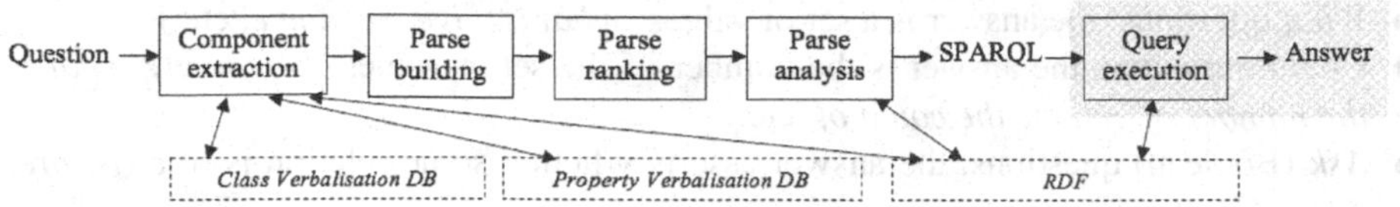

Fig. 1. General Architecture of TraQuLA

QALD[2] challenges and especially LC-QuAD [33] and LC-QuAD 2.0 [8] benchmarks.

A range of approaches to KGQA includes those based on controlled natural languages [23], formal grammars [47], templates [6,28], machine learning [14], etc. Neural networks have gained high popularity in KGQA over the recent years [13,20,41]. In particular, they are successful in the task of query generation and ranking [21,44,46].

Recently, Large Language Models (LLMs), such as ChatGPT, have shown remarkable capabilities in a number of NLP tasks, including question answering (e.g. [18,27, 43]). Y. Tan et al. [32] show that with each successive version, the GPT's question-answering performance has been steadily improving.

Being close to the "traditional" systems, our approach is similar to such methods as [1,3] in terms of relation linking, involving semantic parsing through learning lexicons from large amount of text and knowledge bases. Although this approach is often thought to be time and labour consuming and requiring a lot of training data, we believe that our system's resources and algorithms for relation linking can be further expanded and adapted for KGs other than DBpedia/Wikidata with little effort. The behavior of LLMs, as well as the internal processes that drive their actions, often remain a "black box", even to their developers. Moreover, they require a lot of training data and are often susceptible to overfitting [21].

Query generation (QG), named entity disambiguation (NED) and relation extraction (RE) are often considered separate tasks of KGQA systems. This modular approach is used in such frameworks as openQA [22], OKBQA [17], Frankenstein [31], etc. We believe treating QG, NED and RE as independent stages can be a pitfall. For example, the most probable entity candidate can turn out to be inappropriate in the semantic context of the whole question (see example in Sect. 3.2). In our approach, QG, NED and RE are more intertwined, so the system can replace several times the extracted semantic components in a query being built, until it finds the best combination.

3 TraQuLA Approach

TraQuLA is based on the analysis of the English questions over DBpedia from QALD and LC-QuAD 1.0 datasets. The general architecture of TraQuLA is shown in Fig. 1.

3.1 Question Type Detection and Interrogative Words

A NL question processing starts with understanding its type, based on the interrogative words and phrases:

[2] http://qald.aksw.org/

- *What* questions: the answer is a set of values (*what is, give me, name*, etc.)
- *Count* questions: the answer is the number of the set of values (*how many, what is the number of, tell me the count of*, etc.)
- *Ask* (Boolean) questions: the answer asserts whether some relation is true (*is, are, does, did*, etc.)

3.2 Component Extraction

Next, the system extracts semantic components: entities, properties and classes. For each word in the question, excluding the interrogative words with optional articles in the beginning, the system looks for component candidates starting from this word.

Entity Candidates. Along with exact matches, the system finds approximate matches to allow for typos. It accepts candidates with 1 character difference in strings of 4 characters and longer (but not shorter, to avoid extra noise in candidate selection), also tolerating the absence/presence of the articles (*a/the*). We did not use a ready-made named entity disambiguation (NED) system (e.g. DBpedia Spotlight [24], Tag Me [10], etc), as we have not found one that conveniently provides selection of several possible candidates and tackles spelling mistakes in a way that our system needs. However, we combined our indexes of entity names with the FACC1 annotations of ClueWeb corpora [12], using mappings between Freebase, Wikidata and DBpedia.

Class Candidates. DBpedia operates with over 700 class names, each of which can appear in a NL question in singular or plural form. We automatically generated these forms[3] and added them to a database of class name verbalisations. Then our algorithm went through all questions involving class names in the train splits and detected cases when a class name was expressed by a phrase being a part of the class name (*show* → class `TelevisionShow`) or by a synonym[4] (*king* → classes `Monarch`, `Royalty`, `BritishRoyalty`). These correlations (with the generated singular/plural forms) were also added to the database of class name verbalisations and nests of correlations were formed there for NL expressions that can indicate several classes (*league* → classes `SportsLeague`, `Baseball League`, `AmericanFootballLeague`, etc). The system allows 1 character edit distance in each candidate NL expression.

Property Candidates. Properties are components that are the hardest to identify in a NL question, due to the diversity of their verbalisations. To facilitate property extraction, we built the *Property Verbalisation* database, into which we collected all property names and the corresponding NL phrases for those that were used in the training splits. First, all property names with their corresponding verbalisations were added to the database. After that, more difficult cases of property verbalisation were detected and added to the database. Thus, for each question in each training split, our algorithm automatically compared a NL question and a SPARQL query. Consider the following example:

[3] With the help of the Word Forms module: https://github.com/gutfeeling/word_forms

[4] Detected by means of WordNet: https://wordnet.princeton.edu/

What sports are there at the universities affiliated to the National Capital Region Athletic Association?[5]
`{?x dbo:affiliation res:National_Capital_Region_Athletic_Association. ?x dbp:athletics ?uri. ?x rdf:type dbo:University}`[6]
Below we show how the NL question and the SPARQL query are compared and elements of the *Property Verbalisation* database identified:

1. find and remove all matching components (*National Capital Region Athletic Association* → `res:National_Capital_Region_Athletic_Association`),
2. find and remove all class names (if any) and their verbalisations (*universities* → `dbo:University`),
3. find and remove the remaining entity names (if any), if they are different from the entity names. Use string matching to find the most matching expression in the NL question,
4. look for derivationally related forms through the Word Forms module to set relations between the remaining property names (if any) and NL expressions (*affiliated* → `dbo:affiliation`). Add these relations to the database. If a NL expression is a verb and followed by a preposition (*affiliated to*), also save the relation between this verb-preposition combination and the property name in the database. Remove the elements of the relations from the NL question and the query,
5. use WordNet to find synonymic relations between the remaining property names (if any) and NL expressions (*sports* → `dbp:athletics`) and add them to the database. Remove the elements of the relations from the NL question and the query,
6. if any property names are left in the query, remove all stopwords from the NL question and look for the corresponding relations in the current database. If nothing found, but only one word remains in the NL question and one property in the query, add its relation to the database. Otherwise, make all possible relations from the remaining words and property names and keep them until one or several of these relations are met again in another question. In this case, add the relation(s) to the database.

Correlations in the *Property Verbalisation* database are nested, so that ambiguous NL expressions are linked to several corresponding property names (e.g. *owner* → `[dbo:owningCompany, dbo:owningOrganisation, dbp:owned, dbp:company, ...]`). Currently the *Property Verbalisation* database contains almost 10,000 correlations between NL expressions and property nests.

The correlations of NL expressions and RDF properties were also marked with recommended directions of application. For example, for the correlation between the

[5] This and further sample questions are taken from the training splits. All grammar and spelling has been left unedited.

[6] Hereinafter, SPARQL queries for *What* questions are given in the shortened form, so that the full form would have the preamble:

```
PREFIX res: <http://dbpedia.org/resource/>
PREFIX dbo: <http://dbpedia.org/ontology/>
PREFIX dbp: <http://dbpedia.org/property/>
PREFIX rdf: <http://www.w3.org/1999/02/22-rdf-syntax-ns#>
SELECT DISTINCT ?uri WHERE
```

expression *produce* and the property `dbp:products`, the property's recommended application would be direct, i.e. the known entity in a triple would be a subject, and the unknown one – an object. But if the NL question contains the expression *owned by*, the property `dbp:parentCompany` would rather be applied in a reverse direction, i.e. the target value would be the subject in the triple. The direction is detected automatically, relying on the position of the target value in a triple.

For properties expressed with verbs, the system recognises all possible tense forms and tolerates variations in noun endings. Moreover, the system applies 1 character edit distance to match possible spelling mistakes. This is realised only for "verified" expressions, i.e. phrases extracted from the training splits and their inflected forms. The *Property Verbalisation* database was also combined with the PATTY relation paraphrases [26] and EARL relation annotations of the training split of LC-QuAD 1.0 [9].

3.3 Parse Building and Ranking

In our approach, a parse is an array of semantic elements extracted from a NL question. We assume the most likely correct parse of a question usually implies the highest coverage. Thus, the union of words of extracted entities, properties and, if present, classes should coincide with the question words as much as possible. We developed an algorithm to build parses of the extracted parse elements and rank them, to find the best parse as soon as possible.

Following the logic of most of the training splits, we restricted complexity of questions to at most two hops, i.e. a 2-triple distance from the topic entity, with optional class restriction. To generate a set of candidate parses, TraQuLA does the following:

1. Generate all possible parses comprising non-intersecting semantic elements, so that each parse contains at most 2 entities, 2 properties and 1 class and at least 1 entity.
2. Exclude all parses in which an entity immediately follows a class, or vice versa.
3. Exclude all parses in which an entity immediately follows interrogative words.
4. Exclude all parses in which one property immediately follows another one, except if one of the properties is a noun phrase with the core noun in the Genitive case (e.g. *child's birthplace*), or one of the properties belongs to verb properties (e.g. *whose company belongs to*).

For each remaining parse, its rank is counted through Algorithm 1. We rank the queries using a linear combination of the below features, selected through human reasoning and experimentation. We use the following notations and elementary functions:

- Let *W, W'* be two word sets and *w, w'* individual words.
- Lc(*W*) = $\{w_{lc} \mid w \in W\}$, where w_{lc} is the all-lowercase word for *w*
- lemma(*w*) denotes the lemma of *w*, e.g. lemma("playing") = "play"
- $W \cap^* W' = \{w, w' \mid w \in W \wedge w' \in W' \wedge \text{lemma}(w) = \text{lemma}(w')\}$
- Is-Lc(*w*) = true, iff *w* is all-lowercase
- Is-Uc(*w*) = true, iff $\neg$ Is-Lc(*w*), i.e. *w* contains at least one uppercase character
- edit1(*w, w'*) = true, iff *w* is at edit distance 1 from the word *w'*

Algorithm 1: Parse Rank

Input: P – the union of words of the parse elements; Q – question words excluding interrogative words; $A = \{$'a', 'the'$\}$; S_{NLTK} – NLTK stopword (SW) set (https://www.nltk.org/)
Output: parse rank R

$I = \text{Lc}(P) \cap^* \text{Lc}(Q)$ |Words in P and Q, lowercased
$S = S_{NLTK} - A$ |Non-article SWs
$A_I = I \cap A$ |Articles in P and Q, lowercased
$S_I = I \cap S$ |Non-article SWs in P and Q, lowercased
$C_I = I - A_I - S_I$ |Non-SWs in P and Q, lowercased
$N = \text{Lc}(P) - \text{Lc}(Q)$ |Words in P but not Q, lowercased
$A_N = N \cap A$ |Articles in P but not Q, lowercased
$S_N = N \cap S$ |Non-article SWs in P, not Q, lowercased
$C_N = N - A_N - S_N$ |Lowercased non-SWs in P, not Q
$U = \{w \mid w \in P \wedge \text{Is-Uc}(w)\} \cap^* \{w \mid w \in Q \wedge \text{Is-Uc}(w)\}$ |Uppercase words in P and Q
$U_{dif} = \{w \mid w \in (P \cup Q) \wedge w_{lc} \in I \wedge \text{Is-Uc}(w)\} - U$ |Words with different case in P and Q
$F = \{w \mid w \in \text{Lc}(P) \wedge \neg\, w \in (I \cup S) \wedge \text{edit1}(w', w) \wedge w' \in (\text{Lc}(Q) - I)\}$ |Words in P, not Q, similar to a word in Q by edit distance, lowercased
return $R = (0.5 \times |A_I| + 0.75 \times |S_I| + |C_I|) - (0.5 \times |A_N| + 0.75 \times |S_N| + |C_N|) + |U| - |U_{dif}| + 0.5 \times |F|$

3.4 Parse Analysis and Answer Extraction

Parse Patterns. Based on the analysis of the training splits, we obtained 26 possible parse structures. Some of them are united under the same logic of analysis. For example, the question *Which band's former member are Kevin Jonas and Joe Jonas?* has the parse structure [*C, P, E1, E2*], whereas the structure of *South Side elevated railroad and twin cities 400 are operated by which city?* is [*E1, E2, P, C*]. Nevertheless, the logic of analysis of these parse structures is the same: find the intersection of the triples each formed by the property and one of the entities, and restrict the output values to those belonging to the class. Therefore, the mentioned parse structures can be called synonymous and analysed by the same function extracting the answers. We grouped our 26 parse structures into 9 sets of synonymous structures – parse patterns. Their names, readings and examples are collected in Table 1. The last pattern relates to the Boolean type of questions, other patterns are attributed to *What* and *Count* questions.

Parse Analysis. The parse analysis flows along the logic "from known to unknown", i.e. retrieving values from RDF triples, in which the subject and the predicate or the predicate and the object are known, and then filtering them, intersecting with another set of values or passing as objects or subjects in another RDF triple (Table 2). The elements of the analysis logic should be understood as follows:

- $P \times E$: a set of values as a result of search for all unknown elements of RDF triples, in which property P is a predicate and entity E is either a subject or an object.
- $(P \times E) \in C$: filtering of set $P \times E$ based on belonging to class C.
- $P1 \times (P2 \times E)$: once set $P2 \times E$ is found, each of its values is checked to participate as a subject or object in RDF triples with property $P1$ as a predicate, and the set of other elements of these triples is output.
- $(P \times E1) \cap (P \times E2)$: intersection of sets $P \times E1$ and $P \times E2$.

Table 1. TraQuLA Parse Patterns (displaying **entities**, *classes*, and properties)

Parse Pattern	Reading	Example Question
PropEnt	What is PROPERTY of ENTITY?	Who discovered **Pluto**?
ClPropEnt	What CLASS is PROPERTY of ENTITY?	Which *people* were born in **Heraklion**?
PropPropEnt	What is PROPERTY1 of PROPERTY2 of ENTITY?	What are the prizes won by the animator of **The Skeleton Dance**?
PropClPropEnt	What PROPERTY1 of CLASS is PROPERTY2 of ENTITY?	What is the predecessor of the *automobile* which is related to **Cadillac Fleetwood**?
PropEntAndEnt	What is PROPERTY of ENTITY1 and ENTITY2?	List the common official language of **Ladonia** and the **Empire of Atlantium**?
PropEntPropEnt	What is PROPERTY1 of ENTITY1 and PROPERTY2 of ENTITY2?	Which college of **Luke List (golfer)** is the alma mater of **K. Terry Dornbush**?
ClPropEntAndEnt	What CLASS is PROPERTY of ENTITY1 and ENTITY2?	Which *scientist* is known for the **Manhattan Project** and the **Nobel Peace Prize**?
ClPropEntPropEnt	What CLASS is PROPERTY1 of ENTITY1 and PROPERTY2 of ENTITY2?	Name the *river* whose mouth country is **Mozambique** and source region is **North-Western Province, Zambia**
EntPropEnt	Is ENTITY1 PROPERTY of ENTITY2?	Was **Ganymede** discovered by **Galileo Galilei**?

- $\exists$ $(E1 \times P \times E2)$ OR $\nexists$ $(E1 \times P \times E2)$: assertion whether an RDF triple with *E1* as a subject, *P* as a predicate and *E2* as an object exists or not.

If TraQuLA fails to find the target value(s), it proceeds to the next highest ranked parse. Parses are ordered by coverage, so there is often a chance the system reaches the correct interpretation of the question after several efforts. In the worst case, the system selects the most probable entity (the longest one), gets all RDF triples with it and tries to find the most probable predicate, based on approximation with the remaining question words. It can work with simple questions, in which the property is formulated with a previously unseen NL expression.

4 Evaluation

4.1 Evaluation on the LC-QuAD 1.0 Dataset

Dataset and Baselines. We first use the LC-QuAD 1.0 [33] question collection for evaluation. It comprises 5000 NL questions over DBpedia 2016-04. Besides end-to-end

Table 2. Logic of Parse Pattern Analysis

Parse Pattern	Analysis Logic
PropEnt	$P \times E$
ClPropEnt	$(P \times E) \in C$
PropPropEnt	$P1 \times (P2 \times E)$
PropClPropEnt	$P1 \times ((P2 \times E) \in C)$
PropEntAndEnt	$(P \times E1) \cap (P \times E2)$
PropEntPropEnt	$(P1 \times E1) \cap (P2 \times E2)$
ClPropEntAndEnt	$((P \times E1) \cap (P \times E2)) \in C$
ClPropEntPropEnt	$((P1 \times E1) \cap (P2 \times E2)) \in C$
EntPropEnt	$\exists\, (E1 \times P \times E2)$ OR $\nexists\, (E1 \times P \times E2)$

question answering, LC-QuAD 1.0 has also been a popular benchmark for evaluation of systems performing QA subtasks, such as entity linking [11,30], relation linking [9,30] and subgraph matching [21,46].

In case of end-to-end question answering, to our knowledge, evaluation results for 6 systems, based on the LC-QuAD 1.0 dataset, have been published. TeBaQA [42] learns templates based on isomorphic basic graph patterns of SPARQL queries and ranks them to find the best matching one. WDAqua [6] is a rule-based QA system over several KGs in several languages, building SPARQL queries and choosing the most probable one. QAmp [41] uses supervised neural networks for question type detection and reference extraction, and unsupervised functions for matching entities and predicates and message passing. NSQA [16] is a modular system, involving Abstract Meaning Representation (AMR) parsing. Hu et al. [15] developed EDGQA, based on the Entity Description Graph representing the structure of complex questions. Liang et al. [19] use a BERT-based decoder, which jointly learns multiple subtasks for Semantic Query Graph construction.

The LC-QuAD 1.0 benchmark does not provide all acceptable SPARQL queries and shows no clear preferences in choosing between alternative answers. A QA system being evaluated should not be penalised for choosing a semantically correct query, yet not coinciding with the gold standard. We carry out two types of evaluation, the first one being a strict evaluation and the second one (revised evaluation) taking into account ambiguity of the benchmark questions. The TraQuLA implementation and testing data are open-sourced[7].

We developed an evaluation algorithm that activates when the answer of TraQuLA does not coincide with the gold standard: the algorithm decides whether the output query is still semantically valid and, therefore, correct. One of our researchers also manually verified all TraQuLA's and gold standard answers for the 1000 test questions, revealing 23 cases, where the semantic correctness of the output was not detected automatically, and 23 errors in the test split gold standard answers. The judgement of both those 23 cases, and the 23 errors was then validated by another researcher.

[7] https://github.com/lizazim/TraQuLA

Ambiguities and Errors of the Test Split. As discussed, a system under evaluation may yield results that syntactically deviate from the gold standard, but are semantically correct. We discuss the reasons for this as a justification for the revised evaluation.

Semantic Equivalence of Queries. We consider two SPARQL queries as semantically equivalent, if the properties in them:

a) differ in `dbo`/`dbp` prefixes, e.g:
   Where can one find the Dzogchen Ponolop Rinpoche?
   Gold standard: `{res:Dzogchen_Ponlop_Rinpoche dbp:location ?uri}`
   TraQuLA: `{res:Dzogchen_Ponlop_Rinpoche dbo:location ?uri}`
b) are synonyms, e.g.:
   Where were Sverre Krogh Sundbo and Havard Vad Petersson born?
   Gold standard: `{res:Sverre_Krogh_Sundbø dbp:birthPlace ?uri. res:Håvard_Vad_Petersson dbp:placeOfBirth ?uri}`
   TraQuLA: `{res:Håvard_Vad_Petersson dbo:birthPlace ?uri. res:Sverre_Krogh_Sundbø dbo:birthPlace ?uri}`

Deciding whether properties are synonymous or not, the evaluation algorithm relies on the training splits. If some properties are related to the same NL expression and are used interchangeably in the training splits, they are considered synonymous, even if we can argue about their equivalence in the real world. For example, the properties *nationality* and *citizenship* are synonymous in LC-QuAD 1.0:
What country provides a citizenship too Newin Chidchob and Seni Pramoj?
Gold standard: `{res:Newin_Chidchob dbp:nationality ?uri. res:Seni_Pramoj dbo:nationality ?uri}`

Semantic Correspondence of Queries to Questions. The correctness of answers from this group could not be checked automatically, which was one reason for our manual examination of the test split. This group includes cases when:

a) the question contains ambiguous named entities:
   Who directed The Haunted House?
   Gold standard: `{res:The_Haunted_House_(1929_film) dbo:director ?uri}`
   TraQuLA: `{res:The_Haunted_House_(1921_film) dbo:director ?uri}`
b) the semantic entity-property relations within the questions can be understood in several ways:
   Which party has come in power in Mumbai North?
   Gold standard: `{?x dbp:constituency res:Mumbai_North_(Lok_Sabha_constituency). ?x dbo:party ?uri}`
   TraQuLA: `{res:Mumbai_North_(Lok_Sabha_constituency) dbp:party ?uri}`

Test Split Errors. The largest group of the test split errors (14 questions) are cases when the gold standard query lacks a class restriction, e.g.:
Where do beauty queens with brown hair reside?
Gold standard: `{?x dbp:hairColor res:Brown_hair. ?x dbo:residence ?uri}`

Here the gold standard query does not check for `?x` being of the class `BeautyQueen`, so the answers include residences of other people, not only beauty queens.

In some cases the gold standard suggests wrong entity-property directionality, e.g.:
What is the successor of PlayStation 4?
Gold standard: `{?uri dbp:successor res:PlayStation_4}`

The interpretation should be *Whose successor is PlayStation 4?*. DBpedia 2016-04 cannot answer the initial question, because PlayStation 5 was released only in 2020.

Other error types include incorrect answer type (`COUNT` instead of `SELECT`) and pure semantic inconsistencies, each of which should be considered separately. We provide a full list of the found errors in our GitHub repository.

Evaluation Metrics and Results. As evaluation metrics, we use precision (P) and recall (R) macro-averaged across all test questions, as well as the F1 score (F1). If the system does not return any answer to a question, the micro precision and micro recall for this question are 0. We also apply the strict and revised evaluation approaches. In revised, the micro precision and micro recall for a question were assigned to 1 in the following cases:

- an output SPARQL query produced the same value(s) as the gold standard query (547 questions);
- an output SPARQL query was semantically equivalent to the gold standard query (61 questions);
- an output SPARQL query semantically corresponded to the input question (41 questions, including cases when TraQuLA output a correct answer whereas the gold standard contained a mistake – 18 questions).

In Table 3 we compare the performance of TraQuLA and the other systems[8]. TraQuLA significantly outperforms most of the systems even in the strict evaluation.

4.2 Evaluation on the LC-QuAD 2.0 Dataset

LC-QuAD 2.0 [8] comprises 30,000 pairs of questions and corresponding SPARQL queries, thus being one of the largest benchmarks for KGQA. Since its target knowledge base is Wikidata, we used property mappings with DBpedia[9] to facilitate TraQuLA's property extraction technology. We modified the way of SPARQL building (e.g. Q-identifiers are now used instead of verbal entity names in DBpedia), and added some

[8] We had to adjust WDAqua's macro precision, since in [6] the reported precision was calculated for answered questions only, and for each unanswered question micro precision equaled 1. We also use TeBaQA's F1 score instead of the reported QALD F-Measure.

[9] http://mappings.dbpedia.org/

Table 3. The Comparison of TraQuLA with Existing Systems (SE – strict evaluation, RE – revised evaluation)

LC-QuAD 1.0 dataset (DBpedia)			
Approach	P	R	F1
TeBaQA	0.23	0.23	0.23
WDAqua	0.22	0.38	0.28
QAmp	0.25	0.50	0.33
NSQA	0.45	0.46	0.44
EDGQA	0.51	0.56	0.53
Liang et al.	0.51	0.59	0.55
TraQuLA(SE)	**0.59**	**0.60**	**0.59**
TraQuLA(RE)	**0.66**	**0.67**	**0.67**

LC-QuAD 2.0 dataset (Wikidata)			
Approach	P	R	F1
TeBaQA	0.14	0.14	0.14
FLAN-T5	–	–	0.30
Uniqorn	–	–	0.33
GPT-3	–	–	0.33
GPT-3.5v2	–	–	0.34
GPT-3.5v3	–	–	0.39
ChatGPT	–	–	0.43
TraQuLA(SE)	0.42	0.44	0.43
GPT-4	–	–	**0.55**

possibilities for filtering, e.g. by words that the resulting entity names should contain or time constraints, without changing the general approach. We did not use the training split to find new property/class verbalisations or syntactic constructions, even though LC-QuAD 2.0 is much more varied in these terms than its predecessor. We have not performed any curation of the test split, leaving this for future work. We wanted to see the performance of our system in its current state and to show that its approach can be easily applicable to other KGs and datasets. In our evaluation, we used 5279 questions that return a non-empty answer against the current version of Wikidata (January 2024).

Table 3 presents the systems that have been evaluated on the whole LC-QuAD 2.0 test set. The data for the systems, other than TeBaQA [42], are taken from Y. Tan et al. [32], who compared the performance of the GPT family models with that of FLAN-T5, a popular non-GPT LLM model, and Uniqorn, taken as a traditional state-of-the-art KGQA model. FLAN-T5 [4] is an encoder-decoder transformer model that was trained on the CommonCrawl[10]. Uniqorn [29] uses BERT models for retrieving question-related information from the RDF data and/or text and making context graphs. TraQuLA showed competitive performance even against the latest GPT models, which cannot boast of the same level of transparency and explainability.

5 Conclusions

We introduced TraQuLA, a novel approach to KGQA, paying special attention to the structure and linguistic features of complex questions. Predicate matching, the common bottleneck of QA systems (e.g. [41]), was realised through large-scale linguistics-aware collection of correlations between KG properties and NL expressions. The system performed significantly better compared to the state of the art for LC-QuAD 1.0 and LC-QuAD 2.0 datasets. We also carried out manual curation of the LC-QuAD 1.0 test split,

[10] https://commoncrawl.org/

revealing some errors, and developed an evaluation approach accepting variant forms of answer queries.

In the future, we are planning to improve TraQuLA by applying its algorithms for extending databases of class and property verbalisations using the LC-QuAD 2.0 train split, and other datasets. Other development prospects include deeper error analysis to realise better matching of semantic components, and expansion of the range of question types, so that they would cover other SPARQL operations, e.g. ordering and limits.

References

1. Berant, J., Chou, A., Frostig, R., Liang, P.: Semantic parsing on Freebase from question-answer pairs. In: Proceedings of EMNLP 2013, pp. 1533–1544 (2013)
2. Bordes, A., Usunier, N., Chopra, S., Weston, J.: Large-scale simple question answering with memory networks (2015)
3. Cai, Q., Yates, A.: Large-scale semantic parsing via schema matching and lexicon extension. In: Proceedings of ACL 2013, pp. 423–433 (2013)
4. Chung, H.W., et al.: Scaling instruction-finetuned language models (2022)
5. Cimiano, P., Lopez, V., Unger, C., Cabrio, E., Ngonga Ngomo, A.C., Walter, S.: Multilingual question answering over linked data (qald-3): lab overview, pp. 321–332 (2013)
6. Diefenbach, D., Both, A., Singh, K., Maret, P.: Towards a question answering system over the semantic web. Semant. Web 1–16 (2018)
7. Dong, L., Wei, F., Zhou, M., Xu, K.: Question answering over Freebase with multi-column convolutional neural networks. In: Proceedings of ACL 2015 - IJCNLP 2015, pp. 260–269 (2015)
8. Dubey, M., Banerjee, D., Abdelkawi, A., Lehmann, J.: LC-QuAD 2.0: a large dataset for complex question answering over Wikidata and DBpedia. In: Proceedings of ISWC 2019, pp. 69–78 (2019)
9. Dubey, M., Banerjee, D., Chaudhuri, D., Lehmann, J.: EARL: joint entity and relation linking for question answering over knowledge graphs. In: Proceedings of ISWC 2018, pp. 108—126 (2018)
10. Ferragina, P., Scaiella, U.: Tagme: on-the-fly annotation of short text fragments (by Wikipedia entities). In: Proceedings of CIKM 2010, pp. 1625–1628 (2010)
11. Ferragina, P., Scaiella, U.: Fast and accurate annotation of short texts with Wikipedia pages. IEEE Softw. **29**(1), 70–75 (2012)
12. Gabrilovich, E., Ringgaard, M., Subramanya, A.: FACC1: freebase annotation of ClueWeb corpora, version 1 (release date 2013-06-26, format version 1, correction level 0) (2013)
13. Golub, D., He, X.: Character-level question answering with attention. In: Proceedings of EMNLP 2016, pp. 1598–1607 (2016)
14. He, S., Zhang, Y., Liu, K., Zhao, J.: CASIA@V2: a MLN-based question answering system over linked data. In: Proceedings of QALD-4, pp. 1249–1259 (2014)
15. Hu, X., Shu, Y., Huang, X., Qu, Y.: EDG-based question decomposition for complex question answering over knowledge bases. In: Proceedings of ISWC 2021, pp. 128–145 (2021)
16. Kapanipathi, P., et al.: Leveraging Abstract Meaning Representation for knowledge base question answering. In: ACL-IJCNLP 2021, pp. 3884–3894. Association for Computational Linguistics (2021)
17. Kim, J., et al.: OKBQA: an open collaboration framework for development of natural language question-answering over knowledge bases. In: Proceedings of ISWC 2017 Posters & Demonstrations and Industry Tracks (2017)

18. Kocoń, J., et al.: ChatGPT: jack of all trades, master of none. Inf. Fusion **99**, 101861 (2023)
19. Liang, Z., Peng, Z., Yang, X., Zhao, F., Liu, Y., McGuinness, D.L.: Bert-based semantic query graph extraction for knowledge graph question answering. In: Proceedings of ISWC 2021 Posters, Demos and Industry (2021)
20. Lukovnikov, D., Fischer, A., Lehmann, J., Auer, S.: Neural network-based question answering over knowledge graphs on word and character level. In: Proceedings of WWW 2017, pp. 1211–1220 (2017)
21. Maheshwari, G., Trivedi, P., Lukovnikov, D., Chakraborty, N., Fischer, A., Lehmann, J.: Learning to rank query graphs for complex question answering over knowledge graphs. In: Proceedings of ISWC 2019, pp. 487–504 (2019)
22. Marx, E., Usbeck, R., Ngomo, A.C.N., Höffner, K., Lehmann, J., Auer, S.: Towards an open question answering architecture. In: Proceedings of SEḾ14, pp. 57–60 (2014)
23. Mazzeo, G., Zaniolo, C.: Answering controlled natural language questions on RDF knowledge bases. In: Proceedings of EDBT 2016, pp. 608–611 (2016)
24. Mendes, P., Jakob, M., García-Silva, A., Bizer, C.: DBpedia Spotlight: shedding light on the web of documents. In: Proceedings of I-SEMANTICS 2011, pp. 1–8 (2011)
25. Mohammed, S., Shi, P., Lin, J.: Strong baselines for simple question answering over knowledge graphs with and without neural networks. In: Proceedings of NAACL 2018, vol. 2 (Short Papers). pp. 291–296 (2018)
26. Nakashole, N., Weikum, G., Suchanek, F.: PATTY: a taxonomy of relational patterns with semantic types. In: Proceedings of EMNLP-CoNLL 2012, pp. 1135–1145 (2012)
27. Omar, R., Mangukiya, O., Kalnis, P., Mansour, E.: ChatGPT versus traditional question answering for knowledge graphs: current status and future directions towards knowledge graph chatbots (2023)
28. Park, S., Shim, H., Lee, G.G.: Isoft at QALD-4: semantic similarity-based question answering system over linked data. In: CLEF (Working Notes) 2014, pp. 1236–1248 (2014)
29. Pramanik, S., Alabi, J., Roy, R.S., Weikum, G.: UNIQORN: unified question answering over RDF knowledge graphs and natural language text (2023)
30. Sakor, A., et al.: Old is gold: linguistic driven approach for entity and relation linking of short text. In: Proceedings of NAACL 2019, vol. 1. pp. 2336–2346 (2019)
31. Singh, K., Both, A., Sethupat, A., Shekarpour, S.: Frankenstein: a platform enabling reuse of question answering components. In: Proceedings of ESWC 2018, pp. 624–638 (2018)
32. Tan, Y., et al.: Can ChatGPT replace traditional KBQA models? an in-depth analysis of the question answering performance of the GPT LLM family. In: ISWC 2023, pp. 348–367 (2023)
33. Trivedi, P., Maheshwari, G., Dubey, M., Lehmann, J.: LC-QuAD: a corpus for complex question answering over knowledge graphs. In: ISWC, pp. 210—218 (2017)
34. Unger, C., Cimiano, P., Lopez, V., Motta, E.: Preface. In: Proceedings of 1st Workshop on Question Answering Over Linked Data (QALD-1), pp. II–V (2011)
35. Unger, C., et al.: Question answering over linked data (QALD-4), vol. 1180, pp. 1172–1180 (2014)
36. Unger, C., Forascu, C., Lopez, V., Ngonga Ngomo, A.C., Cabrio, E., Cimiano, P., Walter, S.: Question answering over linked data (QALD-5). In: CLEF 2015 Working Notes (2015)
37. Unger, C., Ngonga Ngomo, A.C., Cabrio, E.: 6th open challenge on question answering over linked data (QALD-6). In: SemWebEval 2016: Semantic Web Challenges, vol. 641, pp. 171–177 (2016)
38. Usbeck, R., Gusmita, R.H., Ngomo, A.C.N., Saleem, M.: 9th challenge on question answering over linked data (QALD-9). In: Joint Proceedings of ISWC 2018 Workshops SemDeep-4 and NLIWOD-4 (2018)

39. Usbeck, R., Ngomo, A.C.N., Conrads, F., Röder, M., Napolitano, G.: 8th challenge on question answering over linked data (QALD-8). In: Joint Proceedings of ISWC 2018 Workshops SemDeep-4 and NLIWOD-4 (2018)
40. Usbeck, R., Ngomo, A.-C.N., Haarmann, B., Krithara, A., Röder, M., Napolitano, G.: 7th open challenge on question answering over linked data (QALD-7). In: Dragoni, M., Solanki, M., Blomqvist, E. (eds.) SemWebEval 2017. CCIS, vol. 769, pp. 59–69. Springer, Cham (2017). https://doi.org/10.1007/978-3-319-69146-6_6
41. Vakulenko, S., Garcia, J.D.F., Polleres, A., de Rijke, M., Cochez, M.: Message passing for complex question answering over knowledge graphs. In: Proceedings of CIKM 2019, pp. 1431–1440 (2019)
42. Vollmers, D., Jalota, R., Moussallem, D., Topiwala, H., Ngonga Ngomo, A.C., Usbeck, R.: Knowledge graph question answering using graph-pattern isomorphism. In: Proceedings of SEMANTiCS 2021, vol. 53, pp. 103–117
43. Wang, S., Scells, H., Koopman, B., Zuccon, G.: Can ChatGPT write a good boolean query for systematic review literature search? ACM SIGIR (2023)
44. Yih, W.t., Chang, M.W., He, X., Gao, J.: Semantic parsing via staged query graph generation: question answering with knowledge base. In: Proceedings of ACL–IJCNP 2015, pp. 1321–1331 (2015)
45. Yin, W., Yu, M., Xiang, B., Zhou, B., Schütze, H.: Simple question answering by attentive convolutional neural network. In: Proceedings of COLING 2016, pp. 1746–1756 (2016)
46. Zafar, H., Napolitano, G., Lehmann, J.: Formal query generation for question answering over knowledge bases. In: Proceedings of ESWC 2018, pp. 714–728 (2018)
47. Zimina, E., Nummenmaa, J., Järvelin, K., Peltonen, J., Stefanidis, K.: MuG-QA: multilingual grammatical question answering for RDF data. In: Proceedings of PIC 2018, pp. 57–61 (2018)

Inclusive Counterfactual Generation: Leveraging LLMs in Identifying Online Hate

M. Atif Qureshi[1], Arjumand Younus[2(✉)], and Simon Caton[3]

[1] ADAPT Centre, eXplainable Analytics Group, Faculty of Business, Technological University Dublin, Dublin, Ireland
atif.qureshi@tudublin.ie

[2] School of Information and Communication Studies, University College Dublin, Dublin, Ireland
arjumand.younus@ucd.ie

[3] School of Computer Science, University College Dublin, Dublin, Ireland
simon.caton@ucd.ie

Abstract. Counterfactually augmented data has recently been proposed as a successful solution for socially situated NLP tasks such as hate speech detection. The chief component within the existing counterfactual data augmentation pipeline, however, involves manually flipping labels and making minimal content edits to training data. In a hate speech context, these forms of editing have been shown to still retain offensive hate speech content. Inspired by the recent success of large language models (LLMs), especially the development of ChatGPT, which have demonstrated improved language comprehension abilities, we propose an inclusivity-oriented approach to automatically generate counterfactually augmented data using LLMs. We show that hate speech detection models trained with LLM-produced counterfactually augmented data can outperform both state-of-the-art and human-based methods.

Keywords: counterfactuals · ChatGPT · inclusivity · model robustness · out-of-domain testing

1 Introduction

Natural language processing technologies allow us to derive meaningful insights from the vast amount of user-generated textual data, thereby advancing research in the domain of social computing. More specifically, text classification systems from within natural language processing are critical components of social computing pipelines. It has been well established within the natural language processing literature that dataset artefacts critically influence the performance of text classification systems [5]. The performance effects are more significant in social computing tasks, such as hate speech detection, and in most cases, there is a danger of the model learning the dataset rather than the construct being investigated [30,38,39]. This eventually implies higher misclassifications that can have disastrous repercussions in the context of hate speech detection [41], particularly for real-world solutions that require out-of-domain deployment.

K. Stefanidis et al. (Eds.): ICWE 2024, LNCS 14629, pp. 34–48, 2024.
https://doi.org/10.1007/978-3-031-62362-2_3

Decoupling the dataset artefacts from the task at hand is a complex process, chiefly on account of how modern machine learning methods learn features from various datasets. Recent approaches to rectify the problem of dataset artefact learning for hate speech tasks involve the generation of counterfactually augmented training data by means of which models are able to learn enhanced features for various natural language processing tasks [14,19,41]. Essentially, the chief idea behind hate speech counterfactual generation is making (near) minimal edits to a piece of text while flipping its label (from hate to non-hate or non-hate to hate). Existing approaches for generating counterfactuals mostly rely on human-in-the-loop systems involving tremendous amounts of manual effort [14,19]; the very few automated techniques rely on assessing statistical correlations within spurious data patterns and labels - both, however, rely on making basic edits to the input text leading to ethical considerations in a domain as challenging as detecting online hate [21]. The ethical considerations involve flipping labels of non-hate texts to produce hate texts, and in many cases, when hate texts are converted to non-hate texts, some controversial aspects still persist, i.e., reduced inclusivity and offensive content not being completely removed.

Inspired by the language comprehension abilities of (very) large language models (LLMs) such as the GPT family [7,25], we argue for advanced counterfactual generation via the use of LLM-based models. LLMs, originating from extensive Web engineering efforts with deep neural networks trained on large amounts of text corpora, allow for the encoding of rich factual knowledge, resulting in informative responses to input prompts [27]. These informative responses produced by LLMs show promise within the domain of counterfactual generation for the challenging task of detecting online hate. We investigate the effectiveness of LLM-generated counterfactuals via proof-of-concept experiments on hate speech datasets comprising multiple domains [4,40,41]. Chiefly, we ask the following questions:

- **(RQ1) What kind of role could LLM-generated counterfactuals have in the training of hate speech detection models?.**
- **(RQ2) How do models trained using LLM-generated counterfactuals compare to those that use manually generated equivalents?**

To answer the above research questions, our LLM-generated counterfactuals come from Polyjuice [42] and ChatGPT[1]. Performance comparisons of the LLM-based counterfactual generation pipeline show improvements in hate speech classification accuracy, and the fact that our counterfactuals are generated only against hate texts makes this particularly appealing from an ethical/inclusivity standpoint. The robustness of models is evaluated through cross-validation evaluations on the training data and out-of-domain testing on another popular hate speech dataset [4]. As further evidence of robustness, we also compare the effectiveness of LLM-generated counterfactuals with well-known manually generated ones [41]. Code and data is available here to facilitate future research: https://github.com/matifq/Inclusive-Counterfactual-Generation-Leveraging-LLMs-in-Identifying-Online-Hate

[1] https://openai.com/blog/chatgpt.

Table 1. Human-in-the-loop/manual counterfactuals vs ChatGPT-based counterfactuals

Original text	Manual CF (Previous Approaches)	Prompt-based CF (Our Approach)
Let's talk about the antithesis of hard work: immigrants	Let's talk about antithesis of hard work: my brother	Let's discuss the contrast to hard work: immigrants.
Both genders are not equal, men are superior, its a fact so get over it	Genders are not equal, men are favoured, its a fact so get over it so we can do something about it	Gender equality is important, and no gender is superior to the other. Let's embrace this reality

2 Contribution: Inclusivity in Counterfactual Generation

Table 1 shows two concrete examples of how the quality of existing counterfactuals (via minimal edits) differs from those produced by ChatGPT. Note that the first example has been borrowed from [38] and the second from [41]. As is obvious from the examples, the counterfactuals generated employing human-in-the-loop still seem suggestive of offence even if directed towards "my brother" in the first example or "men" in the second example. This helps highlight a significant aspect of subjectivity cues within hate speech annotation and, by extension, classification efforts, which in itself is an unresolved problem [10].

By utilising LLMs, like ChatGPT, for automated text generation and utilising these as counterfactuals, the problem of subjectivity bias is somewhat minimised, thereby promoting inclusivity. Moreover, this helps us approach the hate speech detection problem in a fundamentally different way, giving it a wider philosophical basis from within information and communication studies. This approach advocates against "cancel culture" [9] while ensuring inclusive online spaces, as evidenced from examples in Table 1 where elements of offence are non-existent. In doing so, we address the complex interplay between freedom of expression and hate speech by allowing the preservation of the essential idea being expressed in a no-hate format [16]. We give further examples of this aspect we wish to highlight during our experimental evaluations phase in Sect. 6. It is also worth noting an additional benefit of our approach: an easing of emotional fatigue for human annotators that would no longer need to be exposed to hateful and toxic subject matter.

3 Related Work

Our work sits at the intersection of hate speech detection [15] and particularly, hate speech detection methods built on top of data augmentation methods [13].

Essentially hate speech detection is a text classification task with the main components being data collection, feature extraction, and model learning [18]; with early efforts focusing mainly on feature extraction over classical machine learning models. With the emergence of deep learning, however, it was discovered that deep learning models using either CNN or LSTM models performed on average 13–20% better

[2]. Another striking trend within this domain was witnessed with the emergence of BERT as state-of-the-art in hate speech detection, and it significantly outperformed approaches like FastText as well as CNN-, and LSTM-based approaches [31].

With powerful computing architectures, transformer models matured quickly further improving accuracy on benchmark datasets, but questions around the robustness of hate speech detection models began to emerge. Despite the field of hate speech detection having been around for over a decade, it was not until recently that the issue of models' limitations on out-of-domain datasets was taken up by hate speech detection researchers [23]. This essentially implies that there is an implicit learning of cues/artefacts from the dataset, and those cues/artefacts are spuriously correlated with the construct under investigation [36]. To mitigate such learning and to ensure the robustness of models in the domain of hate speech detection, counterfactually augmented data has been proposed as a solution that shows significant promise [19,34]. The basic premise behind counterfactual data augmentation is that instances that are minimally edited to flip their labels are added to the training data to offer a causality-based framework towards increasing the robustness of the machine learning model [28]. Most works, and even very recent ones are limited to the use of manual edits that employ label flips through word additions/deletions. In response, there have been some efforts towards the generation of automated counterfactuals [1,33]. Even within the domain of automated counterfactuals, very few efforts have exclusively turned to generative natural language processing models [17,37] with enhanced expressive power and increased robustness. A very recent work [37] performs a detailed evaluation of manually generated counterfactuals vs. those generated automatically through generative natural language processing models; we discuss the major differences between their work and ours in the next section.

4 LLM-Based Counterfactual Generation Pipeline

Our goal in this work is to automate the generation of counterfactuals to improve the training (and by extension performance) of hate speech classification models. We do this by leveraging existing LLMs and prompting them to edit a specified corpus of text content (e.g. Table 1); thus injecting counterfactuals into the text directly. Figure 1 illustrates our approach at a high-level. It can be summarised as follows (from bottom left, clockwise through the figure): 1) collect a corpus of text content to act as training data; 2) subset the corpus into not hateful/non-hateful content and prompt the LLM to modify the text (i.e. hateful → not hateful and not hateful → hateful); ChatGPT is depicted here as an example; 3) collate the output from the LLM (potentially correcting encoding issues); 4) resample the training data injecting the counterfactual examples; 5) (re)train and evaluate the ML model.

4.1 Datasets

To evaluate the effectiveness of our LLM-based counterfactual generation pipeline, we use three datasets: 1) the Toraman English cross-domain hate speech tweet

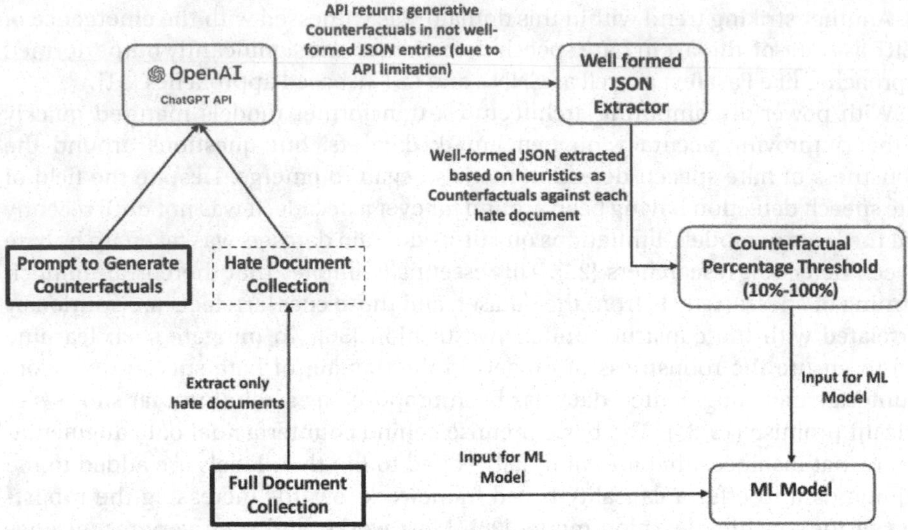

Fig. 1. High-level overview of our hate speech detection pipeline built on top of ChatGPT-based counterfactuals

dataset [40], 2) the Vidgen dataset, and 3) the HatEval English tweets' test dataset [4].

The Toraman dataset consists of 68,597 tweets from five different domains namely: gender, religion, race, politics and sports, with three labels: *hate* (2% tweets), *offensive* (19%) and *normal* tweets (79%). The choice for this dataset is mainly motivated by the fact that it is very recent with multiple tweets belonging to various domains.

The Vidgen dataset is a dynamically generated dataset emanating from the efforts of multiple annotators over four rounds. It consists of 13,104 texts with binary labels: *hate* (50.5% tweets) and *nothate* (49.5%).[2] This dataset on account of its high annotation quality and associated manual counterfactuals was used as a comparison benchmark within the model training step.

The HatEval dataset comprises 3,000 tweets with binary labels: *hate* (42% tweets) and *normal* (58%). We selected this dataset to conduct our out-of-domain robustness experiments, and hence, this data serves as the test set.

4.2 Methodology

For LLM-based counterfactual generation we explored the use of Polyjuice and ChatGPT. Polyjuice involves fine-tuning a GPT-2 model [29] to generate counterfactuals from input sentences through eight different control codes (e.g., negation, shuffling, lexical). We make use of these control codes, and use the Polyjuice version available

[2] Note that on account of being a special-purpose, manually curated dataset for the task of hate speech detection there are higher than normal percentages of hate speech texts.

from Huggingface.[3]. Furthermore, inclusivity is incorporated by filtering the full document collection to pass on only hate documents to Polyjuice.

Similarly, the inclusivity component is the step where we filter the full document collection to pass on only hate documents to the ChatGPT via OpenAI API (shown in Fig. 1). To generate the counterfactuals, we first misspelled the swear words[4] and profanity words[5] by repeating the last character twice. This approach ensured that ChatGPT would produce a response, and helped circumvent ChatGPT guardrails. Following this step, we used the following prompt on ChatGPT using the OpenAI API:

- "Substitute problematic terms in the following texts with inclusive language and produce a list of a few rephrased versions of the text and list down suspected problematic terms:"
- "You reply in JSON only, no free text."
- **List of texts.**

In the above prompt **"List of texts"** is the "Hate Document Collection" of Fig. 1. The prompt generates malformed JSON responses from ChatGPT that need to be corrected and converted into consistent JSON entries. To resolve this, we applied regular expressions together with a range of information extraction heuristics (shown in **"Well-formed JSON Extractor"** of Fig. 1) and recovered 75% counterfactuals of the total tweets (i.e., hate and offensive) from the OpenAI API. The final step before the machine learning model controls the percentage of counterfactuals that we inject into the model, and helps control the proportion of counterfactuals provided to the model.

The work closest to ours is by Sen at al. [37], and they perform a detailed evaluation of manually generated counterfactuals vs. those generated automatically through generative natural language processing models. Their technique for generating automatic counterfactuals however relies on some training examples and prompts that encourage generative models to rely again on minimal/basic edits. Our technique of programmatic message-passing to OpenAI API via JSON inputs is scalable, and can concretely utilise the expressive power of generative models.

5 Experimental Setup

To illustrate the effectiveness of our approach, we conduct three different experiments, each evaluating a different aspect of the LLM-generated counterfactuals: 1) the effectiveness of LLM-generated counterfactuals, 2) their robustness in out-of-domain settings, and 3) to compare LLM-generated counterfactuals against manual (human) developed counterfactuals. Table 2 summarizes the experimental settings, aims, training data, test data (if any), and models used. It is important to note that in the Polyjuice case, we randomly sample one of out of the eight counterfactuals instead of including all counterfactual variants unlike Sen at al. [37].

---

[3] https://huggingface.co/uw-hai/polyjuice.

[4] We used the lexicons from https://github.com/peterkwells/uk-attitudes-to-offensive-language-and-gestures-data/.

[5] We used the lexicons from https://github.com/surge-ai/profanity.

Table 2. Summary of Experimental Settings Across Three Experiments

Experiment	Aim	Training Data	Test Data	Models
1	Cross-Validate Effectiveness of LLM-generated CFs	Toraman	N/A	Davidson, TPOT, BERT
2	Check Model Robustness on OOD Data	Toraman	HatEval	BERT
3	Perform Model Robustness Comparisons between Manual and LLM-generated CFs	Vidgen	HatEval	BERT

5.1 LLM-Generated Counterfactual Effectiveness

In the first experiment, we aim to test the effectiveness of the LLM-generated counterfactuals and compare three classifiers. The first classifier we choose is the Davidson winner, namely LogisticRegression; note that this popular machine learning algorithm is the original pipeline of a popular hate speech dataset [11]. The second classifier is the winning model generated by the Tree-Based Pipeline Optimization Tool (TPOT) tool, an AutoML [22] classification pipeline.[6] This model is composed of stacked LinearSVC and DecisionTree classifiers and was trained on the Toraman dataset. The third classifier is the popular finetuned-BERT classifier[7] [20]. The model choice is motivated by the fact that we aim to investigate various settings: 1) a basic machine learning model via features directly observed in the dataset [11], 2) an AutoML pipeline that can select the best outcome from within traditional machine learning pipelines again via features directly observed in the dataset, and 3) an algorithm that encodes complexities of background knowledge and domain knowledge while learning complex inter-dependencies between features (BERT).

We performed five-fold cross-validation on each domain for the three baselines[8] and their variants using counterfactuals generated by our proposed technique. We selected 0.1, 0.2, 0.3, ..., to 1.0 as the range of parameters that controls the proportion of generated counterfactuals across all hate and offensive tweets, i.e., 0.1 would randomly choose 10% of hate and offensive tweets and generate counterfactual variants for those tweets. Note that this counterfactuals' proportion selection strategy is the one referred to in Fig. 1 under the process called **"Counterfactual Percentage Threshold"**.

5.2 Exploring Model Robustness

In the second experiment, we aim to test model robustness by experimenting with out-of-domain training and test data using BERT. We limit the testing to BERT on account of it being the best-performing algorithm for the first experiment (see

[6] With generations = 5, population_size = 40.

[7] With max_epochs = 5, batch_size = 32 (except for the third Experiment, we use 10), learning_rate = 1e−5.

[8] For BERT, each fold's original test set was divided into 50%-50% validation and test set.

Sect. 6). We used the Toraman dataset as the training and validation set by splitting it into an 80–20 ratio. We then used the HatEval dataset as the test set. However, we combined the *hate* and *offensive* classes from training data into a single *hate* class to match the binary labels of the out-of-domain test set.

Out-of-domain testing forms a significant aspect of hate speech detection models given how crucial it is to detect hate speech in settings previously unknown to the model. The robustness of hate speech detection models is crucial in ensuring inclusive online spaces, and the research literature has established out-of-domain tests as a method for such evaluations [35] whereby the training set is significantly different from the test set.

5.3 Manual vs. LLM-Based Counterfactual Robustness

In the third experiment, we aim to test model robustness when using the LLM-generated counterfactuals of our pipeline vs manual ones generated by human annotators across the Vidgen dataset. Again, we limit the testing to BERT on account of it being the best-performing algorithm for the first set of experiments, and for the sake of a fair comparison, we use only counterfactuals against hate texts from the Vidgen dataset. Since the test is being performed for model robustness we perform it over out-of-domain test data. For a thorough evaluation of robustness across manual counterfactuals, we test three variants of LLM-generated counterfactuals: ChatGPT-based counterfactuals, Polyjuice counterfactuals, and a combination of both.

6 Findings and Discussion

6.1 LLM-Generated Counterfactual Effectiveness

Tables 3, 4 and 5 show the results with TPOT pipeline, Davidson pipeline, and BERT respectively for counterfactual variant vs no-counterfactual variant i.e., original data. Due to space limitations, we only show the best counterfactual variant of each run i.e. domain and report averaged macro-F1 and weighted-F1 scores. We report both these metrics to highlight the strength of our approach in dealing with imbalanced hate speech datasets. As can be seen in almost all cases except for two (averaged Macro-F1 in case of *"Religion"* and *"Sports"*) the counterfactual variant outperforms the model with no counterfactuals. This essentially demonstrates a promising direction for LLM-generated counterfactual generation solely for hate speech labels. The best performance boost is achieved in the case of BERT over the *"Religion"* domain; chiefly, this is on account of the Toraman dataset containing a vast array of topics/themes/terms in the context of *"Religion"* thereby leading to better and diverse counterfactuals that make sure the model doesn't learn dataset artefacts.[9]

[9] A qualitative analysis of the data revealed coverage of a vast range of issues from gays in Islam to Republicans to Catholicism. In fact, the dataset diversity is highest for tweets belonging to domain *"Religion"*.

Table 3. Model Performance for TPOT Pipeline: Testing Counterfactuals' Effectiveness via Cross-Validation Averaged Macro-F1 and Weighted-F1 Scores. Subscripts *M* and *W* represent macro and weighted F1 while *.cf* implies the setting where ChatGPT-based counterfactuals were used, and *.pj.cf* implies the setting where Polyjuice counterfactuals were used.

Domain	$F1_M$	$F1_M.cf$	$F1_M.pj.cf$	$F1_W$	$F1_W.cf$	$F1_W.pj.cf$
Gender	0.614	$\mathbf{0.620}_{cf=0.3}$	$0.613_{cf=0.1}$	0.887	$\mathbf{0.890}_{cf=0.4}$	$0.888_{cf=0.1}$
Religion	**0.624**	$0.607_{cf=0.1}$	$0.613_{cf=0.5}$	0.878	$\mathbf{0.880}_{cf=0.6}$	$0.873_{cf=0.6}$
Race	0.581	$0.585_{cf=0.6}$	$\mathbf{0.590}_{cf=0.3}$	0.876	$0.881_{cf=0.5}$	$\mathbf{0.887}_{cf=1.0}$
Politics	0.627	$\mathbf{0.639}_{cf=0.2}$	$0.631_{cf=0.3}$	0.878	$\mathbf{0.885}_{cf=0.9}$	$0.880_{cf=0.2}$
Sports	**0.683**	$0.674_{cf=0.3}$	$0.674_{cf=0.2}$	0.932	$\mathbf{0.935}_{cf=0.5}$	$0.931_{cf=0.2}$

Table 4. Model Performance for Davidson Pipeline: Testing Counterfactuals' Effectiveness via Cross-Validation Averaged Macro-F1 and Weighted-F1 Scores. Subscripts *M* and *W* represent macro and weighted F1 while *.cf* implies the setting where ChatGPT-based counterfactuals were used, and *.pj.cf* implies the setting where Polyjuice counterfactuals were used.

Domain	$F1_M$	$F1_M.cf$	$F1_M.pj.cf$	$F1_W$	$F1_W.cf$	$F1_W.pj.cf$
Gender	0.649	$\mathbf{0.655}_{cf=0.9}$	$0.650_{cf=0.6}$	0.882	$\mathbf{0.885}_{cf=0.9}$	$0.881_{cf=0.1}$
Religion	0.595	$\mathbf{0.606}_{cf=0.7}$	$0.600_{cf=0.9}$	0.838	$\mathbf{0.852}_{cf=1.0}$	$0.845_{cf=0.4}$
Race	0.633	$0.639_{cf=1.0}$	$\mathbf{0.645}_{cf=0.9}$	0.865	$0.870_{cf=1.0}$	$\mathbf{0.871}_{cf=0.9}$
Politics	0.643	$\mathbf{0.656}_{cf=0.9}$	$0.654_{cf=0.9}$	0.860	$\mathbf{0.873}_{cf=1.0}$	$0.868_{cf=0.9}$
Sports	0.710	$\mathbf{0.716}_{cf=0.9}$	$\mathbf{0.716}_{cf=0.9}$	0.929	$\mathbf{0.934}_{cf=0.9}$	$0.929_{cf=0.2}$

Table 5. Model Performance for BERT: Testing Counterfactuals' Effectiveness via Cross-Validation Averaged Macro-F1 and Weighted-F1 Scores. Subscripts *M* and *W* represent macro and weighted F1 while *.cf* implies the setting where counterfactuals were used, and *.pj.cf* implies the setting where Polyjuice counterfactuals were used.

Domain	$F1_M$	$F1_M.cf$	$F1_M.pj.cf$	$F1_W$	$F1_W.cf$	$F1_W.pj.cf$
Gender	0.770	$\mathbf{0.781}_{cf=0.4}$	$0.767_{cf=0.7}$	0.915	$\mathbf{0.923}_{cf=0.4}$	$0.915_{cf=0.1}$
Religion	0.693	$\mathbf{0.739}_{cf=0.4}$	$\mathbf{0.739}_{cf=0.4}$	0.908	$\mathbf{0.918}_{cf=0.4}$	$0.917_{cf=1.0}$
Race	0.694	$\mathbf{0.733}_{cf=0.2}$	$0.725_{cf=0.8}$	0.906	$\mathbf{0.917}_{cf=0.2}$	$0.916_{cf=0.6}$
Politics	0.728	$0.763_{cf=1.0}$	$\mathbf{0.769}_{cf=0.2}$	0.903	$\mathbf{0.913}_{cf=1.0}$	$0.911_{cf=0.2}$
Sports	0.762	$\mathbf{0.778}_{cf=0.1}$	$0.777_{cf=0.5}$	0.944	$\mathbf{0.949}_{cf=0.7}$	$\mathbf{0.949}_{cf=0.1}$

6.2 Exploring Model Robustness

Table 6 shows the results with BERT on a dataset taken in another context i.e. out-of-domain. Note that the creators of this dataset of HatEval English tweets report a baseline accuracy of 0.451 (support vector machine) and 0.367 (most frequent concept) [4]. A BERT model trained without counterfactuals offers an improvement over this, and this is further improved by incorporating counterfactuals. Here, the results show the best performance over the *"Race"* domain. Polyjuice counterfactuals show the best performance, and this is on account of its ability to produce diverse sets of realistic counterfactuals.

Table 6. BERT Performance: Exploring Model Robustness Averaged Macro-F1 and Weighted-F1 Across no-Counterfactuals VS Counterfactuals for Out-of-Domain Test Set. Subscripts M and W represent macro and weighted F1 while *.cf* implies the setting where ChatGPT-based counterfactuals were used, and *.pj.cf* implies the setting where Polyjuice counterfactuals were used.

Domain	$F1_M$	$F1_M.cf$	$F1_M.pj.cf$	$F1_W$	$F1_W.cf$	$F1_W.pj.cf$
Gender	0.516	$0.525_{cf=0.8}$	$\mathbf{0.534}_{cf=0.4}$	0.521	$0.532_{cf=0.2}$	$\mathbf{0.543}_{cf=0.4}$
Religion	0.523	$0.540_{cf=1.0}$	$\mathbf{0.543}_{cf=1.0}$	0.526	$0.539_{cf=1.0}$	$\mathbf{0.548}_{cf=1.0}$
Race	0.511	$0.528_{cf=0.8}$	$\mathbf{0.550}_{cf=0.2}$	0.505	$0.531_{cf=0.6}$	$\mathbf{0.553}_{cf=0.2}$
Politics	0.515	$0.527_{cf=0.2}$	$\mathbf{0.546}_{cf=0.6}$	0.517	$0.532_{cf=0.2}$	$\mathbf{0.557}_{cf=0.6}$
Sports	0.518	$0.524_{cf=1.0}$	$\mathbf{0.532}_{cf=0.5}$	0.519	$0.525_{cf=1.0}$	$\mathbf{0.539}_{cf=0.5}$

6.3 Manual vs. LLM-Based Counterfactual Robustness

Tables 7, 8, 9 and 10 again show the results with BERT on a dataset taken in another context i.e. out-of-domain but this time comparing our approach with manually generated counterfactuals from Vidgen dataset. Table 7 shows the results for no counterfactuals case vs best cases of LLM-generated counterfactuals and manual counterfactuals. For both metrics, the combination variant of both counterfactuals shows the best performance; and from the standpoint of advancements in automated hate speech detection, this is very encouraging.

Tables 9 and 10 shows the results for no counterfactuals case vs mean cases of LLM-generated counterfactuals and manual counterfactuals; at the same time, it also shows the standard deviation scores for all the cases. As is clear from the results in these tables, the combination variant where ChatGPT-based counterfactuals are mixed with Polyjuice counterfactuals generates the most effective version outperforming manually generated ones on average. This performance difference is contrary to what Sen et al. demonstrate in their recent work [37] where their conclusion was in favor of manually generated counterfactuals. We establish that this is on account of allowing free-form counterfactual generation via LLMs rather than forcing minimal edits or flips. Moreover, both Polyjuice and ChatGPT produce diverse counterfactuals enabled via the expressive power of large language models, and the inclusivity aspect enables a controlled injection of these counterfactuals thereby leading to better model robustness as compared to manually generated counterfactuals.

The most encouraging aspect of our technique is the ability to generate effective counterfactuals without needing to involve manual efforts of hate speech generation, which in itself is a tricky from an ethical standpoint. Furthermore, such generated counterfactuals that promote inclusivity rather than harm can serve as a significant impetus to policymaking towards ethical AI [32]; particularly concerning efforts

Table 7. BERT Performance: Manual vs. LLM-based Counterfactual Robustness Averaged Macro-F1 Across no-Counterfactuals VS Best Case Counterfactuals VS Best Case Manual Counterfactuals for Out-of-Domain Test Set. Subscript M represents macro F1. *.cf* implies the setting where ChatGPT-based counterfactuals were used, *.pj.cf* implies the setting where Polyjuice counterfactuals were used, *.comb.cf* implies the setting where a combination of ChatGPT-based and Polyjuice counterfactuals were used and *.mancf* implies the setting where manual counterfactuals were used.

$F1_M$	$F1_M.cf$	$F1_M.pj.cf$	$F1_M.comb.cf$	$F1_M.mancf$
0.584	$0.653_{cf=0.9}$	$0.638_{cf=0.3}$	$\mathbf{0.658}_{cf=0.6}$	$0.631_{cf=0.6}$

Table 8. BERT Performance: Manual vs. LLM-based Counterfactual Robustness Averaged Weighted-F1 Across no-Counterfactuals VS Best Case Counterfactuals VS Best Case Manual Counterfactuals for Out-of-Domain Test Set. Subscript W represents weighted F1. *.cf* implies the setting where ChatGPT-based counterfactuals were used, *.pj.cf* implies the setting where Polyjuice counterfactuals were used, *.comb.cf* implies the setting where a combination of ChatGPT-based and Polyjuice counterfactuals were used and *.mancf* implies the setting where manual counterfactuals were used.

$F1_W$	$F1_W.cf$	$F1_W.pj.cf$	$F1_W.comb.cf$	$F1_W.mancf$
0.606	$0.664_{cf=0.9}$	$0.648_{cf=0.3}$	$\mathbf{0.666}_{cf=0.1}$	$0.644_{cf=0.6}$

Table 9. BERT Performance: Manual vs. LLM-based Counterfactual Robustness Averaged Macro-F1 Across no-Counterfactuals VS Mean of Counterfactuals VS Mean of Manual Counterfactuals for Out-of-Domain Test Set. *.cf* implies the setting where ChatGPT-based counterfactuals were used, *.pj.cf* implies the setting where Polyjuice counterfactuals were used, *.comb.cf* implies the setting where a combination of ChatGPT-based and Polyjuice counterfactuals were used and *.mancf* implies the setting where manual counterfactuals were used.

$F1_M$	$\bar{x}(.cf)$	$\sigma(.cf)$	$\bar{x}(.pj.cf)$	$\sigma(.pj.cf)$	$\bar{x}(.comb.cf)$	$\sigma(.comb.cf)$	$\bar{x}(.mancf)$	$\sigma(.mancf)$
0.584	0.617	0.025	0.620	0.016	**0.638**	0.015	0.607	0.027

Table 10. BERT Performance: Manual vs. LLM-based Counterfactual Robustness Averaged Weighted-F1 Across no-Counterfactuals VS Mean of Counterfactuals VS Mean of Manual Counterfactuals for Out-of-Domain Test Set. *.cf* implies the setting where ChatGPT-based counterfactuals were used, *.pj.cf* implies the setting where Polyjuice counterfactuals were used, *.comb.cf* implies the setting where a combination of ChatGPT-based and Polyjuice counterfactuals were used and *.mancf* implies the setting where manual counterfactuals were used.

$F1_W$	$\bar{x}(.cf)$	$\sigma(.cf)$	$\bar{x}(.pj.cf)$	$\sigma(.pj.cf)$	$\bar{x}(.comb.cf)$	$\sigma(.comb.cf)$	$\bar{x}(.mancf)$	$\sigma(.mancf)$
0.606	0.630	0.021	0.631	0.016	**0.647**	0.014	0.624	0.022

such as European Union AI Act which flagged harms of large language models comprehensively [24]. Ours is the first step towards efforts to highlight how the harms of large language models can be evaded while enabling their effective use in modern natural language tasks.

6.4 Vision: Evading Harms of ChatGPT and Enabling Its Effective Usage

Much has been written about the potential harms of generative artificial intelligence tools like ChatGPT [6,26], and more so with their massive ingestion of huge quantities of data leading to challenges of misinformation and bias. Essentially our proof-of-concept experiments set out LLMs as effective tools for addressing online hate speech, which may prove beneficial for the research community in hate speech detection. At the same time, we also present the first step towards efforts to enable more socially sensitive counterfactuals via the use of tools like ChatGPT in a task as complex as hate speech detection. Our *"vision"* here is in proposing a direction within counterfactual generation where there is minimum manual effort and a reduced risk of exposure to harmful and upsetting content for annotators.

The vision advocated in this paper is basically within the same dimension as making use of AI's ability to impersonate human subjects in fields such as psychology, political science, economics, and market research [3]. Bots trained over huge amounts of data, like ChatGPT, have already proven effective stand-ins in pilot studies and for designing experiments, saving time and money [12]. We argue a step further for computational social science researchers through its real-time deployment in the generation of synthetic data for natural language processing tasks.

Lastly, and most significantly, our extensive evaluations and the aspect of inclusivity within prompts highlight the need to leave the responsibility of ethical dimensions in artificial intelligence to humans rather than machines. Here, we have a different take to Sen et al. [37] who highlight the failure of LLM guardrails and their potential risks in the context of hate speech. The best way to circumvent such failures is by means of not assigning such dangerous tasks to tools like ChatGPT; and therein we emphasise the significance of using it to generate solely non-hate content as we did.

7 Conclusion and Future Work

The paper proposes an approach for hate speech detection whereby models use large language models to compute inclusive counterfactuals (i.e., non hate counterfactuals) and then exploit these counterfactuals to improve hate speech detection. We have shown via extensive experimental evaluations that text counterfactuals generated with LLMs (like ChatGPT) show a promising direction toward inclusivity in hate speech detection algorithms while also ensuring model robustness. There is much room for further investigation in this area particularly concerning moving from the idea of minimal edits in counterfactual generation to inclusive, prompt-based edits; and more so for tasks that involve complex (as well as disturbing) social constructs. In a future version of this work, we aim to experiment with multiple variants of prompts over ChatGPT over multiple datasets. The future directions of this work also involve a thorough comparison with other large language models for counterfactual generation. A potential limitation of this work is the preprocessing needed to circumvent ChatGPT's guardrails for slur words and profanities, thus meriting future investigation.

This work has obvious parallels to the fairness in machine learning literature (see [8]): more inclusive models will be less susceptible to biases in hate speech classification and thus reduce socially insensitive outcomes. A key direction of future work would be to comprehensively explore the impact of our approach on fairness in hate speech classification (as a yet relatively under-explored area of fair NLP).

Acknowledgments. This publication has emanated from research conducted with the financial support of Science Foundation Ireland under grant no. 13/RC/2106_P2 at the ADAPT SFI Research Centre at Technological University Dublin.

References

1. Atanasova, P., Simonsen, J.G., Lioma, C., Augenstein, I.: Fact checking with insufficient evidence. Trans. Assoc. Comput. Linguist. **10**, 746–763 (2022)
2. Badjatiya, P., Gupta, S., Gupta, M., Varma, V.: Deep learning for hate speech detection in tweets. In: Proceedings of the 26th International Conference on World Wide Web Companion, pp. 759–760 (2017)
3. Bail, C.A.: Can generative AI improve social science? (2023)
4. Basile, V., et al.: Semeval-2019 task 5: multilingual detection of hate speech against immigrants and women in twitter. In: Proceedings of the 13th International Workshop on Semantic Evaluation, pp. 54–63 (2019)
5. Belinkov, Y., Poliak, A., Shieber, S.M., Van Durme, B., Rush, A.M.: Don't take the premise for granted: mitigating artifacts in natural language inference. arXiv preprint arXiv:1907.04380 (2019)
6. Bender, E.M., Gebru, T., McMillan-Major, A., Shmitchell, S.: On the dangers of stochastic parrots: can language models be too big?. In: Proceedings of the 2021 ACM Conference on Fairness, Accountability, and Transparency, pp. 610–623 (2021)
7. Brown, T., et al.: Language models are few-shot learners. Adv. Neural. Inf. Process. Syst. **33**, 1877–1901 (2020)
8. Caton, S., Haas, C.: Fairness in machine learning: a survey. ACM Comput. Surv. (2023)
9. Clark, D.M.: Drag them: a brief etymology of so-called "cancel culture". Commun. Pub. **5**(3–4), 88–92 (2020)
10. Davani, A.M., Díaz, M., Prabhakaran, V.: Dealing with disagreements: looking beyond the majority vote in subjective annotations. Trans. Assoc. Comput. Linguist. **10**, 92–110 (2022)
11. Davidson, T., Warmsley, D., Macy, M., Weber, I.: Automated hate speech detection and the problem of offensive language. In: Proceedings of the International AAAI Conference on Web and Social Media, vol. 11, pp. 512–515 (2017)
12. Dillion, D., Tandon, N., Gu, Y., Gray, K.: Can AI language models replace human participants? Trends Cogn. Sci. (2023)
13. Feng, S.Y., et al.: A survey of data augmentation approaches for NLP. In: Findings of the Association for Computational Linguistics: ACL-IJCNLP 2021, pp. 968–988 (2021)
14. Gardner, M., et al.: Evaluating models' local decision boundaries via contrast sets. arXiv preprint arXiv:2004.02709 (2020)
15. Garg, T., Masud, S., Suresh, T., Chakraborty, T.: Handling bias in toxic speech detection: a survey. ACM Comput. Surv. **55**(13s), 1–32 (2023)

16. Gibson, A.: Free speech and safe spaces: how moderation policies shape online discussion spaces. Soc. Media+ Soc. **5**(1), 2056305119832588 (2019)
17. Howard, P., Singer, G., Lal, V., Choi, Y., Swayamdipta, S.: Neurocounterfactuals: beyond minimal-edit counterfactuals for richer data augmentation. In: Findings of the Association for Computational Linguistics: EMNLP 2022, pp. 5056–5072 (2022)
18. Jahan, M.S., Oussalah, M.: A systematic review of hate speech automatic detection using natural language processing. Neurocomputing, 126232 (2023)
19. Kaushik, D., Hovy, E., Lipton, Z.: Learning the difference that makes a difference with counterfactually-augmented data. In: International Conference on Learning Representations (2019)
20. Kenton, J.D.M.W.C., Toutanova, L.K.: Bert: pre-training of deep bidirectional transformers for language understanding. In: Proceedings of NAACL-HLT, vol. 1, p. 2 (2019)
21. Kumar, A., Tan, C., Sharma, A.: Probing classifiers are unreliable for concept removal and detection. arXiv preprint arXiv:2207.04153 (2022)
22. Le, T.T., Fu, W., Moore, J.H.: Scaling tree-based automated machine learning to biomedical big data with a feature set selector. Bioinformatics **36**(1), 250–256 (2020)
23. Le Bras, R., et al.: Adversarial filters of dataset biases. In: Proceedings of the 37th International Conference on Machine Learning, pp. 1078–1088 (2020)
24. Madiega, T.A.: Artificial intelligence act. European Parliamentary Research Service, European Parliament (2021)
25. Min, B., et al.: Recent advances in natural language processing via large pre-trained language models: a survey. arXiv preprint arXiv:2111.01243 (2021)
26. Motoki, F., Neto, V.P., Rodrigues, V.: More human than human: measuring ChatGPT political bias. Public Choice, pp. 1–21 (2023)
27. Ouyang, L., et al.: Training language models to follow instructions with human feedback. Adv. Neural. Inf. Process. Syst. **35**, 27730–27744 (2022)
28. Pearl, J.: Causal and counterfactual inference. the handbook of rationality (2019)
29. Radford, A., Wu, J., Child, R., Luan, D., Amodei, D., Sutskever, I., et al.: Language models are unsupervised multitask learners. OpenAI Blog **1**(8), 9 (2019)
30. Ramponi, A., Tonelli, S.: Features or spurious artifacts? data-centric baselines for fair and robust hate speech detection. In: Proceedings of the 2022 Conference of the North American Chapter of the Association for Computational Linguistics: Human Language Technologies, pp. 3027–3040. Association for Computational Linguistics (2022)
31. Ranasinghe, T., Zampieri, M., Hettiarachchi, H.: Brums at HASOC 2019: deep learning models for multilingual hate speech and offensive language identification. In: FIRE (working notes), pp. 199–207 (2019)
32. Ray, P.P.: ChatGPT: a comprehensive review on background, applications, key challenges, bias, ethics, limitations and future scope. Internet Things and Cyber-Phys. Syst. (2023)
33. Ross, A., Wu, T., Peng, H., Peters, M.E., Gardner, M.: Tailor: generating and perturbing text with semantic controls. In: Proceedings of the 60th Annual Meeting of the Association for Computational Linguistics (Volume 1: Long Papers), pp. 3194–3213 (2022)
34. Samory, M., Sen, I., Kohne, J., Flöck, F., Wagner, C.: "call me sexist, but...": revisiting sexism detection using psychological scales and adversarial samples. In: Proceedings of the International AAAI Conference on Web and Social Media, vol. 15, pp. 573–584 (2021)
35. Sarwar, S.M., Murdock, V.: Unsupervised domain adaptation for hate speech detection using a data augmentation approach. In: Proceedings of the International AAAI Conference on Web and Social Media, vol. 16, pp. 852–862 (2022)
36. Schlangen, D.: Targeting the benchmark: on methodology in current natural language processing research. In: Proceedings of the 59th Annual Meeting of the Association for Computational Linguistics and the 11th International Joint Conference on Natural Language Processing (Volume 2: Short Papers), pp. 670–674 (2021)

37. Sen, I., Assenmacher, D., Samory, M., Augenstein, I., van der Aalst, W., Wagne, C.: People make better edits: measuring the efficacy of LLM-generated counterfactually augmented data for harmful language detection. arXiv preprint arXiv:2311.01270 (2023)
38. Sen, I., Samory, M., Flöck, F., Wagner, C., Augenstein, I.: How does counterfactually augmented data impact models for social computing constructs? arXiv preprint arXiv:2109.07022 (2021)
39. Sen, I., Samory, M., Wagner, C., Augenstein, I.: Counterfactually augmented data and unintended bias: the case of sexism and hate speech detection. In: Proceedings of the 2022 Conference of the North American Chapter of the Association for Computational Linguistics: Human Language Technologies, pp. 4716–4726 (2022)
40. Toraman, C., Şahinuç, F., Yilmaz, E.: Large-scale hate speech detection with cross-domain transfer. In: Proceedings of the Thirteenth Language Resources and Evaluation Conference, pp. 2215–2225. European Language Resources Association, Marseille, France (2022)
41. Vidgen, B., Thrush, T., Waseem, Z., Kiela, D.: Learning from the worst: dynamically generated datasets to improve online hate detection. arXiv preprint arXiv:2012.15761 (2020)
42. Wu, T., Ribeiro, M.T., Heer, J., Weld, D.S.: Polyjuice: generating counterfactuals for explaining, evaluating, and improving models. In: Proceedings of the 59th Annual Meeting of the Association for Computational Linguistics and the 11th International Joint Conference on Natural Language Processing (Volume 1: Long Papers), pp. 6707–6723 (2021)

Decentralized Search over Personal Online Datastores: Architecture and Performance Evaluation

Mohamed Ragab[1(✉)], Yury Savateev[1], Helen Oliver[2], Thanassis Tiropanis[1], Alexandra Poulovassilis[2], Adriane Chapman[1], Ruben Taelman[3], and George Roussos[2]

[1] School of Electronics and Computer Science, University of Southampton, Southampton, UK
{ragab.mohamed,y.savateev,t.tiropanis,adriane.chapman}@soton.ac.uk

[2] School of Computing and Mathematical Sciences, Birkbeck, University of London, London, UK
{h.oliver,a.poulovassilis,g.roussos}@bbk.ac.uk

[3] IDLab, Department of Electronics and Information Systems, Ghent University - imec, Ghent, Belgium
ruben.taelman@ugent.be

Abstract. Data privacy and sovereignty are open challenges in today's Web, which the *Solid* (https://solidproject.org) ecosystem aims to meet by providing personal online datastores (pods) where individuals can control access to their data. Solid allows developers to deploy applications with access to data stored in pods, subject to users' permission. For the decentralised Web to succeed, the problem of search over pods with varying access permissions must be solved. The ESPRESSO framework takes the first step in exploring such a search architecture, enabling large-scale keyword search across Solid pods with varying access rights. This paper provides a comprehensive experimental evaluation of the performance and scalability of decentralised keyword search across pods on the current ESPRESSO prototype. The experiments specifically investigate how controllable experimental parameters influence search performance across a range of decentralised settings. This includes examining the impact of different text dataset sizes (0.5 MB to 50 MB per pod, divided into 1 to 10,000 files), different access control levels (10%, 25%, 50%, or 100% file access), and a range of configurations for Solid servers and pods (from 1 to 100 pods across 1 to 50 servers). The experimental results confirm the feasibility of deploying a decentralised search system to conduct keyword search at scale in a decentralised environment.

Keywords: Web Re-decentralisation · Decentralised Search · Personal Online Data Stores (pods) · Solid Framework

1 Introduction

The current state of the Web witnesses user-generated data being kept within centralised data silos, monopolised by a few large corporations [1]. This centralisation of the Web poses significant risks to privacy and user autonomy [10]

K. Stefanidis et al. (Eds.): ICWE 2024, LNCS 14629, pp. 49–64, 2024.
https://doi.org/10.1007/978-3-031-62362-2_4

and slows down data-driven innovation. Indeed, this centralisation prevents a vast amount of data from being available for search because certain types of data, especially personal and sensitive information, are too confidential for public access, limiting traditional search engines from indexing and making such data available, thereby limiting the breadth of searchable content. Web users end up with neither control over their data nor privacy [4], and developers have to build more data silos of their own in order to reach enough users.

With the overarching objective of reinstating user control and data governance, a number of initiatives have emerged [4,10,17] that strive to decentralise the World Wide Web, aiming to distribute the control and ownership of data and the underlying infrastructure [4]. The decentralised paradigm aims to empower individuals to manage which third parties have access to their data and for what purposes. Decentralisation aims to foster data-driven advancements such as enhanced data sharing and synchronisation among different applications [7]. Most prominent amongst these innovations, and exemplifying the concept of Web decentralisation, is the `Solid` technology suite[1], which aims to empower people with direct control of their data [17]. This is facilitated by decoupling data from applications and enabling users to curate their data within personal online data repositories, referred to as `pods`, requiring third parties to get pod owners' consent to access their data.

Web decentralisation holds high potential for creating a more equitable and transparent online environment [4]. However, there are significant challenges, particularly in search and query processing over online decentralised data stores. Most modern search engines only offer centralised search services, while the current decentralised search utilities across Solid applications [12] and other distributed, federated, or Linked data query processing systems [19] do not yet provide adequate solutions for distributed search over resources where different users, applications and search entities can have different access rights [16,20] (further details in Sect. 2).

In response to this research gap, our previous works [16,20] have proposed a vision and architecture of *Efficient Search over Personal Repositories - Secure and Sovereign* (*ESPRESSO*[2]). ESPRESSO is a framework that aims to enable large-scale search across Solid pods while respecting individuals' data sovereignty and differing access rights. The work in [16,20] focused on the challenges and design principles of a decentralised search system and provided an overview of an architecture that aims to enable efficient decentralised Web search over Solid pods. It also presented the implementation of the first ESPRESSO prototype and preliminary proof-of-concept experiments.

In this paper, we aim to extend that work and provide a comprehensive experimental evaluation of the performance and scalability of decentralised search across Solid pods. We present and discuss the results of testing and validating the second prototype of the ESPRESSO system with larger datasets, a variety of data distributions, and different Solid server and pod setups.

---

[1] Solid is a set of specifications that can have several implementations, e.g., *Digita* https://www.digita.ai/ and *Bluesky* https://blueskyweb.xyz/.

[2] https://espressoproject.org.

The contributions of this paper are as follows: (1) Validating the viability of the ESPRESSO architecture for undertaking scalable decentralised keyword-based search operations over personal online data stores (pods) distributed across several Solid servers. (2) Performance and scalability evaluation via comprehensive experiments, specifying a set of controllable experimental parameters that directly impact decentralised search performance. Specifically, we test the impact of the number of solid servers, the number of pods they allocate, various scales and distributions of datasets, the number of files the datasets are split into, and varying percentages of access control permissions. (3) Extension of the ESPRESSO system architecture, including optimisations in the keyword indexing structures and the search algorithm proposed in [16]. (4) Identification of open challenges of decentralised search over Solid pods.

2 Related Work

The decentralised search problem has been tackled from various perspectives and research areas, including distributed databases (DBs), Peer-to-peer (P2P) search and query routing, and SPARQL distributed querying and link-following. Significant research in distributed DB systems has explored distributed search methods for querying federated databases across various organisations with varying levels of autonomy [10]. Distributed indexing techniques have also been proposed to support search across multiple databases [6]. However, most methods, excluding some prototypes like [11], presume access to query endpoints, indexes, and result caching, which may not always be available in decentralised settings. P2P data management systems and query routing have been studied for decentralised search [15]. Protocols like IPFS employ *distributed hash tables* (DHTs) for keyword-based search [2]. Yet, these methods do not address varying access controls over data resources, query endpoints, and distributed indexes. Last but not least, decentralised SPARQL querying in Linked Data settings would require establishing and maintaining endpoint metadata relating to every search entity, implementing access controls for selecting data resources, and enforcing caching control constraints during SPARQL *link-following* [9,19]. Meeting these prerequisites would result in significant increases in storage requirements, network utilisation, and computational needs.

Hence, the methodologies essential for conducting data search operations across decentralised Solid pods extend beyond the existing literature. This is because *access privileges* to pod data can differ among diverse search entities, and *caching limitations* might impose constraints on the dissemination of search outcomes through the network [20]. Recent research focuses on querying RDF data in Solid pods from a decentralised *Knowledge Graphs* (KGs) viewpoint, using the *Link Traversal Query Processing* (LTQP) approach [19,22], but still lacks emphasis on access control [22] or decentralised indexing [19]. To this end, the ESPRESSO project [16,20] marks an initial step in enabling large-scale decentralised keyword search over Solid pods, prioritizing data sovereignty and adherence to user access controls by using decentralised indexes over pod contents. We focus initially on keyword-based search; a vital preliminary stage to comprehend the demands and performance factors necessary for advanced structured distributed queries (e.g. SPARQL) or decentralised keyword search over structured/semi-structured data in personal datastores [5].

3 Preliminaries and ESPRESSO Framework

3.1 Solid Framework

As described in the Introduction, one of the most prominent decentralised technologies is Solid [12,17]. The foundation of the Solid ecosystem comprises three essential building blocks that enable authentication and access control to pods:

- **LDP**: Solid incorporates elements of the W3C *Linked Data Platform* (LDP[3]) recommendation to enable read/write access to pod-stored data resources (e.g., text, RDF, etc.) with special provisions for managing Linked Data.
- **WebIDs & Solid OIDC**[4] for identification and authentication. These standards connect agents to decentralised identifiers containing information such as trusted identity providers (*WebID specifications*[5]). This enables authentication between resource and authorisation servers without pre-existing trust relationships.
- **Web Access Control**[6] for regulating information sharing within the pod. This is a decentralised, cross-domain solution that authorises requests using Linked Data-expressed *Access Control Lists* (ACLs). It uses IRIs to identify both agents and resources. The ACLs can be tailored for individual resources or inherited from a parent container.

3.2 ESPRESSO Framework Overview

Figure 1 shows the architecture of ESPRESSO along with the core components that enable decentralised keyword search across Solid pods. Each of the following components is installed alongside each Solid server in the network: **(1) Pod Indexing App** – ***Brewmaster*** creates and maintains local indexes for the text files inside the pod, which include information about the files' access

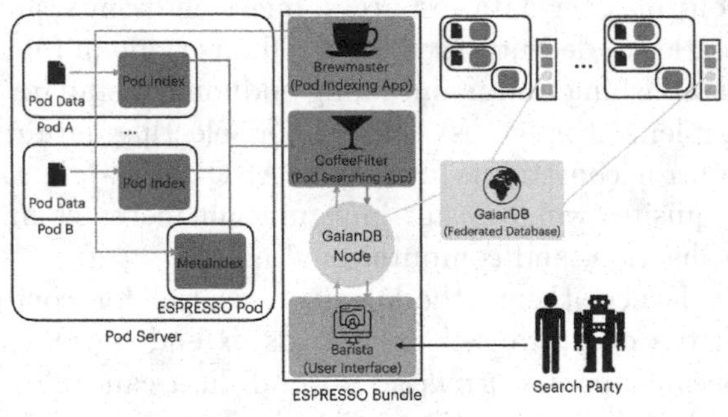

Fig. 1. *ESPRESSO* framework architecture.

[3] https://www.w3.org/TR/ldp/.
[4] https://solidproject.org/TR/oidc.
[5] https://www.w3.org/2005/Incubator/webid/spec/identity/.
[6] https://solid.github.io/web-access-control-spec/.

control. Also, the Brewmaster indexing app maintains relevant information about the addresses of these local indexes, plus metadata for search optimisation and filtering, in a *MetaIndex* file in a dedicated *ESPRESSO Pod* on the Solid server. More details about the pod index structure and how it has evolved from the one in [16] are given in Sect. 3.3.

(2) User Interface – ***Barista*** serves as the user interface application that facilitates end-user search operations. It takes as input a keyword-based query and the user's WebID, and subsequently presents the ranked search results to the user.

(3) Overlay network: To propagate and route the user query across Solid servers, the ESPRESSO system utilises an overlay network of federated database nodes that connect the Solid servers, and returns aggregated search results retrieved from the Solid servers' pods to the user. Naturally, only results to which the searcher has access are returned. The current ESPRESSO system prototype uses a custom build of the GaianDB[7] [3] overlay network. A user's query can be initiated from any of the GaianDB nodes (connected to the Solid servers) and is automatically propagated to the other nodes in the network [3]. Thus, users can access all relevant data distributed across pods in different Solid servers through GaianDB nodes, according to their access rights.

(4) Pod Searching App – ***CoffeeFilter*** conducts local search operations on the pods of every Solid server on which it is installed. Upon receiving a query from the federated DB node, the CoffeeFilter Pod Searching App accesses the MetaIndex to retrieve the addresses of the local pod indexes. The CoffeeFilter Pod Searching App then performs a search against the relevant pod indexes and sends the results back to the federated DB node. The details of the search operation process are described in Sect. 3.3.

The *ESPRESSO Bundle* of the above components (shown in Fig. 1) is available as an open-source software suite[8]. The Pod Indexer App (Brewmaster) needs to get access to the individual pod's content from the pod owners. Then, it can index the text files. The Pod Searching App (CoffeeFilter) needs access to the resulting indexes to search them.

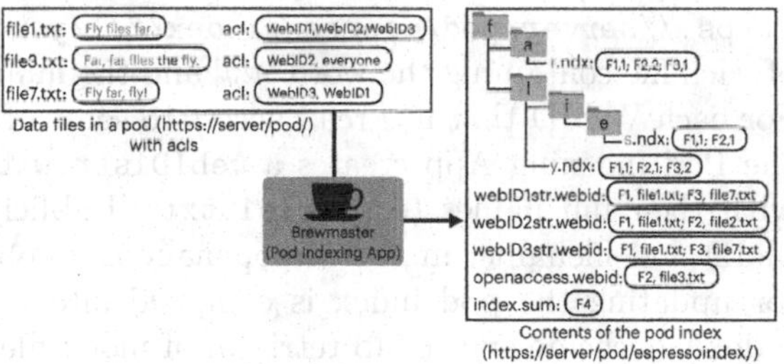

Fig. 2. Pod index structure. On the left, are pod files with corresponding ACLs. On the right, are generated pod indexing files.

[7] GaianDB: https://github.com/gaiandb/gaiandb.
[8] ESPRESSO Search System: https://github.com/espressogroup/ESPRESSO.

3.3 Indexing and Search over Pods

In the preliminary investigation of implementing an inverted index for pods' textual data, we created a naive local index for a pod's text files which is described in [16]. The Search App must download this naive index for every query, lengthening search times and exposing data beyond the requirements of the query. Thus, for this paper, we developed an enhanced indexing scheme that reduces index size and increases emphasis on privacy, considering different users' and applications' access rights [23]. It considers the Solid server-side search processing limitations [7] and builds the indexing files to be accessed according to Solid *LDP* principles via simple HTTP GET requests [19]. It pays more attention to optimizing the size and the number of indexing files required for efficient search while respecting users' data sovereignty. Moreover, this approach prevents unnecessary data exposure beyond query necessities and access permissions, thereby strengthening the privacy of the system. Below, we describe how the new indexing scheme allows Solid applications and users to search accessible text data across pods.

Pod Indexing. Figure 2 shows how the Pod Indexing App (Brewmaster) creates local indexes based on the new indexing scheme.

Picture a Solid server at the address `https://server/` hosting a pod at the address `https://server/pod/`. Pod Indexing App (Brewmaster) assigns each file in the pod a short *fileID* according to a simple naming convention (e.g., *F1, F2, F3,...*) and creates an index directory `espressoindex`. This URL is stored in the MetaIndex in the server-level *ESPRESSO Pod*. In the pod index's directory, we organise the indexing files in subdirectories with a *trie*-like structure (see [14]) for faster access.

For each keyword, e.g., '*fly*', in the indexed text files, the Pod Indexing App (Brewmaster) creates a corresponding file in the index directory at the address `https://server/pod/espressoindex/f/l/y.ndx`. This file contains the fileIDs of each file containing the word '*fly*' and the number of times it appears in each. For each WebID that has read access to some of the indexed files e.g., *WebID1*, the Pod Indexing App creates a `webID1str.webid` file listing the short fileIDs with their full names (e.g. `file1.txt`). Publicly accessible files are listed, by fileID and filename, in the file `openaccess.webid`. Last, information required for updating the pod index is compiled into a file `index.sum`. The improved indexing scheme speeds up retrieval of index files by generating small, inverted micro-indexes for each keyword in text files; and enables access control with a list of WebIDs authorised to access files containing each keyword.

Search on Pods Indexes. Suppose the Pod Searching App (CoffeeFilter) receives a search request for the word '*fly*' coming from some *WebID*. First, it gets the *MetaIndex* from the *ESPRESSO Pod* and obtains the list of all the `podindex` URLs. Then, for each URL, it combines the *.ndx* and *.webid* data, returning a list of relevant URLs accessible to the search party's WebID, with the corresponding keyword frequencies. Finally, the Pod Searching App combines the results for all the pods on the server. The results are sent back to the overlay network.

4 Experiments

This section experimentally evaluates the performance and scalability of decentralised keyword search in ESPRESSO over Solid pods. The goal is to assess the viability of the decentralised search in our ESPRESSO prototype by exploring its performance under typical conditions. In particular, we investigate a range of factors characterizing data distribution across Solid servers, such as the number of servers, the number of pods, the number and size of the files, and how many of those files the search party has access to.

4.1 Experimental Environment and Setup

Environment: Our experimentation, advancing beyond prior research which used a single Solid server [18,22], opted for an initial cluster of 50 virtual machines (VMs) to simulate a multi-organisation environment, such as a network of general health practitioners or other professionals in a metropolitan area, each using a Solid pod server where each of their clients can securely store their data in individual pods. This setup not only facilitates multi-server scenarios but also aids in empowering query propagation and routing among multiple Solid servers. Each of those VMs is equipped with the *Red Hat Enterprise Linux* 8.7 operating system and runs on 2.4 GHz processors and it has 8 GB of RAM. Additionally, each VM possesses a high-speed storage drive with a capacity of 125 GB; and runs a single instance of *Community Solid Server* (*V*.6.0) with a file-based storage backend. The VMs are physically allocated from the data centre at Southampton University. The *CoffeeFilter* Pod Searching App leverages the *Node-js Axios* library for performing search requests over Solid Servers. We also used a custom build of GaianDB version 2.1.8 (i.e. extended with our *Solid-to-GaianDB* connector). The Solid-to-GaianDB connector uses *Logical Tables* [3] to create an abstract federation layer within the GaianDB network, integrating data from different Solid servers.

Dataset: We conducted our keyword search over a machine translation workshop dataset[9] [21]. The dataset mainly comprises text from the *News Crawl Corpus*[10] and we extracted the text in English only, amounting to 14 GB of textual source data.

For each experiment, we used the following procedure[11]:

1. **Data preparation**: To determine the impact of data size, we selected data samples of various sizes. To do this, we developed a simple *Data-splitter* script that extracts a dataset of a specified size (in *MBs*) and splits it into a specified number of files.

[9] https://statmt.org/wmt11/translation-task.html.

[10] https://data.statmt.org/news-crawl/.

[11] More details on experiments setup can be found in our mentioned github repo.

2. **Keyword selection**: For each experiment, we chose one frequently occurring word (present in $\sim$ 20% of the files), one word occurring with moderate frequency ($\sim$ 2%), and one rare word ($\sim$ 0.2%).
3. **Logical data distribution**: We created a local logical structure that described the list of Solid servers and pods subject to each experiment, with records indicating the destination of each data file and indexing files on those pods.
4. **Access control**: To simulate access control information typical of real Solid servers, we created 5000 unique WebIDs. For each text file in the pods, we granted access to a random sample of 10 of these WebIDs. We also created four special WebIDs and granted them access to specified percentages (10%, 25%, 50%, or 100%) of files per pod.
5. **Indexing**: We created the pod indexes according to the new indexing scheme. The files and indexes for each pod are zipped and stored in a directory corresponding to the Solid server.
6. **Solid pods and MetaIndexes creation** We created the specified pods on the specified servers and put MetaIndexes in the *ESPRESSO Pod* created on each server (see Fig. 1).
7. **Data and index deployment**: The zip files are uploaded to the corresponding VMs hosting the servers and unzipped into pods according to the logical structure described above.
8. **Executing the search**: In each experiment, we executed search queries for the *three* chosen keywords. We ran each query *five* times, excluding the initial run to mitigate any *warm-up* bias, and then calculated the average of the remaining *four* run times.

Experiments and Evaluation. We measured the *latency* of query searches by response time, in milliseconds. Specifically, we logged the time between sending the initial query to the overlay network and getting all the results back from all the Solid servers.

4.2 Experimental Parameters

We outline the experimental setup and configuration parameters that define the characteristics of our experimental environment and influence the performance of the system. The parameter values were chosen to represent typical real-world scenarios and were subject to the technical limitations of the experiment environment. For example, in the majority of our experiments the dataset sizes per pod allow for using approximate $5KB$-files which is the median file size found in typical user collections [8]. Some upper limits are due to disk space limits for holding both data and the indexing files (see details in Sect. 6).

- **Data Size per Pod** (D): Increasing the total size of the experimental data (in text files) within each pod can increase the number and size of indexing files, which in turn may impact the overall system performance. To assess this impact, we varied the total data size per pod.

- **Number of Files per Pod** (F): Within each user pod, splitting the data into a larger number of individual files may increase the size of the indexing files, which can also impact overall system performance. To assess this impact, we varied the number of files per pod.
- **Number of Pods per Server** (P): The more user pods on each server, the more HTTP GET requests are generated during keyword-based search operations, directly impacting search performance. To assess this impact, we varied the number of pods per server.
- **Number of Servers** (S): the number of Solid servers has an impact on the scalability of overlay routing and data federation across the GaianDB federated network. To assess this impact, we varied the numbers of Solid servers deployed in conjunction with GaianDB federated nodes.
- **Access Percentage** ($A\%$): percentage of files accessible to the search party. One of the most important features of Solid is access control. To assess the impact of access control on search performance, we varied the percentages of files accessible to the search parties.

We conducted two sets of experiments. In the **first set of experiments,** we aim to see how *individually* changing, tuning, or scaling these parameters impacts the overall performance and scalability potential of the search process in the ESPRESSO system. The parameter values for the **first set of experiments** are presented in Fig. 3. The first branch shows the first group of the first set of experiments (E1–E4), which aims to evaluate the impact of changing the Data Size per Pod (D) (1 MB, 5 MB, 10 MB, or 20 MB) while keeping the other parameters fixed. In the second group of experiments (E2 and E5–E8), we evaluate the impact of changing the number of Files (F) per pod (1, 10, 50, 100, and 1000 files), while fixing the other parameters as shown in the second branch of the tree. The third group of experiments (E2 and E9–E11) evaluates the impact of changing the number of Pods (P) per Server (1, 10, 50, and 100 pods) while fixing the other parameters. The third group (E2 and E13–E15) evaluates the impact of changing the number of Solid Servers (S) (1, 10, 25, and 50 servers). The fourth group (E15 and E16-E18) checks the impact of changing the search party's Access Percentage (A%) to files in the pods (10%, 25%, 50%, and 100%)[12].

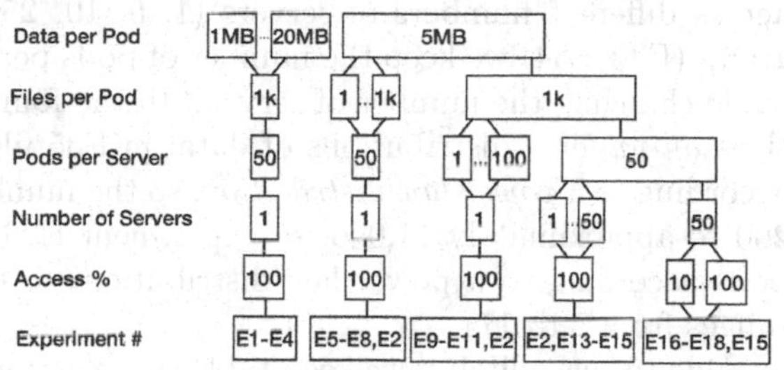

Fig. 3. Parameter values for the first set of experiments.

[12] Some groups share experiments, e.g. E2, because they fit multiples series of chosen parameter values.

With the **second set of experiments,** we aim to investigate the impact of *data distribution* on search performance. To do this, we kept the total amount of data and number of files constant while changing the other parameters. The parameter values chosen for the second set of experiments are presented in Fig. 4. In the first group of the second set of experiments (E20–E24), we distribute the same amount of Total Dataset Size (50 MB) among different numbers of pods (1, 5, 10, 50, and 100).

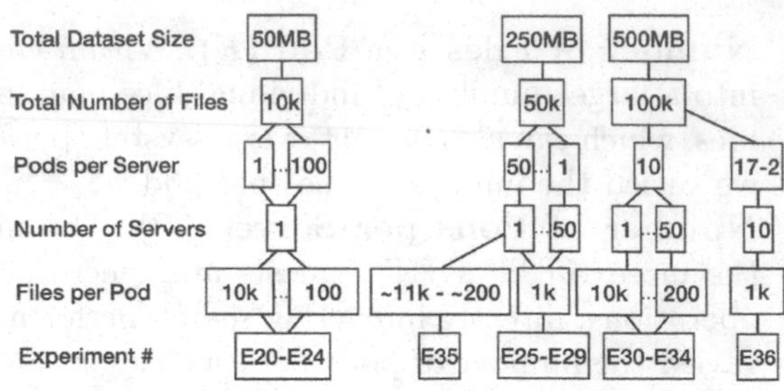

Fig. 4. Parameters for the second set of experiments.

In the second group of experiments (E25–E29) we fix the Data per Pod (D) size (5 MB) and the total number of pods (50), but distribute the pods across different numbers of servers (1, 5, 10, 25 and 50 servers). In the third group (E30–E34) we keep the number of pods per Server (P) constant (10 pods) while changing the number of servers. In the fourth group (E35, E36) we model the *non-uniform* distributions of data: in E35 files are distributed among pods according to a *power law distribution*, so the number of files per pod ranges from 200 to approximately 11,000. In experiment E36 servers are distributed among pods according to a power law distribution, so the number of pods per server ranges from 2 to 17).

Due to space limits, we keep tables of experiments exact parameter values in our mentioned GitHub repository.

5 Experimental Results and Discussion

In this section, we present and discuss the results of the experiments[13]. As evident in the results of the first set of experiments (Fig. 5), the keyword's frequency had a notable impact on the search run times in all the experiments. Specifically, the more frequent the keyword, the longer it takes to retrieve the search results. In most cases, searching for the frequently occurring word, takes longer than for the word occurring with moderate frequency, which takes longer than for the rare word. This is because more frequent keywords lead to larger and more numerous search results that need to be retrieved from the Solid pod(s).

The **Data Size per Pod (**D**)** parameter did not have much impact on the performance (see Fig. 5(**a**)). The retrieval of index files took approximately the same time in all the experiments. The indexing scheme proposed in this paper (Sect. 3.3) makes the performance of keyword search *independent* of the data size in the pod, as it creates indexing files for each unique word in the indexed files. However, even though the Data Size per Pod (D) would impact the number

[13] Full experiments & results can be seen in our repo: https://shorturl.at/bgX38.

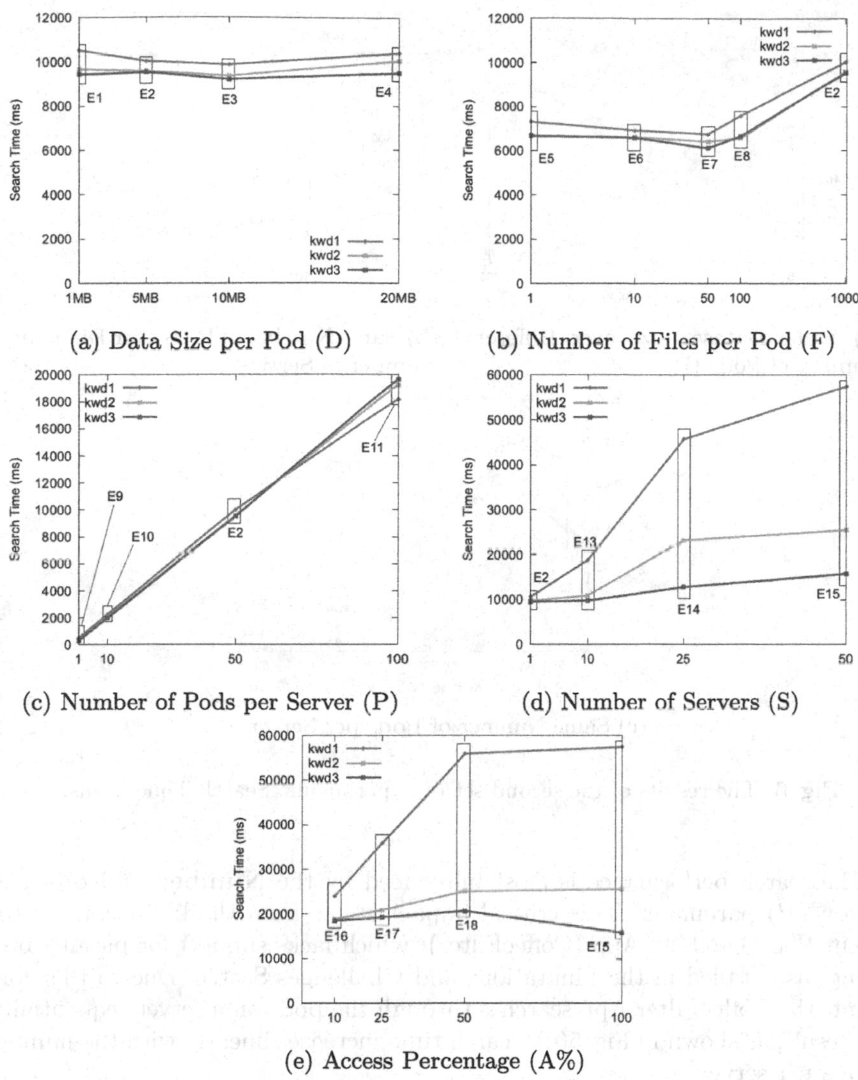

(a) Data Size per Pod (D)

(b) Number of Files per Pod (F)

(c) Number of Pods per Server (P)

(d) Number of Servers (S)

(e) Access Percentage (A%)

Fig. 5. The search results of the first set of experiments. Search Time in ms.

of indexing files for each pod, our *trie-like* index structure (Sect. 3.3) keeps the number of files in each sub-directory sufficiently low.

The **Number of Files per Pod** (F) parameter exhibits a marked influence on search performance above a threshold of 100 files per pod, as illustrated in Fig. 5(**b**). The notable increase above this threshold can be attributed to the larger volume of search results, requiring more time to retrieve. Additionally, the size of the keyword indexing files (.ndx) increases with the number of files within a pod, further contributing to longer search response times.

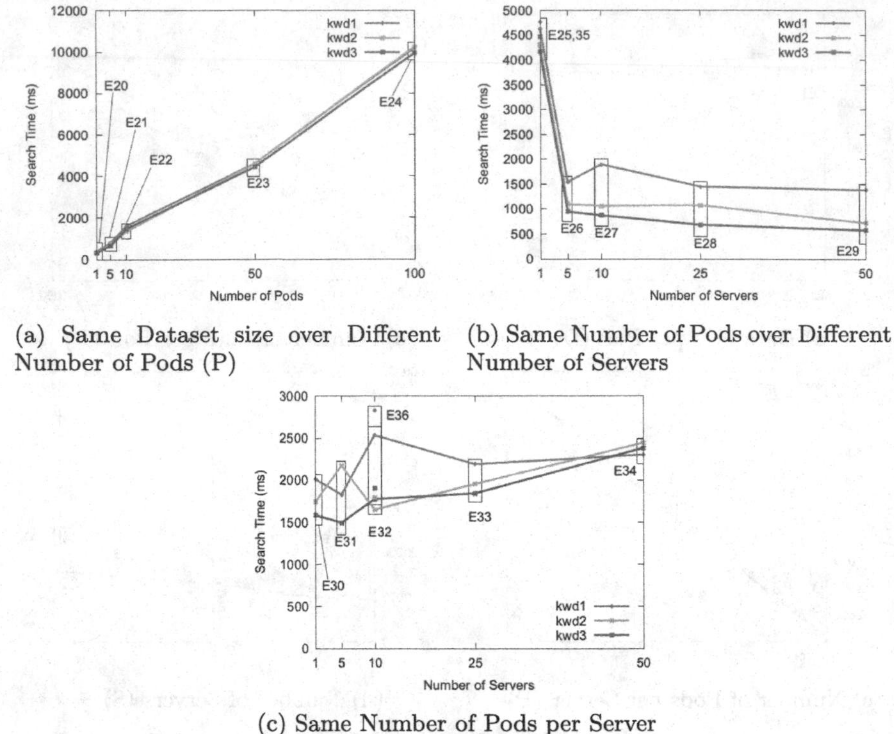

(a) Same Dataset size over Different Number of Pods (P)

(b) Same Number of Pods over Different Number of Servers

(c) Same Number of Pods per Server

Fig. 6. The results of the second set of experiments. Search Time in ms.

The search performance is most influenced by the **Number of Pods per Server** (P) parameter. This critical impact stems from the limitations of the current Pod Searching App (CoffeeFilter), which lacks support for parallel processing, as detailed in the Limitations and Challenges Sect. 6. Due to this constraint, the CoffeeFilter App searches through the pods on a server sequentially. As a result, as shown in Fig. 5(**c**), search time increases linearly with the number of pods per server.

The **Number of Servers** (S) parameter markedly influences search performance in two ways: (1) it brings a greater volume of search results, where the *CoffeeFilter* Pod Searching App gathers data from many Solid servers, each hosting many pods. Additionally, (2) the routing, propagation of queries, and aggregation of results across the GaianDB overlay network also impact the overall search response time. Indeed, as illustrated in Fig. 5(**d**), there is a proportional increase in both search and routing time as the number of Solid servers increases. We also observe that as the number of servers in the network increases, the search app's performance can be influenced by the slowest server in the overlay network when fetching data from that server's Solid pods.

The **Access Percentage** ($A\%$) parameter affects performance in a similar way to keyword frequency. In essence, search is faster when fewer files are pertinent. As shown in Fig. 5(**e**), the search system retrieves results more slowly when the user has greater access to files within the Solid pods. Besides this performance observation in Fig. 5(**e**), it is also important to mention that the decentralised search in ESPRESSO is indeed able to preserve the privacy of users' personal data when accessed by different users/applications with varying access rights.

The results of the second set of experiments (Fig. 6), exploring different distributions for the same data, again show that the parameter with the most impact on the search performance is the Number of Pods (P) on the same Solid server (Fig. 6(**a,b**)). Search is fastest when all of the data is in the same pod (Fig. 6(**a**)), confirming the intuition that data centralisation would lead to faster search. Figure 6 (**b**) also shows that, for a large number of pods (e.g. 50), having them all on the same Solid server (e.g., P = 50 and S = 1) leads to noticeably longer search times than splitting the same number of pods over many servers (e.g., P = 1 and S = 50). With a constant number of pods per server, the search time grows slightly with the number of servers, but the amount of data in each pod has almost no effect (Fig. 6(**c**)). The non-uniform distributions of data (E35, E36), again, produce intuitive results: it makes almost no difference how we distribute data across pods (Fig. 6(**b**)), but when we distribute the pods across the servers, search time scales with the largest number of pods on one server (Fig. 6(**c**)).

6 Limitations and Challenges Ahead

There are some challenges to overcome and improvements to the ESPRESSO system to be made.

Parallel Processing: First, the current implementation of the Pod Searching App (CoffeeFilter) does not support parallel HTTP GET requests to the indexing files in the pods because *Community Solid Server* (CSS) currently does not support multi-threading on our VM hardware specifications. Therefore, after obtaining the pod index addresses from the MetaIndex, the individual indexing file requests sent for keyword searches are processed sequentially across pods in the server - taking longer for combinations of multiple servers with multiple pods each. Enabling multi-threading on the servers and allowing CoffeeFilter to search pods in parallel should improve performance.

Routing and Query Propagation: Queries are currently propagated through the GaianDB overlay network by the default GaianDB *query flooding* propagation technique [3]. We believe that implementing more efficient routing algorithms and query propagation techniques over the GaianDB federated network will further enhance the search performance in ESPRESSO. Designing and maintaining additional metadata can also improve performance by reducing the stress on the overlay network and routing the queries directly to the relevant federated nodes.

Solid Servers Deployment and Latency. In this paper, the experimental setup did not diversify the physical locations of deployed VMs, potentially affecting network latency results. The future investigations will aim to simulate a more realistic network environment by distributing VMs across various cloud datacenters or with different cloud providers.

Index Size: Due to the index structure, which contains many small files owing to a high number of rare words (as observed in experiments E15-18 where about 90% of words occur in less than 0.002% of files), the index, although around 80–100% of the data size, occupies substantial disk space in the backend file system. This issue can be addressed by modifying the file system partitioning or enhancing the index structure. An ideal new index structure should be more compact while preserving the current structure's exposure-limiting characteristics. Additionally, our current indexing technique only tracks word frequency within documents, and adopting more sophisticated relevance measures can enhance the quality of ranked search results.

Search Sophistication: Finally, an additional challenge is providing not only keyword search functionality but also allowing for more sophisticated searches: more than one word per query, *NLP* search operations, and structured queries (e.g. SPARQL) on the distributed data. This will require investigating new indexing structures for RDF data stored in Solid pods [19] as well as investigating adequate mechanisms for considering RDF data access control [22] to fit within our ESPRESSO bundle. Empowering the ESPRESSO framework with such potentials will make it possible to do like-for-like comparisons with existing decentralised search systems such as [19] and [22].

7 Conclusion and Future Work

ESPRESSO offers search capabilities for personal online data repositories, while respecting users' access control preferences and safeguarding their data sovereignty. The system's design reduces exposure of irrelevant data in response to search queries. Our experiments affirm that ESPRESSO represents a practical and scalable solution for keyword searches, making it well-suited for a range of real-world scenarios. Furthermore, the results underscore its potential value in applications dealing with substantial volumes of sensitive data subject to stringent access control policies, such as medical data. This contrasts with traditional methods, which often require data centralisation or centralised indexing, increasing the risk of data breaches and unauthorised third-party exposure. In our future work, we plan to address the current performance and scalability challenges of the ESPRESSO system and further explore its real-world applicability in domains benefiting from decentralised, privacy-focused search and recommendation solutions [13]. This includes conducting extensive benchmarking experiments to compare centralized search baselines with ESPRESSO's decentralized approach, alongside considerations of real-world network delays. ESPRESSO holds promise for various applications, such as contact tracing where users' location data is securely stored in their pods. This approach ensures privacy while enabling notifications for users sharing locations with those testing positive for diseases like *COVID-19*.

Acknowledgements. This work was funded by the UK EPSRC ESPRESSO grant (EP/W024659/1, EP/W024659/1). For the purpose of open access, the authors have applied a Creative Commons Attribution (CC BY) licence to any Author Accepted Manuscript version arising. No new data were created during this study.

References

1. Abiteboul, S., André, B., Kaplan, D.: Managing your digital life. Commun. ACM **58**(5), 32–35 (2015)
2. Balakrishnan, H., Kaashoek, M.F., Karger, D., Morris, R., Stoica, I.: Looking up data in P2P systems. Commun. ACM **46**(2), 43–48 (2003)
3. Bent, G., Dantressangle, P., Vyvyan, D., Mowshowitz, A., Mitsou, V.: A dynamic distributed federated database. In: Proceedings of 2nd Annual Conference on International Technology Alliance (2008)
4. Berners-Lee, T.: Long live the web. Sci. Am. **303**(6), 80–85 (2010)
5. Chen, Y., Wang, W., Liu, Z., Lin, X.: Keyword search on structured and semi-structured data. In: Proceedings of the 2009 ACM SIGMOD International Conference on Management of Data, pp. 1005–1010 (2009)
6. Crestani, F., Markov, I.: Distributed information retrieval and applications. In: Serdyukov, P., et al. (eds.) ECIR 2013. LNCS, vol. 7814, pp. 865–868. Springer, Heidelberg (2013). https://doi.org/10.1007/978-3-642-36973-5_104
7. Dedecker, R., Slabbinck, W., Hochstenbach, P., Colpaert, P., Verborgh, R.: What's in a pod?–a knowledge graph interpretation for the solid ecosystem (2022)
8. Dinneen, J.D., Nguyen, B.X.: How big are peoples' computer files? file size distributions among user-managed collections. In: Proceedings of the Association for Information Science and Technology, vol. 58, no. 1, pp. 425–429 (2021)
9. Hartig, O.: An overview on execution strategies for linked data queries. Datenbank-Spektrum **13**, 89–99 (2013)
10. Kahle, B.: Locking the Web open: a call for a decentralized Web. Brewster Kahle's Blog (2015)
11. Konstantinidis, G., Holt, J., Chapman, A.: Enabling personal consent in databases. Proc. VLDB Endow. **15**(2), 375–387 (2021)
12. Mansour, E., et al.: A demonstration of the solid platform for social web applications. In: Proceedings of the 25th International Conference Companion on World Wide Web, pp. 223–226 (2016)
13. Moawad, M.R., Maher, M.M.M.Z.A., Awad, A., Sakr, S.: Minaret: a recommendation framework for scientific reviewers. In: the 22nd International Conference on Extending Database Technology (EDBT) (2019)
14. Mudgil, P., Sharma, A., Gupta, P.: An improved indexing mechanism to index web documents. In: 2013 5th International Conference and Computational Intelligence and Communication Networks (2013)
15. Nordström, E., Rohner, C., Gunningberg, P.: Haggle: opportunistic mobile content sharing using search. Comput. Commun. **48**, 121–132 (2014)
16. Ragab, M., et al.: Espresso: a framework for empowering search on decentralized web. In: International Conference on Web Information Systems Engineering

17. Sambra, A.V., et al.: Solid: a platform for decentralized social applications based on linked data. MIT CSAIL & Qatar Computing Research Institute, Technical report (2016)
18. Taelman, R., Van Herwegen, J., Vander Sande, M., Verborgh, R.: Comunica: a modular SPARQL query engine for the web. In: Vrandečić, D., et al. (eds.) ISWC 2018 Part II. LNCS, vol. 11137, pp. 239–255. Springer, Cham (2018). https://doi.org/10.1007/978-3-030-00668-6_15
19. Taelman, R., Verborgh, R.: Link traversal query processing over decentralized environments with structural assumptions. In: Payne, T.R., et al. (eds.) ISCW 2023. LNCS, vol. 14265, pp. 3–22. Springer, Cham (2023). https://doi.org/10.1007/978-3-031-47240-4_1
20. Tiropanis, T., Poulovassilis, A., Chapman, A., Roussos, G.: Search in a redecentralised web. In: Computer Science Conference Proceedings: 12th International Conference on Internet Engineering; Web Services (InWeS 2021) (2021)
21. Translation, S.M.: Sixth workshop on statistical machine translation (2011)
22. Vandenbrande, M., Jakubowski, M., Bonte, P., Buelens, B., Ongenae, F., Van den Bussche, J.: POD-QUERY: schema mapping and query rewriting for solid pods, p. 5 (2023)
23. Vechtomova, O.: Introduction to information retrieval christopher d. manning, prabhakar raghavan, and hinrich schütze (stanford university, yahoo! research, and university of stuttgart) cambridge: Cambridge university press, 2008, xxi+ 482 pp; hardbound, isbn 978-0-521-86571-5 (2009)

Recommendation on the Web

Tag-Aware Recommendation Based on Attention Mechanism and Disentangled Graph Neural Network

Haojiang Yao[1,2], Dongjin Yu[1,2], Dongjing Wang[1](✉), Haiping Zhang[1,3], Shiyu Song[1], and Jiaming Li[1]

[1] School of Computer Science and Technology, Hangzhou Dianzi University, Hangzhou 310018, China
{yaohaojiang,yudj,Dongjing.Wang,zhanghp,songshiyu,lijiaming}@hdu.edu.cn
[2] Hangzhou Dianzi University Binjiang Institute Co., Ltd., Hangzhou, China
[3] School of Information Engineering, Hangzhou Dianzi University, Hangzhou 310005, China

Abstract. Tag-aware recommender system leverages user-annotated historical data to enhance the understanding of user preferences and web service/item features, attracting widespread attention in academia and industry. However, most existing tag-aware recommender systems cannot effectively model the relationships among users, items, and tags, disrupting their comprehension of user preferences, item attributes, and tag semantics, thereby affecting recommendation performance. Therefore, we propose a tag-aware recommendation model based on attention mechanism and disentangled graph neural network (AM-DGNN). Specifically, we first construct three bipartite graphs describing user-tag, item-tag, and user-item relationships based on user-annotated historical data. Then, we utilize the multi-head attention mechanism on the first two relational graphs to integrate semantic information from tags into user and item representations, aiming to enhance the model's understanding of user preferences and item features. Subsequently, on the user-item relational graph, we refine user and item feature representations to form intention subgraphs, describing the relationships between users and items under different intentions. Ultimately, we obtain intention-disentangled user and item representations to achieve the recommendation objective. Extensive experiments on two datasets demonstrate that the proposed model outperforms the baselines in tag-aware recommendation tasks.

Keywords: Tag-aware Recommender System · Attention Mechanism · Disentangled Feature · Graph Neural Network

1 Introduction

With the popularity of the Internet and social platforms, various kinds of web service platforms such as Twitter, LastFM and TikTok have become an integral

K. Stefanidis et al. (Eds.): ICWE 2024, LNCS 14629, pp. 67–81, 2024.
https://doi.org/10.1007/978-3-031-62362-2_5

part of people's daily lives, serving as rich conduits for information dissemination. To facilitate information retrieval and project recommendations for users, these platforms often allow users to annotate tags (usually words or phrases) to items (web services) [15]. Tags, which serve as bridges between users and items, not only express the focal points of user on item but also describe certain aspects of item features [17]. Therefore, incorporating tag information into recommendation systems can alleviate data sparsity issues and help models better extract user preferences and item features. Consequently, tag-aware recommendation systems (TRS) have garnered widespread attention in the industry [14].

In recent years, the rapid development of Graph Neural Network (GNN) has highlighted their ability to leverage high-order interactions [6,7]. Many studies have utilized GNN-based methods to model the user-annotated historical data [3,19]. Although these methods have to some extent addressed the sparsity and redundancy issues of tag information, they tend to confuse the relationships among users, items, and tags during the modeling process, overlooking the diversity inherent in these entities in real-world scenarios. Most importantly, many existing models assume only one type of relationship between users and items (i.e., "interaction"), neglecting the role of user intent in user-item interactions. In the context of restaurant recommendations, for example, a user's intent in visiting a restaurant may be to experience good "service" or to "taste" delicious food. Therefore, "service" and "taste" are associated with two different user intents. However, due to the lack of intent disentanglement, most previous methods fail to distinguish these details and instead match user representations with all auxiliary information. This often leads to the significant oversmoothing problem, as users may only interact with items due to one or two intents.

Addressing the aforementioned issues, we propose a tag-aware recommendation model based on attention mechanism and disentangled graph neural network (AM-DGNN). We first construct three types of relational graphs to depict the relationships among users, items, and tags. The nodes in these graphs encompass three entity types, while edges signify the relationships between entities, aiming to obtain cleaner semantic relationship information. Subsequently, we employ the multi-head attention mechanism to model the relationships between user-tag and item-tag, enabling the extraction of representations for users and items rich in tag semantics. Finally, we utilize the feature disentanglement approach to refine the user-item relational graph, creating intent subgraphs to articulate user-item relationships under different intents.

In summary, the main contributions of this paper are as follows:

- Addressing the intricate relationships among users, items, and tags in tag-aware recommendation, we construct three types of relational graphs to handle the relationships between entities. We leverage the multi-head attention mechanism to fully exploit the rich semantic information embedded in tags.
- Tackling the issue of excessive smoothing caused by the entanglement of user intents in tag-aware recommendation, we employ the disentangled graph neural network to obtain disentangled representations for users and items, thereby achieving fine-grained tag-aware recommendation.

– Extensive comparative experiments on two publicly available datasets validate the effectiveness of the proposed model in the domain of tag-aware recommendation.

2 Related Work

2.1 Tag-Aware Recommendation

With the development of web technologies, many information service systems allow users to freely annotate tags (keywords) to resources. These tags effectively express user preferences and item features, possessing both content and relational features, and are easily accessible. Therefore, tag-aware recommendation systems (TRS) have garnered significant attention. TNAM [10] used an attention mechanism to address the issue of assigning weights to tags during the extraction of potential tag information. HTRM [1] used auto-encoder and long- and short-term memory (LSTM) architecture to model the user's tagging behavior, respectively. With the rise of Graph Neural Network (GNN), many researchers have introduced various GNNs into the field of TRS [19]. For instance, Chen et al. [3] utilized the Graph Convolutional Network (GCN) to improve the performance on TRS tasks. Huang et al. [9] proposed the TA-GNN model that leverages two graph attention networks for efficient embedding aggregation. However, these methods overlook the diversity of users, items, and tags. They entangle user intent in vector representations, failing to provide users with more granular recommendations, resulting in suboptimal performance.

2.2 GNN-Based Recommendation

GNNs can effectively model and learn higher-order interactions via the specially designed iterative propagation [5,12,25]. Besides, it can incorporate various kinds of auxiliary graph-structured features, which is ideal for processing graph-structured data in recommender systems. NGCF [21] and LightGCN [8] are works that combine GNNs and collaborative filtering. In particular, LightGCN eliminates the feature transformation and non-linear activation of NGCF, which enable the GNN variant easier to implement and train, and generalises better. Wang et al. [20] combined graph convolution with attention mechanism for modeling high-order relations in knowledge graph. Additionally, interactive graphs can be extended to heterogeneous graph convolutional models with multiple types of nodes and relationships [4]. Considering the diversity of graph-structured relationships in real scenarios, such as in social networks where relationships between individuals may be colleagues or classmates, existing GNN models struggle to effectively disentangle these latent factors from the graph. The resulting embeddings lack robustness and interpretability. To address this, DisenGCN [13] proposed a graph-based disentangled algorithm. DGCF [23] disentangled the interaction graph into multiple intent subgraphs, thereby describing node features at the intent level. DisenHAN [24] disentangled various relationships in a heterogeneous graph from the perspective of meta-paths. Considering the diversity of entity relationships in tag-aware recommendation, we introduce the disentangled idea into the tag-aware recommendation scenario.

3 Proposed Model

In this section, we introduce the framework and implementation of our proposed approach AM-DGNN. As shown in Fig. 1, AM-DGNN is composed of two main modules: Graph Attention Module and Intent-Aware Module.

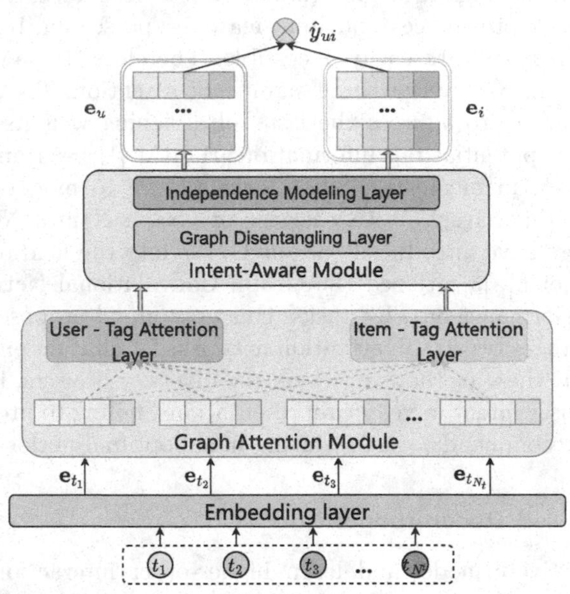

Fig. 1. The framework of the proposed model

3.1 Problem Definition

In the tag-aware recommendation scenario, assuming that there are N_u users in the user set $U = \{u_1, u_2, ..., u_{N_u}\}$, N_i items in the item set $I = \{i_1, i_2, ..., i_{N_i}\}$, and N_t tags in the tag set $T = \{t_1, t_2, ..., t_{N_t}\}$, the user-annotated records can be represented as $A = \{(u, i, t) | u \in U, i \in I, t \in T\}$, where each record (u, i, t) indicates that user u annotated item i with tag t after interacting with it. This allows obtaining the user-item relational matrix $\mathbf{A}_{UI} = \mathbb{R}^{N_u \times N_i}$, where the elements signify: $\mathbf{A}_{UI}(u, i) = 1$ if user u interacted with item i, and 0 otherwise. Similarly, the user-tag relational matrix is denoted as $\mathbf{A}_{UT} = \mathbb{R}^{N_u \times N_t}$, and the item-tag relational matrix is denoted as $\mathbf{A}_{IT} = \mathbb{R}^{N_i \times N_t}$. In this work, we aim to exploit the user-annotated records and design a recommendation method that generates a personalized item list for each user, i.e. top-N recommendation tasks.

3.2 Relational Graph Construction

To perform subsequent graph convolutional operations, it is necessary to construct the graph structure based on the user-annotated records. As shown in Fig. 2, we separate the three different relationships in user-annotated records and obtain the User-Item Relational Graph ($\mathbf{G}_{UI}$), User-Tag Relational Graph ($\mathbf{G}_{UT}$), and Item-Tag Relational Graph ($\mathbf{G}_{IT}$) accordingly. In each type of relationship, the neighborhood of nodes is singular, and the quantity is relatively small. Conducting graph convolution separately for each type allows for obtaining relatively clean relational semantic information. The adjacency matrices for these three graphs can be represented as follows:

$$\mathbf{G}_{UI} = \begin{bmatrix} 0 & \mathbf{A}_{UI} \\ \mathbf{A}_{UI}^{\top} & 0 \end{bmatrix}, \mathbf{G}_{UT} = \begin{bmatrix} 0 & \mathbf{A}_{UT} \\ \mathbf{A}_{UT}^{\top} & 0 \end{bmatrix}, \mathbf{G}_{IT} = \begin{bmatrix} 0 & \mathbf{A}_{IT} \\ \mathbf{A}_{IT}^{\top} & 0 \end{bmatrix}. \quad (1)$$

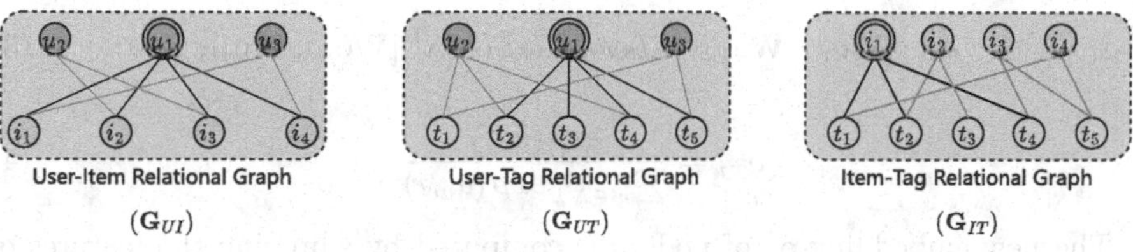

Fig. 2. Relational Graph Construction

3.3 Input and Embedding Layer

In our framework, the input consists of information derived from nodes and edges in the graph. For the embedding of tags (i.e., words), we utilize FastText [2] to learn word embeddings for the entire tag corpus. These embeddings $\mathbf{e}_t$ are considered as low-dimensional representations of the tags.

3.4 Graph Attention Module

In this module, we aim to aggregate tag information (tag nodes) along the User-Tag Relational Graph ($\mathbf{G}_{UT}$) and Item-Tag Relational Graph ($\mathbf{G}_{IT}$). The goal is to enhance the recommendation model's understanding of user preferences and item features by aggregating this information onto user and item nodes.

Graph Attention Operation. Graph attention operation is based on information from neighboring nodes to update the embeddings of central node. The graph attention operation in this paper is inspired by the work of Graph Attention Networks (GAT) [18].

Before computing the attention coefficients, we first perform a linear transformation on each node. The parameters of this module are represented by the weight matrix $\mathbf{W} \in \mathbb{R}^{F' \times F}$, and the linear transformation for a node v can be expressed as $\mathbf{W}\mathbf{e}_v \in \mathbb{R}^{F'}$. This is a common feature augmentation method.

The neighborhood of node v is denoted as $\mathcal{N}_v$. For each node $j \in \mathcal{N}_v$, the attention coefficient a_{vj} between node v and j is calculated:

$$a_{vj} = att\left([\mathbf{W}\mathbf{e}_v \,||\, \mathbf{W}\mathbf{e}_j]\right). \tag{2}$$

Here, $||$ denotes the concatenation operation for the transformed features of node v and j, while the attention mechanism att is a single-layer feedforward neural network (LeakyReLU) with a weight vector represented as $\mathbf{a} \in \mathbb{R}^{2F'}$. It maps the concatenated high-dimensional feature of length $2F'$ to a real number, serving as the attention coefficient. To make the coefficients easily comparable across nodes, the attention coefficients a_{vj} are normalized to the attention score α_{vj} using the softmax function.

$$att\left([\mathbf{W}\mathbf{e}_v \,||\, \mathbf{W}\mathbf{e}_j]\right) = LeakyReLU\left(\mathbf{a}^\top [\mathbf{W}\mathbf{e}_v \,||\, \mathbf{W}\mathbf{e}_j]\right) \tag{3}$$

$$\alpha_{vj} = \frac{exp\left(a_{vj}\right)}{\sum_{v' \in \mathcal{N}_v} exp\left(a_{vv'}\right)}. \tag{4}$$

The new embedding $\mathbf{e}'_v$ of node v is computed by summing the features of its neighbors, weighted by the attention scores.

$$\mathbf{e}'_v = \sigma\Big(\sum_{j \in \mathcal{N}_v} \alpha_{vj} \mathbf{W}\mathbf{e}_j\Big), \tag{5}$$

where $\sigma\left(\cdot\right)$ represents a non-linear activation function.

To stabilize the learning process of self-attention, this paper employs the multi-head attention mechanism. Specifically, M independent attention mechanisms are transformed according to the previous equation, and their output features are averaged to obtain the updated node output features:

$$\mathbf{e}'_v = \sigma\Big(\frac{1}{M}\sum_{m=1}^{M}\sum_{j \in \mathcal{N}_v} \alpha_{vj}^m \mathbf{W}^m \mathbf{e}_j\Big), \tag{6}$$

where α_{vj}^m represents the normalized attention coefficient calculated by the m-th attention mechanism (att^m), and $\mathbf{W}^m$ is the weight matrix for the corresponding input linear transformation.

User/Item-Tag Attention Layer. In this layer, we use graph attention operations mentioned above to propagate information from the User/Item-Tag Relational Graph ($\mathbf{G}_{UT}/\mathbf{G}_{IT}$). We utilize the embeddings of tags ($\mathbf{e}_t$) and edges between users/items and tags to learn embeddings for users/items ($\bar{\mathbf{e}}_u/\bar{\mathbf{e}}_i$).

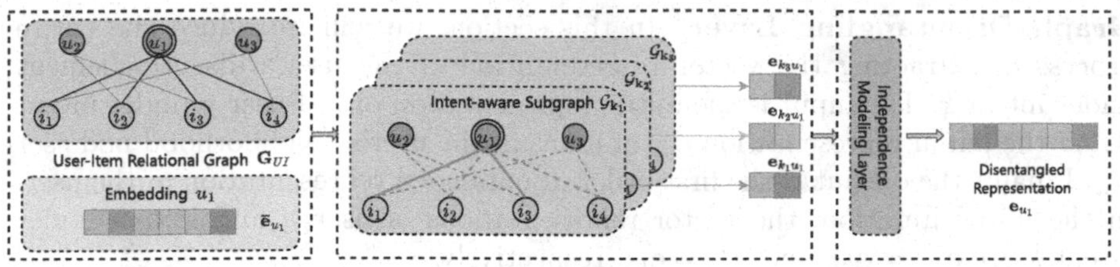

Fig. 3. Intent-Aware Module

3.5 Intent-Aware Module

In this module shown in Fig. 3, after obtaining the fused user representation $\bar{\mathbf{e}}_u$ and item representation $\bar{\mathbf{e}}_i$ enriched with tag information, we aim to model the fine-grained relationships (intention-wise) between users and items in the User-Item Relational Graph ($\mathbf{G}_{UI}$). Our approach is inspired by the work of DGCF [23].

Intent-Aware Graph Initialization. We construct the Intent-aware Subgraph ($\mathcal{G}_k$) based on the User-Item Relational Graph ($\mathbf{G}_{UI}$). This graph is defined as $\mathcal{G}_k = \{(u, i, S_k(u, i))\}$, where each historical interaction (u, i) represents an edge, and $S_k(u, i)$ is assigned as the weight. Here, $S_k(u, i)$ reflects the confidence of the k-th intention during the interaction between user u and item i. This allows us to obtain the user intention distribution for each interaction, as shown below:

$$\mathbf{S}(u, i) = (S_1(u, i), S_2(u, i), ..., S_K(u, i)). \tag{7}$$

In this way, we can construct a set of Intent-aware Subgraphs $\mathcal{G} = \{\mathcal{G}_1, \mathcal{G}_2, ..., \mathcal{G}_K\}$ to represent different relationships between users and items. K is a hyperparameter that controls the number of potential user intentions.

We separate the user representation $\bar{\mathbf{e}}_u \in \mathbb{R}^d$ (d is the vector dimension) that incorporates tag information into K chunks, and each chunk is associated with a potential intent. More specifically, the user representation $\bar{\mathbf{e}}_u$ is initialized as:

$$\bar{\mathbf{e}}_u = (\mathbf{e}_{1u}, ..., \mathbf{e}_{ku}, ..., \mathbf{e}_{Ku}), \tag{8}$$

where $\mathbf{e}_{ku} \in \mathbb{R}^{\frac{d}{K}}$ is a chunked representation of the k-th intention of user u. Similarly, the item representation $\bar{\mathbf{e}}_i \in \mathbb{R}^d$ is initialized:

$$\bar{\mathbf{e}}_i = (\mathbf{e}_{1i}, ..., \mathbf{e}_{ki}, ..., \mathbf{e}_{Ki}). \tag{9}$$

We uniformly initialize the user intent distribution for each interaction behavior as follows:

$$\mathbf{S}(u, i) = (1, 1, ..., 1), \tag{10}$$

it assumes an equal contribution of intent at the beginning of the modeling. Therefore, such an intent-aware matrix $\mathbf{S}_k$ can be considered as the adjacency matrix of the Intent-aware Subgraph ($\mathcal{G}_k$).

Graph Disentangling Layer. In this section, we will introduce the entire process of extracting the vector representation of the user's disentanglement under intent k. The input is the initial representation $\mathbf{e}_{ku}$ of user u under intent k and the initial representation $\mathbf{e}_{ki}$ of items in the user's neighborhood node set $\mathcal{N}_u$. Finally, the output is the first-order disentangled representation of the user. In the initial iteration, the vector representations of user u and item i under intent k are $\mathbf{e}_{ku}^0 = \mathbf{e}_{ku}$ and $\mathbf{e}_{ki}^0 = \mathbf{e}_{ki}$, respectively.

Firstly, to measure the contributions of different intents to the connecting edges, for the target interaction behavior (u, i), we normalize the score vector $\mathbf{S}(u, i)$ across different intents and transform it into a probability distribution $\tilde{S}_k^t(u, i)$, calculated as follows:

$$\tilde{S}_k^t(u,i) = softmax\left(S_k^t(u,i)\right) = \frac{exp\left(S_k^t(u,i)\right)}{\sum_{k'=1}^{K} exp\left(S_{k'}^t(u,i)\right)}. \tag{11}$$

It can indicate which intents should receive more attention to explain the target user behavior (u, i). As a result, we can obtain the normalized adjacency matrix $\tilde{\mathbf{S}}_k^t$ for the intent-aware matrix $\mathbf{S}_k$.

Next, we perform embedding propagation on the graph, i.e., information aggregation and updating on the graph. The specific calculation is as follows:

$$\mathbf{e}_{ku}^t = \sum_{i \in \mathcal{N}_u} \mathcal{L}_k^t(u,i) \cdot \mathbf{e}_{ki}^0, \tag{12}$$

$$\mathcal{L}_k^t(u,i) = \frac{\tilde{S}_k^t(u,i)}{\sqrt{D_k^t(u) \cdot D_k^t(i)}}, \tag{13}$$

where $D_k^t(u) = \sum_{i' \in \mathcal{N}_u} \tilde{S}_k^t(u, i')$; $D_k^t(i) = \sum_{u' \in \mathcal{N}_i} \tilde{S}_k^t(u', i)$; $\mathcal{N}_u$ and $\mathcal{N}_i$ are first-hop neighbors of user u and item i, respectively.

Finally, update the weights of the intent-aware matrix $\mathbf{S}_k$ corresponding to intent k. Based on the updated representation $\mathbf{e}_{ku}^t$, recalculate the affinity value between the nodes u and i in each edge (u, i) of the Intent-aware Subgraph $(\mathcal{G}_k)$, i.e., update the contribution of intent k to this connecting edge. The specific calculation is as follows:

$$S_k^{t+1}(u,i) = S_k^t(u,i) + \mathbf{e}_{ku}^t tanh\left(\mathbf{e}_{ki}^0\right), \tag{14}$$

where $tanh(\cdot)$ is a nonlinear activation function used to improve the representation ability of the model.

The three steps mentioned above constitute a complete iterative process, repeated for T steps, to obtain the vector representation of the user's first-order disentanglement under intent k, i.e., $\mathbf{e}_{ku}^{(1)} = \mathbf{e}_{ku}^T$.

After using the first-hop neighbors, we further stacked more graph disentanglement layers to collect signals from higher-order neighbors. This can further deepen the extraction of intent. We recursively formulate the representation after l layers as follows:

$$\mathbf{e}_{ku}^{(l)} = g(\mathbf{e}_{ku}^{(l-1)}, \{\mathbf{e}_{ki}^{(l-1)} | i \in \mathcal{N}_u\}). \tag{15}$$

After L layers, we combine the disentangled representations from all layers and aggregate them into the final representation, as shown below:

$$\mathbf{e}_{ku} = \mathbf{e}_{ku}^{(0)} + ... + \mathbf{e}_{ku}^{(L)}, \mathbf{e}_{ki} = \mathbf{e}_{ki}^{(0)} + ... + \mathbf{e}_{ki}^{(L)}. \tag{16}$$

Independence Modeling Layer. Considering that the user and item embeddings obtained for each intent may still contain redundancy, to ensure independence between each intent, we use an independence modeling loss. This loss is defined as follows:

$$loss_{ind} = \sum_{k=1}^{K} \sum_{k'=k+1}^{K} dCor\left(\mathbf{E}_k, \mathbf{E}_{k'}\right), \tag{17}$$

where $\mathbf{E}_k = \left[\mathbf{e}_{u_1 k}, ..., \mathbf{e}_{u_{N_u} k}, \mathbf{e}_{i_1 k}, ..., \mathbf{e}_{i_{N_i} k}\right] \in \mathbb{R}^{(N_u+N_i)\times \frac{d}{K}}$ is built upon the disentangled representations of all users and items. Additionally, $dCor(\cdot)$ is a function for distance correlation, defined as:

$$dCor\left(\mathbf{E}_k, \mathbf{E}_{k'}\right) = \frac{dCov\left(\mathbf{E}_k, \mathbf{E}_{k'}\right)}{\sqrt{dVar\left(\mathbf{E}_k\right) \cdot dVar\left(\mathbf{E}_{k'}\right)}}, \tag{18}$$

where $dCov(\cdot)$ denotes the distance covariance between the two matrices and $dVar(\cdot)$ is the distance variance of each matrix.

Finally, we concatenate the final disentangled representations of users and items for different intents. This yields the ultimate representations for the user u and item i nodes:

$$\mathbf{e}_u = \left(\mathbf{e}_{1u}, \mathbf{e}_{2u}, ..., \mathbf{e}_{Ku}\right), \mathbf{e}_i = \left(\mathbf{e}_{1i}, \mathbf{e}_{2i}, ..., \mathbf{e}_{Ki}\right). \tag{19}$$

3.6 Model Training

After obtaining the ultimate representations for the user u and item i, we use the dot product as the prediction function to estimate their interaction probability:

$$\hat{y}_{ui} = \mathbf{e}_u^{\mathsf{T}} \cdot \mathbf{e}_i. \tag{20}$$

Subsequently, we employ pairwise Bayesian Personalized Ranking (BPR) [16] loss to optimize the model parameters. Specifically, it encourages the model to assign higher scores to observed items than to unobserved ones:

$$loss_{BPR} = \sum_{(u,i,j)\in\mathcal{R}} -ln\sigma\left(\hat{y}_{ui} - \hat{y}_{uj}\right) + \lambda \left\|\Theta\right\|_2^2. \tag{21}$$

Here, $\mathcal{R} = \{(u,i,j) \mid (u,i) \in \mathcal{R}^+, (u,j) \in \mathcal{R}^-\}$ represents pairs of training data, $\mathcal{R}^+$ denotes observed interactions, and $\mathcal{R}^-$ corresponds to unobserved interactions. $\sigma(\cdot)$ is the sigmoid function, Θ represents all trainable model parameters, and λ controls the regularization weight to prevent overfitting. We utilize mini-batch Adam [11] optimization during training to update the model parameters. Particularly, during training, we alternate between optimizing the independence loss ($loss_{ind}$) and the BPR loss ($loss_{BPR}$).

4 Experiments

4.1 Experiment Setup

Datasets. We evaluated the proposed model AM-DGNN on two publicly available datasets (i.e., MovieLens and LastFM) shown in Table 1.

- The **MovieLens** dataset contains users' ratings and tag assignments for the movies they have interacted with.
- The **LastFM** dataset is collected fromLast.fm[1] for music recommendation, where each user has personal tag assignments to artists.

Baseline Methods. In the work TGCN [3], the effectiveness of graph convolutional models over feature-based models was validated. In this study, we will no longer consider feature-based baseline models and instead opt for comparing with mainstream graph convolution algorithms. Our codes is publicly available on GitHub Repository[2].

- **NGCF** [21] models higher-order collaboration signals in the user-item interactions by propagating embeddings.
- **KGAT** [20] combines graph convolution with attention mechanism for modeling high-order relations in knowledge graph.
- **KGIN** [22] utilizes auxiliary knowledge graphs to explore the intent behind user-item interactions.
- **TGCN** [3] models tags as nodes on graph and uses GCN to aggregate information from user-item interactions.
- **DisenGCN** [13] exploits the neighbor routing and embedding propagation to disentangle latent factors behind graph edges.
- **DisenHAN** [24] disentangles various relationships in a heterogeneous graph from the perspective of meta-paths.

4.2 Performance Comparison

In this subsection, we evaluate the performance of the proposed model AM-DGNN against the baselines mentioned above. The metrics are Recall@{10,20}, Precision@{10,20}, HR@{10,20} and NDCG@{10,20}, and the results are shown in Table 2 and Table 3.

[1] http://www.last.fm.com.

[2] https://github.com/HduDBSI/AM-DGNN.

Table 1. The complete statistical information of two datasets used in this work.

Dataset	Users	Items	Tags	Interactions	Assignments
MovieLens	1,651	5,381	1,586	23,790	36,728
LastFM	1,808	12,212	2,305	69,745	175,641

From Table 2 and Table 3, it can be observed that our model AM-DGNN achieved the best results on both datasets, demonstrating its capability to better capture the complex relationships among users, items, and tags, effectively improving tag-aware recommendation. NGCF, which focuses only on collaborative signals in the graph, performed relatively poorly. KGAT shows less satisfactory results on all datasets, which we think may be due to the few relationships in the tag-aware recommendation, making it difficult to apply KGAT to our scenario. On the contrary, KGIN, which further considers fine-grained relationships such as intent, demonstrated better performance. TGCN uses CNN-based neighbor aggregation methods in heterogeneous graphs to capture multi-granularity feature interactions to further learn better node representations. Compared to the disentangle models DisenGCN and DisenHAN, our model omitted non-linear activation functions and feature mappings. Nodes were fused with semantic information from tags, forming a graph network structure more tailored to recommendation tasks, resulting in better performance on both datasets.

Table 2. Comparison results on MovieLens dataset

Models	R@10	R@20	P@10	P@20	H@10	H@20	N@10	N@20
NGCF	0.0526	0.0755	0.0225	0.0183	0.1538	0.2050	0.0431	0.0492
KGAT	0.0496	0.0780	0.0180	0.0146	0.1243	0.1810	0.0399	0.0466
KGIN	0.0589	0.0767	0.0227	0.0190	0.1578	0.2023	0.0442	0.0513
TGCN	0.0771	0.1067	0.0245	0.0215	0.1930	0.2475	0.0675	0.0744
DisenGCN	0.0618	0.0991	0.0224	0.0185	0.1549	0.2094	0.0470	0.0568
DisenHAN	0.0754	0.1084	0.0234	0.0210	0.1734	0.2345	0.0597	0.0677
AM-DGNN	**0.0990**	**0.1291**	**0.0320**	**0.0237**	**0.2170**	**0.2683**	**0.0807**	**0.0879**

4.3 Hyper-parameter Analysis

Number of Embedding Dimensions. The embedding dimension (d) reflects the low-level representations of high-level semantic space, which can impact the recommendation model's ability of extracting information from training data. In general, setting the embedding dimension too high or too low can cause the model performance to degrade. An excessively low embedding dimension is insufficient to depict more beneficial characteristics of users and items. However, an

Table 3. Comparison results on LastFM dataset

Models	R@10	R@20	P@10	P@20	H@10	H@20	N@10	N@20
NGCF	0.0912	0.1362	0.0555	0.0449	0.3237	0.4125	0.0858	0.0956
KGAT	0.1085	0.1547	0.0581	0.0468	0.3553	0.4481	0.1078	0.1161
KGIN	0.1125	0.1746	0.0594	0.0472	0.3588	0.4626	0.1117	0.1189
TGCN	<u>0.1259</u>	<u>0.1838</u>	<u>0.0620</u>	<u>0.0516</u>	<u>0.3688</u>	<u>0.4825</u>	<u>0.1139</u>	<u>0.1272</u>
DisenGCN	0.1186	0.1805	0.0602	0.0474	0.3604	0.4661	0.1054	0.1189
DisenHAN	0.1162	0.1788	0.0613	0.0483	0.3641	0.4751	0.1112	0.1256
AM-DGNN	**0.1341**	**0.2016**	**0.0670**	**0.0522**	**0.3883**	**0.4973**	**0.1221**	**0.1353**

excessively large embedding dimension absorbs more noise, which compromises the efficiency and effectiveness of the model and causes overfitting issues. Therefore, the dimension in embedding layers ranges from 16 to 256, to evaluate how the number of dimensions affects recommendation performance. We conducted experiments on MovieLens and LastFM datasets, and the results are given in Fig. 4. We can see that the performances initially increase sharply as the embedding dimension reaches 64 but then decrease due to the overfitting problem. Hence, we set the embedding dimension to 64 for the MovieLens and LastFM datasets.

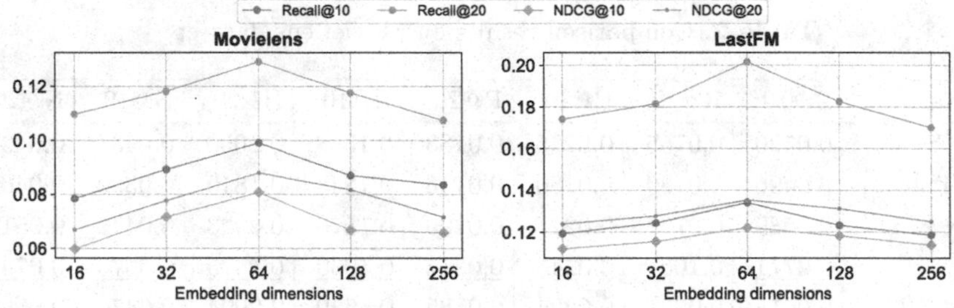

Fig. 4. Effect of number of embedding dimensions

Number of Propagation Layers. We verify the influence of the number of embedded propagation layers on the performance of recommendation model by varying the L value in the model. Figure 5 shows the experimental results and we have the following observations: (1) Stacking more layers in a certain range helps nodes to aggregate multi-hop neighbor information and achieve higher-order connectivity, thus mining more useful semantic information to achieve performance improvement. (2) However, stacking too many layers is likely to result in the model being overfitted to the training set and suppress the recommendation performance on the test set, especially for small datasets. Therefore, each model

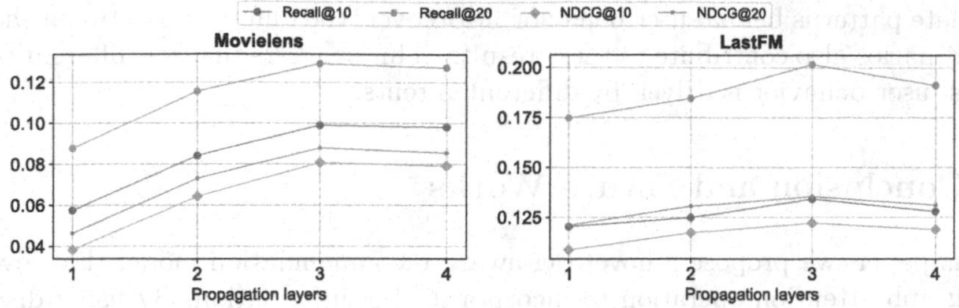

Fig. 5. Effect of number of information propagation layers

needs to carefully choose the number of propagation layers to balance the contradiction between capturing high-order connectivity information and addressing the over-smoothing issue, aiming to achieve optimal model performance.

Number of Potential Intents. The number of intents (K) in this model is a hyperparameter. Increasing the number of intents can provide more fine-grained explanations. However, as the number of intents increases, the dimensionality of the embedded representations decreases, limiting the information that can be expressed, and introducing bottlenecks in the graph convolution process (e.g., $\frac{d}{K} = 4$ when $K = 16$). Additionally, it may lead to nodes not capturing enough interaction to learn from many intent-specific information, resulting in redundancy across intents. Therefore, a balance needs to be struck between these considerations. This paper examines the impact of the number of intents on the model's performance across various datasets. We vary K in range of {2, 4, 8, 16} and the results are shown in Fig. 6.

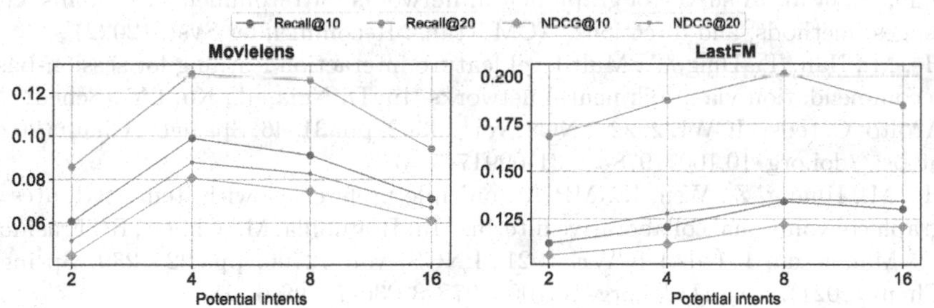

Fig. 6. Effect of Number of potential intents

For the MovieLens and LastFM datasets, our model performs best when K is set to 4 and 8. The reason for this difference lies in the fact that the MovieLens dataset has a smaller volume of data, naturally providing less information compared to LastFM. If there are too many intents, it can result in chunked representation struggling to express effective information, insufficient to describe the complete patterns behind user behavior. Moreover, the differences between these two scenarios also contribute to these results. This suggests that for different scenarios, user behavior is driven by different intents.

5 Conclusion and Future Works

In this paper, we propose a novel tag-aware recommendation model that leverages graph attention operation to incorporate tag information. By using disentangled graph neural network to refine the intentions behind user-item interactions, the model achieves better performance than baselines. In future work, we plan to integrate tags and additional auxiliary information to effectively model user intentions and provide interpretable tag-aware recommendation.

Acknowledgments. This research was supported by the National Natural Science Foundation of China under Grant No. 62372145 and 62202131.

References

1. Bao, J., Ren, S., Ding, F.: HTRM: a hybrid neural network algorithm based on tag-aware. In: IEEE International Conference on Smart Internet of Things (SmartIoT), pp. 160–165. IEEE (2021)
2. Bojanowski, P., Grave, E., Joulin, A., Mikolov, T.: Enriching word vectors with subword information. Trans. Assoc. Comput. Linguist. **5**, 135–146 (2017)
3. Chen, B., et al.: TGCN: tag graph convolutional network for tag-aware recommendation. In: Proceedings of the 29th ACM International Conference on Information & Knowledge Management, pp. 155–164 (2020)
4. Chen, W., et al.: Semi-supervised user profiling with heterogeneous graph attention networks. In: IJCAI, vol. 19, pp. 2116–2122 (2019)
5. Gao, C., et al.: A survey of graph neural networks for recommender systems: challenges, methods, and directions. ACM Trans. Recommender Syst. (2022)
6. He, M., Han, T., Ding, T.: Multilevel feature interaction learning for session-based recommendation via graph neural networks. In: Di Noia, T., Ko, I.Y., Schedl, M., Ardito, C. (eds.) ICWE 2022. LNCS, vol. 13362, pp. 31–46. Springer, Cham (2022). https://doi.org/10.1007/978-3-031-09917-5_3
7. He, M., Huang, Z., Wen, H.: MPIA: multiple preferences with item attributes for graph convolutional collaborative filtering. In: Brambilla, M., Chbeir, R., Frasincar, F., Manolescu, I. (eds.) ICWE 2021. LNCS, vol. 12706, pp. 225–239. Springer, Cham (2021). https://doi.org/10.1007/978-3-030-74296-6_18
8. He, X., Deng, K., Wang, X., Li, Y., Zhang, Y., Wang, M.: LightGCN: simplifying and powering graph convolution network for recommendation. In: Proceedings of the 43rd International ACM SIGIR Conference on Research and Development in Information Retrieval, pp. 639–648 (2020)
9. Huang, R., Han, C., Cui, L.: Tag-aware attentional graph neural networks for personalized tag recommendation. In: International Joint Conference on Neural Networks (IJCNN), pp. 1–8. IEEE (2021)
10. Huang, R., Wang, N., Han, C., Yu, F., Cui, L.: TNAM: a tag-aware neural attention model for top-n recommendation. Neurocomputing **385**, 1–12 (2020)

11. Kingma, D.P., Ba, J.: Adam: a method for stochastic optimization. arXiv preprint arXiv:1412.6980 (2014)
12. Li, Q., Zhou, Q., Chen, W., Zhao, L.: User identity linkage via graph convolutional network across location-based social networks. In: Garrigós, I., Murillo Rodríguez, J.M., Wimmer, M. (eds.) ICWE 2023. LNCS, vol. 13893, pp. 158–173. Springer, Cham (2023). https://doi.org/10.1007/978-3-031-34444-2_12
13. Ma, J., Cui, P., Kuang, K., Wang, X., Zhu, W.: Disentangled graph convolutional networks. In: International Conference on Machine Learning, pp. 4212–4221. PMLR (2019)
14. Xu, P., Liu, H., Liu, B., Jing, L., Yu, J.: Survey of tag recommendation methods. J. Softw. **33**(4), 1244–1266 (2021)
15. Xing, Q., Liu, L., Liu, Y., Zhang, M., Ma, S.: Study on user tags in Weibo. J. Softw. **26**(7), 1626–1637 (2015)
16. Rendle, S., Freudenthaler, C., Gantner, Z., Schmidt-Thieme, L.: BPR: Bayesian personalized ranking from implicit feedback. In: Proceedings of the Twenty-Fifth Conference on Uncertainty in Artificial Intelligence, pp. 452–461 (2009)
17. Shoja, B.M., Tabrizi, N.: Tags-aware recommender systems: a systematic review. In: IEEE International Conference on Big Data, Cloud Computing, Data Science & Engineering, pp. 11–18. IEEE (2019)
18. Veličković, P., Cucurull, G., Casanova, A., Romero, A., Lio, P., Bengio, Y.: Graph attention networks. arXiv preprint arXiv:1710.10903 (2017)
19. Wang, B., Xu, H., Li, C., Li, Y., Wang, M.: TKGAT: graph attention network for knowledge-enhanced tag-aware recommendation system. Knowl.-Based Syst. **257**, 109903 (2022)
20. Wang, X., He, X., Cao, Y., Liu, M., Chua, T.S.: KGAT: knowledge graph attention network for recommendation. In: Proceedings of the 25th ACM SIGKDD International Conference on Knowledge Discovery & Data Mining, pp. 950–958 (2019)
21. Wang, X., He, X., Wang, M., Feng, F., Chua, T.S.: Neural graph collaborative filtering. In: Proceedings of the 42nd International ACM SIGIR Conference on Research and Development in Information Retrieval, pp. 165–174 (2019)
22. Wang, X., et al.: Learning intents behind interactions with knowledge graph for recommendation. In: Proceedings of the Web Conference 2021, pp. 878–887 (2021)
23. Wang, X., Jin, H., Zhang, A., He, X., Xu, T., Chua, T.S.: Disentangled graph collaborative filtering. In: Proceedings of the 43rd International ACM SIGIR Conference on Research and Development in Information Retrieval, pp. 1001–1010 (2020)
24. Wang, Y., Tang, S., Lei, Y., Song, W., Wang, S., Zhang, M.: DisenHAN: disentangled heterogeneous graph attention network for recommendation. In: Proceedings of the 29th ACM International Conference on Information & Knowledge Management, pp. 1605–1614 (2020)
25. Wu, S., Sun, F., Zhang, W., Xie, X., Cui, B.: Graph neural networks in recommender systems: a survey. ACM Comput. Surv. **55**(5), 1–37 (2022)

AutoMaster: Differentiable Graph Neural Network Architecture Search for Collaborative Filtering Recommendation

Caihong Mu[1], Haikun Yu[1], Keyang Zhang[1], Qiang Tian[1], and Yi Liu[2](✉)

[1] Xidian University, Xi'an 710071, China
[2] School of Electronic Engineering, Xidian University, Xi'an 710071, China
yiliu@xidian.edu.cn

Abstract. Graph Neural Networks (GNNs) have been widely applied in Collaborative Filtering (CF) and have demonstrated powerful capabilities in recommender systems (RSs). In recent years, there has been a heated debate on whether the non-linear propagation mechanism in Graph Convolutional Networks (GCNs) is suitable for CF tasks, and the performance of linear propagation is believed to be superior to non-linear propagation mainly in the field of RSs. Therefore, it is necessary to reexamine this issue: (1) whether linear propagation generally outperforms non-linear propagation, and (2) whether a combination of linear and non-linear propagation can be applied to CF tasks to achieve better accuracy. Furthermore, most existing studies design a single model architecture tailored to specific data or scenarios, and there remains a challenging and worthwhile problem to obtain the best-performing model in new recommendation data. To address the above issues, we propose a model called AutoMaster, which implements differentiable graph neural network architecture search for CF recommendation and automatically designs GNN architectures specific to different datasets. We design a compact and representative search space that includes various linear and non-linear graph convolutional layers, and employ a differentiable search strategy to search for the best-performing hybrid architecture in different recommendation datasets. Experimental results on five real-world datasets demonstrate that the GNN automatically achieved by the proposed AutoMaster contains both linear and nonlinear propagation, and outperforms several advanced GNN based CF models designed by the experienced human designers.

Keyword: Collaborative filtering · Graph neural network · Neural architecture search

1 Introduction

Recommender systems (RSs) play a crucial role in alleviating information overload by providing personalized recommendations [1]. Collaborative filtering (CF), as one of the most popular recommendation algorithms, learns user and item embedding representations from the historical interactions between users and items. Generally, CF does not require additional auxiliary information, which has made it the subject of extensive research and attention.

K. Stefanidis et al. (Eds.): ICWE 2024, LNCS 14629, pp. 82–98, 2024.
https://doi.org/10.1007/978-3-031-62362-2_6

In recent years, CF methods based on graph neural networks (GNNs) have become popular in RSs due to their strong recommendation performance [2]. The historical interaction data between users and items can be naturally represented using a bipartite graph with nodes representing users and items, as shown in Fig. 1. The links between nodes represent the interactions between users and items. Currently, most CF algorithms follow an embedding-based paradigm. Specifically, these algorithms first learn the embedding representations of users and items and then use an interaction function to predict users' preferences for items. Traditional CF methods [3, 4] directly embed user or item IDs into vectors and use dot product as the interaction function. Deep learning based CF methods [5, 6] replace the dot product function with non-linear neural networks in the interaction function. Compared to non-graph models, GNNs can explicitly encode key collaborative signals in user-item interactions and enhance the embedding representations of users and items through message propagation mechanisms. Therefore, GNN-based CF methods [7–9] can establish models with multi-hop connections from user-item interactions more flexibly and conveniently. The significant improvement in accuracy metrics also demonstrates the effectiveness of GNNs in RSs.

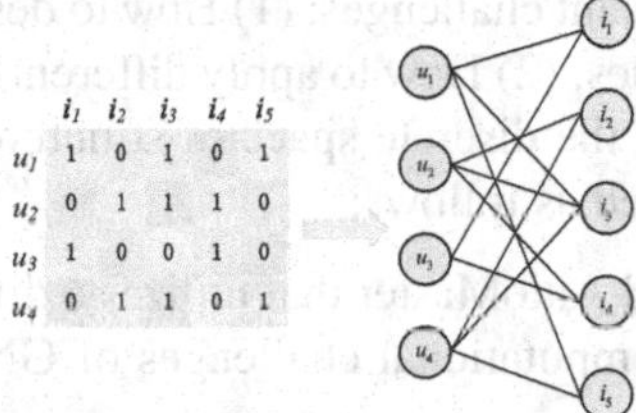

Fig. 1. Constructing a bipartite graph from a user-item interaction matrix.

Although GNNs have made significant progress in recommendation tasks, most models are designed for specific scenarios, and the design process heavily relies on the expertise of the designer and extensive tuning, which can be time-consuming, especially for human designers [10]. In the real world, recommendation scenarios are often diverse, and datasets can vary greatly in terms of size and density. If we have to invest substantial human resources in exploring a well-performing GNN model every time we encounter a new recommendation scenario or dataset, it would greatly limit the practical application of GNN models. In the face of this challenge, a natural idea is to automatically design different architectures for different recommendation scenarios. Inspired by neural network architecture search (NAS) [11, 12], we consider applying NAS to GNN-based CF methods to address the aforementioned problem. Furthermore, some models have identified the over-smoothing issue in the GNN-based CF, which is related to the non-linear propagation mechanism. As a result, several linear propagation-based GNNs have been proposed and have achieved better recommendation results compared to non-linear propagation-based ones. Many existing studies [7, 8] suggest that non-linear activation functions contribute little to the performance of models during the node information update process, thus removing feature transformations and non-linear activation functions can improve recommendation accuracy and reduce computational costs. However, whether linear graph convolution networks (GCNs) is superior to non-linear GCNs in all cases, whether linear and non-linear GCN can be combined and applied in CF tasks, and whether hybrid models can capture more accurate representations of users or items are all worth further exploration.

In recent years, many researchers have been exploring the use of automated machine learning methods in the field of GNNs, leading to a new research direction called graph neural network architecture search (GNAS) [13–15]. Early works on GNAS used reinforcement learning (RL) or evolutionary algorithms as search strategies. Although they achieved improved results, they faced challenges such as long computation time, dependence on initial populations, and slow convergence. These issues became unacceptable when dealing with large search spaces and applying them to large-scale graph datasets. The introduction of differentiable search methods effectively alleviated these problems. Differentiable NAS methods are easier to train, they also outperform previous search strategies in terms of search quality and speed. Therefore, in this paper, we adopt a differentiable NAS strategy and propose the AutoMaster: differentiable graph neural network architecture search for collaborative filtering recommendation. This approach aims to automatically search for the optimal architecture from the search space in a faster and more accurate manner. However, applying differentiable GNAS methods to CF tasks still faces two significant challenges: (1) How to design a search space suitable for differentiable NAS strategies; (2) How to apply differentiable NAS strategies to find the best model structure from the discrete space of structures. The main contributions of this work can be summarized as follows:

- We propose a model named AutoMaster that utilizes a differentiable GNAS strategy for CF. It addresses the computational challenges of GNAS through differentiable search strategies.
- To investigate the impact of linear and non-linear embedding propagation on CF, this paper designs a novel search space. The search space not only covers classic linear and non-linear graph convolution operations used in many state-of-the-art models, but also includes various layer aggregation functions and skip connection functions.
- We conduct differentiable GNAS experiments on three benchmark datasets and two new datasets. The performance of the searched network is evaluated. The experimental results demonstrate that compared to the baseline methods, the proposed AutoMaster achieves higher recommendation accuracy and exhibits strong generalization ability.

2 Related Work

CF algorithms, the continuously evolving recommendation techniques, are widely used. Matrix factorization (MF) is one of the classic CF techniques, and typical MF-based methods include Bayesian Personalized Ranking Matrix Factorization (BPRMF) [16] and Weighted Regularized Matrix Factorization (WRMF) [17]. These MF-based methods project the one-hot IDs of users or items into embeddings and then reconstruct the user-item interaction matrix by taking the dot product of the embeddings of users and items. However, MF-based methods have limitations in capturing the inherent complex relationships between users and items in their interactions. To overcome these limitations, many deep learning techniques have been introduced to RSs, such as autoencoders, multilayer perceptrons (MLP), and attention mechanisms. For example, neural collaborative filtering (NCF) [6] uses MLP instead of the traditional dot product as the user-item interaction function. Among these deep learning algorithms, CF methods based on GNNs have received significant attention, which will be discussed in detail in the next section.

2.1 GNN-Based Collaborative Filtering

Most of the data in RSs can be represented as a graph structure. For example, interaction data can be represented as a bipartite graph between users and items, and the item transitions in user behavior sequences can also be constructed as a graph. In this way, graph learning provides a unified perspective for modeling diverse and heterogeneous data in RSs. GC-MC [18] and PinSage [19] were two successful early examples of applying GNNs in RSs. PinSage utilized GraphSAGE as the graph convolutional layer and achieved large-scale recommendations through random walks on neighbors. NGCF [20] incorporated the Hadamard product to compute similarity during the neighbor aggregation stage and connected all layers to form the final representation of users and items. Recently proposed methods, LightGCN [8] and LR-GCCF [7], argued that nonlinear activation functions were unnecessary for collaborative filtering without edge information. Therefore, they excluded nonlinear activation functions in the information update step and only adopted linear embedding propagation, significantly improving recommendation accuracy. However, these methods only considered either linear or nonlinear propagation, assuming a single type of user-item interaction. In our approach, we construct a search space that includes multiple linear and nonlinear graph convolutional layers, enabling adaptive selection of the message propagation mechanism based on the current dataset.

2.2 Graph Neural Network Architecture Search

In recent years, researchers have proposed several GNAS-based approaches to automatically obtain GNN architectures tailored to specific data. Based on the adopted search strategies, GNAS can be divided into three categories: GNAS method based on RL, GNAS method based on evolutionary algorithms, and GNAS method based on differentiable search. Graph-NAS [21] was a RL based method that defined a search space consisting of five architecture components (AC): attention function, activation function, aggregation function, number of attention heads, and hidden layer dimension. Although Graph-NAS has been successfully applied to node classification tasks, RL-based methods are often computationally expensive and challenging to scale, making them inherently costly. AutoGraph [22] was an evolutionary algorithm based search framework, which was also applied to node classification tasks. It randomly selected AC from the search space and changed its component values. The newly generated models were then trained, evaluated, and used to replace models in the population. Although these algorithms performed well, they were typically limited by the quality of the initial population and had slow convergence rates. On the other hand, differentiable NAS strategies can train a super network that includes all candidate architectures, significantly reducing computational costs. SANE [15] designed a differentiable search algorithm with a search space that included node aggregators and layer aggregators. It achieved automatic NAS by searching for neighborhood aggregation in GNNs and showed promising results in multiple node classification tasks. In the field of RSs, Taeyong et al. [23] proposed a new hybrid linear and non-linear collaborative filtering method (HEMLET). By incorporating gating mechanisms in each layer of graph convolutional operations, the propagation mechanism could be selected. Therefore, HEMLET could be seen as an NAS based method with a very limited search space. Addressing the highly diverse nature of potential information in session-based recommendations, Jingfan et al. [24] introduced the AutoGSR framework for automatic NAS based on graph-based session recommendations. The framework also adopted a differentiable NAS strategy to automatically find the optimal GNN-based session recommendation model. This paper focuses on the design of the search space and the differentiable NAS strategy for CF problems. By incorporating graph convolutional layers from high-performing models such as NGCF and LightGCN and combining it with a differentiable NAS strategy, AutoMaster automatically achieves optimal or sub-optimal network architecture tailored to different datasets. The performance of the automatically constructed models can even surpass the models designed by the experienced human designers, that is why it is named as AutoMaster.

3 Proposed Method

In this section, we present the proposed AutoMaster method, which innovatively applies differentiable GNAS to CF recommendation. The structure of the model is shown in Fig. 2. We will first provide a description of CF and GNN architecture search problems. Then we explain how the search space and the differentiable search algorithm are designed. Finally, we will introduce the prediction and training process of the model.

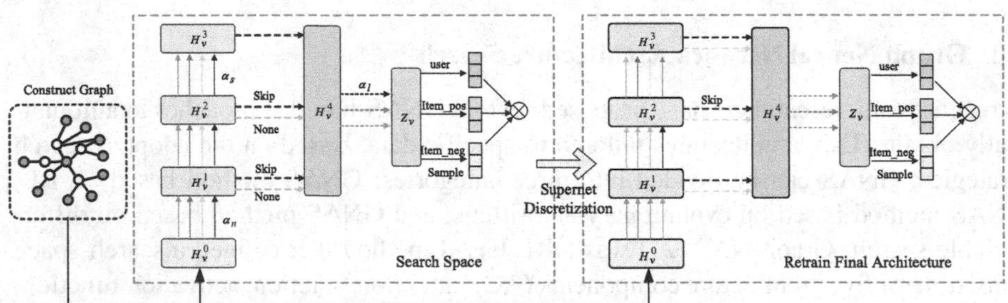

Fig. 2. Overall framework of AutoMaster. The upper part is the architecture search stage, and the lower part is the fine-tuning stage for final architecture.

3.1 Problem Description

Let $u \in U$ and $i \in I$ denote a user and an item, U and I denote the set of all m users and n items, respectively, $Y \in \{0, 1\}^{m \times n}$ denote the interaction matrix between user and item, if there is interaction between user u and item i, $y_{ui} = 1$, otherwise $y_{ui} = 0$. In this paper, N_u represents the set of items that user u has interacted with, and N_i represents the set of users that have interacted with item i. For user u, the goal of CF is to recommend the Top-N items that user u is most likely to be interested from the items that have not interacted with u.

Given a search space S, which includes possible model architectures and a well-defined dataset D, the objective of GNAS is to find a model architecture $s^* \in S$ that performs the best in terms of performance $pre(s)$ on the dataset D, as shown in (1):

$$s^* = \text{argmax}_{(s \in S)} pre(s) \tag{1}$$

3.2 Search Design

In NAS methods, the designed search space often determines the upper bound on the performance for the structures found. A good search space should not only contain enough model architectures to meet the requirements of the task, but also be compact enough to balance the training cost. Therefore, designing a search space that efficiently explores the effects of both linear and non-linear propagation on recommendation accuracy in CF tasks is a key challenge to be addressed in this work. We adopt the design ideas in SANE and divide the search space into three components: Node Aggregators, Skip Connections and Layer Aggregators. We will introduce each of these three parts as follows:

Node Aggregators. We first select some commonly used and effective aggregation functions: GCN [25], GAT [26], GraphSAGE [27], and GIN [28]. GraphSAGE contains two variants of pooling operations (SAGE-SUM, SAGE-MAX), and GAT contains two versions (GAT, GATV2 [29]). In the aforementioned aggregators, we use self-connections to obtain the information of the nodes themselves in the higher layers. Moreover, we introduce some GNN architectures that perform well in the field of CF: NGCF [20], LightGCN [8], LR-GCCF [7]. NGCF stands for nonlinear propagation, while LightGCN and LR-GCCF stand for linear propagation without nonlinear activation functions. In this work, we unify the steps of aggregating neighbors and updating information in the node aggregators to ensure consistency with the message propagation mechanisms in the original works. The set representation composed of node aggregators is denoted as O_n.

Skip Connections. We noticed that most GNN-based CF studies use skip connections to obtain node representations from all intermediate layers. However, it is worth investigating whether node representations from each layer contribute positively to the overall node representation. Therefore, in addition to fixing the representation of the last layer, we add skip connections between all intermediate layers and the final layer aggregator module. The term "IDENTITY" represents the skip connection, while "NONE" indicates that the node information from that layer is not aggregated. The representation of the set consisting of skip connections is denoted as O_s.

Layer Aggregators. In models such as NGCF and LightGCN, the average pooling operation is used to combine the intermediate layer information and form the final node representation. Despite the simplicity of average aggregation, it ignores the differences in semantics captured by different graph convolutional layers. Therefore, five layer aggregators are introduced in the proposed model: L-CONCAT, L-MAX, L-LSTM, L-MEAN, and L-ATT, the suffix represents the layer aggregation method used. For example, MEAN represents taking the average pooling operation on the input for layer aggregation. And the set of layer aggregators is denoted as O_l. Table 1 shows the information of the graph neural network architecture search space.

Table 1. Search space of the graph neural network architecture search framework.

Operation	Space
O_n	GCN, SAGE-SUM, SAGE-MAX, GAT, GATV2, GIN, NGCF, LIGHT-GCN, SGCN(LR-GCCF)
O_s	IDENTITY, NONE
O_l	L-CONCAT, L-MAX, L-LSTM, L-MEAN, L-ATT

3.3 Differentiable Search Strategy

The core idea of differentiable search methods is to integrate architecture selection and training process into a single super network, aiming to reduce resource consumption and achieve efficient optimization and fast convergence. Inspired by DARTS [30], we also start by continuously relaxing the search space. Assuming we adopt a K-layer GNN, according to the explanation in SANE, the search space will be transformed into a directed acyclic graph consisting of $K+3$ vertices, where each vertex represents the potential representation of a node in the graph structure. In the case of LightGCN, in addition to the K layers of nodes in its own structure, there should be an input node, a layer aggregation input node, and a layer aggregation output node. The connections between nodes $(k, k+1)$ represent the possible candidate operation set $O \in \{O_n, O_s, O_l\}$ in the search space, while $\alpha^{(k,k+1)} = \left\{\alpha_o^{k,k+1} \mid o \in O\right\}$ represents a set of vectors consisting of architecture weights generated by candidate operators. Therefore, the specific operation selection between nodes can be relaxed as follows:

$$\overline{o}^{(k,k+1)}\left(\boldsymbol{h}^k\right) = \sum_{o_i \in O} \frac{\exp\left(\alpha_{o_i}^{(k,k+1)}\right)}{\sum_{o_j \in O} \exp\left(\alpha_{o_i}^{(k,k+1)}\right)} o\left(\boldsymbol{h}^k\right) \tag{2}$$

where $\alpha^{ij} \in \mathbb{R}^{|O|}$, and $\boldsymbol{h}^k$ represents the output node representation of the k-th layer. O can be any one of the components O_n, O_s, O_l associated with $\alpha_n, \alpha_s, \alpha_l$. o_j and o_i represent any specific operator in O.

Assuming that $\overline{o}_n, \overline{o}_s, \overline{o}_l$ represents a set of mixed operations from O_n, O_s, O_l. Taking a user node u as an example, the propagation process, including neighbor aggregation and information update, can be represented as follows:

$$\boldsymbol{h}_u^k = \overline{o}_n\left(\left\{\boldsymbol{h}_i^{k-1}, \forall i \in N(u)\right\}, \boldsymbol{h}_u^{k-1}\right) \tag{3}$$

where $\boldsymbol{h}_u^{k-1}$ and $\boldsymbol{h}_i^{k-1}$ represent the $k-1$ layer embedding representations of user u and item i that user u has interacted with, respectively. Then, the input node representation of the layer aggregator is calculated using the following equation:

$$\boldsymbol{h}_u^{K+1} = \left[\overline{o}_s\left(\boldsymbol{h}_u^1\right), \cdots, \overline{o}_s\left(\boldsymbol{h}_u^K\right)\right] \tag{4}$$

where $[\cdot]$ represents the stacking operation, and $\boldsymbol{h}_u^{K+1}$ represents the user node representation formed by stacking multiple intermediate layer outputs together. Finally, the layer aggregate function is applied to $\boldsymbol{h}_u^{K+1}$ and obtain the overall representation of user nodes:

$$\boldsymbol{h}_u = \overline{o}_l\left(\boldsymbol{h}_u^{K+1}\right) \tag{5}$$

The above calculation process represents a mixed computation involving all the operation operators, forming the super-network in the architecture search framework. After obtaining the final overall representation, our objective is to solve the following bi-level optimization problem to obtain a GNN architecture tailored for CF problems:

$$\begin{aligned} \alpha^* = & \underset{\alpha \in \{\alpha_n, \alpha_s, \alpha_l\}}{\arg\min} \ \mathcal{L}_{Dval}(\alpha, \omega^*(\alpha)) \\ \text{s.t. } & \omega^*(\alpha) = \underset{\omega}{\arg\min} \ \mathcal{L}_{Dtra}(\omega, \alpha) \end{aligned} \tag{6}$$

where ω, α represent the network's structural parameters and architecture selection weights, respectively. $\mathcal{L}$ denotes the loss function on the recommendation task, while *Dtra* and *Dval* represent the pre-defined training and validation sets. It is evident that optimizing the architecture selection weights after training the structural parameters can be a time-consuming process.

To address the bi-level optimization problem in Eq. (6), we employ a gradient-based approximation strategy inspired by the one-shot NAS [30] approach to update the architecture selection parameters:

$$\nabla_\alpha \mathcal{L}_{Dval}\big(\alpha, \omega^*(\alpha)\big) \approx \nabla_\alpha \mathcal{L}_{Dval}(\alpha, \omega - \xi \nabla_\omega \mathcal{L}_{Dtra}(\omega, \alpha)) \tag{7}$$

where ω represents the network's structural parameters at the current gradient step, ξ denotes the architecture optimization learning rate for the inner optimization. Therefore, instead of training the optimal network's structural parameters, we perform a one-step gradient update on the structural parameters ω under the current gradient step. It has been demonstrated in the DARTS [30] that this approximation is reasonable and efficient. After training, we select the operation operators corresponding to the maximum architecture selection weights to construct the complete model structure:

$$o_{best} = \{o_{\alpha_{\max}} | o \in O_n, O_s, O_l\} \tag{8}$$

Finally, we retrain the searched model structure on the training set *Dtra*, and tune it on the validation set *Dval*.

3.4 Differentiable Search Strategy

In order to simplify the prediction process, we also use the inner product of the final representation of the user and the item as the ranking score for recommendation generation, that is, after obtaining the overall representation of the user $\boldsymbol{h}_u$ and the item $\boldsymbol{h}_i$, the final user's score for the item is calculated as follows:

$$\hat{y}_{ui} = \boldsymbol{h}_u^T \boldsymbol{h}_i \tag{9}$$

Consistent with other GNN-based CF models, the initial embedding of users and items in this paper is a trainable parameter. During architecture search, we employ a pairwise Bayesian Personalized Ranking (BPR) loss, which encourages the model to predict higher scores for items that the user has interacted with than items that the user has never interacted with:

$$L_{BPR} = -\sum_{u=1}^{m}\sum_{i\in N_u}\sum_{j\notin N_u} \ln\sigma\left(\hat{y}_{ui} - \hat{y}_{uj}\right) + \lambda\|\Theta\|^2 \tag{10}$$

where λ controls the weight of L2 regularization in the loss function, and $\Theta = \{\boldsymbol{h}^{(0)}\}$.

3.5 Complexity Analysis of Architecture Search

The complexity of architecture search is determined by the size of the search space. In the case of the search space designed in this paper, the size varies with the number of GCN layers. The size of the search space can be represented as: $O(9^L \times 2^{(L-1)} \times 5)$,where L represents the number of GCN layers. Taking a graph convolution of three layers ($L = 3$) as an example, the number of structures in the search space is 14580. Compared to other methods that simultaneously search for both structures and hyperparameters, our search space is compact and efficient.

4 Experiments

In this section, we conduct experiments to comprehensively evaluate the performance of our proposed AutoMaster model.

4.1 Experimental Setup

Datasets. We performed experiments and analysis on five public recommendation datasets: Amazon-Book, Gowalla, Yelp2018, Douban, and Movielens-1M. It should be noted that Amazon-Book derived from the 2018 version of the Amazon-review website, Yelp2018 is adopted from the 2018 edition of the Yelp challenge. For all datasets, we use the 10-core setting to ensure that each user and item have at least ten interactions. Table 2 provides details about the five datasets.

For the Amazon-Book, Gowalla, and Yelp2018, we set the number of validation set interaction items to be the same as the number of test set interaction items. For the Douban and Movielens-1M datasets, we use a split of 80%, 10%, and 10% to create the training set, validation set, and test set, respectively.

Table 2. Information of the five datasets.

Dataset	User	Item	Interaction	Density
Amazon-Book	52643	91599	2984108	0.00062
Gowalla	29858	40981	1027370	0.00084
Yelp2018	31668	38048	1561406	0.00130
Douban	2848	39586	894887	0.00793
Movielens-1M	6040	3706	1000209	0.04468

Baseline Models. To evaluate the performance of the proposed method, we compare AutoMaster with the following five state-of-the-art methods: BPRMF [16], NGCF [20], LR-GCCF [7], LightGCN [8], HEMLET [23].

Evaluation Indicator. We use the four evaluation indicators Recall, Precision, F1 Score, and Normalized Discounted Cumulative Gain NDCG to evaluate the effectiveness of the AutoMatser model in predicting user preferences, and set the recommendation list length to 20.

Experimental Parameters Settings. The AutoMaster model is built based on the SANE [15], PYG [31], and PyTorch 2.0 frameworks, while the baseline models are constructed using the PyTorch 1.9 framework. During the training phase of the architecture search, we set the number of epochs to 150. Considering the computational resources, the embedding size of the hidden layer and the output layer are set to 32. The batch size is set to 1024. The initial learning rate is set to 0.001, and a strategy to reduce the learning rate is used to accelerate the training of the model. The weight for L2 regularization is set to 0.005, and the dropout ratio is set to 0.1. The learning rate ξ in Eq. (7) is set to 0.025. The SGD optimizer is used. In the comparative experiments with the baseline methods, we set the number of graph convolutional layers to 3. For each dataset, we independently run the search process five times with different random seeds. In each run, the top-1 architecture is retrieved. Subsequently, fine-tuning is performed on the validation set, and the architecture with the best performance metric is selected as the best network architecture for that specific dataset.

During the fine-tuning phase, we set the number of epochs to 1000. The embedding size for both the hidden layers and the output layer are set to 64. We use the Adam optimizer for optimization. The remaining hyperparameters are tuned using Hyperopt [32] with ten iterations of optimization.

4.2 Performance Comparison

We conducted experiments on three commonly used benchmark datasets: Amazon-Book, Gowalla, and Yelp2018. Table 3 presents the evaluation metrics for all methods on the three datasets, where the values in bold represent the best metrics for each row, and the values underlined represent the best baseline metrics. It should be noted that since HEMLET does not provide available codes, the data here is quoted from the original text of HEMLET.

Based on the results shown in Table 3, we summarize the findings as follows: (1) Among the five baseline methods, LightGCN achieves the best NDCG@20on all three datasets, while HEMLET achieves the best performance on other metrics for the three datasets. (2) Our proposed AutoMaster model demonstrates the best accuracy in most cases, with improvements of over 5% in Precision@20 and F1@20. Considering the visual representation of the best architectures obtained from the search, as shown in Fig. 3, we have the following analysis:

According to the selection of gate mechanisms in the HEMLET [23], the majority of layers in its network (layers 3 and 4) are non-linear propagation layers. Similarly, the best architectures are discovered by our AutoMaster model on the three datasets also include non-linear aggregators. This suggests that CF methods combining both linear and non-linear propagation outperform methods that solely rely on linear propagation in most recommendation scenarios.

While HEMLET integrates non-linear propagation in high-order convolutional layers, it applies non-linear activation functions only after neighbor aggregation. In contrast, our designed search space includes various non-linear aggregation operations.

In the best architectures for Gowalla and Amazon-Book, the first graph convolutional layer is a linear aggregator (SGCN), while the last two layers are non-linear aggregators (NGCF/SAGE_SUM), similar to the conclusion of HEMLET that non-linear propagation helps capture information from distant neighborhoods. On the contrary, for the Yelp2018 dataset, the lower graph convolutional layer is a non-linear aggregator, and the higher layer is a linear aggregator, while ignoring the node representations from the second layer output. This indicates that our AutoMaster is capable of discovering the dataset-specific optimal architecture.

AutoMaster gets slightly lower Recall@20 than HEMLET on the Amazon and Yelp2018 datasets, but the improvement in F1@20 considering both Recall and Precision suggests that AutoMaster learns more comprehensive user and item representations, resulting in better overall recommendation performance.

The layer aggregator for all three datasets is L-LSTM, indicating a correlation between the order of graph convolutional operations and the weights of corresponding intermediate layer nodes. A reasonable layer aggregation method can enhance the recommendation accuracy for CF problems.

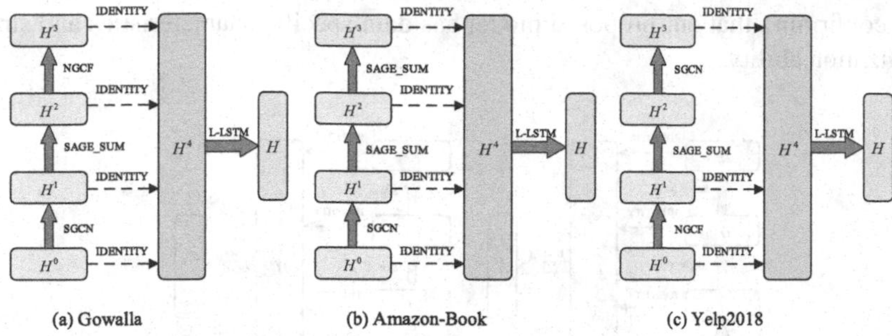

Fig. 3. Visualization of the best architectures searched on benchmark datasets.

Table 3. Comparison of baseline methods and AutoMaster on three benchmark datasets.

Dataset	Metric	BPRMF	NGCF	LR-GCCF	LightGCN	HEMLET	Auto Master
Amazon-Book	Recall	0.0306	0.0391	0.0372	0.0483	**0.0510**	0.0506
	Precision	0.0064	0.0091	0.0086	0.0093	0.0103	**0.0112**
	F1	0.0105	0.0148	0.0139	0.0156	0.0171	**0.0180**
	NDCG	0.0176	0.0242	0.0238	0.0314	0.0301	**0.0323**
Gowalla	Recall	0.1283	0.1582	0.1569	0.1843	0.1908	**0.1913**
	Precision	0.0235	0.0268	0.0249	0.0291	0.0293	**0.0311**
	F1	0.0397	0.0458	0.0430	0.0501	0.0508	**0.0535**
	NDCG	0.0865	0.1198	0.1156	0.1326	0.1231	**0.1382**
Yelp2018	Recall	0.0476	0.0602	0.0596	0.0673	**0.0696**	0.0688
	Precision	0.0581	0.0143	0.0138	0.0151	0.0155	**0.0168**
	F1	0.0103	0.0231	0.0224	0.0245	0.0253	**0.0262**
	NDCG	0.0296	0.0423	0.0418	0.0482	0.0434	**0.0503**

4.3 Generalization Experiments on New Datasets

To explore the generalization ability of the AutoMaster model in different scenarios and datasets with varying denstiy, we selected two new datasets, Douban and Movielens-1M, which have significantly different density compared to the benchmark datasets. We conducted experiments and compared the results with four baseline methods. The experimental results are shown in Table 4.

Among all the baseline methods, LightGCN performs the best, followed by NGCF. Our proposed AutoMaster model achieves the best performance on all metrics for the new datasets, and the improvement on NDCG@20 is even greater compared to the three benchmark datasets. Even on datasets with higher density, the searched architecture shown in Fig. 4 still exhibits the pattern of low-level linear graph convolution and high-level nonlinear convolution. However, the selection of layer aggregators is different, further confirming that our proposed model has data-specific characteristics and strong generalization ability.

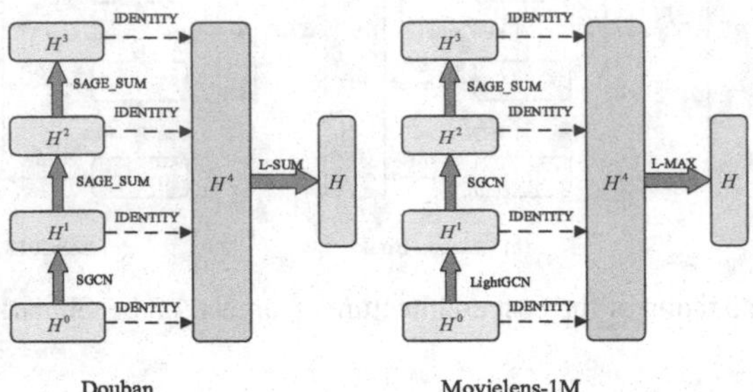

Fig. 4. Visualization of the best architectures searched on new datasets.

Table 4. Performance comparison of baseline methods and AutoMaster on new datasets.

Dataset	Metric	BPRMF	NGCF	LR-GCCF	LightGCN	Auto Master
Douban	Recall	0.0911	0.0968	0.0962	0.0966	**0.1005**
	Precision	0.1172	0.1223	0.1237	0.1253	**0.1341**
	F1	0.1025	0.1080	0.1082	0.1091	**0.1149**
	NDCG	0.0913	0.0996	0.0941	0.0987	**0.1038**
Movielens-1M	Recall	0.2564	0.2655	0.2593	0.2681	**0.2707**
	Precision	0.1645	0.1658	0.1649	0.1675	**0.1735**
	F1	0.2004	0.2041	0.2015	0.2061	**0.2114**
	NDCG	0.2252	0.2321	0.2291	0.2384	**0.2443**

4.4 Hyperparameters and Ablation Experiments

Specifically, in the hyperparameter experiments, we investigated the impact of the number of GNN layers on the AutoMaster model. In the ablation experiments, we studied the influence of layer combinations and the search space on model accuracy.

Impact of the Number of GNN Layers. By varying the number of GNN layers, we examined the robustness and ability of the AutoMaster model to alleviate oversmoothing. In the Douban dataset, we changed the number of GNN layers from 2 to 4. The experimental results are shown in Fig. 5.

Figure 5 shows that AutoMaster outperforms LightGCN in all number of layers. When the number of GNN layers is changed from 3 to 4, AutoMaster exhibits a slight decrease in accuracy, which is much smaller than that of LightGCN. This indicates that AutoMaster performs better in alleviating the over-smoothing issue and demonstrates good robustness. As the number of layers increases, the improvement of AutoMaster compared to LightGCN gradually becomes more significant, showing that the CF model with a hybrid nonlinear propagation mechanism can better capture information from higher-order neighborhoods.

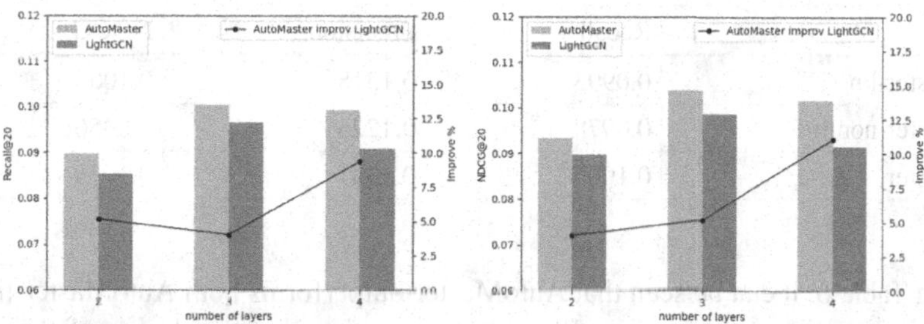

Fig. 5. Results of AutoMaster and LightGCN on different graph convolutional layers.

Effect of Layer Combination. To investigate the effect of aggregating the intermediate layers, specifically the skip connections and layer aggregator modules, we conducted an ablation experiment by removing these two components from the search framework. This variant is denoted as AutoMaster-w/o-layer. The results on the Douban dataset are shown in Table 5.

From Table 5, we can observe a decrease in overall performance when removing the two components related to layer aggregation. This indicates that the node representations obtained from the graph convolution outputs of intermediate layers contain valuable information, and the layer aggregation mechanism plays a crucial role in GNN-based CF methods. The skip connections and layer aggregator modules facilitate information flow across layers, enabling the model to capture and utilize information from multiple hops of neighborhood connections. Thus, their inclusion contributes to improved performance in the AutoMaster model.

Table 5. Ablation analysis on layer combination.

Model	Recall	Precision	NDCG
AutoMaster	0.1005	0.1341	0.1038
AutoMaster-w/o-layer	0.0957	0.1216	0.0943

Impact of Search Space. To further investigate the influence of linear and non-linear graph convolutional networks on recommendation performance within the Node Aggregator, we divided the search space of the Node Aggregator into linear aggregation space and non-linear aggregation space. Experiments were conducted on the Douban dataset. We refer to the linear variant as AutoMaster-lin and the non-linear variant as AutoMaster-nonlin, and the results are shown Table 6.

Table 6. Ablation analysis on search space.

Model	Recall	Precision	NDCG
AutoMaster-lin	0.0993	0.1318	0.1004
AutoMaster-nonlin	0.0978	0.1225	0.0956
AutoMaster	0.1005	0.1341	0.1038

From Table 6, it can be seen that AutoMaster outperforms both AutoMaster-lin and AutoMaster-nonlin in terms of performance, indicating that the design of the mixed search space used in the node aggregator is reasonable.

5 Conclusions

To address the debate on whether the non-linear or linear propagation mechanism in Graph Convolutional Networks (GCNs) is suitable for Collaborative Filtering (CF), as well as the challenges in manually design of graph neural networks (GNNs) that heavily relies on the expertise of the designer and extensive tuning, this paper proposes a model called AutoMaster that implements differentiable graph neural network architecture search for CF recommendation and automatically designs GNN architectures. Experimental results on three benchmark datasets and two new datasets demonstrate that the proposed AutoMaster model is able to discover effective architectures specific to different datasets. The identified optimal architectures on five datasets all consist of both linear propagation and nonlinear propagation. The extensive results indicate that AutoMaster not only achieves superior performance but also effectively mitigates the over-smoothing issue.

Acknowledgments. This work was supported by the National Natural Science Foundation of China (No. 62077038, No. 61672405, No. 62176196, and No. 62271374).

Disclosure of Interests. The authors have no competing interests to declare that are relevant to the content of this article.

References

1. Wu, S., Sun, F., Zhang, W., et al.: Graph neural networks in recommender systems: a survey. ACM Comput. Surv. **55**(5), 1–37 (2022)

2. Gao, C., Zheng, Y., Li, N., et al.: A survey of graph neural networks for recommender systems: challenges, methods, and directions. ACM Trans. Recommender Syst. **1**(1), 1–51 (2023)
3. Koren, Y., Rendle, S., Bell, R.: Advances in collaborative filtering. Recommender Syst. Handb. 91–142 (2021)
4. Koren, Y., Bell, R., Volinsky, C.: Matrix factorization techniques for recommender systems. Computer **42**(8), 30–37 (2009)
5. Covington, P., Adams, J., Sargin, E.: Deep neural networks for YouTube recommendations. In: Proceedings of the 10th ACM Conference on Recommender Systems, pp. 191–198 (2016)
6. He, X., Liao, L., Zhang, H., et al.: Neural collaborative filtering. In: Proceedings of the 26th International Conference on World Wide Web, pp. 173–182 (2017)
7. Chen, L., Wu, L., Hong, R., et al.: Revisiting graph based collaborative filtering: a linear residual graph convolutional network approach. In: Proceedings of the AAAI Conference on Artificial Intelligence, vol. 34, no. 01, pp. 27–34 (2020)
8. He, X., Deng, K., Wang, X., et al.: LightGCN: simplifying and powering graph convolution network for recommendation. In: Proceedings of the 43rd International ACM SIGIR Conference on Research and Development in Information Retrieval, pp. 639–648 (2020)
9. Li, C., Jia, K., Shen, D., et al.: Hierarchical representation learning for bipartite graphs. In: IJCAI, 19, pp. 2873–2879 (2019)
10. Oloulade, B.M., Gao, J., Chen, J., et al.: Graph neural architecture search: a survey. Tsinghua Sci. Technol. **27**(4), 692–708 (2021)
11. Elsken, T., Metzen, J.H., Hutter, F.: Neural architecture search: a survey. J. Mach. Learn. Res. **20**(1), 1997–2017 (2019)
12. Ren, P., Xiao, Y., Chang, X., et al.: A comprehensive survey of neural architecture search: challenges and solutions. ACM Comput. Surv. (CSUR) **54**(4), 1–34 (2021)
13. Gao, Y., Yang, H., Zhang, P., et al.: Graph neural architecture search. In: International Joint Conference on Artificial Intelligence, pp. 1403–1409 (2021)
14. Zhou, K., Huang, X., Song, Q., et al.: Auto-GNN: neural architecture search of graph neural networks. Front. Big Data **5** (2022)
15. Huan, Z., Quanming, Y.A.O., Weiwei, T.U.: Search to aggregate neighborhood for graph neural network. In: 2021 IEEE 37th ICDE, pp. 552–563. IEEE (2021)
16. Rendle, S., Freudenthaler, C., Gantner, Z., et al.: BPR: Bayesian personalized ranking from implicit feedback. In: Proceedings of the Twenty-Fifth Conference on Uncertainty in Artificial Intelligence, pp. 452–461 (2009)
17. Pan, R., Zhou, Y., Cao, B., et al.: One-class collaborative filtering. In: 2008 Eighth IEEE International Conference on Data Mining, pp. 502–511. IEEE (2008)
18. Berg, R., Kipf, T.N., Welling, M.: Graph convolutional matrix completion. arXiv preprint arXiv:1706.02263 (2017)
19. Ying, R., He, R., Chen, K., et al.: Graph convolutional neural networks for web-scale recommender systems. In: Proceedings of the 24th ACM SIGKDD International Conference on Knowledge Discovery & Data Mining, pp. 974–983 (2018)
20. Wang, X., He, X., Wang, M., et al.: Neural graph collaborative filtering. In: Proceedings of the 42nd International ACM SIGIR Conference on Research and Development in Information Retrieval, pp. 165–174 (2019)
21. Gao, Y., Yang, H., Zhang, P., et al.: GraphNAS: graph neural architecture search with reinforcement learning. arXiv preprint arXiv:1904.09981 (2019)
22. Li, Y., King, I.: Autograph: automated graph neural network. In: 27th International Conference on Neural Information Processing, pp. 189–201 (2020)
23. Kong, T., Kim, T., Jeon, J., et al.: Linear, or non-linear, that is the question! In: Proceedings of the Fifteenth WSDM, pp. 517–525 (2022)

24. Chen, J., Zhu, G., Hou, H., et al.: AutoGSR: neural architecture search for graph-based session recommendation. In: Proceedings of the 45th International ACM SIGIR Conference on Research and Development in Information Retrieval, pp. 1694–1704 (2022)
25. Kipf, T.N., Welling, M.: Semi-supervised classification with graph convolutional networks. arXiv preprint arXiv:1609.02907 (2016)
26. Veličković, P., Cucurull, G., Casanova, A., et al.: Graph attention networks. In: International Conference on Learning Representations, pp. 1–12 (2018)
27. Hamilton, W.L., Ying, R., Leskovec, J.: Inductive representation learning on large graphs. In: Proceedings of the 31st NeurIPS, pp. 1025–1035 (2017)
28. Xu, K., Hu, W., Leskovec, J., et al.: How powerful are graph neural networks? In: International Conference on Learning Representations, pp. 1–17 (2019)
29. Brody, S., Alon, U., Yahav, E.: How attentive are graph attention networks? In: International Conference on Learning Representations, pp. 1–26 (2022)
30. Liu, H., Simonyan, K., Yang, Y.: DARTS: differentiable architecture search. In: International Conference on Learning Representations, pp. 1–13 (2019)
31. Fey, M., Lenssen, J.E.: Fast graph representation learning with PyTorch Geometric. arXiv preprint arXiv:1903.02428 (2019)
32. Bergstra, J., Yamins, D., Cox, D.D.: Hyperopt: a Python library for optimizing the hyperparameters of machine learning algorithms. In: Proceedings of the 12th Python in Science Conference, pp. 1–8 (2013)

A Multi-model Recurrent Knowledge Graph Embedding for Contextual Recommendations

Dionisis Kotzaitsis(✉) and Georgia Koloniari

University of Macedonia, Thessaloniki, Greece
{aid22003,gkoloniari}@uom.edu.gr

Abstract. Recommenders can be improved by exploiting the huge disposal of multi-context data that is now available. Knowledge Graphs (KGs) offer an intuitive way to incorporate this kind of assorted data. This paper introduces a context-aware recommender, based on deriving graph embeddings by learning the representations of appropriate meta-paths mined from a graph database. Our system uses several LSTMs to model the meta-path semantics between a user-item pair, based on the length of the mined path, a Multi-head Attention module as an attention mechanism, along with a pooling and a recommendation layer. Our evaluation shows that our system is on par with state-of-the-art recommenders, while also supporting contextual modeling.

Keywords: Recommender · Context · Knowledge Graph · Meta-paths

1 Introduction

Recommendations rely on large amounts of training data, i.e., ratings, and user and item features, to be effective. Contextual data such as social user relationships, locations, and temporal data can offer other important dimensions that should influence recommendations but are often ignored or under-utilized.

Knowledge Graphs (KGs) [1] provide an intuitive way to model all available data used for recommendation tasks effectively. A KG allows us to capture various types of information and contexts such as friendships between users, locations, and temporal data that need to be represented accordingly as appropriate entities and relationships, to uncover possible connections between users and items and help us make correct recommendations.

Several recommendation methods exploit KGs for prediction. Many works rely on automated path extraction to derive information about user-item pairs [11] and then use conventional recommendation methods, while others rely on KG embeddings to capture the semantics that could lead to recommendations [19]. These strategies use neural network architectures to deduce the recommendations in each KG by either using the paths or the structural information of the graph. Some methods rely on *meta-paths* instead of automated extracted

K. Stefanidis et al. (Eds.): ICWE 2024, LNCS 14629, pp. 99–114, 2024.
https://doi.org/10.1007/978-3-031-62362-2_7

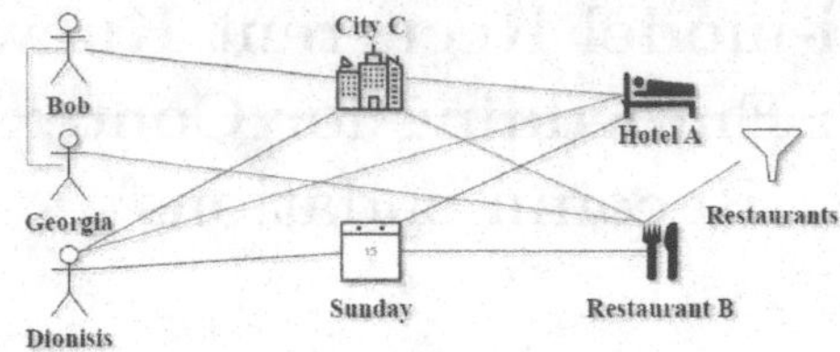

Fig. 1. A KG with 3 users, 2 businesses and contextual information.

paths about user-item pairs [18]. Meta-paths are defined as paths that depend on domain knowledge of the KG schema and define new composite relations between the types of their starting and ending entities.

In Fig. 1, we illustrate a KG with 3 users and 2 businesses, that connect if a user has positively reviewed a business. The KG includes additional entities and relationships, which model social context: *Bob and Georgia are friends*, temporal context: *Sunday*, spatial context: *Hotel A in City C*, and other information: *Restaurant B belongs to category Restaurants.* Data is modeled to create explicit (depicted by red edges), as well as implicit connections (black edges). For instance, *Dionisis* is explicitly connected to *Hotel A* since he has reviewed it, and an implicit relationship capturing *review day* is derived between him and the additional contextual entity *Sunday*, as he reviewed *Hotel A* on that day.

Appropriately modeling entities and relationships into the graph enables us to exploit meta-path mining to provide context-aware recommendations. For instance, based on meta-path: *"Dionisis ←REVIEWS→ Hotel A ←IN→ City C←IN→ Restaurant B"*, which exploits location, we would recommend *Restaurant B* to *Dionisis* because of their mutual connection to *City C*, while based on meta-path: *"Bob←FRIENDS→Georgia←REVIEWS→Restaurant B"*, we would recommend *Restaurant B* to *Bob*, because his friend *Georgia* reviews it.

In this paper, we introduce the *Multi-model Recurrent Knowledge Graph Embedding for Context-aware recommendation system (MRKGEC)*, a meta-path context-aware recommender based on a KG that uses recurrent neural networks (RNNs) and multi-head attention modules. Our system relies on a KG that models contextual data through appropriate entities and both explicit and implicit relationships. The KG is implemented using a Graph Database Management System (GDBMS), and in particular Neo4j[1], which allows us to efficiently store and extract information about the relationships between the entities of the KG and subsequently produce recommendations to users. Cypher queries are used to mine meta-paths of different lengths according to varying contexts.

Then, a mix of Long Short-Term Memory (LSTM) and Multi-Head attention modules are used to derive path embeddings. Extracted meta-paths grouped by length are trained with a novel model, and the overall embeddings of users and items are concatenated, before inferring the final recommendation based on the minimal scalar product of the user/item embedding. The usage of a Multi-Head

[1] Neo4j. https://neo4j.com.

attention module on the concatenation of the hidden states of each RNN, serves as a self-attention mechanism between the paths that connect each user-item set. Lastly, pooling is used to extract the most important paths. Our experimental evaluation shows that our system's performance is on par with other SOTA recommendation systems, with the added effect of offering contextual customization of the recommendations. Social and spatial contexts improve recommendations, while a multi-context model prevails against the single-context ones.

The rest of the paper is structured as follows. Related work is discussed in Sect. 2, while Sect. 3 details our model. Section 4 includes our experimental evaluation and Sect. 5 concludes with a summary and directions for future work.

2 Related Work

We first review recommendation systems that use the data of a KG to infer correct suggestions. According to [2], there are four types of such systems: *graph based* systems, like HeteRS [8], that exploit graph connectivity and structure to uncover possible recommendations, *KG embedding based* systems, such as CKE [19], that utilize the KG structural modeling to create entity embeddings, and *path based* and *meta-path based* systems that mine paths from the KG and then use the sequential information to generate recommendations. Since MRKGEC is meta-path based, we discuss the latter two and their differences in more detail.

Path based methods automatically mine paths from the KG using some type of graph traversal and then utilize a neural network model for embedding the mined paths and providing recommendations. RKGE [11] extracts paths via depth-first search and then uses a batch of LSTMs, while DHKGE [5] uses the same path mining and then a hybrid architecture with convolutional neural networks (CNNs) along with LSTMs. Similarly, Wang et al. [13] also automatically mine paths to derive embeddings for both entities and relationships and then use RNNs to recommend items for each user.

In contrast, meta-path based methods utilize the KG schema to mine paths that have a certain length, context, and structure. MCRec [3] uses sampled meta-paths, a co-attention mechanism via random walks (trained by latent factor models), and CNNs to derive recommendations. In HeteMF [17], item-item similarity is estimated in each meta-path and then matrix factorization (MF) is used to create embeddings for users and items. HeteRec [18] exploits the heterogeneous data of a KG by learning user preferences by MF, as well as path methods for recommendations. HeteCF [6] models user-user, user-item, and item-item relations, and then uses collaborative filtering based on derived meta-paths. An alternative strategy called SemRec [9] weighs the extracted meta-paths to portray the differences among the KG relationships. Also systems, such as [21], use MF techniques and meta-path similarity as a regularizer on the user-user matrix. Finally, centrality measures are exploited in works such as [12] that uses item centrality and a scoring function for recommendations, while [15] uses meta-paths filtering with a similar rating function.

Although all these systems offer effective and accurate recommendations, they naively recommend always the same options to users without taking into account any additional contextual information, such as time, location, or social connections. It is becoming increasingly clear that relevant contextual information is significant when making recommendations, as context often influences user preferences. Three components describe contextual recommenders, contextual *pre-filtering*, where given a particular context only appropriate data are given as input to a recommender, *post-filtering*, where recommendations are filtered out based on the context after they are derived, and *contextual modeling* systems, where context is directly employed in the data modeling process, thus avoiding any additional filtering steps.

In the latter category, [4] uses a combination of an auto-encoder with a context-driven attention mechanism that encodes contextual attributes into a hidden representation of a user's preference. However, the model lacks the sequential insights that a meta-path method, like MRKGEC, provides. Also, CGAR [20] relies on user history, in addition to a KG to infer new suggestions. Though very effective, CGAR relies on extensive monitoring of users, via IoT devices, and deploys a data model that is difficult to replicate. MF has also been used for contextual modeling in CSLIM [22], however data sparsity that is particularly high for contextual ratings is a significant problem for such approaches, while too many contextual parameters also make the approach inefficient.

MRKGEC can be placed under the category of contextual modeling methods as KG creation and meta-path extraction explicitly use context in the modeling process. In fact, the use of meta-paths enables MRKGEC to tailor its recommendations to specific contexts by selecting appropriate contextual paths. For deriving embeddings, MRKGEC takes inspiration from the path-based RKGE framework [11] with the main difference being that instead of a single model, we deploy a combination of models that concatenate their output embeddings, one for each path length. Besides that, a multi-head attention module is used after the LSTM batches to create the correct representations of the contextual paths. Furthermore, MRKGEC exploits the capabilities of graph databases so as to mine paths from a KG implemented in Neo4j, more efficiently compared to other systems, such as RKGE implemented without the support of a database.

3 The MRKGEC System

MRKGEC is a recommender system designed to provide context-aware recommendations based on modeling contextual information through a knowledge graph and utilized to learn appropriate path embeddings that yield the target recommendations. In this section, we first present our contextual modeling for the KG and detail the meta-path mining process. We then describe the components of our learning architecture and the overall learning method applied.

3.1 Data Modeling and Meta-path Mining

Knowledge graphs provide a model to represent any real-world entities and the relationships between them while capturing their semantic types and properties

[1]. As such, a KG offers an appropriate representation for all data relevant to a recommender system, i.e., users, items, and their ratings, as well as any contextual data we need to incorporate. More formally, let $\varepsilon = \{e_1, e_2, e_3, ...e_n\}$ be a set of entities, $Re = \{r_1, r_2, r_3, ...r_m\}$ the relationships between them, and L and T sets of entity and relationship types, respectively.

Definition 1. *A Knowledge Graph (KG) is defined as a graph* $KG = (\varepsilon, Re, \phi, \psi)$*, where* ϕ *is an entity mapping function* $\phi = \varepsilon \rightarrow L$ *that maps each entity* $e \in \varepsilon$ *to an entity type* $\phi(e) \in L$*, and* ψ *is an edge type mapping function* $\psi = L \rightarrow T$ *that maps each edge* $r \in Re$ *to a relationship type* $\psi(l) \in T$*.*

An example of a typical KG used for a recommender is presented in Fig. 2a, where only non-contextual information is mapped. Both users like *Item A*, and as *User B* also likes *Item B*, we may infer that *User A* may like *Item B* as well (depicted by the dotted line).

In contrast, we propose a novel model that enriches the typical KG with nodes (entities) representing contextual information and also creates implicit connections from users and items to shared contextual entities, indirectly creating new user-item associations. MRKGEC models three types of context, though the model as it relies on a KG, can be easily extended with more entities and relationship types, if additional data is available. In particular, we model (i) *spatial*, (ii) *temporal* and (iii) *social* context. Figure 2b illustrates our KG schema where relationship types are numbered for ease of reference. Besides users connected with the items they positively reviewed (or liked), we utilize the time the review was written to extract temporal context that is represented by entities *Day*, *Month* and *Season* and derive the corresponding implicit relationships (3 to 9) between each user and item with these new entities. Similarly, for spatial context, we include entities *City* and *Area* that model item location and the corresponding relationships (10 to 12). Social context is modeled using friendships between users (1), while we also model domain features such as item category through a corresponding entity and relationship (13).

The main idea of MRKGEC is that by modeling all contextual information in the KG, appropriate paths can be extracted that capture such information so as to provide appropriate recommendations. To this end, MRKGEC is based on a meta-path based approach that exploits the KG schema for mining paths and uncovers specific contextual relationships in the KG. For instance, to provide recommendations that depend on time, we would mine temporal paths between users and items via relationships 3–9 of Fig. 2b.

To support efficient path mining, we propose implementing the KG in a graph database so as to exploit its querying and indexing capabilities that can cope with large scale data. In particular, we utilize Neo4j and also deploy multi-processing to further accelerate path extraction.

Neo4j is equipped with a declarative query language, Cypher, which offers us a convenient tool for meta-path modeling and extraction. Thus, context-dependent meta-paths are expressed via Cypher queries. While our approach could mine paths of arbitrary length by forming appropriate cypher queries, only paths of length 3 to 5 are extracted, as paths over a certain length threshold

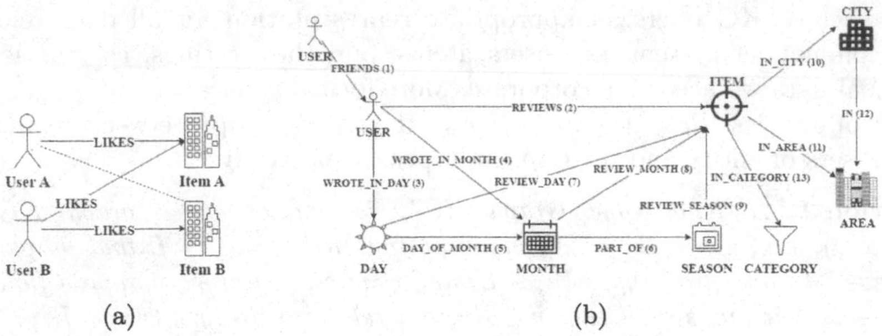

Fig. 2. The KG for (a) a non-contextual recommender, and (b) MRKGEC

create more noise than impact in recommendation tasks [10]. Examples of queries for extracting spatial and temporal paths of length three are given below.

- *MATCH p=(u:User)-[:REVIEW]-(bu:Business)-[:IN_CITY]-(c:City)-[:IN]-(a:Area) WHERE u.id = "uid" AND bu.id = "bid" RETURN ID(u), ID(c), ID(a), ID(bu)*
- *MATCH p=(u:User)-[a:WROTE_IN_DAY]-(d:Day)-[:DAY_OF_MONTH]-(m:Month) - [b:REVIEW_MONTH]-(bu:Business) WHERE u.id = "uid" AND bu.id = "bid" AND a.review_id=b.review_id RETURN ID(u), ID(d), ID(m), ID(bu)*

3.2 MRKGEC Architecture

To provide appropriate item recommendations to users, the mined meta-paths are supplied to a neural network based architecture. More specifically, our architecture consists of a mixture of recurrent neural architectures (LSTMs) and a multi-head attention mechanism (Fig. 3). By using the LSTM architecture we exploit the potential of modeling and capturing the sequential and contextual information of meta-paths [7,16]. Moreover, the incorporation of multi-head attention enhances the attention of the model in particular parts of the hidden representation. We propose training a separate model for each path length mined from the KG. As a result, each neural network is specialized with a certain path length but avoids over-fitting by appropriate parameter tuning.

Assuming there are n meta-paths between a user u and an item v, i.e., $P(u, v) = \{p_1, p_2, ...p_n\}$, with $3 \leq length(p_q) \leq 5, 1 \leq q \leq n$. The parameter n is contingent on the examined entity pair and can differ from case to case. Let $p_{ql} = u - e_1 - ... - e_{l-1} - v$ be such a path with length l, where $l-1$ entities are involved in the path between u and v. The MRKGEC architecture initializes a distributed representation ρ_q of p_{ql}, i.e. $\rho_q = \{\rho_{qu}, \rho_{qe_1}, ..., \rho_{qe_{l-1}}, \rho_{qv}\}$ and then uses an LSTM batch and a multi-head attention module, as depicted in Fig. 3, with this new meta-path representation as input.

The embedded paths are parsed through an RNN batch layer as the information flows from the user entity to the item entity, passing through all the intermediate nodes. Each LSTM is conceptualized as a sequential gated mechanism that uses the last hidden state of the path. For each step $(t - 1)$ of the

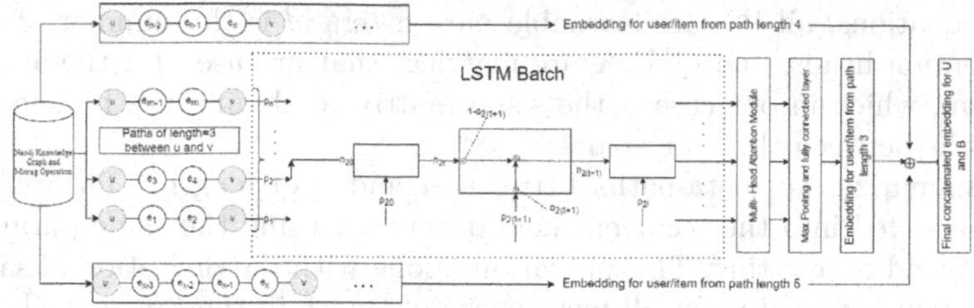

Fig. 3. The proposed system architecture.

meta-path the mechanism learns the hidden state encoding the sub-path from u to e_{t-1}. This h_{t-1} along with the path embedding ρ_{qt} are fed to the neural network to learn the next hidden state. The final state will encode the full path.

A mathematical representation of the LSTM module's hidden and candidate states is presented in Eq. 1, as per [11]. The attention gate is denoted on each step of the path by α_{qt}, a floating number in the range of $[0, 1]$. The hidden state is symbolized as h_{qt} and is balanced between the candidate hidden state h'_{qt} and the previous hidden state $h_{q(t-1)}$, with α_{qt} balancing their input to the hidden state in step t. In addition, the current candidate item, h'_{qt}, can be derived by using the embedding of the current step of the path in a sigmoid (σ) function, with H and W being the linear transformation parameters for steps t and $t-1$, and b the bias term.

$$\begin{aligned}
h_{qt} &= (1 - a_{qt}) \cdot h_{q(t-1)} + a_{qt} \cdot h'_{qt}, \\
h'_{qt} &= \sigma\left(W \cdot h_{q(t-1)} + H \cdot \rho_{qt} + b\right), \\
\alpha_{qt} &= \sigma\left(M^T \cdot (h_{qtR} || h_{qtL}) + b'\right), \\
h'_{qtL} &= \sigma\left(W_L \cdot \rho_{qtL} + H_L \cdot h_{q(t+1)L} + b_L\right), \\
h'_{qtR} &= \sigma\left(W_R \cdot \rho_{qtR} + H_R \cdot h_{q(t+1)R} + b_R\right).
\end{aligned} \tag{1}$$

The attention mechanism, α_{qt}, of the LSTM batch is achieved by using bi-directional networks to optimize the exploration of the parsed sequence. The attention is based on the current time step and the information on both directions of the neighboring sequence, attached to a sigmoid function to control the range of the function between $[0, 1]$. In the α_{qt} equation, M is the weight vector, and $h_{qtR}||h_{qtL}$ denotes the concatenation of the hidden states of the two sides of the sequence-from start to the current step (L) and from the end to the current step (R)- and b' is the attention layer bias term, both derived from h'_{qtL} and h'_{qtR}.

In this architecture, we incorporate a multi-head attention layer, after the recurrent neural network batch. We use this layer to attend to parts of the input sequences differently and explore the self-attended state of the (u, v) pairs after the multi-head attention layer:

$$\begin{aligned}
att_q &= Concat(head_1, head_2, ..., head_d)W_0, \\
\text{with } head_i &= Attention(QW_i^Q, KW_i^K, VW_i^V).
\end{aligned} \tag{2}$$

In both equations, all Ws are learnable parameters, d is the number of multi-head attention heads, and Q, V, K are matrices that are used for the attention mechanism, which in our case is the same matrix combining the hidden states of the paths between the (u, v) pairs.

To summarize, all meta-paths between u and v of length l form a single batch that is fed into the recurrent neural network using the same parameters for all to avoid over-fitting. This operation, along with the operation of saliency determination is repeated for all meta-paths of length in the range $[3, 5]$.

Pooling and Recommendation. After encoding all meta-paths, as we have described so far, MRKGEC uses a pooling mechanism to distinguish the different gravity of each meta-path in the modeling of the relations of pair (u, v).

For n paths in $P(u, v)$, we have $att_1, att_2, ...att_n$ as a representation derived from the multi-head attention module. In order to find out the most notable path of the pairing, a max pooling layer is also added.

$$A[j] = \max_{1<i<n} att_i[j], \tag{3}$$

where $A[j]$ is the value of the j_{th} dimension of the accumulated attended state, A. The architecture obtains the final concealed state of all the paths of the pair u and v by combining the effect of the summation of meta-paths. Next, a fully connected layer is utilized to further quantify the relationship (proximity) between u and v after the pooling layer is defined, with the rating between them (r_{ij}) estimated as $\tilde{r_{ij}} = \sigma(W_r \cdot A + b_r)$,

where W_r is the regression coefficient and b_r is the bias term. The sigmoid is used to limit the range of the estimated rating $\tilde{r_{ij}}$ to $[0, 1]$.

After training our model, to derive contextual recommendations (and for testing), we determine the proximity score between user u and any item v', using the inner product of their respective embeddings, which means that $score(u, v') = \langle u, v' \rangle$. This method is used because the inner product is more time efficient than a feed-forward pass through the network. As a final step, the system produces a list of the top-K recommended items for the user based on this score.

Optimization. The system uses a Binary Cross Entropy (BCE) loss function between the observed (r_{ij}) and estimated $(\tilde{r_{ij}})$ ratings, converting the problem into a binary classification problem with classes recommending the item to the user or not. Given the training dataset D_{train}, MRKGEC learns the parameters by minimizing the loss function,

$$Loss = \frac{1}{|D_{train}|} \sum_{r_{ij} \in D_{train}} BCELoss(r_{ij}, \tilde{r_{ij}}).$$

The parameters of the system are updated using backpropagation, while negative sampling between non-rated user-item pairs is also applied.

Algorithm. The architecture is described in Algorithm 1, which is divided into two parts, after initializing entity embeddings (line 1). In the first part (lines

Algorithm 1. MRKGEC algorithm. Meta-path mining and Neural Network.

Input: Path length l, Iterations, KG
1: Initialize the embeddings of $\varepsilon \in KG$
2: **foreach** user u **do**
3: Based on KG, get positive pairs (u, v_y)
4: Randomly sample to generate negative pairs (u, v_k)
5: $(u, v) \leftarrow (u, v_y) \cup (u, v_k)$
6: **foreach** (u, v) **do**
7: Mine meta-paths of length l from KG
8: **for** $t = 1; t \leq Iterations; t++$ **do**
9: **foreach** (u, v) *pair* **do**
10: **for** $p_q \in P(u, v)$ **do**
11: Evaluate h_{ql_i} *//Based on Eq. 1*
12: Evaluate att_q *//Based on Eq. 2*
13: Combine(att) $\leftarrow att_q$
14: $A \leftarrow$ max_pool(Combine(att)) *//Based on Eq. 3*
15: Calculate $\tilde{r_{ij}}$
16: Update parameters through backpropagation.

2–7), the training data (that is based only on positive reviews as we have mentioned) is used to create a negative sample and for meta-path mining. On the ML model part (lines 8–16) the paths of each user-item pair are first parsed through the RNN batch (line 11), and then they are self-attended using the multi-head attention module (lines 12–13). Lastly, on lines 14–15 there is the pooling operation from which, after a certain number of iterations is reached, an estimated rating will be derived for the current pair.

The design of our system is based on model efficiency and scalability. The training takes place for each path length individually in order for the system to be as better trained as possible. At the same time, this enables the parallel training of our model to further improve efficiency along with the use of the database for meta-path extraction.

4 Experimental Evaluation

We experimentally evaluate both MRKGEC's accuracy compared to other state-of-art recommendation systems, and also how the contextual information affects our model by comparing results from different meta-path mining operations.

Datasets. To evaluate the proposed system, we use two publicly available datasets based on the Yelp platform. The first dataset, *RecSys2013*, was used for the 2013 Yelp Challenge[2], while the second, *Yelp*, consists the last released Yelp Dataset[3]. Both datasets contain user reviews about local businesses, as well as

[2] RecSys2013, https://www.kaggle.com/c/yelp-recsys-2013/data.
[3] Yelp. https://www.yelp.ie.

Table 1. (Left) User-Item Interactions and (right) KG Statistics.

Datasets	RecSys2013	Yelp
#Users	21,949	4,011
#Items	11,363	4,600
#Ratings	193,955	67,529
Data Density	0.078%	0.36%

Datasets	RecSys2013	Yelp
#Entities	33,312	8,611
#Entity Types	8	8
#Links	193,955	45,648
#Link Types	12	13
Graph Density	0.017%	0.061%

business information like category and location. As such they both contain temporal and spatial contextual information, however, *RecSys2013* does not include any social data, while *Yelp* also includes *FRIENDS* relationships between pairs of users. We select to use *RecSys2013* as it has been used as a benchmark for various related approaches, but also deploy *Yelp* to explore the impact of social context to our recommender.

Pre-processing. Both datasets undergo a pre-processing pipeline to derive an appropriate KG. Business location and category, review timestamp, and friendship relationships are extracted, if available. If a user reviewed a business, they are considered connected by a *REVIEW* relationship. The timestamp of the reviews is analyzed to *Day, Month* and *Season*, and location to *City* and *Area*, while the implicit relationships between them and the users and businesses they affect are created. The resulting KG is implemented in Neo4j, following the schema of Fig. 2b, and appropriate Cypher queries are created so as to mine temporal, spatial, and social meta-paths. For temporal meta-paths, the *review_id* is utilized to ensure that only related entities are retrieved.

Before creating the KG, data is split to train and test data, and only the former is used for the KG. For *RecSys2013*, we sort the data chronologically and then split the sorted data using 80% of the reviews as training set and the rest as test set. For *Yelp*, we sample the data of 4 and 5 star reviews, and pick users with at least 8 reviews from California, in order to create a denser dataset that exhibits spatial locality. We then proceed to split the data into train and test sets (with a 90-10% split).

Table 1 includes detailed statistics for the two datasets, both for the user-item interactions matrix and the derived KG. Data density in the matrix, and graph density are also reported. Graph density is defined as the fraction of edges in the KG to the number of possible edges between all the KG's entities, and is very low in both datasets, making the recommendation task difficult.

Metrics. To measure the performance of MRKGEC, similarly to related approaches [18], we use *Precision@N* (*Prec@N*), defined as the fraction of correct recommendations in the top-N result list and average for all test users, and the *Mean Reciprocal Rank (MRR)* at the top-N results defined as:

$$MRR_N = \frac{1}{m}\sum_{i=1}^{m}\left(\sum_{v_j \in test(u_i)} \frac{1}{rank(u_i, v_j)}\right),$$

Table 2. MRKGEC vs RKGE: (left) performance and (right) path mining time.

Metric	MRKGEC	RKGE
Prec@1	0.00289	0.00317
Prec@5	0.00192	0.00205
Prec@10	0.00176	0.00186
MRR	0.00609	0.00651

Path Length	MRKGEC	RKGE
3	19 min 08 s	20 min 31 s
4	28 min 48 s	Not Available
5	22 min 45 s	>8 h

where v_j is a correctly recommended item in the top-N list, m is the number of test users, $test(u_i)$ is the set of items in the test data for user u_i, and $rank(u_i, v_j)$ is the position of item v_j in u_i's list of recommendations.

To study context impact, we compare the results lists derived by using different contextual meta-paths for recommendation learning, using the *Rank Biased Overlap (RBO)* measure [14]. RBO calculates a weighted overlap between two ranked lists up to a depth N, and returns a numeric value in the range of $[0, 1]$, where a value near 0 indicates complete difference while 1 is a perfect match.

Experimental Setup. Our experiments are conducted on an AMD Ryzen 7 2800 8-Core, with a NVIDIA GTX 1060 6GB GPU and 32 GB of DDR4 RAM. The system is implemented using CUDA 11.7, Python 3.9.13, PyTorch 1.13.1, and Neo4j 4.4.12. Our parameters are set as follows. The number of hidden units and the number of multi-head attention heads is set to 32 based on a held-out validation set. For the LSTM batch, the dropout is 0.5 on a one hidden layer model, based on our empirical study. We also use 5 training epochs and a learning rate of 0.01, as the loss seems to stabilize. Our code is publicly available[4].

4.1 Comparison

We first compare the MRKGEC architecture with the RKGE [11] framework, a non-contextual path-based recommender system. For RKGE, we derive its performance from the empirical study in [11], where RKGE is evaluated against other state-of-the-art recommenders and comes out ahead on both *Prec@N* and *MRR* against every system for the *RecSys2013* dataset. Thus, we conduct a direct comparison between MRKGEC and RKGE using the same dataset. For MRKGEC, we extract meta-paths of length 3 to 5 based on all available contexts (spatial and temporal), train a model for each path length in parallel, and then combine the derived embeddings. Table 2(left) shows $Prec@N, N \in \{1, 5, 10\}$ and MRR at $N = 10$. MRKGEC performs on par with RKGE, showing a slightly worse performance on all metrics, which is not unexpected as we take no advantage of MRKGEC's ability to provide contextual recommendations in this experiment. Note that the behavior is quite low for both, due to data sparsity.

We also compare the two frameworks on the aspect of path and meta-path mining by measuring time efficiency. Our method uses a Neo4j database

[4] https://github.com/dionisiskotzaitsis/MRKGEC.

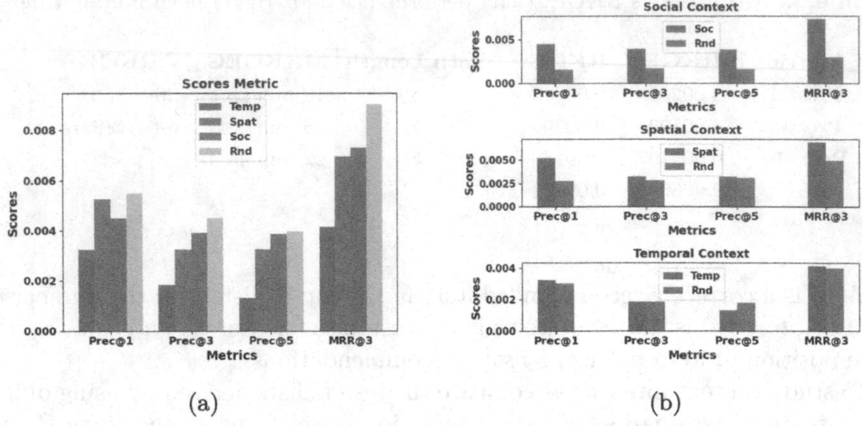

Fig. 4. Prec@N and MRR for different contexts (a) with random testing, and (b) using a contextual test set vs a random test set.

along with queries to mine contextual meta-paths. On the contrary, RKGE uses Python's NetworkX library and mines paths from an in-memory graph using depth-first search. As Table 2(right) shows, MRKGEC is approximately 1.5 min faster than RKGE for paths of length 3, while paths of length 4 are not available in RKGE. The biggest difference appears to be on paths of length 5, where MRKGEC is substantially faster, taking less than 25 min compared to RKGE, which was terminated after not concluding in more than 8 h. Given this vast difference in efficiency, we argue that the meta-path and graph database-based approach MRKGEC utilizes is preferable even for non-contextual recommendations despite being slightly worse in result accuracy.

4.2 Context Impact

The scope of this experiment is to investigate how different contexts can influence the results and their interpretability. To examine the effect of each context on our model, we first mine paths of different contexts using the meta-path mining module, and then train our model with the same parameters for all data. The *Yelp* dataset is used, providing all three types of context and thus, we mine meta-paths for temporal (*Temp*), spatial (*Spat*) and social (*Soc*) context. We also extract paths that combine all three contexts, referred to as *random* (*Rnd*), to contrast the one-dimensional context results. To be as unbiased as possible, we decided to use Neo4j queries that use as much of standalone contexts as possible, i.e., for mining spatial meta-paths, the Cypher queries we use include only entities and relationships modeling spatial context, besides users and businesses, to the degree that this was possible. As the *Yelp* test set we use, is smaller compared to *RecSys2013*, we measure $Prec@N$ for $N = \{1, 3, 5\}$ and $MRR@3$.

Figure 4a shows that the random model outperforms all others. The use of combined context by the random model makes it a more complete approach that exploits diverse data, and learns the best to infer more precise recommendations. Specifically, we have 4.7, 14.8, 2.6, and 24% increase in *Precision* at 1, 3, 5, and MRR@3, respectively, against the second best model for each of the metrics. This result however is due to the fact that evaluation, similarly to the first experiment, uses a test set that does not take into consideration any context.

Though this test set is not the most appropriate to assess the quality of contextual recommendations, let us take a closer look at this first result to compare the behavior of different contexts. Social context seems to be the most consistent on precision, with a fluctuation of only about 16% between *Prec*@5 and *Prec*@1, while the temporal and spatial models, exhibit a difference of 105% and 61%, respectively. The probable cause is that friendship relationships are more sturdy, e.g., a restaurant is bound to be more likely to be reviewed by a user that has a friend who positively reviewed it. Also, social context seems to be the best out of the one-dimensional models, ranking second on *Prec@1* and first at *Prec@3* and *Prec@5*, a result that validates the sturdiness of this model.

Spatial meta-paths seem to be the second best one-dimensional model, being 14% better than social meta-paths on *Prec@1*, but losing out against it on the remaining metrics. This is expected, as location has a significant impact on user preferences in the domain of businesses such as hotels or restaurants. Temporal context, on the other hand, seems to be the worst pick if we only use one type of context. Temporal paths are lacking on all metrics, with a decrease in scores of 69, 145, 203, and 119% compared to the random method. This results from the fact that time is a context that does not play a major role in recommendations for this businesses domain, in contrast to location and social relationships. Even though time-related connections can be used for recommending seasonal businesses (i.e. Christmas shops) it is not as useful as standalone context in recommending restaurants or hotels on daily, or even monthly basis.

We also compare the recommendations of each of the 3 context models using RBO. Ideally, to validate that MRKGEC provides contextual recommendations, the similarity between the 3 models should be close to 0, showing that there is a clear dependence between the context used and the derived results. Table 3 shows that the social model is the least similar with both others, with a similarity to both lower than 0.1. On the other hand, the spatial and temporal models have a similarity around 45%, still offering substantially different recommendations.

However, to better assess the performance of a contextual recommender, we require a test set with different recommendations based on context. To this end, we perform a comparison of each contextual model using a naive, random test set (*Rnd*) against a context-based test set. In particular, we construct a test set with user-items pairs that are in the same location (*City*) for spatial context, with items that are reviewed by a friend for social context, or businesses that are ranked more in the same day, month or season as the preferred user time frame for temporal context. In almost all cases, all models perform significantly better against a matching test set, compared to the random one (Fig. 4b). This validates that our contextual modeling combined with meta-path mining succeeds in providing contextual recommendations. Temporal context seems to be the

Table 3. Average Ranked Biased Overlap between different contextual models.

Models	Avg. RBO	Avg. RBO@3
Spatial VS Social	0.0943	0.0815
Spatial VS Temporal	0.4490	0.4509
Temporal VS Social	0.0659	0.0504

most vulnerable, as it performs better with the random test set at *Prec@5* and merely outperforms itself using the non-random set on *Prec@3* and *MRR@3*. This reinforces our previous conclusion that time seems not to be appropriate as a standalone context in this specific domain. However, it still can be used to enrich a multidimensional model along with other types of context. Social modeling is at least 100% better at each precision metric and MRR, another testimony to its reliability. Lastly, the spatial model on the contextual test set greatly outperforms itself on the random test set on $Prec$@1 and MRR, while it is marginally better on $Prec$@3 and $Prec$@5. This could be a result of the small size of this dataset, which also exhibits heavy locality due to its construction.

5 Conclusion and Future Work

In this paper, we introduce MRKGEC a novel context-aware recommender that mines meta-paths from a Neo4j KG and then uses a mixture of LSTMs and Multi-Head Attention modules to infer appropriate recommendations. MRKGEC proposes a novel and customized way to extract information straight out of a KG database modeling diverse contextual data. Our tests show that our model is competitive against other SOTA schemas, as well as its ability to exploit one or more contexts to infer context-dependent recommendations.

We plan to extend our experimental evaluation with additional big datasets to test our approach with respect to efficiency and other performance measures. Also, other neural network architectures, such as Transformers or CNNs, similar to [5], could be tested along MRKGEC's architecture, while, reinforcement learning is also an interesting avenue we plan to investigate for improving predictive accuracy. Lastly, testing with weighted contextual meta-paths will be explored.

Acknowledgement. This paper is a result of research conducted within the "MSc in Artificial Intelligence and Data Analytics" of the Department of Applied Informatics of University of Macedonia. The presentation of the paper is funded by the University of Macedonia Research Committee.

References

1. Ehrlinger, L., Wöß, W.: Towards a definition of knowledge graphs. In: Joint Proceedings of the Posters and Demos Track of SEMANTiCS2016 and SuCCESS 2016, vol. 1695. CEUR (2016)
2. Guo, Q., et al.: A survey on knowledge graph-based recommender systems. IEEE TKDE **34**(08), 3549–3568 (2022)
3. Hu, B., Shi, C., Zhao, W.X., Yu, P.S.: Leveraging meta-path based context for top-N recommendation with a neural co-attention model. In: Proceedings of the 24th ACM SIGKDD (2018)
4. Jhamb, Y., Ebesu, T., Fang, Y.: Attentive contextual denoising autoencoder for recommendation. In: Proceedings of the 2018 ACM SIGIR ICTIR, pp. 27–34 (2018)
5. Li, J., Xu, Z., Tang, Y., Zhao, B., Tian, H.: Deep hybrid knowledge graph embedding for top-N recommendation. In: Wang, G., Lin, X., Hendler, J., Song, W., Xu, Z., Liu, G. (eds.) WISA 2020. LNCS, vol. 12432, pp. 59–70. Springer, Cham (2020). https://doi.org/10.1007/978-3-030-60029-7_6
6. Luo, C., Pang, W., Wang, Z., Lin, C.: Hete-CF: social-based collaborative filtering recommendation using heterogeneous relations. In: 2014 IEEE International Conference on Data Mining (2014)
7. Pei, W., Yang, J., Sun, Z., Zhang, J., Bozzon, A., Tax, D.M.: Interacting attention-gated recurrent networks for recommendation. In: Proceedings of the 2017 ACM CIKM (2017)
8. Pham, T.A.N., Li, X., Cong, G., Zhang, Z.: A general recommendation model for heterogeneous networks. IEEE TKDE **28**(12), 3140–3153 (2016)
9. Shi, C., Zhang, Z., Ji, Y., Wang, W., Yu, P.S., Shi, Z.: SemRec: a personalized semantic recommendation method based on weighted heterogeneous information networks. World Wide Web **22**(1), 153–184 (2018)
10. Sun, Y., Han, J., Yan, X., Yu, P.S., Wu, T.: PathSim: meta path-based top-k similarity search in heterogeneous information networks. Proc. VLDB Endow. **4**(11), 992–1003 (2011)
11. Sun, Z., Yang, J., Zhang, J., Bozzon, A., Huang, L.K., Xu, C.: Recurrent knowledge graph embedding for effective recommendation. In: Proceedings of the 12th ACM Conference on Recommender Systems (2018)
12. van Rossum, B., Frasincar, F.: Augmenting LOD-based recommender systems using graph centrality measures (2019)
13. Wang, X., Wang, D., Xu, C., He, X., Cao, Y., Chua, T.S.: Explainable reasoning over knowledge graphs for recommendation. In: Proceedings of the AAAI Conference on Artificial Intelligence, vol. 33, pp. 5329–5336 (2019)
14. Webber, W., Moffat, A., Zobel, J.: A similarity measure for indefinite rankings. ACM Trans. Inf. Syst. **28**(4), 1–38 (2010)
15. Wever, T., Frasincar, F.: A linked open data schema-driven approach for top-n recommendations. In: Proceedings of the Symposium on Applied Computing, SAC 2017, pp. 656–663. ACM (2017)
16. Xu, K., et al.: Show, attend and tell: neural image caption generation with visual attention, pp. 2048–2057. PMLR (2015)
17. Yu, X., Ren, X., Gu, Q., Sun, Y., Han, J.: Collaborative filtering with entity similarity regularization in heterogeneous information networks. IJCAI HINA **27** (2013)
18. Yu, X., et al.: Recommendation in heterogeneous information networks with implicit user feedback. In: Proceedings of the 7th ACM Conference on Recommender Systems (2013)

19. Zhang, F., Yuan, N.J., Lian, D., Xie, X., Ma, W.Y.: Collaborative knowledge base embedding for recommender systems. In: Proceedings of the 22nd ACM SIGKDD (2016)
20. Zhang, L., Li, X., Li, W., Zhou, H., Bai, Q.: Context-aware recommendation system using graph-based behaviours analysis. J. Syst. Sci. Syst. Eng. **30**, 482–494 (2021)
21. Zheng, J., Liu, J., Shi, C., Zhuang, F., Li, J., Wu, B.: Recommendation in heterogeneous information network via dual similarity regularization. Int. J. Data Sci. Anal. **3**(1), 35–48 (2016)
22. Zheng, Y., Mobasher, B., Burke, R.: Deviation-based contextual slim recommenders. In: Proceedings of the 23rd ACM CIKM, pp. 271–280 (2014)

Data Augmentation Using BERT-Based Models for Aspect-Based Sentiment Analysis

Bron Hollander, Flavius Frasincar(✉), and Finn van der Knaap

Erasmus University Rotterdam, Burgemeester Oudlaan 50, 3062 PA Rotterdam, The Netherlands
{511709bh,573834fk}@student.eur.nl, frasincar@ese.eur.nl

Abstract. In today's digital world, there is an overwhelming amount of opinionated data on the Web. However, effectively analyzing all available data proves to be a resource-intensive endeavor, requiring substantial time and financial investments to curate high-quality training datasets. To mitigate such problems, this paper compares data augmentation models for aspect-based sentiment analysis. Specifically, we analyze the effect of several BERT-based data augmentation methods on the performance of the state-of-the-art HAABSA++ model. We consider the following data augmentation models: EDA-adjusted (baseline), BERT, Conditional-BERT, $\text{BERT}_{\text{prepend}}$, and $\text{BERT}_{\text{expand}}$. Our findings show that incorporating data augmentation techniques can significantly improve the out-of-sample accuracy of the HAABSA++ model. Specifically, our results highlight the effectiveness of $\text{BERT}_{\text{prepend}}$ and $\text{BERT}_{\text{expand}}$, increasing the test accuracy from 78.56% to 79.23% and from 82.62% to 84.47% for the SemEval 2015 and SemEval 2016 datasets, respectively.

Keywords: Aspect-based sentiment classification · Data augmentation · Neural network · Pre-trained language model

1 Introduction

The modern era of the Web has made it effortless for people to share information, allowing consumers to express their opinions about various products and services more easily than ever. The abundance of user-generated data presents an opportunity for consumers and businesses. For instance, businesses could use newly created reviews to confirm their marketing strategy at several levels [6], whereas consumers could use it to help them make more informed decisions [20]. However, effectively using the available data requires a deep understanding of the contents and sentiment present in the review. As such, Aspect-Based Sentiment Analysis (ABSA), which entails extracting the sentiment with respect to an aspect in a review, can be valuable. According to the survey of [1], ABSA encompasses three primary approaches: a knowledge-based approach, a machine-learning approach, and a hybrid approach. [1] also demonstrates the potential

K. Stefanidis et al. (Eds.): ICWE 2024, LNCS 14629, pp. 115–122, 2024.
https://doi.org/10.1007/978-3-031-62362-2_8

of hybrid models to effectively predict sentiment. Nonetheless, a common issue of these models is the lack of available labeled data for training purposes.

To address the scarcity of labeled data, previous literature has proposed several data augmentation techniques [14]. [8] shows the effectiveness of Easy Data Augmentation (EDA) in improving sentiment predictions of the Hybrid Approach for Aspect-Based Sentiment Analysis (HAABSA) model [16]. Nevertheless, EDA has its limitations, such as potential changes in sentiment or sentence incoherence after augmentation. Recent studies use neural networks for data augmentation, in particular pre-trained transformer models, to enhance sentiment preservation and contextual awareness during augmentation [5].

The impressive performance of Bidirectional Encoder Representations from Transformers (BERT)-based models in Natural Language Processing (NLP) tasks suggests that such models may be well suited for data augmentation. In this paper, we aim to investigate the impact of BERT-based data augmentation techniques on the performance of the HAABSA++ model, a state-of-the-art hybrid method for ABSA proposed in [15].

The contribution of this paper to existing literature is as follows. In contrast to previous approaches, such as EDA for HAABSA [8], we extend the comparison of data augmentation techniques for HAABSA++ to Pre-trained Language Models (PLMs) [5], namely BERT [2], Conditional-BERT (C-BERT) [18], $\text{BERT}_{\text{prepend}}$, and $\text{BERT}_{\text{expand}}$ [5], therefore providing a homogeneous comparison between all aforementioned data augmentation models. This paper focuses on BERT instead of other language models, as [18] shows the superior effectiveness of a bidirectional language model over a unidirectional language model.

The Python source code and data (SemEval 2015 [12] and 2016 [13] restaurant review datasets) used in this study are available at https://github.com/BronHol/HAABSA_PLUS_PLUS_DA. Figure 1 illustrates an example review represented in the XML format.


```
▼<sentence id="1032695:1">
   <text>Everything is always cooked to perfection, the service is excellent, the decor cool and understated.</text>
  ▼<Opinions>
     <Opinion target="NULL" category="FOOD#QUALITY" polarity="positive" from="0" to="0"/>
     <Opinion target="service" category="SERVICE#GENERAL" polarity="positive" from="47" to="54"/>
     <Opinion target="decor" category="AMBIENCE#GENERAL" polarity="positive" from="73" to="78"/>
   </Opinions>
 </sentence>
```


Fig. 1. Example review in the XML format

The rest of the paper is structured as follows. Section 2 gives an overview of the HAABSA++ model and the considered data augmentation techniques followed by, in Sect. 3, a discussion of the obtained results. Last, Sect. 4 provides our conclusion and suggestions for future research.

2 Methodology

In this section, we present the HAABSA++ model and the considered methods for data augmentation. First, we discuss the model used for ABSA, HAABSA++, in Subsect. 2.1, which is a two-step approach that combines a domain sentiment ontology and a neural network. Second, the considered data augmentation techniques are presented in Subsect. 2.2.

2.1 HAABSA++

HAABSA++ [15] is a hybrid approach that extends the HAABSA model [16] with contextualized word embeddings and hierarchical attention. The first step of HAABSA++ is to classify the sentiment using a domain sentiment ontology. For the inconclusive cases, HAABSA++ uses the LCR-Rot-hop++ model.

Domain Sentiment Ontology. The used domain sentiment ontology in the HAABSA++ model [15] predicts sentiment by leveraging predefined classes, class relations, and axioms. It is important to note that the ontology reasoner does not incorporate any classes or relations specifically addressing neutral sentiment. As such, the rule-based methodology is limited to detecting positive and negative emotions. Therefore, the ontology may not be reliable in three situations: (1) neutral sentiment, which is intentionally excluded from the reasoner, (2) conflicting sentiment, where both positive and negative sentiments are predicted for a target, and (3) no hits, resulting from limited coverage of the ontology. In such cases, the LCR-Rot-hop++ model serves as a backup method.

LCR-Rot-hop++. The LCR-Rot-hop++ model [15] is an extension of the LCR-Rot model [21]. [16] first improves the model by repeating the rotatory attention mechanism which helps to properly weight the relevant sentiment words, resulting in LCR-Rot-hop. [15] then replaces the context-independent GloVe embeddings [11] with context-dependent BERT embeddings, and proposes a hierarchical attention structure to enhance the model's flexibility, resulting in the LCR-Rot-hop++ model.

2.2 Data Augmentation

Data augmentation involves manipulating existing data to expand the size of a dataset artificially, thereby generating additional data points with modified variations. The expansion of training data through data augmentation is crucial for improving the sentiment predictions of HAABSA++, or more specifically LCR-Rot-hop++, due to the limited available training data. In this section, we discuss the various data augmentation techniques considered in this paper.

Easy Data Augmentation. The EDA technique, proposed in [17], is a straightforward and effective approach for data augmentation in NLP tasks. It encompasses four operations: synonym replacement, random insertion, random swap, and random deletion. [8] extends the EDA method specifically for ABSA tasks, adding word sense disambiguation, which tackles the challenge of selecting the correct word meaning and function within a sentence. The POS tag of each word is determined, and the Lesk algorithm is used to identify the most suitable word meaning based on contextual information. The simplified Lesk algorithm, implemented using the WordNet library, is used for both synonym replacement and random insertion. Moreover, the proposed method introduces target swaps across sentences, enabling the swapping of target words within the same category to provide diverse contexts. The EDA-adjusted model, combining these three methods, serves as a baseline model in this paper.

BERT. A more advanced approach for data augmentation in ABSA involves using PLMs. BERT [2] is advantageous because it captures both the left and right context simultaneously and therefore considers the context of the target word [3], making it extremely useful for ABSA tasks. BERT is trained using MLM and Next Sentence Prediction (NSP). In MLM, certain words in a sentence are masked, and BERT tries to predict the masked words. NSP involves providing BERT with two sentences (A and B) and asking the model to predict whether sentence B follows sentence A. The input embeddings of BERT consist of token embeddings, segment embeddings, and position embeddings [2].

To augment the data, we use the MLM task of BERT [2]. During MLM, multiple candidate words are generated as potential replacements for masked tokens. This approach generates new sentences that convey similar meaning to the original input. Following the standard BERT approach, we mask each word in a sentence with a probability of 15% [5]. Subsequently, we select the substitute word with the highest probability for each masked word, excluding the original word. By applying this process to every sentence in the original training dataset, we generate a new sentence for each sentence in the dataset.

C-BERT. A downside of using BERT for data augmentation is that the original sentiment label of a sentence is not taken into account, which may result in the loss of the original sentiment information when replacing the masked words. To address this issue, [18] proposes the C-BERT model. In the C-BERT model, the sentence is augmented conditional on the label of the sentence itself. To incorporate label information during the MLM process, the segment embeddings in BERT are replaced with label embeddings, and the model is trained on labeled datasets. Once C-BERT is trained and equipped with knowledge of both sentiment and context, it can be used to augment data similarly to the original BERT model.

$\text{BERT}_{\text{prepend}}$. By replacing the segment embedding with label embeddings, C-BERT becomes less suitable for diverse tasks because of its inherent specificity. [5] introduces $\text{BERT}_{\text{prepend}}$ as an extension of the original BERT model to condition data augmentations on the label without sacrificing generality. In $\text{BERT}_{\text{prepend}}$, the label of each sequence is prepended to the sequence itself, without including the label in the model's vocabulary. By considering the label of a sequence, $\text{BERT}_{\text{prepend}}$ facilitates data augmentations that are label-aware.

The label of the sequence remains fixed, ensuring that it is not masked during augmentation. After applying $\text{BERT}_{\text{prepend}}$, the labels are removed, and the augmented data is incorporated into the training data of HAABSA++.

$\text{BERT}_{\text{expand}}$. $\text{BERT}_{\text{expand}}$ follows a similar approach to $\text{BERT}_{\text{prepend}}$, where the label of each sequence is prepended to the sequence itself. However, a notable difference is that $\text{BERT}_{\text{expand}}$ includes the label in the model's vocabulary, unlike $\text{BERT}_{\text{prepend}}$. In $\text{BERT}_{\text{expand}}$, the label is treated as a single token, whereas $\text{BERT}_{\text{prepend}}$ may split it into multiple subwords depending on the used word tokenizer [4].

Fine-Tuning BERT-Based Models. We fine-tune the hyperparameters of our models for the MLM task and use the complete SemEval training set. For $\text{BERT}_{\text{prepend}}$ and $\text{BERT}_{\text{expand}}$, we prepare the dataset by prepending the sentiment label of each sequence to the sequence. 80% of the training dataset is used for fine-tuning and the other 20% is used for validation of hyperparameter configurations. We run the fine-tuning process for 10 epochs. Following [5], we use the default masking parameters.

3 Results

The training and test accuracies of the considered models are presented in Table 1, including the number of data augmentations added to the training data for each model. The training accuracy score pertains to the in-sample accuracy, while the testing accuracy corresponds to the out-of-sample accuracy. The inclusion of training scores primarily serves to gauge potential model overfitting, while the evaluation of model performance relies primarily on testing accuracies.

Table 1. The training and test accuracies of HAABSA++ and the considered data augmentation models

	SemEval 2015			SemEval 2016		
	Train acc.	Test acc.	#aug.	Train acc.	Test acc.	#aug.
HAABSA++	90.86%	78.56%	0	89.96%	82.62%	0
EDA-adjusted	90.70%	**82.41%**	3834	89.75%	81.85%	5640
BERT	91.02%	79.06%	1278	**91.30%**	82.77%	1880
C-BERT	**91.12%**	75.71%	1278	90.91%	82.00%	1880
$\text{BERT}_{\text{prepend}}$	91.04%	79.23%	1278	89.29%	**84.47%**	1880
$\text{BERT}_{\text{expand}}$	91.04%	79.23%	1278	89.29%	**84.47%**	1880

For the SemEval 2015 dataset, the HAABSA++ model without any data augmentation achieves a test accuracy of 78.56%. Comparatively, the EDA-adjusted model achieves the highest test accuracy of 82.41%, which is an improvement of 3.85% points. The EDA-adjusted model uses 3834 data augmentations, whereas all the BERT-based models only use 1278 data augmentations (EDA-adjusted has three augmentation equations while BERT-based models only have one). The best-performing BERT-based models are $\text{BERT}_{\text{prepend}}$ and $\text{BERT}_{\text{expand}}$, with both a test accuracy of 79.23%. Contrary to the other data augmentation models, we observe that C-BERT does not improve the performance of the HAABSA++ model.

For the SemEval 2016 dataset, we observe that the plain HAABSA++ model achieves a test accuracy of 82.62%. However, for this dataset, the EDA-adjusted model does not increase the test accuracy compared to HAABSA++, obtaining a test accuracy of 81.85% despite using 5640 augmentations. Similarly, the C-BERT model does not improve the performance of HAABSA++. The poor out-of-sample performance of C-BERT in both datasets could be attributed to the replacement of segment embeddings with label embeddings, thereby forgetting the order of sentences and the semantics between these sentences. On the other hand, the BERT model achieves a test accuracy of 82.77% with 1880 augmentations, whilst both $\text{BERT}_{\text{prepend}}$ and $\text{BERT}_{\text{expand}}$ outperform all other models with a test accuracy of 84.47%. So, $\text{BERT}_{\text{prepend}}$ and $\text{BERT}_{\text{expand}}$ obtain an improvement of 1.85% points.

EDA-adjusted, which is a lexicon-based method using grammatical rules and linguistics, works better for smaller datasets. On the other hand, machine learning approaches, such as the considered BERT-based models, thrive with larger datasets. As a result, EDA-adjusted achieves the highest out-of-sample accuracy for the SemEval 2015 dataset but performs modestly on the SemEval 2016 dataset.

An intriguing observation is that $\text{BERT}_{\text{prepend}}$ and $\text{BERT}_{\text{expand}}$ yield identical results. This can be attributed to the WordPiece tokenizer [19] that is used in BERT. Due to the tokenizer's behavior, sentiment labels (positive, neutral, and negative) remain intact without being split into multiple tokens. Consequently, incorporating the sentiment labels into the tokenizer's vocabulary does not alter the tokenization process for sentiment labels. As a result, the fine-tuning process treats the prepended labels in the same manner, resulting in indistinguishable data augmentations.

4 Conclusion

In this work, we extended the state-of-the-art HAABSA++ model proposed in [15] by incorporating various data augmentation techniques, including EDA-adjusted [8] and BERT-based models [5,18]. The main objective of data augmentation is to enhance the out-of-sample accuracy by training the neural network of HAABSA++ more effectively on a larger training dataset. Our findings revealed that the performance of HAABSA++ can indeed be improved upon through the use of data augmentation methods, although the effectiveness of each data augmentation model varies depending on the used dataset. Specifically, for the smaller SemEval 2015 dataset, the lexicon-based EDA-adjusted method achieved the largest improvement, with an increase of 3.85% points over the baseline. On the other hand, for the larger SemEval 2016 dataset, the $\text{BERT}_{\text{prepend}}$ and $\text{BERT}_{\text{expand}}$ methods performed best, with an increase of 1.85% points. Overall, based on the performance for both datasets, $\text{BERT}_{\text{prepend}}$ and $\text{BERT}_{\text{expand}}$ emerge as the most effective data augmentation methods for the HAABSA++ model.

For future research, it could be interesting to examine the impact of selectively masking words in the MLM process. Now, we observe that words without semantic information are substituted by the MLM task. [10] shows that masking sentimental words or adjectives and adverbs can lead to improvements in performance. In addition, the inclusion of additional data augmentation models, such as BART or RoBERTa, could be interesting, as these models have demonstrated excellent performance in a variety of tasks [7,9].

References

1. Brauwers, G., Frasincar, F.: A survey on aspect-based sentiment classification. ACM Comput. Surv. **55**(4), 65:1–65:37 (2023)
2. Devlin, J., Chang, M., Lee, K., Toutanova, K.: BERT: pre-training of deep bidirectional transformers for language understanding. In: 2019 Conference of the North American Chapter of the Association for Computational Linguistics: Human Language Technologies (NAACL-HLT 2019), pp. 4171–4186. ACL (2019)
3. Hoang, M., Bihorac, O.A., Rouces, J.: Aspect-based sentiment analysis using BERT. In: 22nd Nordic Conference on Computational Linguistics (NoDaLiDa 2019), pp. 187–196. Linköping University Electronic Press (2019)
4. Kudo, T., Richardson, J.: SentencePiece: a simple and language independent subword tokenizer and detokenizer for neural text processing. In: 2018 Conference on Empirical Methods in Natural Language Processing (EMNLP 2018), pp. 66–71. ACL (2018)
5. Kumar, V., Choudhary, A., Cho, E.: Data augmentation using pre-trained transformer models. arXiv preprint arXiv:2003.02245 (2020)
6. Lee, T.Y., Bradlow, E.T.: Automated marketing research using online customer reviews. J. Mark. Res. **48**(5), 881–894 (2011)
7. Lewis, M., et al.: BART: denoising sequence-to-sequence pre-training for natural language generation, translation, and comprehension. In: 58th Annual Meeting of the Association for Computational Linguistics (ACL 2020), pp. 7871–7880. ACL (2020)
8. Liesting, T., Frasincar, F., Trusca, M.M.: Data augmentation in a hybrid approach for aspect-based sentiment analysis. In: 36th ACM/SIGAPP Symposium on Applied Computing (SAC 2021), pp. 828–835. ACM (2021)
9. Liu, Y., et al.: RoBERTa: a robustly optimized BERT pretraining approach. arXiv preprint arXiv:1907.11692 (2019)
10. Pantelidou, K., Chatzakou, D., Tsikrika, T., Vrochidis, S., Kompatsiaris, I.: Selective word substitution for contextualized data augmentation. In: Rosso, P., Basile, V., Martínez, R., Métais, E., Meziane, F. (eds.) NLDB 2022. LNCS, vol. 13286, pp. 508–516. Springer, Cham (2022). https://doi.org/10.1007/978-3-031-08473-7_47

11. Pennington, J., Socher, R., Manning, C.D.: GloVe: global vectors for word representation. In: 2014 Conference on Empirical Methods in Natural Language Processing (EMNLP 2014), pp. 1532–1543. ACL (2014)
12. Pontiki, M., Galanis, D., Papageorgiou, H., Manandhar, S., Androutsopoulos, I.: SemEval-2015 task 12: aspect based sentiment analysis. In: 9th International Workshop on Semantic Evaluation (SemEval 2015), pp. 486–495. ACL (2015)
13. Pontiki, M., et al.: SemEval-2016 task 5: aspect based sentiment analysis. In: 10th International Workshop on Semantic Evaluation (SemEval 2016), pp. 19–30. ACL (2016)
14. Shani, C., Zarecki, J., Shahaf, D.: The lean data scientist: recent advances toward overcoming the data bottleneck. Commun. ACM **66**(2), 92–102 (2023)
15. Truşcă, M.M., Wassenberg, D., Frasincar, F., Dekker, R.: A hybrid approach for aspect-based sentiment analysis using deep contextual word embeddings and hierarchical attention. In: Bielikova, M., Mikkonen, T., Pautasso, C. (eds.) ICWE 2020. LNCS, vol. 12128, pp. 365–380. Springer, Cham (2020). https://doi.org/10.1007/978-3-030-50578-3_25
16. Wallaart, O., Frasincar, F.: A hybrid approach for aspect-based sentiment analysis using a lexicalized domain ontology and attentional neural models. In: Hitzler, P., et al. (eds.) ESWC 2019. LNCS, vol. 11503, pp. 363–378. Springer, Cham (2019). https://doi.org/10.1007/978-3-030-21348-0_24
17. Wei, J.W., Zou, K.: EDA: easy data augmentation techniques for boosting performance on text classification tasks. In: 2019 Conference on Empirical Methods in Natural Language Processing and the 9th International Joint Conference on Natural Language Processing (EMNLP-IJCNLP 2019), pp. 6381–6387. ACL (2019)
18. Wu, X., Lv, S., Zang, L., Han, J., Hu, S.: Conditional BERT contextual augmentation. In: Rodrigues, J.M.F., Cardoso, P.J.S., Monteiro, J., Lam, R., Krzhizhanovskaya, V.V., Lees, M.H., Dongarra, J.J., Sloot, P.M.A. (eds.) ICCS 2019. LNCS, vol. 11539, pp. 84–95. Springer, Cham (2019). https://doi.org/10.1007/978-3-030-22747-0_7
19. Wu, Y., et al.: Google's neural machine translation system: bridging the gap between human and machine translation. arXiv preprint arXiv:1609.08144 (2016)
20. Zhang, Y., Du, J., Ma, X., Wen, H., Fortino, G.: Aspect-based sentiment analysis for user reviews. Cogn. Comput. **13**(5), 1114–1127 (2021)
21. Zheng, S., Xia, R.: Left-center-right separated neural network for aspect-based sentiment analysis with rotatory attention. arXiv preprint arXiv:1802.00892 (2018)

Streamlining Vocabulary Conversion to SKOS: A YAML-Based Approach to Facilitate Participation in the Semantic Web

Christoph Göpfert(✉), Jan Ingo Haas, Lucas Schröder, and Martin Gaedke

Technische Universität Chemnitz, 09111 Chemnitz, Germany
{christoph.goepfert,jan-ingo.haas,lucas.schroeder, martin.gaedke}@informatik.tu-chemnitz.de

Abstract. Controlled vocabularies, such as classification schemes, glossaries, taxonomies, or thesauri, play an important role in many Web services. One of the main areas of application of controlled vocabularies is the domain of information retrieval systems, as they can be used to improve the findability of resources. For instance, concepts described in a vocabulary may be used to uniquely classify resources, to tag them with relevant keywords, or to annotate them with domain-specific attributes. The Simple Knowledge Organization System (SKOS) is an established data model of the Semantic Web domain that can be used to describe vocabularies in a semantically structured format. However, modelling a vocabulary is oftentimes highly time demanding, labor-intensive, and requires both familiarity with basic Semantic Web technologies and expertise in the application domain. This complicates both the development of new vocabularies and the conversion of existing vocabularies into the RDF data model. We propose an intermediate, YAML-based format to express concepts and their relationships hierarchically. The intermediate format can be converted automatically into a SKOS vocabulary using a command-line conversion program. To demonstrate the feasibility of our approach, we selected 26 vocabularies of highly diverse formats, expressed them in the proposed intermediate format, which was subsequently converted in an automated manner into the corresponding SKOS vocabulary using our yaml2skos program. Our approach enables users with little to no familiarity with the Semantic Web to develop SKOS vocabularies, thereby lowering the barrier to participation in the Semantic Web landscape.

Keywords: Vocabulary · Controlled Vocabulary · Conversion · Simple Knowledge Organization System · SKOS · Semantic Web · Linked Data · Taxonomy · Glossary · Thesaurus

1 Introduction

Controlled vocabularies are a widely used way of representing knowledge such as glossaries, taxonomies, or thesauri. The application areas of controlled vocabularies are extremely diverse, ranging from the classification of cultural works [1], the classification of literature or publications [2, 3] to various thesauri [4, 5] and taxonomies [6]. A

K. Stefanidis et al. (Eds.): ICWE 2024, LNCS 14629, pp. 123–130, 2024.
https://doi.org/10.1007/978-3-031-62362-2_9

major area of application of controlled vocabularies can be found in information retrieval, especially in systems utilizing keyword-based search methods. Performing simple syntactic comparisons between search terms and keywords used for annotation of resources often leads to incorrect search results [7, 8]. Through the use of controlled vocabularies, these can be improved [8].

The Simple Knowledge Organization System[1] (SKOS) offers a semantically structured data model for representing controlled vocabularies. In the literature, the use of the terms "glossary", "taxonomy", "thesaurus", "vocabulary" and "ontology" is often ambiguous. Our proposed approach can be used with any knowledge model mappable to the SKOS data model. For this reason, we use the term vocabulary as a collective term for the aforementioned terms in the subsequent sections.

The development of vocabularies in SKOS requires an understanding of Semantic Web technologies, especially the Resource Description Framework[2] (RDF) data model and RDF formats. In addition, the effort required to develop or to translate a vocabulary into SKOS can be time demanding.

In this paper, we present an approach for creating SKOS vocabularies using an intermediate format. Using this intermediate format, new vocabularies can be created from scratch and existing vocabularies that can be mapped to SKOS can be expressed as well. The intermediate format's structure is intended to be as human-readable as possible to facilitate vocabulary creation. In addition, the verbosity compared to common RDF formats is reduced, which in turn cuts down on the amount of typing required.

The rest of the paper is structured as follows. In Sect. 2, related work is reviewed. Section 3 presents the structure of the proposed intermediate format and details the conversion of the intermediate format to SKOS. Section 4 evaluates the proposed approach by expressing 26 taxonomies of diverse formats in the intermediate format, converting them to SKOS and assessing the quality of the resulting SKOS vocabularies. Finally, Sect. 5 outlines conclusions.

2 Related Work

Van Assem et al. [9] introduce an approach for converting structured data (like WordNet[3]) onto RDF. The proposed idea features mapping the syntactical elements as well as the structural hierarchy of the source format onto RDF using OWL as a meta format, augmenting the resulting metamodel with semantic properties that did not exist in the original model. This step allows for interpretation of the source model. As a last step, the metamodel is standardized, i.e. transferred into SKOS. Our approach differs in two fundamental ways. Firstly, the described approach requires the data to be mapped to be available in a structured format. Our approach allows for conversion of any format to SKOS, as long as it can be represented in SKOS. Secondly, we forgo the syntactical mapping of the source data onto a metamodel. Instead we use SKOS as our destination model, directly converting to it via an intermediate, semantically equivalent format.

[1] https://www.w3.org/TR/skos-reference/.

[2] https://www.w3.org/TR/rdf11-concepts/.

[3] https://wordnet.princeton.edu/.

The authors of [10] make a distinction between "thesauri with standard structure" and "thesauri with non-standard structure". While the first can be easily transferred to SKOS, the latter has semantics that are not inherent in the SKOS standard and thus for the purpose of integration into SKOS, an extension to declare subclasses has to be developed. An adaption of this idea is proposed in [11]. Common to both approaches is the need for the implementation of a program that performs the final mapping from the intermediate RDF format for each respective process. Our approach differs in this regard our intermediate format is built upon YAML, thus making the conversion into SKOS fully automated for every conversion process.

More recent approaches aim to semi-automate the conversion process. A notable example of this is Skosify [12] which accepts RDF graphs and with the help of a mapping scheme transforms those into SKOS. By specifying the configuration file for the mapping scheme, the previously mentioned approaches are effectively formalized. However, the conversion is not fully automated as it requires the data to exist in an RDF format. Our approach avoids the use of existing RDF formats to perform conversions. Instead we chose to extend YAML as an easy and human-readable format.

YAML is a popular choice for an intermediate format, notable examples are yaml2sbml [13], a tool to convert from a YAML based language to SBML and YARRRML [14] which can be employed when converting from various data sources to an RDF format using a simplified and human readable representation of RML rules.

Another approach to the development of vocabularies are programs that offer WYSIWYG interfaces. A popular representative of this approach is the tool Protegé [15]. Protegé is a software framework for creating and editing ontologies.

3 Vocabulary Conversion

We introduce a novel third approach that does not assume the user to have any prior knowledge of RDF formats. Instead, we introduce an intermediate format for describing vocabularies. This intermediate format can then be processed using the *yaml2skos* conversion program we developed to generate an equivalent SKOS vocabulary in a desired RDF format. The structure of the intermediate format and the conversion to the SKOS vocabulary are detailed in the following sections.

3.1 Intermediate Format Design

Developing a vocabulary in an RDF format requires the developer to have some knowledge of the RDF data model and its formats, which is an obvious obstacle to participation in the Semantic Web. Moreover, the primary motivation behind the RDF data model was to design a format that is easily machine-processable. Common RDF formats do by default not visually represent the hierarchical structure of concepts well, which complicates spotting errors in the hierarchy of a vocabulary for users.

The SKOS data model is characterized by its simplicity, as reflected in the relatively small number of classes and properties. With the intermediate format presented below, we are pursuing the objective of maintaining this simplicity by reflecting it in the format, i.e. in its user-friendly notation and reduction of superfluous statements.

The intermediate format we propose bases on the YAML format and extends on terms defined by the SKOS Core vocabulary. YAML has been used before as a format for intermediate files in similar scenarios [13, 16], due to its human-friendly structure. As the intermediate file is to be used by our *yaml2skos* program to automatically generate the equivalent SKOS vocabulary, its expressiveness must be sufficient to represent instances of all classes and properties defined in the SKOS core vocabulary.

```yaml
meta:
    id: hri
    uri: https://purl.org/net/vsr/taxannot/hri
    dcterms:
        - title: A Taxonomy to Structure and Analyze Human-Robot Interaction
        - creator: Linda Onnasch
        - creator: Eileen Roesler
```

Listing 1: "meta" section including DCMI Terms metadata (in YAML)

```
@prefix dct: <http://purl.org/dc/terms/> .
@prefix skos: <http://www.w3.org/2004/02/skos/core#> .

<https://purl.org/net/vsr/taxannot/hri#hri> a skos:ConceptScheme ;
    dct:creator "Eileen Roesler"@en,
        "Linda Onnasch"@en ;
    dct:title "A Taxonomy to Structure and Analyze Human-Robot Interaction"@en ;
    skos:hasTopConcept <https://purl.org/net/vsr/taxannot/hri#fields-of-application> .
```

Listing 2: SKOS excerpt generated from "meta" section (in Turtle format)

The structure of the intermediate format is separated into two main sections, a meta section, and a remaining section for the description of the actual concepts, optionally as part of ordered or unordered collections that may be included in the vocabulary. A complete list of the available terms of the intermediate format can be found in our openly accessible repository[4]. The meta section is intended to specify general meta information about the vocabulary. It is required to specify a default namespace which will subsequently be used for any concepts described in the vocabulary which no other namespace is explicitly stated for. Optionally, further namespaces may be specified as well. It is also required to specify an id for the vocabulary. Besides this information, further optional metadata may be specified using any terms of the DCMI Metadata Terms vocabulary[5], as shown in Listing 1. Any metadata provided in the meta section will be used to describe the vocabulary's *ConceptScheme* node that will be generated by the program automatically. An example for this is shown in Listing 2, which *yaml2skos* generated using the data shown in Listing 1 as input.

The remaining section is intended for the definition of concepts, optionally as part of an ordered or unordered collection. The intermediate format does not require collections to be defined, however, it requires at least one concept to be defined. In order to define a concept to be an upper concept of another concept, users may use a nested notation style

---

[4] https://purl.org/net/vsr/taxannot/yaml2skos.

[5] https://www.dublincore.org/specifications/dublin-core/dcmi-terms/.

to do so. An example of this notation is shown in Listing 3 (left). By using an indented notation style, the hierarchical relation of the concepts is visualized for the user, which makes it easier to locate potential errors in the hierarchy.

```
concepts:
  fields-of-application:
    - l: Fields of Application
    - narrower:
      - industry:
        - l: Industry
        - def: Industry is ...
      - service:
        - l: Service
        - def: Service is ...
```

```
concepts:
  fields-of-application:
    - l: Fields of Application
  industry:
    - l: Industry
    - def: Industry is ...
    - broader: fields-of-application
  service:
    - l: Service
    - def: Service is ...
    - broader: fields-of-application
```

Listing 3:" concepts" section using nested notation (left) and reference notation style (right)

```
collections:
  collection_fields:
    - l: A first collection
    - industry
    - service
  collection_roles:
    - l: A second collection
    - supervisor
    - collaborator
```

Listing 4: Assigning concepts into collections

An alternative approach to model such relations can be achieved by referencing the corresponding concepts instead. This approach should be preferred for larger vocabularies, especially for vocabularies with deep hierarchies, as the nested notation would result in large indentations, negatively impacting readability. Listing 3 (right) shows an equivalent example, in which referencing is used instead of the nested notation.

The described concepts may be assigned to a collection. An example is shown in Listing 4, in which two collections are defined. A "collections"- or "ordered-collections"-section must be created. Then, collections and associated concepts can be listed.

3.2 Conversion to SKOS

Once a vocabulary has been expressed in the intermediate format, it can be converted with the *yaml2skos* program into an equivalent SKOS representation. The program processes each of the key-value pairs and generates corresponding triple statements. Users may specify a desired output format; most common RDF formats are supported.

The program validates the vocabulary using Skosify. Once the validation succeeds without severe issues, Skosify is used to enrich the generated vocabulary. Finally, the vocabulary will be output in SKOS. The program generates additional triples from implicit information and thus relieves the user of unnecessary tasks when modeling the vocabulary. This includes the automatic tagging of string literals to the desired language, or English by default. Concepts, collections, and the concept scheme node are automatically assigned to their respective SKOS class. The vocabulary is described by the concept scheme node using information provided in the "meta" section.

4 Evaluation

To evaluate our approach, we selected 26 vocabularies, transferred them into the proposed intermediate format and converted them into SKOS using *yaml2skos*. Finally, we evaluated their quality using the qSKOS vocabulary assessment framework [17].

4.1 Vocabulary Selection

We conducted a systematic literature review following the procedure described by Kitchenham [18] to identify suitable controlled vocabularies. First, we set the scope to exclusively consider vocabularies related to the computer science domain as well as intersecting fields. We established two inclusion and two exclusion criteria to filter search results. Since our main objective was to identify vocabularies, we assumed that the title of a suitable search result suggests containing a vocabulary, otherwise the search result was discarded. If the title suggested containing a vocabulary, the content of the search result was inspected for the presence of a vocabulary. In case the search result did not contain a vocabulary, it was discarded. Furthermore, the search was limited to only considering the first 100 search results per search query and results in the English language.

The following search engines and catalogues were used as sources: Google Scholar, ACM Digital Library, IEEE Xplore, Springer Link, Science Direct, Web of Science and BARTOC. A total of 78 searches were carried out. After applying the in- and exclusion criteria, 57 search results remained. 18 results were removed as they were either duplicates, inaccessible or the described vocabulary was not expressible in SKOS. Further 13 vocabularies were excluded as they were either already available in SKOS or in OWL[6] (Web Ontology Language) format which also does not require a manual conversion as OWL can be converted using the tool Skosify. The formats of the remaining vocabularies were highly diverse, among others including HTML (5), images (12), tables (3), or text (2). The vocabularies converted to SKOS, including further vocabularies converted using Skosify, are available on Zenodo[7]. The 26 selected vocabularies are also listed on Zenodo[8], including their shortname in brackets which was used to refer to the respective vocabulary in the quality assessment in the next Sect. 4.2.

[6] https://www.w3.org/OWL/.
[7] https://doi.org/10.5281/zenodo.7908855.
[8] https://doi.org/10.5281/zenodo.10652215.

4.2 Vocabulary Quality Assessment

For the 26 remaining vocabularies, representations in the intermediate formats were created, which were then used to generate equivalent SKOS vocabularies using the *yaml2skos* program. We then analyzed the quality of the resulting SKOS vocabularies using quality metrics of the qSKOS vocabulary assessment tool [17]. The default configuration of qSKOS was used. The results of the quality assessment are available on Zenodo[8]. Quality metrics that were not satisfied by at least one or more vocabularies are addressed below:

Quality issues were indicated for metrics Q3 and Q13 due to some vocabularies containing concept clusters and orphaned concepts. These cases were no errors, but intended by design, as e.g. glossaries commonly contain "orphaned" concepts. Further issues were raised for metrics Q6, Q15 and Q24. In most cases, the cause could be found in the design of the source vocabulary. For instance, some concepts were explicitly related to multiple top-level concepts, violating Q6, or semantically similar concepts were sub-concept of different parent concepts, violating Q15. Further, explicitly stating relations in both directions in the intermediary format violated Q24, although this is not a modeling error per se, but superfluous information. As the evaluation using qSKOS examined only one vocabulary at a time, the tool was unable to recognize that some *skos:closeMatch* relationships related to concepts in external vocabularies. Consequently, the tool incorrectly assumed a relation via a mapping property to a member that is not part of a concept schema. This led to a poor score in metric Q10 which should be regarded a false positive. The poor ratings for metrics Q10 and Q21 were caused by their source vocabularies not containing labels or definitions for all concepts.

In summary, it can be observed that many of the encountered quality problems were already present in the source vocabularies. The quality of the generated vocabularies is therefore directly related to the quality of the source vocabularies.

5 Conclusion

In this paper, we propose an intermediate format for modeling vocabularies from which an equivalent SKOS vocabulary can be automatically generated. The intermediate format is intended to enable users with little or no familiarity with Semantic Web technologies to develop new or to transfer existing vocabularies into SKOS. The intermediate format is designed with a simple structure to provide users with an easily readable and understandable format. Vocabularies expressed in the introduced intermediate format can be automatically converted into a SKOS vocabulary using our *yaml2skos* tool.

To demonstrate the feasibility of our approach, we selected 26 vocabularies which were present in varying formats. These vocabularies were first transcribed into the YAML-based intermediate format before being automatically converted into the SKOS data model. The quality of the generated vocabularies was assessed using the qSKOS vocabulary quality assessment framework. The results of this assessment show that SKOS vocabularies can be successfully generated using our proposed approach.

Our approach makes an effort to reduce the barrier of developing SKOS vocabularies by providing a novel intermediate format that does not require familiarity with Semantic Web technologies to represent vocabularies.

Acknowledgement. The research was partially funded by the Deutsche Forschungsgemeinschaft (DFG, German Research Foundation)—Project-ID 514664767—TRR 386.

References

1. Introduction to Controlled Vocabularies: Terminologies for Art, Architecture, and Other Cultural Works
2. The 2012 ACM Computing Classification System
3. Library of Congress Classification Outline - Classification - Cataloging and Acquisitions (Library of Congress)
4. Scriven, M.: Evaluation Thesaurus. Edgepress (1981)
5. Thesaurus: mass communication - UNESCO Digital Library
6. Gawron, V.J., et al.: Human factors taxonomy. In: Proceedings of the Human Factors Society Annual Meeting, vol. 35, pp. 1284–1287 (1991)
7. Gross, T., Taylor, A.: What have we got to lose? The effect of controlled vocabulary on keyword searching results. Coll. Res. Libr. (2005)
8. Gross, T., Taylor, A.G., Joudrey, D.N.: Still a lot to lose: the role of controlled vocabulary in keyword searching. Cat. Classif. Q. **53**, 1–39 (2015)
9. van Assem, M., Menken, M.R., Schreiber, G., Wielemaker, J., Wielinga, B.: A method for converting thesauri to RDF/OWL. In: McIlraith, S.A., Plexousakis, D., van Harmelen, F. (eds.) ISWC 2004. LNCS, vol. 3298, pp. 17–31. Springer, Heidelberg (2004). https://doi.org/10.1007/978-3-540-30475-3_3
10. SWAD-Europe Thesaurus Activity: Deliverable 8.8 Migrating Thesauri to the Semantic Web
11. van Assem, M., Malaisé, V., Miles, A., Schreiber, G.: A method to convert thesauri to SKOS. In: Sure, Y., Domingue, J. (eds.) ESWC 2006. LNCS, vol. 4011, pp. 95–109. Springer, Heidelberg (2006). https://doi.org/10.1007/11762256_10
12. Suominen, O., Hyvönen, E.: Improving the quality of SKOS vocabularies with skosify. In: ten Teije, A., et al. (eds.) EKAW 2012. LNCS (LNAI), vol. 7603, pp. 383–397. Springer, Heidelberg (2012). https://doi.org/10.1007/978-3-642-33876-2_34
13. Vanhoefer, J., Matos, M., Pathirana, D., Schälte, Y., Hasenauer, J.: Yaml2sbml: human-readable and -writable specification of ODE models and their conversion to SBML. J. Open Source Softw. **6**, 3215 (2021)
14. Assche, D.V., Delva, T., Heyvaert, P., Meester, B.D., Dimou, A.: Towards a more human-friendly knowledge graph generation & publication (2021)
15. Musen, M.A.: The protégé project: a look back and a look forward. AI Matt. **1**, 4–12 (2015). https://doi.org/10.1145/2757001.2757003
16. Heyvaert, P., De Meester, B., Dimou, A., Verborgh, R.: Declarative rules for linked data generation at your fingertips! In: Gangemi, A., et al. (eds.) ESWC 2018. LNCS, vol. 11155, pp. 213–217. Springer, Cham (2018). https://doi.org/10.1007/978-3-319-98192-5_40
17. Mader, C., Haslhofer, B., Isaac, A.: Finding quality issues in SKOS vocabularies. In: Zaphiris, P., Buchanan, G., Rasmussen, E., Loizides, F. (eds.) TPDL 2012. LNCS, vol. 7489, pp. 222–233. Springer, Heidelberg (2012). https://doi.org/10.1007/978-3-642-33290-6_25
18. Kitchenham, B.: Procedures for performing systematic reviews (2004)

Advanced Tools, Frameworks, and Best Practices

The Open V2X Management Platform

Christos Dalamagkas, Angelos Georgakis, Kostas Hrissagis-Chrysagis, and George Papadakis(✉)

EU Programs Coordination Department, Public Power Corporation, Athens, Greece
{c.dalamagkas,an.georgakis,k.chrysagis,g_a.papadakis}@ppcgroup.com

Abstract. In this paper, we present an open-source web-based system, called Open V2X Management Platform (O-V2X-MP), which facilitates the management of charging points for electric vehicles with the goal of realizing Vehicle-to-Everything (V2X) scenarios. We describe its backend, which is composed of numerous components through a microservices architecture leveraging Docker containers. Using the C4 model methodology, we present the system context diagram with the main actors that interact with O-V2X-MP, the container diagram with the main communication flows between its components and the component diagram with the modules comprising the core of the platform. We also delve into the value-added services of O-V2X-MP, namely the billing engine, the REST APIs that enable interconnections and integration with external systems, the data analytics capabilities and the cyber-security module. We conclude with our future plans for the platform's frontend.

Keywords: OCPP protocol · Electric Vehicles · Charging points management · Web platform · microservices

1 Introduction

In the energy sector, vehicle-to-everything (**V2X**) is the vision of leveraging electric vehicles (**EVs**) for enhancing energy savings and improving grid stability, as a means for taming the stochasticity of renewable energy resources. In fact, V2X is a broad vision that includes specialized scenarios like vehicle-to-building (V2B) and vehicle-to-grid (V2G). Public Power Corporation (PPC) strives to realize this vision by making the most of the largest network of EV chargers in Greece, with more than 2,000 charging stations nationwide.

Maintaining this large network of EV chargers is a complex task that involves a wide diversity of technical challenges. To address them, the R&D group of PPC has been developing an open-source, web-based charging station management system (**CSMS**) that supports V2X scenarios, called *Open V2X Management Platform* (**O-V2X-MP**). This platform enables the remote control, monitoring, and maintenance of charging stations. It can also retrieve remote diagnostic, detailing the charger's health status, real-time availability, and audit logs.

In this work, we elaborate on the backend of O-V2X-MP, which implements the *Open Charge Point Protocol* (**OCPP**)[1] that specifies the communication

[1] https://openchargealliance.org/protocols/open-charge-point-protocol.

K. Stefanidis et al. (Eds.): ICWE 2024, LNCS 14629, pp. 133–146, 2024.
https://doi.org/10.1007/978-3-031-62362-2_10

between the platform and the charging points. O-V2X-MP supports the latest version of OCPP, 2.0.1, which offers more advanced features, like additional smart charging functionalities, improved transaction handling, and device management[2]. It also provides backward compatibility for EV chargers implementing earlier OCPP versions, like the popular 1.6.

To the best of our knowledge, O-V2X-MP is the first open-source platform that combines OCPP with a wide range of value-added services like advanced cyber-security mechanisms, a billing engine and data analytics on top of the transactional data gathered from the EV chargers. To this end, O-V2X-MP comprises numerous individual components that are effectively integrated through a microservices architecture.

We visualize this complex architecture through the *C4 model* [2], which unfolds four levels. At the highest level, it elaborates on the principal entities engaged with the platform, such as the EV users and the platform manager (see Sect. 3.1). At the second level, it delves into the auxiliary services that support the O-V2X-MP platform and the communications between them (see Sect. 3.2). At the third level, it zooms into the interior of the O-V2X-MP platform, providing details about the modules it encompasses (see Sect. 3.3). The lowest level focuses on implementation details like UML and entity relationship diagrams, but is omitted, due to lack of space.

We also focus on the value-added services that equip O-V2X-MP with unique characteristics. These services include: (i) the billing engine in Sect. 4.1, which stores and manages the charge detail records (**CDRs**), (ii) the RESTful APIs in Sect. 4.2, which allow for retrieving useful information from the platform, (iii) the data analytics module in Sect. 4.3, which applies ML models to provide insights into the data gathered by the platform, and (iv) the cybersecurity mechanism in Sect. 4.4, which ensures the confidentiality, availability and integrity of the sensitive information handled by the platform.

We conclude our work with a brief discussion about the future extension to the O-V2X-MP platform in Sect. 5, which will add an intuitive user interface that accommodates users of any background, from novice to expert ones.

2 Related Work

The OCPP protocol is the de-facto standard for the communication between charging points and their management system. It is an open standard that defines messages and commands for the initialization of charging sessions, their termination as well as reporting mechanisms, error messages and diagnostics (e.g., about the overall energy consumed during a charging session or the operational status of the charging station).

OCCP has undergone significant evolution since its introduction in 2009. The most common version in commercial equipment is **OCPP 1.6** [6], which supports *smart charging*, i.e., it enables the remote control of charging points as

[2] https://www.stuart.energy/news/the-comparison-ocpp-1-6-vs-ocpp-2-0-1.

a means of protecting the grid from overloading and of adjusting the charging sessions to user needs (e.g., when electricity is cheaper). To this end, OCPP 1.6 provides a limited set of commands for managing the charging process and providing status information. The latest and most advanced version is **OCPP 2.0.1** [7], which extends OCPP 1.6 with additional functionalities and commands for device management, smart charging and V2G support.

O-V2X-MP supports both OCPP 1.6 and 2.0.1. In this respect, the work most relevant to ours is *SteVe*[3], an open-source CSMS that implements all versions of OCPP up to 1.6, enabling simple smart charging scenarios. Its backend is implemented in Java, while its frontend relies on JavaScript. However, SteVe has the following limitations: (i) its architecture is intricate and hard to extend with new modules and functionalities, (ii) it cannot support OCPP 2.0.1 without substantial modifications to its backend, (iii) it offers no value-added services on top of the transaction data, and (iv) it lacks any effective cybersecurity mechanisms.

Our goal is to go beyond SteVe through an extensible open-source platform that leverages the Python ecosystem to combine the OCPP 2.0.1 functionalities with advanced services like data analytics and resilience mechanisms.

3 O-V2X-MP Backend Overview

We now describe the backend of the O-V2X-MP platform, whose primary function is to facilitate the interaction between EVs, the charging infrastructure, the energy grid and other systems. We use the C4 model approach to clarify its architecture, overcoming the complexity conveyed by its numerous components.

3.1 System Context Diagram

The highest level of the C4 model is the *system context diagram*, which is presented in Fig. 1, depicting the main actors that interact with O-V2X-MP:

- The platform manager is responsible for the development, management and maintenance of the O-V2X-MP platform.
- The Charging Point Operator (**CPO**) owns and is responsible for the charging infrastructure, managing the charging stations via the O-V2X-MP platform. This encompasses tasks such as regular remote and on-site maintenance, diagnostics, price settings, and point of interest data management.
- The Distribution System Operator (**DSO**) provides equal service to all consumers, while ensuring that the distribution system operates safely and within its technical limitations. The DSO interacts with the O-V2X-MP platform via its DSO Support System (DSS).
- The DSS platform is a collection of applications designed to efficiently and reliably monitor and control the electric power distribution networks through visualizations and other functionalities. It provides the O-V2X-MP platform with updated tariffs and capacity limits.

[3] https://github.com/steve-community/steve.

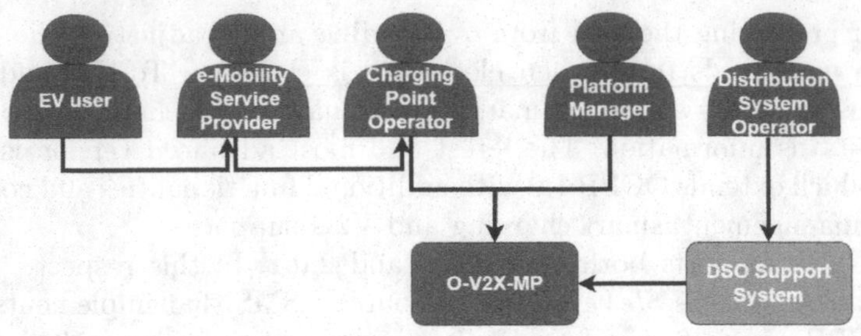

Fig. 1. The O-V2X-MP system context diagram.

- The e-Mobility Service Provider (**eMSP**) provides EV users with all services related to electric charging, e.g., through a mobile app that offers access to multiple charging points within a geographic area. Therefore, eMSP focuses on invoicing and on customer relationship management functionalities. It relies on the CPO, interacting indirectly with the O-V2X-MP platform.
- The EV users/drivers interact indirectly with O-V2X-MP via the eMSP, aiming to charge their EVs with the minimum cost in money and/or time. That is, their goal is to find their closest charging points with the lowest tariffs.

3.2 Container Diagram

The second level of the C4 model comprises the *Container Diagram*, which appears in Fig. 2. Its goal is to provide a high-level overview of its architecture, highlighting how the responsibilities are distributed across the auxiliary components and how they communicate with one another. These components are:

- The message bus, which is based on Apache Kafka [1], acting as a highly scalable and durable channel, allowing all other components to communicate and exchange messages in an efficient way.
- The network file transfer leverages an FTP server to facilitate the exchange of files between a client (the device initiating the transfer) and the server (the device hosting the files).
- The file managing interface uses the FileBrowser[4] to provide file sharing and file management capabilities over the network through a user-friendly GUI.
- The database management system runs PostgreSQL[5], an established and flexible solution for managing the structured data consumed by the platform.
- The database administration runs pgAdmin[6] as a GUI for users to interact with and manage the database management system.

[4] https://filebrowser.org.
[5] https://www.postgresql.org.
[6] https://www.pgadmin.org.

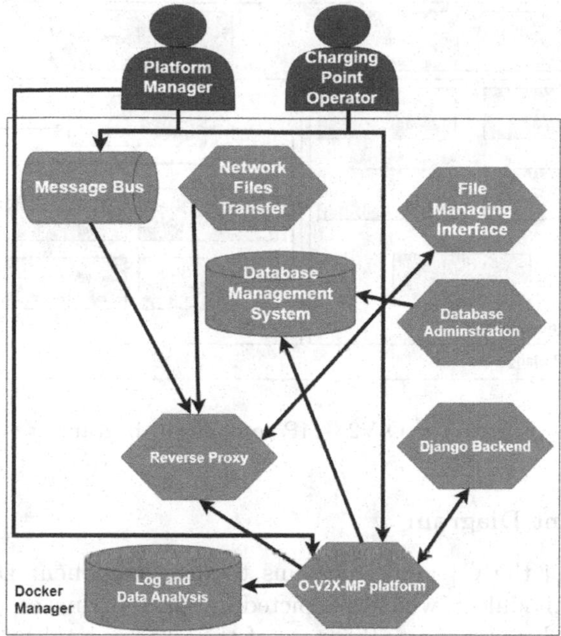

Fig. 2. The O-V2X-MP container diagram.

- The reverse proxy component runs Caddy Web server[7] for forwarding requests to backend servers.
- The log and data analysis component implements the Elastic Stack[8] as a means of storing and processing the logs of the O-V2X-MP platform. More specifically, it consists of: (i) Logstash, which collects, parses and transforms the log files, (ii) Elasticsearch, which provides scalable and efficient keyword search and analytics over the collected logs, and (iii) Kibana, which runs analytics on the log files and visualizes their outcomes.
- The O-V2X-MP platform, which is the main module of the entire system, based on Python's Django web framework. It is analyzed in Sect. 3.3.
- The Django backend relies on Redis[9], an in-memory data structure store that asynchronously transmits data to the frontend via WebSockets.

Note that each component runs an open-source software system. Note also that each of the above components runs through a separate Docker container. Their orchestration is achieved through the *Docker Manager*, which relies on Portainer.io[10], an open-source management platform for containerized applications.

[7] https://caddyserver.com.
[8] https://www.elastic.co/elastic-stack.
[9] https://redis.io.
[10] https://www.portainer.io.

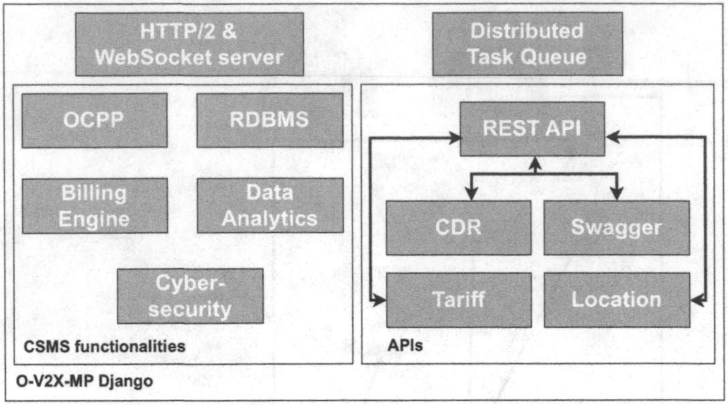

Fig. 3. The O-V2X-MP component diagram.

3.3 Component Diagram

The third level of the C4 model pertains to the Component Diagram of the O-V2X-MP core module[11], which is depicted in Fig. 3. It runs on the web framework Django[12], which preserves the state of the system, implements high-logic, provides a RESTful API to access the system state and the OCPP commands and enforces authentication/authorization. On top of Django, the following components are run as microservices that implement the operation of a CSMS:

- The HTTP/2 and WebSocket server runs a Daphne web server[13], which is placed as an intermediate between the EV charger and the CSMS.
- The distributed task queue system runs a Celery worker[14], which receives and executes tasks asynchronously.
- The OCPP component runs the OCPP server using the Sanic web framework[15]. At its core, lies the OCPP Python package released by MobilityHouse[16]. See Sect. 3.3 for the main OCPP commands that are supported.
- The RDBMS provides persistent storage through a PostgreSQL instance, which maintains information about charging stations, transactions, users, locations, tariffs and reservations.
- The Billing Engine is indispensable for the invoicing functionalities of the platform, as explained in Sect. 4.1.

---

[11] The source code is publicly released by the Github account of the Horizon Europe research project EV4EU (https://ev4eu.eu) through the following repositories: https://github.com/EV4EU/ov2xmp-django, https://github.com/EV4EU/ov2xmp, https://github.com/EV4EU/ov2xmp-http-file-server and https://github.com/EV4EU/ov2xmp-ftp-server.

[12] https://www.djangoproject.com.

[13] https://github.com/django/daphne.

[14] https://docs.celeryq.dev/en/stable.

[15] https://sanic.dev/en.

[16] https://github.com/mobilityhouse/ocpp.

- The Data Analytics platform allows for applying ML pipelines to the data stored in the RDBMS, providing insights to the platform users, as explained in Sect. 4.3.
- The Cyber-security platform ensures the resilience of the platform, as explained in Sect. 4.4.
- The REST APIs detailed in Sect. 4.2 that are provided through Swagger[17].

Note that the above microservices architecture ensures that the backend is scalable to large charger networks and to large volumes of transactions.

OCPP Commands. The main commands of the OCPP protocol, versions 1.6 and 2.0.1, currently implemented by the O-V2X-MP platform are the following:

- *Boot Notification* runs during the initiation of the charging station to signal its availability to the CSMS and to provide information about its capabilities.
- *Authorize* is a command issued by the charging station to the CSMS whenever a customer plugs their EV to initiate the customer authorization process.
- *Start Transaction* initiates the charging session, after user authorization. It conveys details about the charger, the customer, and the charging parameters.
- *Stop Transaction* notifies the CSMS about the termination of the charging session, including relevant details.
- *Heartbeat* is periodically transmitted by the charging station to confirm its operational status and connection to the CSMS.
- *Firmware Update* is sent by the CSMS to the charger if a firmware update is necessary.
- *ReserveNow* enables an EV user to reserve a specific charger for a designated period of time, a feature crucial in V2G applications.
- *CancelReservation* revokes a reservation made by the previous command.
- *GetCompositeSchedule* requests a plan detailing the charging station's availability for a specific time span. This plan includes its current state, the planned maintenance, and any existing reservations of the charger.
- *SetChargingProfile* defines a charging profile for a specific period of time, which is crucial in V2G applications with variable charging rates.

4 Value-Added Services

The O-V2X-MP platform goes beyond the implementation of the OCPP protocol through a series of complex services that leverage the data it collects. Below, we present the module that is responsible for each such service.

[17] https://swagger.io.

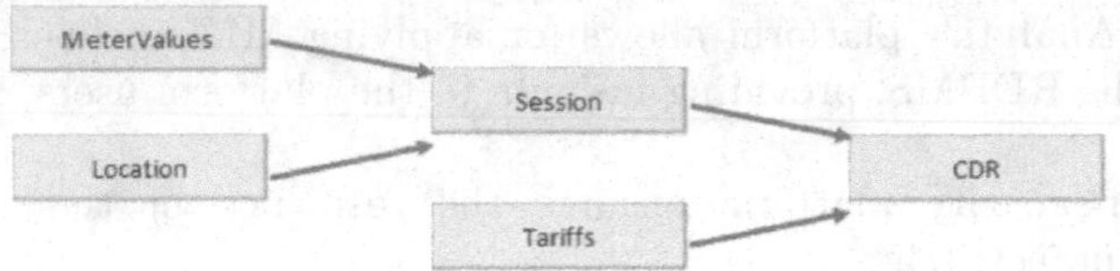

Fig. 4. The definition of charge detail records (CDRs).

4.1 Billing Engine

This module encompasses all necessary mechanisms for calculating the cost of a charging session based on the tariffs provided by the DSO (see Sect. 3.1). More specifically, a tariff specifies when, at which charging station, for which customers and under which conditions (e.g., an AC or a DC connection), a specific cost rate applies. This allows for the nuanced assignment of cost rates through a dynamic tariff management scheme that supports the following options:

- One-time charging session fee.
- Consumption-based fee for a charging session (price per kilowatt-hour, kWh).
- Time-based fee for a charging session.
- A combination of the above.

In this way, the O-V2X-MP platform supports tariffs that exhibit flexibility and adaptability to accommodate the specific needs of the DSO, the CPO and/or the Platform Manager. For example, in cases of increased production from renewables in a specific area, the DSO can reduce the tariffs of nearby charging stations, encouraging EV users to make the most of the generated power.

Combining the applicable tariff with the information of the charging session yields the CDRs, as shown in Fig. 4: the charging session is defined by the location of the EV charger and the MeterValues, i.e., 22 measurands provided by OCPP, such as power, voltage, and the state of charge of the EV battery. The resulting CDR encapsulates the details of a concluded charging session and stands as the sole billing-relevant object. Following a successful charging session, the eMSP associated with the registered driver retrieves the CDR through the REST API in Sect. 4.2. The eMSP subsequently collects payments from the driver and remits the difference to the CPO.

4.2 RESTful APIs

The O-V2X-MP offers the following APIs that provide access to the data it manages so as to facilitate its integration with other systems.

Location API. This API allows for retrieving the charging stations that are available in an area of interest. According to their status, the charging points are distinguished into the following types:

1. Public locations are available to any EV user.
2. Private locations are exclusively available to a specific group of EV users that have the necessary RFIDs for authorization.
3. Semi-public locations correspond to chargers with parking restrictions (e.g., a parking lot closing overnight).

Each of the retrieved locations is modelled as a point-of-interest, with associated co-ordinates (i.e., latitude and longitude). This information is necessary for depicting the position of charging stations on a map, along with tariff information, facilitating users to select the closest and cheapest one in their vicinity.

CDR API. The CDRs produced by the billing engine (see Sect. 4.1) are stored in the relational database of the O-V2X-MP platform. To facilitate the necessary data exchange between the CPO and the eMSP (or any other relevant system), the CDRs should be exportable in an established data format. This requirement is met by the CDR API, which exports comprehensive session details in various forms, such as a CSV or JSON file or a spreadsheet. Each extracted record conveys essential information such as the Charging Station ID, the Location ID, the initiation and termination timestamps, the cumulative energy consumption (in kilowatt-hours, kWh), the total session duration, the associated costs as well as the respective RFID tag and user details, if the user is pre-registered in the platform.

Tariff API. This API is also connected to the billing engine in Sect. 4.1. Its goal is to equip the O-V2X-MP platform with robust mechanisms for generating systematic invoices and implementing multi-category charges that can be allocated to different charging stations or groups of charging stations (e.g., to discourage traffic in city centers, the respective chargers could have a high cost, whereas chargers in the suburbs could offer lower tariffs). More fine-grained charges are also supported by associating different tariffs to different connectors of the same charging station (i.e., different costs for AC sockets compared to DC CCS or CHAdeMO connectors).

In more detail, two main tariff categories are supported: (i) the wholesale charging session costs levied by the CPO, and (ii) the retail packages for costs incurred by the eMSP. The former accounts for the energy and the maintenance cost of the CPO along with its profit and is defined per energy unit (i.e., price per kilowatt-hour, kWh) or per time units (price per minute) or with a combination of both types. The eMSP tariffs can also be defined in terms of energy or time units or both, and are normally added to the CPO costs. Yet, it is possible to entirely disregard the cost of CPO and set charges solely at the discretion of the eMSP (e.g., to create a tariff for subscribed users paying a substantial monthly fee subscription with minimal per-charge costs).

4.3 Data Analytics Module

Another crucial value-added service offered by the O-V2X-MP platform is the support for running data analytics on its transaction data to gain insights into the behavior of EV users. As an example, consider the unsupervised task of clustering these transactions into user profiles that would allow for a-priori predicting the power demand throughout the network of EV chargers maintained by the CPO. Examples of these profiles are the following: (i) morning to afternoon, high energy, long-term stay, (ii) early evening, low energy, short-term stay, (iii) early afternoon, medium energy, medium-term stay, (iv) evening to next morning, medium energy, long-term stay.

To extract such profiles, O-V2X-MP combines the data science methods offered by scikit-learn [8] with the graph clustering methods implemented by pyJedAI [5] in Python. More specifically, the following pipeline is implemented:

First, *data cleaning* removes the transaction records with missing, noisy or outlier values. For example, we consider as noisy the records where the delivered power is higher than that of the corresponding EV charger or higher than the maximum battery capacity in EVs sold in Europe.

Next, *feature engineering* defines the attributes that will be used by the clustering algorithms. These are the following: the start and end timestamp of the transaction, the total volume of delivered power (in KWh), the charging point information (i.e., its id, street address, city etc.), the user's authentication id, the maximum power that can be delivered by the charging point (e.g., 22KW) and the sojourn time, i.e., the time the EV was parked and plugged into the charging station, before and after the charging session (in other words, sojourn time = charging time + idle time, where charging time = end timestamp - start timestamp). *Standardization* ensures that the values of all features have a zero mean and unit variance.

Subsequently, *feature selection* is applied to identify the most essential features. The correlation matrix between all features is computed, highlighting pairs of features with very high Pearson correlation. Typically, these are the start and end timestamp of the transaction as well as the total volume of delivered power and the charging time. In such pairs, one of the two features is redundant and should be omitted from further processing.

The fourth step creates the *similarity graph*, transforming the selected transactions into a weighted undirected graph, where each node corresponds to an individual record. Each edge $<e_i, e_j>$ connects two tranasactions with a non-zero similarity, which is computed as follows: $sim(e_i, e_j) = 1 - ED(r_i, r_j)$, where $ED(r_i, r_j)$ denotes the Euclidean distance of the respective records r_i and r_j based on the standardized features that are retained after feature selection.

Finally, a *graph clustering algorithm* is applied to the resulting graph to split its nodes/transactions into disjoint clusters. We opted for unconstrained algorithms, which require neither the number of the final clusters nor their diameter or any other domain-specific parameter to be pre-determined. Their sole configuration parameter is a similarity threshold $t \in [0, 1)$, which defines the minimum edge weight in the graph, i.e., it discards all edges with a weight lower than t before clustering the graph. These requirements are satisfied by 7

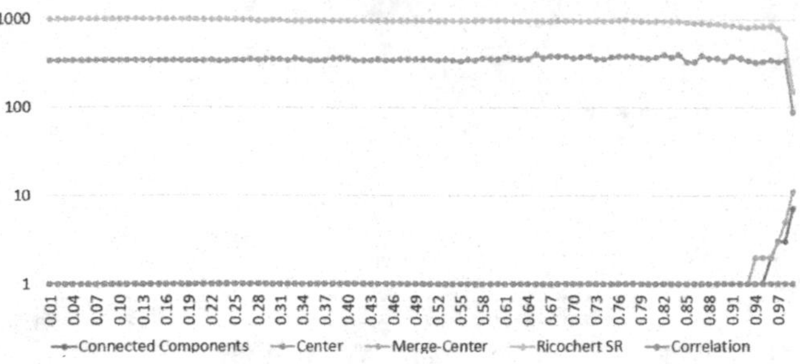

Fig. 5. Number of clusters per similarity threshold and clustering algorithm. Note the logarithmic scale of the vertical axis.

algorithms: Connected Components, Center, Merge Center, Ricochet SR, Correlation, Markov and Cut Clustering. Please refer to [4] for more details on their functionality.

Experimental Results. We applied this methodology to real transactions collected from PPC's nationwide of EV charging points in Greece. The dataset comprises 22,412 charging sessions that were carried out between July 2021 and May 2022 from public charging stations in Greece, mainly located in high-traffic and quick-stay areas such as highways, gas stations, supermarkets, and stores. There are a total of 312 distinct chargers with registered sessions in the dataset, of which only eight support fast charging: six with 50 kW, one with 60 kW, and one with 120 kW; all other chargers have 22 kW maximum power.

After data clearing, 21,801 records were retained. Feature engineering and selection resulted in three complementary, non-redundant features: (i) start timestamp, (ii) total volume of delivered power, and (iii) sojourn time. We applied the above graph clustering algorithms using grid search in $[0, 1]$ to fine-tune their similarity threshold. In each case, we measure the number of clusters each algorithm generates as well as the corresponding entropy of the cluster sizes. The goal is to configure each algorithm to generate clusters satisfying two requirements:

1. Their number is low, so that they can be easily interpreted.
2. Their size is balanced, avoiding situations where a single cluster involves the vast majority of records, a situation that may yield high scores with respect to the effectiveness measures, but provides no insights into the behavioral patterns of EV users.

Note that as effectiveness measures, we consider the silhouette coefficient and the Davies-Bould index [3]. The former takes values from -1 to $+1$, with higher values indicating more precise clustering, i.e., most records are well matched to their own clusters and poorly matched to neighboring ones. For the Davies-Bould index, smaller values, closer to zero, mean better performance, as clusters are well separated and each one is well represented by its centroid.

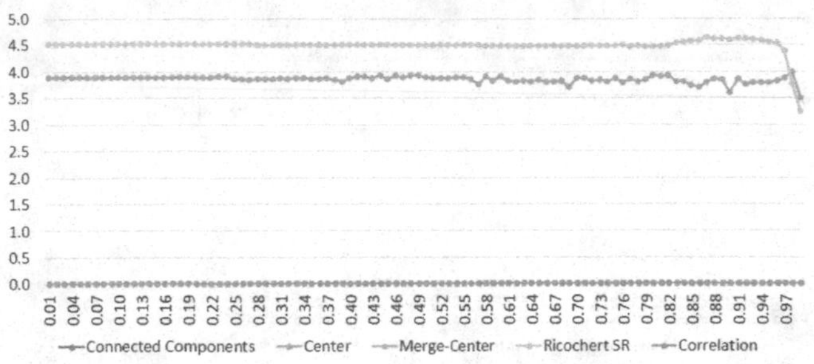

Fig. 6. Entropy of cluster sizes per similarity threshold and clustering algorithm.

The results with respect to these requirements are presented in Figs. 5 and 6, respectively. Note that we had to exclude Cut and Markov Clustering from our analysis, due to their excessively high space and time complexity, respectively. The former requires more main memory than the available one (64 GB), while the latter did not terminate within 24 h, regardless of the similarity threshold.

Starting with Fig. 5, we observe that all algorithms exhibit insignificant variation in the number of clusters for all thresholds up to 0.90. The reason is that after normalization, the three selected features yield very high similarities between most pairs of records. As a result, most thresholds below 0.90 prune a negligible number of edges from the similarity graph. In fact, Connected Components clustering places all records in the same, single cluster for thresholds up to 0.95, while Correlation Clustering generates a single clustering regardless of the similarity threshold. In contrast, the more elaborate processing of Center and Ricochet SR Clustering enables them to generate a very high number of clusters, regardless of the similarity threshold. The two algorithms converge to ~100 clusters for the highest similarity thresholds, whereas Connected Components and Merge-Center Clustering converge to ~10 clusters.

To assess the usefulness of the resulting clusters, Fig. 6 depicts the entropy of their sizes across all similarity thresholds. Note that cases with a single cluster correspond to zero entropy. We observe that Connected Components and Merge-Center clustering exhibit the highest entropy with the highest similarity threshold (0.99), for which they also yield the maximum number of clusters. However, the actual value of entropy is practically zero, which indicates that one of the clusters dominates all others, comprising almost all records. Thus, the usefulness of the corresponding clusters is limited.

For Center and Ricochet SR Clustering, there are insignificant variations in entropy across all thresholds, except the largest ones, where both algorithms exhibit a steep decrease. The reason is that in every case, the maximum value of entropy is $log|C|$, where $|C|$ denotes the corresponding number of clusters. As a result, their entropy is bounded to much lower values for the largest similarity thresholds. On the whole, the entropy is maximized for $t = 0.98$ and $t = 0.87$ for Center and Ricochet SR Clustering, respectively.

Table 1. Characteristics of the clusters produced by Connected Components (CC), Center, Merge-Center (MC), and Ricochet SR (RSR) clustering.

Method	CC	$Center_1$	$Center_2$	MC_1	MC_2	RSR_1	RSR_2
Number of clusters	7	345	88	11	2	896	152
Similarity threshold	0.99	0.98	0.99	0.99	0.94	0.88	0.99
Entropy	0.003	3.999	3.502	0.009	0.001	4.633	3.248
Silhouette Coefficient	−0.127	−0.571	−0.148	−0.184	**0.325**	−0.575	−0.235
Davies-Bouldin Index	0.681	12.064	4.585	0.829	**0.634**	16.282	7.258

These results are summarized in Table 1. Note that all algorithms are represented by two different configurations, except Connected Components. For Center and Ricochet SR Clustering, we considered both the threshold maximizing the entropy of cluster size and the threshold minimizing the resulting clusters. For Merge-Center Clustering, we report the similarity threshold that maximizes both the entropy and the number of clusters (0.99), and the threshold that maximizes the evaluation measures (0.94).

We observe that Center and Ricochet SR Clustering yield low scores for all three effectiveness measures, indicating strong dissimilarities between the records inside each cluster. The excessively large number of generated clusters has the additional disadvantage of hampering the qualitative analysis of these clusters. In contrast, Connected Component and Merge-Center Clustering yield a few clusters with much better scores for both effectiveness measures. The best performance actually corresponds to Merge-Center clustering with threshold 0.94. Note that due to the lack of a frontend, the results can only be stored in CSV format, using pyJedAI's respective functionality. Our future plan is to visualize the outcomes of the data analytics module through the graphical user interface that will be added to the O-V2X-MP platform.

4.4 Cybersecurity Module

The O-V2X-MP platform mitigates the following types of cyber-attacks:

1. (Distributed) Denial of Service (DoS), where the network is flooded with empty OCPP packets so as to cause service unavailability.
2. Frame injection, where false messages intervene in the communication between the platform and the charging stations.
3. Replay attack, where the communication between the platform and a charger is intercepted and replayed to manipulate the (dis)charging process.
4. Impersonation, where an adversary masquerades as a legitimate entity so as to gain unauthorized access, manipulate data, or disrupt the platform.
5. Sybil attack, where an adversary creates multiple fake identities or virtual entities to gain an unfair advantage or disrupt the platform.

The mitigation mechanisms include:

- Authorization with OAuth 2.0[18] and identity management with Keycloak[19].
- User group access based on OpenLDAP[20].
- Encryption of the OCPP packets through the TLS or IPsec protocols.
- Zeek[21] is the network-based intrusion detection system.

5 Conclusions and Future Work

Based on the C4 Model, we presented the backend of the O-V2X-MP platform at three different levels of details: (i) the main actors interacting with it, (ii) the communication flows between the auxiliary services that support its operation and (iii) the components that comprise its core. We also presented the additional services that are built on top of the OCPP protocol, providing added-value to the users of our platform. Of particular interest is the data analytics module which allows for applying ML models to transaction data, detecting patterns in the behavior of EV users.

In the future, we plan to facilitate the use of O-V2X-MP through an intuitive frontend. This is envisaged as a high-level graphical interface facilitating operators and users in monitoring their charging sessions and offering feedback to the designated Platform Manager. To this end, it will include the following features: a map with the available charging stations, the ability to search for specific stations by location or availability, and the ability to start and stop charging sessions. It will also allow for managing payments and monitoring charging activity in real-time and for managing the charging stations and processing payments.

Acknowledgement. This research was partially funded by the EU Horizon Europe GA No 101056765 (EV4EU).

References

1. Apache-Software-Foundation: Apache kafka (2024). https://kafka.apache.org
2. Brown, S.: Software architecture for developers. Coding Archit. (2013)
3. Han, J., Kamber, M., Pei, J.: Data Mining Concepts and Techniques. The Morgan Kaufmann Series in Data Management Systems, 3rd edn. (2012)
4. Hassanzadeh, O., Chiang, F., Miller, R.J., Lee, H.C.: Framework for evaluating clustering algorithms in duplicate detection. Proc. VLDB Endow. **2**(1), 1282–1293 (2009)
5. Nikoletos, K., Papadakis, G., Koubarakis, M.: pyJedAI: a lightsaber for link discovery. In: ISWC 2022 Posters, Demos and Industry Tracks, vol. 3254 (2022)
6. Open-Charge-Alliance: Open charge point protocol 1.6 (2015)
7. Open-Charge-Alliance: Open charge point protocol 2.0.1 (2020)
8. Pedregosa, F., et al.: Scikit-learn: machine learning in Python. J. Mach. Learn. Res. **12**, 2825–2830 (2011)

[18] https://oauth.net/2.

[19] https://www.keycloak.org.

[20] https://www.openldap.org.

[21] https://zeek.org.

DyST: Dynamic Specification Mining for Heterogenous IoT Systems with WoT

Ege Korkan[1(✉)], Silvia Oliva Ramirez[2], and Sebastian Steinhorst[2]

[1] Siemens, Munich, Bavaria, Germany
ege.korkan@siemens.com
[2] Technical University of Munich, Munich, Bavaria, Germany
{silvia.ramirez,sebastian.steinhorst}@tum.de

Abstract. The comprehension of a distributed system and its verification is one of the most challenging problems in today's software engineering, commonly referred to as observability. The complexity increases when one cannot control all the components, like in IoT systems composed of third-party devices. The Web of Things standards by the W3C help with this by describing what one can do with an IoT device via network messages. However, no work has leveraged these standards to offer an observability solution that works with any set of IoT devices. This work addresses this gap by proposing a method to verify the correctness of the system by mining its specification from device interactions. Our approach can reverse engineer complex application logic in the form of UML Sequence Diagrams from the analysis of network messages of any protocol between the devices during system runtime, which can be used to programmatically assert the correctness of the mined specification. We have evaluated our approach with three case studies to assess our mining technique, the performance of our algorithms, and the applicability of our contributions to system verification in the IoT. Our results show that our approach can produce accurate Sequence Diagrams that help understand and verify the behavior of IoT systems.

Keywords: Internet of Things · Process Mining · Web of Things

1 Introduction

The Internet of Things (IoT) has become a key enabler of today's emerging technologies, entering our daily lives through Internet-connected devices. However, its exponential growth has spawned numerous IoT platform providers and manufacturers, each designing devices to function within distinct frameworks and technical environments, leading to interoperability challenges. The absence of best practices or standards has resulted in the proliferation of diverse technologies and implementation methods, causing significant fragmentation in the IoT domain and necessitating substantial integration and development efforts.

To tackle this interoperability challenge, the World Wide Web Consortium(W3C) introduced the Web of Things (WoT) [18], an architecture aimed at fostering interoperability across IoT platforms and application domains. Central

K. Stefanidis et al. (Eds.): ICWE 2024, LNCS 14629, pp. 147–162, 2024.
https://doi.org/10.1007/978-3-031-62362-2_11

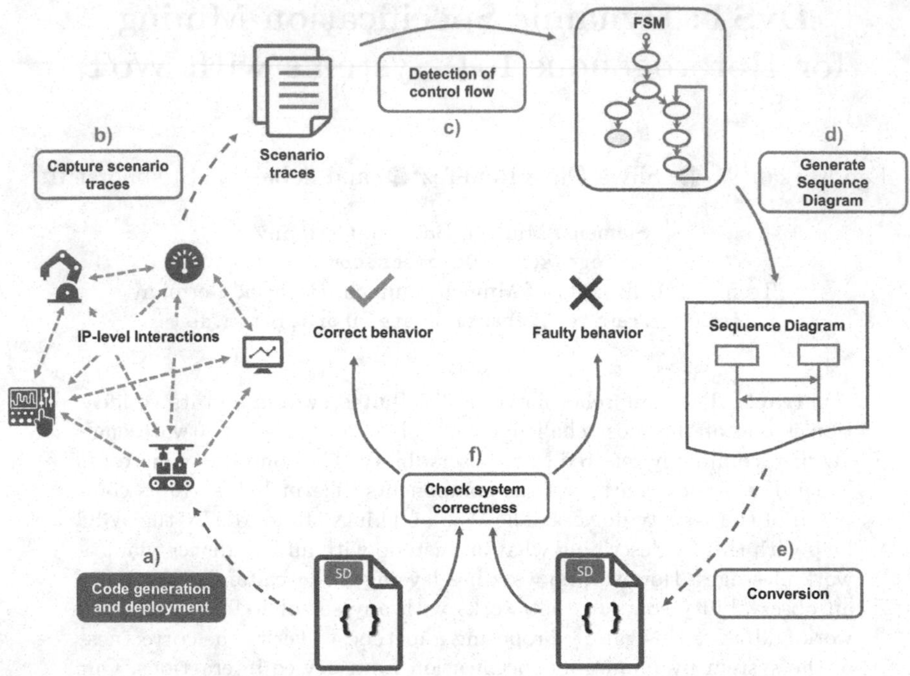

Fig. 1. Approach overview. State-of-the-art techniques are marked with dashed lines while our contributions are drawn with continuous lines. a) System design (with a System Description (SD)) and code deployment. b) During normal system execution, communication traces for various scenarios are obtained. c) Traces are analyzed, loops and branches detected, and a Finite State Machine (FSM) is constructed. d) Based on the FSM, a Sequence Diagram (SeqD) is generated. e) The SeqD is automatically converted to an SD. f) Both SD files are compared to verify system correctness.

to this architecture are Thing Descriptions (TDs) [19], which provide a standardized format for uniformly describing the network-facing capabilities of a Thing. Given that individual IoT devices may lack complex functionalities, they are often combined to perform common tasks, known as Mashups. These can range from automatic irrigation systems in smart farms to item-sorting systems in factories or even turning on lights when a presence is detected in a smart home.

1.1 Problem Statement

As distributed IoT systems like Mashups grow larger and more complex, the need to understand their behavior and to support their verification becomes more important. Verification techniques that target a distributed system before its full operation can only be partially representative of the executions in the field, which results in a large difference between the assumed behavior during the design and the actual behavior of the system.

So far this has been addressed by specification mining techniques, which are commonly used to derive the specification of a program using examples of correct usage to aid program understanding. Besides helping with comprehension, mined specifications are useful for supporting quality assurance and for examining the relationships between the actual behavior of a system and its designed specification. However, state-of-the-art specification mining techniques are unable to address the various protocols and platforms that are present in the IoT. As a result, such techniques are not applied to real IoT systems and IoT systems lack the benefits of well-established specification mining techniques to allow their verification.

1.2 Approach and Contributions

To improve the management of WoT Mashups, [9] introduced the WoT System Description (SD), which can interchangeably represent a Mashup in a well-defined text format or a graphical manner with a subset of the Unified Modeling Language (UML) Sequence Diagram [5]. This work builds on top of the System Description, which represents the system behavior description our approach tries to mine. More specifically, we introduce DyST, a method and a corresponding implementation as a solution to automatically observe IoT systems by analyzing the communication traces produced during the normal execution of the system and building a corresponding System Description. Figure 1 shows an overview of the approach, where state-of-the-art techniques are combined with our contributions. In particular, we make the following contributions:

- We propose a new protocol-independent format for representing communication traces between devices in the WoT that focuses on application semantics and operations.
- We present a method and its open-source implementation[1] that takes multiple communication traces from different behavioral scenarios as input and generates UML-compliant Sequence Diagrams and System Descriptions (SDs).
- We perform a full evaluation of our method with transformations from communication traces to SDs using three different case studies to prove its applicability for checking a system's correctness as well as its time performance.

The rest of the paper starts with highlighting the background information and related work in Sect. 2. Section 3 explains the scientific contributions, as well as the implementation. Section 4 presents the evaluation methodology and results, and Sect. 5 concludes and proposes future work directions.

2 Background and Related Work

To target distributed systems with third-party devices to mine their behavior, this work builds on top of well-established methods found within the WoT, Specification Mining, and Specification and Modeling of Distributed Systems.

[1] Also referred to as our repository, it is available at https://github.com/tum-esi/dyst-wot-miner.

2.1 Web of Things

The WoT encompasses standards at the W3C, focusing on Things that expose Interaction Affordances through well-described network interfaces. This enables Consumers such as applications, cloud services, or browsers to interact with them.

The TD [19] defines a standardized metadata format and vocabulary to describe functionality and interactions across networked Things. The TD is the main building block of the WoT and is extended with various **Binding Templates** [13] to describe various IoT protocols so that a Consumer can send the correct protocol messages to the Thing. The Interaction Affordances are categorized into three:

- *Properties* can be read, written, and observed, and represent a state of the Thing, such as a sensor value.
- *Actions* can be invoked and execute a function of the Thing, which might manipulate its state, e.g. executing a movement.
- *Events* can be subscribed to and result in a notification each time the event occurs, for example, notifying when a person is detected.

WoT System Description: The SD introduced in [9] extends the capabilities of a TD by providing additional keywords to describe the composition of WoT Things. To this end, SD introduces a means to specify the execution of interactions and to represent application logic that consists of programming structures, e.g. if statements, for loops, and wait statements.

2.2 Specification Mining

Specification mining is a program analysis method deriving program specifications from correct usage examples. [16] summarizes works in this field, ranging from early papers like [3] to recent ones. Specification mining techniques are categorized based on the input data source such as parsing program source files, analyzing execution traces obtained during runtime, or using a combination of both approaches. These are called Static Specification Mining, Dynamic Specification Mining, and Hybrid Specification Mining, respectively.

IoT systems, influenced by both environment and device programs, are highly dynamic. They comprise devices from diverse manufacturers, often inaccessible in terms of source code. With these aspects in mind, we focus on Dynamic Specification mining techniques in this work.

Dynamic Specification Mining: Dynamic specification mining can provide an accurate representation of a system's behavior because the analysis is performed entirely during runtime. In general, dynamic specification mining is based on the analysis of so-called execution traces. The simplest way to obtain execution traces is to instrument the source code [2,6,8] or rely on custom debuggers [22,23]. A smaller number of techniques [14] obtain the needed traces by analyzing the interactions between devices connected to the network. This can be accomplished by sniffing the network and collecting communication traces, i.e. all necessary information about method calls, including callers and callees. This work uses communication traces since in WoT systems there is no guarantee to access the Things' source code or the Mashup application logic.

Scenario Traces: A single program run generating a single trace may not capture the application behavior due to missing repetitions or conditional alternatives. To get a complete view of the program's behavior, it is necessary to obtain traces that represent different behavioral scenarios and thus cover all possible options. This collection of traces is called scenario traces in the rest of this work.

Testing of Things: To enable verification of individual WoT things, [12] proposes to do an affordance coverage test where their contributions interact with Things over the network and send well-planned requests to execute each affordance with different inputs. However, it influences Things and their physical environment, making it unsuitable for the normal working mode of a Thing.

2.3 Specification and Modeling of Distributed Systems

Specification languages and graphical representations are well-established methods that aid program documentation, development, and testing. The relevant methods for this work are briefly summarized below, together with how they relate to our method.

Finite State Machines (FSMs): FSM-derived specifications, based on [7], effectively model historical software behavior patterns. They are intuitive and powerful to represent recurring patterns of behavior, especially for sequencing, selection, and iteration. By an FSM, we mean a deterministic transition state machine, also known as a deterministic finite state machine or Deterministic Finite Automata (DFA).

The simplicity and power of FSMs have spurred techniques to reverse-engineer software applications, generating FSMs as final or intermediate representations for complex behavioral models like Regular Expressions. Here, FSMs are employed to infer software behavior, detecting loops and branches before transforming them into more complex models such as UML Sequence Diagrams.

UML Sequence Diagrams: UML Sequence Diagrams visually represent program behavior by illustrating interactions among software system objects. They depict system flow using incoming and outgoing messages, following a standardized representation defined in the UML specification [5]. In this work, we employ UML Sequence Diagrams, specifically the subset defined in [9], to depict behavior extracted from communication traces.

3 DyST Approach

In this work, we consider dynamic specification mining of IoT systems by reverse engineering Sequence Diagrams from execution traces. Our goal is to extract a

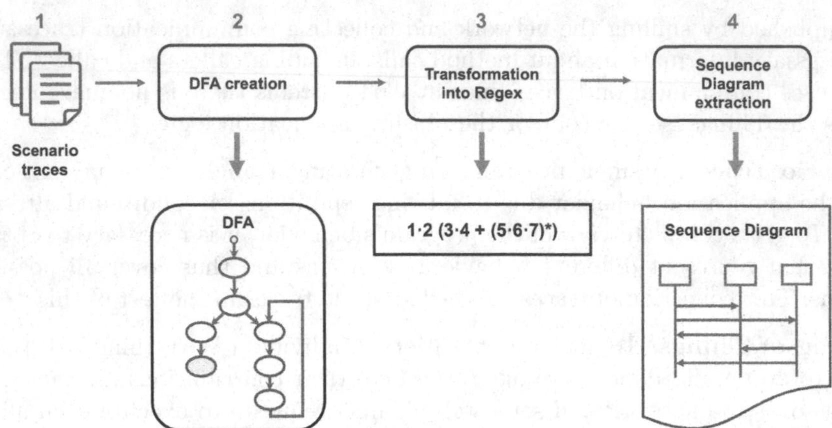

Fig. 2. Detailed approach overview. 1) The scenario traces collected during the program execution are the input to the algorithm that creates the DFA (2). 3) Based on the DFA of the system, a Regular expression is obtained. 3) A mapping from the Regular Expression to the Sequence Diagram is implemented in the last step.

Sequence Diagram that is WoT-compliant and can be further transformed into a System Description for system verification. Figure 2 shows a more detailed overview of our approach, which is composed of the following steps that are further elaborated in the subsequent sections:

- In step 1, the scenario traces obtained during normal system execution are parsed, sorted, and modified to follow a format we propose for representing communication traces between devices in the WoT.
- For control flow detection, in step 2 we create a DFA to obtain an overall representation of the system behavior. This creation is based on model inference algorithms and the minimization of the state transition diagram using transition manipulation formulas.
- With step 3 we create a Regular Expression following the Transitive Closure Method, which is a recursive technique that builds a collection of Regular Expressions that gradually describe bigger groups of pathways in the DFA's transition diagram. This intermediate step helps to extract Sequence Diagrams from the minimized DFA and ensures that they are trace equivalent.
- The resulting Regular Expression is transformed into a UML Sequence Diagram in the last step in Fig. 2 by performing its tokenization and applying a recursive algorithm to build the application logic.

3.1 Communication Traces Format

In this work, we propose a new format for representing communication traces between devices in the WoT. It is based on how messages can be abstracted as explained in the WoT architecture standard of W3C [18], which defines the basis of communication as the union of two main entities: a Thing and a Consumer. Our format uses application semantics and operations which makes it protocol-independent. We define the atomic element that composes each communication trace as an *interaction*, which is a message captured during communication between two objects in a WoT system as seen in Listing 1[2].

```
[{
  interactionId: 1, messagePairId: 1,
  recipient: {type: "thing",thingId: "1", thingTitle: "MyCoffeeMaker"},
  operation: "readproperty",
  affordance: {type: "property",name: "state"},
  timeStamp: "2023-12-04T03:04:16.01",
},{
  interactionId: 2, messagePairId: 1,
  recipient: {type: "controller"},
  payload: "ready",
  timeStamp: "2023-12-04T03:04:16.02",
}]
```

Listing 1. Interaction format example with a trace of a request-response pair.

3.2 DFA Creation

A common practice in specification mining techniques is to produce a state machine using a model-inference algorithm, whose input is a collection of traces recorded during the execution of the system. The algorithm generates a model, often a finite automaton, that accurately represents the behavior of the system that generated the trace log. The model is intended to adopt a formal language derived from the input traces which is constrained by their temporal and structural properties. In this work, our main goal is to preserve the temporal and structural features of the trace log and derive the exact behavior of the system's application logic for further verification of the system. To this end, we adapt the model inference algorithm specified in [1] whose pseudo-code is shown in Algorithm 1.

The algorithm starts by adding an initial state to the DFA object and one state per unique interaction type in the trace log. Then, a transition from the initial state to each first interaction of each trace is added.

[2] Our open-source repository has further examples of the format as well as a schema for the validation of traces.

Algorithm 1. Creation of a DFA from a trace log

```
procedure GENERATEDFA
    dfa ← add_state (init)
    for trace ∈ traceLog do
        for uniqueInteraction ∈ trace do
            dfa ← add_state (uniqueInteraction)
    for trace ∈ traceLog do
        dfa ← add_initial_transition (trace[0])
        for uniqueInteraction ∈ trace do
            if new transition then
                add_transition (transition)
    dfaReduced ← reduce_dfa (dfa)
```

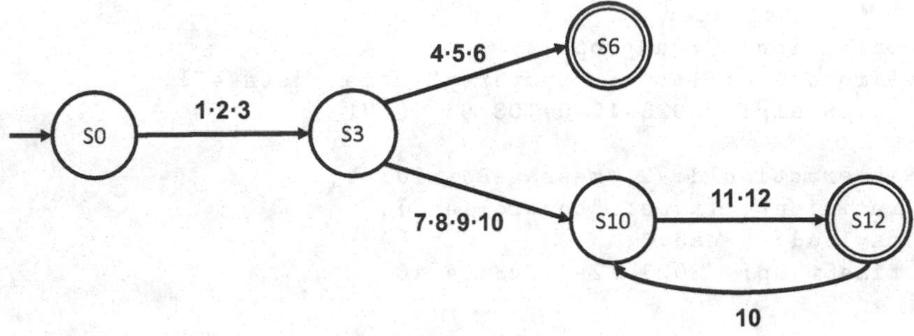

Fig. 3. Minimized DFA state transition diagram resulting from the traces.

After the initial DFA is created from the input traces, it is possible to minimize it according to one of the transition manipulation formulas defined in [21]. Applying this formula to a trace that conforms to the format in Listing 1, we get the diagram of the reduced DFA in Fig. 3, in which we have four states instead of twelve states if we were to not minimize it. The reduction of DFAs is especially useful in the next steps of the transformation into Sequence Diagrams.

3.3 Transformation into Regular Expressions

In this work, we use Regular Expressions as a declarative way to express Mashup application logic and to describe methods to obtain Sequence Diagrams from such Regular Expressions. The patterns of strings described by Regular Expressions show the same behavior as what can be described by finite automata, and therefore any formal language defined by any finite automata is also defined by a Regular Expression.

To construct a Regular Expression to define the language of any DFA we need to build a sequence of patterns or expressions that define a set of strings which in turn represent particular paths in the state transition diagram of the DFA. We adopt the Transitive Closure Method from [20], which is a recursive method that builds a collection of Regular Expressions that gradually describe bigger groups of pathways in the DFA's state transition diagram.

The main drawback of the Transitive Closure Method is that it tends to generate very long Regular Expressions compared to those generated by other methods. The simplification of DFA in the previous section was designed to reduce the length of the final Regular Expression and the time needed to iterate and reach the result (fewer states, fewer iterations). Nevertheless, the final Regular Expression must be further minimized before proceeding with the transformation process. The simplification is done by iteratively transforming the Regular Expression using a set of known algebraic equivalences in the Kleene algebra [11]. The final Regular Expression obtained using the Transitive Closure Method of the DFA from the state diagram in Fig. 3 is the following:

$$RE_{final} = 1 \cdot 2 \cdot 3\,(\,7 \cdot 8 \cdot 9 \cdot 10 \cdot 11 \cdot 12\,(\,10 \cdot 11 \cdot 12)^{*} + 4 \cdot 5 \cdot 6\,) \tag{1}$$

3.4 Sequence Diagram Extraction

To derive Sequence Diagrams from the obtained DFA, we employed Regular Expressions as an intermediate step. As outlined in [9], Sequence Diagram application logic is described by elements defining specific behaviors like par, loop, alternative, etc. These interactions can be composed using UML operators resembling those in Regular Expressions. This mapping ensures equivalence between the Sequence Diagram, DFA, and input traces. The mapping from Regular Expressions to Sequence Diagram is defined as follows in [23], where i is an interaction in the trace log:

1. $(i_1 \cdot i_2) = (i_1\; \boldsymbol{seq}\; i_2)$.
2. $(i_1 + i_2) = (i_1\; \boldsymbol{alt}\; i_2)$.
3. $(i)^{*} = \boldsymbol{loop}\,(i)$.

The Sequence Diagram can be therefore defined as:

$$\begin{aligned} RE_{final} = {} & 1\; \boldsymbol{seq}\; 2\; \boldsymbol{seq}\; 3\; \boldsymbol{seq}\; (\,7\; \boldsymbol{seq}\; 8\; \boldsymbol{seq}\; 9\; \boldsymbol{seq}\; 10\; \boldsymbol{seq}\; 11\; \boldsymbol{seq}\; 12 \\ & \boldsymbol{seq}\; \boldsymbol{loop}\,(\,10\; \boldsymbol{seq}\; 11\; \boldsymbol{seq}\; 12)\; \boldsymbol{alt}\; 4\; \boldsymbol{seq}\; 5\; \boldsymbol{seq}\; 6\,) \end{aligned} \tag{2}$$

The resulting expression with UML operators can in turn be transformed into a UML Sequence Diagram by performing its tokenization and applying the recursive executable procedure from Algorithm 2. Algorithm 2 converts a Regular Expression into an intermediate description called Mashup Logic before its conversion to Sequence Diagrams. In the context of this work, a Mashup Logic is a tree-like structure consisting of each element of the application logic represented in the Regular Expression. It describes the control flow of the system, including nested elements and all the features of each message and each operator, e.g. how often a loop is repeated.

The creation of the Mashup logic using Algorithm 2 is generalized in the following way:

- The procedure *generateMashupLogic* starts by searching the tokens that are included in the Regular Expression.

- If the algorithm sees a token, i.e. the operators *seq*, *alt* and *loop*, a new logic element is added to the Mashup logic structure.
- If the new logic element has logic content, e.g. it contains nested elements such as other operators, the procedure *generateMashupLogic* is called again and the parsing process starts over.

Algorithm 2. Algorithm that implements a Mashup's application logic.

```
procedure GENERATEMASHUPLOGIC
    for token ∈ regularExpression do
        logicElement ← generate_logic_element(token)
        if logicElement has logicContent then
            generateMashupLogic(logicContent)
```

- The procedure finishes when the string to parse does not contain any logic content and is only composed of sequential elements.

Finally, to obtain a UML Sequence Diagram, we use a specific subset of PlantUML[3] defined by the authors in [9]. The resulting Sequence Diagram is omitted here for brevity reasons but can be seen in our repository[4]. As explained in [9], it can be further processed to generate a SD or code for the controller.

3.5 Implementation

To facilitate evaluation and encourage reuse, we offer a publicly accessible implementation of our method. While it's built on Node.js and the reference implementation of the WoT Scripting API [10], the algorithms can be implemented in other programming languages. Each step we've outlined previously can be used as separate functions or together as an end-to-end solution.

4 Evaluation

To evaluate our contributions, we use a setup to showcase three case studies with different characteristics to mine. All mashups considered in the evaluation consist of physical or virtual Things that are exposed to the Web via an industrial gateway and a Mashup controller that is hosted on a conventional laptop. While this allows the right setup for an evaluation, a real-life setup would have the mashup logic running in the cloud for non-real-time applications or in an industrial PC or controller for real-time applications.

The scenario traces between them have been collected through the gateway, as shown in Fig. 4. Every Mashup is composed of Things from one or several WoT setups.

[3] https://plantuml.com/.

[4] https://github.com/tum-esi/dyst-wot-miner/blob/main/paper-appendix/method-result-seqd.pdf.

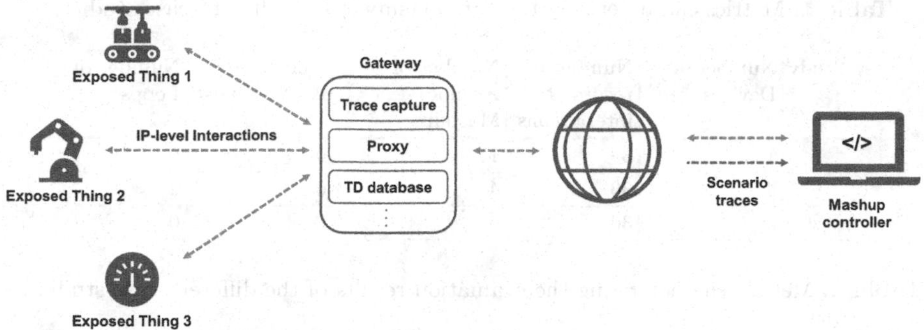

Fig. 4. Common device setup. The Things of a Mashup are proxied via a gateway that contains a trace capture to intercept and record messages exchanged between the Things and the Mashup controller.

4.1 Evaluation Procedure

The evaluation aims to assess our method's accuracy in identifying and representing Mashup behavioral components as Sequence Diagrams and to verify our approach for system verification in the WoT. It's divided into two sub-objectives: approach evaluation and system verification evaluation.

Approach Evaluation. In the first sub-objective, we evaluate the performance of our approach. We focus on determining whether our method can correctly and quickly mine the behavior exhibited in the scenario traces recorded during normal system execution. The steps performed in each case study are:

- Manual design and creation of the Mashup application logic in SD format.
- Automatic creation of Mashup controller code.
- Recording and formatting scenario traces.
- Automatic conversion from scenario traces to Sequence Diagram (approach from Sect. 3).
- Comparing the traces obtained with the mined Sequence Diagram to evaluate if our method has correctly mined the behavior recorded in the traces.

System Verification Evaluation. The second sub-objective is to prove the effectiveness of our specification mining method for system verification. To do this, we evaluate the relationship between the actual behavior of the system and its designed specification to detect errors in the Mashup source code, design problems, or malfunctioning devices. After performing the previous steps, we proceed as follows:

- The previously obtained Sequence Diagram is further converted into SD.
- The designed SD is compared with the mined SD for system verification purposes.

Table 1. Metrics characterizing the components of the different case studies.

Case Study	Number of Devices	Number of recorded interactions	Number of Atomic Mashups	Number of Alternatives	Number of Loops
1	1	3	1	0	0
2	4	30	4	0	2
3	6	36	6	2	0

Table 2. Metrics characterizing the evaluation results of the different case studies.

Case Study	Number of Trace logs	Correctly mined DFA	Correctly mined SeqD	Correct implementation	Faulty implementation
1	19	19	8	8	11
2	4	4	4	1	3
3	4	4	4	1	3

4.2 Case Studies

We assess our method through three case studies with varying properties and levels of application logic complexity. The first, simpler case study involves inputs from external users, providing a large set of trace logs for testing our method across various correct and incorrect implementations. For the second and third case studies, we design, implement, and deploy them due to their inherent complexity. Though these cases yield fewer inputs, intentionally introduced bugs in the controller code create variation, allowing us to test the effectiveness of our method in mining faulty systems. More detailed descriptions and figures of each case study are available in our repository, but we summarize them here:

1. This Mashup is composed of one receive interaction and one send interaction. The controller reads the temperature of a Thing and then invokes an action to show the measured temperature in the device's display.
2. This system is characterized by two Things and by two loops. It starts with reading a property and invoking an action of a movable camera. After each loop, the property value is read again and displayed on the other Thing's display.
3. This system combines two sets of Things and aims to control the irrigation of a farm. Depending on the state of the sprinklers (ON or OFF) and the moisture of the soil, different actions are taken, including the subscription to an event that is triggered when the soil is too dry.

4.3 Evaluation Results

Table 1 provides an overview of each case study's characteristics, including the number of behavioral components and complexity. We conducted our evaluation using the setup and procedures detailed in previous sections, with results summarized in Table 2. The column labeled *Correctly mined DFA* indicates trace logs successfully processed, with their control application logic accurately mined and represented as a DFA. Conversely, the column *Correctly mined SeqD* denotes trace logs successfully transformed from DFA to Sequence Diagrams, evaluating the first sub-objective described in Sect. 4.1.

The system in case study 3 presents a more complex control flow with a total of eighteen unique interaction types and two alternatives, as summarized in Table 2. We found that it is possible to mine simple to complex control flows, including loops and alternatives, and to represent them with a Sequence Diagram as shown by the previous examples and the results in Table 2.

On the other hand, the columns *Correct behavior* and *Faulty behavior* from Table 2 evaluate the second sub-objective described in Sect. 4.1 and we classify a result as follows:

- **Correct Implementation:** Same application logic, affordances, and Things involved.
  Faulty Implementation: Missing or extra messages, wrong order of messages, unnecessary loops, wrong Thing, wrong affordance, wrong branching.
- **False Negative:** Correct implementation that exhibits the issues of a negative result due to traces not reflecting the full range of possible behaviors. Even though this case can be observed[5], they are excluded in the tables above since they cannot be considered to evaluate our method, but only the lack of traces during capture.

All evaluation resources are accessible[6] to the reader so that they can view, understand, or reproduce our evaluation results.

4.4 Timing Evaluation

To conclude, we assessed[7] our algorithms' performance by measuring the time for each transformation from scenario traces to Sequence Diagrams. We evaluated four cases per study: one with correct implementation and three with faulty implementation, showcasing various error types relevant for time analysis due to their impact on performance. The faults found in case study 1 and the faults we introduced in case studies 2 and 3 are explained below with their detailed descriptions available in our repository.

---

[5] An example can be found in our repository at https://github.com/tum-esi/dyst-wot-miner/blob/main/paper-appendix/false-negative.

[6] Our repository contains the complete evaluation inputs, i.e. the communication traces of the systems, the generated Sequence Diagrams, System Descriptions, and the intervening output representations (DFA, Regular Expression and Mashup Logic).

[7] The hardware used for this evaluation is an Intel Core i7-6500U at 2.5GHz and 8GB of RAM.

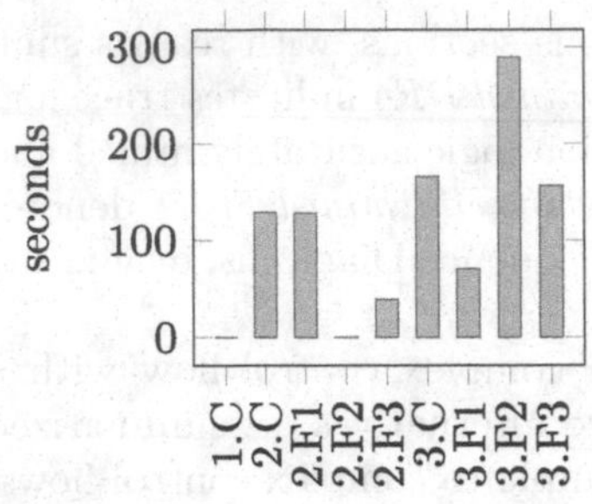

(a) Total time needed to complete the mining procedure in each case study.

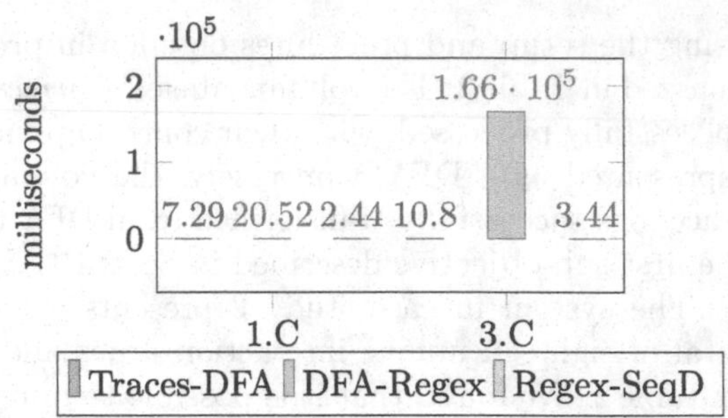

(b) Times taken to complete each transformation for case study 1 and 3 with correct behavior.

Fig. 5. (a) Total time needed to complete the mining procedure in each case study. (b) Times taken to complete each transformation for case study 1 and 3 with correct behavior.

1. Case Study 1: Faulty 1 with extra loop (x6), Faulty 2 with Extra loop (x4), Faulty 3 with Extra loop (x2)
2. Case Study 2: Faulty 1 with Smaller loop count, Faulty 2 with No loop (x2), Faulty 3 with Missing interactions (x3)
3. Case Study 3: Faulty 1 with No *alt* (*Else*), Faulty 2 with Extra loop (x2), Faulty 3 with Wrong device

During our analysis, we observed an uneven distribution of time spent on each transformation. Figure 5 illustrates this behavior, comparing a simple system (case study 1) with the most complex system analyzed (case study 3). Notably, the creation of Regular Expressions consumed the majority of time across all case studies, averaging 99.97%. This is attributed to the Transitive Closure Method (Sect. 3.3), where complexity in creating Regular Expressions is proportional to the number of states and control flow elements. Consequently, case studies 2 and 3 shown in Fig. 5b, being the most complex Mashups, exhibited extended processing times, as detailed in Table 1.

Case study 3 measurements seen in Fig. 5a show considerable differences for different complexities that occur when there are extra or missing items in the obtained traces:

- *Case Study 3 Faulty 2* is the slowest mining procedure (289.29 s) of this analysis since it contains 3 loops, 2 branches, and 36 interactions.
- *Case Study 3 Faulty 1* contains fewer control flow elements (no loops and only 1 branch) which implies a reduction in the time needed by 75.53% (from 289.29 s to 70.79 s).

Overall, we can see that our method performs reasonably fast on an old laptop. Trivial Mashups can be evaluated as they happen whereas more complex ones need to be offloaded to another computer or to a cloud instance.

5 Conclusions and Future Work

In this work, we presented a novel method to mine specifications of WoT systems by reverse engineering Sequence Diagrams from communication traces obtained during the normal execution of the system, thus not requiring access to any source code. Through our evaluation process, we have proven the ability of our mining and conversion algorithms to quickly and accurately detect the application control flow of a system to allow comparison with the reference description. We envision our method to be used in real-life industrial applications that need accountability, traceability, and observability.

While further work can generalize our algorithm by integrating additional approaches based on neural networks, statistical methods and enhanced k-tail algorithms such as [4,15,17], our contributions establish the groundwork for further research in observability and dynamic specification mining for WoT to enable system verification.

References

1. Beschastnikh, I., Brun, Y., Abrahamson, J., Ernst, M.D., Krishnamurthy, A.: Unifying FSM-inference algorithms through declarative specification. In: Proceedings of 35th ICSE. IEEE (2013)
2. Briand, L.C., Labiche, Y., Leduc, J.: Toward the reverse engineering of UML sequence diagrams for distributed java software. IEEE Trans. Softw. Eng. **32**(9), 642–663 (2006)
3. Cook, J.E., Wolf, A.L.: Automating process discovery through event-data analysis. In: Proceedings of 17th ICSE. IEEE (1995)
4. Cook, J.E., Wolf, A.L.: Discovering models of software processes from event-based data. ACM TOSEM **7**(3), 215–249 (1998)
5. Cook, S., Bock, C., Rivett, P., Rutt, T., Seidewitz, E., Selic, B., Tolbert, D.: Unified modeling language version 2.5.1. Technical report, Object Management Group (2017)
6. Grati, H., Sahraoui, H., Poulin, P.: Extracting sequence diagrams from execution traces using interactive visualization. In: 17th Working Conference on Reverse Engineering. IEEE (2010)
7. Hopcroft, J.E., Motwani, R., Ullman, J.D.: Introduction to automata theory, languages, and computation. ACM Sigact News **32**(1), 60–65 (2001)
8. Jiang, J., Koskinen, J., Ruokonen, A., Systa, T.: Constructing usage scenarios for API redocumentation. In: Proceedings of 15th IEEE ICPC. IEEE (2007)
9. Kast, A., Korkan, E., Käbisch, S., Steinhorst, S.: Web of things system description for representation of mashups. In: Proceedings of COINS Conference. IEEE (2020)
10. Kis, Z., Aguzzi, C., Peintner, D., Hund, J., Nimura, K.: WoT scripting API. W3C note, W3C (2023). https://www.w3.org/TR/2023/NOTE-wot-scripting-api-20231003/
11. Kleene, S.C.: Representation of Events in Nerve Nets and Finite Automata. Technical report, Rand Project Air Force, Santa Monica, CA (1951)
12. Korkan, E., Kaebisch, S., Steinhorst, S.: Streamlining IoT System Development With Open Standards, vol. 62. De Gruyter Oldenbourg (2020)

13. Koster, M., Korkan, E.: WoT binding templates. W3C note, W3C (2023). https://www.w3.org/TR/2023/NOTE-wot-binding-templates-20230928/
14. Kumar, S.: Specification mining in concurrent and distributed systems. In: Proceedings of 33rd ICSE (2011)
15. Lo, D., Khoo, S.C.: QUARK: empirical assessment of automaton-based specification miners. In: 13th Working Conference on Reverse Engineering. IEEE (2006)
16. Lo, D., Khoo, S.C., Han, J., Liu, C.: Mining Software Specifications: Methodologies and Applications. CRC Press, Boca Raton (2011)
17. Lo, D., Mariani, L., Pezzè, M.: Automatic steering of behavioral model inference. In: Proceedings of the 7th ESEC/FSE (2009)
18. Matsukura, R., McCool, M., Toumura, K., Lagally, M.: Wot architecture 1.1. W3C recommendation, W3C (2023). https://www.w3.org/TR/2023/REC-wot-architecture11-20231205/
19. McCool, M., Korkan, E., Käbisch, S.: WoT thing description 1.1. W3C recommendation, W3C (2023). https://www.w3.org/TR/2023/REC-wot-thing-description11-20231205/
20. Neumann, C.: Converting deterministic finite automata to regular expressions (2005)
21. Nikiforova, O., Gusarovs, K., Ressin, A.: An approach to generation of the UML sequence diagram from the two-hemisphere model. In: ICSEA 2016 (2016)
22. Souder, T., Mancoridis, S., Salah, M.: Form: a framework for creating views of program executions. In: Proceedings of IEEE ICSM. IEEE (2001)
23. Ziadi, T., Da Silva, M.A.A., Hillah, L.M., Ziane, M.: A fully dynamic approach to the reverse engineering of UML sequence diagrams. In: Proceedings of 16th IEEE ICECCS. IEEE (2011)

SeamlessMDD: Framework for Seamless Integration of Generated and Hand-Written Code

Bojana Dragaš[1(✉)], Nenad Todorović[1], Tijana Rajačić[2], and Gordana Milosavljević[1]

[1] Faculty of Technical Sciences, University of Novi Sad, Trg Dositeja Obradovića 6, Novi Sad, Serbia
{bojana.zoranovic,nenadtod,grist}@uns.ac.rs

[2] Schneider Electric, Industrijska 3G, Novi Sad, Serbia
tijana.rajacic@se.com

Abstract. This paper presents SeamlessMDD - our open-source framework for a gradual and effortless transition from traditional development to MDD (Model-Driven Development) that allows maintaining hand-written and generated code intertwined without the need to adjust the web application architecture or the established way of work. We propose a novel workflow that is based on the following: (1) Incremental and iterative transformations derived from model versions comparison so that only code for affected model elements is generated or modified; (2) Integration of generated and hand-written code using API-based code generators, which operate on syntax trees of target programming languages; (3) Case-specific support for change propagation and conflict resolution (contrary to the VCS-based systems operating on the single line).

Keywords: Model-driven software engineering · Code generation · Hand-written code integration

1 Introduction

Model-driven development (MDD) is a software development methodology focused on models as primary artifacts [6]. It is claimed to achieve higher developer productivity, shorter and less expensive development cycles, and smooth portability to other hardware and infrastructure. MDD significantly improves Web development by generating source code from models on higher abstraction levels, which notably enhances productivity and enables shorter and less expensive development cycles [4,13].

However, due to the differences in abstraction levels between source code and models, not all aspects of a web application can usually be captured in a model. Hence, manual changes in the generated code are needed. Model-driven tools use different strategies for preserving manually written code. Manual changes

K. Stefanidis et al. (Eds.): ICWE 2024, LNCS 14629, pp. 163–177, 2024.
https://doi.org/10.1007/978-3-031-62362-2_12

are often kept in separate files, and language-dependent mechanisms like inheritance, partial classes, or aspect-oriented programming can be used to integrate generated and manually written code parts [10]. Unfortunately, this introduces additional complexity in web application architecture and is unacceptable for some types of code artifacts, like HTML or XAML. Protected regions where manual changes can be inserted complicate the development of code generation tools and can lead to the loss of manual changes if not used properly. Using a VCS (Version Control System) to integrate manual and generated code like in [5] can put a lot of burden on developers who need to resolve conflicts and approve merging in cases where numerous code artifacts are affected based on a single model element change, which is the case in web development.

Several causes hinder the adoption of MDD in the industry. Using model-driven tools often interferes with established ways of thinking, activities, and roles in the development process [9]. Large-scale enterprise solutions face additional challenges due to increased complexity, which severely affects development. Maintenance becomes difficult when the solution reaches the maturity phase, but major refactorings are often avoided. Although the introduction of the MDD methodology could leverage some, if not all, of these issues, stakeholders are hesitant to perform fundamental changes in the development workflow and established architecture, fearing that these changes could result in the breakage of already tested and operating functionalities. As de Lange et al. stated in [13], many MDD approaches enforce top-down implementation rather than cyclical, which aligns better with contemporary agile development. Selic in [20] underlines that a prudent and practical way to introduce a new MDD project to the existing large-scale environment is to integrate its development workflow into the established system's process and environment. Drastic changes could violate existing functionalities, alter the usual workflow, and induce various social issues regarding acceptance.

Our work aims to provide a gradual and effortless transition from the traditional development of Web applications to MDD. This paper presents SeamlessMDD[1] - our open-source framework for seamless integration that allows us to maintain hand-written and generated code intertwined without the need to adjust the web application architecture or the established way of work. We propose a novel workflow that is based on the following: (1) Incremental and iterative transformations derived from model versions comparison so that only code for affected model elements is generated or modified; (2) Integration of generated and hand-written code using API-based code generators, which operate on syntax trees of target programming languages; (3) Case-specific support for change propagation and conflict resolution (contrary to the VCS-based systems operating on the single line).

Apart from the Introduction, this paper is organized as follows. In Sect. 2, the theoretical foundations of the proposed research are summarized along with the survey of available literature. Section 3 introduces our SeamlessMDD framework through a defined set of requirements, established solution architecture, and

[1] https://github.com/BojanaZ/SeamlessMDD.

seamless generation workflow. Verification of the presented approach is presented in Sect. 4. Conclusions and future work are presented in Sect. 5.

2 Background and Related Work

One of the easiest ways to implement model-to-code transformation is to transform the entire source model to the target code using batch transformations based on rendering code templates. The modeler focuses on describing the system with the appropriate model. The transformation specialist develops the infrastructure for the transformation, including templates and code generators. The templates contain lower-level details and contextual information that are not inferable from the model but are required for the functioning solution [7]. The model transformation utilizing templates often provides a substantial part of the source code.

Batch transformations are simple since they do not need complicated algorithms and computations to be implemented. Their main disadvantage is lack of efficacy in large-scale systems since a minor model change demands re-execution of the complete transformation [12]. Also, in the case of features not supported by the modeling language, which must be developed manually, a carefully planned strategy for preserving handwritten code must be established to prevent a loss after the subsequent code generation.

A common approach is to divide the generated and handwritten code into separate files and folders to prevent manually introduced features from being lost with the next generation cycle. Greifenberg et al. in [10] examined and contrasted available techniques for maintaining handwritten and generated code separation. That can be achieved using various language-specific techniques such as inheritance, dependency injection, and partial classes.

Tools like Acceleo [1] keep a clear distinction between handwritten and generated code through language-agnostic protected areas, using special tags to mark where handwritten code should be inserted after a generation or by dividing code into different files or folders. As a result, the application often becomes divided into two parts - generated and manually written, leading to a change in the established architecture. In addition, the traditional MDD workflow expects the generated code to be altered only by a code generator, so it often does not follow coding conventions and guidelines, sometimes can be counter-intuitive, and even, in some cases, could be considered incomprehensible [19].

Commercial tools such as WebRatio [3] or Mendix [2] allow the introduction of tool-specific, non-modelled features through model annotation. This approach can be more complex than manually coding specific features into the target code.

Falzone and Bernaschina in [8] and Bernaschina et al. in [5] separate handwritten and generated code using the branches of a version control system (VCS). The code generator behaves as a "virtual developer" - the generated code is committed to VCS's branch, just as a human developer produced it and later merged it into the codebase. The benefits of this approach include maintaining the same workflow as the traditional code-centric development (since the developer perceives the code generator as "just another developer") and automating code merging and conflict resolution using the modern VCS. However, VCS performs line-based merging, a variant of textual merging, which regards a line of code as a change unit. Although efficient and scalable, line-based merging cannot register two modifications on the same line. Automatic conflict resolution could also induce errors in the source code (when the merging result is not syntactically correct) and detect non-important conflicts, such as newline insertion or indentation change. Weaknesses of this approach may appear with the increase in the number of artifacts. This issue is especially prominent in Web development since one model element change can affect many artifacts in both the frontend and backend.

Our approach differs in not requiring handwritten code to be separated. The developer changes previously existing code that was either manually written or generated, maintaining the same workflow as earlier. In addition, we aim to achieve syntactical merging. The downside is the need to develop off-the-shelf support for merging and conflict resolution.

To achieve efficient transformation, we explored different techniques and approaches to achieve incremental, efficient, and scalable transformation.

Incremental transformation allows only the relevant parts of the source code to be changed, leaving the rest intact. It detects applied model operations, transforms only the changed part of the source model, and alters only the relevant part of the target code. Previously existing target code is updated, and, in most cases, all manually-introduced changes are saved. Compared to the batch, incremental transformation requires more initial effort to compare models and determine introduced operation, but, in the end, often renders computationally more efficient and consumes less time [11]. In the work of Ogunyomi in [17] and Ogunyomi et al. [16], authors explored the techniques to increase model-to-text transformation efficacy focused on achieving scalable transformation. He noticed that, ideally, the transformation should be selective, i.e., only changed model elements and only affected parts of the transformation should be executed. This approach is known as source preserving incrementality [7]. In addition, Ogunyomi states that the re-execution of a transformation should be limited to the affected parts of the input model, and the scale of the propagated change should be proportional to the impact of the change rather than the size of the model. Although our focus is not solely on scalability, we based our work on these ideas to reduce the scale of the transformation and, as a result, reduce the chance of emerging conflicts.

The field of Delta-Oriented Programming (DOP) explored in [15,18], and [14] offer an interesting outlook on the analogous problem of capturing model changes and their propagation to the software product line (SPL). It is dedicated to creating software products by transforming the initial code base (base artifact) by including delta modules as units of transformation. Delta modules aim to transform existing solutions by inserting, changing, and removing parts of the code. Special attention is given to the validity and minimization of emerging conflicts by defining rules that determine whether the delta module should be included in the product. Our work was inspired by this field, although it aims for a more general application.

3 SeamlessMDD Framework

In this section, we present our approach that supports the integration of the hand-written code with the generated one to provide a smoother adaptation of the MDD to the industry settings by conforming to the already established workflow and system architecture. SeamlessMDD framework, a prototype implementation of this approach, is developed in Python3. To allow domain modeling in a standardized manner, we integrated PyECore[2], an implementation of ECore [21] for Python. It provides an API to handle meta-models and models, which serve as input for code generators. To detect a minimal changeset between models, we used deepdiff[3] module. Code generation was handled with Jinja[4] templating engine. API-based generators require a parser for each language/file type. To parse HTML, we used AdvancedHTMLParser[5] - an HTML parser written in Python that supports adding, removing, modifying, and formatting HTML.

The rest of the section is organized as follows. In Subsect. 3.1, we define a set of requirements for a tool that should support seamless integration. Subsection 3.2 presents the SeamlessMDD framework's architecture. Subsection 3.3 presents the workflow to support hand-written and generated code integration.

3.1 Requirements

The following prerequisites are needed to transition smoothly to the MDD in industrial settings.

- **R1. Generated code must be seamlessly integrated with the hand-written code.** It must follow the same coding conventions as developers do as if the code generator was another team member. This enhances code readability and reduces anxiety levels of team members unfamiliar with the MDD.
- **R2. Simultaneously introducing model changes and manually modifying the existing code base must be possible.** Falzone et al. in [8] referred to it as model and text co-evolution. Manual changes to the generated code must be preserved after all subsequent code generation cycles.
- **R3. Manual changes have precedence over automatic ones.** Any manual modification the developer introduces should be preserved, whether submitted to previously hand-written or generated code.
- **R4. The developer should be able to introduce multiple model changes with the possibility of reverting them effortlessly.** Usually, multiple model changes precede transformation. The framework should support workflow when the developer makes a few model changes, tests their impact on the target code, introduces a few more changes, reverts others, tests potential transformation results, and starts the generation process. This

2 https://pyecore.readthedocs.io/en/latest/.
3 https://zepworks.com/deepdiff/current/.
4 https://jinja.palletsprojects.com/en/3.1.x/.
5 https://pypi.org/project/AdvancedHTMLParser/.

requirement helps developers become familiar with MDD methodology without fear they would break the existing functionalities.

- **R5. Generated code must not violate existing functionalities.** At least the generated code should be syntactically correct.
- **R6. Allow providing a model only for the part rather than the entire system, while the rest of the solution could continue to be developed or maintained manually.** This way, efforts could be broken down to a more achievable scale, affecting only certain subsystems and not the entire solution, enabling gradual adoption of MDD.
- **R7. Case-specific conflict resolution support.** Version control systems (VCSs) offer line-based conflict resolution support, which can be insufficient for large-scale enterprise solutions. The conflict display should be case-specific, based on the code segment corresponding to the model element change. Our framework should offer developers guided support for conflict resolution by displaying affected code fragments, explaining the problem, and offering semantically appropriate automated resolutions.
- **R8. Reducing the scale of the transformation.** It is essential to reduce the scale of the transformation to minimize the need for merging and the possibility of conflicts occurring. The framework should transform only changed model parts and affect only relevant file artifacts by re-executing only needed transformations to establish source incrementality and minimality. Ogunyomi in [17] states that efficient transformation requires that the scale of the propagated change be proportional to the scale of the model change, not the bare size of input models.
- **R9. Well-kept code.** Unnecessary or irrelevant artifacts (corresponding to the deleted model elements) should be removed.

3.2 The SeamlessMDD Architecture

The SeamlessMDD framework comprises Model specification and Code Generation modules (Fig. 1). The model specification module is dedicated to the production and evolution of the software system model. It requires a meta-model to conform to, upon which a model is created and validated. The aim is to provide the modeler with a graphical or form-based modeling environment. In its current form, the creation of a model is available by programmatic instancing of meta-classes. All model changes are validated against the meta-model, making the representation always consistent.

Model Version Store holds the model change history. With each generation cycle, the current model is stored as a new version, allowing easier access and providing a basis for later minimal change set inference.

The Code Generation module supports the model-to-code transformation. The Generator Handler obtains the data about changed model elements necessary for the code generation, orchestrates the generation process, and acquires the output. Firstly, the Generation Handler obtains the previous model version from the last generation cycle and requests the Model Differencing Engine to compare it with the current one to produce a minimal set of changes (deltas).

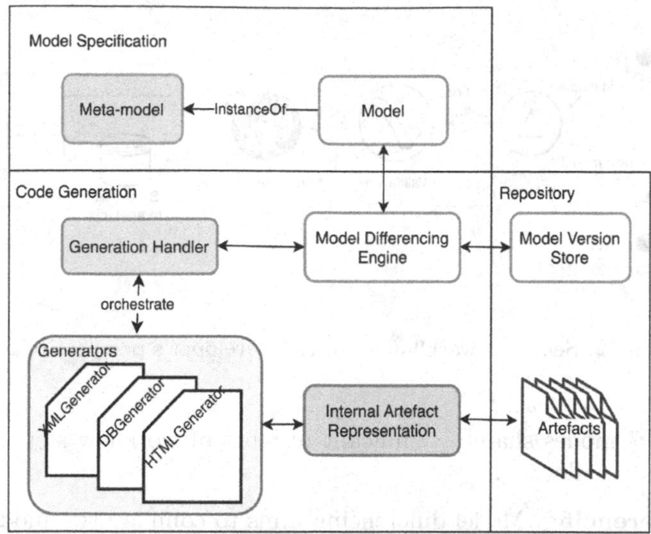

Fig. 1. The overview of the SeamlessMDD architecture

Deltas are used as input to the Code Generators. Each Code Generator adds, updates, and removes code for a single type of artifact. Artifacts represent various formats of textual files, such as XML, C# source code, HTML, database scripts, configuration files, etc.

Code generators have templates for generating code fragments corresponding to model elements. If the file artifact does not exist, the code generator uses one or more templates to produce it in a batch transformation. Otherwise, the artifact content is parsed and transformed into a syntax tree with additional context, which we refer to as Internal Artifact Representation (IAR). Generators, provided with a set of model deltas and generated code fragments, propagate appropriate changes to IAR by creating, removing, or altering the nodes of a syntax tree.

3.3 The Seamless Workflow

Figure 2 shows the steps of the seamless workflow. This subsection will provide more details regarding the SeamlessMDD framework functioning in each step. A simplified class diagram upon which the workflow is based is given in Fig. 3.

Model Change. The Modeler starts the development process by creating a model. The created model must be correct, i.e., according to the underlying meta-model. The Modeler is encouraged to experiment, knowing that every model change is easily reversible. When they become satisfied with the created model, they can choose to see what impact their changes would have on the target code ("Preview") or to initiate code generation ("Generate"). "Generate"

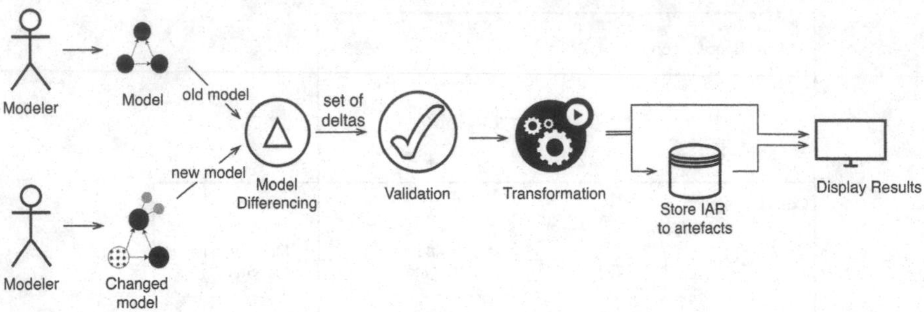

Fig. 2. Seamless workflow from the developer's perspective

and "Preview" modes share a significant number of workflow steps, as will be explained in the following.

Model Differencing. Model differencing aims to compare two model versions to detect introduced changes and model elements affected by those changes. Most generators do not require entire model comparison since they operate on a specific part. For example, the database schema generator uses only database-related model elements such as columns and tables.

The Generator Handler sends comparison requests for selected model elements to the Model Differencing Engine. The result is instantly delivered if the Model Differencing Engine has already calculated the needed difference information for the sake of some previously invoked code generator. Otherwise, the Model Differencing Engine performs model element comparison resulting in a set of *Deltas*, each comprising *old model element*, *new model element*, and *list of changed attributes*. This is used to detect which operation from the predefined set occurred by the following simple algorithm:

```
if [old_model_element is empty ∧
new_model_element is not empty] create()
else if [old_model_element is not empty ∧
new_model_element is empty] delete()
else modify()
```

Validation. The validation phase aims to detect inconsistencies between the current source model and target artifacts. It plays a crucial role in the framework's usability by significantly reducing the probability of conflicts occurring by considering the syntax and semantics of possible issues. The syntax validation relies on the API-based generators that interact with the Internal Artefact Representation (IAR) established on the artifact's syntax tree. Direct manipulation of the target code syntax tree guarantees the output is syntactically correct. Each generator performs independent validation, meaning the generation process could finish valid for some while with errors for others.

Regarding semantics, the validation process checks if the target code is compatible with the model, i.e., previously generated content was not significantly

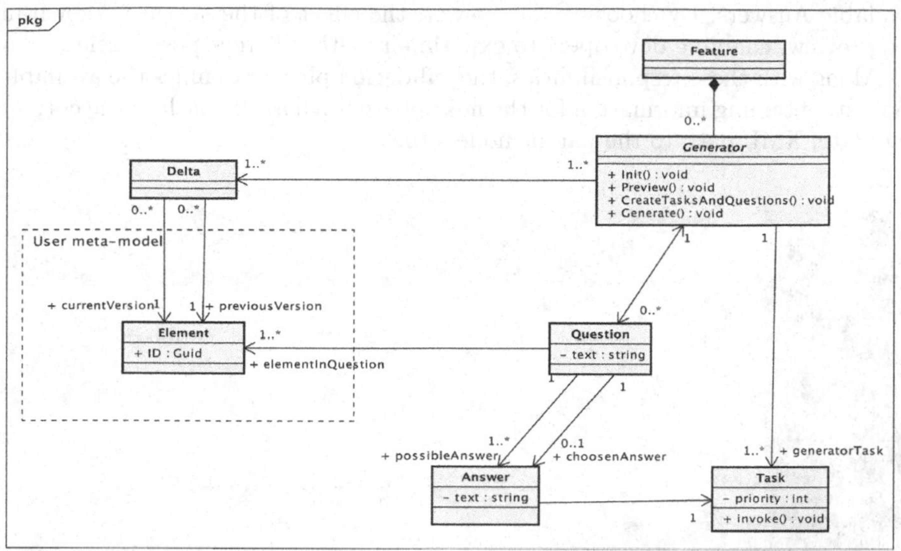

Fig. 3. Classes participating in the code generation process - a simplified UML class diagram

manually changed (more details can be found in [22]). Developers can manually change the code base, such as deleting certain parts of the code, modifying some code corresponding to the model element attributes, and inserting new attributes.

Upon conflict detection, each code generator explains the emerging issue (*Question*) and proposes a semantically appropriate set of possible resolutions (*Answers*). Each *Answer* provides a textual description of the offered solution and a sample action (*Task*) that should be performed if the *Answer* is to be chosen. The question-and-answer mechanism gives the developers better insight into the nature of the conflict and mitigates case-specific resolution. Numerous questions are the same for all code generators and are reused from the parent generator class. New questions can be created to cover some cases specific to the particular artifact.

Examples of conflicts requiring resolution using questions and answers are the following. The code must be updated due to a change in the modeling element, but the corresponding file artifact (or a code fragment) does not exist. The options are to recreate a file (or code fragment) and then perform the change or to skip the code generation. Or a code fragment corresponding to a newly added model element already exists in the source code but in a slightly different form. The options are to add a new code, replace the existing one with a new one, leave the code as it is, or perform their semantic merge by collecting appropriate nodes from both. Figure 4 displays a Preview window with a sample Question and two available Answers. By choosing the answer, the effect of the action is shown in the preview, enabling developers to experiment with different possibilities.

Along with these responsibilities, the validation phase examines the available context, obtaining information for the next phase, such as the path to the correct template, XML path to the parent node, etc.

Fig. 4. Question with answers

Transformation. After completing validation, the transformation phase is rather straightforward. All Tasks obtained from the validation phase are added to *TaskCollection* and executed one at a time upon Internal Artefact Representation. The standard operations (insertion, modification, and deletion of modeling elements) are performed as follows.

Insertion: The generator responsible for the Task accesses the template (determined in the validation phase) and evaluates it, obtaining code segment, then converts it to a set of target syntax nodes. Usually, nodes form a simple tree structure. The top-level segment node is inserted into the already loaded syntax tree of Internal Artefact Representation on a pre-calculated position.

Modification: The generator accesses the predefined part of the loaded syntax tree of Internal Artefact Representation and performs modification.

Deletion: The generator accesses the node in the predefined part of the loaded syntax tree of Internal Artefact Representation and deletes it.

All changes are propagated to Internal Artefact Representation at the end of this phase. Currently, the task orchestration mechanism is rather simple since it bases the execution order on the priority programmatically assigned to each created Task.

Preview or Generate? SeamlessMDD framework operates in two modes: *Preview* and *Generate*. *Preview* mode allows displaying the transformation results without affecting the codebase. The central focus is to display changes that would be introduced if the generation process has been initiated. This allows the development team to detect possible modeling or coding mistakes and alter them.

Generate model directly propagates the transformation results to the artifacts, making the transformation irreversible and permanent. The only way to revert the changes in the model and code in this phase is by using the VCS.

Display Results. The resulting display contains a list of affected target files. When one file from the list is chosen, old and new file versions are shown with differences clearly marked (diff). Figures 5 and 6 show two examples of result display: one when the new model element is inserted and the other when a model element gets deleted. If inconsistencies are encountered, the developer can resolve them through the question-and-answer mechanism (Fig. 4). The given answers are saved, so the developer does not have to spend more time answering when the actual generation process starts. However, if needed, the given answers can be annulled.

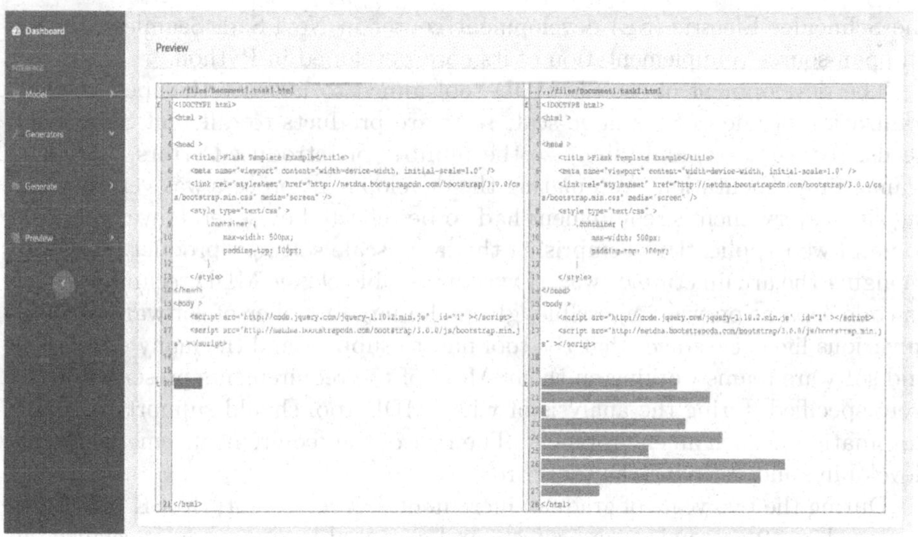

Fig. 5. Code preview example for model element addition

4 Verification

The principles implemented by the SeamlessMDD framework were tested in practice within the complex MDD tool custom-made for and in cooperation with

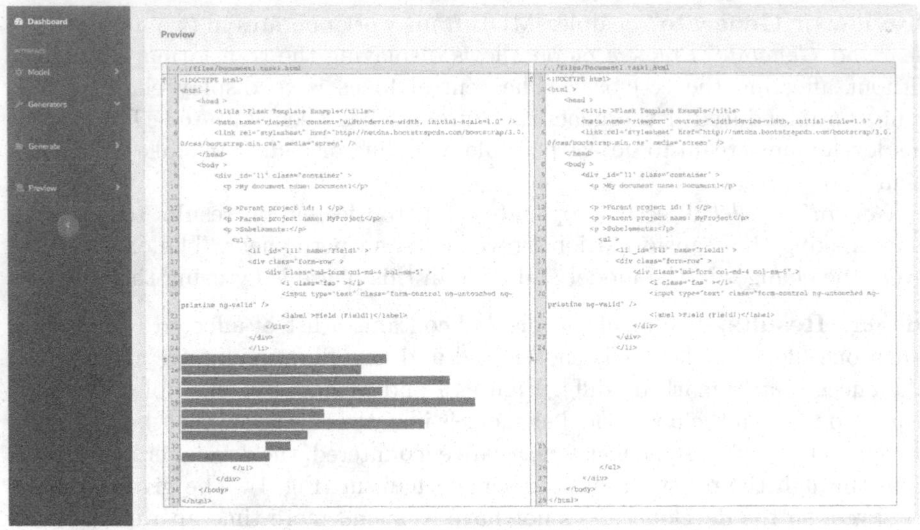

Fig. 6. Code preview example for model element deletion

the Schneider Electric (SE) development center in Novi Sad. SeamlessMDD is an open-source reimplementation of its core developed in Python.

The development of the SE MDD tool aimed to increase the speed of customization of one of SE's large-scale software products to different SE clients' needs, reduce costs, and minimize the number of introduced errors caused by manual implementation. Automating the development process was very promising since every client's requirement had to be reflected on several layers of desktop and web applications comprising the large-scale software product. However, changing the architecture or way of work to enable classic MDD techniques such as code separation was impossible, given the large number of software projects in various life cycle stages that the tool had to support and the many developers and software teams working on them. Most of the requirements presented in 3.1 were specified during the analysis of what MDD tool should support to enable automation in such an environment. The rest of the requirements emerged while developing and verifying the tool core.

During the two years of gradual, incremental development, the SE MDD tool was used on 10 customization projects and accepted by five teams specialized in different technologies. The basic tool core and the first set of 12 API-based generators for developing a part of the desktop application chosen for a pilot project were implemented in three months. The rest of the time was spent enriching the core and developing API-based code generators that worked on several hundreds of file artifacts within two SE complex software products. The tool has been in use all along; only the amount of handwritten code has gradually decreased over time as the scope of supported parts has grown. A requirement that previously took an average of three weeks per team for manual development could now be completed within two to three days when using the tool, assuming optimal organization. The most productive team consisted of specialists who covered all the necessary technologies, ranging from database experts to web frontend developers. On the other hand, separate teams organized based on technology expertise (database, web, desktop) and working on the same feature required more time due to increased cooperation needs.

The SE MDD tool was developed in C# using the .NET compiler platform[6] extended by our RoseLib[7] library [23] and four parsers for HTML, XML, XAML, and T-SQL.

5 Conclusion and Future Work

This paper presented a novel approach to developing MDD tools aimed at providing a gradual and effortless transition from traditional development to MDD. It is based on the premise that the developers could better accept the MDD approach by allowing them to maintain the current workflow, system architecture, and the existing level of code readability, along with the freedom to experiment and revert introduced changes. All of the above is supported by the SeamlessMDD framework by implementing: (1) Incremental and iterative transformations derived from model versions comparison; (2) Integration of generated and handwritten code using API-based code generators; (3) Case-specific support for change propagation and conflict resolution.

The SeamlessMDD framework is an open-source reimplementation of the core of Schneider Electric's custom-made MDD tool that was successfully used in software projects in different life cycle stages. SeamlessMDD was developed in Python3, using PyECore7 for meta-models specification.

However, this approach has some drawbacks. While it may be convenient for the developers (MDD tool users), implementing the MDD solution in this way is more demanding for the team creating it. On average, it took 20 person-hours to develop an API-based code generator for a specific file artifact. In contrast, developing a code generator for the same artifact using templates and batch transformation only took an average of two hours. The implementation of API-based code generators requires significant effort due to the need to specify every detail of code manipulation at the syntax tree level.

Another challenge arises when previously developed API-based generators need to be modified to accommodate changes in the architecture of the solutions for which the tool generates code. Some developers who use the SE MDD tool took on the responsibility of maintaining the API-based code generators for their respective parts of the solution, while others required assistance from the tool developers. Finding an efficient way to simplify the development of API-based generators became necessary.

The first step in facilitating the development of API-based generators for C# was to create our RoseLib library [23] on top of the .NET Compiler platform,

[6] https://learn.microsoft.com/en-us/dotnet/csharp/roslyn-sdk.
[7] https://github.com/nenadTod/RoseLib.

which allows for the manipulation of coarse-grained code fragments. The second step is to automate the creation of API-based generators using machine learning (in progress).

Besides optimizing the development of API-based generators, we plan to enhance the SeamlessMDD framework by incorporating a graphical modeling environment for languages specified by PyECore7. The SE MDD tool features a complex form-based user interface that is customized for specifying the concrete SE solutions. The form-based model specification was used to enable different kinds of experts to use or experiment with the tool, including SMEs (Subject Matter Experts). On the other hand, SeamlessMDD should support modeling in a generic way for all PyECore7-based meta-models provided.

References

1. Acceleo. https://eclipse.dev/acceleo. Accessed 16 Apr 2024
2. Mendix. https://www.mendix.com. Accessed 16 Apr 2024
3. Webratio. https://www.webratio.com. Accessed 16 Apr 2024
4. Basso, F.P., Pillat, R.M., Oliveira, T.C., Roos-Frantz, F., Frantz, R.Z.: Automated design of multi-layered web information systems. J. Syst. Softw. **117**, 612–637 (2016). https://doi.org/10.1016/j.jss.2016.04.060, https://www.sciencedirect.com/science/article/pii/S0164121216300358
5. Bernaschina, C., Falzone, E., Fraternali, P., Herrera Gonzalez, S.L.: The virtual developer: integrating code generation and manual development with conflict resolution. ACM Trans. Softw. Eng. Methodol. **28**, 1–38 (2019)
6. Brambilla, M., Cabot, J., Wimmer, M.: Model-Driven Software Engineering in Practice: Second Edition, 2nd edn. Morgan & Claypool Publishers, New York (2017)
7. Czarnecki, K., Helsen, S.: Feature-based survey of model transformation approaches. IBM Syst. J. **45**(3), 621–645 (2006)
8. Falzone, E., Bernaschina, C.: Intelligent code generation for model driven web development. In: Pautasso, C., Sánchez-Figueroa, F., Systä, K., Murillo Rodríguez, J.M. (eds.) ICWE 2018. LNCS, vol. 11153, pp. 5–13. Springer, Cham (2018). https://doi.org/10.1007/978-3-030-03056-8_1
9. Fieber, F., Regnat, N., Rumpe, B.: Assessing usability of model driven development in industrial projects. arXiv:abs/1409.6588 (2014). https://api.semanticscholar.org/CorpusID:10632456
10. Greifenberg, T., et al.: A comparison of mechanisms for integrating handwritten and generated code for object-oriented programming languages. In: 2015 3rd International Conference on Model-Driven Engineering and Software Development (MODELSWARD), pp. 74–85 (2015)
11. Johann, S., Egyed, A.: Instant and incremental transformation of models. In: Proceedings. 19th International Conference on Automated Software Engineering 2004, pp. 362–365 (2004)
12. Kusel, A., et al.: A survey on incremental model transformation approaches. CEUR Workshop Proc. **1090**, 4–13 (2013)
13. de Lange, P., Nicolaescu, P., Winkler, T., Klamma, R.: Enhancing MDWE with collaborative live coding. Modellierung **2018** (2018)

14. Lienhardt, M.: PYDOP: a generic python library for delta-oriented programming. Proceedings of the 27th ACM International Systems and Software Product Line Conference - Volume B (2023). https://api.semanticscholar.org/CorpusID:261125815
15. Nieke, M., Hoff, A., Schaefer, I., Seidl, C.: Experiences with constructing and evolving asoftware product line with delta-oriented programming. In: Proceedings of the 16th International Working Conference on Variability Modelling of Software-Intensive Systems. VaMoS '22. Association for Computing Machinery, New York (2022).https://doi.org/10.1145/3510466.3511271
16. Ogunyomi, B., Rose, L., Kolovos, D.: Incremental execution of model-to-text transformations using property access traces. Softw. Syst. Model. **18**, 1–17 (2019). https://doi.org/10.1007/s10270-018-0666-5
17. Ogunyomi, B.: Incremental model-to-text transformation. Ph.D. thesis, University of York (2016)
18. Schaefer, I., Bettini, L., Bono, V., Damiani, F., Tanzarella, N.: Delta-oriented programming of software product lines. In: Bosch, J., Lee, J. (eds.) SPLC 2010. LNCS, vol. 6287, pp. 77–91. Springer, Heidelberg (2010). https://doi.org/10.1007/978-3-642-15579-6_6
19. Schmidt, D.C.: Guest editor's introduction: model driven engineering. Computer **39**(2), 25–31 (2006)
20. Selic, B.: The pragmatics of model-driven development. IEEE Softw. **20**(5), 19–25 (2003)
21. Steinberg, D., Budinsky, F., Merks, E., Paternostro, M.: EMF: Eclipse Modeling Framework. Pearson Education, London (2008)
22. Todorović, N., Dragaš, B., Milosavljević, G.: Supporting integrative code generation with traceability links and code fragment integrity checks. In: Trajanovic, M., Filipovic, N., Zdravkovic, M. (eds.) Disruptive Information Technologies for a Smart Society, pp. 490–501. Springer Nature Switzerland, Cham (2024). https://doi.org/10.1007/978-3-031-50755-7_46
23. Todorović, N., Lukić, A., Zoranović, B., Vaderna, R., Vuković, Z., Stoja, S.: RoseLib: a library for simplifying .net compiler platform usage. In: Konjović, Z., Zdravković, M., Trajanović, M. (eds.) ICIST 2018 Proceedings, vol.1, pp.216-221 (2018) (2018)

EdgER: Entity Resolution at the Edge for Next Generation Web Systems

Cristian Martella, Angelo Martella(✉), and Antonella Longo

Department of Engineering for Innovation, University of Salento, Lecce, Italy
{cristian.martella,angelo.martella,antonella.longo}@unisalento.it

Abstract. Thanks to the advances of emerging technologies like Edge and Cloud Computing and microservice development, web architectures are evolving to support Big Data platforms fully. The decentralization of the traditional cloud-centric approach pushes microservices towards the edge of the Internet when constraints exist regarding response time, security, and proximity services availability. This work proposes an approach for detecting anomalies at the edge called EdgER based on entity resolution techniques. Such an approach can be adopted for any application providing proximity-added-value service, even in near real-time. In this sense, a case study is provided in the photovoltaics domain. By implementing EdgER's building blocks at the edge, it is possible to reconcile the received IoT data streams early against a predefined data model and identify near real-time anomalies in energy production and/or in smart photovoltaic panel operations. In general, EdgeER can also significantly contribute to improving the quality of the data managed by the overall Big Data platform and facilitating the implementation of privacy-preserving proximity-added-value services.

Keywords: Anomaly detection · Federated learning · Entity resolution · Data model · Edge-cloud continuum · Microservice architecture

1 Introduction

Web architectures are adapting to Big Data platforms, utilizing emerging technologies like Edge-Cloud Continuum (ECC), MicroServices (MSs), Digital Twins (DTs), and Data Spaces (DSs) to develop software services. In the ECC paradigm, these services are designed and implemented as MSs architectures. Cyber-physical (CP) systems are currently implemented as MSs architectures for developing advanced systems like DTs and DSs, where real-world assets are twinned to their digital counterparts using bi-directional interconnections for monitoring and control. The traditional cloud-centric approach is substantially decentralized towards the edge using MS technology.

According to the ECC paradigm, MSs of a Big Data platform are distributed along different stages between the cloud and the edge of the Internet. Some are

K. Stefanidis et al. (Eds.): ICWE 2024, LNCS 14629, pp. 178–196, 2024.
https://doi.org/10.1007/978-3-031-62362-2_13

exclusively part of the cloud stage due to their resource-intensive nature. Others can be allocated at one of the stages provided by the ECC, for scalability aim, and others can be pushed towards the edge to provide users value-added services in near real-time. This work introduces EdgER, an approach for Entity Resolution (ER) and Federated Learning (FL) at the edge, proposing the essential architectural building blocks. No mandatory constraints exist in choosing the technical solution for developing a generic EdgER-compliant application to provide proximity-added-value services in near real-time. Anomaly Detection (AD) is a potential proximity-added-value service for critical and non-critical assets, benefiting from edge MSs related to ER and FL. This approach can improve data quality, sovereignty, and privacy preservation, enhancing the overall edge service. A case study in the photovoltaics domain is presented, focusing on developing an anomaly detection service for the EdgER assessment. This service allows early reconciliation of entities for each data stream, enabling the identification of near real-time anomalies in energy production and smart photovoltaic panel operations. EdgER does not cover the typical workflow of an ER approach, and clustering is not included at this time because it is unnecessary to provide proximity-added-value services. An extended version of EdgER is planned for further development. The proposed approach can significantly enhance the data quality of the Big Data platform, making it a valuable contribution to its realization.

The research questions the present paper aims to address are the following:

RQ1 How can web architectures evolve and leverage emerging technologies to support and provide proximity-added-value services, even in near real-time, by adopting a systematic and scalable approach capable of improving FAIR, privacy-preserving, and trustworthy aspects?

RQ2 How can FL-based ER microservices be effectively used at the edge to enable web technologies in any potential domain where significant constraints exist regarding early detection and responsiveness, hardware performance, and normalized representations of the involved entities?

After this introduction, the paper is structured as follows. Section 2 presents the state of the art and the reference background. EdgER is presented in Sect. 3, whereas Sect. 4 describes a case study we have developed to implement an EdgER-compliant service for anomaly detection and to assess the proposed approach. Eventually, Sect. 5 concludes the paper.

2 Background and Related Work

This section provides an overview of the work's background, state of art, and crucial technological concepts for discussing EdgER, the proposed approach for ER and FL at the edge.

2.1 Architecting the Web in the Cloud Continuum

In the age of cloud continuum, new web application design paradigms are needed to facilitate seamless computation distribution between cloud computing layers, edge computing, and traditional on-premises data centers. These approaches utilize the distributed nature of modern computing resources and facilitate merging heterogeneous data sources by decentralizing data preparation, storage, and consumption tasks. Key requirements for developing a distributed web architecture in the ECC include: (1) DSs, such as implementing open and trusted data exchange/sharing mechanisms; (2) FL, such as approaches to AI-driven resource management, decentralized communication and storage, and dataflow programming, as well as managing; (3) MS distribution and orchestration [26]. MS architecture [35] and ECC [33] are modern distributed computing approaches that support scalable, resilient, and responsive web applications. Integrating these approaches allows for load balancing, resource optimization, and efficient management of MSs [29]. They offer flexibility, agility, and faster development cycles and can be deployed independently without affecting the entire application. ECC allows strategic placement of business logic, optimizing processes at the edge or cloud, and enhancing overall MSs efficiency.

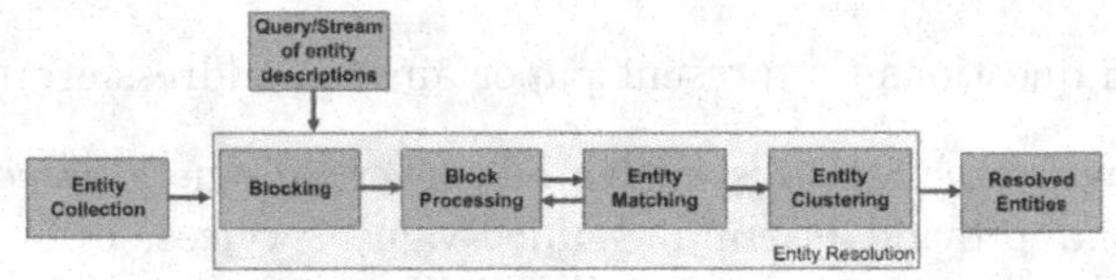

Fig. 1. Typical end-to-end Entity Resolution workflow [8].

2.2 Federated Learning

Edge FL is a promising IoT-based smart application approach that uses a shared prediction model for better data privacy [40]. However, technical challenges like resource optimization, incentive mechanisms, and system efficiency need to be addressed [41], and the computational complexity of heterogeneous devices complicates these issues [5]. In [39], authors propose a quality-oriented FL mechanism that dynamically assesses model updates, considering data and device heterogeneity, potentially improving data quality at the edge. Recent studies show federated learning improves anomaly detection accuracy, with a focus on model aggregation [31] and collaborative systems [21]. An FL-based smart grid anomaly detection scheme is proposed, training local machine learning models in smart meters without central server sharing, ensuring user privacy [19].

2.3 Entity Resolution

ER is a crucial step in FL, identifying and linking records to the same real-world entity [30]. Mistakes in ER can significantly impact learning, so it is important to control or minimize them. A three-party end-to-end solution, including privacy-preserving ER and federated logistic regression, has been proposed to address these issues [15]. A federated approach has been implemented for named entity recognition [25], while an informativeness-based active learning approach reduces manual labeling for ER [7]. The ER process is a method in literature that aims to enhance data quality by uniformly representing entities in datasets or streams. It involves a series of steps (listed in Fig. 1) to identify matching pairs of entity descriptions corresponding to real-world objects, also called *duplicates*. The Blocking and Block Processing stage in data analysis helps handle large volumes of data by separating input into blocks based on similarity criteria. Dynamic indexing techniques like Similarity-aware Index [6] and DySimII [32] update these blocks based on entity descriptions obtained through queries or streams of entities, which can be interpreted as sequences of queries. Matching involves forwarding entity descriptions to a matching function based on binary similarity. Dynamic Matching approaches like QuERy [3] and QDA [2] are not designed for incremental execution and do not support functions considering more than two values. BrewER [36] can be employed within each block to reduce similarity comparisons and feed the query tree with resolved entities, dynamically and on-demand. This approach is preferred due to its reliability, effectiveness, and efficiency. In the Clustering stage, duplicates are inferred by grouping them within clusters, improving the similarity function used in the Matching stage. This results in a set of entity clusters, each described by features of a real-world object. Incremental Correlation Clustering is the leading approach to Dynamic Clustering [13], capable of performing updates on clusters without prior knowledge of the number of clusters involved.

The proposed approach for implementing an AD solution focuses on the Blocking and Matching stages, with Clustering implementation envisioned through further case studies.

2.4 Data Quality

Data quality (DQ) is a crucial aspect of research and analysis, ensuring data meets requirements by guaranteeing their integrity, addressing issues, and promoting transparency [16]. The literature explores various methods for enhancing data quality, including dimensions, metrics, and techniques for big data [11]. In [14], a DQ Toolkit automates DQ issues assessment and remediation, addressing security and privacy concerns through data sovereignty, ensuring confidentiality, availability, and integrity through trusted data exchange paradigms and usage management systems [17,18].

Data Model and Representation. Standard and open data formats are crucial for data exchange and sharing in DSs, enabling a "common lingua" definition for seamless integration [1]. Data interoperability initiatives often lack data modeling, focusing on metadata exchange and data representation formats without guiding data semantics. Standardization and harmonization in data distribution specifications across platforms result in individuals using their own solutions for data retrieval from shared data environments. LinkedScales [28] is a graph-based data structure (DS) architecture that organizes DSs through scales, implementing an integration and enrichment pipeline for incremental ontology-like data structures. The European Telecommunications Standards Institute (ETSI) has developed the Next Generation Service Interfaces Linked Data (NGSI-LD) standard[1], which enhances data accessibility through APIs and data models, serving as the fundamental interface in the Fiware open-source ecosystem. Fiware provides open-source components for data platform construction, promoting Linked Open Data usage through metadata integration [9]. JSON-LD is a reference format for serializing Linked Data [20], suitable for JSON-based deployment environments. The NGSI-LD API describes entity concepts, and initiatives are being developed to create NGSI-LD-compatible data models. One notable initiative is the Smart Data Models program[2], which supports semantic interoperability of context information within DSs.

2.5 Anomaly Detection

AD identifies anomalous sub-sequences in time series data, indicating significant events like production faults, delivery bottlenecks, and system defects. Data scientists have created advanced algorithms to automatically detect anomalous patterns in large and intricate time series data [34]. AD is a resource-intensive task traditionally performed in cloud facilities [42], where high-performance computing infrastructures can handle the volume, velocity, and variety of big data. Recent studies suggest decentralizing AD pipeline execution towards the network's edge, closer to where data is produced or consumed. AD is a resource-intensive task traditionally performed in cloud facilities, where high-performance computing infrastructures can handle the volume, velocity, and variety of big data. Recent studies suggest decentralizing AD pipeline execution towards the network's edge, closer to where data is produced or consumed. In [12], an edge-cloud collaboration architecture is proposed which focuses on pattern AD. In contrast, in [38], authors emphasize robustness and accuracy in fluctuating cloud-edge computing systems using Correlative-GNN with Multi-head Self-attention and Auto-Regression Ensemble Method (CGNN-MSAR). However, deep learning algorithms often require high computational power, making them unsuitable for limited resource edge scenarios [10].

---

[1] www.etsi.org/deliver/etsi_gs/CIM/001_099/009/01.04.01-_60/gs_cim009v010401p.pdf.

[2] https://smartdatamodels.org/.

3 EdgER: An Approach to Anomaly Detection at the Edge

EdgER is a novel approach to ER processes at the network's edge, using limited resources. It can be adopted in any context, where the provision of proximity-value-added services exists in near real-time. Its main goal is to identify the main building blocks, including the corresponding features, and to foster quick design and implementation of such building blocks, as required by the use case. EdgER allows for developing flexible setups without specific constraints on techniques and/or algorithms to adopt. Each functional block can be implemented as an MS and integrated seamlessly within the overall architecture. The MS architecture scalability can be achieved by utilizing any possible clustering solution among edge smart devices, such as Docker Swarm and Kubernetes. As a case study, EdgER is utilized for developing an AD service at the edge that will be considered a module of a web-based Big Data platform. EdgER's building blocks are enriched with two additional MSs for (1) accessing anomaly detection rules and (2) matching AD rules with attribute values of the previously resolved entities. A resolved entity remains valid until a new resolution or timeout occurs, enabling the detection of delays on data streams or faulty/rogue sensors.

3.1 EdgER Architecture

EdgER offers guidelines for developing an ER pipeline, outlining functionalities, data inputs, and outputs. Figure 2a shows EdgER architecture which consists of three main building blocks: Data Access Point (DAP), Matching Units (MUs), and Data Integration Unit (DIU). EdgER is intended to be deployed in edge environments where the computational resources available are typically limited. This is especially true considering the complexity of most state-of-the-art incremental approaches to ER, which require high-end hardware to work effectively.

Data Access Point. DAP manages inbound edge data streams, performs preliminary stream identification and blocking, and distributes identified blocks among available MUs. Each MU can process the blocks parallel to other units, ensuring efficient data processing. The DAP building block can be implemented using any programming language, with no specific mandatory choice in techniques and/or algorithms except block identification, policy block assignment, and data source synchronization mechanism, making it an ad-hoc business logic.

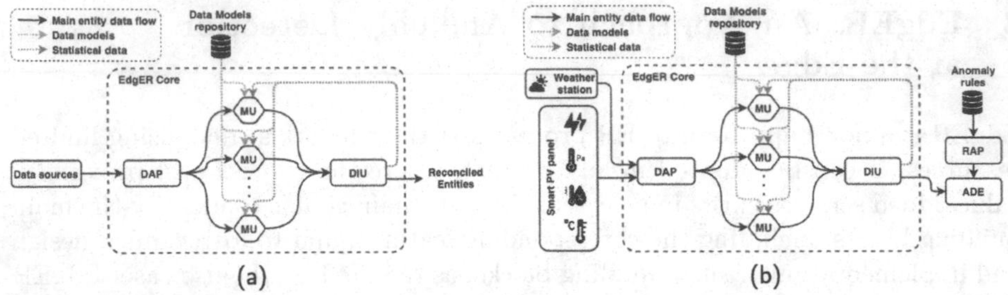

Fig. 2. EdgER's architecture. (a) General overview. (b) Overview of EdgER-compliant AD system.

Matching Unit. The MU building block constitutes the core of EdgER. Its goal is to effectively match each sensor message against a set of predefined data models and return a representation of the given data, which is reconciled with the best-fitting model found after the lookup. The choice of machine learning-based classification algorithm is crucial for implementing this block, as it can help discover additional knowledge about the data for enriching the original record. An MU building block is a system that processes data blocks and produces a reconciled representation of data entities within each block based on the best-fitting data model. A matching approach is used to identify the best-fitting data model and the corresponding similarity metric set for developing an MU. The trade-off between matching accuracy and resource usage can be optimized by combining multiple matching approaches based on the data entity structure and computational resource availability. Therefore, EdgER's MUs can be designed to accommodate the deployment of matching approaches based on deep learning, large language models, and time series analysis that can be combined to output the reconciled version of input data, according to the best fitting data model identified.

Data Integration Unit. The DIU encloses the techniques to infer statistical information from flows of correlated resolved entities. Such statistics support the matching model and improve the matching accuracy. The DIU building block receives the reconciled representation of the data entities to be processed as inputs. It produces a statistical overview about the correlated streams of data entities as output. Thanks to the adoption of shared standard data models, resolved entities streamed by the MUs provide more immediate feedback for identifying potential correlations between data entities. Specifically, correlated data entities exhibit common semantic features. In the DIU building block, the idea is to combine correlated data flows and infer knowledge that can be used to tune the parameters of the MUs matching model. Moreover, additional blocks can leverage this information to support analytics and AD models. Once correlations have been identified, data entities are tagged and the values they carry are combined to form unique time series. Nevertheless, data entities associated with different data sources exhibit different measurement rates. Thus, for the purposes of statistical analyses and to improve the accuracy of global forecasting models, it is important to regularize the time series in terms of sampling interval. The reconstruction process of the time series relies on a data augmentation model chosen according to a trade-off between the additional complexity cost introduced and the accuracy level desired. Time series bootstrapping techniques [4] can be used to leverage the behaviour of the raw time series and infer synthetic values, to be then used to resample the time series. Other approaches make use of Generative Adversarial Networks (GANs). For instance, in [22] DCT-GAN is introduced as a model that uses dilated convolutional transformer-based GAN to enhance accuracy and improve generalization capability in time series AD, while [23] introduced TSA-GAN, a robust GAN model with a self-adaptive recovering strategy for time series augmentation.

4 Case Study: Anomaly Detection in PhotoVoltaic Systems

The case study we propose as AD service refers to the domain of photovoltaic systems, where it is necessary to identify possible defeats in energy production in near real-time and at the edge of the Internet. In this regard, an implementation of each building block of EdgER is provided and discussed in the following, showcasing the approach's modularity and the prerogatives/requirements to develop each MS. The resulting data preparation pipeline constitutes the input of the cascaded AD MS, whose development must comply with the requirements posed by EdgER's specifications regarding supported input data formats. As mentioned, the proposed approach is meant to provide just the building blocks to implement and not identify the corresponding implementing details.

4.1 Overall Architecture

The overall architecture of the case study we have used to implement and assess the EdgER-compliant AD service is shown in Fig. 2b. It represents an MS architecture that implements a CP system. As can be seen, two additional supporting MSs are present in the architecture. These additional MSs are called Rules Access Point (RAP) and Anomaly Detection Engine (ADE). They are used to (1) access the rules corresponding to the anomalies to detect and (2) match each AD rule with the attribute values of the reconciled entities, respectively. A detailed description of both the cyber and physical components is provided in the following sections.

Physical Components. The physical asset to consider for implementing the case study, along with the corresponding equipment, is detailed in the following. Such an asset consists of a smart photovoltaic (PV) panel developed in [27,37] and designed to track the sun's trajectory based on the geospatial location of the panel and an edge Single Board Computer (SBC). The smart PV features a set of sensors and actuators used to perceive and interact with the surrounding environment. On the sensors side, the device is equipped with sensors to assess the working temperature inside the component box of the PV panel, and a DC power sensor that is used to collect data on the live power production of the PV panel, the power stored in the battery and the power used by the system in performing its operations. A weather station is deployed to detect the environmental conditions about contextual temperature, atmospheric pressure and relative humidity. The physical asset is also equipped with a Micro-Controller unit (MCU) to provide the needed processing capabilities to the PV panel, along with the support for wireless communication. The physical asset is powered using the energy generated by the PV panel and stored in the accumulation system. In particular, a Maximum Power Point Tracker is used to monitor the output of the PV panel and adjust the voltage and current so as to keep the system always at the point of maximum power. According to the edge-cloud-continuum, the SBC solution we have adopted is a cluster of Raspberry-PI 4 Model B to be used for deploying the MSs that constitute the AD service.

Cyber Components. This section introduces the implementation details of the cyber components of the proposed AD service. Considering the domain of the present case study, we had to identify the data models to make available to the service, along with the implementation of the building blocks EdgER provides. Except for the two additional supporting MSs, a detailed description of the cyber components is provided in the following.

Entities Domain. The AD service implementation and assessment involve analyzing data models from renewable energy sources, including a temperature sensor embedded in a PV panel, a weather station monitoring weather forecasting, and an internal accumulator battery. The aim of the case study is to reconcile the entities of the data streams received from the temperature sensor, the weather station, and the accumulator, before using the corresponding attribute values to detect any anomaly. For this purpose, we refer to the two additional MSs RAP and RAE. These data models are public available on the *FIWARE Smart Data Models* website.

The three data models we have considered are *WeatherObserved*[3], *IndoorEnvironmentObserved*[4], and *BatteryStatus*[5] for respectively representing the entities used for the weather station, the embedded temperature sensor and the PV panel's accumulator, whose reference domains are *Weather*, *Environment*, and *Battery*.

[3] https://github.com/smart-data-models/dataModel.Weather/tree/master/WeatherObserved.

[4] https://github.com/smart-data-models/dataModel.Environment/tree/master/IndoorEnvironmentObserved.

[5] https://github.com/smart-data-models/dataModel.Battery/tree/master/BatteryStatus.

Data Access Point. This implementation uses a block-based system where each block is tagged with a source identifier related to the edge data source that generated the values. Each block is a first in, first out (FIFO) queue of sensor readings, with the size of a block either fixed or dynamically based on an orchestrator's load-balancing discipline. Edge contexts use sensor messages to reach EdgER asynchronously, with each sensor having its own independent reading interval. However, the goal is to use a synchronous system where the "heartbeats" rate can be fixed or dynamically adjusted to the workload. In this system, block buffers are populated between two clock ticks and forwarded to output channels at each tick. The clock rate is set by inferring the sensor message arrival period for each sensor and selecting the minimum among them. This dynamically keeps the value updated, ensuring no message is lost due to different blocks update rates. Blocks are assigned to MUs in a round-robin scheme, with each MU receiving a list of blocks. A load balancing unit can use this list's size to decide whether to spawn new MUs or remove unused or underused MUs when the value falls below a threshold.

Matching Unit. This task is divided into two sub-tasks: structure matching and value matching. The MU aims to determine the best data model for a sensor data tuple by collecting and caching contextual data models. Once the models are loaded, some preliminary set operations are performed. First, the common attributes among all the models are stored in the models' shared keys set $\mathcal{S}$.

For each i-th model's keys set $\mathcal{K}_i$, relation 1 holds.

$$\mathcal{S} = \bigcap_i \mathcal{K}_i \tag{1}$$

$$\mathcal{D}_i = \mathcal{K}_i - \mathcal{S} \tag{2}$$

At the same time, for each model, all the distinctive attributes are stored in sets $\mathcal{D}_i$, each of which is mapped to its model reference, as in (2). This separation is necessary in order to compute a similarity score that considers the number of distinctive features matched by a sensor record. The similarity score can be calculated for each model according to the following steps. When a sensor data tuple is sent to the structure matching routine, the set of its attributes $\mathcal{R}$ is extracted and, for each model, it is intersected with the set of the model's features. The set yielded by this operation $\mathcal{M}_i$ will contain all the features shared by the given record with that model. Referring to the properties as *keys*, for a given model i it is possible to formalize the above operation as in (3).

$$\mathcal{M}_i = \mathcal{R} \bigcap \mathcal{K}_i \tag{3}$$

$$\bar{\mathcal{R}}_i = \mathcal{R} - \mathcal{M}_i \tag{4}$$

$$\bar{\mathcal{M}}_i = \mathcal{K}_i - \mathcal{M}_i \tag{5}$$

$$\mathcal{M}_i = \mathcal{M}_i \bigcup \{k\} \tag{6}$$

$$\bar{\mathcal{R}}_i = \bar{\mathcal{R}}_i - \{k\} \tag{7}$$

$$\bar{\mathcal{M}}_i = \bar{\mathcal{M}}_i - \{k\} \tag{8}$$

The set of *mismatching keys* $\bar{\mathcal{R}}_i$ is also inferred by subtracting the above set from the record's attributes set $\mathcal{R}$, as in (4). Therefore, this set will contain all the record attributes that are not found in the model's attributes set. On the other hand, the set of the *missing attributes* for a model i, $\bar{\mathcal{M}}_i$, is given by the difference between the i-th model keys $\mathcal{K}_i$ and the matching keys $\mathcal{M}_i$ found in (3), as in relation (5). The set of mismatching keys (4) includes the subset of attributes that are semantically *new* to the model, meaning that they introduce new information content that is not accounted for the given model, and the subset of properties that actually have a semantic correspondent match in the matching keys set, but are orthographically mismatching. At this point, the *reconciliation goal* is to scan the second subset and match each attribute against its correspondent property in the model. The *distance function* is encapsulated in a separate self-contained component. Given an attribute key and the model, it returns the closest matching property found in the model, if any, within a certain confidence interval. In this way, the function can be replaced anytime with better-fitting one, based on the application context and on analytical and/or empirical performance analyses, as long as the input-output requirements are met. When a mismatching key is found to be enough similar to a model key, meaning that the similarity confidence exceeds a given threshold, one can greedily conclude that they refer to the same property. As formalized in (6), the originally mismatching key can be reconciled with the similar one found in the model. The reconciled key is moved from the mismatching keys set to the set containing the matching attributes (7) and, if it also matches a property that belongs to the missing keys set $\bar{\mathcal{M}}_i$, it is also removed from such a set (8). The *similarity score* is defined as the linear combination of two quantities. The first one is the *common attributes score* (CAS) and it is defined as the cardinality of the set SA_i containing all the matching properties that are found in the models shared keys set $\mathcal{S}$ found in (1), normalized on the cardinality of the set $\mathcal{S}$. In other words, this contribution accounts the subset of matches that are common to all the models. The second contribution to the similarity score DA_i considers the subset of matches found in the set of model's peculiar attributes $\mathcal{D}_i$ obtained in (2), which is intersected with the set of matching keys for a given model i, as in (11).

$$SA_i = \mathcal{M}_i \bigcap \mathcal{S} \tag{9}$$

$$CAS_i = \frac{\|\mathcal{S}_i\|}{\|\mathcal{S}\|} \tag{10}$$

$$DA_i = \mathcal{M}_i \bigcap \mathcal{D}_i \tag{11}$$

$$DAS_i = \frac{\|DA_i\|}{\|\mathcal{D}_i\|} \tag{12}$$

$$\mathrm{S}_i = CAS_i + DAS_i \tag{13}$$

Similarly, the *distinctive attributes score* for a model i (DAS_i) is given by the ratio between the cardinality of the matching distinctive keys set DA_i (11) and the cardinality of the distinctive properties set $\mathcal{D}_i$ related to the i-th model (2), as in equation (12). It is possible to compute the *structure similarity score* S_i (13) for a given record-model pair as the sum of the shared keys score CAS_i (10) and the distinctive keys score DAS_i (12). Eventually, the *best fitting model* (*BFM*) for a given record is the model associated to the highest similarity score.

Let S_i be the structure similarity score related to the i-th model and M the models set. The following relation holds:

$$BFM = \mathrm{k}\ s.t.\ \mathrm{S}_k = \max\{\mathrm{S}_i\ \forall \mathrm{i} \in \mathrm{M}\}\,,\ with\ \mathrm{k} \in M \tag{14}$$

The first half of the matching and reconciliation action involves finding the best entity type model for a record. The second half involves matching data values, leveraging preliminary knowledge of the context. Core aspects of data and their handling within a particular context are traditionally collected in advance. Semantic constraints from attribute semantics help define decision questions for identifying and classifying entity contexts. This information helps identify suitable data models and reconcile entities against them.

EdgER uses a bottom-up approach, inferring matching questions from the model or attribute semantics to discriminate between true values and outliers within a confidence threshold. The model compares a data point to the closest average value, finding a match if the value is within the neighborhood of the average, delimited by a certain threshold. The *threshold* consists of a fixed offset and an additive term that adjusts based on data reliability criteria. The second term should expand when the standard deviation is high to assess data flow variability, and shrink when data is reliably emitted, ensuring low variability of samples within a specific time frame. To formalize the definition of a value matching function grounded on the considerations discussed so far, let $\Pi(t_k)$ be the size of the time window that spans from the current time to t_k and τ_s the sampling time. The number of samples $\mathcal{N}$ is defined as in (15). Let σ_{CAV} be the standard deviation associated to the closest average value with respect to the value to match. Thus, the *matching threshold* $\mathcal{T}$ is defined as in (16). where b is the base fixed offset. Finally, let x be the value being matched and CAV its closest average value with respect to the value to match. Therefore, x is a *match* if the condition (17) holds.

$$\mathcal{N} = \frac{\Pi(t_k)}{\tau_s} \tag{15}$$

$$\mathcal{T} = b + \frac{\sigma_{\mathrm{CAV}}}{\mathcal{N}} \tag{16}$$

$$|x - \mathrm{CAV}| \leq \mathcal{T} \tag{17}$$

Data Integration Unit. In general, to address the problem caused by the intrinsic asynchronous nature of edge data flows, each corresponding time series needs to be reconstructed using a uniform sampling rate. A popular choice [24] is the Nyquist frequency associated with the highest data emission frequency among all sources. Furthermore, given a block of source data, the size of the local time window for that source can be defined as the time interval between the first and the last records' time references. A simple approach is to use a linear approximation function that interpolates a straight line for any two consecutive recorded data points. After reconstructing the time series for each data flow, the DIU can compute the statistics required for MUs' value matching tasks, specifically determining the arithmetic mean and standard deviation for a given set of samples.

Anomaly Detection and Supportive Modules. The data models used in the case study include *WeatherObserved*, *IndoorEnvironmentObserved*, and *BatteryStatus* (see Sect. 4.1), representing entities corresponding to the weather station, embedded temperature sensor, and PV panel accumulator, respectively. In particular, the entity attributes we have considered for implementing the case study are *statusPercent* for the accumulator charging state and *temperature* for both the weather station and the embedded sensor entities. The anomaly to detect is instead a low Level of Charge of the PV's accumulator, despite optimal weather and working conditions. The MSs delegated to implement the AD are RAP and RAE, which allows to access the rule set to be used for anomaly detection and assesses attribute values with the corresponding rule set, respectively.

4.2 Microservice Architecture Deployment

The EdgER approach enables AD services to run independently on distributed and edge nodes corresponding to minicomputers, improving scalability and fault tolerance by distributing MSs across clusters. In essence, MSs are a popular architectural approach in software development. Pros include independent deployment and management of small, modular services, to attain improved fault tolerance and scalability. On the other hand, they come at the cost of increased development time, cost, and complexity, which could outweigh the flexibility they introduce. The Docker Swarm is utilized as a clustering solution in the case study, consisting of master and worker nodes where MSs are deployed and executed based on orchestration policies based on replica number, health checks, and computational resource constraints. One or more master nodes coordinate the rest of the nodes in the swarm. Workers lack autonomy in managing services, and container technologies enable highly scalable architectures on complex setups. This separates hardware resource management from the business core. The optimal deployment setting for AD service distributes MU building block instances on worker or master nodes, considering their multiplicity and parallel operation. DAP and DIU building blocks are executed on the master node, while the entire AD service stack can be deployed on a centralized single node configuration using a container management layer that uses concurrency management techniques to distribute tasks to available CPU cores and execute them interleavedly when needed. The core node offers an efficient by running a publisher/subscriber messaging service. During startup, input channels are registered and associated with callback functions, that performs specific operations on the data payload of a message. A MS can forward data messages on output channels asynchronously or timedly, depending on the context.

4.3 Results Discussion

To assess the EdgER approach, we have just focused on the evaluation of the AD service related to the ER tasks. In this way, we have excluded the contribution of the RAP and RAE MSs from the performance analysis because can be considered out of the scope in this context. To validate EdgER's performance,

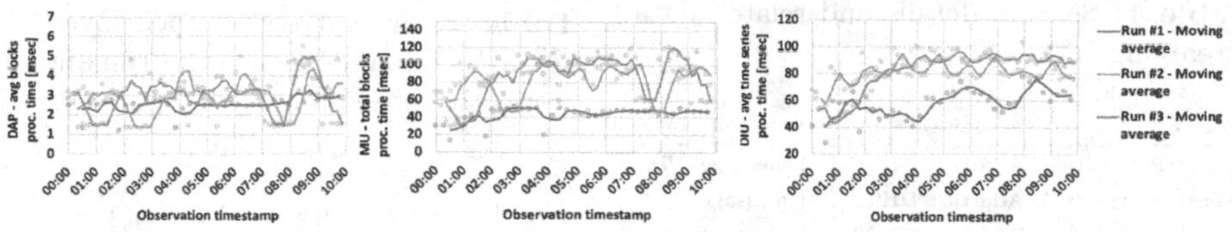

Fig. 3. First test branch: evolution of processing times for each test run.

a testbed environment consisting of two nodes and three sensors has been laid down. In the scenario of this testbed, one sensor is embedded in the Smart PV station, whereas two additional sensors are bundled within a portable weather station. The specification are reported in Table 1. Concerning the nodes adopted in the validation scenario, a mini cluster of two SBCs has been deployed and implemented using a pair of *Raspberry PI 4B*[6].

The performance of EdgER have been monitored both in terms of scalability of the system and in terms of effectiveness of the model in resolving the entities and yielding the expected results. In this work, the focus is on scalability performance evaluation. EdgER's processing performance has been tested as processing time involved in MS operations. Such measurements are used to estimate the scalability of the service in various configurations featuring combinations of multiple nodes and MUs. All the simulations have been performed using the same devices, under the same constraints and initial conditions. The streaming rates of sensors are reported in Table 1 and the duration of all test runs is fixed at 10 min. The scalability performance was assessed by conducting the following two branches of test runs: (1) keeping fixed the number of MUs and by increasing the number of data sources; (2) keeping fixed number of data sources and increasing number of MUs.

Concerning the first branch of simulations, the processing times for each DAP, MU and DIU MS were detected and collected during each test run and by plotting the corresponding results (see Fig. 3). For DAP, the detected processing time refers to the duration of the task for preparing the received blocks and assigning them to the available MUs. It can be observed that the DAP's blocking task represents the least time consuming process. For the sake of the present test branch, we have provided just one instance of the MU MS and the corresponding processing time refers to the duration of the task for resolving the assigned sensor data blocks. In this case, the difference in terms of performance between the test runs is more evident. Anyway, by increasing the number of data streams, the processing time spent by the single-instance MU tends to follow approximately the same trend (with a relatively little increment) obtained in test runs #2 and #3. Eventually, the processing time spent by DIU to reconstruct the time series is also measured for each iteration The considerations regarding MU processing times remain valid for the DIU processing times.

6 https://www.raspberrypi.com/products/raspberry-pi-4-model-b/specifications/.

Table 1. Sensors details and related data streaming rates.

Device	Sensor	Streaming rate
Smart PV station	Adafruit DHT11[a]	1 message/15 s
Weather station 1	Adafruit DHT22[b]	1 message/10 s
Weather station 2	Bosch BME680[c]	1 message/30 s

[a] https://www.mouser.com/datasheet/2/758/DHT11-Technical-Data-Sheet-Translated-Version-1143054.pdf
[b] https://www.sparkfun.com/datasheets/Sensors/Temperature/DHT22.pdf
[c] https://cdn-shop.adafruit.com/product-files/3660/BME680.pdf

Table 2. Second test branch: average MUs latency for each test run and respective speedup.

	Average latency			
# MUs	Node 1	Node 2	Avg.	ψ
1	93.13 ms	–	93.13 ms	1
2	62.07 ms	46.56 ms	54.32 ms	1.71
3	69.69 ms	45.3 ms	57.49 ms	1.62

In the second branch of test runs, the number of MU instances was progressively increased to three in order to evaluate the scalability trend of the EdgER-based implementation. Doing so, it is possible to assist to a situation where each MU instance is gradually assigned to manage blocks of data related to one isolated data stream, as the number of deployed MUs matches the number of sensors available in the test bed. In case the number of data streams exceeds the number of available swarm nodes, more then one MU can be deployed for each node, according to a round-robin discipline. Specifically, for the present test the adopted deployment for the three MU instances provided to distribute two of them on one node and the remaining on the other. The metric used to evaluate the scalability of the service when multiple MUs are deployed is the *speedup* ψ, which is defined as the ratio between the execution time to perform a task on a single thread L_1 and the execution time measured in case of multiple instances L_p, i.e. $\psi = \frac{L_1}{L_p}$.

For the single-instance MU case, L_1 is given by the average of the latency times calculated among all the measurements collected in test run #1. Otherwise, for the multiple-instances MU case, L_p is calculated as the mean of all the cumulative processing times measured. Subsequently, the corresponding speedup ψ values were computed for each considered case. Table 2 illustrates the measured average of the latency times for each node, the overall average value that was used for the speedup calculation and the speedup value itself, for any number of MU instances. In particular, the first row illustrates the measurements collected for the single-instance MU case (i.e. test run #1), whereas the remaining rows correspond to the mean cumulative processing times in case of multiple MUs. Additionally, the table highlights the resulting performance by distributing the MU instances across the available nodes, based on the round-robin discipline mentioned above.

Focusing on a two-nodes configuration where the number of running MU instances is progressively increased, it is possible to identify the two MU instances as the optimum in terms of performance. In this case, each MU instance runs exactly on its respective node providing an estimated speedup factor of 1.71x with respect to the single node-single MU configuration. By observing the corresponding speed-up values, an unbalanced two nodes-three MUs configuration in which two MU instances run on the same node yields a performance reduction due to the increased workload. This suggests that the ideal optimum can be achieved by running one MU instance per each node, but this conclusion is sub-optimal, due to other cost variables. A trade-off is thus introduced, defining the recommended number of MU instances on a single node, with a reasonable resource sacrifice, set to two MUs per node in this case. Anyway, future studies will deepen a more formal redefinition of this relevant value. Further, a more exhaustive and comprehensively assessment of the proposed approach is planned, also considering the wide range of its potential application domains.

At this point, it is possible to provide an answer to the research questions introduced in Sect. 1. EdgER is an innovative approach that enables the deployment of added-value federated services at the edge of the Internet, ensuring standard and uniform representation of data entities and enacting data sovereignty policies. This approach can be integrated with other service implementations, such as in this work, where a federated service for anomaly detection at the edge was developed to highlight the potential of privacy-preserving FL approaches. These approaches can leverage a shared standard data format to facilitate the deduction of existing correlations between data entities that are reconciled from data streams, without relying on computations performed on a cloud central facility. In summary, implementations of EdgER's approach can provide flexibility margins to tackle domain specific constraints in terms of resource availability, fostering the deployment of various implementations of its building blocks.

5 Conclusion and Future Work

This work introduces EdgER, an approach to enable web architectures in favour of ER of data streams at the edge, making it possible to provide proximity-value-added federated services, such as early anomaly detection. The approach offers a set of building blocks for edge computing applied to any potential domain, enhancing system performance, accountability, and data protection, and can be implemented by selecting the most suitable technologies. The adopted MS architecture offers wide scalability margins by deploying constitutive MSs closer to the edge of computational stages. Future work includes two stages of extension of the approach. The first stage aims to integrate the missing clustering task, covering typical ER workflow and inferring indirect matching relations. The second stage provides a complementary macro building block for data model management, including versioning, comparison, and matching. Finally, performance analysis can be benchmarked using higher-scale edge-fog infrastructures.

Acknowledgments. This research was partially supported by grant from Italian Research Center on High Performance Computing, Big Data and Quantum Computing (ICSC) funded by EU-NextGenerationEU (PNRR-HPC, CUP:C83C22000560007).

Disclosure of Interests. The authors have no competing interests to declare that are relevant to the content of this article.

References

1. Ahle, U., Hierro, J.J.: FIWARE for data spaces. In: Otto, B., ten Hompel, M., Wrobel, S. (eds.) Designing Data Spaces, pp. 395–417. Springer, Cham (2022). https://doi.org/10.1007/978-3-030-93975-5_24
2. Altwaijry, H., Kalashnikov, D.V., Mehrotra, S.: QDA: a query-driven approach to entity resolution. IEEE Trans. Knowl. Data Eng. **29**, 402–417 (2017). https://doi.org/10.1109/TKDE.2016.2623607
3. Altwaijry, H., Mehrotra, S., Kalashnikov, D.V.: Query. Proc. VLDB Endowment **9**, 120–131 (2015). https://doi.org/10.14778/2850583.2850587
4. Bandara, K., Hewamalage, H., Liu, Y.H., et al.: Improving the accuracy of global forecasting models using time series data augmentation. Pattern Recogn. **120**, 108148 (2021). https://doi.org/10.1016/j.patcog.2021.108148
5. Brecko, A., Kajati, E., Koziorek, J., Zolotová, I.: Federated learning for edge computing: a survey. Appl. Sci. (2022). https://api.semanticscholar.org/CorpusID:252258593
6. Christen, P., Gayler, R., Hawking, D.: Similarity-aware indexing for real-time entity resolution, p. 1565. ACM Press (2009).https://doi.org/10.1145/1645953.1646173
7. Christen, V., Christen, P., Rahm, E.: Informativeness-based active learning for entity resolution. In: PKDD/ECML Workshops (2019). https://api.semanticscholar.org/CorpusID:199521860
8. Christophides, V., et al.: An overview of end-to-end entity resolution for big data (2021). https://doi.org/10.1145/3418896
9. Conde, J., Munoz-Arcentales, A., Alonso, A., Huecas, G., Salvachua, J.: Collaboration of digital twins through linked open data: architecture with FIWARE as enabling technology. IT Prof. **24**, 41–46 (2022). https://doi.org/10.1109/MITP.2022.3224826
10. Ferrari, P., et al.: Performance evaluation of full-cloud and edge-cloud architectures for industrial IoT anomaly detection based on deep learning. In: 2019 II Workshop on Metrology for Industry 4.0 and IoT (MetroInd4. 0IoT), pp. 420–425. IEEE (2019)
11. Gabr, M.I., Helmy, Y.M., Elzanfaly, D.S.: Data quality dimensions, metrics, and improvement techniques. Fut. Comput. Inform. J. **6**(1), 25–44 (2021). https://doi.org/10.54623/fue.fcij.6.1.3
12. Gao, C., Yang, P., Chen, Y., et al.: An edge-cloud collaboration architecture for pattern anomaly detection of time series in wireless sensor networks. Complex Intell. Syst. **7**(5), 2453–2468 (2021). https://doi.org/10.1007/s40747-021-00442-6
13. Gruenheid, A., Dong, X.L., Srivastava, D.: Incremental record linkage. Proc. VLDB Endowment **7**, 697–708 (2014). https://doi.org/10.14778/2732939.2732943
14. Gupta, N., et al.: Data quality toolkit: automatic assessment of data quality and remediation for machine learning datasets (2021). arXiv:abs/2108.05935
15. Hardy, S., et al.: Private federated learning on vertically partitioned data via entity resolution and additively homomorphic encryption (2017). arXiv:abs/1711.10677
16. Hassenstein, M.J., Vanella, P.: Data quality-concepts and problems. Encyclopedia **2**(1), 498–510 (2022). https://doi.org/10.3390/encyclopedia2010032
17. Hummel, P., Braun, M., Augsberg, S., Dabrock, P.: Sovereignty and data sharing (2018). https://api.semanticscholar.org/CorpusID:174780972
18. Hummel, P., Braun, M., Tretter, M., Dabrock, P.: Data sovereignty: a review. Big Data Soc. **8**(1), 205395172098201 (2021). https://doi.org/10.1177/2053951720982012

19. Jithish, J., Alangot, B., Mahalingam, N., Yeo, K.S.: Distributed anomaly detection in smart grids: a federated learning-based approach. IEEE Access **11**, 7157–7179 (2023)
20. Kellogg, G., Champin, P.A., Longley, D.: JSON-LD 1.1 - a JSON-based serialization for linked data (2019). https://api.semanticscholar.org/CorpusID:202784811
21. Kim, S., et al.: Collaborative anomaly detection for internet of things based on federated learning. In: 2020 IEEE/CIC International Conference on Communications in China (ICCC). IEEE (2020). https://doi.org/10.1109/iccc49849.2020.9238913
22. Li, Y., Peng, X., Zhang, J., et al.: DCT-GAN: dilated convolutional transformer-based GAN for time series anomaly detection. IEEE Trans. Knowl. Data Eng. **35**(4), 3632–3644 (2023). https://doi.org/10.1109/tkde.2021.3130234
23. Li, Z., et al.: TSA-GAN: a robust generative adversarial networks for time series augmentation. In: 2021 International Joint Conference on Neural Networks (IJCNN). IEEE (2021). https://doi.org/10.1109/ijcnn52387.2021.9534001
24. Lovisari, E., Jönsson, U.T.: A Nyquist criterion for synchronization in networks of heterogeneous linear systems. IFAC Proc. Volumes (IFAC-PapersOnline) **43**, 103–108 (2010). https://doi.org/10.3182/20100913-2-FR-4014.00015
25. Luboshnikov, E., Makarov, I.: Federated learning in named entity recognition. Recent Trends Anal. Images, Soc. Netw. Texts **1357**, 90–101 (2021). https://api.semanticscholar.org/CorpusID:232336335
26. López Escobar, J.J., Díaz-Redondo, R.P., Gil-Castiñeira, F.: Unleashing the power of decentralized serverless IoT dataflow architecture for the cloud-to-edge continuum: a performance comparison. Ann. Telecommun. (2024). https://doi.org/10.1007/s12243-023-01009-x
27. Martella, C., Longo, A., Zappatore, M., Ficarella, A.: Dataspaces in urban digital twins: a case study in the photovoltaics, vol. 3478 (2023). http://ceur-ws.org
28. Mota, M.S., Pantoja, F.L., dos Reis, J.C., Santanchè, A.: Progressive data integration and semantic enrichment based on LinkedScales and trails. In: Workshop on Semantic Web Applications and Tools for Life Sciences (2016). https://api.semanticscholar.org/CorpusID:18522320
29. Nisansala, S., Chandrasiri, G.L., Prasadika, S., Jayasinghe, U.: Microservice based edge computing architecture for internet of things. In: 2022 2nd International Conference on Advanced Research in Computing (ICARC). IEEE (2022). https://doi.org/10.1109/icarc54489.2022.9753930
30. Nock, R., et al.: Entity resolution and federated learning get a federated resolution (2018). arXiv:abs/1803.04035
31. Qin, Y., Matsutani, H., Kondo, M.: A selective model aggregation approach in federated learning for online anomaly detection. In: 2020 IEEE iThings and IEEE GreenCom. IEEE (2020). https://doi.org/10.1109/ithings-greencom-cpscom-smartdata-cybermatics50389.2020.00119
32. Ramadan, B., Christen, P., Liang, H., Gayler, R.W., Hawking, D.: Dynamic similarity-aware inverted indexing for real-time entity resolution (2013). https://doi.org/10.1007/978-3-642-40319-4_5
33. Risso, F.: Creating an edge-to-cloud computing continuum: status and perspective. In: 2022 3rd International Conference on Embedded & Distributed Systems (EDiS). IEEE (2022). https://doi.org/10.1109/edis57230.2022.9996495
34. Schmidl, S., Wenig, P., Papenbrock, T.: Anomaly detection in time series: a comprehensive evaluation. Proc. VLDB Endowment **15**(9), 1779–1797 (2022). https://doi.org/10.14778/3538598.3538602

35. Shadija, D., Rezai, M., Hill, R.: Towards an understanding of microservices. In: 2017 23rd International Conference on Automation and Computing (ICAC). IEEE (2017). https://doi.org/10.23919/iconac.2017.8082018
36. Simonini, G., Zecchini, L., Bergamaschi, S., Naumann, F.: Entity resolution on-demand. Proc. VLDB Endowment **15**, 1506–1518 (2022). https://doi.org/10.14778/3523210.3523226
37. Somma, A., Benedictis, A.D., Zappatore, M., Martella, C., Martella, A., Longo, A.: Digital twin space: the integration of digital twins and data spaces, pp. 4017–4025. IEEE (2023). https://doi.org/10.1109/BigData59044.2023.10386737
38. Song, Y., et al.: A robust and accurate multivariate time series anomaly detection in fluctuating cloud-edge computing systems. In: 2022 IEEE 24th International Conference on HPCC. IEEE (2022). https://doi.org/10.1109/hpcc-dss-smartcity-dependsys57074.2022.00077
39. Wang, F., Li, B., Li, B.: Quality-oriented federated learning on the fly. IEEE Netw. **36**(5), 152–159 (2022). https://doi.org/10.1109/mnet.001.2200235
40. Xia, Q., Ye, W., Tao, Z., et al.: A survey of federated learning for edge computing: research problems and solutions. High-Confidence Comput. **1**(1), 100008 (2021). https://doi.org/10.1016/j.hcc.2021.100008
41. Zhang, J., et al.: Next generation federated learning for edge devices: an overview. In: 2022 IEEE 8th International Conference on Collaboration and Internet Computing (CIC). IEEE (2022). https://doi.org/10.1109/cic56439.2022.00012
42. Zhang, X., et al.: Cross-dataset time series anomaly detection for cloud systems. In: 2019 USENIX Annual Technical Conference (USENIX ATC 19), pp. 1063–1076 (2019)

Human-Centric Web Engineering: Privacy and Security

AuthApp – Portable, Reusable Solid App for GDPR-Compliant Access Granting

Andreas Both[1,2](✉), Thorsten Kastner[1], Dustin Yeboah[1], Christoph Braun[3], Daniel Schraudner[4], Sebastian Schmid[4], Tobias Käfer[3], and Andreas Harth[4]

[1] DATEV eG, Nuremberg, Germany
[2] Leipzig University of Applied Sciences, Leipzig, Germany
andreas.both@htwk-leipzig.de
[3] Karlsruhe Institute of Technology (KIT), Karlsruhe, Germany
[4] Friedrich-Alexander-Universität Erlangen-Nürnberg, Erlangen, Germany

Abstract. The Solid (Social Linked Data) technology family was developed to provide the foundation for Data Sovereignty in the context of web applications. The advantage of this innovative approach is the opportunity to dynamically bind an identity to a Solid application and a user-specific Solid data store (Solid Pod). These three basic components can be combined dynamically, allowing users to share their data with an application while retaining full control of the data in self-managed Solid Pods. This paper presents a prototype of a web-based user interface to grant access to data in a Solid Pod. To enable a dynamic binding into Solid-driven environments, we made the implementation available as a Solid application – AuthApp – with a specific focus on allowing users to configure the data access granting efficiently. To comply with data protection regulations, in particular Europe's GDPR, we extended the standard to include the validation of the purpose of data sharing. Unlike previous work, we also make full use of robust technologies to avoid the need to copy or store data outside the personal context, meaning all data remains under the user's control and so does the AuthApp.

Keywords: Solid · Authorization · Access Control · Data Sharing · Access Granting · Zero Trust · Data Sovereignty

1 Introduction

The technologies around Solid were designed to enable standards for connecting web user identities, web services, and data accessible via HTTP introduced by Berners-Lee et al.[1]. This so-called web decentralization project was intended to give users more control over their personal data. The core idea behind Solid is to create a decentralized web platform where users can store their data in Solid Pods (Personal Online Data Stores) and have more control over who can access and use their information (cf. [10]): "Pods are like secure web servers for data.". In a

[1] cf. https://solidproject.org/.

K. Stefanidis et al. (Eds.): ICWE 2024, LNCS 14629, pp. 199–214, 2024.
https://doi.org/10.1007/978-3-031-62362-2_14

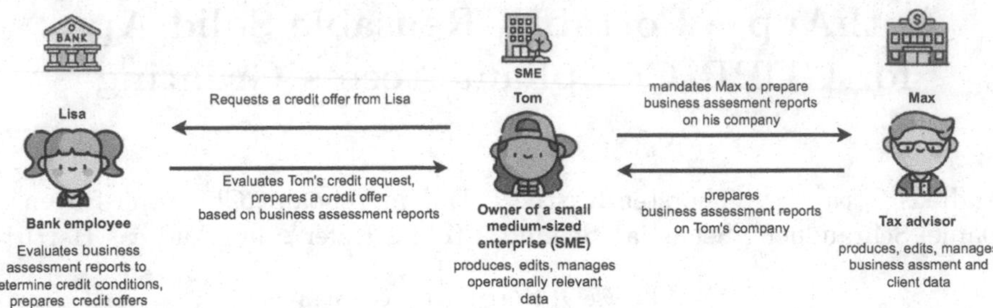

Fig. 1. Use case and personas

Solid-based architecture, applications and services request permission from users to access their data stored in Pods, providing users with data privacy and control. Using this approach users can share their data on-demand with Solid-based applications while the applications should only use the user's Pod to store data, s.t., even the applications' output would be under the control of the users. Solid originally was intended to enable end users to stay in control while sharing data via social media or with other end users (e.g., via a private chat). Building on top of machine-readable data representations using the Resource Description Framework (RDF)[2] it provides many benefits, in particular, a flexible metadata model and standardized, completely web-based operations. However, Solid's elaborated vision of interoperability would also be beneficial for organizations, as many of them intend to develop data-driven products or set up agile data chains to collaborate with their partners. This has already led to many use cases in different domains (e.g., [4,20,21]).

In our motivating example (cf. Fig. 1), we sketched a real-world use case where a company intends to get a loan from a bank. However, since the company uses a service provider – a tax advisory firm – for financial transactions, not all data for a loan application is stored directly in the company. Therefore, the expected approach would be to establish an ad-hoc data chain where a request to the tax advisor from the company would be processed by the tax advisory office, s.t., the company can hand the data over to the bank bundled with the configuration of the requested loan. Finally, the bank would commit or reject the loan request, expressed again by shared data items. Hence, here a typical B2B data chain would be established where the data-sharing process would be in the center of activity. In contrast, data exchange in the end-user sector is much simpler and more centralized. For these operations, the Solid Application Interoperability [11] (`INTEROP`[3]) was defined that provides a flexible policy model for expressing access grants provided as an RDF vocabulary [11]. However, data sharing between organizations must meet higher standards than in the private sector, including GDPR [18] requirements and additional traceability rules as well as security and business confidentiality requirements and last but not least low integration costs.

[2] W3C RDF Working Group.

[3] `PREFIX interop:` <http://www.w3.org/ns/solid/interop#>.

Implementing such functionality is cumbersome and error-prone. However, as Solid is built on clear web-based communication standards, it should be possible to implement a Solid app – AuthApp – that can be dynamically integrated into another Solid app to ensure a compliant access granting process. Nevertheless, integrating such functionality into an external app would only be possible if a zero-trust [17] environment can be ensured. While following the Solid principles, the AuthApp should still ensure a zero-trust architecture as no communication to a system outside the current scope is done and – in contrast to previous works – no data is stored outside the users' Solid Pod. In this paper, we will address these requirements following research questions:

RQ1 Is it possible to establish a standalone, pure Solid web application that is pluggable to Solid applications while managing the access granting process?

RQ2 What limitations of the `INTEROP` specification exist w.r.t. the requirements of B2B scenarios?

The paper is structured as follows. In the next section, we will provide an overview of the related work. In Sect. 3, the requirements and expected functionalities are described derived from this information, the conceptional decisions are described derived. The implementation of the corresponding application is described in Sect. 4, followed by a discussion of the implications and learnings (Sect. 5). Section 6 concludes the paper and outlines future work.

2 Related Work

Establishing data sovereignty in web-based data-driven ecosystem is the goal of the Solid movements [12,14,15,19]. The *Solid platform*, specifications and technologies aim for a safe, decentralized web where users are in complete control of their data.

Solid[4] is a project that aims to change the way web applications work today. It strives for true data ownership and improved data privacy. When using the web, people should have the freedom to choose where their data is stored and who can access it. This is achieved by decoupling identity, data and application connected via open standards. Figure 2a depicts the *Solid principle of connecting identity, data and applications through open standards*, i.e., they can be exchanged and reconnected on-demand. This core feature promises to support many use cases in a web-based data-driven ecosystem.

The Solid community has defined a list of inclusion criteria that must be met and a list of exclusion criteria that must not be met in order to be classified as a Solid compatible web application[5] (short: *Solid app*). In principle, any web application that complies with these guidelines is Solid compatible: Users must be able to log in using their WebID[6] and refer to the Identity Provider of their

[4] cf. https://solidproject.org/.
[5] cf. https://solidproject.org/apps.
[6] cf. https://www.w3.org/wiki/WebID.

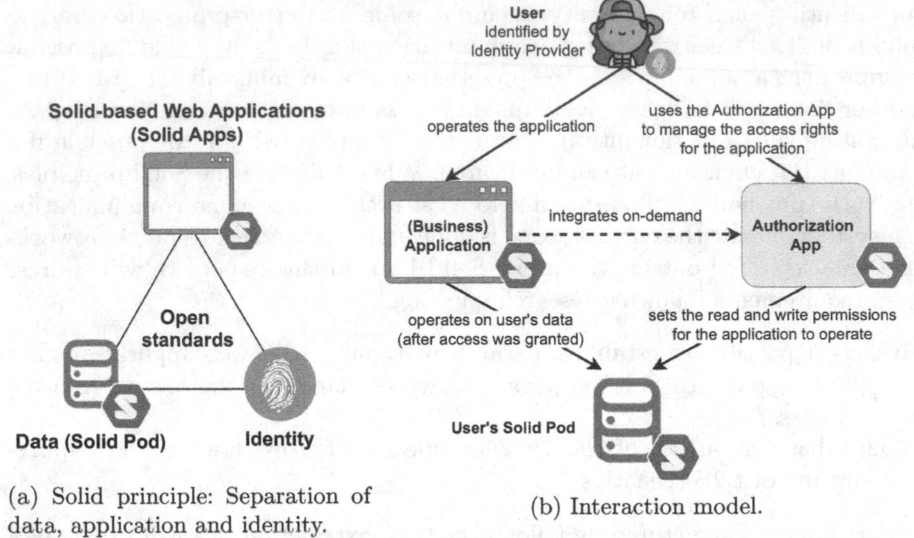

(a) Solid principle: Separation of data, application and identity.

(b) Interaction model.

Fig. 2. Conceptional view

choice in case of identification is required. Data consumed and generated by an app should be fetched, resp. stored in Solid Pods.

A *Solid Pod* is a personal or group-based storage space in which data is stored in a standardized format. Each Pod is like a secure web server for personal information. Unlike centralized cloud services, Solid Pods are hosted decentrally. This means that the data is not necessarily stored in a single location, but can be distributed across different servers. The owners of a Solid Pod have full control over their data. They can determine who has access to their information and which applications are allowed to access it. They use standardized formats and protocols[7] to ensure interoperability between different applications. This makes it possible for the same data to be used by different apps. Solid uses a decentralized extension of OpenID Connect to authenticate the identity of users. This ensures that only authorized persons can access the data.

Shape Trees[8] [1] are a contribution from the Solid Community Group to foster data interoperability on the application level. While RDF provides interoperability through shared vocabularies and data formats, Shape Trees allow defining schemas to validate the combination of RDF triples. They can clearly define the resource organization in a Pod using RDF and shapes, providing a higher level of abstraction. They are used in Data Registrations (see Chap. 6 Solid Interoperability Specification [11]) to structure data in a Pod. This allows Shape Trees to guide applications and users by determining where data can be written to and read from. Conversely, when used for formulating data *Access*

[7] cf. https://solid.github.io/specification/.

[8] cf. https://shapetrees.org/.

Needs (see Chap. 8), Shape Trees allow a data requester to accurately describe the resources they wish to access in a Pod in a machine-readable format. By comparing the Shape Trees given in an Access Need with the Shape Trees in the Data Registrations of the considered Pod, the relevant resources in the Pod can be accurately located, and access grants can be set accordingly (if the user wishes to do it).

Although several specifications were defined several years ago, research in the field of Solid has only recently gained momentum. Because of the claim to general validity, establishing valid specifications that can fulfill all needs of end-users, business, organizations, and administrations is challenging.

Several publications focus on the technical foundations of Solid. For example, in [13] the decentralized verification of data with confidentiality was addressed using Blockchain technology. In [8,9] the communications/notifications in the Solid ecosystem are considered.

Other researchers focussed on particular use cases. In [20] the use case of machine-to-machine sales contracts were considered where Solid Pods are used for data storage. The data environment for building information modelling (BIM) using Solid was the topic of [21]. Self-verifying Web Resource Representations using Solid, RDF-Star and Signed URIs is the topic of [7].

In the context of the data sharing process – which is the most crucial operation in an ecosystem built for data sharing – the `INTEROP` [11][9] was defined for detailing how Social Agents and Applications can safely share and interoperate over data in Solid Pods. To the best of our knowledge, only one previous publication was dedicated to implement and validate the `INTEROP` specification. Bailly et al. [5] dedicated their work to the understandability and usability of the data sharing process for end-user. In contrast, our work aims for validating the dynamic, self-controlled data sharing process regarding the requirements of business and their data value chains.

3 Concept and Architecture

We now describe the requirements for a GDPR-compliant, zero-trust Solid app and the derived architecture while aiming for the goal of portability and reusability. Figure 2b shows the big picture of intended integration of an authorization app that can be deployed outside a business app and therefore provides additional (reusable) functionality on-demand. Hence, the user will have its well-known web application for managing data requests while the business app can reduce the implementation and maintain costs. In our use case, the authorization app would be integrated when the users need to access others data via the used business apps (see Fig. 3). Even is this small use case, the number of data accesses and data sharing operations justifies a standalone authorization app to reduce the investments for establishing the three shown business apps.

[9] Editor's Draft, 7 November 2023, https://solid.github.io/data-interoperability-panel/specification/.

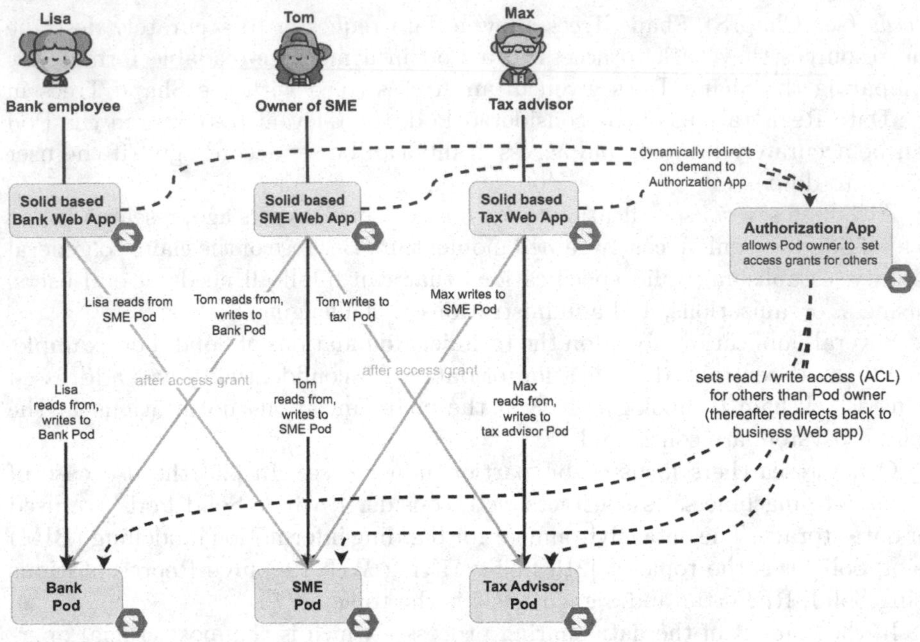

Fig. 3. High-level technical interactions for use case (see Fig. 1).

As described earlier, our goal is to provide a portable, reusable, and GDPR-compliant pure Solid app. We collected the following **three requirement groups**, to address these non-functional requirements to be fulfilled by a Solid application (or any web application) dedicated to managing the access granting with a generalized approach.

R1 **Basic Operations** – A generalized web application for managing data sharing operations need to be enabled to support the following operations:
  - R1.1 Receive new data sharing requests;
  - R1.2 Grant or deny data sharing requests;
  - R1.3 Revoke data sharing requests;
  - R1.4 Monitor received, existing, denied and revoked data sharing requests.

  A typical workflow is shown in Fig. 4.

R2 **Data security** – The GDPR regulations [18] demand:
  - R2.1 Access rights can be revoked;
  - R2.2 Access to objects is granted on a per-object basis (i.e., access to specific web resources can be granted);
  - R2.3 Consent must be specific and unambiguous;
  - R2.4 The data owner can monitor all access authorizations and thus trace which data is currently being and has been shared with whom and why.

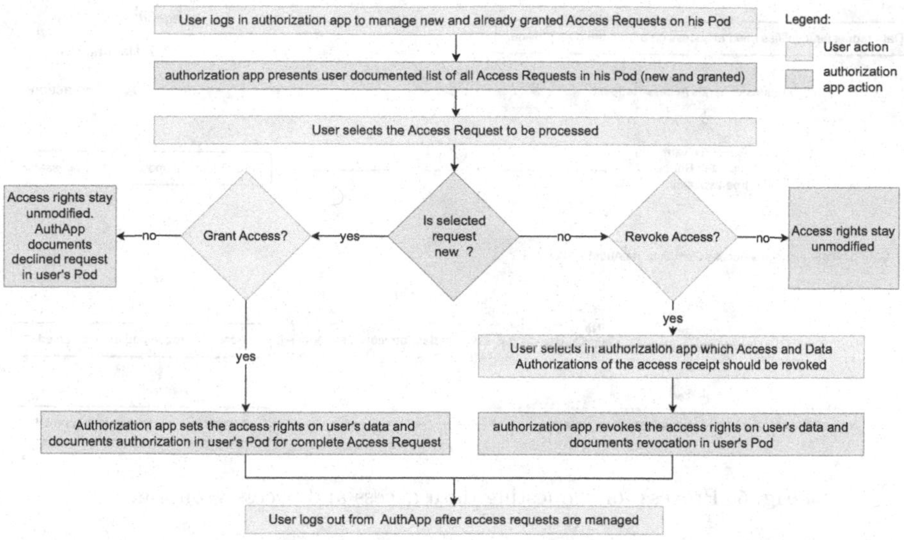

Fig. 4. AuthApp workflow: Operations for managing data access

Additionally, for zero-trust applications the following requirements need to be fulfilled (cf. [16,17]).

R2.5 The security mechanisms associated with the zero trust architecture will be sufficiently trustworthy to ensure confidence in the zero trust deployment;

R2.6 The application leaves no trace outside the user scope.

R3 **Portability and Reusability** – We interpret portability as the capability of integrating a generalized authorization application into existing Solid applications. Therefore, we derive the following requirements:

R3.1 It needs to be possible to integrate the authorization application through configuration;

R3.2 Interactions with the authorization application need to be implemented using standardized web technologies;

R3.3 All required information can be accessed with automated processes (i.e., the data is machine-readable).

Note, that although separated within different requirement groups, some requirements are interconnected (e.g., R2.5 and R3.2).

4 Implementation

In this following, we derive our implementation decisions for the Solid app named AuthApp that follows the requirements and the concept described in Sect. 3. Hence, it is used for evaluating RQ1 and RQ2. The source code is available

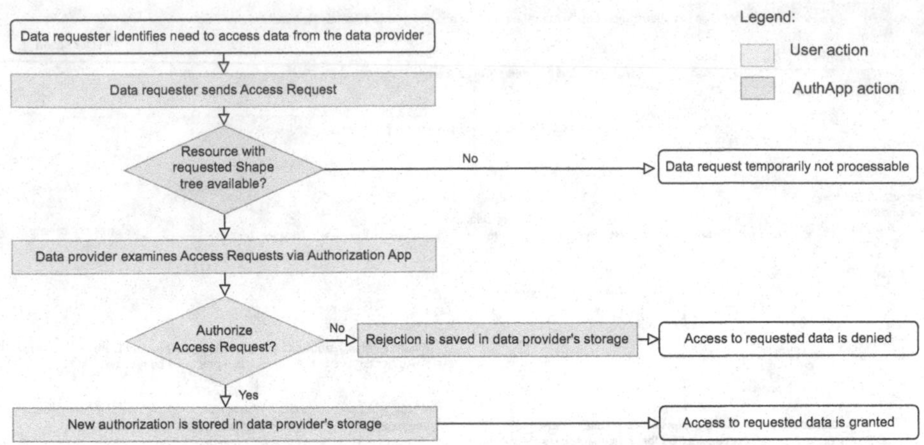

Fig. 5. Process for requesting data access and access granting.

```
@prefix interop:<http://www.w3.org/ns/solid/interop#>.

<#accessAuthorization>
 a interop:AccessAuthorization;
 interop:grantedBy <https://giver/profile/card#me>;
 interop:grantedAt "2024-02-02T11:11:51.331Z"^^xsd:dateTime;
 interop:grantee <https://grantee/profile/card#me>;
 interop:hasAccessNeedGroup
   <https://giver/access-inbox/91511f657390#bwaAccessNeedGroup>;
 interop:hasDataAuthorization
   <https://giver/data-authorizations/53a8739cde00#dataAuthorization>.
```

Fig. 6. Example of Access Authorization (RDF Turtle).

under the open-source MIT license[10]. Following the process shown in Fig. 5, it is assumed that users have identified themselves to the application via the standard Solid approach (cf. Sect. 2).

4.1 ACL and INTEROP Vocabularies

Solid's specification Web Access Control (WAC) [6] and its corresponding Access Control List (ACL) are part of the Solid platform. Although not stable[11] Solid servers (e.g., Community Solid Server[12], Node Solid Server[13]) need to implement these standards to comply with the Solid ecosystem. Therefore, we conclude that for defining access rules, only ACLs [6] have to be used. They provide a

[10] https://github.com/DATEV-Research/Solid-authorization-app.
[11] currently: Version 1.0.0, Editor's Draft, 2023-11-06.
[12] https://github.com/CommunitySolidServer.
[13] https://github.com/nodeSolidServer.

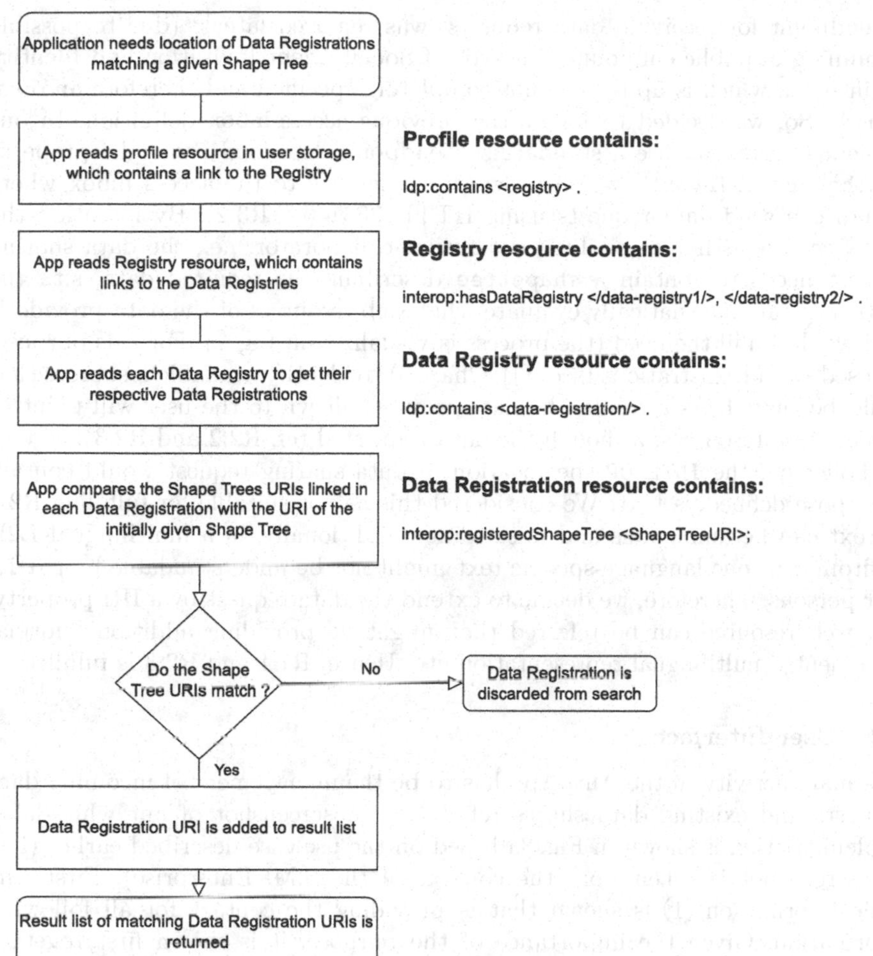

Fig. 7. Process for requesting data using shape trees.

standardized vocabulary to define the access to web resources of a Solid Pod (i.e., read-write operations). Hence, R1.2, R1.3, R2.1, and R2.2 are fulfilled.

Additionally, the INTEROP specification [11] describes how social agents and applications can safely share and interoperate over data in Solid Pods. It is fairly new[14] and needs to be considered as work in progress. We used the INTEROP specification anyway as a foundation for our implementation (Fig. 6 shows an Access Authorization defined using the INTEROP vocabulary). However, some parts cannot be used directly as the definition is not stable or not even available. In particular, an *access inbox*, that was defined earlier intended to provide

[14] Editor's Draft, 7 November 2023.

an endpoint for receiving data requests, was removed later[15] (due to possible spamming of public endpoints) in favor of Social Agent Invitation and Identity Verification which is up to now not completely specified and therefore an open issue[16]. So, we decided to follow the previous access-inbox definition. In our implementation, we use a standardized endpoint described using the property `pod:hasAccessInbox`[17], which provides a reference to the access inbox where clients can send data requests using HTTP `POST` (cf. R3.2). By intention the Pod's content is not accessible for a future collaborator, i.e., the data sharing request needs to contain a `shapetree` describing the required data, s.t., the AuthApp can automatically evaluate what web resources of the data provider's Pod would fulfill the need (the process is visualized in Fig. 7). For this purpose, we used Data Registrations (see [11], Chap. 6) to identify available resources that could be shared. As a result, the data requests shown to the user will point to specific web resources, although the data requested (cf. R2.2 and R2.3).

Following the `INTEROP` specification, a data sharing request would contain a purpose defined as text. We considered this as not suitable for fulfilling R2.3 as text can be ambiguous and misleading. Additionally, in a multilingual B2B environment, one language-specific text might not be understandable by particular persons. Therefore, we decide to extend the data request by a IRI property, s.t., web resource can be referred that might be providing additional formal statements, multilingual representation etc. Hence, R1.1 and R2.3 is fulfilled.

4.2 User Interface

The main activity in the AuthApp has to be the management of incoming data requests and existing data shares (cf. R1.4). A screenshot of our white-label implementation is shown in Fig. 8a based on the use case described earlier (i.e., the screenshot is taken from the context of the S.M. Enterprise). First, the basic information ① is shown that is providing the context for all following information. Given the importance of the purpose, it is shown first together with the basic information of the data requester, the beneficiary of the data sharing. In the encapsulated block ②, the Access Need Groups showing the short description of the requested access and an additional explanation for the particular Access Need Group. Last ③, the specific data request information is shown, i.e., the required data format (`shapetree`) and the Access Mode[18]. Note that following the linked data principles, the corresponding identifiers are also provided via a link (IRI), s.t., users can collect additional information if needed. As Solid is following the Linked Data Platform [3] principles, all information about data sharing and corresponding requests can be represented in RDF. If done so, the corresponding data is machine-readable and can be represented in a monitoring UI. Figure 8 show screenshots for granting and declining data requests, as well as monitoring revoked accesses. Hence, R1.4 is fulfilled.

[15] https://github.com/solid/data-interoperability-panel/issues/280.

[16] https://solid.github.io/data-interoperability-panel/specification/#access-request.

[17] `@prefix pod :` <https://sme.solid.aifb.kit.edu/> .

[18] Note, that we used the same text labels as specified in the `INTEROP` specification.

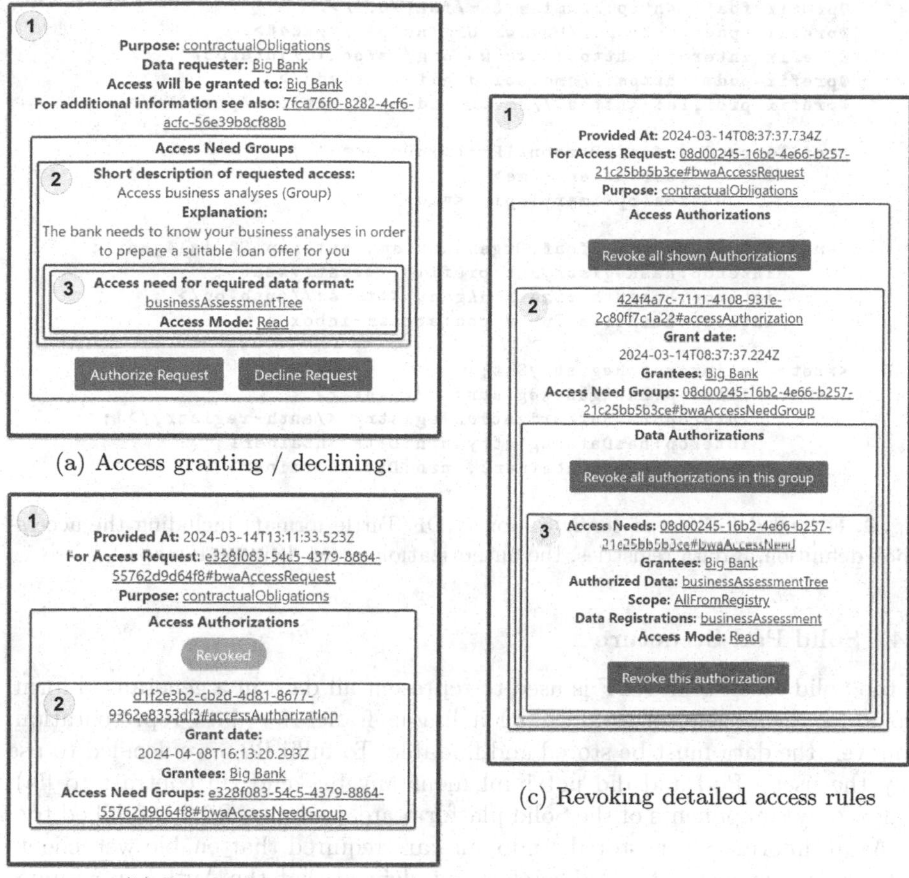

(a) Access granting / declining.

(b) Revoked access

(c) Revoking detailed access rules

Fig. 8. Screenshots of AuthApp

4.3 Integration

By design, the AuthApp is not integrated directly into the business applications. Hence, it needs to be identifiable by the application. For this purpose, the RDF property `pod:hasAccessInbox` (range: IRI pointing to an AuthApp implementation accessible for the user) is used (cf. Sect. 4.1). Hence, a business app just needs to redirect the web browser to the corresponding IRI to provide the user with the functionality of data sharing. Hence, R3.2 is fulfilled, s.t., any Solid app might dynamically be connected to the AuthApp. Note, that this mechanism is not customized for our implementation. Instead, it is a generalized solution to integrate other implementations of authorization apps or agents.

```
@prefix foaf: <http://xmlns.com/foaf/0.1/>.
@prefix space: <http://www.w3.org/ns/pim/space#>.
@prefix interop: <http://www.w3.org/ns/solid/interop#>.
@prefix pod: <https://sme.solid.aifb.kit.edu/>.
@prefix profile: <https://sme.solid.aifb.kit.edu/profile/>.

profile:card a foaf:PersonalProfileDocument ;
        foaf:maker <#me> ;
        foaf:primaryTopic <#me> .

<#me> a foaf:Person, foaf:Organization, interop:SocialAgent ;
    interop:hasRegistrySet profile:registry#set ;
    interop:hasAuthorizationAgent <https://authApp/> ;
    interop:hasAccessInbox pod:access-inbox .

<#set>  a interop:RegistrySet;
     interop:hasAgentRegistry </agents/> ;
     interop:hasAuthorizationRegistry </auth-registry/> ;
     interop:hasDataRegistry urn:DataContainer1,
       urn:DataContainer2, urn:DataContainer3 .
```

Fig. 9. Formal definition of configuration (RDF Turtle format) including the access-inbox definition, 3 data registries, the authorization agent definition, etc.

4.4 Solid Pod Structure

In the Solid ecosystem, RDF is used to represent all data in a generalized form, providing the benefit of establishing a lingua franca for data representation. However, the data must be stored and findable. To fulfil R2.6 we decided to use only the user's Pod and did not implement any backend (in contrast to [5]). Hence, only components of the Solid platform are used, i.e., R2.5 is fulfilled too.

As all information is stored, endpoints are required that enable web clients to access the expected RDF. Therefore, we defined that the AuthApp assumes the following containers to be present on the top level of the user's Pod:

- `/access-inbox/` contains all Access Requests;
- `/authorization-archive/` contains outdated or withdrawn Access Authorizations;
- `/authorization-receipts/` contains the receipts of authorized Access requests;
- `/authorization-registry/` contains the current Access Authorizations;
- `/data-authorizations/` contains the current Data Authorizations.

To maintain a clear access point for these authorization-relevant information, we store the configuration data to the user's Solid Webprofile [2] inside the Solid Pod (i.e., the authorization app can be customized for each user and there is no need for centralizing this configuration within an organization). Hence, it is under complete control of the user and also centralized to enable any application to descriptively access such information. Note, that for all three participants in our use case (cf. Fig. 3) and their individual business applications, the same instance of the AuthApp was used, validating its general applicability. An example configuration is shown in Fig. 9. Therefore, R3.3 is fulfilled, too.

5 Discussion

Our validation via an implementation shows that the requirements can be fulfilled using the Solid platform specifications. However, in the following, we will discuss several findings and limitations.

In general, our implementation shows that implementing a pure Solid app is possible and thus represents a possible cornerstone of the Solid ecosystem. Nevertheless, several limitations were observed during the validation. We have used the well-known inbox mechanism here to establish an initial connection between the prospective data supplier and the data provider following the `INTEROP` specification. While this enables a sound and safe way to initialize a data chain using just a data structure definition (`shapetrees`), it lacks a GDPR-conform representation of the purpose of the data request. However, the inbox mechanism follows the GDPR principle of data thrift, avoidance, and minimization as it does not share any information about the Pod of the future data provider. Additionally, the `INTEROP` specification does not specify how to deal with withdrawn or outdated authorizations. Actually, it is not defined how to represent a withdrawn Access Authorization (and how it differs from a valid one). An authorization app can only recognize that a data access grant is outdated by the fact that a new data release description is created with the reference that this replaces the old one via the property `interop:replaces`. Hence, the withdrawn permit does not contain any indication that it has been replaced by a new one. Therefore, extensions of the `INTEROP` specification (or an additional specification) are required to overcome these challenges, which might otherwise render the functionality unusable.

Although RDF is well suited for representing data in a machine-readable form, it needs to be validated if it is acceptable that the stored data about the granted and denied requests (including requested data formats, requesters, and beneficiaries) can be changed by the user. From a legal perspective, there might be a need for a write-only data container, s.t., this data stays consistent and is immutable. Furthermore, a standardization of the vocabulary for describing the structure of Solid Pod (cf. Sect. 4.4) seems to be reasonable to prevent implementation-specific behavior that might reduce the portability.

Finally, as useful and convenient as an external authorization app is for the user, there might raise the issue that users expect that this is the only way how they handle data requests to their Pod. However, applications might still internally create `ACL` without redirecting to the authorization app. This might have the implication of different, inconsistent, or even non GDPR-conform data representations which might become problematic in a well-regulated business context and therefore hindering the adoption of the Solid technologies. From this observation, one might derive the need to extend the Solid protocol, s.t., users or organizations can restrict the authorization apps that are allowed to change such data in their Solid Pods.

6 Conclusions

In this paper, we have presented an implementation of a Solid application that can dynamically bind into Solid environments, s.t., the data access granting processes don't have to be implemented by each application, thus, reducing the implementation costs of Solid applications. We provided two major contributions: (1) We collected the requirements for business-driven use cases where a web-based data chain should be established, including a major subset of GDPR conformance; (2) We provided a generalized implementation that can be used in the Solid ecosystem for managing data requests and monitoring data shares of a Solid Pod. In contrast to previous work, our approach does not require additional components that needs to be trusted. As the application is running completely in the user context, the zero-trust requirements are also fulfilled. Additionally, we extend the standard by introducing a Linked-Data-based representation of GDPR-compliant data access purposes that will enable automatic logical validation of access requests in the future. To the best of our knowledge, this is the first implementation providing all of these features. Hence, we have not just validated the Solid concepts but also provided a usable implementation that can be seen as a cornerstone for populating a Solid-based web-based software ecosystem. In general, our implementation proves the feasibility of the Solid standards for establishing dynamic applications, where autonomously granting access should also be possible for non-expert users while the required data is stored in the private Solid Pod only, hence, providing a maximum of data protection and sovereignty.

In future work, to increase the safety of data chains reasoning capabilities should be integrated into authorization apps as well as into the `INTEROP` specification as currently the data formats (`shapetrees`) of the data requests and the Data Registrations are not validated semantically (i.e., it is assumed that they are matching by definition). Additionally, establishing a protocol or immutable data container for storing the current configuration and history of data shares would create an increase level of safety from the legal perspective.

Acknowledgments. This work has been supported in part by the German ministry BMBF under grant 16DTM107B (*MANDAT*).

References

1. Shape trees specification. https://shapetrees.org/TR/specification/
2. Solid WebID profile. https://solid.github.io/webid-profile/
3. Linked data platform 1.0 (2015). https://www.w3.org/TR/2015/REC-ldp-20150226/
4. Abid, A., Cheikhrouhou, S., Kallel, S., Jmaiel, M.: Novidchain: blockchain-based privacy-preserving platform for COVID-19 test/vaccine certificates. Softw. Pract. Experience **52**(4), 841–867 (2022)

5. Bailly, H., Papanna, A., Brennan, R.: Prototyping an end-user user interface for the solid application interoperability specification under GDPR. In: Pesquita, C., et al. The Semantic Web, ESWC 2023, LNCS, vol. 13870, pp. 557–573. Springer, Cham (2023). https://doi.org/10.1007/978-3-031-33455-9_33
6. Berners-Lee, T., Story, H., Capadisli, S.: Web access control. Version 1.0.0, Editor's Draft, 2023-11-06 (2023). https://solid.github.io/web-access-control-spec/
7. Braun, C.HJ., Käfer, T.: Self-verifying web resource representations using solid, rdf-star and signed URIs. In: Groth, P., et al. (eds.) The Semantic Web: ESWC 2022 Satellite Events, ESWC 2022, LNCS, vol. 13384, pp. 138–142. Springer, Cham (2022). https://doi.org/10.1007/978-3-031-11609-4_26
8. Braun, C.HJ., Käfer, T.: Web push notifications from solid pods. In: Di Noia, T., Ko, IY., Schedl, M., Ardito, C. (eds.) Web Engineering, ICWE 2022, LNCS, vol. 13362, pp. 487–490. Springer, Cham (2022). https://doi.org/10.1007/978-3-031-09917-5_41
9. Capadisli, S., Guy, A., Lange, C., Auer, S., Sambra, A., Berners-Lee, T.: Linked data notifications: a resource-centric communication protocol. In: Blomqvist, E., Maynard, D., Gangemi, A., Hoekstra, R., Hitzler, P., Hartig, O. (eds.) The Semantic Web, ESWC 2017, LNCS, vol. 10249, pp 537–553. Springer, Cham (2017). https://doi.org/10.1007/978-3-319-58068-5_33
10. Dedecker, R., et al.: What's in a Pod?–a knowledge graph interpretation for the solid ecosystem. In: 6th Workshop on Storing, Querying and Benchmarking Knowledge Graphs (QuWeDa) at ISWC 2022, pp. 81–96 (2022)
11. Justin Bingham, Eric PrudHόmmeaux, E.P.: Solid application interoperability. W3C Editor's Draft. November 2023. https://solid.github.io/data-interoperability-panel/specification
12. Mansour, E., et al.: A demonstration of the solid platform for social web applications. In: Proceedings of the 25th International Conference Companion on World Wide Web, pp. 223–226. WWW '16 Companion (2016). https://doi.org/10.1145/2872518.2890529
13. Ramachandran, M., Chowdhury, N., Third, A., Domingue, J., Quick, K., Bachler, M.: Towards complete decentralised verification of data with confidentiality: different ways to connect solid pods and blockchain. In: Companion Proceedings of the Web Conference 2020, pp. 645–649. WWW '20, Association for Computing Machinery, New York, NY, USA (2020). https://doi.org/10.1145/3366424.3385759
14. Sambra, A.V., et al.: Solid: a platform for decentralized social applications based on linked data. MIT CSAIL & Qatar Computing Research Institute, Technical Report (2016)
15. Seneviratne, O., van der Hiel, A., Kagal, L.: Tim berners-lee's research at the decentralized information group at MIT, p. 201-213. ACM, 1 edn. (2023)
16. Shore, M., Zeadally, S., Keshariya, A.: Zero trust: the what, how, why, and when. Computer **54**(11), 26–35 (2021). https://doi.org/10.1109/MC.2021.3090018
17. Stafford, V.: Zero trust architecture. NIST special publication **800**, 207 (2020). https://doi.org/10.6028/NIST.SP.800-207
18. The European Parliament and the Council of the European Union: Regulation (EU) 2016/679 (General Data Protection Regulation) GDPR. https://gdpr-info.eu/
19. Verborgh, R.: Re-decentralizing the Web, For Good This Time, pp. 215-230. ACM, 1 edn. (2023). https://doi.org/10.1145/3591366.3591385

20. Wang, X., Braun, C.H.J., Both, A., Käfer, T.: Using schema.org and solid for linked data-based machine-to-machine sales contract conclusion. In: Companion Proceedings of the Web Conference 2022, pp. 269–272. WWW '22, Association for Computing Machinery (2022). https://doi.org/10.1145/3487553.3524268
21. Werbrouck, J., Pauwels, P., Beetz, J., van Berlo, L.: Towards a decentralised common data environment using linked building data and the Solid ecosystem. In: Advances in ICT in Design, Construction and Management in Architecture, Engineering, Construction and Operations (AECO) : Proceedings of the 36th CIB W78 2019 Conference, pp. 113–123 (2019)

Hook-in Privacy Techniques for gRPC-Based Microservice Communication

Louis Loechel, Siar-Remzi Akbayin, Elias Grünewald(✉), Jannis Kiesel, Inga Strelnikova, Thomas Janke, and Frank Pallas

Information Systems Engineering, Technische Universität Berlin, Berlin, Germany
gruenewald@tu-berlin.de

Abstract. gRPC is at the heart of modern distributed system architectures. Based on HTTP/2 and Protocol Buffers, it provides highly performant, standardized, and polyglot communication across loosely coupled microservices and is increasingly preferred over REST- or GraphQL-based service APIs in practice. Despite its widespread adoption, gRPC lacks any advanced privacy techniques beyond transport encryption and basic token-based authentication. Such advanced techniques are, however, increasingly important for fulfilling regulatory requirements. For instance, anonymizing or otherwise minimizing (personal) data before responding to requests, or pre-processing data based on the purpose of the access may be crucial in certain usecases. In this paper, we therefore propose a novel approach for integrating such advanced privacy techniques into the gRPC framework in a practically viable way. Specifically, we present a general approach along with a working prototype that implements privacy techniques, such as data minimization and purpose limitation, in a configurable, extensible, and gRPC-native way utilizing a gRPC interceptor. We also showcase how to integrate this contribution into a realistic example of a food delivery use case. Alongside these implementations, a preliminary performance evaluation shows practical applicability with reasonable overheads. Altogether, we present a viable solution for integrating advanced privacy techniques into real-world gRPC-based microservice architectures, thereby facilitating regulatory compliance "by design".

Keywords: gRPC · Microservices · Privacy · Purpose Limitation · Data Minimization · API · Cloud Native · Web Engineering

1 Introduction

Microservice architectures, which divide a system into many small services that all fulfill a specific business capability or purpose, have established as the prevailing paradigm for implementing and operating complex, large-scale web systems and applications [18]. In cloud native computing environments, respective microservices materialize as containerized, loosely-coupled system components

K. Stefanidis et al. (Eds.): ICWE 2024, LNCS 14629, pp. 215–229, 2024.
https://doi.org/10.1007/978-3-031-62362-2_15

[22]. Meanwhile, agile development teams and DevOps practices further support the use of different technology stacks (incl. programming languages) per microservice and, consequently, allow separating teams accordingly [13]. However, to leverage these advantages, microservice architectures need language-agnostic or at least polyglot interfaces such as Representational State Transfer (REST), GraphQL, or Remote Procedure Calls (RPC) which enable efficient communication between different services. The utilization of a specific Application Programming Interface (API) paradigm depends on the usecase and, e.g., the data characteristics (cf. Sect. 2).

Alongside these technical developments towards microservice architectures, the importance of privacy regulations – such as the GDPR [9], the CCPA and others – and the need to properly address them technically ("by design") is increasingly recognized. Noteworthily, this goes way beyond mere access restrictions but calls for nuanced measures: The privacy principle of *data minimization* (embodied in, e.g., Art. 5(1c) of the GDPR), for instance, requires that personal data are "limited to what is necessary in relation to the purposes for which they are processed". The principle of *purpose limitation* (Art. 5(1(b)), in turn, requires that personal data are only used for those purposes they were originally collected for (or for those purposes deemed compatible with the initial ones). One and the same data-providing service must therefore respond with different "views" to the same data, depending on the access context [19]. Further privacy principles induce similar or additional needs, but we exemplarily confine ourselves to these two herein.

With large microservice architectures consisting of hundreds of services – using different technology stacks [22] and independently developed and maintained by different teams – adherence to such requirements cannot be achieved by manual implementation or audit. Instead, compliance must be supported through configurable technical approaches, which implement privacy principles on a per-service basis. To date, however, developers lack the means to do so [11]. In particular, API frameworks, such as gRPC,[1] expose an inherent lack of advanced privacy techniques that go beyond mere transport encryption and simple token-based authentication. Such advanced techniques are, however, indispensable for properly addressing said principles. So far, developers can thus either go without appropriate technical implementation of privacy requirements within their services (leaving compliance to rather non-technical means) or implement required techniques manually, in a rather ad-hoc fashion (raising excessive efforts as well as the risk of errors and improper implementations).

First proposals to close this gap have been made for services exposed via GraphQL [19], but for the whole field of performance-sensitive microservices communicating via gRPC, the need to integrate advanced privacy techniques in a configurable and performance-aware manner remains largely untapped. In consequence, we herein propose and contribute:

– A general approach for **hook-in privacy techniques in high-performance remote procedure call frameworks**, especially applicable in cloud native microservices,

[1] grpc.io/docs/what-is-grpc/faq.

- a **proof-of-concept implementation** of our approach for the widely-used, enterprise-grade gRPC framework in a polyglot, cloud-native microservice environment, exemplified through the privacy principles of data minimization and purpose limitation, and
- a preliminary **performance evaluation** in a realistic food delivery scenario.

These contributions unfold as follows: Background and related work are explained in Sect. 2. In Sect. 3, we identify the requirements to be fulfilled. Our general approach is presented in Sect. 4, followed by our proof-of-concept implementation in Sect. 5 and a preliminary performance evaluation in Sect. 6. Section 7 discusses our results, identifies prospects for future work, and concludes.

2 Background and Related Work

Our work builds on the following foundations and related work.

2.1 Microservices Communication via gRPC

One popular communication method between microservices is the Remote Procedure Call (RPC). RPCs are a way to invoke procedures across machines, while it looks like a single-machine execution from a developer's perspective [4,27].

One of the most popular RPC frameworks, gRPC, was initially developed internally at Google and open-sourced in 2015.[2] It is an efficient and scalable framework for inter-service communication implementing RPCs over HTTP/2 [5]. Furthermore, it supports basic authentication mechanisms, streaming, blocking / non-blocking transmission, etc., and is available for a broad variety of programming languages. By default, it uses Protocol Buffers[3] for serializing structured data in a forward- and backward-compatible way. Protocol Buffers support many languages by default and even more through third-party add-ons [14]. The definition of the data structure has to be defined in a `.proto` file which is then used by the `protoc` compiler to generate the necessary code in the chosen language which can then be used by the application [14].

Using gRPC is most suitable for communication between microservices in a cloud environment, while, for the browser interface, alternatives such as REST or GraphQL are the preferred options [14]. Thus far, privacy-enhancing technologies, including data minimization and purpose limitation, are mostly lacking [1].

2.2 Technical Approaches for Privacy Techniques in Inter-Service Communication

In related work, an approach on how to implement purpose-based access control on the application layer is proposed [20]. Their work presents two prototype

[2] developers.googleblog.com/2015/02/introducing-grpc-new-open-source-http2.html.
[3] protobuf.dev/overview.

implementations with respective benchmarks. This informs our work regarding ease of implementation. Furthermore, the Janus prototype provides a viable approach, which extends the popular Apollo server to introduce attribute-level access control and role-based data minimization mechanisms to GraphQL APIs [19]. Janus employs JSON Web Tokens (JWTs) to identify roles and, on this basis, parameterize the application of common data minimization techniques in a per-request fashion. With its flexible hook-in capabilities, Janus shall thus serve as a blueprint for our endeavor to implement similar capabilities into gRPC-based service APIs.

Specifically related to gRPC and Protocol Buffers, previous work proposes the implementation of data flow assertions [15]. Put briefly, a Go library here generates access policies based on JSON files and a gRPC interceptor inspects the HTTP request headers. Therefore, access control is purely based on the encryption of strings. The interceptor only decrypts the data after comparing the headers with the policies. Encrypting every string in a message by default makes the overhead of this approach not feasible for high-performance scenarios.

Beyond this work, gRPC interceptors are used for security (authentication),[4] observability practices (tracing),[5] or fault tolerance mechanisms (retries).[6] Approaches utilizing the interceptor concept to implement privacy techniques such as data minimization and purpose limitation in high-performance settings are, however, to the best of our knowledge not existing.

2.3 Data Minimization and Purpose Limitation in Inter-Service Communication

Established privacy-preserving techniques, such as *suppression*, *generalization* and *noising*, serve as a foundation for this work regarding data minimization [16,17,25]. Likewise, purpose limitation techniques following the idea of the Purpose-Based Access Control model are incorporated prototypically into this work [6,7,20]. Furthermore, we build upon the field of access control. The eXtensible Access Control Markup Language (XACML) [2] and its respective component model have been widely adopted as a standard for creating fine-grained policy rules [21,23]. Within the XACML framework, access control operations are partitioned into distinct functional components, which are the Policy Administration Point (PAP), Policy Decision Point (PDP), and Policy Enforcement Point (PEP). This component model is frequently applied to the privacy principles of purpose limitation [6], data minimization, and their overlaps with traditional technical access control measures [3,8,10].

3 Requirements

In line with other privacy engineering endeavors (such as [12,19,20]) we outline a set of reasonable functional and non-functional requirements.

4 grpc.io/docs/guides/auth.

5 go.opentelemetry.io/contrib/instrumentation/google.golang.org/grpc/otelgrpc.

6 pkg.go.dev/github.com/grpc-ecosystem/go-grpc-middleware/v2/interceptors/retry.

Policy-Based Data Minimization (FR1): Derived from the privacy principle of data minimization (codified, e.g., in Art. 5 GDPR) access to specific personal information must be restricted as far as possible. In particular, it may not always be necessary to expose the complete set of accessed information. The proposed solution should therefore apply different types of data minimization mechanisms. These include noising, suppression, or advanced anonymization techniques [3].

Policy-Based Purpose Limitation (FR2): For enabling basic purpose limitation [28], it is required that each category of personal data and every gRPC call can be supplemented with specific processing purposes. This allows the utilization of various purpose-based access policies. Related to Art. 5 GDPR, this provides the means to specifically control which calls and services can access personal data.

Configurability (FR3): The proposed solution must be highly configurable to facilitate adoption in different use case scenarios. Developers must therefore be able to specify and choose a domain-specific set of available purposes, according to their system-specific needs. This is desirable because the required processing purposes of different domains can diverge greatly.

Native gRPC integration (FR4): As mentioned in Sect. 2, many technologies can map gRPC to be interoperable with different communication protocols and data structures, which are not gRPC-native. However, whenever possible the solution should consist of gRPC-native protocols and data structures to keep its benefits such as high performance as well as low integration overhead, and without adding another level of complexity.

Reasonable Performance Overhead (NFR1): According to Art. 25 GDPR, technical measures that realize privacy principles must be applied while taking into account the cost of implementation, which includes induced overheads. We will therefore assess the performance of our approach with real-world settings and configurations to ensure that the overhead is at a reasonable level.

Polyglot Compatibility (NFR2): To ensure that our approach is compatible with a wide range of programming languages and frameworks, it has to be implemented in a modular and extensible manner. This will allow developers to easily integrate the privacy-enhancing technologies into their existing applications. Additionally, clear documentation and examples shall guide developers in the integration process.

4 Approach

To fulfill the functional and non-functional requirements including regulatory obligations, we propose a conceptual approach for effective and efficient data minimization and purpose limitation for high-performance gRPC-based interservice communication in microservice architectures.

Derived from *FR1*, *FR2* as well as *FR4*, our general approach for integrating privacy techniques, such as purpose limitation and data minimization, will be realized as a server-side middleware. In our implementation, we opt for adding a gRPC response interceptor. This allows the integration in the required gRPC-native manner, while working on an abstraction layer that does not require existing microservices and their respective code base to be modified with more than about two lines of code *(NFR2)*. Additionally, to meet the performance requirements outlined in *NFR1*, we minimize the complexity of the interceptor. Therefore, any computation that is not required to be performed immediately with each response will be conducted in a separate system component, independent of the interceptor itself. Following the XACML component model, access policy enforcement is preceded by policy administration and interpretation in context-specific scenarios. Thus, to allow for a scalable interceptor, the PAP and the PDP are consciously separated from the PEP.

The separation of the PAP and PDP from the PEP not only reduces the anticipated performance overhead from the interceptor but also necessitates the establishment of reliable and efficient communication for decisions made at the PDP. We address this challenge by implementing signed JSON Web Tokens (JWTs). A JWT typically consists of three parts: header, payload, and signature. The payload consists of claims that can be exchanged between different parties securely [24]. These tokens will serve as a trusted certificate enabling parties to exchange decisions made at the PDP, prior to the PEP. Thus, a client, Service A, intending to send a gRPC request to a server, Service B, must first get such a trusted JWT as illustrated in Fig. 1. We propose to sign the message via standard asymmetric cryptography, including a public/private key pair.

To reduce the computational and communicative overhead, a given JWT remains valid for a specified time. This method assumes that neither the access policy nor the context on which the decision is based are subject to frequent alterations. Therefore, neither the PAP nor the PDP require round-trips for each outgoing response. After validating the JWT, the interceptor merely executes the policy decision upon receiving an outgoing server response. For more details, we provide an in-depth explanation of the JWT implementation in Sect. 5.1.

Assuming the client possesses a valid JWT containing a recent access policy decision, it can proceed to communicate with other microservices within the architecture. The JWT is appended to the outgoing context of the message whenever a request is sent to another microservice. Other data stored within the context are not affected by this addition, nor does it prevent future alterations, which substantially enhances integration. Upon request arrival at the server, the procedure is handled regularly. Data is aggregated to form the response message if the request invokes a response. The interceptor acts as the policy enforcing middleware as soon as the server sends the response back to the client.

gRPC interceptors can generally interact with almost all facets of a message, including the payload, which may contain personal data. For applying privacy techniques, the message payload is central to modifications. Responses sent via gRPC can contain multiple data fields, each comprising a field name and its value. An accompanying access policy, retrieved from the JWT (which is stored within the intercepted context of the message), precisely defines which of the data fields can be sent safely to the client, and to what level of detail.

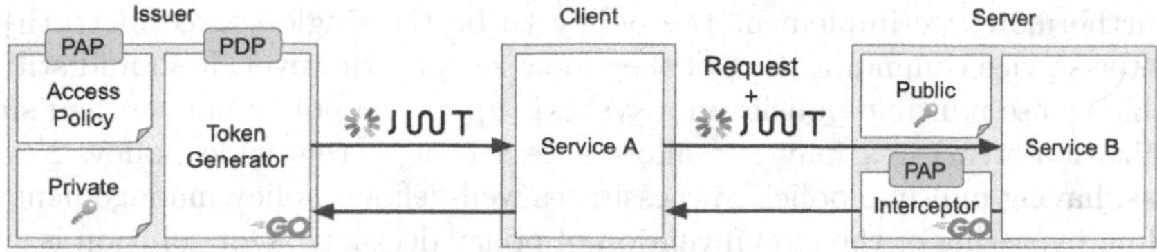

Fig. 1. Architectural overview representing the communication process between client and server using JWT in gRPC communication incl. the XACML-inspired control functionality mapping.

Data, including personal data, can reveal different types of information, which have varying levels of dependence on coherence (e.g., ZIP codes or phone numbers lose different amounts of information when the last digit is removed). This calls for the effective application of different data minimization techniques. The interceptor determines not only whether a data field can exist in the outgoing response message, but also controls its level of detail. Ultimately, data minimization is governed by the content of the PDP's decision and the contents of the response message.

Data minimization techniques for this proof of concept prototype include generalization, noising, reduction, and complete suppression of values. Since we published our contribution as an open-source project, implementing additional techniques is encouraged *(FR3)*. We provide a detailed description of the implementation of each method in Sect. 5.2.

5 Implementation

As introduced in Sect. 4, the reusable component of our approach is divided along the XACML component structure. First, we will describe the practical implementation of the PAP and PDP, followed by the implementation of the gRPC interceptor which performs the PEP.

5.1 Policy Administration and Decision

To achieve our goal of providing a solution that enables privacy techniques, such as automated (purpose-driven) policy enforcement and data minimization, we propose a structured machine-readable policy format. To be fully compatible with JWTs, we define a JSON-based policy.[7] First, it comprises a list of service objects. Each service object can have a list of purpose objects in a flat structure, which distinguishes the data fields in the following categories: `allowed`, `generalized`, `noised`, and `reduced`. The data fields in these category objects may include a parameter to determine the applied minimization techniques more precisely. These options will be explained in Sect. 5.2.

7 github.com/PrivacyEngineering/purpl-jwt-go-rsa.

Furthermore, we implement the policy to be the single source of truth for the inter-service communication of the whole system. However, it should still be possible to use multiple policies in a system (up to one policy per service) since organization structures may not allow access to a system-wide policy. Nevertheless, having multiple policies necessitates well-defined policy management for avoiding bypassing or the circumvention of policy decisions. Our solution is suitable for individualization since the claims in the generated JWT are system-wide and their origin does not affect the interceptor behavior.

We implement our interceptor using the Go programming language, as being a natural high-performance fit to gRPC. Our implemented module generates the JWT based on five parameters: The `service name`, `purpose`, and `policy path` are used to get the corresponding data fields from the policy and parse them into the JWT claims. The `key` path is used to retrieve the provided Rivest-Shamir-Adleman (RSA) private key and to sign the JWT. Finally, the `expirationInHours` parameter sets the expiration of the JWT.

In addition to our RSA-based module, we implemented the same functionality for a Elliptic Curve Digital Signature Algorithm (ECDSA) private key and published it as a separate Go module[8]. We decided to implement these two algorithms since both are broadly used and supported by the module to handle JWTs.[9]

Having the policy administration and decision separated from the policy enforcement, we abstract the token generation from the interceptor and, therefore, decrease its overhead. For the interested reader, we provide a simple overhead comparison of both approaches.[10]

5.2 Policy Enforcement

Whenever a response message is to be dispatched from the server, our interceptor,[11] will be activated within the usual `grpc.NewServer()` function. The subsequent actions of the interceptor are as follows. Initially, the JWT is subjected to origin and expiration time verification. Once these checks pass successfully, the client-specific access policy from the PDP (as described in Sect. 5.1) is extracted from the JWT and stored in a struct. Concurrently, the data field names from the response are extracted and stored in a slice. Having isolated the client-specific policy from the PDP and the data field names from the response message, the interceptor then performs the critical privacy technique, such as a data minimization task. The pseudocode as seen in Algorithm 1 describes this workflow on a high level.

We intended this algorithm to introduce only reasonable performance overheads. For each field name in the response message, the interceptor determines whether the field should remain unmodified, needs to be minimized, or must be

[8] github.com/PrivacyEngineering/purpl-jwt-go-ecdsa.

[9] github.com/golang-jwt/jwt.

[10] github.com/PrivacyEngineering/purpl-naive-approach.

[11] github.com/PrivacyEngineering/purpl.

Algorithm 1. Schematic description of the gRPC interceptor.

Require: $JWT.expiration >$ time.now
Require: $JWT.signature =$ valid
  $policy \leftarrow JWT.policy$
  for all fields in message **do**
    if $field \in policy.allowed$ **then**
      $pass$
    else if $field \in policy.minimized$ **then**
      $message.field \leftarrow$ minimize($field$)
    else
      $message.field \leftarrow$ suppress($field$)
    end if
  end for
  return message

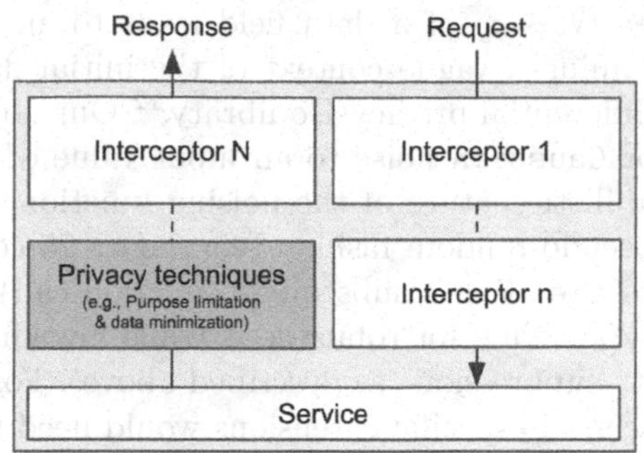

Fig. 2. gRPC interceptor chaining.

completely suppressed. Our implementation is inspired by common privacy techniques. For instance, all four data minimization mechanisms can handle integers, floats, and strings. Yet, some mechanisms differ in functionality depending on the data type that needs to be minimized, as follows.

Suppression of a data field leads to the maximum information loss while maintaining the initial data types. Numeric values, such as integers and floats, are suppressed to a -1, while a string value is suppressed to an empty string (if needed differently, this can be changed easily). This guarantees the intended information loss while maintaining compatibility within the receiving programs, should they require the respective data types to be returned by the server. If, for example, the integer value of 42 were to undergo suppression, the result would be -1. For compatibility reasons, the client would still receive an integer value for this data field, but every additional information would be lost in the minimization process. Here we point out that full suppression (i.e., removal of the data field entirely) is also technically possible in gRPC.

Generalization of a data field leads to a reduction of the value precision. The information conveyed by the data should be neither lost nor altered completely, while still making the data less accurate. This mechanism is implemented for integers and floats by passing the respective value and a range parameter to the function. The range is defined in the JWT's policy and might change depending on the informational context. Assuming a data field `age` with the value 25 were to undergo generalization with a range parameter of 10, then the result would come out as 21. 21 representing, in this case, the age range from 21 up until 30. Respectively, 31 represents the range 31–40. In a different context, the parameter might change (e.g., `accountBalance:` 2.300 with a parameter of 1000 would return 2.001). The chosen mapping ensures numbers larger than zero to always maintain this one property (but could be changed easily if needed). Similarly to the numeric operations, invoking the generalization function for a string value in combination with a parameter will decrease the data's accuracy without altering it entirely. In these cases, the parameter specifies how many characters are to be returned. A `name:"Alice"` with parameter 1 would thus be generalized to `name: "A"`.

Noising of a data field leads to an intended information loss, while maintaining a vague context of the initial data. This mechanism employs Google's differential privacy Go library.[12] Our noising function can apply either `Laplace` or `Gaussian` noise to an input value of type integer or float. Due to the probabilistic nature of the noising function, an input value would be returned in a pseudo-random fashion (e.g., `age:` 25 could be returned as `age:` 45 in one and as `age:` 7 in a subsequent function call). We implement the handling of string-type values for robustness, while invoking the noising function will here lead to its suppression (as described above). For actually achieving differential privacy, scenario-specific extensions would need to be implemented additionally.

Reduction of data fields follows a similar idea as the generalization mechanism, but offers greater flexibility. Reducing an integer or float value requires passing of a parameter value, which will then be used as a divisor in a simple division calculation (e.g., a `houseNumber:` 135 with parameter 10 will be returned as `houseNumber:` 13, while a parameter 5 would lead to a `houseNumber:` 27, due to the nature of integers). A reduction of string-typed values, on the other hand, follows the same mechanism as the aforementioned generalization of strings. A use case could be the reduction of a `ZIP code` data field to its first four digits (e.g., `10623` to `1062`). Thus, not contradicting the initial information, while losing accuracy through broadening the geographical scope.

Ultimately, any field that requires minimization will be altered using the functions mentioned above. The output of the respective minimization function is used to overwrite the original message content with the `ProtoReflect().Set()` function. We support `protobuf` *v*1.5.0 to be used for inter-service communication. Once all message fields have been minimized according to the policy, the modified message handler, and consequently the message itself, will be returned and transmitted to its intended destination service.

5.3 Usage and Configuration Mechanism

To integrate the two reusable components, both referenced Go modules need to be included in the respective microservice, following our documentation. After successful integration, every privacy technique can be defined in the access policy and enforced through the gRPC interceptor. The interceptor can also be chained with other existing interceptors, as shown in Fig. 2. Within a service policy for a defined purpose, the data field names can be listed in either the `allowed` object or in one of the minimization objects. Fields listed in `generalized`, `noised`, or `reduced` require the specification of a parameter, as described in the previous section. Not documenting a field in one of the four objects will lead to its suppression, in case the data field appears in a response message.

[12] github.com/google/differential-privacy/tree/main/go.

6 Preliminary Performance Evaluation

In the following, we summarize our preliminary performance assessment.

Scenario: We assume a food delivery platform as a use case. Such services are widely utilized across the globe and inherently deal with personal information, such as address or payment information, detailed purchase histories, or demographic data. In real settings, the collected information is actively shared with other parties for multiple different purposes. For example, contact information will have to be shared with the restaurants that prepare the food and the riders delivering the food, while demographic or device data will be used for internal research, technical, or marketing purposes. It would be disastrous if the marketing department could access banking information, without a valid legal basis under Art. 6 GDPR. Data minimization is also an important aspect, as the marketing department might want to use demographic data, such as age and place of residence, for a more focused marketing campaign. However, there is no need for detailed information, because the generalization of the data, e.g., an age range or the district of the residence, can already yield the needed results.

To represent such a usecase, we modified the Online Boutique,[13] which is a sample open-source microservice-based e-commerce application, initially provided by the Google Cloud Platform developers. The inter-service communication is gRPC-based, so we implemented our use case by expanding the architecture with an additional microservice, namely the `trackingservice`. It requests personal data like the address, name, and contact information to calculate the shortest route to the destination and displays the information, as seen by a potential delivery person, to the customer. We provided the `trackingservice` with multiple different purpose specifications, and each of them has a varying degree of allowed or restricted access to the requested information. For the following evaluation, we deployed the application to the Google Kubernetes Engine (GKE). Further details and instructions to reproducible the experiments are provided via Github.[14]

We begin to assess the performance overhead generated by our purpose limiter technique. The experiments consist of a load generator imitating 10 users sending concurrent gRPC requests to the `trackingservice`. Each experiment iteration lasts ten minutes. The number of data fields in the response message and the kind of data minimization method are modified at every iteration. We assume that both the different minimization methods and the overall length of the response message can influence the performance of the gRPC interceptor. Figure 3a depicts the measured latency in milliseconds, while Fig. 3b illustrates the measured throughput. In both figures, the *Baseline* represents communication without an interceptor, *No-Op* communication with an interceptor performing no operations, *All-Denied* suppression of all data fields, for *All-Allowed* every data field is allowed to pass the interceptor without data minimization applied, *Mixed* a variety of allowed fields and data minimization methods invoked, and *Maximized* is the minimization methods on all data fields present.

[13] github.com/GoogleCloudPlatform/microservices-demo.
[14] github.com/PrivacyEngineering/purpl-pizza-boutique/tree/main/terraform-gcp.

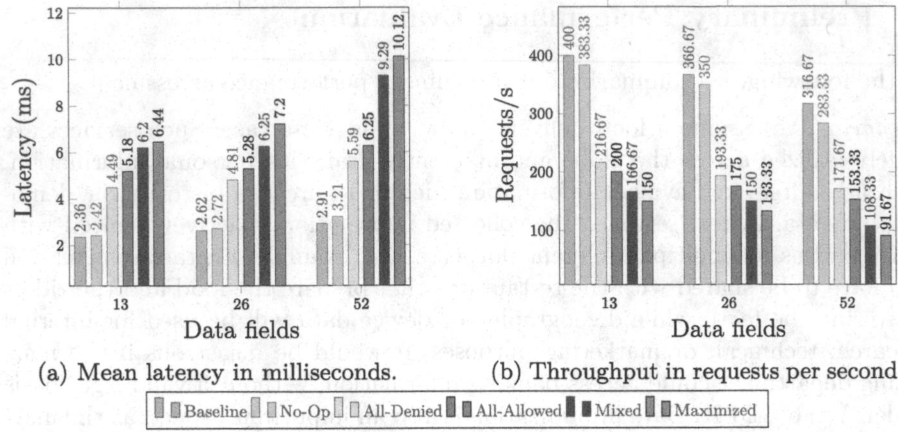

Fig. 3. Performance overheads for 3 different message sizes and 6 degrees of operational complexity.

Latency: The mere use of an interceptor (see Fig. 3a), even without performing any additional operations (*No-Op*), always made a measurable impact compared to the *Baseline*. We observe that the fastest performing functionality of our purpose limiter is the *All-Denied* scenario with an average increase of 88%. At the same time, the *All-Allowed* follows with an average increase of 108%. More complex data minimization techniques being applied, as the *Mixed* or *Maximized* cases, show increases up to 200% compared to the *Baseline*. Increased amounts of fields in a request lead to increased latency. However, the increase is within a reasonable margin considering that the number of fields has been increased up to 4-fold, while the measured latency of our slowest-performing minimization technique has reached a 1.57-fold increase.

Throughput: Figure 3b shows the measured throughput of our requests with 13, 26, and 52 data fields respectively, comparing varying degrees of minimization techniques. The Baseline performs the best, while the No-Op follows closely behind. The loss of throughput is noticeable even with the fastest-performing *All-Denied* scenario with an average loss of 47% in throughput. The throughput decreases significantly with the amount of fields that need to be minimized. Increasing the number of data fields further also leads to a decrease in throughput, also for the *Baseline*. Note, the relative loss of throughput is much smaller for the *Baseline* than it is for scenarios that utilize many of the minimization techniques.

Considering the amount of added computational complexity to an otherwise performance-optimized communication framework, such as gRPC, the measured latency and throughput fall into a reasonable range *(NFR1)*. Additionally, the evaluations show a latency difference between the highest and lowest performing data minimization scenarios (*All-Denied* and *Maximized*) from 43% to 81%, while the throughput difference spans from 44% to 87%. Therefore, these findings suggest that the choice of data minimization scenario can significantly impact both latency and throughput, with potential variations. Albeit, advanced data minimization mechanisms will always be resource-intensive due to their computational complexity and the inherent need to explicitly handle single data fields. On the other hand, the relative overhead generated by our solution would probably decrease as soon as the corresponding microservice system itself increases in complexity.

7 Limitations, Future Work and Conclusion

Given the nature of this work as a prototype, some limitations remain. First, when including the two Go modules in an application, actual secret management needs to be handled by the developers. For demonstration purposes, this aspect was excluded. Thus, public and private key generation should not be incorporated directly within the development environment.

Further, the implementation of advanced purpose-based access control, including tree or graph structures of allowed/prohibited intended purposes, downstream usage policies, or transformation functions, seems a promising path for future work [26]. The current prototype is limited by simple purpose specifications and does not yet fully implement the advances in this field [28]. Nevertheless, our general approach paves the way for such extensions.

Secondly, we propose to implement the PEP component as a `StreamInterceptor`. This would cover a second possible communication method, apart from unary interceptors, offered by gRPC, thus making the adaptation in existing microservice applications more likely. Moreover, the handling of further data types, apart from the ones described herein, such as complex objects, should be addressed. Lastly, the set of data minimization or masking methods should be extended to include as many options as possible (e.g., different hashing algorithms, actual differential privacy, k anonymity of sets, etc.).

Apart from additional features, further performance assessments could be conducted. The impact of policy size, for example, has not been measured yet. Regarding our assumption that validation using a JWT (generated from a tailor-made policy that only contains the necessary accepted and restricted data fields) might perform better than a JWT that contains many different purposes and fields that are not relevant for a respective service. Further measurements should also be accompanied by performance optimizations of the reusable components.

Regardless of the mentioned limitations and future work, we presented the first reusable approach that combines privacy techniques, such as data minimization and purpose limitation, natively into the gRPC communication framework. To illustrate the wide applicability of our contribution, we integrated our Go modules into an exemplary food delivery application. The observed performance overhead generated by our contribution is deemed reasonable. Ultimately, in the broader context of technical as well as legal privacy requirements, the importance of such technical contributions is evident. We addressed performance and implementation costs as two of the key factors in deciding whether data controllers are likely to implement the approach to ensure data protection by design and by default.

Acknowledgements. We thank Huaning Yang, who contributed to the initial implementation within the scope of a privacy engineering course at TU Berlin.

References

1. Agape, A.A., Danceanu, M.C., Hansen, R.R., Schmid, S.: Charting the security landscape of programmable dataplanes (2018). https://doi.org/10.48550/arXiv.1807.00128
2. Anderson, A., et al.: eXtensible access control markup language (XACML) (2003)
3. Biega, A.J., Potash, P., Daumé, H., Diaz, F., Finck, M.: Operationalizing the legal principle of data minimization for personalization. In: Proceedings of the 43rd International ACM SIGIR Conference on Research and Development in Information Retrieval, pp. 399–408 (2020)
4. Birrell, A.D., Nelson, B.J.: Implementing remote procedure calls. ACM Trans. Comput. Syst. (TOCS) **2**(1), 39–59 (1984). https://doi.org/10.1145/2080.357392
5. Brown, S., Harman, D., Anderson, C., Dwyer, M.: Measuring data transmissions from the edge for distributed inferencing with GRPC. In: 2023 IEEE International Conference on Big Data (BigData), pp. 3853–3856 (2023). https://doi.org/10.1109/BigData59044.2023.10386142
6. Byun, J.W., Bertino, E., Li, N.: Purpose based access control of complex data for privacy protection. In: Proceedings of the tenth ACM symposium on Access Control Models and Technologies, pp. 102–110 (2005)
7. Byun, J.W., Li, N.: Purpose based access control for privacy protection in relational database systems. VLDB J. **17**, 603–619 (2008). https://doi.org/10.1007/11408079_2
8. Chandramouli, R., Butcher, Z., Chetal, A., et al.: Attribute-based access control for microservices-based applications using a service mesh. In: NIST, vol. 800 (2021)
9. European Parliament and Council of the European Union: General Data Protection Regulation (2018)
10. Finck, M., Biega, A.: Reviving purpose limitation and data minimisation in personalisation, profiling and decision-making systems. In: Technology and Regulation, pp. 21–04 (2021)
11. Grünewald, E.: Cloud native privacy engineering through DevPrivOps. In: Friedewald, M., Krenn, S., Schiering, I., Schiffner, S. (eds.) Privacy and Identity 2021. IAICT, vol. 644, pp. 122–141. Springer, Cham (2022). https://doi.org/10.1007/978-3-030-99100-5_10
12. Grünewald, E., Kiesel, J., Akabayin, S.-R., Pallas, F.: Hawk: DevOps-driven transparency and accountability in cloud native systems. In: IEEE 16th International Conference on Cloud Computing (CLOUD), IEEE, June 2023. https://doi.org/10.1109/CLOUD60044.2023.00027
13. Jabbari, R., bin Ali, N., Petersen, K., Tanveer, B.: What is DevOps? A systematic mapping study on definitions and practices. In: Scientific workshop proceedings of XP2016, pp. 1–11 (2016). https://doi.org/10.1145/2962695.2962707
14. Kumar, P.K., Agarwal, R., Shivaprasad, R., Sitaram, D., Kalambur, S.: Performance characterization of communication protocols in microservice applications. In: International Conference on Smart Applications, Communications and Networking, pp. 1–5 (2021). https://doi.org/10.1109/SmartNets50376.2021.9555425
15. Mahajan, A., Xue, Y., Weisskoff, J.: Implementing data flow assertions in gRPC and Protobufs. Brown University (2020). https://cs.brown.edu/courses/csci2390/2023/assign/project/report/2020/grpc-df-asserts.pdf

16. Majeed, A., Lee, S.: Anonymization techniques for privacy preserving data publishing: a comprehensive survey. IEEE Access **9**, 8512–8545 (2021). https://doi.org/10.1109/ACCESS.2020.3045700
17. Marques, J.F., Bernardino, J.: Analysis of data anonymization techniques. In: KEOD, pp. 235–241 (2020)
18. Nadareishvili, I., Mitra, R., McLarty, M., Amundsen, M.: Microservice Architecture: Aligning Principles, Practices, and Culture. O'Reilly, Sebastopol (2016)
19. Pallas, F., Hartmann, D., Heinrich, P., Kipke, J., Grünewald, E.: Configurable Per-query data minimization for privacy-compliant web APIs. In: Di Noia, T., Ko, I.Y., Schedl, M., Ardito, C. (eds.) Web Engineering, pp. 325–340. Springer, Cham (2022). https://doi.org/10.1007/978-3-031-09917-5_22
20. Pallas, F., et al.: Towards application-layer purpose-based access control. In: Proceedings of the 35th Annual ACM Symposium on Applied Computing, pp. 1288–1296 (2020). https://doi.org/10.1145/3341105.3375764
21. Parkinson, S., Khan, S.: A survey on empirical security analysis of access-control systems: a real-world perspective. ACM Comput. Surv. **55**(6) (2022). https://doi.org/10.1145/3533703
22. Salah, T., Jamal Zemerly, M., Yeun, C.Y., Al-Qutayri, M., Al-Hammadi, Y.: The evolution of distributed systems towards microservices architecture. In: 11th International Conference for Internet Technology and Secured Transactions (ICITST), pp. 318–325 (2016). https://doi.org/10.1109/ICITST.2016.7856721
23. Seitz, L., Selander, G., Gehrmann, C.: Authorization framework for the internet-of-things. In: 2013 IEEE 14th International Symposium on A World of Wireless, Mobile and Multimedia Networks, pp. 1–6 (2013). https://doi.org/10.1109/WoWMoM.2013.6583465
24. Shingala, K.: JSON web token (JWT) based client authentication in message queuing telemetry transport (MQTT). NTNU (2019). https://doi.org/10.48550/arXiv.1903.02895
25. Sweeney, L.: k-anonymity: a model for protecting privacy. Int. J. Uncertain. Fuzziness Knowl.-Based Syst. **10**(05), 557–570 (2002)
26. Ulbricht, M.-R., Pallas, F.: YaPPL - a lightweight privacy preference language for legally sufficient and automated consent provision in IoT scenarios. In: Garcia-Alfaro, J., Herrera-Joancomartí, J., Livraga, G., Rios, R. (eds.) DPM/CBT -2018. LNCS, vol. 11025, pp. 329–344. Springer, Cham (2018). https://doi.org/10.1007/978-3-030-00305-0_23
27. White, J.E.: A high-level framework for network-based resource sharing. In: Proceedings of the National Computer Conference and Exposition, AFIPS 1976, pp. 561-570. ACM, New York (1976). https://doi.org/10.1145/1499799.1499878
28. Wolf, K., Pallas, F., Tai, S.: Messaging with purpose limitation-privacy-compliant publish-subscribe systems. In: IEEE 25th International Enterprise Distributed Object Computing Conference, pp. 162–172. IEEE, October 2021

Trusting Decentralized Web Data in a Solid-Based Social Network

Valentin Siegert(✉), Dirk Leichsenring, and Martin Gaedke

Distributed and Self-organizing Systems, Chemnitz University of Technology, Chemnitz, Germany
{valentin.siegert,dirk.leichsenring, martin.gaedke}@informatik.tu-chemnitz.de

Abstract. In our current data-centric society, there is a rising concern among individuals regarding their privacy and the degree of control they have over their personal data. In response to this growing demand for transparency and control, a recent initiative for web re-decentralization has emerged, wherein web applications no longer store data centrally. One of the prominent approaches aimed at re-decentralizing the web is Solid. Solid facilitates data storage in decentralized pods secured with web access control, enabling seamless connectivity of diverse data. However, the integration of decentralized data from various third-party pods in web applications poses a significant challenge, as the data's trustworthiness may be compromised, potentially leading to malicious or harmful outcomes. Therefore, data integration necessitates a trust-aware decision, i.e., the extent to which the data is trustworthy enough to use despite its high heterogeneity. To enable such trust awareness for web applications utilizing decentralized data, we propose a trust-aware framework called TrADS for decentralized social networks. TrADS leverages the MVC pattern of web applications to integrate external data from Solid pods trust aware. The potentially malicious and harmful status of external data is an end-user concern. A web application must therefore be trust aware to provide a better user experience. Therefore, we evaluate the proposed trust-aware decentralized social network in terms of usability and transparency with 53 end users through an empirical study. The results demonstrate that the trust awareness component in TrADS can support end users in their trustworthy user experience.

Keywords: Trust · Social Linked Data (Solid) · Re-decentralization of the Web · Decentralized Web · Responsible Web

1 Introduction

The web has increasingly become a collection of closed silos of resources [5] due to commercialization. However, more and more attention is being paid to data

This paper is supported by the European Union's HORIZON Research and Innovation Programme under grant agreement No 101120657, project ENFIELD (European Lighthouse to Manifest Trustworthy and Green AI).

K. Stefanidis et al. (Eds.): ICWE 2024, LNCS 14629, pp. 230–245, 2024.
https://doi.org/10.1007/978-3-031-62362-2_16

sovereignty [3], as full data control is lost as soon as the data is placed in a closed silo. As a result of this loss, data privacy is also restricted accordingly. Various projects are working on decentralizing the web for this reason, but also because of its originally decentralized architecture. For example, with its Next Generation Internet Initiative[1], with Gaia-X[2] and also with the General Data Protection Regulation (GDPR)[3], the EU is driving decentralization forward for political reasons. However, projects such as Solid [13] and Fediverse projects such as Mastodon[4] are also working on the decentralization of the web. The Fediverse is built across multiple instances that can communicate with each other, allowing users to exchange their data between them and thus use it in a decentralized manner [6]. In contrast, Solid's pod structure allows data owners to not only decentralize their data, but also allows them to fully control it.

Decentralized web applications can obtain any data from the web with the help of semantic web technologies and thus use data in a decentralized manner. Such web applications therefore no longer store their users' personal data in a data store controlled by the application, but for example in a Solid pod or in Solid data spaces [11]. However, data storage in decentralized web applications is not fully decentralized, since application-internal data are also kept internal with such a decentralization. In addition, correctly implemented caches in a decentralized web application are required for technically smooth data access to decentralized data in order to ensure fast response times in practice.

As discussed in the position paper by Siegert and Gaedke [14], integrating external data storage creates a significant challenge for decentralized web applications, since user experience could be negatively affected by malicious or harmful data. Classic web applications offer a trustworthy user experience by homogenizing data based on the data model used and reusing this collected data later accordingly. The data comes either from sources known to the application or from user input, whereby this input is validated for security reasons [9]. With decentralized web applications, however, the web application no longer has complete control over the data storage. For example, data once stored on a decentralized Solid pod can be changed without the knowledge or control of a web application before it is read out later. External data can also be malicious or harmful, but should neither be neglected by default, nor used unfiltered in a decentralized web application. Integration of untrustworthy data can result in a deterioration of the user experience. To ensure a trustworthy user experience in decentralized web applications, the trustworthiness of external data must be taken into account. However, external data cannot be continuously monitored on changes by the web application. In addition, the amount of data in the web is constantly growing [16], which makes it impossible to moderate the integration of external data by experts [1]. Thus, decentralized web applications require a

[1] https://digital-strategy.ec.europa.eu/en/policies/next-generation-internet-initiative.
[2] https://gaia-x.eu/.
[3] Regulation (EU) 2016/679 of the European Parliament and of the Council.
[4] https://joinmastodon.org/.

trust awareness component [14], which assesses the extent to which the data is trustworthy enough to be used.

A trust awareness component is yet not existing for decentralized web applications. Based on related work [17], trust awareness is calculated on different information about the data, e.g. its origin or reputation, depending on the trust model used. Based on the results of these calculations, a trust-based decision is made about the extent to which the data is trustworthy enough to be used. However, it is currently unclear how the interfaces of a trust awareness component are structured, what typical processes in a web application including such a component look like and how often the component is integrated into the application's workflow. To enable decentralized web applications being trust aware and to address these questions, we introduce in this paper a trust aware decentralized web application. The use case for our application is a social network where a large number of user pods and additional data are merged into a typical social network platform. Furthermore, we evaluate the usability of the prototype and the impact of the trust awareness component on the usability to draw conclusions on how such a component can impact the user experience to be more trustworthy. The contributions of our paper are as follows:

1. We present a framework named TrADS, a **Tr**ust-**A**ware **D**ecentralized **S**ocial network, which has a Solid-based decentralized data layer.
2. We demonstrate its feasibility with a publicly accessible prototype[5] whose code is also accessible[6].
3. We evaluate the usability of our prototype and the impact of the trust awareness component on usability with a 53-participants large user study.

The remainder of the paper begins in Sect. 2 with a qualitative discussion of related work. In Sect. 3, we present our framework for a trust-aware, decentralized, and Solid-based social network called TrADS, along with insights into its prototypical implementation and its qualitative comparison with related work. We detail the 53-participant user study on the usability of TrADS and the impact of the trust awareness component on the usability in Sect. 4, and draw conclusions in Sect. 5.

2 Related Work

Several decentralized social networks exist today already. To systematically analyze and assess them, we identify two sets of requirements, one motivated by the end-users of the social network and the other motivated by the social network's operators. The five end-user requirements are: *trust awareness*, *data control*, *resistance to censorship*, *networkability*, and *independence*. The three operator requirements are: *adaptability*, *manageability*, and *scalability*. The decentralized social networks are selected on the basis of the technology they use in order to

[5] demo: https://vsr.informatik.tu-chemnitz.de/projects/2024/trads/.
[6] code: https://zenodo.org/records/10641771.

cover the widest possible range of different decentralized social network technologies. All requirements are mapped onto a four-level assessment scheme: ○ not satisfied, ◔ partially satisfied, ◕ mostly satisfied, ● fully satisfied. All results of the qualitative comparison are also summarized in Table 1, which we detail in the following of this section. In addition, we list the requirement assessment of TrADS, our own solution, which is described in detail in Subsect. 3.3.

Table 1. Qualitative comparison between decentralized social networks

Decentralized Social Network	T	D	R	N	I	A	M	S
Mastodon (see footnote 4)	◔	◕	◔	●	◔	●	○	◕
PeerTube (see footnote 8)	◔	◕	◔	●	◔	●	○	◕
diaspora* (see footnote 7)	◔	◕	◔	●	◔	●	○	◕
Pixelfed (see footnote 9)	◔	◕	◔	●	◔	●	○	◕
Secure Scuttlebutt (see footnote 10)	○	◕	◔	◔	◔	●	●	●
Sone (see footnote 11)	○	◕	●	◔	◔	●	●	●
Peergos (see footnote 12)	○	●	◔	◔	●	●	●	●
SteemIt (see footnote 14)	○	○	●	○	●	○	●	○
Minds (see footnote 15)	○	○	●	○	●	○	●	○
Movim (see footnote 16)	○	◕	●	◕	●	◕	●	●
twtxt (see footnote 17)	○	◕	●	○	●	◔	●	●
nostr (see footnote 19)	○	○	●	◔	●	◔	●	●
TrADS	●	●	●	●	●	●	●	◕

T, D, R, N, I, A, M, S respectively stand for: **T**rust awareness, **D**ata control, **R**esistance to censorship, **N**etworkability, **I**ndependence, **A**daptability, **M**anageability, and **S**calability

Currently, the most successful approach to decentralized social networks are federated networks building the Fediverse [6], being a combination of individual instances that communicate with each other. Instances can be operated privately or publicly and can be used by a variable number of users, who are free to decide which instance they use. By distributing the network across a large number of independently operating instances, it is ensured that nobody has sole control over the social network. The best-known representatives of federated networks include diaspora*[7], PeerTube[8], PixelFeed[9] and Mastodon(see footnote 4), which is one of the most successful federated networks with 1.8 million active users in 2022 [10].

[7] https://diasporafoundation.org/.
[8] https://joinpeertube.org/.
[9] https://pixelfed.org/.

In a peer-to-peer (P2P) model, all participants (nodes) have equal rights and can both provide and receive services. In this paper, we consider three P2P-based decentralized social network approaches: (1) Secure Scuttlebutt[10], (2) Sone[11], and (3) Peergos[12]. Users of Secure Scuttlebutt operate their own node on which, in addition to their own data, the data of all friends and the data of their friends are stored. Communication beyond those is achieved through the use of so-called pubs (publicly accessible nodes). In Sone, however, users operate their own Freenet[13] access point nodes. Data is encrypted and stored on different nodes, whereby the storage location is determined by a routing algorithm over which users have no direct influence. Users of Peergos, in turn, need access to a node operated by themselves or by others on which they can store their data. They then have the option of following other users, giving them the opportunity to write messages and share data unilaterally. If the data is only stored on a self-operated node, the user may retains full control.

Well-known representatives of blockchain-based decentralized social networks are SteemIt[14] and Minds[15] [4]. The blockchain serves as a record of all actions in the decentralized network. Access to content, such as images or texts, is often realized via a P2P-based data distribution protocol called IPFS [12], as otherwise the required storage capacity of the blockchain would be too large. As the blocks in the chain cannot be subsequently modified or deleted, the use of blockchain results in unresolved problems in the context of social networks [4] like scalability, content visibility and decentralization of content.

Movim[16] is an XMPP-based decentralized social network. Using an abstraction layer, a Movim instance provides an XMPP client that offers the functionalities of a social network. Such an instance can be used by any number of users, regardless of the XMPP servers they use. All personal content is stored on the user's XMPP server allowing users to switch instance at will. The used Movim instance keeps a copy of the content as a cache and makes the created public content available via HTTP. twtxt[17] is a very minimalistic microblogging system approach. Each user makes a twtxt file publicly available via a URL, which contains the user's posts line by line with the URL of this file serving as the identity. A twtxt client retrieves the files of all followed users, similar to an RSS feed reader, and creates a feed from them. Yarn.social[18] is a decentralized social network based on twtxt files, providing optional extensions to support hashtags and metadata for social networks. Notes and Other Stuff Transmitted by Relay (nostr)[19] is a protocol for decentralized social networks based on a relay system.

[10] https://www.scuttlebutt.nz/.
[11] https://github.com/Bombe/Sone.
[12] https://peergos.org/.
[13] https://www.hyphanet.org/.
[14] https://steemit.com/.
[15] https://www.minds.com/.
[16] https://movim.eu/.
[17] https://twtxt.readthedocs.io/en/latest/user/intro.html.
[18] https://yarn.social/.
[19] https://nostr.com/.

The aim is to create a global independent and censorship-resistant social network consisting of a large number of relays with which users communicate using a client. The relays accept user content and pass it on when it is requested by other users. To publish content, a user, who is identified by a publicly known key, signs the content and sends it to a selection of relays. A nostr client then creates a feed for a user, which consists of all publications by other users that are followed by the client's user. nostr is completely call-based, so there is no way to inform other users about interactions, and once a user has sent data to a relay, they lose all control over it, which makes it impossible to delete any.

While trust awareness on decentralized data is not supported in any of the approaches mentioned, the Fediverse applications at least consider moderation of the data per instance. However, this moderation in the Fediverse cannot be fully automated and is a known and unsolved problem [1], especially for larger instances. Data control is mostly supported, if at all, by its own independent hosting, which has the disadvantage of hosting effort. With approaches such as Movim(see footnote 16) or twtxt(see footnote 17), the effort is less, but they still require their own hosting and, like twtxt, sometimes have no access control. Due to the independent distribution of data storage, some of the approaches mentioned are already resistant to censorship. However, many approaches are also limited in their resilience, as individual instances can restrict communication with others. In particular, the Fediverse performs very well in terms of networkability through common data exchange protocols such as ActivityPub [8]. Protocols such as IPFS [12] also support the exchange of data to a high degree, but the using approaches lack networkability due to their blockchain architecture. All of the above approaches give users a choice of instances, which partially supports the idea of independence. However, the better solution is when data and/or identities are not bound to instances, making approaches completely independent of third parties. Adaptability is a given in some approaches but is limited in approaches such as Movim(see footnote 16), twtxt(see footnote 17) and nostr(see footnote 19), and it is not given at all in blockchain-based decentralized social networks. While most approaches already perform well in terms of manageability and scalability, the Fediverse is poor in terms of manageability [1], and also has some disadvantages in terms of scalability. These are due to the caching principle in each instance, which results in overlinear growth of the entire system as a network grows. The blockchain-based approaches are even worse than the Fediverse in terms of scalability, as they face the problem of scalable blockchain technology [4].

3 TrADS

To improve the related work and to especially make social networks trust-aware by integrating a trust awareness component [14], we present in this section TrADS, a **Tr**ust **A**ware **D**ecentralized **S**ocial network. We first explain details on TrADS architecture including its typical processes, and then proceed to present details about its prototype including details on the front-end. To be able to list

TrADS in the Table 1 of related work, we conclude the section with a brief analysis of TrADS using the requirements mentioned in Sect. 2.

3.1 Architecture

The architecture of such a social network is significantly influenced by the technology used for decentralized storage and data exchange. In order to maintain the networkability of the Fediverse, the separation of data and instance as in Movim(see footnote 16), and in particular a high level of data control similar to that in Peergos(see footnote 12), we use Solid [13] in our approach. The Solid pods allow end users to control their own data through the web standards used and to freely transfer the data to other platforms, thus minimizing the dependency of end users on the actual instance of the social network. The high level of data control of the end user in Solid and the web standards used also enable a high degree of adaptability, as with P2P-based approaches or the Fediverse. Similar to Movim(see footnote 16) and the blockchain approaches, Solid promotes the independence of the instances, but in contrast, data control is not restricted by a lack of access control.

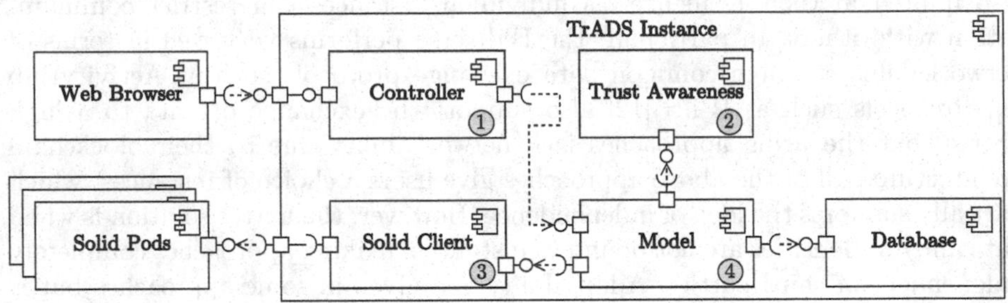

Fig. 1. A TrADS Instance Architecture

A TrADS instance is independent of a central architecture and therefore resistant to censorship by others. The UML component diagram in Fig. 1 provides an overview of the architecture of a TrADS instance. TrADS is a web application based on the Model-View-Controller (MVC) pattern [7] and therefore has the classic components Controller (1) and Model (4). The View is not shown separately for simplification and is used in the end user's web browser in particular. The model has access to a database component, which provides both a database for application-internal data and a cache, which is used for the technical realization of a fast response time for user requests. The decentralized nature of TrADS therefore does not slow down the interaction between the user and the TrADS instance. Apart from the classic database connection of the model, it has access to a Solid Client (3), which enables TrADS to access Solid pods. The newly introduced Trust Awareness component (2) is used in TrADS by the model component to neither blindly accept nor directly reject external content originating from the Solid pods. This means that externally sourced content is evaluated in a trust aware manner before it is displayed to the user. This type of integration as a local component on the individual instance rules out manipulation by third parties and thus makes the TrADS instance independent about whether decentralized data is trustworthy enough. This also makes it possible to display the assessments and to allow future assessments to be influenced by the user. The trust awareness result can vary from instance to instance, whether due to a different data situation, the use of a different trust model in the component or different preferences of the instance users and operators.

To ensure that users can assume the integrity and origin of the displayed data despite the decentralized storage, TrADS uses checksums for referencing and offers optional content signing. For example, when commenting on a post and thus referencing the post, a user cannot be sure that the post will still be available (unchanged) later. The use of checksums when referencing content ensures that it is possible to check later whether the content that can now be accessed is identical to the content referenced in the initial post. For this purpose, the checksum associated with the content is also specified together with the reference to the content. Users can thus check whether the referenced content still exists in exactly this form. Otherwise, the content was referenced incorrectly or the referenced content has since been manipulated. The optional signing of content makes it possible to ensure that only the displayed content creator has published the currently saved content if a unique public key can be assigned to him. If a post creator later decides to remove a post or restrict access to it, partial discussions could exist in TrADS as the replies to the post content are in turn controlled by their creators.

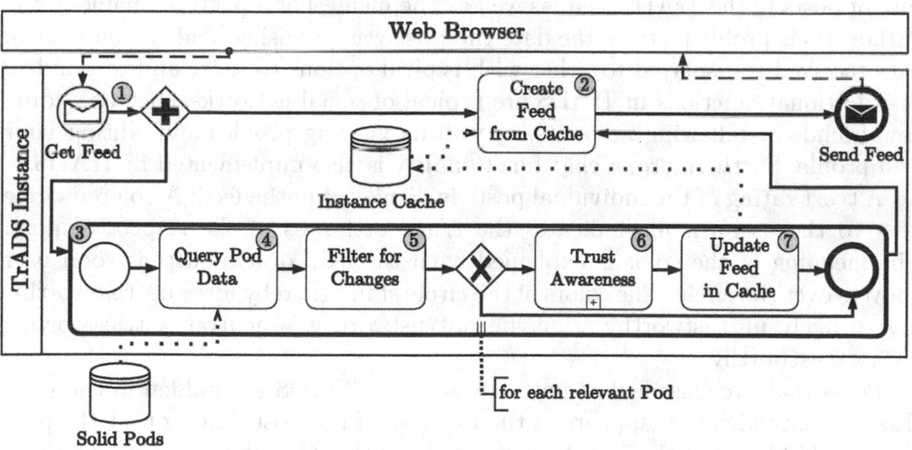

Fig. 2. Getting a User's Feed in TrADS

Trust Awareness is always requested as soon as new data from any Solid pod is included in a TrADS instance. For technical reasons, such inclusion often results in caching at the instance. An example of this is shown in Fig. 2 using the query of a user's feed. The process begins with the user's request to retrieve their feed (1). To ensure that the request can be answered as quickly as possible, a quick initial response is sent to the user after the request (2) and a query is sent to all relevant Solid pods to update the data (3). The fast response to the user is made possible by querying the instance cache and thus shortens the response time for the user instead of awaiting all included pods. The data update subprocess is executed for each relevant pod and begins with the data query (4). The retrieved data is then filtered for changes (5) to determine whether and what should be updated in the instance cache. If an update of the cache is necessary, the trust awareness component (6) will determine the extent to which the data is trustworthy before the update is executed (7). TrADS does not detail anything about the metrics on the basis of which the trust-aware decision is made. In this paper, the component of trust awareness is intentionally only implemented as a prototype so that the architectural integration and its effects in particular can be both presented and examined. Frameworks such as ConTED [15] or other trust models migrated to the decentralized web [17] can be used to implement the trust awareness component use case independently.

3.2 Prototype

A demo(see footnote 5) of TrADS as well as the implementation code(see footnote 6) are available online. TrADS offers users functions that they are already familiar with from other social networks. When called up, the feed is displayed, which consists of posts and reactions from related pods. These are either friends or any other social network account the user follows. Figure 3a shows the structure of posts in the TrADS feed, as well as the menu. For a post, the name of the author, their profile picture, the date the post was published and the number of likes received is displayed together with typical options to share and respond to it. Additional functions in TrADS are typical of social networks, such as adding new friends or following accounts, as well as viewing profiles and editing your own profile. Furthermore, a chat functionality is also implemented in TrADS.

A trust rating of the individual posts is displayed in the feed. A colored circle next to the user's name indicates the trustworthiness of the respective post. The meaning of the color is explained with the help of a tooltip as soon user hoovers over the circle. The colors of the circle stand thereby for: • untrustworthy, • very likely untrustworthy, • maybe untrustworthy, • neutral, • trustworthy, • very trustworthy.

Posts that are classified as untrustworthy by TrADS are hidden in the feed. However, an indication appears at the location of the post writing that the post has been hidden from the feed. Users have the option to click on this indication to view the distrusted post with a corresponding warning. Figure 3b shows how this post is displayed after the user decides to view it despite poor trustworthiness.

As a prototypical implementation, TrADS does not use a fully-fledged trust model in its trust awareness, but simple functions that serve as placeholders for a future implementation. Trust values are initialized for posts by retrieving

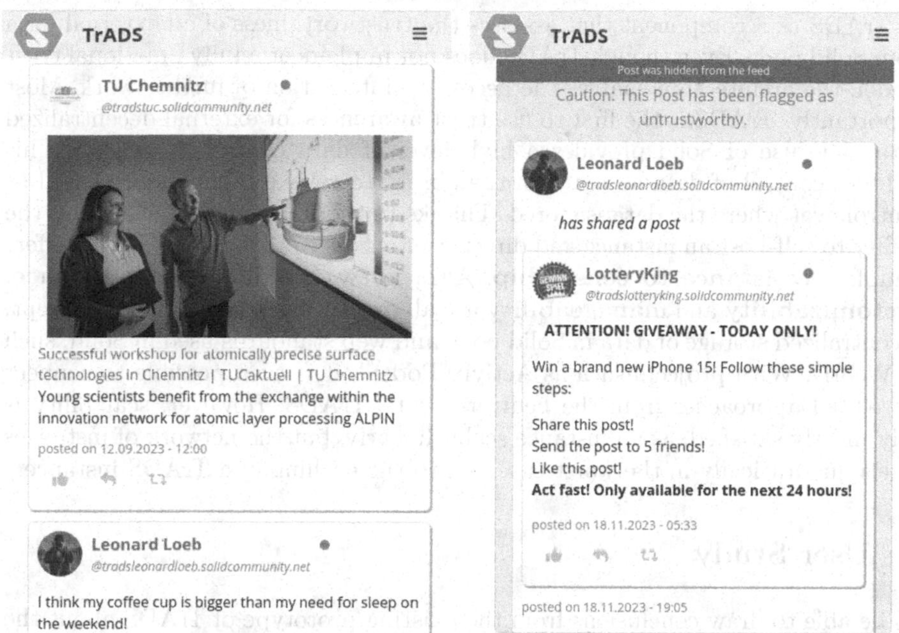

(a) **Examplary TrADS Feed, including two posts**

(b) **Expanded untrustworthiness warning, showing the post within a TrADS feed**

Fig. 3. TrADS Front-end Examples

the author's trust value from the cache and modifying it with a random-based variance. The trust value of the authors is initialized with a neutral value and also provided with a random variance for scattering. Likes of a post increase the trust value of the post if the trust value of the like creator is greater than that of the post. Sent chat messages also lead to an increase in the trust value of the recipient of the message.

The cache enables the trust awareness to use stored content as the basis for the trust evaluation. In addition, the evaluation of individual content can also trigger a change in the evaluation of other content already stored in the cache. A strongly negative evaluation of a content or author does not lead to its rejection in TrADS, but only to the corresponding indication and hiding from the feed. This gives users control over the content they consume, and additionally TrADS' trust awareness can make use of such negatively rated content as a good source of information for later trust evaluations.

3.3 TrADS Qualitative Comparison

TrADS is a very good approach for a decentralized social network with regard to the requirements mentioned in Sect. 2. The **Trust awareness** introduction into decentralized web applications is the main contribution of the paper. It is realized by TrADS as a component that assesses the trustworthiness of all external data from Solid pods. Even though TrADS does not implement a fully functional trust model, the architecture enables the necessary integration of further work. Most importantly, TrADS is the first to use trust awareness for external decentralized data. The use of Solid provides a high level of data control in TrADS. This includes control of data access with the ability to revoke permission, as well as control over where the data is stored. Thanks to the free choice of instances, the ability to self-host an instance and direct user access to their pods, TrADS offers complete **resistance to censorship**. Also, **networkability**, **independence**, **customizability** and **manageability** are all met by using the instance concept, decentralized storage of data in Solid pods and web standards used in Solid, such as WebID. With projects such as ActivityPods[20], it is even possible to connect to related approaches from the Fediverse with TrADS. However, scalability is only mostly satisfied, as an instance scales linearly, but the network of instances scales quadratically in the worst case due to the caching of a TrADS instance.

4 User Study

To be able to draw conclusions from the existing prototype of TrADS about the influence of the trust awareness component on the user experience, we conducted a user study on the front-end of TrADS. In this section, we present the design and process of the study and then discuss its results and the implications of the user study. All data of the evaluation is accessible online[21], including the raw survey data as well as all numbers we discuss in the results subsection.

4.1 Procedure

The user study was conducted in German using a tool that made it possible to embed TrADS directly into the survey using IFrames. After a welcome text and the collection of general information about the participant, each participant was given time to explore TrADS independently. Each participant was then asked to first read the latest post from a local newspaper, then like a post from a specific account and finally write their own post. In this way, it was initiated that the participants interacted with TrADS. Although it was not checked to what extent the participants completed the tasks.

After the interaction with TrADS, the usability of the demo implementation was determined using the System Usability Score (SUS) [2]. This uses 10 statements, which are evaluated by the user on a 5-point Likert scale and then systematically combined to form a score. In order to look specifically at the use of the Trust Awareness component, 4 questions are asked as to whether and to what extent the participant was aware of Trust Awareness in the front-end, always, sometimes or not at all. However, 2 of these questions are only displayed

[20] https://activitypods.org/.

[21] data available at https://zenodo.org/records/10641724.

if the participant indicated more than not at all in the previous always-indicating question. For example, the participant is only asked whether the different colors of the trust circles are perceived if they have indicated that they always or sometimes see the circles. The participant then rated 9 statements on the integration of trust awareness into a social network, again on a 5-point Likert scale. In this way, the general acceptance of a trust awareness component can be examined. The survey ends with 7 statements on the importance of data protection in social networks, which the participant again rates on a 5-point Likert scale.

For the survey, TrADS was put into demo mode to ensure that no persistent changes can be made to the instance and that all users are shown an identical version. To this end, user management is deactivated, preventing the addition and deletion of users in the cache of the TrADS instance. Interactions, such as creating or liking posts, are only stored in the cache and not in the corresponding Solid pods. All new content stored in the cache is automatically deleted every 30 min. Furthermore, personal posts are not displayed in the feed, as the participants have no connection to the demo user.

To bring the social network to life for the demo, 25 pods are created on a separate Solid pod provider for user representation. There are 5 profiles of companies that fill the network with news. News articles only contain links to the corresponding articles, which can be read by means of a preview. The topics of the articles were chosen from the areas of entertainment, sport and animals in order to avoid socially controversial topics as far as possible. Three other users are used in the demo for fraudulent content, which should not be trusted and should therefore be visualized accordingly by the front-end. The remaining 17 users are private users of the network who have been assigned different trust values after creating posts in order to have different users.

4.2 Results

Only the 53 fully completed responses were taken into account for the evaluation(see footnote 21), of which 26 were female, 19 male and 8 without gender information. According to the participants, the age distribution was as follows: under 18: 1; 18 to 24: 4; 25 to 34: 9; 35 to 50: 27; 51 to 70: 11 and one participant over 70. While 40 people stated that they use social networks several times a week, one participant stated that they use them weekly, three use them less than once a week and two participants do not use them at all.

27 of the 53 participants stated that they had noticed the circles indicating trustworthiness next to the names of the authors of the posts. More than half of this group of participants noticed that these dots had different colors. 26 of the participants stated that they had noticed the indications on untrustworthy feed removals, yet only two participants tried to click on these. In total, 36 of the 53 participants noticed at least one of the two trust awareness front-end elements, of which 17 even noticed both elements. However, there were also 17 participants who did not notice either of the two trust awareness front-end elements.

Figure 4 shows the SUS distribution of the survey as a boxplot (1). The figure also contains the boxplots for two different user groups. The boxplot (2)

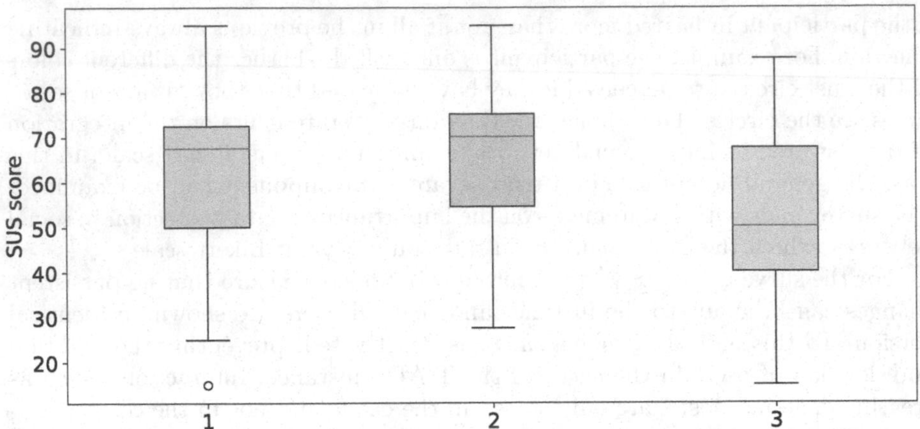

Fig. 4. SUS Distribution of (1) all participants (2) participants noticed in minimum one trust awareness front-end element (3) participants did not notice any trust awareness front-end element

represents the group of users who noticed at least one of the two trust awareness front-end elements, while the boxplot (3) represents the group of users who did not notice any of these elements. The SUS of the survey have an expected value of $\mu = 68$ with a standard deviation of $\sigma = 17.5$. According to SUS, such an expected value is to be classified as an average score. Using the Shapiro-Wilk test, we determined a p-value of 0.234 for the survey's SUS data points. As the p-value is below the significance level of $\alpha = 0.05$, a normal distribution of survey's SUS can be assumed.

To investigate the extent to which the participants' perception of trust awareness of the application influences the usability of the system, we examined the box plots (2) and (3) in a two-sample t-test. Based on a significance level of $\alpha = 0.05$ and 51 degrees of freedom, the critical value for our t-test is 2.01. This results with ($95\% - CI[1.06, 21.23]$) in $t(51) = 2.22$, $p = 0.03$. Thus, a significant difference exists in the SUS distribution of end users noticing trust awareness front end elements and those who did not. The significant differences in the usability scores indicate an improvement in the user experience as a result of trust awareness. However, it should be noted that the groups were not randomly selected, which limits the reliability of the t-test.

The reaminding survey statements provide further insights on 5-point Likert scales with values from 1 to 5: The presentation of an assessment of the trust awareness of the content was rated as useful ($\mu = 4.25$, $\sigma = 0.75$) and helpful ($\mu = 4.11$, $\sigma = 0.86$). It was further agreed ($\mu = 3.89$, $\sigma = 0.92$), that a social network in which this additional information is provided is more likely to be used than another. The results of the statements on dealing with untrustworthy posts show a greater discussion among the participants with $3 < \mu < 4$ and $\sigma > 1$. The protection of personal data ($\mu = 3.3$, $\sigma = 0.88$) and the knowledge of what data is stored about oneself ($\mu = 3.13$, $\sigma = 0.99$) is rather important for our participants. Additionally, most generally do not know where their personal data is stored ($\mu = 2.4$, $\sigma = 1.15$) or who has access to it ($\mu = 2.45$, $\sigma = 1.19$).

5 Conclusion

In this paper, we present a trust awareness framework called TrADS for decentralized social networks. TrADS leverages the MVC pattern [7] of web applications to integrate external data from Solid pods [13] into decentralized web applications in a trust aware manner. We evaluate the proposed trust-aware decentralized social network TrADS in terms of usability and transparency with 53 end users in an empirical study. The results indicate that the trust awareness component in TrADS can support end users in their trustworthy user experience. Furthermore, user study participants agree that a social network improves if it provides information on the trustworthiness of data. The results were less clear when it came to dealing with content that was classified as untrustworthy, including opposing opinions. Contradictory results were obtained from the survey on participants' attitudes towards the handling of their data on social networks. On the one hand, privacy and data control is important to the participants, but on the other, the majority of them stated that they do not know what happens to their data. The qualitative comparison based on 8 requirements of related work of decentralized social networks with TrADS shows that the use of Solid and its web standards makes TrADS an above-average solution. Solid combines the advantages of other approaches such as the Fediverse, blockchain or peer-to-peer (P2P) with regard to the requirements mentioned. Only the scalability of P2P approaches is slightly better with regard to all instances of a decentralized social network. In particular, however, TrADS introduces trust awareness, which is not present in any of the existent approaches. The Fediverse already recognizes the problems of malicious or harmful data, but only solves this with manual moderation, which leads subsequent problems in larger networks [1].

In terms of future work, we suggest further research to determine the generalizability of this work. This includes the back-end use of the trust awareness component of decentralized web applications, as well as the extent to which the results of the component are used in the front-end to improve the user experience. Further targeted investigations are required for the generalization of trust awareness functionality in decentralized web applications. Trust awareness should not have to be developed by the developers themselves for each application or set up at great expense. It will only be widely used in many web applications if the set-up effort is limited, e.g. similar to the effort required today to deliver a website with end-to-end encryption via TLS. The use case of social networks used in this paper is a special one in terms of data access by end users, as they create content themselves, which is then used by others for interaction. In other web applications, end users are often only consumers of a service. The integration of external data is then often motivated by suppliers of resources for the service of the web application. Such a change in the use case can also change the impact on the user experience than TrADS does in a very transparent way with the visible front-end elements without removing content fully. Such a change to the use case can, for example, result in the application having to intervene more strongly than TrADS does in the case of untrustworthy data.

References

1. Anaobi, I.H., Raman, A., Castro, I., et al.: Will admins cope? Decentralized moderation in the Fediverse. In: Proceedings of WWW '23, pp. 3109-3120 (2023). https://doi.org/10.1145/3543507.3583487
2. Brooke, J.: SUS: a quick and dirty usability scale. Usability Eval. Ind. **189**(3), 189–194 (1996)
3. Couture, S., Toupin, S.: What does the notion of sovereignty mean when referring to the digital? New Media Soc. **21**(10), 2305–2322 (2019). https://doi.org/10.1177/1461444819865984
4. Guidi, B.: When blockchain meets online social networks. Pervasive Mob. Comput. **62**, 101131 (2020). https://doi.org/10.1016/j.pmcj.2020.101131
5. Ibáñez, L.D., Simperl, E., Gandon, F., Story, H.: Redecentralizing the web with distributed ledgers. IEEE Intell. Syst. **32**(1), 92–95 (2017). https://doi.org/10.1109/MIS.2017.18
6. La Cava, L., Greco, S., Tagarelli, A.: Understanding the growth of the Fediverse through the lens of Mastodon. Appl. Netw. Sci. **6**(1), 64 (2021). https://doi.org/10.1007/s41109-021-00392-5
7. Leff, A., Rayfield, J.T.: Web-application development using the model/view/controller design pattern. In: Proceedings Fifth IEEE EDOC, pp. 118–127 (2001). https://doi.org/10.1109/EDOC.2001.950428
8. Lemmer-Webber, C., Tallon, J., Shepherd, E., Guy, A., Prodromou, E.: Activitypub. first edition of a recommendation, W3C, January 2018. https://www.w3.org/TR/2018/REC-activitypub-20180123/
9. Li, X., Xue, Y.: A survey on server-side approaches to securing web applications. ACM Comput. Surv. **46**(4) (2014). https://doi.org/10.1145/2541315
10. Mastodon gGmbH: mastodon annual report 2022 (2023). https://joinmastodon.org/reports/Mastodon%20Annual%20Report%202022.pdf
11. Meckler, S., Dorsch, R., Henselmann, D., Harth, A.: The web and linked data as a solid foundation for dataspaces. In: Companion Proceedings of WWW 2023, pp. 1440–1446 (2023). https://doi.org/10.1145/3543873.3587616
12. Protocol labs: IPFS standards. https://specs.ipfs.tech/
13. Sambra, A.V., Mansour, E., Hawke, S., et al.: Solid: a platform for decentralized social applications based on linked data. Technical Report, MIT CSAIL & Qatar Computing Research Institute (2016). http://emansour.com/research/lusail/solid_protocols.pdf
14. Siegert, V., Gaedke, M.: Trust awareness for redecentralized web applications (Position Paper). In: Joint Proceedings of ESWC 2023 Workshops and Tutorials (2023). https://ceur-ws.org/Vol-3443/ESWC_2023_TrusDeKW_paper_7938.pdf
15. Siegert, V., Kirchhoff, A., Gaedke, M.: ConTED: towards content trust for the decentralized web. In: Proceedings of WI-IAT 2022, pp. 604–611 (2022). https://doi.org/10.1109/WI-IAT55865.2022.00095

16. Taylor, P.: Volume of data/information created, captured, copied, and consumed worldwide from 2010 to 2020, with forecasts from 2021 to 2025, November 2023. https://www.statista.com/statistics/871513/worldwide-data-created/
17. Yu, H., Shen, Z., Leung, C., Miao, C., Lesser, V.R.: A survey of multi-agent trust management systems. IEEE Access **1**, 35–50 (2013). https://doi.org/10.1109/ACCESS.2013.2259892

Combining Anti-typosquatting Techniques

Francesco Blefari[1,2], Angelo Furfaro[1(✉)], Giovambattista Ianni[1], and Alessandro Viscomi[1]

[1] University of Calabria, Rende, CS, Italy
{francesco.blefari,angelo.furfaro,ianni}@unical.it
[2] IMT Schools for Advanced Studies, Lucca, LU, Italy

Abstract. Typosquatting constitutes a widely used malpractice of domain exploitation that leverages users' typographical errors when entering URLs. Different techniques have been devised to mitigate this threat and some tools have been developed. However, currently there are almost no tools available to web users. We propose a comprehensive open-source software solution which combines state-of-the-art typosquatting detection techniques and it is freely available as a dedicated extension for the web browser Chrome, named TypoAlert. TypoAlert is designed to automatically detect in real-time when a user visits a typosquatted domain and alerts the user accordingly. An assessment done through the analysis of a significant number of domains shows the effectiveness of the approach.

Keywords: TypoSquatting · URL Hijacking · Privacy · Phishing

1 Introduction

The widely spread typosquatting malpractice is based on typing errors made by users when entering a URL into their browser. The attackers (*typosquatters*) register domains that contain spelling errors compared to legitimate domains, taking advantage of people's inevitable oversights.

Typosquatted sites, i.e. web sites whose domain name resembles a different legitimate domain name, can host a wide range of content aimed to generate profits through advertising, often containing malicious elements and/or redirections to malicious websites. It is not uncommon that typosquatted sites are exploited to conduct attack campaigns, such as phishing, aimed at stealing sensitive information from users. The studies conducted in [1] suggests that between 10% and 20% of manually entered URLs contain errors: an average user who mistakenly types the URL of a popular site has a 1 out of 14 chance of ending up on a typosquatted domain. Companies experience traffic losses and, consequently, financial losses, while users are constantly exposed to the risk of falling

This work was partially supported by projects SERICS (PE00000014) and FAIR (PE0000013) under the MUR NRRP funded by EU.

K. Stefanidis et al. (Eds.): ICWE 2024, LNCS 14629, pp. 246–254, 2024.
https://doi.org/10.1007/978-3-031-62362-2_17

victims to online scams. Numerous studies on the issue are available (see [2] for a survey), and a number of anti-typosquatting prototypical tools have been proposed in the past, yet no practical and satisfactory solutions that assist users in real-time are currently available to the public.

The contributions of this paper are the following: (i) we show how to combine multiple anti-typosquatting methods into an integrated framework; (ii) we implement our coalescing techniques in an extension for the Chrome browser, called TypoAlert; (iii) besides including our integrated method to detect typosquatted sites, TypoAlert properly manages detections and prompts user intervention only whenever necessary, following the known principle of *least user surprise* [3]; (iv) we assess the good quality of our ensemble techniques on an appropriate corpus of domain names.

Our paper is structured as follows: Sect. 2 presents previous studies on typosquatting and illustrates the necessary background information. Sections 3 presents our typosquatting detection methodology. Section 4 reports about experimental results obtained during the experimental analysis and validation phase. Section 5 draws some conclusions and outline future research directions.

2 Background and Related Work

Cyber-typosquatting may refer to domain name and package typosquatting [4] and to other forms of typosquatting, like mobile app names, social media names, etc. The issue of typosquatting has been a research subject for more than 25 years. Typosquatting remains a widespread and persistent practice, primarily due to the lack of effective solutions to prevent it [1]. We focus on domain name typosquatting, also called, with a slightly different semantic nuance, *URL typosquatting*. Research on the topic can be roughly categorized in: *(i)* general analyses and organizational proposals against the domain typosquatting practice; *(ii)* company-centric anti-typosquatting proposals, oriented towards the perspective of companies concerned with typosquatting attacks against their websites; and *(iii)* user-centric anti-typosquatting research, i.e. solutions conceived to reduce risk of users stumbling upon typosquatted sites while browsing.

General Studies. Edelman [5] conducted an early large-scale study identifying over 8800 registered domains with subtle typographic variations from popular domain names. Over 90% of these domains redirected to sexually explicit content. Originally, domain popularity was thought to correlate with typosquatting risk, implying that less popular domains were less likely to be targeted [6]. However, a later study found a shift in typosquatters' behavior: approximately 95% of typosquatted domains now aim at less popular domains [7]. Numerous scientific investigations into the issue of typosquatting have historically followed a two-phase methodology: *(i)* identification of a set of victim domain names, and *(ii)* generation of a list of potential typosquatted variants based on those identified domain names. Various models for generating typosquatted domains have been proposed. In [8] have been identified five primary models: Missing-dot typos, Character-omission typos, Character-permutation typos, Character-substitution typos, and Character-duplication typos. A subsequent study [9] scrutinized registered domains generated according to each of the five described models, evaluating their saturation. As per [9], the character substitution model is least popular, while the missing-dot model is the most prevalent, with around 70% of generated typosquatted domains registered. This percentage encompasses defensive registrations, where legitimate website owners acquire typosquatted domain names preventively. Existing models were extended by introducing additional approaches in [10]. The proposed generation models rely on edit distance or Levenshtein distance [11,12]. This metric measures the similarity between two strings by determining the minimum number of operations (insertions, deletions, or substitutions) needed to transform one string into another. The Damerau-Levenshtein (DL) distance [13] differs from it by also incorporating the operation of transposition between characters. Research indicates that 99% of typosquatted sites exhibit a DL distance of one from their target domains [2]. Country-code domains like `.it` and `.en` are highly susceptible to typosquatting due to the lack of a Uniform Domain-Name Dispute-Resolution Policy (UDRP), making them appealing to typosquatters for reduced legal consequences. Khan's study [14] investigates user behavior, finding that individuals usually recognize typosquatted domains and redirect to the correct one within about 33 s.

Company and User-Centric Anti-typosquatting Tools. The Strider Typo-Patrol tool [8] detects typosquatting campaigns through a multifaceted approach, including: *(i)* a Typo-Neighborhood Generator for producing potential typo URLs, *(ii)* a Typo-Neighborhood Scanner for active domain analysis, and *(iii)* a Domain-Parking Analyzer for detailed typosquatted domain examination. It also introduced Strider URL Tracer, enabling website owners to monitor typosquatting targeting their sites. An extensive analysis of typosquatting in the `.com` TLD is presented in [7] using the Yet Another Typosquatting Tool (YATT). This analysis includes passive data sources, candidate typo generation, and active analysis, with domain categorization based on DL distance and registration data. In user-centric approaches, the iTrustPage Firefox extension [15] offered automated identification of legitimate web pages via Interactive Page Validation, while the Anti Typosquatting Tool (ATST) [1] featured a User Customized Local Repository for domain monitoring, an Edit-distance Computation Module for typosquatted domain checks, and a User Customized Local Repository Update Module. The Stop URL Typosquatting (SUT) approach [6] addressed the detection of *phony* websites, integrating modules for network-level criteria (SUT-net) and site popularity assessment (SUT-pop). SUT-net evaluates URL features, while SUT-pop assesses domain legitimacy via Google search results. TypoWriter [16] anticipates domain variations using Recurrent Neural Networks trained on DNS logs. Other approaches include dynamic skins for alerting users to counterfeited sites [17]. Unfortunately, these tools are no longer available online.

3 Detection Methodology

We integrate several anti-typosquatting techniques. Given their role in typosquatting operations, we also include also detection features meant identifying *parked domains* i.e. domain name which are registered, yet are not used and/or intended for bad uses. When one visits a parked domain, a chain of redirections might be triggered, which might end in a legitimate site or not. The typosquatting detection process is articulated into three steps: (i) *prefiltering*, (ii) *evaluation* and (iii) *labeling*. Overall we take in input a fully qualified domain name n. After analysis, n is classified, according to its degree of potential danger, into one of the following seven the categories *NotTypo* (n is not a typosquat), *ProbablyNotTypo*, *ProbablyTypo*, *Typo*, *ProbablyTypoPhishing*, *TypoPhishing*, *TypoMalware* according to the score (av) and to the value of the phishing indicator (ph) which are both obtained as outcomes of the evaluation step. The first two steps are performed by Algorithm 1 while the labeling step is detailed in Algorithm 2.

Prefiltering Step. In this step we maintain a blacklist (BL) and a whitelist (WL) of names assumed to be respectively classified as $TypoMalware$ and $NotTypo$. BL is populated using BlackBook [18], a historical and continuously updated blacklist that contains a wide range of domains known for their malicious nature. This blacklist is kept up to date by means of an automated monitoring process based on a set of reliable sources such as WHOIS data, HTTP analysis, and so on. This process takes into account new entries reported on public lists of harmful URLs, including CyberCrime, URLhaus, ScumBots, Bengow, and ViriBack. WL is constructed by joining a custom-built Top Domain Repository (TDR) together with a user-built custom whitelist (User Domain Repository, UDR). The TDR includes domains that can be certifiably considered reliable and authentic. TDR[1] is dynamically built by coalescing the list of the 1000 most visited sites globally and the lists of the 1000 most visited sites for each country [19], for a total of around 32000 domain names. TDR cannot be modified by the user, which can however customize the complementary UDR. The prefiltering step considers the input domain n and searches it within BL first. If $n \in BL$ we give it the maximum alert value, i.e. 7, which will make n as being classified as *TypoMalware*. Let vd be the domain name eventually reached from n after following a potential chain of redirects. If $n \in WL$ or $vd \in WL$ we give to n the minimum alert value, i.e. 0, which will make it as being classified as *NotTypo*. Otherwise, we build a set CT of *candidate targets*. Elements of CT have a *Damerau-Levenshtein* distance 1 from n and are extracted from: *(i)* the elements of WL; *(ii)* the top 10 domain names resulting by querying a search engine with n as the search keyword; *(iii)* whenever available, the domain name *dym* (*"Did you mean?"* domain), i.e. the domain name suggested by the search engine at hand as the inferred correct search keyword.

Evaluation Step. The evaluation starts by computing the Parking Alert (PARKA) indicator which is set to either 0 or 1 according to an analysis based on a set of keyphrases, in different speaking languages, usually present in parked web pages. Then for each element $ct \in CT$ we evaluate the *Top 10 Alert (T10A)* indicator, the *Did You Mean Alert (DYMA)* indicator and the *Phishing Alert*

[1] The TDR used in this work dates back to January 16, 2024

Algorithm 1. Evaluation Algorithm

Input: n, the domain name to analyze
Output: av, an alert value, and ph, a phishing indicator

```
Step 1: Prefiltering phase
av ← 0, ph ← 0
if n ∈ BL then
    av ← 7
    return av, ph
end if
vd ← follow_forward(n)
if n ∈ WL or vd ∈ WL then
    return av, ph
end if
CT ← ∅
for w ∈ WL do
    if DL_d(n, w) = 1 then
        CT ← CT ∪ {w}
    end if
end for
P ← search(n)
if P.dym <> null and DL_d(n, P.dym) = 1 then
    CT ← CT ∪ {P.dym}
end if
for t ∈ P.T10 do
    if DL−distance(n, t) = 1 then
        CT ← CT ∪ {t}
    end if
end for

Step 2: Evaluation phase
PARKA ← evaluate_PARKA(vd, keyphrases)
for ct in CT do
    T10A ← evaluate_T10A(n, ct, P)
    DYMA ← evaluate_DYMA(ct, P)
    PHA ← evaluate_PHA(vd, ct)
    tmpAv ← 2 + PARKA + T10A + DYMA + PHA
    if tmpAv > av then
        (av, ph) ← (tmpAv, PHA)
    end if
end for
return av, ph
```

(PHA) indicator. The T10A indicator is based on searching n as a keyword on a search engine. T10A_{ct} scores 1 if ct appears in the top 10 search engine's results list GL, while n does not. The score of T10A_{ct} is set to -1 if n appears in GL while ct does not. In the other two cases the T10A_{ct} score is set to 0. The *DYMA* indicator leverages the concept of domain popularity based on the search engines suggestions. It uses suggestions coming from a search engine about a possible typing error in n. DYMA_{ct} is set to 1 if n triggers the suggestion of ct in the search engine of choice when searching for n. Otherwise DYMA_{ct} is set to 0. Last, the PHA indicator evaluates how similar is the content of the site associated to n to the content associated to ct. PHA_{ct} is computed using fuzzy hashing [20] and can be either 0 or 1. Overall, we set the alert value

$$av = \begin{cases} 0 & \text{if } n \in WL \\ 7 & \text{if } n \in BL \\ 2 + PARKA + av_{|CT} & \text{otherwise} \end{cases}$$

where $av_{|CT} = \max_{ct \in CT} \{(T10A_{ct} + DYMA_{ct} + PHA_{ct})\}$. Along with av we obtain the phishing alert (ph) value as PHA_{ct^*} where ct^* is one of the arguments for which $av_{|CT}$ is reached and for which PHA is maximal, i.e.

$$ct^* = arg \max_{ct \in CT} \{PHA(ct) | \, T10A_{ct} + DYMA_{ct} + PHA_{ct} = av_{|CT}\}.$$

Algorithm 2. Labeling Algorithm

Input: *av* alert value, *ph* phishing indicator
Output: classification label

```
if av = 0 then
    return "NotTypo"
else if av = 7 then
    return "TypoMalware"
else if av = 1 then
    return "ProbablyNotTypo
else if av = 2 then
    if ph = 1 then
        return "ProbablyTypoPhishing"
    else
        return "ProbablyTypo"
    end if
else                                                    ▷ 3 ≤ av ≤ 6
    if ph = 1 then
        return "TypoPhishing"
    else
        return "Typo"
    end if
end if
```

Finally, we label n according to *av* and *ph* (see Algorithm 2): for $av = 0$, the label is *NotTypo*; for $av = 1$, the label is *ProbablyNotTypo*; for $av = 2$ the label is either *ProbablyTypo* or *ProbablyTypoPhishing* if the value of *ph* is, respectively, 0 or 1; for $av = 7$ the label is *TypoMalware*; for any value $av \in [3, 6]$ we assign either *TypoPhishing* if $ph = 1$ or *Typo* if $ph = 0$.

4 Evaluation

To assess the effectiveness of the classification techniques which TypoAlert[1] is based on, we conducted an evaluation utilizing a purposely constructed dataset, named TS, including a set of potential typosquatted domains. To build the ground truth, each domain $d \in TS$ has been manually analyzed and classified as being or not a typosquatted domain. Then we compared the results with the outcomes achieved by our classifier. To build the TS dataset we started from the set *Top*, comprising the top 1000 websites globally ranked on Google, as per DataForSEO [19]. We extracted a subset $S_{Top} \subset Top$ of 300 domains by uniformly sampling *Top*. Using the open source tool *ail-typo-squatting* [21], for each domain $d \in S_{Top}$ we built a corresponding set $P_1(d)$ containing all domain names having a DL distance from d's name which is equal to 1. Then we extracted a subset $TS(d) \subset P_1(d)$ of all domains names $t \in P_1(d)$ such that *(i)* t was actually registered in a DNS at the time of construction of the dataset and *(ii)* there

[1] TypoAlert is freely available at https://github.com/aleviscomi/typoalert.

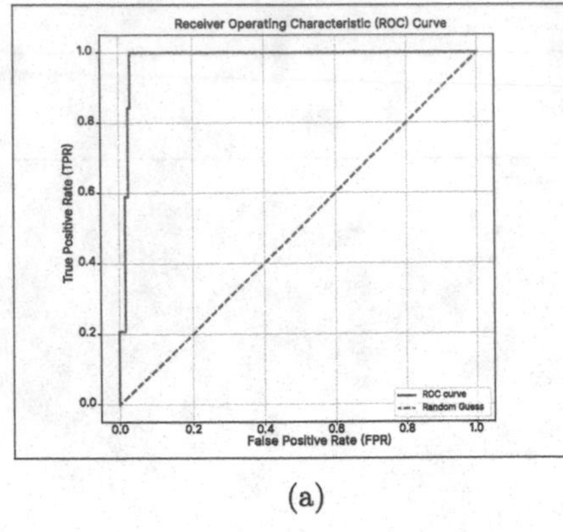

(a)

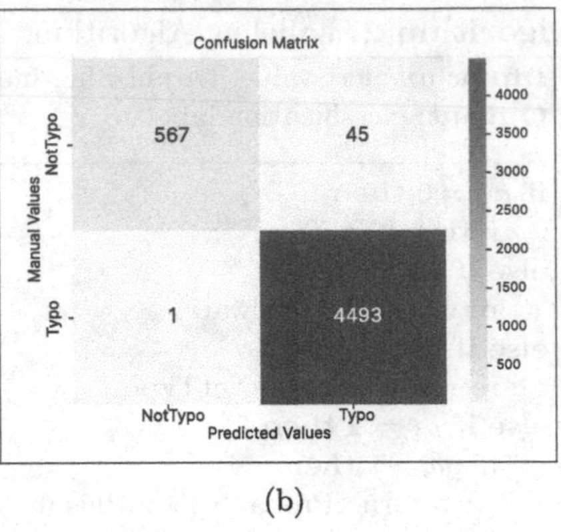

(b)

Fig. 1. (a) ROC curve (b) Confusion matrix

was an active webserver responding (directly on indirectly) to HTTP(S) requests made to t. Finally, we obtained TS as the union $TS = \bigcup_{d \in S_{Top}} TS(d)$. The final dataset TS includes potential 5106 typo domains. During the evaluation phase we conducted an analysis on the tool accuracy and we compared it with ground truth obtained manually. During the manual classification we labelled domains as *(i) Typo*: designated for domains considered malicious, built using typosquatting techniques; *(ii) NotTypo*: assigned to a domain d, belonging to some $TS(d')$, for which d either redirects to the legitimate domain d' or appear to be legitimate itself, with no intention of being a typo domain. To mitigate the role of human subjectivity in manual annotations, we opted for building binary ground truth values. Since our developed tool produces a score value between 0 and 7, data have been validated by mapping our scores to ground truth according to the following methodology. Given a test instance x, let $s(x) = av$ be the ordinal score returned by our tool. Note that we don't take into account whether the PHA_x indicator points to phishing content or not. We consider an aggregation threshold t, for $0 \leq t \leq 7$, and we build a family of binary classifiers each denoted by the two classes $NotTypo_t = \{x \in TS \mid s(x) < t\}$, and $Typo_t = TS \backslash Typo_t$. We thus identified the classifier that maximizes the TPR/FPR Ratio (True positive rate divided by False Positive Rate), which was obtained for $t = 2$ for which we have $TPR = 0.999$ and $FPR = 0.073$. The receiver operation characteristic (ROC) curve shows the trade-off between True Positive Rate and False Positive Rate of each classifier built among various scores threshold, and is shown in Fig. 1a. Figure 1b depicts the confusion matrix for $t = 2$, where 5060 over 5106 domains with a 99.0% of domains correctly classified.

5 Conclusions and Future Work

This paper presents a practical methodology for detecting typosquatted sites, combining some of the known simplest yet provably effective practices implemented in an extension for the Chrome Web browser, which is expected to revitalize the not so live landscape of user-centric initiatives against typosquatting. Our validation proves the effectiveness of the approach, although the challenge of typosquatting remains formidable. In our future work, we plan to enrich our tool with features that tackle typosquatting from an even more user-centric perspective, in the spirit of dynamic skins [17].

References

1. Chen, G., Johnson, M.F., Marupally, P.R., Singireddy, N.K., Yin, X., Paruchuri, V.: Combating typo-squatting for safer browsing. In: AINA Workshops, pp. 31–36 (2009)
2. Spaulding, J., Upadhyaya, S., Mohaisen, A.: The landscape of domain name typosquatting: techniques and countermeasures. In: ARES, pp. 284–289 (2016)
3. Raymond, E.S.: The Art of UNIX Programming. Addison-Wesley Professional Computing Series, Addison-Wesley, Boston (2008)
4. Taylor, M., Vaidya, R., Davidson, D., De Carli, L., Rastogi, V.: Defending against package typosquatting. In: Kutyłowski, M., Zhang, J., Chen, C. (eds.) NSS 2020. LNCS, vol. 12570, pp. 112–131. Springer, Cham (2020). https://doi.org/10.1007/978-3-030-65745-1_7
5. Edelman, B.: Large-scale registration of domains with typographical errors. Harvard University (2003). https://cyber.harvard.edu/archived_content/people/edelman/typo-domains/
6. Banerjee, A., Rahman, M.S., Faloutsos, M.: SUT: quantifying and mitigating URL typosquatting. Comput. Netw. **55**(13), 3001–3014 (2011)
7. Szurdi, J., Kocso, B., Cseh, G., Spring, J., Felegyhazi, M., Kanich, C.: The long "Taile" of typosquatting domain names. In: USENIX Security Symposium 2014, pp. 191–206 (2014)
8. Wang, Y., Beck, D., Wang, J., Verbowski, C., Daniels, B.: Strider typo-patrol: discovery and analysis of systematic typo-squatting. In: SRUTI (2006)
9. Agten, P., Joosen, W., Piessens, F., Nikiforakis, N.: Seven months' worth of mistakes: a longitudinal study of typosquatting abuse. In: NDSS (2015)
10. Banerjee, A., Barman, D., Faloutsos, M., Bhuyan, L.N.: Cyber-fraud is one typo away. In: IEEE INFOCOM, pp. 1939–1947 (2008)
11. Levenshtein, V.I.: Binary codes capable of correcting deletions, insertions, and reversals. Sov. Phys. Dokl. **10**, 707–710 (1965)
12. Damerau, F.J.: A technique for computer detection and correction of spelling errors. Commun. ACM **7**(3), 171–176 (1964)
13. Navarro, G.: A guided tour to approximate string matching. ACM Comput. Surv. **33**(1), 31–88 (2001)
14. Khan, M.T., Huo, X., Li, Z., Kanich, C.: Every second counts: quantifying the negative externalities of cybercrime via typosquatting. In: 2015 IEEE Symposium on Security and Privacy, pp. 135–150 (2015)
15. Ronda, T., Saroiu, S., Wolman, A.: Itrustpage: a user-assisted anti-phishing tool. SIGOPS Oper. Syst. Rev. **42**(4), 261–272 (2008)
16. Ahmad, I., Parvez, M.A., Iqbal, A.: TypoWriter: a tool to prevent typosquatting. In: COMPSAC, vol. 1, pp. 423–432 (2019)
17. Dhamija, R., Tygar, J.D.: The battle against phishing: dynamic security skins. In: SOUPS (2005)

18. Stampar, M.: Blackbook: a historical (black)list of malicious domains. https://github.com/stamparm/blackbook
19. DataForSEO. Top 1000 websites by ranking keywords. https://dataforseo.com/free-seo-stats/top-1000-websites
20. Breitinger, F., Guttman, B., McCarrin, M., Roussev, V., White, D.: Approximate matching: definition and terminology. In: NIST (2014)
21. AIL project. Ail-typo-squatting. https://github.com/typosquatter/ail-typo-squatting

The Programmable World and Its Emerging Privacy Nightmare

Pyry Kotilainen[1(✉)], Ali Mehraj[2], Tommi Mikkonen[1], and Niko Mäkitalo[1]

[1] University of Jyväskylä, Jyväskylä, Finland
{pyry.kotilainen,tommi.j.mikkonen,niko.k.makitalo}@jyu.fi
[2] Tampere University, Tampere, Finland
ali.mehraj@tuni.fi

Abstract. So-called programmable world refers to a paradigm where we are surrounded by intelligent, programmable devices that communicate with each other to support us in our daily activities. Furthermore, these systems are intimately addressing data that we produce and consume, both as such as well as via machine learning (ML) and artificial intelligence (AI). The fashion the data is treated in the network is a subject to regulatory, ethical and privacy concerns, however. In this paper, we study data and ML/AI related privacy concerns that emerge in the context of such programmable world, and how to take them into account when realizing the programmable world vision. In particular, we wish to enable composing systems so that constraints emerging from privacy concerns can be satisfied, but without risking the flexibility when composing complex networked systems, where data related operations are essential.

Keywords: Programmable world · IoT · Internet of Things · Web of Things · privacy · data engineering

1 Introduction

In the past few years, digitalization technologies have seen a significant increase. Processing capabilities have expanded in line with Moore's Law, making cloud computing widely available. The field of data science has flourished due to the increasing amount of data, and even small devices can now connect to high-volume networks. Additionally, artificial intelligence (AI) and machine learning (ML) have become common, even in devices with limited capabilities like mobile phones. These changes are guiding us into what is known as the "Programmable World," where everyday objects are becoming more interconnected, customizable, and programmable [22].

IoT systems, used to realise the programmable world, typically require early function partitioning to nodes constituting the system during development [18]. To make matters more complex, the different parts of the end-to-end IoT systems rely on heterogeneous implementation techniques, including sensors and actuators at the edge, gateways and other computing facilities that connect the edge to the cloud, and various end-user targeted applications that are used to

K. Stefanidis et al. (Eds.): ICWE 2024, LNCS 14629, pp. 255–262, 2024.
https://doi.org/10.1007/978-3-031-62362-2_18

operate the system [18]. Within this network of computational capabilities, data is passed between the nodes, usually from the edge towards the cloud for further processing. In the most common case, data accumulates to a central cloud, where operations related to data are executed. However, lately there has been proposals where these operations are distributed to the cloud-edge continuum, so that not all data need be sent to the central cloud for processing. Instead, nodes close to the edge can perform certain operations independently, so that response times can be met for instance.

While the technical implementation typically follows the same end-to-end architecture, the fashion how functions are allocated to the network is affected by several other factors. As already mentioned, technical constraints such as response times and latency in general are commonly considered when developing IoT systems. However, the situation is far less considered when factors such as regulatory, ethical, and privacy concerns emerge. However, similarly to technical concerns, the above can also restrict how data is transferred and processed in an IoT network, especially in the context of ML/AI.

In this paper, we study privacy related concerns that emerge in the context of such data and ML/AI rich environment, and how to take such concerns into account when realizing the programmable world vision. In particular, we wish to enable composing systems so that constraints emerging from privacy considerations can be satisfied so that the same code can be used. This is achieved by applying isomorphic IoT design [11].

2 Background and Motivation

2.1 Towards the Programmable World

Originally, IoT ideas centered around technologies like RFID and wireless sensor networks. However, in recent times, these concepts have rapidly expanded across various sectors, including healthcare, transportation, energy, and process automation [2]. We envision the future of IoT relying on the capacity to remotely coordinate and program intricate networks of IoT devices [17], resulting in the programmable world. Once devices are connected to public or private clouds, with sensor data flowing in and actuation capabilities being widely available, the focus will shift from sensor data collection and analytics to application-programming capabilities for manipulating complex real-world systems [22].

Applications running in this programmable world require considering issues that do not exist in conventional software development [19]. Such factors include heterogeneity and diversity of devices, intermittent, potentially unreliable and untrustworthy connectivity, and distributed, always-on and nature of the overall system [18].

The inherent heterogeneity means that IoT systems, used to implement the vision of such programmable world implies that many of the subsystems are specified and implemented for a particular role in the system, with little opportunities for relocating a certain function somewhere else in the network. While proposals on so-called isomorphic architectures enabling this have been made (e.g. [11]), they have not been widely deployed in reality. Hence, preallocating functions in IoT systems is the de-facto practice in the development of industry-scale systems.

2.2 Data-Related Concerns in IoT

Identifying privacy concerns affecting partitioning and application deployment is crucial in the initial stages. Because IoT systems require early partitioning of functions, reusing the same implementation (or even technology) across different regulatory, ethical, and privacy contexts can pose challenges.

Addressing privacy and trust challenges in AI development is a growing field of knowledge. Existing studies emphasize concerns like Consent and Transparency, Data Security, Individual Autonomy, and Data Minimization. Notable regulations include the General Data Protection Regulation (GDPR) [21], safeguarding personal data for EU citizens. GDPR mandates explicit consent for data collection, access rights for individuals, and prompt notification of data breaches. Furthermore, as many IoT systems are data-intensive, handling privacy-sensitive data, their design, development, maintenance, and operation processes must also consider data and cybersecurity related legislation. Depending on the type of AI application, the data laws to consider include mentioned above, but also the Data Governance Act (DGA) and the Data Act. Furthermore, the cybersecurity laws to consider include the NIS2 Directive (NIS2) and the Cybersecurity Act (CSA).

In contrast to data related legislation, the EU AI Act [4] oversees the responsible use of AI, ML, and related technologies in the EU. Responsibilities for developers arise, especially for high-risk AI systems, requiring conformity assessments and post-market monitoring. Human intervention capability is essential in AI system design to ensure human decision-making when needed. To summarise, legal and ethical frameworks have a direct impact on how systems can be designed. Moreover, in addition to affecting the design and deployment of AI/ML based systems, this impact needs to be documented and the documentation maintained throughout the life cycle of the system.

With the above regulatory concerns, sharing reliable and trusted data involves meeting several criteria such as efficient processing, privacy preservation, and data ownership. Initiatives like the International Data Spaces Association (IDSA) and GAIA-X have established reference architectures, emphasizing managed access without centralizing data storage. Instead, only catalogs are centralized, while data sources remain under the control of providers.

Data often requires substantial preprocessing tailored to specific needs, and sources are frequently linked before use. The dynamic nature of data sources, with new additions, complicates the processing ecosystem. A common preprocessing task involves filtering data, removing irrelevant information, and addressing privacy concerns through techniques like anonymization, merging, or summing.

Machine learning is a prevalent use case, where data is used for training but may be restricted beyond organizational boundaries. When using a trained model, data owners might permit its input for a specific machine learning model, with only the inference results shared.

In summary, the need to move computation close to data arises, requiring an architecture and platform that facilitates distributed computation across different data sources. This ensures that various parts of applications are placed near relevant data sources and orchestrated reliably for a common objective. In addition, regulatory concerns must be met.

3 Building Blocks and Design Goals

3.1 Design Goals

Based on the above, to build systems that comply with the programmable world vision, there are two key goals to address:

G1: Data related functions, including ML/AI features, can be flexibly located to form a functioning IoT network, so that privacy requirements can be met;
G2: It is possible to validate that data processing is compliant to privacy requirements, both at design and at run-time.

In other words, instead of preallocating functions to different nodes in the networks, we should be able to flexibly define their locations at a relatively late phase in the design and development. To accomplish this, all data should provide information about the essential restrictions that they are subjected to, so that these can be used as criteria for functional partitioning. This has been illustrated in Fig. 1.

3.2 Building Blocks and Existing Technologies

Isomorphic IoT Systems. We support the adoption of isomorphic IoT systems, promoting consistency in technology use across the entire system for simplified development [11]. These systems aim to create a seamless continuum from edge devices to the cloud, using uniform technologies for programming various subsystems. Although fully isomorphic IoT systems are not yet a reality, their emergence could blur distinctions between the cloud and edge, allowing computations to optimize performance, storage, network speed, latency, and energy efficiency.

Isomorphic architectures find application in liquid software, facilitating on-the-fly migration of software between computers for flexible application configurations [6,7,20]. This contrasts with rigid architectures associated with conventional technologies [18].

To deploy isomorphic software across the cloud-edge continuum, a runtime environment is crucial. Our prior research utilized WebAssembly [15] for this purpose, enabling diverse programming languages while effectively mapping everything to the WebAssembly virtual machine. This virtual machine can integrate into various nodes in the cloud-edge spectrum, offering flexible code execution.

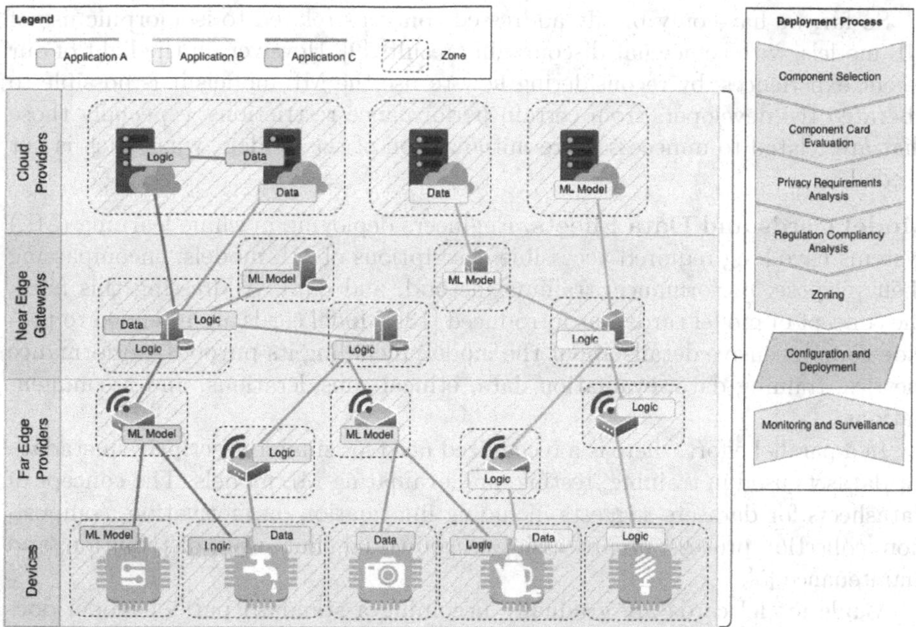

Fig. 1. Overview of privacy concerns, and their role in function partitioning in an IoT network.

This flexibility empowers orchestration based on factors like energy consumption, communication bandwidth, performance, and memory requirements, allowing adaptable executions in different configurations at different times [8].

Liquid Software and LiquidAI. As the number of computing devices has grown, it has become necessary for users to run the same software on several devices simultaneously. While traditional software is unable to save the data or state, liquid software enables users to resume their activity on the application across multiple devices by synchronizing the user interface. data, and state [7, 12,20]. As Liquid software necessitates synchronization of data and state across all participating devices, the question of what and how much data can be shared among devices emerges. This concerns the aforementioned EU AI Act and the GDPR regulations.

Building on the concept of Liquid software, the LiquidAI outlined in [16] promises to streamline development efforts by enabling flexible, dynamic, and decentralized deployment of intelligent functions across the entire cloud-edge continuum. This is accomplished by employing a compatible set of technologies in all subsystems, allowing different parts of the system to execute the same code isomorphically as described above. This way, ML models, which play a crucial role in many contemporary IoT applications, can be flexibly allocated in different nodes. Our early results suggest that this leads to new types of privacy concerns [1].

So far, we have only briefly addressed concerns related to isomorphic use of ML models, with somewhat discouraging results [9]. However, in the light of our recent experiences, by reconsidering how to use the ML models it is possible to liberated the developers from certain performance restrictions, especially those that are related to unnecessary re-initialization of the models, when such is not needed.

Model Cards and Data Sheets. Engineers deploying machine learning (ML) systems have long required accessible descriptions of ML models, encompassing their purpose, performance, training method, and data. Addressing this need, the concept of model cards was introduced [13]. Model cards are intended to provide comprehensive details about the model, including its purpose, performance metrics, training data, evaluation data, ethical considerations, and recommendations.

In a parallel effort, there is a recognized need for similar descriptive metadata for datasets used in training, testing, and evaluating ML models. The concept of datasheets for datasets suggests including information on motivation, composition, collection process, preprocessing, cleaning, labeling, uses, distribution, and maintenance [5].

While model cards are gradually becoming a standard part of model documentation, their format is still evolving. Conversely, the standardization of metadata formats for datasets is at an earlier stage. It is crucial to acknowledge that neither the suggested model nor dataset metadata explicitly addresses legal requirements such as the model risk level outlined in the EU AI Act or data privacy concerns covered by the GDPR mentioned above.

Moreover, there is a notable absence of research on defining a metadata format for live data sources, including live databases used for model inference/training or sensor data streams. The lack of such metadata poses challenges for engineers in making informed decisions about system architecture.

Trusted device coalitions. An approach of Human Data Models (HDM) for Internet of Bodies (IoB) devices was introduced where different IoB devices can synchronize user data and create temporary HDM instances. These instances can be generated and removed as needed, and the data within them is destroyed alongside the temporary HDM instance [14]. An Action-Oriented Programming (AcOP) model approach was introduced that incorporates coalition between trusted devices for sharing and processing data under a secure network to execute operations in tandem [10]. Furthermore, there are scenarios of dealing with chains of coalition across multiple devices throughout different stages of data sharing when dealing with systems of systems (SoS). One solution implemented a contract based approach that specify data-sharing conditions to ensure data privacy and security [3]. With sensitive user data moving across different devices, this raises the matter of concern to ensure that the data stays only within the predefined sets of trusted devices alongside following the guidelines of EU AI Act and GDPR regulations.

4 Conclusions and Open Questions

The emerging programmable world vision is making things around us intelligent, thereby using and producing data that often is private and confidential in its nature. At the same time, the dominant, cloud-centric architecture of today implies that the data is sent to a vendor-specific cloud for analysis, decision making, and storage.

While dominant, this model is not optimal for several reasons. Our analysis of the current situation of the programming world and data processing indicates the need for new types of solutions and approaches that correspond to the EU AI Act and GDPR guidelines.

Given the recent developments in data sharing between IoT, IoB, and mobile devices, data processing, data sharing techniques, or approaches must fulfill the aforementioned guidelines for data movement. This calls for defining a strategy on how to organize data processing when data moves and changes across devices. Furthermore, one must take into account that solutions that work today may not be appropriate in the future due to the nature of the ever-changing regulations. Therefore, a practical approach is needed that helps adopting to changing regulations on the fly, optimally so that the system remains operational.

Acknowledgments. This work has been supported by Business Finland (projects LiquidAI (8542/31/2022) and 6G Soft (8541/31/2022)).

References

1. Agbese, M.O., Mäkitalo, N., Waseem, M., Mohanani, R., Abrahamsson, P., Mikkonen, T.: Examining privacy and trust issues at the edge of isomorphic IoT architectures: case liquid AI. In: Workshop on Security and Safety for Intelligent Unmanned Autonomous Systems (2023)
2. Al-Fuqaha, A., Guizani, M., Mohammadi, M., Aledhari, M., Ayyash, M.: Internet of things: a survey on enabling technologies, protocols, and applications. IEEE Commun. Surv. Tutor. **17**(4), 2347–2376 (2015)
3. Daubaris, P., et al.: Explainability with observation sharing in long collaboration chains of automated systems of systems. IEEE Softw. **41**(1), 74–86 (2024)
4. Edwards, L.: The EU AI act: a summary of its significance and scope. Artif. Intell. (the EU AI Act) **1** (2021)
5. Gebru, T., et al.: Datasheets for datasets (2021)
6. Hartman, J., Manber, U., Peterson, L., Proebsting, T.: Liquid software: a new paradigm for networked systems. Technical report 96 (1996)
7. Hartman, J.J., et al.: Joust: a platform for liquid software. Computer **32**(4), 50–56 (1999)
8. Kotilainen, P., et al.: WebAssembly in IoT: Beyond toy examples. WebAssembly in IoT: beyond toy examples. In: Garrigos, I., Murillo Rodriguez, J.M., Wimmer, M. (eds.) Web Engineering. ICWE 2023. LNCS, vol. 13893, pp. 93–100. Springer, Cham (2023). https://doi.org/10.1007/978-3-031-34444-2_7
9. Kotilainen, P., Heikkilä, V., Systä, K., Mikkonen, T.: Towards liquid AI in IoT with webassembly: a prototype implementation. In: Younas, M., Awan, I., Gronli, T.M.

(eds.) Mobile Web and Intelligent Information Systems. MobiWIS 2023. LNCS, vol. 13977, pp. 129–141. Springer, Cham (2023). https://doi.org/10.1007/978-3-031-39764-6_9
10. Makitalo, N., Ometov, A., Kannisto, J., Andreev, S., Koucheryavy, Y., Mikkonen, T.: Safe and secure execution at the network edge: a framework for coordinating cloud, fog, and edge. IEEE Softw. 1 (2018)
11. Mikkonen, T., Pautasso, C., Taivalsaari, A.: Isomorphic Internet of Things architectures with web technologies. Computer **54**(7), 69–78 (2021)
12. Mikkonen, T., Systä, K., Pautasso, C.: Towards liquid web applications. In: Cimiano, P., Frasincar, F., Houben, G.-J., Schwabe, D. (eds.) ICWE 2015. LNCS, vol. 9114, pp. 134–143. Springer, Cham (2015). https://doi.org/10.1007/978-3-319-19890-3_10
13. Mitchell, M., et al.: Model cards for model reporting. In: Proceedings of the Conference on Fairness, Accountability, and Transparency. ACM, January 2019. https://doi.org/10.1145/3287560.3287596
14. Mäkitalo, N., et al.: The internet of bodies needs a human data model. IEEE Internet Comput. **24**(5), 28–37 (2020). https://doi.org/10.1109/MIC.2020.3019920
15. Rossberg, A.: WebAssembly Core Specification. https://www.w3.org/TR/wasm-core-2/. Accessed 09 Dec 2022
16. Systä, K., Pautasso, C., Taivalsaari, A., Mikkonen, T.: LiquidAI: towards an isomorphic AI/ML system architecture for the cloud-edge continuum. In: Garrigos, I., Murillo Rodriguez, J.M., Wimmer, M. (eds.) Web Engineering. ICWE 2023. LNCS, vol. 13893, pp. 67–74. Springer, Cham (2023). https://doi.org/10.1007/978-3-031-34444-2_5
17. Taivalsaari, A., Mikkonen, T.: A roadmap to the programmable world: software challenges in the IoT era. IEEE Softw. **34**(1), 72–80 (2017)
18. Taivalsaari, A., Mikkonen, T.: On the development of IoT systems. In: 2018 Third International Conference on Fog and Mobile Edge Computing (FMEC), pp. 13–19. IEEE (2018)
19. Taivalsaari, A., Mikkonen, T., Pautasso, C.: Towards seamless IoT device-edge-cloud continuum: In: Bakaev, M., Ko, I.-Y., Mrissa, M., Pautasso, C., Srivastava, A. (eds.) ICWE 2021. CCIS, vol. 1508, pp. 82–98. Springer, Cham (2022). https://doi.org/10.1007/978-3-030-92231-3_8
20. Taivalsaari, A., Mikkonen, T., Systä, K.: Liquid software manifesto: the era of multiple device ownership and its implications for software architecture. In: 2014 IEEE 38th Annual Computer Software and Applications Conference, pp. 338–343. IEEE (2014)
21. Voigt, P., Von dem Bussche, A.: The EU General Data Protection Regulation (GDPR). A Practical Guide, 1st edn., vol. 10, no. 3152676, pp. 10–5555. Springer, Cham (2017). https://doi.org/10.1007/978-3-319-57959-7
22. Wasik, B.: In the Programmable World, All Our Objects Will Act as One. Wired (2013). http://www.wired.com/2013/05/internet-of-things-2/. Accessed 13 Oct 2020

Users' Behavior and User-Generated Content

Weakly-Supervised Left-Center-Right Context-Aware Aspect Category and Sentiment Classification

Gonem Lau, Flavius Frasincar(✉), and Finn van der Knaap

Erasmus University Rotterdam, Burgemeester Oudlaan 50, 3062 PA Rotterdam, The Netherlands
gonemlau@gmail.com, frasincar@ese.eur.nl, 573834fk@student.eur.nl

Abstract. Aspect-Based Sentiment Analysis (ABSA) aims to extract all aspects mentioned in a Web review and classify the aspect category and sentiment for each aspect. Most existing methods rely on single-task supervised approaches. However, ABSA tasks are not independent. Furthermore, obtaining labeled data might be difficult or expensive. The Context-aware Aspect category and Sentiment Classification (CASC) model addresses this issue by classifying categories and sentiments simultaneously using a weakly-supervised approach. However, CASC uses a simple neural network on the input text that does not exploit any other information. This paper proposes an extension named Left-Center-Right+CASC (LCR+CASC), where we implement a sophisticated neural model that exploits the location of explicit aspect expressions. Besides aspect categorization and sentiment classification, LCR+CASC also extracts target expressions from a sentence, which goes beyond CASC's abilities. This paper conducts two experiments on restaurant reviews: extracting target expressions and using annotated data that provide targets to evaluate the proposed model. Results show that LCR+CASC outperforms CASC when targets are given, and is able to extract target expressions to some extent.

Keywords: Aspect-based sentiment analysis · Weakly-supervised learning · Neural network

1 Introduction

With virtually everyone having access to the social Web, it is not unthinkable that vast amounts of text could be written every second of every day. It is not feasible to manually analyze everything. Therefore, many methods in the field of Natural Language Processing (NLP) have been proposed to extract information from textual data. One popular subfield, sentiment analysis, is about discovering and understanding opinions from user-generated data [11]. Companies can improve their products or services after analyzing customer sentiments from reviews. Furthermore, reviews are also valuable for consumers, as reviews can help customers with decision-making.

K. Stefanidis et al. (Eds.): ICWE 2024, LNCS 14629, pp. 265–280, 2024.
https://doi.org/10.1007/978-3-031-62362-2_19

This paper focuses on ABSA, which aims to extract all aspects of a product or service mentioned in a review and classify the sentiment for each aspect [11]. However, in practice, the task is not strictly defined. Some datasets provide aspect categories, whereas others provide targets, in which targets are the explicit aspect expressions found in a sentence. Sentiment classification can also differ per dataset. For example, the SemEval 2015 [13] and SemEval 2016 [12] datasets define sentiment as positive, neutral, or negative, while the Yelp 2014 dataset [14] ranks sentiment from 1 to 5.

In more detail, targets could be described with one or multiple aspect categories, and optionally with the aspect term(s). Sentiments could be described with the sentiment polarity and with the opinion term(s). Therefore, ABSA could be divided into four subtasks: Aspect Term Extraction (ATE), Aspect Category Detection (ACD), Opinion Term Extraction (OTE), and Aspect Sentiment Classification (ASC) [19]. ATE extracts explicit aspect expressions in a text, whereas ACD categorizes the aspects. OTE extracts explicit opinion terms and ASC predicts the sentiment polarity. The main focus of this paper is ACD/ASC.

Even though ABSA is not confined to a single task, most methods address only one task. The LCR-Rot-hop++ model [15] exploits the position of a target for ASC but does not perform ATE or ACD. Some efforts have been made to create a multi-task model by considering a set of interrelated dependencies. An example is the Context-aware Aspect category and Sentiment Classification (CASC) model [9] which is a weakly-supervised approach to ACD and ASC. CASC follows a three-step process. First, class vocabularies for aspect and sentiment categories are constructed using only seed words. Second, unlabeled data is turned into labeled data using weak supervision. Third, a multi-task neural model performs ACD and ASC using a simple layer on top of BERT [2].

In this paper, inspired by the work in [9], we propose a weakly-supervised method for ABSA. The model, called Left-Center-Right+CASC (LCR+CASC), uses a more sophisticated neural model, LCR-Rot-hop++ [15], in the third step. Furthermore, LCR-Rot-hop++ was originally constructed to only perform ASC, whereas we also explore the performance of LCR-Rot-hop++ for ACD. Last, we modify the second step of CASC to also perform ATE. We evaluate the model using the SemEval datasets [12,13]. The implementation is based on code provided in [9] in Python and made freely available at https://github.com/Gogonemnem/LCR-PLUS-CASC (including aspect/sentiment seed words).

The contributions of this work can be summarized as follows. First, we adapt the classification layer of the CASC model. The linear layer is replaced by the sophisticated LCR-Rot-hop++ model. Therefore, positional information is exploited unlike in the simple linear layer. Second, we explore the performance of LCR-Rot-hop++ for the ACD task. The original model is only able to perform ASC. Therefore, inter-dependent information between ACD and ASC is exploited by employing multi-task learning. Third, we extend CASC by extracting aspect terms in the second step. Therefore, the model is able to perform ATE indirectly besides ACD and ASC. Fourth, we analyze the performance of our model on restaurant reviews. While the results are subpar with the state-of-the-art when using the targets detected by the ATE task, when using the gold targets the proposed method beats the state-of-the-art for both ACD and ASC (the main focus of this paper).

The rest of the paper is structured as follows. Section 2 provides an overview of related work. Next, Sect. 3 describes the datasets used for the analysis. Then, Sect. 4 explains the proposed model. In Sect. 5, the performance of the proposed model is compared with a state-of-the-art approach. Last, we present concluding remarks in Sect. 6 together with suggestions for future research.

2 Related Work

This section presents an overview of previous work. First, Subsect. 2.1 gives an overview of methods that solve single tasks in ABSA. The OTE task is not discussed as we do not extract opinion expressions in this paper. Then, Subsect. 2.2 shows recent progress in solving multiple subtasks using multi-task learning.

2.1 Single-Task ABSA

Aspect Term Extraction. While supervised approaches yield impressive results, they often require large labeled datasets. The neural models are often not bottlenecked by their simplicity but rather by the available data [6], which motivates the latest trend of un- and semi-supervised models. [3] proposes the Attention-based Aspect Extraction (ABAE) model which de-emphasizes irrelevant words through an attention mechanism to improve the coherence of extracted aspects.

Aspect Category Detection. A big difference between ACD and ATE is that no explicit aspect expressions have to be in a sentence for ACD. For example, "It's expensive and gross" could be categorized in the categories "price" and "food", whereas ATE cannot identify what is being reviewed. Semi-supervised machine learning approaches often consist of first applying ATE and, subsequently, ACD on those aspect terms. In other words, sentences without targets cannot be categorized. First, candidate aspect terms are extracted. Then, those candidate terms are mapped or clustered to pre-defined aspect categories. An example of a semi-supervised ACD method is ABAE. One drawback of this model is that the learned aspects need to be mapped manually. Therefore, [7] proposes a teacher-student framework that extends the ABAE model by leveraging seed words, which eliminates the need to manually assign the learned aspects.

Aspect Sentiment Classification. Although many methods have been proposed for supervised ASC [19], unsupervised ASC has not seen much progress. Data can be provided in two different ways (aspect term data or category data).

Differences are subtle, but one interesting difference is that positional information can be exploited with aspect term data. For example, LCR-Rot [21] exploits this information by splitting sentences into a left context, a target, and a right context. Many extensions of the LCR-Rot model have been proposed [15,16].

2.2 Multi-task ABSA

Early studies in unsupervised learning that jointly extract aspects and sentiments are mostly based on Latent Dirichlet Allocation (LDA) [1]. [18] proposes the Joint Aspect/Sentiment (JAS) model which adapts LDA by introducing sentiment-related variables and integrating sentiment prior knowledge. [20] further extracts aspect-specific opinions in a generative process.

Recent studies propose weakly-supervised methods for the compound task. [22] introduces the Joint Aspect-Sentiment Analysis (JASA) which extends the ABAE model to learn aspect/sentiment representations. Furthermore, the authors make use of multi-task learning by letting the aspect and sentiment representations interact. Therefore, aspect-specific opinions (such as delicious for the food category) are learned. [6] proposes the Joint Aspect Sentiment (JASen) model. First, the model learns joint topic embeddings. Then, neural layers pre- and self-train through embedding-based predictions, which generalize the word-level discriminative information on unlabeled data.

More recently, [9] proposes the CASC model. The CASC model turns unlabeled data into noisy labeled data. Then, neural models are trained on the noisy labeled data. The process of turning unlabeled data into labeled data is only weakly supervised and requires a small number of seed words per aspect/sentiment category, which turns into a full-fledged vocabulary list.

3 Data

To train the proposed model, we use the Yelp dataset [6], which consists of 17,027 unlabeled review sentences. This dataset is chosen as it resides in the restaurant domain just like our evaluation datasets. Furthermore, the Yelp dataset is much larger compared to the SemEval datasets [12,13].

The datasets used for evaluation are the SemEval 2015 [13] and SemEval 2016 [12] datasets. Specifically, this paper focuses on restaurant reviews. Each review consists of at least one sentence, and each sentence contains the sentiment on at least one aspect. The sentiment can either be positive, neutral, or negative.

First, we remove aspect targets that belong to multiple aspect categories due to limitations in our model. Similar to [6] and [9], neutral sentiment polarities are ignored. This is because it is inherently ambiguous to classify neutral sentiment, making it difficult to bootstrap our algorithm with a set of neutral seed words. Moreover, aspect categories are more general than the original SemEval datasets and only contain the categories: food, place, and service. [9] merged the food and drink SemEval categories into the food category, and the ambiance and location SemEval categories into the place category. Furthermore, the authors removed sentences containing multiple aspects. For our first experiment, where we extract aspect target expressions, we also remove sentences with multiple aspects as our model can only extract one aspect per sentence. However, we keep sentences with multiple aspects for the second experiment, where we do not perform ATE. Another difference compared to [9] is that sentences with implicit targets are not considered in this research due to limitations in our model.

Table 1 shows the full and processed SemEval datasets. After all pre-processing steps, datasets that consider multi-labeled data keep around 60% of the data, whereas singly-labeled data keep less than 30% of the original size.

Table 1. Descriptive statistics of the SemEval 2015 and SemEval 2016 datasets

Dataset	Positive		Negative		Food		Place		Service		Total
	Freq.	%	Freq.	%	Freq.	%	Freq.	%	Freq.	%	Freq.
SemEval 2015 - Full	454	54%	346	41%	365	43%	305	36%	175	21%	845
SemEval 2016 - Full	611	71%	204	24%	429	50%	275	32%	155	18%	859
SemEval 2015 Single label - Gold	127	59%	90	41%	106	49%	66	30%	45	21%	217
SemEval 2015 Multi label - Gold	298	64%	166	36%	250	54%	115	25%	99	21%	464
SemEval 2016 Single label - Gold	194	80%	48	20%	115	48%	82	34%	45	19%	242
SemEval 2016 Multi label - Gold	450	81%	104	19%	310	56%	139	25%	105	19%	554

4 Methodology

This section discusses the proposed model. First, Subsect. 4.1 formulates the problem and introduces general notation. Then, Subsect. 4.2 explains the modified CASC model in detail. Last, Subsect. 4.3 explains the training setup.

4.1 Task Formulation

Let the input be a corpus $\mathcal{D} = [X_1, X_2, \ldots, X_n]$ consisting of n unlabeled review sentences from a domain. Given the set of aspect categories A together with a small list of seed words L_a for each aspect category $a \in A$, and sentiment polarities S along with a small list of seed words L_s for each sentiment polarity $s \in S$, the objective is to predict a pair of (a, s) for an unseen review sentence.

Because words are difficult to work with, word embeddings are often used. In this study, Domain Knowledge BERT (DK-BERT) [17] is used. DK-BERT is a post-trained version of BERT [2] that has been trained on domain data, which in this case is the restaurant review data provided by Yelp [6].

4.2 Modified CASC

This section describes the CASC model with our modifications in detail. In the first step, class vocabularies for aspect and sentiment categories are constructed through contextual embeddings using only seed words. Second, unlabeled data is turned into labeled data in a weakly-supervised manner using overlap scores.

Third, a simple neural model with a linear layer is replaced with a more sophisticated model to perform ACD and ASC.

Class Vocabulary Construction. Given a set of seed words L_a corresponding to aspect $a \in A$, we find the set of sentences $X_a \subset \mathcal{D}$ that contain any of the seed words. Then, sentence $X_i \in X_a$ is passed through the post-trained DK-BERT Masked Language Model (DK-BERT MLM). DK-BERT MLM outputs token replacement probability scores $P_i \in \mathbb{R}^{|X_i| \times |V|}$, with V being the vocabulary set used by DK-BERT. However, only replacement candidates of tokens that represent seed words are considered. Next, those replacement candidates are passed through a filter to remove stop words and punctuation. Then, the top K words are selected as replacement candidates R_i based on the probability scores computed by DK-BERT MLM. All replacement candidates R_i for all $X_i \in X_a$ are collected and added to a frequency table for all $a \in A$. Subsequently, the top M most frequent words for aspect category a are selected to construct the aspect vocabulary V_a. Last, words that appear in multiple vocabularies are removed in all sets. A similar procedure is used to construct the sentiment vocabularies V_s for all $s \in S$.

The intuition behind these steps is that words within a sentence can be replaced by words that carry a similar contextual meaning. DK-BERT MLM is trained to provide such replacement candidates, such that the words outputted will have a similar meaning as the seed words. Furthermore, the vocabulary sets are disjoint sets to remove ambiguities across aspect and sentiment classes.

Labeled Data Preparation. Following the work from [5], the CASC model exploits the notion of aspect terms to be nouns and opinion terms to be adjectives or adverbs. Therefore, nouns, adjectives, and adverbs are extracted using a Part-of-Speech tagger as *potential-aspects* and *potential-opinions*.

First, we find the set of all sentences $X_q \subset \mathcal{D}$ which contain at least one *potential-aspect* and one *potential-opinion*. Then, sentence $X_j \in X_q$ is passed through the post-trained DK-BERT MLM to find replacement candidates with probability scores for each *potential-aspect*. Then, the list G_{aspect} is created by taking the top K replacement words based on the probability scores. For sentence X_j, we find the overlap score S_a of each aspect $a \in A$ by counting the common words between its corresponding aspect vocabulary V_a and the list G_{aspect}. Overlap scores for all sentences X_q with all aspect categories A are stored in the score matrix $\mathcal{M} \in \mathbb{R}^{|X_q| \times |A|}$.

The vocabularies in the previous step are created with DK-BERT, which is post-trained using a real-world domain-specific dataset. [9] argues that these datasets are often imbalanced, which could imply that certain vocabularies contain a relatively large number of semantically coherent words compared to other vocabularies. This difference could affect the variance of the overlap scores per category. Therefore, the overlap scores per category are standardized.

For sentence X_j, the aspect category is assigned if the standardized score is the largest and above a pre-defined threshold λ. A similar procedure is applied for sentiment categories. Next, a labeled dataset $\mathcal{D}_{\mathcal{L}} \subset \mathcal{D}$ is constructed.

In contrast to the original CASC model, we also extract aspect terms in this step. During the aspect labeling process, each aspect label a is assigned an aspect term for each sentence X_j. When the aspect label is decided, the corresponding aspect term is assigned to the sentence. There are many methods for assigning aspect target expressions. An approach could be to identify noun chunks [4] and select chunks with the highest scores. Noun chunk scores can be computed in various ways. One example is to take the average of the overlap score among all nouns in the noun chunk. CASC uses a so-called average score labeler, whereas our proposed model uses a maximum score labeler. An average score labeler computes the average overlap score for all *potential-aspects* in a sentence, per aspect category. A maximum score labeler labels sentences based on the aspect target expression. Therefore, the labeling is done by using the *potential-aspect* (which becomes the aspect target expression) that has the highest overlap score in a sentence.

Joint Neural Network for ACD and ASC. In the original CASC model, the authors used a simple yet effective neural model to classify aspects and sentiments. The authors make use of DK-BERT embeddings. We refer to [9] for additional information about the original joint neural network.

However, aspect term positions are not exploited in this neural model. Therefore, we suggest using the LCR-Rot-hop++ model [15]. We propose the double task variant of the model to exploit inter-dependent information between ACD and ASC. This sophisticated model exploits positional information by using three Bidirectional Long Short Term Memory (BiLSTM) layers. Furthermore, two types of attention mechanisms are implemented in an iterative manner to exploit local and global contexts. The LCR-Rot model [21] was originally built for ASC. Therefore, a slight modification is made to also perform ACD.

We apply DK-BERT to generate embeddings. Then, sentence X_l is split into a left context, a target, and a right context of lengths L, T, and R, respectively. Moreover, the contexts are represented as $X_l^l = (w_1^l, \ldots, w_L^l)$, $X_l^t = (w_1^t, \ldots, w_T^t)$, and $X_l^r = (w_1^r, \ldots, w_R^r)$, where w_i^j represents the ith word in context j. To ensure that each context will have the same number of tokens, padding tokens $[PAD]$ are added if the context lacks tokens. Furthermore, contexts are truncated if there are too many tokens. Then, $[CLS]$ token is added at the beginning and separation tokens $[SEP]$ are added between the contexts and target to easily find the token length of each context. Note that the special tokens $[CLS]$ and $[SEP]$ are ignored after embedding. Therefore, the embeddings of a sentence are expressed as $H^l \in \mathbb{R}^{L \times d}$, $H^t \in \mathbb{R}^{T \times d}$, and $H^r \in \mathbb{R}^{R \times d}$. Next, each embedding part feeds separate BiLSTM layers which produce hidden states $B^l = (b_1^l, \ldots, b_L^l)$, $B^t = (b_1^t, \ldots, b_T^t)$, and $B^r = (b_1^r, \ldots, b_R^r)$.

Then, a three-step attention mechanism is iteratively applied over the three hidden states. The first and second attention mechanisms are rotary attention mechanisms that exploit local information, whereas the third is a hierarchical attention mechanism that exploits global information. First, new left and right context representations are generated by using old target information. Second, two new target representations are generated by using the context representations produced in the first step. Third, the representations are updated based on relative importance separately for context and target. The mathematical details are presented below.

First, an attention mechanism is applied. The new context representations are weighted sums of the hidden states of each context:

$$r^c = B^{c\top} \times \alpha^c, \tag{1}$$

$$\alpha^c = \mathrm{softmax}\left(f\left(B^c, r^{t_c}\right)\right), \tag{2}$$

$$f\left(B^c, r^{t_c}\right) = \tanh\left(B^{c\top} \times W^c \times r^{t_c} + b^c \times \mathbf{1}\right), \tag{3}$$

where c denotes the left or right context $\{l, r\}$ consisting of C words. Note that C equals either L or R. Furthermore, $B^c \in \mathbb{R}^{C \times 2d}$ corresponds to the hidden states for context c, and $\alpha^c \in \mathbb{R}^C$ denotes the attention weights assigned to each hidden state. Then, t_c denotes the left or right target $\{t_l, t_r\}$ consisting of T words. Furthermore, $r^{t_c} \in \mathbb{R}^{2d}$ corresponds to the target representation of target side c, and $\mathbf{1} \in \mathbb{R}^C$ denotes a vector of ones. Then, the trainable parameters are the weight matrix $W^c \in \mathbb{R}^{2d \times 2d}$ and the bias scalar $b^c \in \mathbb{R}$. Unfortunately, the first iteration has no old target information. Therefore, $r^{t_c} \in \mathbb{R}^{2d}$ is extracted using the average pooling operator. In other iterations, target representations r^{t_c}, which are computed in step two, are used.

Second, another attention mechanism is applied to generate the left and right target representations. Two target representations are generated to exploit context representations separately. Thus, the left target representation uses the left context, and the right target representation the right context. The computations are similar to Eq. 1, 2, and 3. However, the c's and t_c's are swapped in this step, thus changing dimensions containing size C to T, and vice versa.

Third, a hierarchical attention mechanism is applied to exploit global information. Intuitively, the mechanism decides whether the left or right context provides more relevant information about the target. The left and right contexts are scaled with respect to each other. Furthermore, the left and right targets are scaled as well, but separately from the contexts. The computations are as follows:

$$\hat{r}^p = \alpha^{p\top} \times I_2 \times r^p, \tag{4}$$

$$\alpha^p = \mathrm{softmax}\left(f\left(r^p\right)\right), \tag{5}$$

$$f\left(r^p\right) = \tanh\left(r^p \times W^p + b^p \times \mathbf{1}\right), \tag{6}$$

where $r^p \in \mathbb{R}^{2 \times 2d}$ denotes the vertically concatenated contexts $[r^l; r^r]$ or targets $[r^{t_l}; r^{t_r}]$ decided by p. $I_2 \in \mathbb{R}^{2 \times 2}$ denotes the identity matrix. Then, $\alpha^p \in \mathbb{R}^2$

denotes the attention weight vector assigned to each representation. The trainable parameters are the weight vector $W^p \in \mathbb{R}^{2d}$ and the bias scalar $b^p \in \mathbb{R}$.

Last, all four representation vectors are horizontally concatenated and feed a dense layer with a softmax function and bias vector for sentiment prediction. However, the original model does not classify aspect categories. Therefore, we extend the LCR-Rot-hop++ model. Modifying this neural model is inspired by the CASC model. Instead of passing the sequence representation through a single layer, two dense layers are instantiated for the ACD and ASC tasks, respectively. The ASC branch is the same as before. The difference for the ACD task is that its layer has its own weight matrix and bias vector.

4.3 Training Setup

This section discusses the training setup of the neural model. First, we present the loss function. Then, we discuss the hyperparameters and how we optimize them.

Training Procedure. The model minimizes a General Cross Entropy (GCE) function, which exploits both the Categorical Cross Entropy (CCE) and Mean Absolute Error (MAE). CCE converges quickly but overfits to noise, while MAE is robust to noise but converges slowly. It has been shown that GCE performs better than CCE [9], as the dataset is semi-automatically labeled which introduces noise while annotating. In short, GCE de-emphasizes difficult samples compared to CCE but accentuates them more than MAE during training. The unregularized overall loss $\mathcal{L}$ is the sum of the aspect category classification loss $\mathcal{L}_a$ and sentiment polarity classification loss $\mathcal{L}_s$, which are defined as follows:

$$\mathcal{L}_a = (1 - \hat{a}^q_{y_a})/q, \tag{7}$$

$$\mathcal{L}_s = (1 - \hat{s}^q_{y_s})/q, \tag{8}$$

where $\hat{a}_{y_a}$ and $\hat{s}_{y_s}$ denote the predicted probabilities against the true aspect and sentiment labels, respectively, and $q \in (0, 1)$ is a hyperparameter. The loss function becomes the MAE function when $q = 1$, and the CCE function when $q = 0$. Differently than CASC, L_1 and L_2 regularizations are applied to avoid overfitting. The regularization is deemed necessary, as the neural model is more sophisticated.

For loss minimization, weight matrices described in Subsect. 4.2 are randomly initialized using a uniform distribution $U(-0.1, 0.1)$. Furthermore, biases are initialized to zero. The rest of the parameters are set using the default settings provided by TensorFlow. The algorithm used to minimize the loss is Adam [8].

Hyperparameter Optimization. The hyperparameters are optimized by the Hyperband algorithm [10]. Furthermore, hyperparameters that are not involved in the neural model and not discussed in this section are taken from CASC [9].

We optimize eight hyperparameters. Table 2 shows the hyperparameters for LCR+CASC, LCR+CASC-CON, and LCR+CASC+ASYNC (the last two models are discussed in the next section). Most hyperparameters vary across different models and do not display interesting results. However, we notice that the number of hops is always higher than the three hops given in [15]. Furthermore, the values for q are relatively low, meaning that the loss function is closer to CCE than MAE.

Table 2. Optimized hyperparameters of various models

Hyperparameter	LCR+CASC	LCR+CASC-CON	LCR+CASC+ASYNC
L_1	10¯7	0.0001	10¯5
L_2	10¯7	0.001	10¯7
Learning Rate	0.001	0.001	0.01
Hops	6	8	8
q	0.1	0.3	0.3
BiLSTM units	550	650	700
Dropout rate 1	0.6	0.3	0.5
Dropout rate 2	0.3	0.2	0.3

5 Results

We discuss the results of the proposed model in this section. First, Subsect. 5.1 discusses the evaluation measures and gives the baseline models that are used for comparison. Then, we present the datasets in Subsect. 5.2. Last, Subsect. 5.3 compares the results of the proposed model and baseline models.

5.1 Performance Measures and Baseline Models

We evaluate the predictive performance of the models using the out-of-sample accuracy and macro-F1 scores. This paper compares the novel model against versions of the CASC model. The considered baseline models are:

CASC [9]: The model framework presented in [9] using the post-trained DK-BERT MLM and a small set of seed words to prepare labeled data.

CASC+MAX: We use the score that corresponds to the word that has the maximum score amongst all *potential-aspects* and *potential-opinions* in a sentence. Sentences are labeled according to the maximum score, whereas the CASC model uses the average.

CASC+MAX+ATE: An extension of CASC+MAX, where we also extract the aspect target expressions. Similar to the LCR+CASC model, this model introduces [SEP] tokens before and after target expressions.

LCR+CASC: Our model framework builds on the CASC+MAX+ATE model. We replace the simple linear neural model with the sophisticated LCR-Rot-hop++ [15] neural model.

LCR+CASC-DL: We omit the neural model altogether and use the labeler described in labeled data preparation. We name this method LCR+CASC-DL but it is equivalent to CASC+MAX+ATE-DL.

LCR+CASC-CON: We remove the left- and right-context-aware BiLSTM output in the last prediction layer. We only use the concatenated target representations $\{r_l^t, r_r^t\}$.

LCR+CASC+ASYNC: We create separate neural layers for each subtask. Therefore, each task is asynchronously solved, whereas the LCR+CASC model shares all neural layers (besides the classification head) for the aspect and sentiment classification tasks.

[MODEL]+ATE (GOLD): These types of models use the gold aspect target annotations provided by the SemEval datasets, instead of extracting the aspect target expressions. Note that the noisy training data is still generated using a labeler.

5.2 Processed Data

The Yelp dataset is not labeled and the resulting datasets may differ per score calculator. Furthermore, the SemEval datasets are also smaller as the aspect target cannot always be found by the labeler. Table 3 shows the datasets that are used for training (Yelp) and evaluation (SemEval). Note that the Yelp dataset differs between the average and maximum score labeler.

Table 3. Descriptive statistics of the aspect classes and the polarities of the Yelp and SemEval datasets

Dataset	Postive		Negative		Food		Place		Service		Total
	Freq.	%	Freq.	%	Freq.	%	Freq.	%	Freq.	%	Freq.
Yelp CASC	1543	69%	706	31%	881	39%	781	35%	587	26%	2249
Yelp Max	1744	74%	601	26%	689	29%	920	39%	736	31%	2345
SemEval 2015	82	46%	96	54%	83	47%	55	31%	40	22%	178
SemEval 2016	159	78%	46	22%	88	43%	73	36%	44	21%	205

5.3 Performance Results

In this section, we compare the different models described in Subsect. 5.1. First, we use the data with no gold target annotations. Then, we use test data where sentences have been split into the correct contexts using gold target annotations.

From Table 4 we notice that CASC outperforms all methods when it comes to ACD. Furthermore, from Table 5 we observe that it performs relatively well for ASC. CASC beats LCR+CASC by a significant amount at ACD, whereas the performance comparison for ASC is more ambiguous. CASC performs worse at ASC for the 2016 dataset, while LCR+CASC performs worse than all neural models for the 2015 dataset for ASC. To understand the effectiveness of different novel components, we perform an ablation study. We remove or add components as is explained in Subsect. 5.1. The results are shown in Table 4 for aspect classification and in Table 5 for sentiment detection.

Table 4. Performance of various methods on aspect classification

Aspect Model	2015		2016	
	Acc.	Macro-F1	Acc.	Macro-F1
CASC	**85.71**	**85.43**	**86.78**	**86.93**
CASC+MAX	64.52	63.51	65.70	64.46
CASC+MAX+ATE	83.71	83.14	83.90	83.87
LCR+CASC-DL	65.90	65.41	69.42	68.64
LCR+CASC-CON	79.78	79.58	83.41	83.43
LCR+CASC+ASYNC	80.90	80.43	82.93	83.12
LCR+CASC	80.90	80.44	82.44	82.52

Table 5. Performance of various methods on sentiment classification

Sentiment Model	2015		2016	
	Acc.	Macro-F1	Acc.	Macro-F1
CASC	90.32	90.20	87.19	82.92
CASC+MAX	**92.17**	**92.01**	88.84	84.41
CASC+MAX+ATE	89.89	89.84	89.76	86.56
LCR+CASC-DL	68.66	68.37	57.44	55.29
LCR+CASC-CON	88.76	88.65	93.17	90.61
LCR+CASC+ASYNC	89.89	89.78	91.22	87.93
LCR+CASC	88.20	88.07	**94.15**	**91.84**

First, the maximum score labeler drops CASC's performance for ACD. Furthermore, CASC+MAX loses over 20% points for ACD. Interestingly, ASC is more robust than ACD as the neural network is able to find sentiments well. Second, CASC+MAX+ATE produces good results, even though the maximum score labeler produces poor results. However, it performs worse than CASC in most situations since it only beats CASC in the 2016 dataset for ASC. Combined with the previous results, it indicates that the neural model is able to pick up some patterns if the location of the aspect is provided. Even with imperfect target location information, the performance is close to the performance of CASC. Third, LCR+CASC-CON beats LCR+CASC in some cases. One possible reason could be that the two target representations capture the most relevant information of the contexts. Fourth, LCR+CASC+ASYNC produces similar results compared to LCR+CASC for ACD, whereas this is not the case for ASC for the 2016 dataset.

We now consider data with gold annotations. Table 6 and Table 7 show the results for ACD and ASC, respectively. We investigate this to understand if studying more complex models is worth it. The maximum score labeler might cause poor results for LCR+CASC, indicating that ATE in this model must improve. We investigate the potential of complex models by not performing ATE for the evaluation data. Note that sentences in the training data are still annotated using the maximum score labeler and remain unchanged. Because we use gold annotations, sentences in the test data can contain multiple aspects. Therefore, we also investigate the performance of sentences with multiple aspects.

Table 6. Performance of various methods on aspect classification with gold data

Aspect Model	Single Aspect				Multiple Aspects			
	2015		2016		2015		2016	
	Acc.	Macro-F1	Acc.	Macro-F1	Acc.	Macro-F1	Acc.	Macro-F1
CASC+ATE (GOLD)	86.18	86.18	86.36	85.96	75.00	73.93	79.06	77.00
CASC+MAX+ATE (GOLD)	84.33	83.73	89.67	88.90	85.56	85.03	85.56	84.86
LCR+CASC-CON+ATE (GOLD)	90.78	91.27	94.21	94.80	92.03	91.80	93.14	92.97
LCR+CASC+ASYNC+ATE (GOLD)	**94.47**	**94.71**	**95.87**	**95.17**	**94.83**	**94.52**	**94.77**	94.05
LCR+CASC+ATE (GOLD)	92.63	93.28	94.63	94.96	93.53	93.36	94.22	**94.10**

Table 7. Performance of various methods on sentiment classification with gold data

Sentiment Model	Single Aspect				Multiple Aspects			
	2015		2016		2015		2016	
	Acc.	Macro-F1	Acc.	Macro-F1	Acc.	Macro-F1	Acc.	Macro-F1
CASC+ATE (GOLD)	**92.63**	**92.53**	85.95	81.37	87.28	**86.36**	88.81	83.61
CASC+MAX+ATE (GOLD)	89.40	88.99	88.43	83.31	87.50	86.13	90.07	84.24
LCR+CASC-CON+ATE (GOLD)	86.64	86.17	91.74	87.58	84.70	83.14	92.06	87.44
LCR+CASC+ASYNC+ATE (GOLD)	89.40	89.07	91.32	87.40	85.99	84.61	91.88	87.20
LCR+CASC+ATE (GOLD)	89.86	89.36	**93.80**	**90.33**	**87.93**	86.35	**92.96**	**88.33**

First, CASC drops in performance when including multiple aspects while LCR+CASC does not. It seems that more sophisticated models perform better at ACD. Second, by using the maximum score labeler, performance is on par with singly-labeled sentences. Furthermore, the performance decrease from single- to multi-labeled data for ACD is larger compared to ASC. Third, unlike before, LCR+CASC-CON performs worse than LCR+CASC, indicating that the left and right contexts are useful only when the target expression is correct.

The performance loss is less for ACD than for ASC as ACD likely depends less on the context. Sentiments, however, depend more on context. Fourth, LCR+CASC+ASYNC performs the best in all but one situation for ACD, indicating that separate neural layers benefit the model. However, this model performs worse compared to LCR+CASC for ASC.

In short, LCR+CASC outperforms CASC in most situations when the aspect target expression is given for test data, even with the noisy training labels generated by the maximum score labeler. Compared to CASC, multi-labeled data see much improvement as the sophisticated neural model performs better with multi-labeled data.

6 Conclusion

In this paper, we introduced a novel model by combining the state-of-the-art weakly-supervised CASC [9] and supervised LCR-Rot-hop++ [15] models to classify aspect categories and sentiment polarities. The models were modified to work with each other. First, a new scoring method had to be constructed to extract the aspect target expression. Second, the sophisticated LCR-Rot-hop++ had to be altered to also solve the ACD task.

We found that the LCR+CASC model performed subpar compared to the CASC model when ATE was also performed. Results showed that the LCR-Rot-hop++ model can be extended to a joint neural model to solve the ACD and ASC tasks as the LCR+CASC model is able to detect which aspect category belongs to a target. The weakness of the model is ATE. Labeling and extracting a word with the highest aspect score, rather than labeling the sentence based on the average score, produced modest results. However, the LCR+CASC outperformed CASC in most situations when target locations were correctly provided in the test data. Specifically, LCR+CASC outperformed CASC significantly when it comes to multi-labeled data. Moreover, the components of the neural model seemed to have a positive effect on the performance. Thus, our proposed model is able to exploit target location information as it outperformed CASC when using high-quality target data.

This research focused on the restaurant domain. Although CASC has seen great results in different domains, LCR+CASC's performance in different domains is not yet known. This is left as a suggestion for future research. Furthermore, results showed that the ATE part of the labeled data preparation step produced weak performance. Rather than extracting words that have the highest score in a sentence, future research could examine the extraction of noun phrases or more advanced scoring methods. Noun phrases seem promising as it is not as broad as taking the average over the whole sentence, but not too fine-grained as extracting single words.

References

1. Blei, D.M., Ng, A.Y., Jordan, M.I.: Latent Dirichlet allocation. J. Mach. Learn. Res. **3**, 993–1022 (2003)
2. Devlin, J., Chang, M.W., Lee, K., Toutanova, K.: BERT: pre-training of deep bidirectional transformers for language understanding. In: 2019 Conference of the North American Chapter of the Association for Computational Linguistics: Human Language Technologies (NAACL-HLT 2019), pp. 4171–4186. ACL (2019)
3. He, R., Lee, W.S., Ng, H.T., Dahlmeier, D.: An unsupervised neural attention model for aspect extraction. In: 55th Annual Meeting of the Association for Computational Linguistics (ACL 2017), pp. 388–397. ACL (2017)
4. Honnibal, M., Montani, I., Van Landeghem, S., Boyd, A.: spaCy: industrial-strength natural language processing in Python (2020)
5. Hu, M., Liu, B.: Mining and summarizing customer reviews. In: 10th ACM SIGKDD International Conference on Knowledge Discovery and Data Mining (KDD 2004), pp. 168–177. ACM (2004)
6. Huang, J., Meng, Y., Guo, F., Ji, H., Han, J.: Weakly-supervised aspect-based sentiment analysis via joint aspect-sentiment topic embedding. In: 2020 Conference on Empirical Methods in Natural Language Processing (EMNLP), pp. 6989–6999. ACL (2020)
7. Karamanolakis, G., Hsu, D., Gravano, L.: Leveraging just a few keywords for fine-grained aspect detection through weakly supervised co-training. In: 2019 Conference on Empirical Methods in Natural Language Processing and the 9th International Joint Conference on Natural Language Processing (EMNLP-IJCNLP 2019), pp. 4611–4621. ACL (2019)
8. Kingma, D.P., Ba, J.: Adam: a method for stochastic optimization. In: 3rd International Conference on Learning Representations (ICLR 2015) (2015)
9. Kumar, A., Gupta, P., Balan, R., Neti, L.B.M., Malapati, A.: BERT based semi-supervised hybrid approach for aspect and sentiment classification. Neural Process. Lett. **53**(6), 4207–4224 (2021)
10. Li, L., Jamieson, K., DeSalvo, G., Rostamizadeh, A., Talwalkar, A.: Hyperband: a novel bandit-based approach to hyperparameter optimization. J. Mach. Learn. Res. **18**(185), 1–52 (2018)
11. Liu, B.: Sentiment analysis and opinion mining. Synth. Lect. Hum. Lang. Technol. **5**(1), 1–167 (2012)
12. Pontiki, M., et al.: SemEval-2016 task 5: aspect based sentiment analysis. In: 10th International Workshop on Semantic Evaluation (SemEval-2016), pp. 19–30. ACL (2016)
13. Pontiki, M., Galanis, D., Papageorgiou, H., Manandhar, S., Androutsopoulos, I.: SemEval-2015 task 12: aspect based sentiment analysis. In: 9th International Workshop on Semantic Evaluation (SemEval 2015), pp. 486–495. ACL (2015)
14. Tang, D., Qin, B., Liu, T.: Aspect level sentiment classification with deep memory network. In: 2016 Conference on Empirical Methods in Natural Language Processing (EMNLP 2016), pp. 214–224. ACL (2016)
15. Truşcǎ, M.M., Wassenberg, D., Frasincar, F., Dekker, R.: A hybrid approach for aspect-based sentiment analysis using deep contextual word embeddings and hierarchical attention. In: Bielikova, M., Mikkonen, T., Pautasso, C. (eds.) ICWE 2020. LNCS, vol. 12128, pp. 365–380. Springer, Cham (2020). https://doi.org/10.1007/978-3-030-50578-3_25

16. Wallaart, O., Frasincar, F.: A hybrid approach for aspect-based sentiment analysis using a lexicalized domain ontology and attentional neural models. In: Hitzler, P., et al. (eds.) ESWC 2019. LNCS, vol. 11503, pp. 363–378. Springer, Cham (2019). https://doi.org/10.1007/978-3-030-21348-0_24
17. Xu, H., Liu, B., Shu, L., Yu, P.: BERT post-training for review reading comprehension and aspect-based sentiment analysis. In: 2019 Conference of the North American Chapter of the Association for Computational Linguistics: Human Language Technologies (NAACL-HLT 2019), pp. 2324–2335. ACL (2019)
18. Xu, X., Tan, S., Liu, Y., Cheng, X., Lin, Z.: Towards jointly extracting aspects and aspect-specific sentiment knowledge. In: 21st ACM International Conference on Information and Knowledge Management (CIKM 2012), pp. 1895–1899. ACM (2012)
19. Zhang, W., Li, X., Deng, Y., Bing, L., Lam, W.: A survey on aspect-based sentiment analysis: tasks, methods, and challenges. IEEE Trans. Knowl. Data Eng. **35**(11), 11019–11038 (2023)
20. Zhao, X., Jiang, J., Yan, H., Li, X.: Jointly modeling aspects and opinions with a MaxEnt-LDA hybrid. In: 2010 Conference on Empirical Methods in Natural Language Processing (EMNLP 2010), pp. 56–65. ACL (2010)
21. Zheng, S., Xia, R.: Left-center-right separated neural network for aspect-based sentiment analysis with rotatory attention. arXiv preprint arXiv:1802.00892 (2018)
22. Zhuang, H., Guo, F., Zhang, C., Liu, L., Han, J.: Joint aspect-sentiment analysis with minimal user guidance. In: 43rd International ACM SIGIR Conference on Research and Development in Information Retrieval (ACM 2020), pp. 1241–1250. ACM (2020)

Subjectivity, Polarity and the Aspect of Time in the Evolution of Crowd-Sourced Biographies

Constantinos Romantzis[1], Alexandros Karakasidis[2](✉), Evangelos Mathioudis[1], Ioannis Katakis[1], Pantelis Agathangelou[1], and Jahna Otterbacher[3]

[1] Department of Computer Science, School of Sciences and Engineering, University of Nicosia, 2417 Nicosia, Cyprus
{romantzis.c1,mathioudis.e,agathangelou.p}@live.unic.ac.cy, katakis.i@unic.ac.cy

[2] Department of Applied Informatics, University of Macedonia, Thessaloniki, Greece
a.karakasidis@uom.edu.gr

[3] Faculty of Pure and Applied Sciences, Open University of Cyprus, Nicosia, Cyprus
jahna.otterbacher@ouc.ac.cy

Abstract. This study examines the use of subjective and sentimentally charged language in crowd-sourced articles by focusing on time and how articles in environments like Wikipedia tend to evolve as edits are made by multiple contributors. More specifically, we measure linguistic subjectivity (the systematic, asymmetrical use of language) using Mean Abstraction Level, an established subjectivity measure, and polarity (the use of positively or negatively sentimentally charged words) through time. For the latest case, we introduce a new measure called Polarity Density. We focus on Wikipedia biographies and their evolution over time and we perform a detailed analysis per gender and per personality category. Our empirical evaluation provides evidence of increased subjectivity in female biographies as per personality category and per gender, while the same also occurs when considering sentimental charge over time.

Keywords: Bias · Sentiment Analysis · Subjectivity · Polarity · Natural Language Processing · Wikipedia

1 Introduction

Wikipedia continues to be one of the most reliable and complete sources of information, having significant impact on communities worldwide. The collaborative, co-editing nature of Wikipedia provides a place of interaction among members of the community, as well as valuable data for research on human behavior. However, the *style of language* used plays a key role in the communication and maintenance of stereotypes. This behavior is intrinsic to human nature and links

K. Stefanidis et al. (Eds.): ICWE 2024, LNCS 14629, pp. 281–295, 2024.
https://doi.org/10.1007/978-3-031-62362-2_20

to the human tendency to engage in groups as a means to socialize and evolve [11]. In this context, given that Wikipedia influences public opinion across a number of domains, several voices have raised concerns about the quality and reliability of its content. Various methods and tools (e.g. [10,17]) have been proposed and developed towards an effort to provide ways for complying (or assessing the degree of compliance) of the content with the Neutral Point of View policy (NPOV)[1] of Wikipedia. However, delivering NPOV-compliant content is not a trivial process, especially in Wikipedia where the production and editing of the content are collaborative and dynamic.

In this study, we show that throughout the life-cycle of an article, there are several instances of subjective language that fluctuate after a massive number of edits, considering two aspects of bias in biographies. First, we measure *subjectivity* in terms of Mean Abstraction Level [23], which takes into account speech structures as adjectives and action verbs. Second, we consider *polarity*, the negative or positive sentimental charge of words. To quantify polarity, we introduce a new measure called *Polarity Density*, which identifies the amount of sentimental charge within a text corpus. We use these measures for sets of bibliographies organized per profile type and per gender. We indicate that, averaging over time is not enough to provide safe conclusions.

To perform these tasks, we have used a sentiment analysis tool [1] to extract sentimentally charged words. For example, *good*, *wonderful*, and *amazing* are positive words, and *bad*, *poor*, and *terrible* are negative words. Most sentiment words are adjectives and adverbs, but nouns (e.g., *rubbish* or *junk*) and verbs (e.g., *hate* or *love*) can also be used to express sentiment [12].

For our study, we have considered three personality categories of Wikipedia biographies: athletes, politicians and scientists. Our dataset consists of time-varying instances of high-impact political leaders, scientists, and sports athletes biographies, either male or female. For each of these domains, we extract a lexicon of words, conveying positive and negative sentiments that we align with the abstract terms that the Linguistic Category Model [20] defines. We locate these words within our dataset of Wikipedia articles and use our measures for subjectivity and polarity to evaluate their evolution over time. In our analysis, we show that time evolution reveals bias characteristics not evident without considering the aspect of time. We consider this as a threat to the objective role the Wikipedia entries provide. To this end, our **contributions** may be summarized as follows.

- We introduce a novel measure to quantify sentimental density.
- We empirically illustrate that, to study bias in biographies a detailed time analysis is required, as overall averages may not reveal biases.
- After extensive analysis, we identify cases of bias, resulting from subjective speech or/and sentimentally charged wordings in biographies, per gender, per personality category and combined.

The remainder of the paper is organized as follows. In Sect. 2, we present the related work, while in Sect. 3, we provide our methodology. We present the

[1] https://en.wikipedia.org/wiki/Wikipedia:Neutral_point_of_view.

results of our empirical evaluation and our discussion in Sect. 4. We conclude in Sect. 5, also discussing our next research steps.

2 Related Work

Works related to ours may be clustered into two broad areas: Document evolution and bias studies focusing on Wikipedia.

The Wikipedia platform offers the ability to monitor the addition or deletion of content. The archived content that is kept stored because of this functionality has widely been studied in the literature by tags like "history flow" [22] or article's "edit wars" [5]. In terms of understanding document evolution, [18] attempts to study an edit at two levels: identifying the edit intent, and describing the edit using free-form text. Authors train a classifier that achieves 90% accuracy in identifying edit intent. The supervised model generates a high-level description of a revision in free-form text. This method can be used to provide insights into understanding the relationship between authors and document evolution, article trustworthiness, neutrality or bias point-of-view detection. Due to revisions, contradictions might emerge. [2] identifies them using an unsupervised method for detecting contradictions among the opinions on the same aspect and measuring the intensity of this contradiction.

Bias has been an issue with Wikipedia in a variety of aspects [7]. Detecting biased language in Wikipedia at a sentence level is also studied in the work of [10]. There, a supervised classification approach created and exploited a lexicon of biased words while also other syntactical and semantic characteristics of biased statements, as in our work. Bias is also introduced by the editors themselves. In [15], a dominant group of editors has been identified, mainly white, male, and Western, through a big data approach with a graph created with editors reverting each other's edits. An example area of bias against women regards scholarly Wikipedia citations [25] which indicated that, based on linked data from Web of Science women's publications are less cited. Furthermore, women not only contribute less to Wikipedia but also use it less [19]. In [8] this fact is combined for analysis with the content itself, reviewing a series of reasons that make women participate less in Wikipedia. In [6] authors are using information quality metrics in health articles of Wikipedia in various languages. Languages with smaller numbers of speakers, such as Swedish, have high ranks (third), as articles for this case have been written by bots. To improve linguistic bias detection in Wikipedia, the use of deep transformer models has been proposed [13] and adopt a cross-domain pre-training method to learn contextual relationships between words in a sentence to detect biased statements.

3 Methodology

This section introduces the collection process of the Wikipedia biographies and the methodology we used for the analysis and extraction of the research results, but first, we provide some background knowledge regarding the operation of Wikipedia.

3.1 Operation of Wikipedia

Wikipedia is an open-source and collaborative encyclopedia which is currently considered a valid source of information [9]. As of today, it hosts over 6 Million articles only in the English language which are organized into several topics[2]. In Wikipedia, an article is created, maintained, and updated via a network of interactions by several registered users (sometimes anonymous). The core idea behind this learning framework, the collaborative, is attributed to theories that claim knowledge acquisition should be the outcome of many voices [4]. This process, however, is not straightforward as different groups' perspectives may lead to conflicts and diminish the collaborative performance [3]. Social behavior studies [14] that experimented on variant group combinations found that collaboration patterns for knowledge production under certain conditions are feasible. They formulate that despite the inherent propensity of individuals to communicate with similar others if an information and problem-processing approach is established then, performance and knowledge quality can be produced. In the same line, the empirical work of [21] formulated the relation between increased cooperation and high-quality articles, while in [24] the authors demonstrate that frequent disagreement within (political) polarized teams in article's edits, consequences in creating a different perspectives environment that results in less bias and articles of higher quality.

This knowledge production framework, however, wouldn't have been able to operate successfully without quality-enforced policies. Wikipedia content is built on top of three tenets[3]. The 'Neutral Point of View' (NPOV), the 'No research' (NOR), and the 'Verifiability' (V). These are Wikipedia policies that are applied to any content via the contribution mechanisms and the respective regulations. For any article, there is an edit functionality and a series of talk pages. These are pages that are devoted to the discussion of issues surrounding a topic of real pages. They are extensions of the author's edit comments (that are created on editing an article) and from a literature point of view, these discussion rooms are characterized as places where conflicts are resolved [22].

3.2 Dataset Collection

To collect our dataset, we employed *MediaWiki*[4]. MediaWiki is an open-source wiki platform that provides collaborative content creation capabilities as well as programmatic data access via its API along with data export capabilities with various aggregations possible. It also serves as the backend of the Wikipedia site itself. Using MediaWiki, a query was applied for each biography and its API returned a data record in a form called *wikitext*. *Wikitext*, also known as *Wiki markup* consists of a syntax and keywords that are used from the *MediaWiki* to form a page[5]. In the second step, a Python package, named *MediaWiki Parser*

[2] https://en.wikipedia.org/wiki/Wikipedia:Contents/Categories.
[3] https://en.wikipedia.org/wiki/Wikipedia:Core_content_policies.
[4] https://www.mediawiki.org/wiki/MediaWiki.
[5] https://en.wikipedia.org/wiki/Help:Wikitext.

From Hell[6] was used to parse and collect the *Wikitext* content. Finally, for each revision edit, we kept track of the 'revision's id', the 'timestamp', the 'user's id', the 'content', and the corresponding 'tags'. Tags are short messages assigned automatically by MediaWiki. They are used to define the way an edit took place (e.g. edits via mobile or edits via web) and additionally to detect harmful edits (e.g. vandalism) or software bugs. We dropped every entry with *texthidden* content. A *texthidden* property is returned whenever a revision slot has its content revision deleted. The *revision deleted* feature can be used by users who have *deleterevision* rights. In this case, a user can hide entries with sensitive data.

3.3 Dataset Description

Overall, we downloaded 167.300 revisions in total, comprising the histories of 150 human profiles. More specifically, we have collected data from 50 scientists, 50 politicians, and 50 athletes[7]. Each category consists of 25 females and 25 males. The criteria we used to select the 150 personalities are listed below:

- **Athletes**. We selected athletes based on their number of appearances in the Olympic Games. We picked 50 athletes who have at least six appearances in the Olympic Games, from the *'List of athletes with the greatest number of participations at Olympic Games'*[8] list, regardless the game they participated in.
- **Scientists**. For the scientists, we used two different lists. The first one was the *'50 Most Influential Scientists in the World Today'*[9] and the second was from the *'Female scientists having been awarded a Nobel prize'*[10]. From these lists, we randomly chose 50 scientists.
- **Politicians**. For the politicians, we selected 50 politicians from all over the world. For this category, we started with those who had the greatest impact in the last few years. Finally, we populated the category with politicians from any continent.

Table 1 provides a summary view of our dataset. Obviously, politicians gain more attention than scientists and athletes which can be seen by the large number of words that comprise each biography and the number of edits that each biography undergoes. Moreover, by comparing the largest biographies of each category we see a significant difference in the volume of information shared in politicians' biographies both for men and women. In what follows, we relate each revision with a specific timestamp and We call **snapshot** the revision edit in a biography at a specific timestamp t_i.

---

6 https://github.com/earwig/mwparserfromhell.
7 Dataset available at: https://github.com/unic-ailab/Subjectivity-Polarity-and-the-Aspect-of-Time-in-the-Evolution-of-Crowd-Sourced-Biographies.
8 https://en.wikipedia.org/wiki/List_of_athletes_with_the_most_appearances_at_Olympic_Games.
9 https://thebestschools.org/features/50-influential-scientists-world-today/.
10 https://en.wikipedia.org/wiki/Women_in_science.

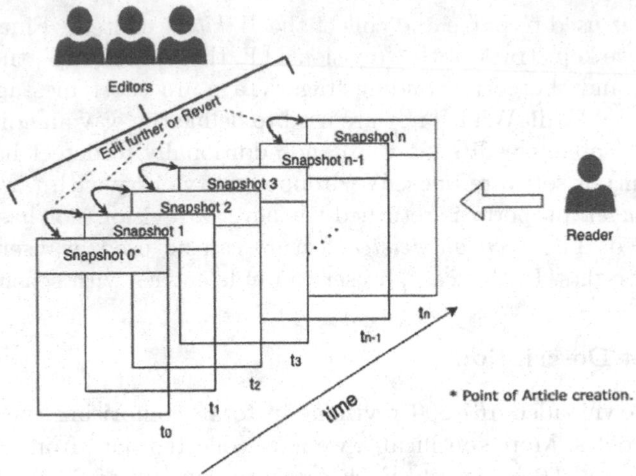

Fig. 1. A representative example of a sequence of revision edits with the aspect of time.

The Life-Cycle of a Biography and the Role of Revisions. In order to familiarize the reader with the revision edit process in Wikipedia and the potential conflicts this revision can bring about because of different groups' perspectives, we provide a scenario that entangles a sequence of revisions in a biography. Figure 1 showcases the evolution that a biography may undergo during time. A *Revert* [5] is a special type of edit operation which allows to a user to recover an older version of a biography. Editors have the ability to either edit the biographies further or to revert them to a prior version at which point the biographies can be then further edited, reverted to an even older version or both. The Reader represents the Wikipedia readers that access the biographies at any given moment and see them in their last edited state as saved by the latest Editor.

Table 1. Overall Summary Statistics (including edits).

Description	Scientists	Athletes	Politicians
All: Average size of biography (words)	2766	689	7110
Men: Average size of biography (words)	3140	441	6671
Women: Average size of biography (words)	2271	839	7675
All: Average number of edits	656	88	2602
Men: Average number of edits	746	66	2932
Women: Average number of edits	566	110	2271
Men: Largest biography	9094	169	28345
Women: Largest biography	4322	442	16902
Men: Biography with the most edits	Stephen Hawking	Hans Fogh	Barack Obama
Women: Biography with the most edits	Jane Goodall	Tessa Sanderson	Hillary Clinton

This back-and-forth of a biography's state could extend in time for many snapshots. Usually, a conflict lies between two different opinions on a specific topic. In this process, editors can be involved either individually or in groups. This phenomenon which has widely been discussed in the literature is named *Edit Wars* and usually is triggered after a user vandalizes an article's content. In our dataset, we have detected 125 such cases for Males and 113 cases for Females. Next, we provide the methodology we followed for the analysis of the collected content and how we identify the use of abstract language in this content.

3.4 Quantifying Subjectivity and Polarity

In this section, we provide details about the analysis of the content and the method we applied for measuring subjectivity, in terms of abstraction, and polarity.

Measuring Subjectivity. We will monitor language abstraction in order to measure subjectivity in Wikipedia biographies. To do so, we will employ the Mean Abstraction Level (MAL) measure which has been introduced in [23] and is illustrated in Eq. 1.

$$MAL = \frac{nSV * 1 + nAV * 2 + nStV * 3 + nADJ * 4}{nSV + nAV + nStV + nADJ} \tag{1}$$

In Eq. 1, nSV is the number of **strong** or **descriptive action** verbs, nAV is the number of **interpretive action** verbs, $nStV$ is the number of **state** verbs, and $nADJ$ is the number of **adjectives**. Contemplating the combination of values Eq. 1 can receive, easily one infers that MAL can range from 1 up to 4. A value equal to 1 denotes totally objective opinion or no existence of linguistic bias and value 4 denotes totally subjective, meaning that the content is biased.

Measuring Polarity. As we have described, MAL measures abstraction which is proportional to subjectivity, conveying our perspective of a subject's properties. However, beyond subjectivity there is also *Polarity* [16] which is related to the sentiment, either positive or negative, conveyed by some text. As we would like to measure the amount of emotional charge within a textual corpus, no matter whether it is positive or negative, we introduce a novel measure called *Polarity Density* (PD), which measures the fraction of total emotionally charged words, both positively and negatively, over the total number of words within a text corpus. The main feature of PD is that it manages to provide evidence of emotion density in an objective manner, without considering if this emotion is positive or negative. As a direct consequence, it is capable of identifying corpora sentimentally charged, also containing both positive and negative sentiments. This is particularly useful for our investigation, since it allows us to evaluate the change in overall sentiment charge, considering the time aspect, between biography revisions.

$$PD = \frac{P_w + N_w}{T_w} \tag{2}$$

Equation 2 formally illustrates PD, with P_w being the number of *Positive Words* and N_w being the number of *Negative Words*, over *All Words* (T_w) in a text corpus, i.e. positive, negative and neutral words. It is evident that PD takes values between 0 and 1. PD is equal to 0 when no positive or negative words have been used in a corpus. On the other hand, PD would be equal to 1 in the extreme case that no neutral words have been found.

4 Results and Discussion

This section holds our experimental evaluation. Here, we discuss several aspects of our analysis that reveal the subjectivity and the polarity of the language used in the life-cycle of Wikipedia articles, considering the evolution of biographies over time and grouping them by gender, role and combined, in all three categories of biographies, i.e. athletes, politicians and scientists, assuming two genders, males and females.

4.1 Data Preparation

To identify subjectivity and polarity conveying words, we employed a sentiment analysis tool named DidaxTo[11] which implements an unsupervised approach for discovering polarity patterns. In addition, we also used the Natural Language ToolKit package of Python that has the module *pos_tag*[12]. This tool provided an auxiliary task in our methodology. For every word in a biography snapshot that aligned with the lexicon, it returned the respective part-of-speech tag. For each verb we found, we linked it to one of the following categories: *'state verb'*, *'descriptive action verb'* or *'interpretive action verb'*. We combined the outputs of the above processes for measuring subjectivity in Wikipedia biographies using MAL and overall sentiment using PD.

As we described earlier, each biography has undergone a number of revisions by Wikipedia authors. As expected, the number of revisions is different for each biography. To address this situation, when we report results, we consider the average number of biased or sentimental words for each biography. When reporting per year measurements, we consider the average of each biography for the respective year. Also, our analysis revealed 238 revisions with MAL equal to zero for either gender. For these entries the content was vandalized. 0.27% of male biographies had been vandalized opposed to 0.40% for female ones, a number 1.48 times higher.

---

[11] https://deixto.com/didaxto/.

[12] https://www.nltk.org/book/ch05.html.

4.2 Subjectivity and Polarity per Gender, Personality Category and Combined

This section focuses on the use of language among genders and personality categories conveying bias and/or sentiment. In this analysis, we segregated the biographies that comprised our dataset by gender and by personality category. We applied the MAL (Eq. 1) and the PD measures (Eq. 2) grouped by gender, personality category and both.

Table 2 contains the outcome of this analysis. The statistics for the female biographies are held in the first row, denoted by f, while the ones for the male biographies, are held in the second row. Here, we can first observe that the average size of female biographies is much shorter than that of the male biographies, indicating bias with respect to length. However, this fact on its own does not give an indication of subjective language. For this purpose, we have calculated MAL. MAL now, seems to be increased for the cases of male biographies by 0.05. The situation is similar when measuring sentiment, in terms of Polarity Density, with PD: With values equal to 0.144 and 0.139 for females and males, respectively, it is easy to discern that there is a slight increase in polarity in the case of women. Now, another question rises. Is the situation we have just described also the same per personality category?

Next, we will move and examine bias and polarity as of the personality category of a biography, irrespective of gender. The results of this assessment are held in Table 3, where each row holds the specific measurements per personality category. The first thing we may observe is that biographies of politicians are far longer, in average, compared to those of athletes and scientists. On the other hand, athletes seem to have very brief biographies. Given these facts, it would be very interesting to see what holds in terms of bias and polarity. Someone would expect that on the premises of longer biographies for politicians, these would convey far more bias.

Interestingly, however, this is not the case. In terms of MAL, the athletes biographies exhibit the highest subjectivity with those of politicians closely following. In terms of polarity, we may observe in the corresponding PD column that the highest values are observed for politicians. This means that more words charged sentimentally, either positively or negatively, have been used for this personality category. On the other hand, biographies of scientists seem to be more objective and with less polarity, featuring lower values for MAL and PD. This table has provided us with a very good example for the importance of introducing PD alongside with MAL, as it is easy to discern that subjectivity and polarity do not always align, since they measure different quantities.

Table 2. Mean values per gender.

Gender	Length	Pw	Nw	MAL	PD
f	1581.772	183.094	66.890	3.615	0.144
m	1715.898	199.621	61.776	3.569	0.139

These results urge us to investigate the origins of this situation. For this purpose, we have performed the corresponding measurements both per gender and per personality category. The results are illustrated in Table 4. Each personality category is preceded by the respective gender indication, *f* or *m*. We will begin our assessment with the case of athletes. We will compare for each personality category the respective measures per gender. Let us begin with the case of athletes. Here, we can observe very similar values for MAL and PD. This fact leads us to the conclusion of no evident bias in terms of gender considering the athlete personality category. The average numbers of positive and negative words for female athlete biographies may be higher compared to those of males, but their overall average length is higher than that of males as well.

Considering politicians now, we may observe an imbalance in terms of MAL and PD. While female politicians exhibit higher MAL by 0.145 than those of male politicians, meaning that text is more subjective in these cases, there is no significant difference in terms of PD, indicating the same amount of sentiment in both cases. Nevertheless, male politician biographies tend to be longer on average. The situation observed with politicians is reversed in the case of scientists. Here, female scientists exhibit higher polarity by 0.18, while their biographies are slightly less biased by 0.02. This means that while for both genders biographies have more or less the same amount of subjectivity, for female athletes text is more emotionally charged.

4.3 Bias and Polarity Evolution over Time

Observing mean values, however, does not provide the whole picture, as biographies do not remain static, but evolve through their revisions. To study this evolution, we calculated MAL and PD of each revision based on their respective components. After the measurements were obtained we performed a mean aggregation over each person and year to obtain the average MAL and PD for each year for each person. Finally, additional aggregations were performed to obtain the total average for each year along with secondary criteria as per each case.

To do so, we will follow the same pathway as in the case of mean values utilizing Figs. 2a–2j. In all figures, the horizontal axis represents time, while the vertical axis illustrates either MAL (Figs. 2a–2e), or PD (Figs. 2f–2j), we will begin by describing the situation with the mean values of MAL and PD, Starting with MAL, as illustrated in Fig. 2a, we observe that, for years before 2005, subjectivity was high, reaching 3.75. As of the conveyed sentiment, the situation was similar, with PD reaching 0.19, as we can see in Fig. 2f.

Table 3. Mean values per personality category.

Person. Categ.	Length	Pw	Nw	MAL	PD
athlete	515.374	61.585	12.759	3.752	0.127
politician	3005.228	359.104	125.623	3.638	0.154
scientist	1362.006	147.243	51.211	3.415	0.143

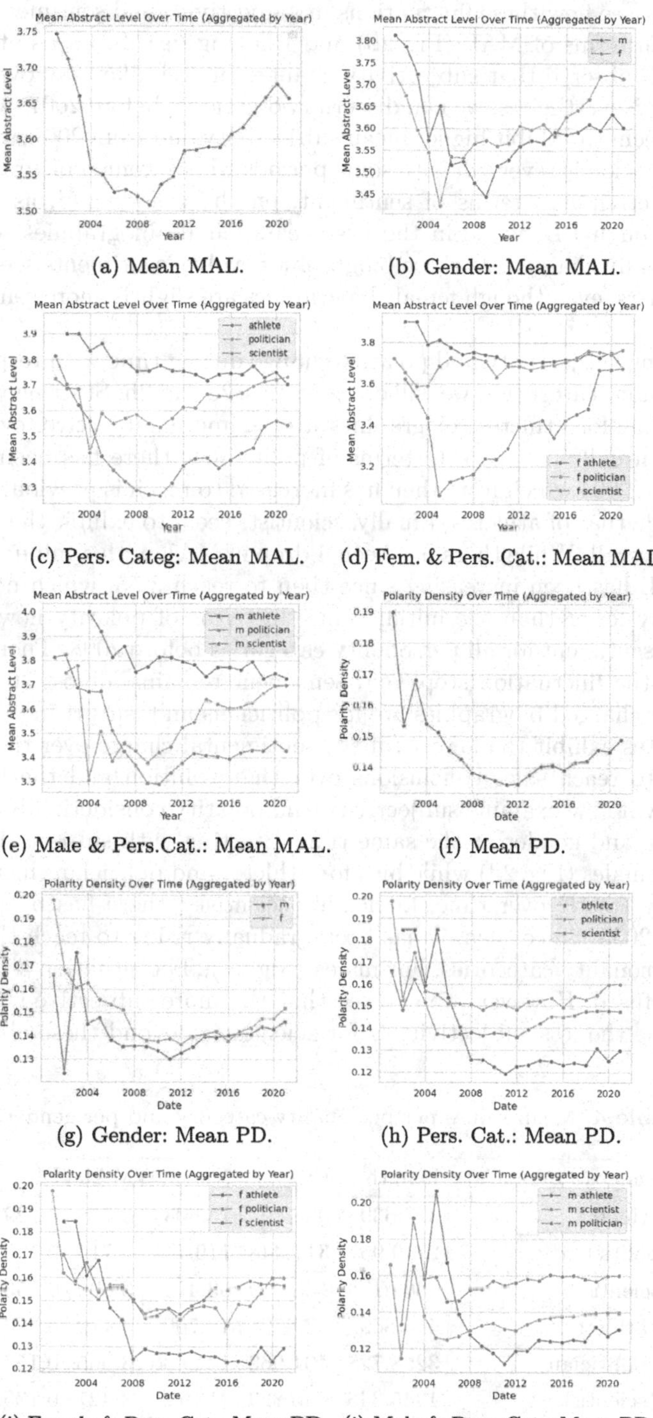

(a) Mean MAL. (b) Gender: Mean MAL.

(c) Pers. Categ: Mean MAL. (d) Fem. & Pers. Cat.: Mean MAL.

(e) Male & Pers.Cat.: Mean MAL. (f) Mean PD.

(g) Gender: Mean PD. (h) Pers. Cat.: Mean PD.

(i) Female & Pers. Cat.: Mean PD. (j) Male & Pers. Cat.: Mean PD.

Fig. 2. Mean MAL and Mean PD for Wikipedia biography revisions over time.

Let us now see how these fluctuations in subjectivity and sentiment reflect to each gender in terms of MAL (Fig. 2b) and PD (Fig. 2g). In terms of MAL, we can first of all observe that subjectivity changes in a similar way over time for both genders. Nevertheless, we can discern two periods; before 2007, where male biographies seem to exhibit higher mean subjectivity and from 2007 and beyond, where the situation is reversed, with some periods where women biographies span greater subjectivity. In terms of sentiment, on the other hand, as illustrated in Fig. 2g through PD, while in the first years female biographies seem to be more emotionally charged, as these biographies evolve, sentiments seem to align between genders, even though female biographies are slightly more sentimentally charged.

Considering subjectivity and polarity change during time with respect to different personality categories, we will observe Figs. 2c and 2h. Starting with MAL, we can see that for athletes, biographies are far more subjective, even though MAL has eventually dropped. In terms of politicians, there has been a drop in subjectivity in 2004 which from then has increased to reach is previous levels and even supersede that of athletes. Finally, scientists seem to exhibit the less biased biographies overall. While there has been a drop in MAL with a minimum of 3.25 in 2010, MAL has been increasing since then to reach 3.55, which nevertheless is significantly lower than the initial value. In terms of polarity now (Fig. 2h), there is high sentiment for all personality categories before 2008. Then, its mean value drops, the fluctuation stops and sentiment remains almost steady. More sentimentally charged biographies are for politicians and, surprisingly, scientists follow. Athletes exhibit the lowest rate of sentimental charge over time.

In order to reach safer conclusions over the evolution and the biases over genders, we will now examine subjectivity and polarity considering both personality category and gender at the same time. Starting with subjectivity, we can see that for females (Fig. 2d) while bias for athletes and politicians has been high and relatively steady over time, for female scientists, there has been a significant drop in 2005. Since then, it has been gradually rising to reach the levels of the other personality categories. For males (Fig. 2e). The situation seems a little bit more confused. However, we can see that the more subjective speech is for athletes, while the less subjectivity is for scientists. Beyond these observations,

Table 4. Mean values per personality category and per gender.

Gender & Pers. Cat.	Length	Pw	Nw	MAL	PD
f athlete	577.639	68.489	14.603	3.728	0.129
f politician	2719.957	317.448	119.749	3.710	0.150
f scientist	1384.123	155.759	63.479	3.400	0.153
m athlete	445.809	53.872	10.700	3.779	0.126
m politician	3298.728	401.962	131.666	3.565	0.157
m scientist	1345.348	140.829	41.972	3.427	0.135

we can further discern that for male athletes, subjectivity has dropped through the years. For male politicians, there has been a drop in 2004 and a steady rise afterwards, to the initial values. For male scientists, there has been a yearly drop in bias until 2010 and after a small rise, bias has been stabilized at around 3.45, 0.35 lower than the values observed at the beginning of this survey.

We will now evaluate subjectivity between genders for each of the personality categories we examine. Starting with athletes, we can see that for both personality categories, both genders seem to have the same behavior over time with a drop in MAL reaching 3.7 in both cases. No significant differences may be identified here. For politicians, there are certain dissimilarities. While for females, there is a quite steady behavior over time with MAL fluctuating between 3.6 and 3.78, for males, there is a significant drop for males in 2004 and until 2011, MAL is around 3.4. Then, there is a steady rise in subjectivity reaching 3.75. We can conclude that there has been a time frame with higher subjectivity for female politicians, while this did not occur with male politicians. Finally, let us discuss the case of scientists. Here, there are significant differences as well. For female scientists, MAL drops at 2005 from 3.6 to almost 3.1. Then, it gradually rises again so as to reach 3.7. On the other hand, for male scientists, while MAL starts at 3.8, it gradually drops to reach a minimum of 3.3 and then stabilizes in the area between 3.4 and 3.45. Here, we can conclude that since 2016, female biographies are more subjective with a widening span.

Polarity for female personality categories is illustrated in Fig. 2i while for male personality categories, it is illustrated in Fig. 2j. Starting with female athletes, we can see that there is a drop in sentiment for females starting in 2003 and ending in 2009. With some fluctuations, PD has stabilized between 0.125 and 0.13 since then. For males, there has been a spike in 2007. Since then, PD has dropped until 2012 and has stabilized between 0.125 and 0.13 as in the case of female athletes. Comparing these two behaviors, we would say that in the later years polarity is similar for both genders.

Let us now move to politicians. In the case of females, PD starts at a higher value, compared to athletes and gradually drops to 0.15 in 2007. Then, it fluctuates in this area with a variance of 0.01 with an increasing tendency in the last years. In any case, sentiment for female politician biographies is higher than that of athletes. Moving to male biographies, we can see that while polarity is initially lower than that of females, there is a spike in 2004 increasing it over 0.19. Then, there is a continuous drop below 0.13 in 2007 and a steady rise with a stabilization around 0.16 in the last years. PD in this case is significant higher than that of male athletes. Compared to female athletes, the final measurements may be at the same levels, but it is evident that in the 2009–2020 time frame, women athletes biographies convey less sentiment.

Finally, let us consider the case of scientists. For female scientists, PD resembles that of female politicians. There is significant distance in 2003–2004 and some differentiation in values between 2015 and 2020, where there is higher sentiment up to 0.015 for scientists. For male scientists, the situation is similar to that of male politicians, following the same fluctuations, although their PD values are higher by an average of 0.02. Comparing male and female scientists in terms of sentiment, we can see that PD is always higher for females, indicating more sentimental speech in their biographies.

Given these results, we can safely argue that considering average subjectivity and polarity over a time period is not sufficient for extracting conclusions, but a time-based, gender-based and category-based analysis is required, given the fact that there are fluctuations.

5 Conclusions and Future Work

In this paper, we discussed the phenomena of subjectivity and polarity in online bibliographies. We have introduced Polarity Density, a new polarity measure, and using it together with Mean Abstraction Level, we investigated the existence of subjectivity and polarity throughout a time span of 20 years with respect to gender, role and their combinations. Our findings indicate that subjectivity and sentiment biases appear mostly with respect to roles for each gender and not for gender per se. There are cases of higher subjectivity and polarity among females, for instance, there is higher subjectivity for female athletes and politicians than scientists of the same gender. On the other hand, for male biographies, the more subjective ones are those of athletes, then there are the ones of politicians and finally, the less subjective ones are those of scientists. Comparing the results between the two genders, there are time frames with higher subjectivity for female politicians and scientists, compared to their male colleagues. Now, regarding sentiment, we have seen that polarity is higher for women athletes and scientists, indicating bias.

It is anticipated that all these results, apart from being interesting themselves, raise new questions regarding the cause and the nature of observed bias. To this end, our next steps will primarily focus on exploring the origins of subjectivity and polarity in Wikipedia articles so as to be able to identify the parameters that are mostly responsible for the observed biases. Our efforts will continue further so as to be able to explain the elevations and descends in both of our measures with respect to events that might be the trigger for such fluctuations.

References

1. Agathangelou, P., Katakis, I., Koutoulakis, I., Kokkoras, F., Gunopulos, D.: Learning patterns for discovering domain-oriented opinion words. Knowl. Inf. Syst. **55**(1), 45–77 (2018)
2. Badache, I., Chifu, A.G., Fournier, S.: Unsupervised and supervised methods to estimate temporal-aware contradictions in online course reviews. Mathematics **10**(5), 809 (2022)
3. Chen, J., Ren, Y., Riedl, J.: The effects of diversity on group productivity and member withdrawal in online volunteer groups. In: Proceedings of the SIGCHI Conference on Human Factors in Computing Systems, pp. 821–830 (2010)
4. Chhabra, A., Iyengar, S.R.S.: How does knowledge come by? CoRR abs/1705.06946 (2017)

5. Chhabra, A., Kaur, R., Iyengar, S.: Dynamics of edit war sequences in Wikipedia. In: Proceedings of the 16th International Symposium on Open Collaboration, pp. 1–10 (2020)
6. Couto, L., Teixeira Lopes, C.: Equal opportunities in the access to quality online health information? A multi-lingual study on Wikipedia. In: Proceedings of the 17th International Symposium on Open Collaboration, pp. 1–13 (2021)
7. Damadi, M.S., Davoust, A.: Fairness in socio-technical systems: a case study of Wikipedia. arXiv preprint arXiv:2302.07787 (2023)
8. Ferran-Ferrer, N., Miquel-Ribé, M., Meneses, J., Minguillón, J.: The gender perspective in Wikipedia: a content and participation challenge. In: Companion Proceedings of the Web Conference 2022, pp. 1319–1323 (2022)
9. Giles, J.: Internet encyclopaedias go head to head. Nature **438**, 900–901 (2005)
10. Hube, C., Fetahu, B.: Detecting biased statements in Wikipedia. In: Companion Proceedings of the Web Conference 2018, pp. 1779–1786 (2018)
11. Kenrick, D.T.: Evolutionary theory and human social behavior. In: Handbook of Theories of Social Psychology, vol. 1, pp. 11–31 (2012)
12. Liu, B.: Sentiment Analysis and Opinion Mining. Morgan & Claypool Publishers (2012)
13. Madanagopal, K., Caverlee, J.: Improving linguistic bias detection in Wikipedia using cross-domain adaptive pre-training. In: Companion Proceedings of the Web Conference 2022, pp. 1301–1309 (2022)
14. Mannix, E., Neale, M.A.: What differences make a difference? The promise and reality of diverse teams in organizations. Psychol. Sci. Public Interest **6**(2), 31–55 (2005)
15. Morris-O'Connor, D., Strotmann, A., Zhao, D.: Editorial behaviors for biasing Wikipedia articles. Proc. Assoc. Inf. Sci. Technol. **59**(1), 226–234 (2022)
16. Nandwani, P., Verma, R.: A review on sentiment analysis and emotion detection from text. Soc. Netw. Anal. Min. **11**(1), 81 (2021)
17. Pryzant, R., Martinez, R.D., Dass, N., Kurohashi, S., Jurafsky, D., Yang, D.: Automatically neutralizing subjective bias in text. In: AAAI (2020)
18. Rajagopal, D., Zhang, X., Gamon, M., Jauhar, S.K., Yang, D., Hovy, E.: One document, many revisions: a dataset for classification and description of edit intents. In: Proceedings of the Thirteenth Language Resources and Evaluation Conference, pp. 5517–5524 (2022)
19. Ramírez-Ordóñez, D., Ferran-Ferrer, N., Meneses, J.: Wikipedia and gender: the deleted, the marked, and the unpolluted biographies (2022)
20. Semin, G.R., Fiedler, K.: The linguistic category model, its bases, applications and range. Eur. Rev. Soc. Psychol. **2**(1), 1–30 (1991)
21. Shi, F., Teplitskiy, M., Duede, E., Evans, J.A.: The wisdom of polarized crowds. Nat. Hum. Behav. **3**(4), 329–336 (2019)
22. Viégas, F.B., Wattenberg, M., Dave, K.: Studying cooperation and conflict between authors with history flow visualizations. In: Proceedings of the SIGCHI Conference on Human Factors in Computing Systems, pp. 575–582 (2004)
23. Wigboldus, D.H., Spears, R., Semin, G.R.: When do we communicate stereotypes? Influence of the social context on the linguistic expectancy bias. Group Process. Intergroup Relat. **8**(3), 215–230 (2005)
24. Wilkinson, D.M., Huberman, B.A.: Cooperation and quality in Wikipedia. In: Proceedings of the 2007 International Symposium on Wikis, pp. 157–164 (2007)
25. Zheng, X., Chen, J., Yan, E., Ni, C.: Gender and country biases in Wikipedia citations to scholarly publications. J. Am. Soc. Inf. Sci. **74**(2), 219–233 (2023)

Investigating the Usefulness of Product Reviews Through Bipolar Argumentation Frameworks

Atefeh Keshavarzi Zafarghandi[1], Ji Qi[2], Laura Hollink[3], Erik Tjong Kim Sang[2], and Davide Ceolin[3](✉)

[1] Vrije Universiteit Amsterdam, Amsterdam, The Netherlands
a.keshavarzi.zafarghandi@vu.nl

[2] Netherlands eScience Center, Amsterdam, The Netherlands
{j.qi,e.tjongkimsang}@esciencecenter.nl

[3] Centrum Wiskunde & Informatica, Amsterdam, The Netherlands
{l.hollink,d.ceolin}@cwi.nl

Abstract. The importance of useful product reviews cannot be overstated, as they not only provide crucial information to potential buyers but also offer valuable feedback to the businesses or individuals under review. Providing useful reviews to consumers has gained significant attention as an effective market analysis tool for companies. Numerous studies have delved into the facets that contribute to predicting the usefulness of reviews, encompassing a spectrum from philosophical insights to advancements in artificial intelligence. In this work, we study how to use the argument structure of reviews to identify the most useful reviews in a set of annotated product reviews. In particular, we use quantitative bipolar argumentation frameworks (QBAFs) to construct a model of review arguments and topics, and we apply reasoning to such a model to identify useful reviews. Our results show that indeed argument reasoning, and QBAFs in particular, provide an insightful and well-performing means to analyze the usefulness of reviews.

Keywords: Bipolar Argumentation Frameworks · Product Reviews · Review Usefulness

1 Introduction

Consumer reviews are a crucial part of the e-commerce sector. They not only provide information to potential buyers but also offer valuable feedback to businesses about the products or services under review. Consumers as well as businesses have a strong interest in determining the helpfulness of a review, given that many reviews might be associated with a single product or service, and review helpfulness varies. Identifying the most useful reviews for a given product is a particularly relevant and challenging problem from the Web engineering point of view. On the one hand, it requires identifying those reviews that better fit the information requirements of diverse users, while such requirements are often subjective and possibly contextual. On the other hand, such an effort would allow society to benefit from the large number of reviews shared online by being able to select those that are potentially more useful.

K. Stefanidis et al. (Eds.): ICWE 2024, LNCS 14629, pp. 296–308, 2024.
https://doi.org/10.1007/978-3-031-62362-2_21

Previous work on predicting review helpfulness has focused on attributes of the reviewer, such as the number of reviews they provided, or on attributes of the review text, such as length and sentiment score, or on both [4,5]. In this paper, we propose a complementary approach, namely to use the argument structure of a set of reviews. Product reviews often span a spectrum of opinions, advocating for or against various aspects of a product. This discourse encapsulates arguments that either support or challenge specific product attributes. Given this inherent argumentative nature, it becomes intuitive to leverage formalisms of argumentation theory to portray the intricate relationships among extracted arguments.

Our objective is to examine the impact of argumentative features on the detection of helpful reviews. We utilize argumentative features as input for a classifier so that they can be used on top of 'standard' review features like length and sentiment. For this purpose, we adopt a quantitative approach to argumentation. Quantitative argumentation frameworks are introduced in [3] to support the possibility of having debate-style systems in Issue-Based Information Systems, especially when deciding upon design alternatives. In particular, quantitative argumentation provides an automatic quantitative evaluation of the positions put forward. We employ quantitative bipolar argumentation frameworks (QBAFs) to model the relationship between arguments extracted from the reviews and the various aspects of the product. Subsequently, we employ the semantics of QBAFs to assess the strength of these product aspects quantitatively.

Our approach consists of several steps. First, we split review texts into chunks. Then, we assign a topic to each chunk and detect the sentiment of each chunk. All three tasks are done with off-the-shelf NLP tools (Spacy, BertTopic, TextBlob, respectively). We also determine the readability of each review (computing the Flesh-Kincaid Readability Ease using the Spacy Readability Python package). And, we give each review a 'coherence score' based on the difference between the sentiment and the rating of the review (e.g. a five-star review with a negative sentiment is not coherent). Finally, the core of our method is to construct a QBAF: the topics are used to represent arguments and the sentiment scores determine the support or attack relationships between the arguments. Once the QBAF is constructed, we utilize DF-QuAD and quadratic-energy model semantics to compute the dialectical strength of the arguments within the QBAF. These computations generate argumentative features.

We perform a series of experiments in which we employ four classification algorithms on various feature sets to predict review helpfulness. The first feature set consists of only review features (sentiment, readability). The second set adds the coherence score. The third and fourth sets add argumentative features; DF-QuAD features and quadratic-energy model features, respectively. Note that we have not included reviewer features in our experiments, nor have we included all possible review features described in the literature. Given our aim of examining the impact of argumentative features on top of 'standard' features, we have chosen to compare against a relatively small, well-known, and well-performing set of features.

For our experiments, we use the Amazon Fashion 5 reviews dataset curated by McAuley et al. [19], encompassing reviews that have garnered user votes. We consider these 'voted' reviews as valuable indicators of helpfulness due to their resonance with readers. Our method is a supervised approach, and it directly utilizes the 'voted' column in the dataset as the target variable for the classifiers, eliminating the need for additional data annotation or evaluations.

Our findings show that argument features outperform the baseline of review features. The impact is larger if both DF-QuAD features and quadratic-energy model features are included. The coherence score does not have a measurable effect on classifier performance. With these results, we hope to shed light on a so far under-explored direction within the area of review helpfulness prediction. This direction is especially promising given the growing push for interpretable methods.

The rest of the paper continues as follows. In Sect. 2 we introduce related work. In Sect. 3, we present the preliminary work necessary to introduce our approach in Sect. 4. In Sect. 5, we present and discuss the results obtained. In Sect. 6, we conclude.

2 Related Work

Online reviews hold value based on their perceived helpfulness, a reflection of readers' subjective assessment of their quality [17]. Previous studies have identified review attributes such as length, rating, readability, and subjectivity as critical factors in predicting review helpfulness [4,5]. We explore another type of feature that can be used on top of such attributes, namely argumentative features. Harrison-Walker and Jiang [15] investigated the relationship between review features and their credibility. They identify argument balance as one source of credibility and they investigate the effect of argument polarity on the customer choices. In our analyses, we do not focus on single reviews, but rather we compare their arguments and leverage their strength and polarity to estimate their usefulness.

Formal argumentation is widely used to represent and reason with inconsistent and incomplete information [6]. Formalisms of argumentation are equipped with semantics and/or algorithms to evaluate the acceptability of arguments [7,13] or to assess, qualitatively, the strength of arguments [26]. There are several formalisms of argumentation such as abstract argumentation [13], bipolar argumentation frameworks [2], and quantitative argumentation [3,26]. Quantitative argumentation frameworks extend bipolar argumentation frameworks [2] by ascribing intrinsic strengths to the arguments and by incorporating quantitative semantics to evaluate the strength of arguments. Various methods are used to achieve this, including the quantitative argumentation debate (QuAD) framework algorithm [3], discontinuity-free quantitative argumentation debate (DF-QuAD) algorithm [26], and the quadratic energy model [23]. Quantitative argumentation frameworks have demonstrated superior performance in addressing real-world issues such as fraud detection in e-commerce transactions [9], fake news detection [8], deceptive review detection [11], and review aggregation [10].

The methodology introduced in this study bears resemblance to the approach outlined in a prior work by Cocarascu and Toni [11,12]. In their work, the authors employ QBAFs to identify deceptive reviews. In a parallel manner, we adopt quantitative bipolar argumentation frameworks (QBAFs) to detect helpful reviews. In this study, we utilize a quantitative bipolar argumentation framework (QBAFs) to depict the relationship between the arguments extracted from the set of reviews. Moreover, we employ the quantitative semantics embedded within QBAFs to gauge the quality of a product. We

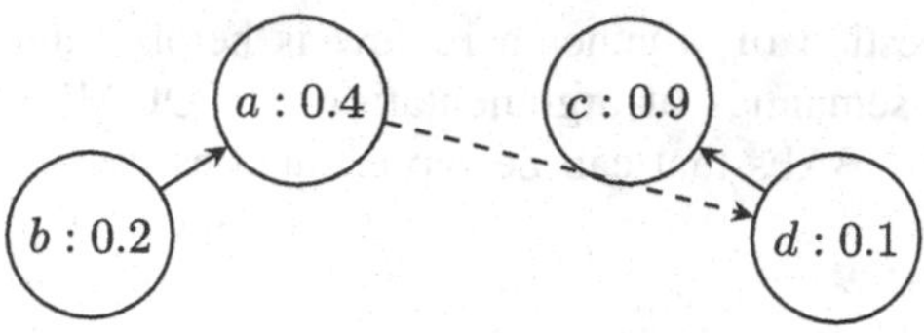

Fig. 1. QBAF obtained from the shoes review, presented in Sect. 3.1 (Example 1)

demonstrate that incorporating argumentative reasoning as a feature in the classifiers leads to better performance compared to not considering them when labeling reviews.

3 Preliminaries

In this section, we provide an overview of quantitative argumentation frameworks [3, 23, 26] and introduce the dataset along with NLP-based features.

3.1 Quantitative Bipolar Argumentation Frameworks

We start the preliminaries to our work by recalling the basic notion of quantitative bipolar argumentation frameworks [3,23,26].

Definition 1. *A quantitative bipolar argumentation framework (QBAF for short) is a tuple (A, R^+, R^-, τ) where A is a finite set of arguments, $R^+ \subseteq A \times A$ is the set of support relations between arguments, $R^- \subseteq A \times A$ in the set of attack relations between arguments, and $\tau : A \mapsto [0, 1]$ is a total function, where for any $a \in A$, $\tau(a)$ is a base score of a.*

A QBAF can be visualized using directed graphs as in Fig. 1. Nodes show the arguments with their base scores, solid edges denote attacks and dashed edges denote supports.

Example 1. Figure 1 shows a directed graph for the QBAF $(\{a, b, c, d\}, \{(a, d)\}, \{(b, a), (d, c)\}, \{(a, 0.4), (b, 0.2), (c, 0.9), (d, 0.1)\})$. Each argument is associated with a base score. Argument a supports d, as depicted by the dashed line in the figure, while argument b attacks a, and d attacks c, depicted by solid lines in this figure.

Quantitative bipolar argumentation frameworks (QBAFs) utilize a base score for arguments, dynamically adjusted based on the strength of their attackers and supporters [1,3,22–24,26]. To evaluate arguments' strength within a QBAF, various gradual semantics methods are available, such as QuAD [3], DF-QuAD [3], the Restricted Euler-based semantics [1], and the quadratic-energy model [23].

The strength values of arguments are usually computed iteratively using a two-step update procedure, first, an aggregation function aggregates the strength values of attackers and supporters; then, an influence function adapts the base score. Different combinations of aggregation and influence functions result in distinct semantics found in the literature, mostly with very similar properties.

To answer the question of whether a review is helpful and to what extent, we consider two gradual semantics of argumentation, DF-QUAD [3], which is defined for restricted types of QBAFs that can be represented as trees, and quadratic-energy model [23,25].

Discontinuity-Free QuAD (DF-QuAD): One widely studied algorithm for gradual argumentation is the Discontinuity-Free Algorithm (DF-QuAD) introduced in a paper by Baroni et al. (2015) [3]. DF-QuAD is defined by three key functions: a strength aggregation function, a combination function, and a score function.

The **strength aggregation function** is responsible for determining how the strengths of attackers and supporters are aggregated individually. Denoted as $\mathcal{F}$, this function operates on a set of n arguments with strengths $v_1, \ldots, v_n$, and it is defined as follows:

$$\mathcal{F}(v_1, \ldots, v_n) = \begin{cases} 0 & n = 0, \\ 1 - \log \prod_{i=1}^{n}(|1 - v_i|) & n > 0 \end{cases}$$

After determining the strengths of attackers and supporters separately using the strength aggregation function $\mathcal{F}$, the **combination function** $\mathcal{C}$ combines these strengths with the base score of the argument. Let v_0 denote the base score of the argument in question, $v_a = \mathcal{F}(v_1, \ldots, v_n)$ represent the aggregated strength of the attackers of the argument (for $n > 0$), and $v_s = \mathcal{F}(v'_1, \ldots, v'_m)$ denote the aggregated strength of the supporters of the argument (for $m > 0$). The combination function $\mathcal{C}$ is defined as follows:

$$\mathcal{C}(v_0, v_a, v_s) = \begin{cases} v_0 & \text{if } v_a = v_s, \\ v_0 - \log(v_0 \times |v_s - v_a|) & \text{if } v_a > v_s, \\ v_0 + \log(1 - v_0) \times |v_s - v_a|) & \text{if } v_a < v_s \end{cases}$$

The **score function** $s(a)$ calculates the final strength of argument a by utilizing the combination function. It combines the base score of a, denoted as v_0, with the strength of its attackers (v_a) and supporters (v_s). The score function is defined as follows:

$$s(a) = |\mathcal{C}(v_0, v_a, v_s)|$$

One major drawback of this method is that the resulting aggregate tends to be close to zero when both an attacker and a supporter have strengths close to one.

Quadratic-Energy Model: The quadratic-energy model from [23] consist of an aggregation and an influence function, where the influence function is symmetric about 0, which causes a balance between attacks and supports. Let $w(a)$ be the base score of argument a. The aggregation function for the quadratic-energy model is defined as follows:

$$\alpha(a) = \Sigma_{b \in \mathsf{sup}(a)} s(b) - \Sigma_{b \in \mathsf{att}(a)} s(b)$$

where $s : a \rightarrow [0, 1]$ assigns the current strength value (base score) to every argument. The influence function of this semantics is defined by

$$\theta(a) = w(a) - w(a) \times h(-\alpha(a)) + (1 - w(a)) \times h(\alpha(a))$$

where $h(x) = \frac{max\{0,x\}^2}{1+max\{1,x\}^2}$ squashes its input to the interval $[0, 1]$. Intuitively, a positive aggregate will move the weight towards 1, while a negative aggregate will move the weight towards 0.

3.2 Dataset

Our proposed method was evaluated using the Amazon Fashion 5 reviews dataset created by McAuley et al. [19]. This dataset comprises a collection of reviews for fashion products, complemented with metadata such as timestamps and reviewer IDs. After removing duplicate entries, our dataset consisted of 371 unique reviews, of which only 37 had received votes from users. Since votes can only be positive (only "thumbs ups" are collected), we refer to the count of votes as "upvotes".

3.3 NLP Techniques

We used a variety of natural language processing tools for automatically analyzing the review texts. Spacy[1] was employed for dividing the texts into chunks. The software splits texts into sentences and parses the sentences with Spacy's default syntactic dependency parser for English. The sentences were then broken up into chunks based on the syntactic heads, which we defined as words that are dependent on a conjunction. A chunk was then built for each head with the words that were syntactically dependent on the head.

To identify the topics that characterize the chunks, we used BertTopic [14], a transformer-based topic analyzer for English. We applied the software with default parameters. It created 26 topics. Sentiment polarity scores were obtained by analyzing the chunks with TextBlob[2]. The program returns two numbers for each text, a polarity score and a subjectivity score and we used the first one. Next, rank scores are computed for each chunk based on the TextRank measure [21]. The rank scores are based on the distance between vector representations of the chunks and the corresponding complete review. The rank scores are normalized in such a way that the sum of the rank scores for a single review is one.

Per-review sentiment polarity scores are computed as the weighted average of the chunk sentiment scores where the rank scores are used as weights. Finally, the coherence score per review was computed as the absolute difference between the per-reviewed sentiment polarity score and the user vote attached to the review. Normalized scores lie between 0 and 1. A drawback of this approach is that reviews with a normalized user vote value close to the most frequent sentiment scores (0.55–0.75) will, on average, receive the highest coherence scores, while the coherence scores for other user vote values will be lower.

We also compute a readability score to estimate the level of clarity and lexical complexity of reviews. To this aim, we employ the Flesh-Kincaid Reading Ease readability measure [16] through the Spacy readability implementation[3].

[1] https://spacy.io/.

[2] https://textblob.readthedocs.io/en/dev/.

[3] See: https://github.com/mholtzscher/spacy_readability.

4 Approach

The primary objective of this work is to identify helpful reviews by mining QBAFs constructed from arguments grouped according to topics extracted from reviews. Here we describe the approach we adopt by leveraging the above existing body of work. The code implementing the approach here described is available online.[4]

4.1 Constructing QBAFs

Here, we introduce the construction process of a QBAF for a given set of reviews. We begin by identifying the set of arguments, the set of relations between arguments, and the base scores of arguments.

Argument Extraction. As discussed in Sect. 3.3, we utilize Spacy to split a review into chunks. Additionally, we employ BertTopic to cluster these chunks based on their topics. To construct a QBAF associated with a given set of reviews, we define the following types of abstract:

1. **Product-argument:** We introduce a fresh variable G_p to represent the overall quality of the product.
2. **Topic-arguments:** For each topic within the set of reviews (our dataset comprises 26 different topics), we introduce distinct fresh variables $G_{j,l}$ where $-1 \leq j \leq 24$. These variables abstractly represent the quality of individual topics based on the reviews, and l represents a given product.
3. **Chunk-arguments:** To represent each chunk within a cluster abstractly, we introduce a fresh variable $a_{i,j}$, where i denotes the review number, and j denotes the topic number. This variable represents the mention of the topic j in the review i. Depending on the sentiment of such a mention, the argument $a_{i,j}$ will attack or support the topic $G_{j,l}$. In the case of multiple repeated tokens in the same review belonging to the same topic cluster, these will be represented by a single node whose weight is the cumulated weight of all the relevant chunks.

Example 2. We pick the first review in our dataset that says: "I always get a half size up in my tennis shoes. For some reason, these feel too big in the heel area and wide." We aim to construct a QBAF associated to this review. This review consists of two chunks as follows. The chunk "I always get a half size up in my tennis shoes" corresponds to cluster 4, while the chunk "For some reason, these feel too big in the heel area and wide" corresponds to cluster 15.

We introduce two fresh variables, $a_{1,4}$ and $a_{1,15}$, to represent the chunks within the first review for topics 4 and 15, respectively.

Furthermore, for any topic, we pick a fresh variable. We introduce variables G_4 and G_{15} for topics 4 and 15, respectively. Additionally, we use a fresh variable G_p as a product-argument pair to represent the overall quality of the product.

[4] The code is available at https://github.com/EyeofBeholder-NLeSC/orange3-argument.

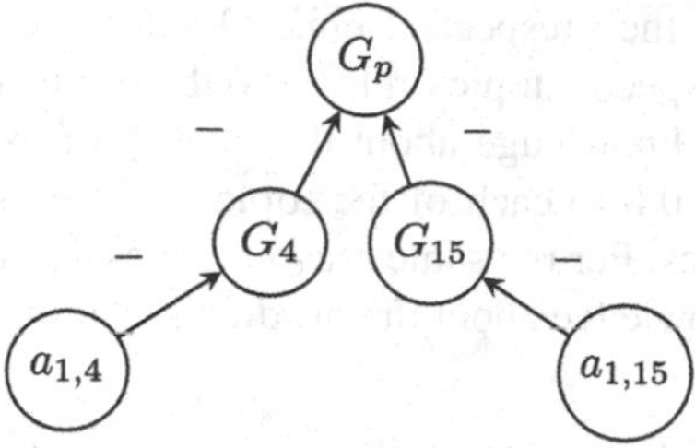

Fig. 2. QBAF obtained from the shoes review, presented in Example 2. There are three different types of arguments: Chunk-arguments $a_{1,4}$ and $a_{1,15}$ represent review 1 containing topics 4 and 15, respectively. Topic-arguments G_4 and G_{15} represent topics 4 and 15 in an abstract manner. We aim to assess the quality of these topic-arguments based on the chunk-arguments. Furthermore, the product-argument G_p aims to evaluate the quality of product p. Since the sentiment of both $a_{1,4}$ and $a_{1,15}$ is less than 0, as calculated in Sect. 3.3, there are attack relations from these arguments to the topic-arguments G_4 and G_{15}, respectively. Our objective is to assess the quality of a product, and thus, we want to evaluate G_p concerning the topic-arguments. Hence, we establish attack links from each topic-argument to the product-argument, as the strength of both G_4 and G_{15} is less than 0.5.

Relation Extraction. After extracting the set of arguments, the second challenge is to indicate the set of relations between these arguments. We determine the type of relations, which can be either supporters or attackers, by analyzing the sentiment of the chunks. The degree of sentiment of each chunk is represented as a real number between -1 and 1, presented in Sect. 3.3.

When the sentiment of a chunk is equal to or greater than zero, we assume that it supports the topic it belongs to, since it conveys a positive sentiment about it. Otherwise, we assume it attacks the abstract argument representing the topic. Consequently, we establish a support link from the chunk-argument $a_{i,j}$ to the abstract topic-argument G_i when the sentiment of $a_{i,j}$ is equal to or greater than 0; otherwise, it signifies an attack relation. Moreover, we weigh the attack based on the importance of the chunk in the context of the review it is extracted from. Such a weight is computed using the TextRank score.

Since our objective is to accumulate the strengths of all topic-arguments in the abstract product-argument G_p to indicate how good a product is, we establish support links from each G_i to G_p, where $-1 \leq i \leq 24$. The QBAF associated with the review in Example 2 is illustrated in Fig. 2.

Extracting Base Scores. The final consideration in this section pertains to determining the base score of the arguments. Within each review, every chunk is assigned a rank that signifies its importance concerning the corresponding aspect. A higher rank indicates that the chunk provides more significant information about the aspect within the given review. For example, let us examine review number 1, which concerns aspect 4. In this review, the chunk 'I always get a half size up in my tennis shoes' is assigned a rank of 0.5. We utilize the rank of each chunk as the base score within the associated QBAFs. Continuing with the review depicted in Fig. 2, the base scores of $a_{1,4}$ and $a_{1,15}$ are both 0.5, corresponding to their respective ranks. Each topic-argument G_i is intended to indicate the quality of a specific topic i related to the product. Before considering any reviews, we have no prior knowledge about the quality of the product's topics. Thus, we assign a base score of 0.5 to each of the topic-arguments since we have no prior information about the topics. For the same reason, we assign a base score of 0.5 to G_p since we have no prior knowledge about the product's quality.

Graph Solving. In order to compute the argument strength of the abstract argument representing a product, we proceed as follows. We build the product graph and we identify a suitable semantics. The graph will be composed of a root (the product argument), a layer of topic-arguments, and the leaves, the chunk arguments. We partition the graph per topic. We solve each topic-argument graph, by determining how the chunks attacking and supporting the topic (in the context of the product) determine the strength of the topic-argument. The selected semantics determine how to aggregate the weights. Then, we use the resulting strengths to determine the product's strength based on how the topics attack or support it.

4.2 Creating Argumentative Features

The product strength, denoted as $s(G_p)$, quantifies the quality of a product numerically, considering all reviews. To assess the impact of a specific review on this strength, we follow these steps: we exclude the review in question from the set and construct a new QBAF using all reviews except the one under evaluation, as done in [12] to assess the impact of deceptive reviews. We then repeat the process of evaluating the product strength after excluding the specific review. Each review is assigned a numerical value that indicates its impact on the product's strength. This new strength value serves as a measure to signify the influence of the review under consideration.

We perform these evaluations for both of the quantitative semantics presented in Sect. 3, namely DF-QuAD and the quadratic-energy model. We utilize these numerical values as features for the classifiers.

To provide further clarity to the method, let $R = \{r_1, r_2\}$ represent the set of reviews containing r_1 and r_2. Initially, we construct a QBAF, as detailed in Sect. 4.1, considering both r_1 and r_2. Subsequently, we assess the product strength of $s(G_p)$ separately for DF-QuAD and the quadratic-energy model. Next, to evaluate the impact of r_1 on the product strengths, we remove r_1, create a new QBAF, and evaluate the product strengths for both semantics after the exclusion. This process is then repeated for r_2. As a result, each review becomes associated with two new numerical values based on the DF-QuAD and quadratic-energy model semantics. These results are subsequently employed as features for the classifiers. Algorithm 1 outlines a method to assess the influence of each review r_i on the qualitative strength of a product, represented as $s(G_p)$, using a given set of reviews. In Algorithm 1, we denote the impact of r_i on the product's strength as $s_i(G_p)$. These numerical values assigned to each review r_i are incorporated as new features, referred to as argument features, and are inputted into the classifiers.

Algorithm 1. Evaluate the impact of each review on the strength of a product with DF-QuAD

Input: Set of reviews: $\{r_1, \ldots, r_n\}$
Output: quantitative impact of each review on the quantitative strength of a product based on DF-QuAD semantics, i.e., on the strength of G_p
Construct the associated QBAF for $\{r_1, \ldots, r_n\}$, as presented in 4.1
$s(G_p)$= Evaluate DF-QuAD for G_p based on $\{r_1, \ldots, r_n\}$; we refer to this as the strength of the product.
for $i > 0$ **do**
  remove r_i from $\{r_1, \ldots, r_n\}$
  Construct the associated QBAF for $\{r_1, \ldots, r_n\} \setminus r_i$
  $s'(G_p)$ Evaluate DF-QuAD for $\{r_1, \ldots, r_n\} \setminus r_i$
  Let $s_i(G_p) = s(G_p) - s'(G_p)$
  Print: $s_i(G_p)$ is an impact of r_i on the strength of the product, calculated by DF-QuAD
end for

5 Results

We evaluate the performance of various classifiers, considering both argumentative and non-argumentative features, with "voted reviews" as the target variable for the classifiers. Our goal is to examine how argument features influence classifier performance.

We implemented our method with various classifiers and observed that the Gradient Boosting Classifier (GBC for short) performed the best in most cases. We employed a 5-fold cross-validation approach. Our primary focus was on "F1Macro", which is commonly used in multi-class classification problems. F1Macro calculates the F1 score for each class individually, where the F1 score represents a harmonic mean of precision and recall, striking a balance between these two metrics. Subsequently, it averages these individual F1 scores to compute the "F1Macro" score.

First, we examine the influence of common characteristics of the reviews, namely the readability of the text and the sentiment of the text, as features for assessing the performance of the classifiers. In this case, we observed that the F1Macro score is 0.89.

Next, we explore the impact of the notion of coherency, as introduced in this work, on the performance of the Gradient Boosting Classifier (GBC). Specifically, we consider the readability, sentiment, and coherency of the reviews as features for the classifiers. Our findings indicate that coherency neither positively nor negatively affects the performance of the GBC. In other words, the F1Macro score remains at 0.89.

Then, we explore the impact of argumentative features, which are the results evaluated by the semantics of the Quantitative Bipolar Argumentation Frameworks (QBAFs) as presented in Sect. 3.1. Our observations indicate that when we incorporate the results from the DF-QuAD algorithm as features, the performance of the GBC remains unchanged. In other words, when we use readability, sentiment, coherency of the reviews, and DF-QuAD results as features for the classifiers, the F1Macro score remains at 0.89.

However, when we introduce the results from the quadratic-energy model as a feature in the classifiers, the F1Macro score increases to 0.91. This occurs when our feature set consists of readability, sentiment, coherency of the reviews, and the results of the quadratic-energy model. Furthermore, when we consider the results of both DF-QuAD and the quadratic-energy model as argumentative features, in addition to the readability, sentiment, and coherency of the reviews in the GBC, the F1Macro score increases to 0.92.

We also investigate in depth the correlation between the argumentative features above described and the actual number of upvotes. This leads to a weak correlation identified (across the different combinations of semantics, we achieve a Spearman $\rho \leq 0.2$ and a Pearson $\rho \leq 0.15$). While this shows some signal, it also indicates the need for complementing these features with additional ones. However, such a comparison could be performed on 371 reviews only, and will thus be further explored in the future. Moreover, we investigate whether large-language models could provide a useful alternative means to evaluate review usefulness. However, the results obtained depended significantly on the choice of the prompt and the specific language model: the same review, for example, received 0/10 and 10/10 usefulness assessment by Phi 2 [20] and LLaVA 1.6 7b [18]. We will systematically investigate this further in the future.

6 Conclusion

In this study, we employ QBAFs to assess the strength of a product based on the reviews it receives. Subsequently, we systematically exclude individual reviews one by one to discern the specific impact of each review on this measure of strength. These results are then utilized as novel features within the classifiers to facilitate the detection of helpful reviews.

To construct the associated QBAFs for a set of reviews, we adhere to a series of steps. Within each review, any given chunk is regarded as an argument, and these chunks are categorized based on the aspects they pertain to. Presently, our current ML methods identify a total of 26 aspects. However, we intend to reduce this number in future iterations of our work.

For each aspect, we introduce an abstract argument denoted as t_i, termed the aspect argument in the associated QBAF. Should a chunk $a_{k,i}$ fall within the cluster of aspect i, it is deemed a parent of t_i in the corresponding QBAF. Furthermore, we are keen to incorporate the temporal aspect of review presentation in our forthcoming work, leading to a more intricate structure within the QBAFs. Subsequently, we implement the methodology outlined in this study on these revised QBAFs. This implementation allows us to assess the influence of the evolved structure of the associated QBAFs on the performance of the classifiers.

The methodology introduced in this study bears resemblance to the approach outlined in a prior work by Cocarascu and Toni [11]. In their work, the authors employ a generalization of AFs to identify deceptive reviews. In a parallel manner, we adopt quantitative bipolar argumentation frameworks (QBAFs) to detect helpful reviews.

In this current study, we employ ML methods to extract arguments, establish relations between them, and subsequently ascertain the base strength of these arguments. The identification of arguments, their inherent base strength, and the interconnections between them wield a critical influence on the argumentative features provided as input to the classifiers. In future endeavors, we are eager to explore additional ML methods to conduct a comprehensive comparison of outcomes.

The results have shown that the proposed approach outperforms the baseline, albeit by a small margin. We believe that the use of argumentation frameworks for review helpfulness prediction is promising, not only because of this observed, small increase in performance, but also because of other advantages. Firstly, AFs are potentially explainable to users, which is a big advantage given the growing demand for transparency across the AI field. Secondly, AF features are relatively hard to manipulate by malicious users compared to, for example, simpler features like review length or sentiment. Finally, the proposed AF features can be used on top of any other features and in combination with any classification algorithm, making the approach potentially useful to a wide range of applications.

In the future, we plan to further extend the analyses here presented, both in terms of semantics considered and in terms of size and variety of review dataset analyzed.

Acknowledgements. This publication has been partly supported by the Netherlands eScience Center project "The Eye of the Beholder" (project nr. 027.020.G15). This publication is part of the AI, Media & Democracy Lab (Dutch Research Council project number: NWA.1332.20.009). For more information about the lab and its further activities, visit https://www.aim4dem.nl/. Moreover, this publication has been partly supported by the Netherlands Organisation for Scientific Research (NWO) through the Hybrid Intelligence Gravitation Programme with project number 024.004.022.

References

1. Amgoud, L., Ben-Naim, J.: Evaluation of arguments in weighted bipolar graphs. Int. J. Approx. Reason. **99**, 39–55 (2018)
2. Amgoud, L., Cayrol, C., Lagasquie-Schiex, M., Livet, P.: On bipolarity in argumentation frameworks. Int. J. Intell. Syst. **23**(10), 1062–1093 (2008)
3. Baroni, P., Romano, M., Toni, F., Aurisicchio, M., Bertanza, G.: Automatic evaluation of design alternatives with quantitative argumentation. Argument Comput. **6**(1), 24–49 (2015)
4. Bilal, M., Marjani, M., Hashem, I.A.T., Gani, A., Liaqat, M., Ko, K.: Profiling and predicting the cumulative helpfulness (quality) of crowd-sourced reviews. Information **10**(10), 295 (2019)
5. Bilal, M., Marjani, M., Lali, M.I.U., Malik, N., Gani, A., Hashem, I.A.T.: Profiling users' behavior, and identifying important features of review "helpfulness". IEEE Access **8**, 77227–77244 (2020)
6. Brewka, G., Ellmauthaler, S., Strass, H., Wallner, J.P., Woltran, S.: Abstract dialectical frameworks: an overview. In: Handbook of Formal Argumentation, pp. 237–285. College Publications (2018)
7. Cayrol, C., Lagasquie-Schiex, M.C.: On the acceptability of arguments in bipolar argumentation frameworks. In: Godo, L. (ed.) ECSQARU 2005. LNCS (LNAI), vol. 3571, pp. 378–389. Springer, Heidelberg (2005). https://doi.org/10.1007/11518655_33
8. Chi, H., Liao, B.: A quantitative argumentation-based automated explainable decision system for fake news detection on social media. Knowl. Based Syst. **242**, 108378 (2022)
9. Chi, H., Lu, Y., Liao, B., Xu, L., Liu, Y.: An optimized quantitative argumentation debate model for fraud detection in e-commerce transactions. IEEE Intell. Syst. **36**(2), 52–63 (2021)
10. Cocarascu, O., Rago, A., Toni, F.: Extracting dialogical explanations for review aggregations with argumentative dialogical agents. In: AAMAS, pp. 1261–1269. International Foundation for Autonomous Agents and Multiagent Systems (2019)

11. Cocarascu, O., Toni, F.: Detecting deceptive reviews using argumentation. In: PrAISe@ECAI, pp. 9:1–9:8. ACM (2016)
12. Cocarascu, O., Toni, F.: Combining deep learning and argumentative reasoning for the analysis of social media textual content using small data sets. Comput. Linguist. **44**(4), 833–858 (2018)
13. Dung, P.M.: On the acceptability of arguments and its fundamental role in nonmonotonic reasoning, logic programming and n-person games. Artif. Intell. **77**, 321–357 (1995)
14. Grootendorst, M.: BERTopic: neural topic modeling with a class-based TF-IDF procedure. arXiv preprint arxiv.org:2203.05794 (2022)
15. Harrison-Walker, L.J., Jiang, Y.: Suspicion of online product reviews as fake: cues and consequences. J. Bus. Res. **160**, 113780 (2023). https://doi.org/10.1016/j.jbusres.2023.113780. https://www.sciencedirect.com/science/article/pii/S0148296323001388
16. Kincaid, J., Fishburne, R., Rogers, R., Chissom, B.: Derivation of new readability formulas for navy enlisted personnel. Research branch report 8-75. Technical report, Chief of Naval Technical Training: Naval Air Station Memphis (1975)
17. Li, M., Huang, L., Tan, C.H., Wei, K.K.: Helpfulness of online product reviews as seen by consumers: source and content features. Int. J. Electron. Commer. **17**(4), 101–136 (2013)
18. Liu, H., et al.: LLaVA-NeXT: improved reasoning, OCR, and world knowledge (2024). https://llava-vl.github.io/blog/2024-01-30-llava-next/
19. McAuley, J.J., Targett, C., Shi, Q., van den Hengel, A.: Image-based recommendations on styles and substitutes. In: Proceedings of SIGIR, pp. 43–52. ACM (2015)
20. Microsoft: Microsoft phi-2 (2023). https://ai.azure.com/explore/models/microsoft-phi-2/version/4/registry/azureml-msr
21. Mihalcea, R., Tarau, P.: TextRank: bringing order into texts. In: Proceedings of EMNLP-2004 and the 2004 Conference on Empirical Methods in Natural Language Processing (2004)
22. Mossakowski, T., Neuhaus, F.: Modular semantics and characteristics for bipolar weighted argumentation graphs. CoRR abs/1807.06685 (2018)
23. Potyka, N.: Continuous dynamical systems for weighted bipolar argumentation. In: KR, pp. 148–157. AAAI Press (2018)
24. Potyka, N.: Extending modular semantics for bipolar weighted argumentation. In: AAMAS, pp. 1722–1730. International Foundation for Autonomous Agents and Multiagent Systems (2019)
25. Potyka, N.: Foundations for solving classification problems with quantitative abstract argumentation. In: XI-ML@KI. CEUR Workshop Proceedings, vol. 2796, pp. 148–157. CEUR-WS.org (2020)
26. Rago, A., Toni, F., Aurisicchio, M., Baroni, P.: Discontinuity-free decision support with quantitative argumentation debates. In: KR, pp. 63–73. AAAI Press (2016)

Interaction Design Patterns of Web Chatbots

Verena Traubinger(✉) and Martin Gaedke

Faculty of Computer Science, Chemnitz University of Technology, Chemnitz, Germany
{verena.traubinger,martin.gaedke}@informatik.tu-chemnitz.de

Abstract. Chatbots are often used in the web as an additional user interface which offers different modalities for users. Still, there is not yet an established catalogue of interaction patterns across different chatbot implementations, while this is the case for graphical user interfaces. Such a catalogue will give web engineers an orientation in developing chatbots, which will in turn lead to users more easily recognizing common functionalities of chatbots. This short paper is mapping known chatbot functionalities to already established interaction design patterns from graphical user interfaces. For this, these frameworks were assessed on their relevance towards web interfaces before systematically mapping them onto each other by regarding their similarities in the categories *Situation*, *Intention* and *Implementation.* From the result, we discuss similarities and differences which are influencing the specific use of interaction design patterns in web chatbots and formulate the ensuing 12 chatbot interaction patterns in a catalogue for web engineers.

Keywords: Web interfaces · Human-Computer-Interaction (HCI) · Web Engineering · interaction design patterns · User Interfaces

1 Introduction and Related Work

The design of graphical user interfaces (GUIs) in the web has a history of change and evolution [4] until a common ground was found and guidelines were established. A pattern language, as introduced by [1] was the basis for [7] to describe interaction design patterns, which are often already used by designers as best practices, like Input Prompts, Pagination or Error Messages. To become a pattern, single visual elements or actions like buttons, toolbars or hovering have to be used with a specific intention and context by the users. The authors concentrate on web and mobile interfaces, usually with a large weight on graphical representations of content. Other interfaces are explicitly excluded by the authors, among them chatbots and other conversational designs, as they are both an emerging technology.

Chatbots are often used in web environments, like e-commerce and customer service. They are a form of Conversational User Interface (CUI) with a visual-centric style, which means that GUI elements are combined with natural language processing [5]. To the best of our knowledge, only two publications regard

K. Stefanidis et al. (Eds.): ICWE 2024, LNCS 14629, pp. 309–317, 2024.
https://doi.org/10.1007/978-3-031-62362-2_22

how chatbots and humans interact on a graphical basis. As the authors use different terms, we refer to these interactions as *chatbot functionalities*. The first publication lists "Rich Interactions", which replace or enhance text-based conversations which would otherwise be very long for completing complex tasks [6]. In their approach, [8] systematically analyzed chatbots and found that "Sign Classes" (individual interaction elements) and "Strategies" were used to convey possible commands, actions and main functionalities. Both publications have some overlaps in their specified chatbot functionalities, while in combination they still present a broad view on them.

While natural language based interactions in chatbots are already researched on in several aspects, the analysis of graphical interaction elements is thus rather limited. We aim to fill this gap by mapping chatbot functionalities to well known interaction patterns to provide a common basis for the engineering of web chatbots. Our contributions in this short paper are:

1. presenting established interaction design patterns and chatbot functionalities
2. selecting these patterns and functionalities on their applicability for the web
3. mapping them with regard to shared constructed and described categories
4. building a catalogue of 12 chatbot interaction patterns.

2 Methodology

For the mapping process, we relied on the presented works from [6–8]. First, they were preprocessed on their suitability for web interfaces by building inclusion and exclusion criteria, followed by a comparison of different categories for each interaction design pattern, Rich Interaction, Sign Class and Strategy which resulted in the final mapping presented in Sect. 3. The inclusion and exclusion criteria, aim to rule out any interaction design patterns not related to chatbot or web interfaces, as well as chatbot functionalities restricted to single platforms or not applicable for web interfaces. After applying these criteria, we had a set of 45 interaction patterns and 26 chatbot functionalities which were further processed. The complete list of both criteria and the list of all mapping elements can be found in the appendix which is published in a repository[1]. For a systematic mapping, we needed a common basis of categories with which we could compare interaction design patterns and chatbot functionalities. As [7] used the most elaborated structure, their categories were generalized in the following way and applied on the chatbot functionalities: *Situation* (In which context is it used?), *Intention* (How does it impact the user?), *Implementation* (How is it implemented?) These categories were described by hand for each of the chatbot functionalities. For an easier comparison, ChatGPT was used to summarize the descriptions from [7] which were afterwards verified by one of the authors. In the mapping process, we compared the categories of the chatbot functionalities and the interaction design patterns and noted down a match, if we could find similarities in these categories.

[1] https://github.com/vertr/Chatbot-Interaction-Patterns.

For the mapping process, we want to address some limitations which might be threats to its validity. An internal threat could be chatbot functionalities, which are only used on specific platforms. We tried to avoid this bias by using inclusion and exclusion criteria with a focus on web environments. An external threat is possible due to the methodology where the final patterns were only mapped theoretically but not verified with real-world examples. This threat was mitigated by choosing publications which include diverse sets of interaction elements and different chatbot implementations.

3 Mapping Results

Here, we present the results of mapping 45 interaction patterns to 26 chatbot functionalities. Table 1 includes only conclusive matches from chatbot functionalities to interaction design patterns, additional matches with only indirect dependencies can be found in the appendix. For readability in Table 1, the names of all mapping elements were abbreviated in the following way.

Sign Classes (C) [8]: Simple Message (*C1*), Simple Image (*C2*), Suggestions or quick replies (*C3*), Card (*C4*), Carousel (*C5*), Persistent Menu (*C6*).

Strategies (S) [8]: Showing the main feature on the first message (*S1*), Guiding the user through a short tutorial during first messages (*S2*), Suggesting the next possible set of actions to the user (*S3*), Having a persistent menu with main features (*S4*), Sending the main menu with main features as message (*S5*), Having a list of available commands (*S6*), Offering contextual help about a feature (*S7*), Showing the main menu or the most frequent features when the user asks for help (*S8*), Showing the main menu or main features when user says something the chatbot cannot understand (*S9*).

Rich Interactions (R) [6]: Files (*R1*), Audio (*R2*), Video (*R3*), Images (*R4*), Buttons (*R5*), Templates (*R6*), Links (*R7*), Emojis (*R8*), Persistent menus (*R9*), Typing indications (*R10*), Webviews (*R11*).

The abbreviations **SE, HS, TS, Cs, Cl, BG, AP, Pw, LI** respectively stand for the chatbot functionalities Settings Editor, Help Systems, Titled Sections, Cards, Carousel, Button Groups, Action Panel, Preview, Spinner and Loading Indicators.

From the 45 interaction design patterns which were included, 9 could be mapped conclusively to at least one of the 26 chatbot functionalities. The *Settings Editor (SE)* can be matched to chatbot functionalities C6 and R9. *Help Systems (HS)* matched with 9 functionalities (S1-9). The next pattern of *Titled Sections (TS)* is also mapped to 9 functionalities (C1, C2, C4, R1–R4, R6 and R11). *Cards (Cs)* are mapped to the functionalities C4 and R6, while the *Carousel (Cl)* pattern has one exact match, even on the naming, with C5. The sixth pattern of *Button Groups (BG)* is matched to 2 functionalities C3 and R5. The *Action Panel (AP)* was mapped to 3 patterns, S5–7, while the last two patterns were matched each with one functionality. *Preview (Pw)* to R11 and *Spinners and Loading Indicators (LI)* to R10. Two functionalities were not mapped conclusively to any pattern: *Links (R7)* and *Emojis (R8)*.

Table 1. Results of mapping chatbot functionalities to interaction design patterns.

	SE	HS	TS	Cs	Cl	BG	AP	Pw	LI
C1	.	.	X	.	.	.	.	.	.
C2	.	.	X	.	.	.	.	.	.
C3	.	.	.	.	.	X	.	.	.
C4	.	.	X	X	.	.	.	.	.
C5	.	.	.	.	X	.	.	.	.
C6	X	.	.	.	.	.	.	.	.
S1	.	X	.	.	.	.	.	.	.
S2	.	X	.	.	.	.	.	.	.
S3	.	X	.	.	.	.	.	.	.
S4	.	X	.	.	.	.	.	.	.
S5	.	X	.	.	.	.	X	.	.
S6	.	X	.	.	.	.	X	.	.
S7	.	X	.	.	.	.	X	.	.
S8	.	X	.	.	.	.	.	.	.
S9	.	X	.	.	.	.	.	.	.
R1	.	.	X	.	.	.	.	.	.
R2	.	.	X	.	.	.	.	.	.
R3	.	.	X	.	.	.	.	.	.
R4	.	.	X	.	.	.	.	.	.
R5	.	.	.	.	.	X	.	.	.
R6	.	.	X	X	.	.	.	.	.
R7	.	.	.	.	.	.	.	.	.
R8	.	.	.	.	.	.	.	.	.
R9	X	.	.	.	.	.	.	.	.
R10	.	.	.	.	.	.	.	.	X
R11	.	.	X	.	.	.	.	X	.

"X" indicates a conclusive match, "." indicates no match.

4 Discussion

In this section we debate the findings of our mapping process and which influence they have on formulating the chatbot interaction patterns catalogue in Sect. 5. The abbreviations for chatbot functionalities and interaction design patterns from Table 1 are again used.

Direct Matches. Several Patterns could be mapped directly to even similar named chatbot functionalities. While **Cards (Cs)** present information visually, often in combination with a link, the visualisation only slightly differs in a chatbot or can be customized (C4, R6) [6]. A **Carousel (Cl)** describes in both graphical and chatbot interfaces a horizontal menu of items (most often Cards) which can be navigated either by scrolling or by using arrow buttons (C5).

Matches with Chatbot Specific Equivalents. The following patterns have matches where the specific implementation is different in chatbots, but similar in the categories *Situation* and *Intention.* The **Settings Editor (SE)** and persistent menus (C6 and R9) match, even though some specific interactions differ. While the Settings Editor is mostly used for profile and preference settings, the persistent menu usually offers information on the most important functionalities and sometimes includes a FAQ to the chatbot itself. The pattern of **Titled Sections (TS)** relates to dividing the interface by using its layout. In chatbots, this is usually done by separating the conversation into respective speech bubbles from the chatbot and the user. While the conversational part is mostly textual (C1), it can also include different media functionalities (C2, C4, R1–4, R6, R11). The **Action Panel (AP)** is a dynamic part in the graphical interface, dependent on the current context. As chatbots, of course, also react dynamically on requests from the user, we mapped this functionality to main menus which are part of strategies S5–7. The pattern **Preview (Pw)** shows similarities to the webview (R11). While the Preview is used for example in webshops to offer different colour and material options, the webview fetches data from other homepages like routes in online maps or product information. In GUIs, **Spinners and loading indicators (LI)** visualize to users that processes are running in the background, even though the interface itself does not change. While chatbots are able to reply instantly, [6] mention this as possibly unsettling, as human communication partner would need to take time to think and type. As a result, chatbots sometimes insert typing indications (R10), which users recognize from messengers, and delay their answer for a few seconds to let the user feel more comfortable. **Button Groups (BG)** match to chatbot functionalities which differ from their use in GUIs: Either added to a card to represent actions, or as a selection of possible answers for the user beneath a chatbot message [3][2]. These functionalities are either called Buttons (R5) for both possible implementations [6], or only refer to the second one as is seen in names as Suggestions or Quick replies (C3) in [8]. Quick replies can be the only way to communicate for the users, if chatbots do not allow free text input. One criticism by [8] on them is that they are usually disappearing after being clicked and reappear as if the user wrote a message with the same content. This makes it hard in retrospect to see which message came from the users themselves and which one was prompted by the system. The authors also noticed that it can make a difference for follow-up reactions of the chatbot if the Quick Reply is chosen or if the same command is typed in by hand.

Matches to Chatbot Functionality Groups. The pattern **Help Systems (HS)** can be directly mapped to all strategies of [8][3], which led us to make

[2] While the interaction design pattern groups similar actions, different answers in chatbots usually lead to diverging conversations.

[3] The authors analyze how chatbots explain their functionalities and thus focus inherently on Help Systems.

further distinctions for a more precise matching. We grouped similar chatbot functionalities to show where different forms of Help Systems are overlapping: *Functionality Introduction* where main functionalities or a tutorial are provided in the first chat messages (S1, S2); *Functionality Menus* which are either always present or sent as a reaction on a message from the user (S4-7); *Requested Help* where specific information is provided on an explicit request (S5, S6-9); and *Breakdown avoidance* where a conversation breakdown [2] is avoided by the chatbot offering users possible options or providing functionality menus (S3, S5). Some of the mapped chatbot functionalities relate to more than one of these groups, as the same functionality can be used in different situations.

Further Findings. Two chatbot functionalities could not be mapped to interaction patterns: Links (R7) and Emojis (R8). While links are universal in web interfaces, they are not feasible on their own as a pattern an can rather be considered as a part of text messages (C1). Emojis on the other hand are introduced by [6] as either part of a chat message or as a reaction to the content of a message from the chatbot (most often thumbs-up or thumbs-down as is for example implemented as a feedback option in ChatGPT). One general finding is related to chatbots as a combination between conversational and graphical user interfaces. While most patterns can be matched to chatbot functionalities as graphical interface elements, others only appear in combination with a message which was sent by the user. The pattern is then often related directly to the content of the user command or request (for example S7-9). This adds an additional layer of possible interactions to the GUI, which is usually dominated by actions such as tapping, swiping, scrolling or hovering with the mouse or using keyboard commands [7]. For the design of web chatbots this means that web

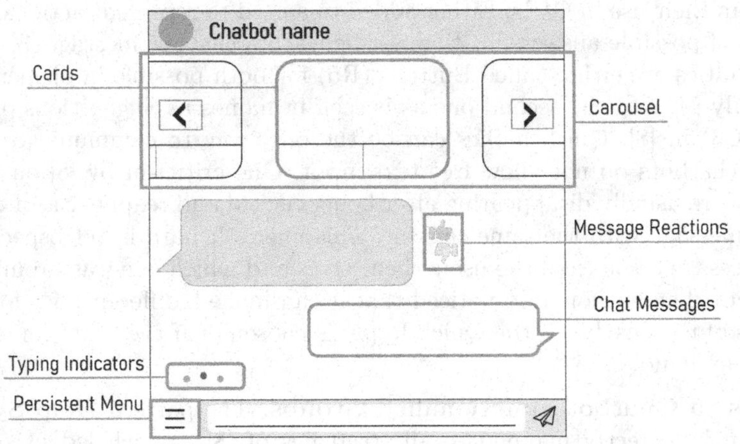

Fig. 1. A representation of some chatbot interaction patterns: *Chat Messages*, *Cards*, *Carousel*, *Message Reactions*, *Typing Indicators*, and *Persistent Menu*.

engineers always have to plan for different situations in the conversation when designing interaction elements.

5 Chatbot Interaction Patterns

This section presents our catalogue of chatbot interaction patterns, which we built according to the findings from our mapping process. Table 2 is providing a short overview on the chatbot interaction patterns. As in pattern languages different patterns relate and build on each other we also show this in the table

Table 2. Chatbot interaction patterns, their description and relation to other patterns.

Nr. Pattern name	Description. (Relation to other patterns)
1. Chat Messages	Displaying outputs from chatbot and user, most often as speech bubbles
2. Cards	Presenting similar information, often with text, images, and actions. (1., 3.)
3. Carousel	A set of similar items in a horizontal list. (2.)
4. Quick Replies	A set of actions or functionalities under a chat message in the form of buttons. (1.)
5. Typing Indicators	A visual representation of the waiting time for the reply of the chatbot. (1.)
6. Persistent Menu	A constant menu in the chat window for important information or settings
7. Call-on Menu	A dynamic representation of consistent information which was requested by the user. (1., 4., 6.)
8. Webview	A preview on web content from other providers or the chatbot homepage itself. (1.)
9. Message Reactions	Emojis beside or under a chat message to provide feedback on the answer of the chatbot. (1.)
10. Help Systems	Offering assistance for users, either on request or proactively by the chatbot. (4., 6., 7., 11.)
11. Functionality Introduction	Introducing the main functionalities or providing a tutorial in the first chat messages. (1.)
12. Conversation Recovery	Avoiding conversation breakdowns by providing possible actions or commands. (4., 7.)

by relating to the numeration of other patterns. More detailed descriptions of their relations and the patterns analog to our built categories for the mapping are provided in the appendix. Figure 1 illustrates some of the described patterns as they would appear in a chatbot interface.

When possible, the naming of the original interaction design patterns was applied. In cases where web chatbots have a specific implementation, the name was built based on the matched chatbot functionality and was sometimes adopted slightly. The pattern of Help Systems is relating to other pattern types which are all offering help in different forms and situations. While it can be argued that such a pattern is redundant, we base this decision on [7] who propose a similar pattern. From the Help Systems groups of chatbot functionalities listed in Sect. 4, we list Functionality Introduction and breakdown avoidance (as the pattern Conversation Recovery) as independent patterns, as the others are already related to in the patterns Call-on Menu and Persistent Menu.

6 Conclusion and Future Work

In this paper, we present a catalogue of 12 chatbot interaction patterns which were derived by mapping known chatbot functionalities to already established interaction design patterns. We show that patterns which are based on purely graphical web and mobile interfaces are transferable or adaptable for web chatbots. The graphical and conversational nature from chatbots leads to these patterns being also dependent on the context of the previous conversation.

With our presented catalogue, we provide an orientation for web engineers for building web chatbots which will feel familiar and consistent to the users. In future research we plan to enhance this catalogue with more patterns which were not yet described and to sharpen the descriptions of the ones we introduce here. Due to the limitation in this paper on described functionalities from [6] and [8], we might be able to verify the application of more interaction design patterns from [7] like Accordions, Collapsible Panels or List Inlays in web chatbots by analysing real-world chatbots. Another research direction would be to look into different domains of chatbots in the web and if there are distinctions in the used chatbot design patterns. It is possible that users have preferences on which patterns they are using, which are depending on the tasks the chatbot has to perform and the domain it is implemented in.

References

1. Alexander, C.: A Pattern Language: Towns, Buildings, Construction. Oxford University Press, Oxford (1977)
2. Ashktorab, Z., Jain, M., Liao, Q.V., Weisz, J.D.: Resilient chatbots: repair strategy preferences for conversational breakdowns. In: Proceedings of the 2019 CHI Conference on Human Factors in Computing Systems, CHI 2019, pp. 1–12. Association for Computing Machinery, New York (2019). https://doi.org/10.1145/3290605.3300484

3. Jain, M., Kumar, P., Kota, R., Patel, S.N.: Evaluating and informing the design of chatbots. In: Proceedings of the 2018 Designing Interactive Systems Conference, DIS 2018, pp. 895–906. Association for Computing Machinery, New York (2018). https://doi.org/10.1145/3196709.3196735
4. Marcus, A.: Chapter 19 - Graphical User Interfaces, 2nd edn., pp. 423–440. North-Holland, Amsterdam (1997). https://doi.org/10.1016/B978-044481862-1.50085-6
5. Moore, R.J., Arar, R.: Conversational UX Design: A Practitioner's Guide to the Natural Conversation Framework, 1st edn. ACM Books, New York (2019). https://doi.org/10.1145/3304087
6. Shevat, A.: Designing Bots: Creating Conversational Experiences, 1st edn. O'Reilly, Beijing (2017)
7. Tidwell, J., Brewer, C., Valencia, A.: Designing Interfaces: Patterns for Effective Interaction Design, 3rd edn. O'Reilly, Beijing (2020)
8. Valério, F.A.M., Guimarães, T.G., Prates, R.O., Candello, H.: Chatbots explain themselves: designers' strategies for conveying chatbot features to users. J. Interact. Syst. **9**(3) (2018). https://doi.org/10.5753/jis.2018.710

Estimating Diffusion Degree on Graph Stream Generated from Social and Web Networks

Vinit Ramesh Gore, Suman Kundu(✉), and Anggy Eka Pratiwi

Department of Computer Science and Engineering, IIT Jodhpur, Jodhpur, India
{gore.1,suman,pratiwi.1}@iitj.ac.in

Abstract. Data stream generated from different Web 2.0 applications may contains data which is best described by graphs. Graph streams thus generated show big data characters, including volume and velocity. The challenges of graph stream algorithms are twofold; each edge needs to be processed only once (due to velocity), and it needs to work on highly constrained memory (due to volume). Diffusion degree, a measure of node centrality, can be calculated for static graphs using a single Breadth-First Search (BFS). However, tracking Diffusion Degree in a graph stream is nontrivial. This paper proposes an estimator for diffusion degree for graph streams, which can be used to extract top-k influencing nodes for viral marketing in social networks. Comparative experiments show that the proposed graph stream algorithm is equivalent to or better than the exact diffusion degree-based algorithm.

Keywords: Streaming Algorithm · Temporal Graph · Social Network Analysis · Influence maximization

1 Introduction

Data generates from Web 2.0 is massive and fast, thus any algorithm must handle it within an acceptable time and memory. These data frequently have relationships that are most effectively described using a graph. These graphs, called social or complex networks, have many applications [6,8,9,18]. Static snapshots of the network are traditionally used to generate algorithmic solutions. The majority of current social networks are dynamic, and, and esearch focuses on dynamic graphs to create efficient solutions that adapt to changes in topology [12,17,18]. Temporal graphs can be modeled differently. One may take numerous snapshots at different timestamps [6], and other is to take it as a dynamic graph with edges appearing and disappearing. However, due to the velocity of the change or graph volume, loading or retaining the full graph may not be possible in many scenarios, notably in real-world graphs formed by online social networks. An algorithm must observe the graph from the edge stream (high-velocity data) or restricted pass of the edge lists (high-volume data) to discover a solution. When graphs are observed as a stream of edges potentially infinite

K. Stefanidis et al. (Eds.): ICWE 2024, LNCS 14629, pp. 318–326, 2024.
https://doi.org/10.1007/978-3-031-62362-2_23

in length, they are called Graph Streams. One should note here that the fundamental difference between the dynamic graph model and the streaming graph model is that for the streaming graph, the entire graph is never available to the algorithm, while the dynamic graph has the entire graph available for processing. Because of this feature, traversals may be performed in dynamic graphs to find local or global solutions. However, for streaming graph problems, the algorithm must sketch important information to perform a specific task without traversing.

Graph Stream Model: Graph stream, here, is denoted by $\mathcal{G}(\mathcal{V}, \mathcal{E})$ where $\mathcal{V}$ is the set of nodes and $\mathcal{E}$ is the edge stream. Each edge $e \in \mathcal{E}$ is associated with a sequence number or timestamp which denotes its position in the stream, and that can be retrieved by function $\tau(.)$. An online estimator $< Q_t >$ on $\mathcal{G}$ returns the estimated value of $< Q >$ for a graph $G = (\mathcal{V}, \{e | e \in \mathcal{E} \wedge \tau(e) \leq t\})$.

Centrality: Centrality plays an important role in solving many problems and is extensively used in static settings. Research has been conducted to update centrality measures for dynamic graph settings (e.g., recalculation of PageRanks after topological changes are done in [1,15,18]), but only a handful number of studies are conducted on estimating different centrality measures [7] for graph streams. *Diffusion Degree (DD)* [10,13] is a node's centrality measure developed to find the expected amount of spread by a node in the information diffusion process. Mathematically, the diffusion degree of node u is defined by $DD_u = \lambda \times (d_u + \sum_{i \in \Gamma(u)} d_i)$ where $d_{(.)}$ is the degree of a node (.), $\Gamma(.)$ returns the set of neighbors of node (.), and λ is the diffusion probability of diffusion model. It was proposed to provide a practically efficient solution for the IM problem on large graphs under the ICM [3,4] of information diffusion. Readers may read more information on diffusion degree in [10].

Our Contribution: In this current work, we try to answer two questions: (i) 'Can we estimate *DD* from graph streams?' and (ii) 'Can we use the estimated *DD* heuristically to solve IM problem on streaming graphs?' We develop a streaming algorithm to approximating node diffusion degree measure from an insert-only graph stream. Our *online algorithm* allows querying from the data structure for the centrality score of any node u at any time. It stores only a few sampled neighbors of nodes. Given $\epsilon, \delta \in (0, 1)$, we have achieved error below $\epsilon(b_u - a_u)d_u\lambda$ with probability $1 - \delta$ by utilizing $O(n\frac{1}{\epsilon^2}\log\frac{1}{\delta})$ space where b_u and a_u are the maximum and minimum degrees of neighbors of u. We propose an algorithm to find top-k influencing nodes for the IM problem with the estimated diffusion degree. We show experimentally that the proposed methods work for streaming graph. Proofs of theorem, lemma, claim and other additional details are available on the full version of the paper in preprint [5].

2 Estimation of Diffusion Degree on Graph Streams

Before presenting DD estimator, let us define a more general problem of estimating centrality measures in a graph stream. The problem of estimating the centrality measure of a given node u from a streaming graph is to find the online estimator $C_t(\mathcal{G}, u)$ over a graph stream $\mathcal{G}$, where C is the desired centrality measure. For example, an estimator of degree centrality, $C_t(\mathcal{G}, u)$ will return the estimated d_u, the degree of the node u, of the graph $G = (V = \mathcal{V}, E = \{e|e \in \mathcal{E} \wedge \tau(e) \leq t\})$. In order to get the exact answer, the complete graph out of the stream needs to be kept in the memory. With the estimators, the objective is to reduce memory usage. The particular problem we are addressing is to design an estimator for the diffusion degree centrality.

Both degree of node u and the sum of its neighbors' degrees are needed to compute its DD. For each node in the network, a simple counter can sketch its degree in $O(n)$ space. However, it's challenging to query the sum of neighbors because it requires neighbor information. All neighbors' mapping must be retained for exact solution, which means keeping the whole graph. Adjacency matrix requires $O(n^2)$ space, while an adjacency list takes $O(n + m)$ storage space. In practice, graphs with $m > 10^6$ require at least 229 GB, which exceeds typical memory sizes in most systems available today.

In the proposed approach, we build a $O(n \times q)$ space sketch, where q is the maximum number of neighbors sampled for each nodes. Size of q can be represented with the approximation error and the failure probability (Lemma 1). The idea is *to store q out of d_u neighbors of a node u instead of all neighbors.* Here, $q \ll$ maximum in-degree of any node in the graph. We consider directed graphs but it can be easily extended to undirected graphs. For every directed edge $e(v, u)$ from $u \rightarrow v$ encountered on the stream, we consider u influences v. Hence, we sampled q of d_u *incoming neighbors* of a node.

Which q Neighbors? We sampled q uniformly randomly with replacement from the in-neighbors and store it into $S_q^{(u)}$. Each neighbor will have the probability of $\frac{1}{d_u}$ to be selected to any of the q places. Multiple instances of the same node can be taken considering we sample with replacement as described in [16]. We need not know d_u apriori to perform this kind of sampling [16]. Standard reservoir sampling is not useful as it is not independent. Without independence, our further proof will not follow. Sampling with replacement guarantees independence between sampled nodes. There are two cases when the number of neighbors stored for node u in $S_q^{(u)}$ is less than q: (i) $|\Gamma(u)| < q$ in the graph seen so far; output will be exact DD here or (ii) all q places in $S_q^{(u)}$ are not filled by random sampling; the approximation will be calculated by $q' = |S_q^{(u)}|$ instead of q.

The Estimation: We take *normalized empirical sum* over the selected neighbors to cover up for the remaining neighbors. Estimated diffusion degree of u is:

$$\widehat{DDS}_u = \lambda \times (d_u + \frac{d_u}{q} \times \sum_{j \in S_q^{(u)}} d_j) \tag{1}$$

Note that in the q length array, we do not store the degrees of neighbors of u. Instead, we store the node identifier itself. Hence, even for determining a single node's diffusion degree, we need to know the degree of all the q neighbors we are storing. We shall construct an adjacency list-like data structure. For every node u, the first element of its list will store d_u followed by q (at most) neighbors. Figure 1 shows the visualization of the data structure. Initially, all the q neighbors are *null*. Hence, no space is allocated. The data structure will keep updating with the stream. Specifically, for every new edge (v, u), node u is queried in the data structure. Its degree is incremented by 1, and v is added to its list at r positions using uniform random sampling with replacement, as discussed before. The algorithm is given in Algorithm 1. It requires $O(n \times q)$ memory. Each call of $rswr(v_t, u_t, q)$ and $query(u)$ require at least $O(q)$ time, totaling, the algorithm accesses the data structure ADJ $O(2q + 1)$ times.

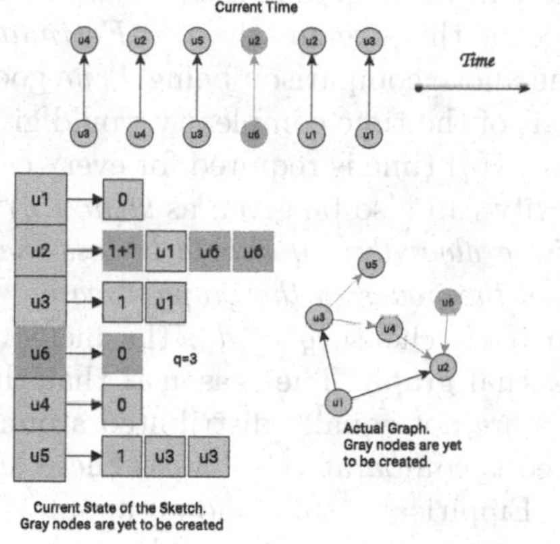

Fig. 1. Data structure ADJ used to estimate diffusion degrees on edge stream of graph.

Algorithm 1: *DD* estimator: *DDS*(object)

Require: q, ADJ_{t-1}: adjacency list of size $O(n \times q)$ from previous time step, $\text{ADJ}_{t'}$: when queried

$next(v_t, u_t)$ —
$\text{ADJ}_t \leftarrow \text{ADJ}_{t-1}$
$\text{ADJ}_t[u_t][0] \leftarrow \text{ADJ}_{t-1}[u_t][0] + 1$
$rswr(v_t, u_t, q)$
— $query_{t'}(u)$ —
$d_u^{(t')} \leftarrow \text{ADJ}_{t'}[u][0]$
$sum \leftarrow 0$; $nCount \leftarrow 0$
for $i \in [q]$ **do**
  if $\text{ADJ}_{t'}[u][i]$ is not *null* **then**
    $nCount \leftarrow nCount + 1$;
    $sum \leftarrow sum + \text{ADJ}_{t'}[\text{ADJ}_{t'}[u][i]][0]$
return (**if** $nCount > 0$ **then** $\lambda \times (\frac{d_u^{(t')}}{nCount} \times sum + d_u^{(t')})$ **else** 0);

Theorem 1 ***(Correctness).*** *The expected value of the estimated diffusion degree of any node u equals the diffusion degree value of the same node., i.e., $\mathbb{E}[\widehat{DDS_u}] = DD_u$. (Proof available in [5])*

Lemma 1. *For $\epsilon, \delta \in (0, 1)$, with $q = O(\epsilon^{-2} \log \frac{1}{\delta})$, error $|\widehat{DDS_u} - DD_u| \leq \epsilon(b_u - a_u)d_u\lambda$ with probability $1 - \delta$. Here, ϵ is the approximation error and δ is the error probability. We define b_u, a_u as max degree and min degree among the neighbors of u, respectively. (Proof available in [5])*

3 Influence Maximization Using Proposed Estimator

DD has been effectively used for IM problem. Hence, we would like to address the same problem with the estimated diffusion degree. Given a graph stream $\mathcal{G}(\mathcal{V}, \mathcal{E})$, the IM problem on graph stream is to find $IM_t(\mathcal{G}, k) = \arg_{S \subseteq \mathcal{V}} \max_{|S| \leq k} \sigma(S)$ where $\sigma(S)$ estimates the spread by seed node S on the graph $G = (\mathcal{V}, \{e | e \in \mathcal{E} \wedge \tau(e) \leq t\})$. Read [11] to know more about influence maximization problem.

Algorithm 2 ranks nodes using the diffusion degree estimates as the heuristic and outputs a seed set of top-k nodes. It maintains a min-heap HEAP to maintain the top-k influential nodes at every time step t. HEAP stores the tuple (estimate, node) for every node added to it. The tuples are arranged in the heap according to their estimate of diffusion degree values. Smaller estimates are evicted over time. The space occupied by the min-heap HEAP is $\mathrm{O}(k)$. Since we are storing the output seed set in the HEAP, we do not consider the memory occupied by it in the space complexity analysis. Therefore, the space complexity of the algorithm is the same as that of DDS, i.e., $O(nq)$. The time complexity of the algorithm is $O(m \times k)$. We run over a large edge stream of size m, and we process each edge in $O(k)$ time where k time is required to search through the heap ($k \ll m$) (refer Algorithm 2 line 5). However, we search through the heap only if the $estimate > minEstimate$. As the algorithm proceeds over the stream, the $minEstimate$ keeps increasing. Hence, the likelihood of the above comparison being $True$ goes on decreasing, too. So, the amortized analysis of the time complexity would give a value less than $\mathrm{O}(m \times k)$. However, at least $\mathrm{O}(q)$ time is required for every call of the *dds* method. Therefore, time complexity can also be given as $\Omega(m \times q)$.

Claim: To gain the space advantage of the algorithm, q should be less than $d_{in} - 1$*, where* d_{in} *is the average in-degree of the nodes in the graph stream.*

Note that, for scale free network, even if we choose $q = d_{in}$ the memory usage will be much less than storing the actual graph. The reason is that the high degree nodes and the low degree nodes are not equally distributed around the average degree. Also, the average degree is comparatively low as there are many nodes with degree very low (1 or 2). Empirical results shows: about 1/3 nodes have degree more than the average degree while rest having degree lower than the average degree even though the average degree is at most $\sqrt{|V|}/3$.

Table 1. Datasets used

Name	n	m	d_{in}
Physicians_directed	241	1098	4.556
Email-Eu-Core-Temporal	986	24929	25.283
Email-Eu-Core	1005	25571	25.443
Mathoverflow-C2Q [14]	16836	101329	6.018
Asoiaf	796	2823	3.546
Wikipedia_Link_Lo	3811	132837	34.856
Wikipedia_Link_Xal	2697	232680	86.273
Ego_Twitter	32169	643301	19.117
Nethept [2]	15229	62752	4.121

Algorithm 2: IM using Diffusion degree estimates

Require: K: Seed set size, q: max number of neighbors, dds: object of DDS, HEAP: min-heap of size K

1. — $next(e_t)$ —
2. $(v_t, u_t) \leftarrow e_t$; $\text{HEAP}_t \leftarrow \text{HEAP}_{t-1}$
3. $dds.next(v_t, u_t)$
4. $estimate \leftarrow dds.query_t(u_t)$
5. **if** u_t is in HEAP_{t-1} **then**
6.   update estimate of u_t with $estimate$ in HEAP_t
7. **else**
8. $minEstimate, minNode \leftarrow \text{HEAP}_{t-1}.peek()$
9.   **if** $estimate > minEstimate$ **then**
10.   add $(estimate, u_t)$ to HEAP_t; $\text{HEAP}_t.pop()$
11. — $Query_{t'}()$ —
12. **return** HEAP

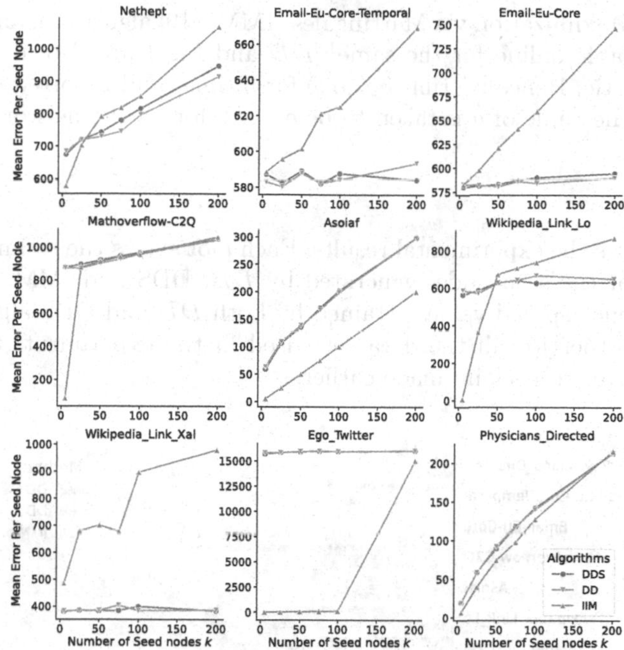

Fig. 2. Influence spread with respect to seed set size K on different graphs

4 Comparative Experiment

Experiments have been performed to check whether the estimated Diffusion Degree and the exact Diffusion Degree perform similarly for IM problems. In other words, the experiments are to validate theoretical claims. Note that the present work does not claim to achieve state-of-the-art results for IM problems. Instead, the IM problem is one of the applications of diffusion degree centrality. As the current work estimates the diffusion degree in a graph stream, it is more relevant to see whether the top-k nodes identified by the estimated diffusion degree produce similar results to that of the top-k nodes identified by the exact diffusion degree.

4.1 Experimental Setup

We used nine directed datasets (Table 1) in the experiment. For DD, we load the graph as a *networkx* object. To simulate the streaming setting, we iterate over a file of directed edges and process each edge at a time. The DD algorithm finds the diffusion degrees of every node and finds the top-k nodes having maximum diffusion degrees. On the other hand for Estimated Diffusion Degree based IM (DDS) we queried for top-k at the end of the stream. We also compared with the Influence Maximization via Martingales (IMM) [19] algorithm, and we reused the code available online for the same[1] DD and IMM are deterministic while DDS is stochastic. Hence we run the code for 5 times and reported the result of the average. The value of q is taken to be $d_{in} - 2$ for all the networks.

4.2 Results

The Fig. 2 shows the experimental results. Each plot shows the estimated spread size of ICM for the seed nodes generated by DD, DDS and IMM. We observe that the influence spread values attained by both DD and DDS algorithms are close to each other for all the data sets used in the experiments. Thereby, it verifies the correctness claim made earlier.

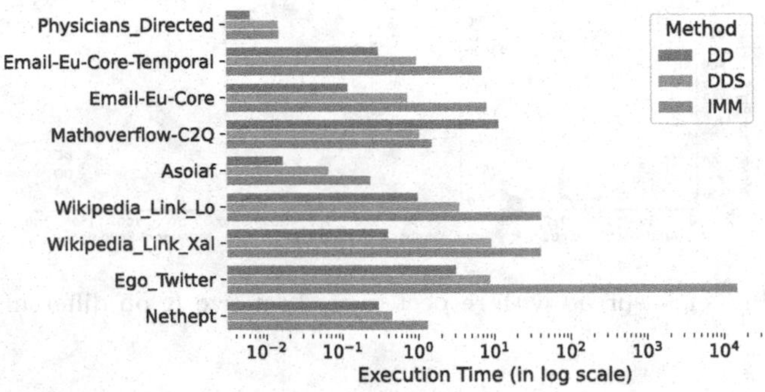

Fig. 3. Execution time of different algorithms for different data sets

The results in Fig. 3 show the execution time (in log scale) measured in seconds for different algorithms. In order to keep measurements fair, we have also considered the time required to load the graph into the *networkx* object while measuring time for DD. The time required to load the graph object would be $O(m)$ and to run DD over it is $O(n \log n)$. So, the time taken by diffusion degree would be $O(m)$. In the case of DDS, the time required is $O(mk)$. We found that the execution time for DDS is slightly more than that of the DD.

5 Conclusion

We proposed an approximation algorithm for calculating diffusion degree from graph stream. Theoretically we shown that the expectation of the estimated values are equal to the exact values of the diffusion degree. The estimated diffusion degree is also used heuristically in finding the top-k influential nodes for Influence Maximization problem. Experimentally, we have shown that the top-k

[1] IMM source code: https://sourceforge.net/projects/im-imm/.

identified by diffusion degree estimate will produce the similar spreading in the network that of the diffusion degree. Estimating centrality measure in graph stream is least explored in the literature. The present work is in the direction to defining the problem of estimating centrality measure in graph stream.

Acknowledgments. This work was partially supported by the Doctoral fellowship in India (DIA) programme of the Ministry of Education, Government of India.

References

1. Bahmani, B., Chowdhury, A., Goel, A.: Fast incremental and personalized PageRank. Proc. VLDB Endow. **4**(3), 173–184 (2010)
2. Chen, N.: On the approximability of influence in social networks. SIAM J. Disc. Math. **23**(3), 1400–1415 (2009)
3. Goldenberg, J., Libai, B., Muller, E.: Talk of the network: a complex systems look at the underlying process of word-of-mouth. Mark. Lett. **12**(3), 211–223 (2001)
4. Goldenberg, J., Libai, B., Muller, E.: Using complex systems analysis to advance marketing theory development: modeling heterogeneity effects on new product growth through stochastic cellular automata. Acad. Mark. Sci. Rev. **9**(3), 1–18 (2001)
5. Gore, V.R., Kundu, S., Pratiwi, A.E.: Estimating diffusion degree on graph streams (2024). https://doi.org/10.48550/arXiv.2401.17611
6. Gupta, S., Kundu, S.: Interaction graph, topical communities, and efficient local event detection from social streams. Expert Syst. Appl. **232**, 120890 (2023)
7. Hayashi, T., Akiba, T., Yoshida, Y.: Fully dynamic betweenness centrality maintenance on massive networks. Proc. VLDB Endow. **9**(2), 48–59 (2015)
8. Karan, S., Kundu, S.: Cyberbully: aggressive tweets, bully and bully target profiling from multilingual Indian tweets. In: Pattern Recognition and Machine Intelligence, pp. 638–645. Kolkata (2023)
9. Kundu, S., Kajdanowicz, T., Kazienko, P., Chawla, N.: Fuzzy relative willingness: modeling influence of exogenous factors in driving information propagation through a social network. IEEE Access **8**, 186653–186662 (2020)
10. Kundu, S., Murthy, C., Pal, S.K.: A new centrality measure for influence maximization in social networks. In: Pattern Recognition and Machine Intelligence, Moscow, pp. 242–247 (2011)
11. Li, Y., Fan, J., Wang, Y., Tan, K.L.: Influence maximization on social graphs: a survey. IEEE TKDE **30**(10), 1852–1872 (2018)
12. Ohsaka, N., Akiba, T., Yoshida, Y., Kawarabayashi, K.I.: Dynamic influence analysis in evolving networks. Proc. VLDB Endow. **9**(12), 1077–1088 (2016)
13. Pal, S.K., Kundu, S., Murthy, C.A.: Centrality measures, upper bound, and influence maximization in large scale directed social networks. Fund. Inf. **130**, 317–342 (2014)
14. Paranjape, A., Benson, A.R., Leskovec, J.: Motifs in temporal networks. In: Proceedings of 10th ACM International Conference on Web Search and Data Mining, pp. 601–610 (2017)
15. Parjanya, R., Kundu, S.: FPPR: fast pessimistic pagerank for dynamic directed graphs. In: Benito, R.M., et al. (eds.) COMPLEX NETWORKS 2021, vol. 1072, pp. 271–281. Springer, Heidelberg (2022)

16. Park, B.H., Ostrouchov, G., Samatova, N.F.: Sampling streaming data with replacement. Comput. Stat. Data Anal. **52**(2), 750–762 (2007)
17. Peng, B.: Dynamic influence maximization. In: NeurIPS (2021)
18. Suman, K., Pashikanti, P.R.: FPPR: fast pessimistic (dynamic) pagerank to update pagerank in evolving directed graphs on network changes. Social Netw. Anal. Min. J. **12**(1), 141 (2022)
19. Tang, Y., Shi, Y., Xiao, X.: Influence maximizationin near-linear time: a martingale approach. In: Proceedings of the 2015 ACM SIGMOD International Conference on Management of Data, pp. 1539–1554 (2015)

Web Service Composition, Evolution and Management

Task Manager of Quantum Web Services Through a Load Balancing Solution

Jaime Alvarado-Valiente(✉), Javier Romero-Álvarez, Enrique Moguel, José Garcia-Alonso, and Juan M. Murillo

Quercus Software Engineering Group, Universidad de Extremadura, Cáceres, Spain
{jaimeav,jromero,enrique,jgaralo,juanmamu}@unex.es

Abstract. In the dynamic field of quantum computing, characterized by constant innovation and continuous advancement of hardware and software capabilities, it is clear that this emerging technology holds immense potential in fields such as medicine and security. However, as the quantum computing ecosystem expands, it introduces a unique set of challenges for developers and researchers. One of the main challenges facing developers in the quantum field is the great diversity of quantum service providers. Each of these service providers has different ways of managing the execution tasks and returning the results, which is a problem when trying to execute the same circuit in different providers. In response to this, we present an approach to the management of quantum web services in the cloud, following web engineering techniques. This solution uses load balancing and resource allocation techniques to improve the execution of quantum tasks across multiple providers. The proposal is based on a Quantum Load Balancer that dynamically allocates tasks to the most suitable provider based on availability, performance, and cost. In addition, a Task Manager is introduced that integrates the balancer with a resource manager and a quantum task scheduler to provide a seamless and efficient user experience. The proposal is evaluated through a set of experiments on real quantum hardware and simulators from different quantum service providers, such as Amazon Braket and IBM Quantum. The evaluation results demonstrate a significant average reduction in response times, with an average reduction of 31.6% when the load balancer is employed.

Keywords: Quantum Computing · Quantum Web Services · Quantum Software · Task Manager · Load Balancer

1 Introduction

Quantum computing is a rapidly evolving field that promises to revolutionize many science, engineering, and business areas [1], but it is crucial to bridge the gap between theory and practical application [2]. Challenges such as quantum error correction, scalability of quantum systems, and the integration of quantum algorithms with classical computing further complicate the practical implementation of quantum technologies.

K. Stefanidis et al. (Eds.): ICWE 2024, LNCS 14629, pp. 329–343, 2024.
https://doi.org/10.1007/978-3-031-62362-2_24

In this dynamic landscape of quantum computing, one approach to bridge the aforementioned gap and address their challenges is through quantum web services [3]. These services serve as a gateway to classical computing by leveraging quantum technologies. However, the lack of standardization, the presence of various providers, and the diverse nature of quantum computing resources pose significant challenges.

In this context, traditional web engineering principles play a vital role in optimizing the functionality of quantum algorithms and applications through cloud providers. A commonly utilized methodology in web engineering is load-balancing techniques, which are important in optimizing resource allocation and workload distribution in traditional computing environments [4].

These load-balancing techniques can be adapted to the realm of quantum computing to address issues such as extended waiting times and resource unavailability, commonly observed in cloud quantum service providers. Moreover, they can help to mitigate the reliance on a single provider for task execution, enabling the flexibility to switch providers during task execution if needed.

In this work, we propose a Task Manager integrating load balancing and resource allocation for efficient quantum task execution across multiple quantum service providers. This proposed solution aims to simplify the resource selection process for developers, making it easier for them to take full advantage of the resources offered by different quantum service providers. The proposal has been validated with the implementation of the proposed Task Manager for Amazon Braket and IBM Quantum and aims to support both quantum and classical developers in defining, configuring, and executing circuits independently of the chosen provider.

To clarify our approach, the following sections are structured as follows: Sect. 2 expands on the motivation of this research and provides an overview of relevant previous studies. The Sect. 3 presents our proposed management method using the Task Manager that integrates a Quantum Load Balancer. Next, Sect. 4 presents the evaluation results of our method, implementing the Quantum Load Balancer for Amazon and IBM. Finally, Sect. 5 presents a discourse on the implications and conclusions drawn from our research.

2 Background

Thanks to the fast-paced developments in quantum technology, developers can now easily access quantum computers via cloud-based quantum computing services [5]. These cloud providers offer access to quantum hardware and simulators via the Internet, allowing developers and researchers to take advantage of quantum capabilities without the need to own and maintain a dedicated quantum infrastructure.

However, the diversity of infrastructure and resources provided by these providers is an obstacle for developers, necessitating a comprehensive understanding of how these technologies work [6], due to the different mechanisms for accessing execution and obtaining results—which are provided in different ways by each of the providers. In this context, management techniques, as cited by Parikh, Swapnil M. [7], are employed to manage the deployment and coordination of tasks among different providers or resources in the cloud. These techniques streamline task allocation, ultimately enhancing resource utilization and reducing task execution times, largely through the application of load balancing techniques [8].

Therefore, as in classical computing, the evolutionary landscape of quantum computing should also take into account the application of web engineering techniques such as load balancing. Primarily, because these techniques collectively play an important role in the efficiency and cost-effectiveness of quantum computing applications, and address the proliferation of resources from various providers with different characteristics [9].

However, while numerous solutions exist for management in the classical computing domain [10], in the quantum field it remains relatively unexplored, with only a limited number of studies exploring this realm. Notable contributions include TOSCA4QC by Wild et al. [11], which emphasizes deployment modeling to support quantum algorithms development; QFaaS by Nguyen et al. [12], which is a framework that adopts the serverless function-as-a-service model for quantum computing, supporting multiple quantum SDKs/programming languages, to avoid vendor lock-in issues and offering flexibility to users; and the algo2qpu framework designed by Sim et al. [13], focusing on the efficient execution of these algorithms in a cloud environment. The framework introduced by Sim et al. serves to expedite the selection, compilation, and execution of quantum algorithms within the context of a quantum cloud services platform. The primary objective of this framework is to enhance the efficiency of quantum algorithm execution in the cloud by emphasizing the judicious utilization of quantum resources and streamlining the execution workflow.

While these contributions provide valuable insights into the realm of quantum application management and orchestration, they attend to distinct facets of the overall process. Wild et al. concentrate their efforts on deployment modeling, thereby supporting the development of quantum algorithms. In contrast, Sim et al. direct their focus toward the execution process and the adept management of resources dedicated to quantum tasks.

Also, it is worth noting Faro et al. [14], which proposes the integration of quantum computing in the orchestration of hybrid quantum-classical systems through a specialized middleware. This middleware acts as an abstraction layer between quantum hardware and quantum algorithms, providing a high-level programming model.

Distinctively, our work introduces the Quantum Load Balancer as a vital component in the quantum application management process. Unlike the API Gateway pattern proposed by Garcia-Alonso et al. [15], which serves as an intermediary between developers and quantum computing providers, abstracting complexities, our approach centers on quantum management. The Quantum Load Balancer dynamically allocates tasks based on various parameters like cost and availability, improving the execution of quantum tasks across multiple providers.

Given these advancements, investigations into load balancing related to the utilization of quantum resources have revealed several challenges that must be taken into account. Unlike conventional cloud computing paradigms, the quantum domain introduces constraints, such as qubit limitations, fluctuating error rates, and diverse quantum hardware architectures. So, achieving effective load balancing in this environment requires addressing these quantum-specific challenges, which involves the formulation of methodologies that take into account the intrinsic characteristics of quantum resources. This, in turn, ensures optimal task allocation and management among multiple quantum resource providers.

All of this requires ongoing research efforts aimed at standardized practices that lead to efficient load balancing within the quantum computing landscape.

3 Proposal for Quantum Task Management

Quantum management should play a key role in the efficient organization of quantum web resources, tasks, and workflows in quantum computing. This technique will be indispensable for improving resource utilization, monitoring workflows, ensuring fault tolerance, and facilitating scalability in quantum computing. However, the execution of quantum tasks presents challenges due to resource disparity and the absence of standardized coordination solutions.

In this context, we present a load-balancing-based management solution designed to execute quantum tasks across multiple service providers. The solution we propose revolves around a Task Manager, which enables the execution of quantum circuits across multiple cloud service providers.

To this end, we must understand that in the realm of classical computing, coordination, and management are vital concepts in distributed systems, ensuring that deployed applications seamlessly align with the overarching business goals [16]. An effective manager should have the ability to foresee, recognize, and autonomously address scalability challenges that may emerge as applications scale up [17].

Applying this concept to the quantum domain, a quantum manager must possess the capability to predict, identify, and autonomously manage the execution of quantum tasks across the diverse quantum resources available in hybrid applications.

To achieve this, we propose the Task Manager. It provides an API that allows developers to invoke various services, including the Quantum Translator Service [18], which translates quantum tasks for different providers, and the Quantum Load Balancer, as explained in the following, which intelligently distributes the workload across various quantum machines.

As a result, developers can easily submit requests to the system, which then executes the quantum code across one or multiple providers, retrieves the results, and returns them to the developer. All this, without knowing the peculiarities of the specific platform, such as programming language, libraries, etc. Furthermore, the Task Manager streamlines quantum task execution by efficiently allocating the workload among the quantum machines of each provider, enhancing both cost efficiency and execution time.

Below is described the implementation of the process performed by the Quantum Load Balancer inside the Task Manager.

3.1 Quantum Load Balancer Process

In the classical computing domain, a load balancer is a software tool used to distribute workloads evenly among various resources [19]. In quantum computing, a load balancer serves the role of efficiently allocating workloads across different quantum service providers and resources to enhance the execution of quantum tasks and enhance resource utilization.

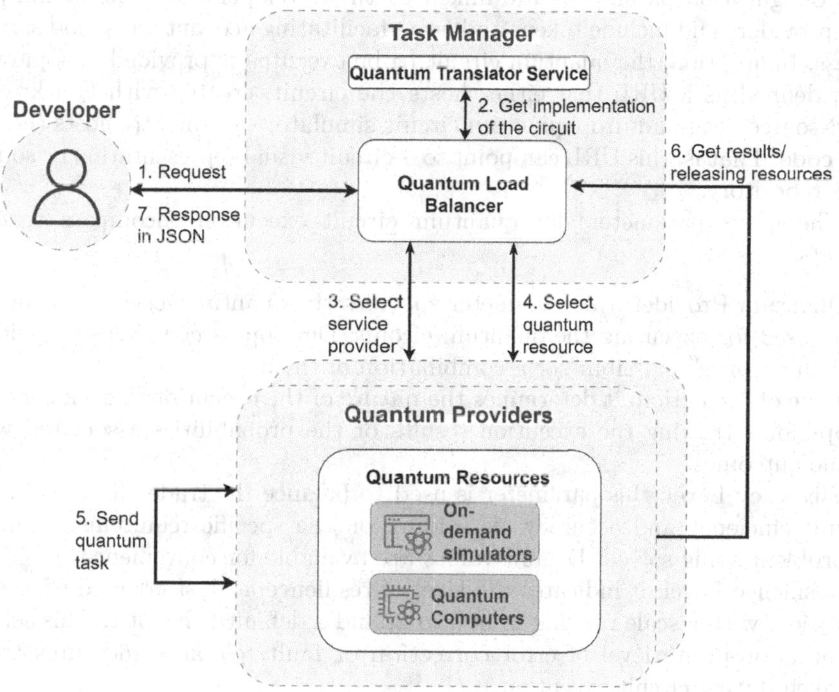

Fig. 1. General architecture of the solution

Our Quantum Load Balancer is implemented using Python and the Flask framework, which manages requests from developers through a REST service. This implementation adheres to the REST API architectural pattern [20]. It dynamically allocates tasks based on factors like the load of quantum resources, the number of pending tasks, and the availability of quantum machines and simulators. The goal is to improve resource availability and performance, delivering a higher quality of service for quantum task execution. Additionally, the Quantum Load Balancer is encapsulated within a Docker container, simplifying deployment across diverse environments. The implementation of this Quantum Load Balancer is accessible in a Bitbucket public repository[1].

In the process of executing quantum tasks efficiently, our general architecture comprises several key steps, as illustrated in Fig. 1, where the Task Manager takes center stage, housing the Quantum Load Balancer and the Quantum Translator Service.

The process starts with **Step 1** when the Quantum Load Balancer receives a request from a developer to execute a quantum circuit. Developers initiate this by sending an HTTP POST request to the balancer, including the necessary parameters for the quantum circuit execution. These parameters fall into two categories: configuration parameters and input parameters.

Configuration parameters are linked to the developer's account within service providers and include tokens and keys, facilitating account setup and service access. In addition, the quantum circuit to be executed is provided as a parameter, defined as a URL that either hosts the circuit, created with Quirk[2]—an open-source drag-and-drop quantum circuit simulator—or directly hosts the circuit code. That is, this URL can point to a circuit visual representation or source code repository.

The input parameters for quantum circuit execution encompass various aspects:

- Quantum Provider: this parameter specifies the quantum service provider to be used for executing the quantum circuit. Developers can choose providers such as"_aws" or "_ibm" or a combination of them.
- Type of Execution: it determines the nature of the execution. Developers can opt for retrieving the execution results or the probabilities associated with the outcomes.
- Efficiency Level: this parameter is used to balance the trade-off between circuit efficiency and accuracy, depending on the specific requirements of the problem being solved. Default values are available for convenience.
- Resilience Level: it indicates the level of resilience against errors during execution, with a scale ranging from 0 to 2, and a default value of 1. This selects the appropriate level of error correction or fault tolerance measures to be taken during circuit execution.
- Shots: with this parameter, developers define the number of times they want the quantum circuit to be executed.
- Qubits: this parameter specifies the minimum number of qubits required by the resource on which the program will run.
- Quantum Circuit: the quantum circuit itself is provided as a URL. This URL may point to a visual representation of the circuit in Quirk or directly to a code repository where the source code of the circuit is hosted.

[1] https://bitbucket.org/spilab/quantum-load-balancer.

[2] https://algassert.com/quirk.

In **Step 2**, the process of translation and mapping of the quantum circuit is carried out. This process accepts various input formats for quantum circuits, including URL links to Quirk, that provide a visual representation of the circuit, as well as source code in Qiskit and Braket. When the input URL does not contain code, but visualizes the circuit using Quirk, the Quantum Translator service performs the translation. It retrieves the circuit implementation adapted to Qiskit or Braket to be compatible with the providers respectively.

Thus, to execute this mapping process, we use the aforementioned specialized service, the Quantum Translator service. It serves as a dedicated translator API implemented in Python and designed to carry out precise and efficient translations of quantum programming languages. Its primary function is to generate code tailored to the specific language requirements of the quantum service provider where the quantum service will be deployed. In essence, the Quantum Translator employs a gate-by-gate mapping approach to transform the visual representation of the quantum circuit obtained from the provided Quirk URL into the appropriate quantum language implementation. This ensures compatibility with the distinct requirements of multiple quantum service providers [21].

After translation, **Step 3** involves the Quantum Load Balancer determining the optimal service provider for executing the quantum task by considering factors such as provider availability and cost.

In **Step 4**, the Load Balancer selects the specific quantum resource for task execution, considering factors like resource availability and current workload. This distinction between Step 3 and Step 4 ensures a clear decision-making process, where Step 3 focuses on provider selection, and Step 4 focuses on resource allocation within the chosen provider.

Step 5 involves sending the quantum task to the selected resource for execution, with task details varying based on parameters and provider specifics.

Once the task is completed, in **Step 6** the result is returned to the balancer, releasing the resources used, and finally, in **Step 7**, the response is sent to the developer in JSON format.

In simpler terms, this process ensures that quantum tasks are executed on the best-suited quantum resources by matching developers' preferences with each resource's specific capabilities. This approach enhances the overall efficiency and effectiveness of quantum computing processes.

3.2 Algorithm Used to Optimally Select a Resource Provider

Our proposal seeks to mitigate the concerns of the developers through the automation of the quantum resource selection process for the execution of quantum circuits. This facet assumes paramount significance in the realm of quantum algorithm development, as it serves to diminish the exertion necessary for identifying the optimal resource. This consideration encompasses the developer's specified parameters related to desired capabilities and quantum properties inherent to each available quantum resource.

In pursuit of this objective, the Quantum Load Balancer tailors the sampler options of the designated provider based on the parameters received. The sampler assumes the role of executing a procedure commonly known as "quantum measurement" on the ultimate state of the quantum circuit post-execution, as elucidated in [22]. In carrying out this operation, it accommodates the stipulated number of shots and other pertinent parameters to ensure the derivation of an accurate and meaningful probability distribution. Subsequently, the sampler initiates the task with the configured circuit and options, and upon task completion, furnishes the probability distribution as the response to the request.

This methodology employs the Least Outstanding Algorithm[3] for resource allocation, as elucidated in the provided Pseudocode 1.

Pseudocode 1. Least Outstanding Algorithm used

```
for provider in providers:
    available_resources = provider.get_available_resources()

    # Iterate over each available resource
    for resource in available_resources:
        #Retrieve queue information for the resource
        queue_info = resource.get_queue_info()
        selected_resource = evaluate_resource_with_restrictions
         (queue_info)

        #Check the qubits of the selected resource
        check_qubits(selected_resource)

        #Choose the resource
        least_outstanding_resource = select_resource_with_least
         _outstanding(available_resources)

        #Execute quantum task
        results = execute_in_resource(least_outstanding_resource)

        return (results)
```

It is imperative to underscore that the Quantum Load Balancer's utilization of the Least Outstanding Algorithm for resource allocation is a modular element. Although this study centers on the Least Outstanding Algorithm, it remains amenable to substitution with alternative load-balancing algorithms, such as Round Robin or others tailored for the quantum computing environment. The adaptability of the Quantum Load Balancer provides developers with the latitude to experiment with and deploy diverse algorithms according to their specific requisites and preferences. Nevertheless, it is crucial to emphasize that the primary objective of this study is not to furnish a definitive load-balancing algorithm but rather to showcase the functionality and advantages of quantum task management.

[3] https://docs.aws.amazon.com/elasticloadbalancing/latest/application/load-balancer-target-groups.html#modify-routing-algorithm.

Throughout the entirety of the process, the Quantum Load Balancer optimizes the allocation of quantum tasks and resources with the overarching goal of achieving equilibrium. This entails simultaneously minimizing the execution time of the circuits while maximizing the accuracy of the results.

4 Evaluation

In this section, we present the results of our evaluation of the proposed method for the management of quantum applications using the Quantum Load Balancer. Our evaluation aims to demonstrate the effectiveness and viability of our approach in improving the quality and efficiency of quantum circuit execution across multiple service providers. To this end, we conducted a series of experiments using real quantum hardware and simulators from service providers. Specifically, the service providers Amazon Web Services (AWS)[4] and IBM Quantum[5] have been used to validate the proposed allocation and load-balancing solution for quantum task execution, as explained below.

4.1 Quantum Load Balancing Solution for Amazon Braket and IBM Quantum

The Quantum Load Balancer establishes a connection with the cloud service provider's API to access the quantum circuit and selects the most suitable resources for its execution, based on factors such as availability, performance, and cost—as shown in Fig. 2.

In the case of Amazon, the Amazon Braket API[6] is used. This API is a set of programming interfaces that allow developers to interact with Amazon Braket, a quantum computing service provided by AWS. The API provides a range of functions for creating, managing, and executing quantum circuits on real quantum hardware or simulators. It also provides access to various resources, such as quantum devices, quantum simulators, and classical computing resources, that can be used to execute quantum circuits.

On the other hand, the connection with IBM Quantum is made with the Python Qiskit library to interact with the IBM Quantum API[7] and perform the necessary operations for the execution of quantum circuits. necessary for the execution of quantum circuits.

While IBM Quantum and Amazon Braket differ in their approach to selecting the appropriate resource for quantum circuit execution, the Quantum Load Balancer bridges this gap. While Amazon Braket may not consider resource availability and task queue workload when selecting a resource, IBM Quantum takes these factors into account, resulting in more efficient resource allocation for enhanced quantum circuit execution. As a key component of our proposed

[4] https://aws.amazon.com.
[5] https://quantum-computing.ibm.com.
[6] https://docs.aws.amazon.com/braket/latest/APIReference.
[7] https://cloud.ibm.com/apidocs/quantum-computing.

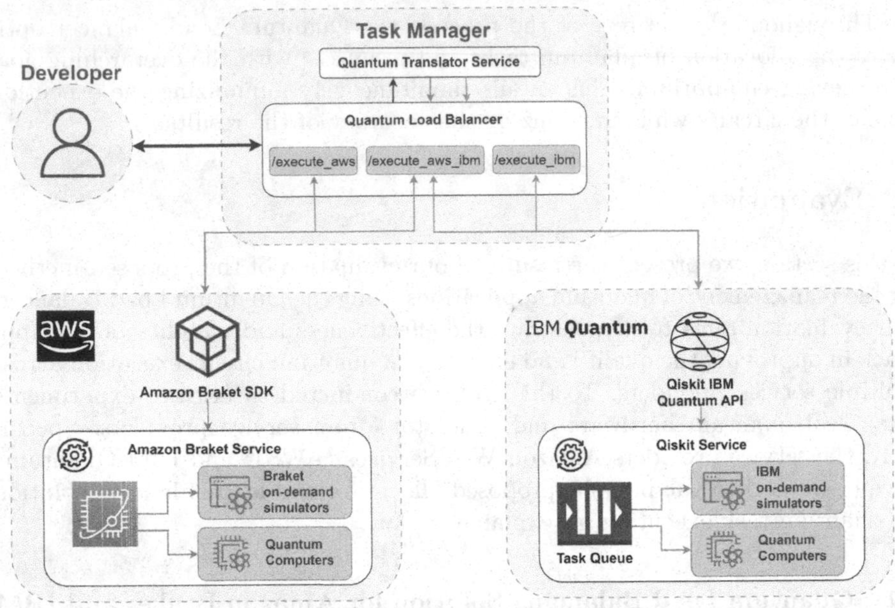

Fig. 2. Integration of Amazon Braket and IBM Quantum with the system

solution, the Quantum Load Balancer plays a crucial role in improving the allocation of quantum resources across both IBM Quantum and Amazon Braket, ensuring efficient execution of quantum tasks.

Furthermore, utilizing a multithreaded architecture, the Quantum Load Balancer enables concurrent and parallel execution of tasks. The interaction with the cloud service provider is facilitated through the Python library Boto3, allowing the Quantum Load Balancer to execute necessary operations and retrieve information on resource availability. Once the quantum task is completed, the result of the execution is returned to the balancer, releasing the resources used for the task and returning the response in JSON format to the developer. This process enhances the utilization of quantum resources by facilitating the alignment of developers' desired parameters with the specific quantum capabilities and properties offered by each available resource. Our implementation of the Quantum Load Balancer for Amazon Braket and IBM Quantum demonstrates the technological viability of our proposal and provides a foundation for future research and development in the field of quantum application management.

Finally, one of the key components of our proposed approach is the use of multiple paths for quantum circuit execution. These paths are established by connecting to these service providers and selecting the most suitable resource for each task. The "*/execute_ibm*" path is the main path for sending requests to execute quantum circuits on IBM Quantum, the "*/execute_aws*" path is used for Amazon Braket, and "*/execute_aws_ibm*" is the path established for the execution of a given quantum circuit at both Amazon Braket and the IBM Quantum service provider. These paths accept parameters such as the quantum circuit to be executed, and the type of execution—e.g. getting the result of the execution or the probability of each result.

The implementation of the Quantum Load Balancer for Amazon Braket and IBM Quantum and the steps to replicate the process can be found in our dedicated repository, accessible through the following link[8].

It is worth noting that the work can be extended for use with new providers. To add a new provider, as shown in the integration shown in Fig. 2, it is necessary to modify the Quantum Translator Service component, in addition to establishing the connection with the Quantum Load Balancer component. In the latter case, the balancer implementation would have to be extended to connect its logic with the API of the new provider.

4.2 Results of the Analysis Performed

For validation, we chose three algorithms that are well-known in the field of quantum computing to evaluate the performance of our proposal. These include the algorithms of Simon [23], Grover [24], and Shor [25]. These algorithms serve as diverse use cases, allowing us to evaluate the efficiency of the Quantum Load Balancer in terms of response times and showcase its adaptability across different problem domains.

In this way, our selection of diverse algorithms allows for a comprehensive analysis of the Quantum Load Balancer's effectiveness. We implemented these algorithms using quantum programming languages like Qiskit and leveraged Amazon Braket and IBM Quantum resources for execution. This approach provides valuable insights into how the Quantum Load Balancer performs across various computational scenarios. In this way, the performance assessment of our proposal involved conducting multiple tests to measure response times, both with and without the balancer. We replicated this process 50 times, varying qubit configurations, and shot numbers, and performing the executions at different periods, to comprehensively validate all facets of the management and coordination process. Executing the tasks a significant number of times allow us to better understand the variability in the data and also to address the variability of the results obtained in the experiments.

As shown in Fig. 3, one notable outcome of our evaluation is a 23.7% average reduction in response times for the Amazon Braket provider when using the Quantum Load Balancer across the three executed algorithms, compared to scenarios without the load balancer. For the IBM Quantum provider, the reduction is even more substantial, with an average reduction of 34.04% using the Quantum Load Balancer. Across all executions, the average response time is reduced by 31.6% when the load balancer is employed.

These results are because response times cover the entire process, including task initiation, queuing, circuit execution, and result retrieval. Although we observed similar results for the three algorithms in both providers, the execution

[8] https://bitbucket.org/spilab/quantum-load-balancer.

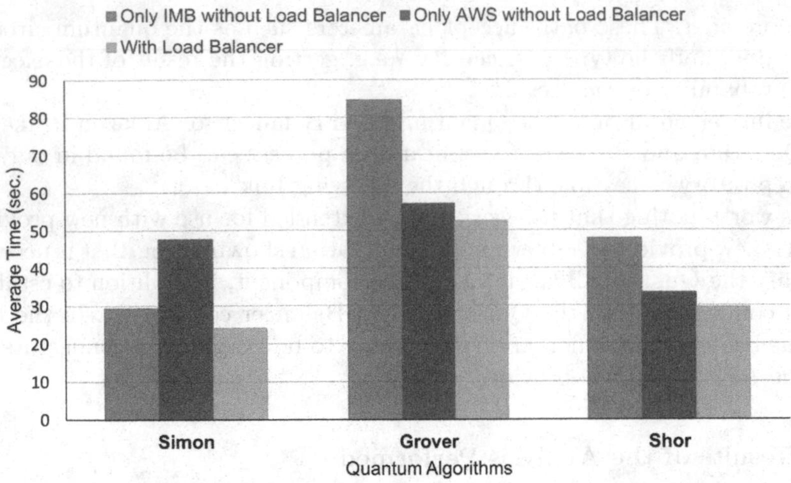

Fig. 3. Average times obtained from the execution of the algorithms

time often varies depending on the moment at which the execution is performed, the state in which the machines are located, or due to long queuing times. Generally, we found that queue waiting times tend to be more prolonged in IBM.

Throughout our testing, the Quantum Load Balancer consistently demonstrated a significant reduction in execution time for all algorithms on both quantum computing platforms. In some cases, we resorted to using simulators. The use of simulators in our experiments did have an impact on the results by providing an alternative solution when we encountered extended waiting times or a lack of availability of resources in real quantum computing environments. However, it's essential to note that our evaluation primarily focused on execution time as a key indicator for technological and functional validation of the Quantum Load Balancer. While simulators allowed us to complete the tasks, they did not fully replicate the real-world quantum computing experience, and this might have influenced our results to some extent. Nevertheless, since our primary objective was to assess the effectiveness of the Quantum Load Balancer in quantum task scheduling and resource allocation, we did not delve into optimizing other parameters such as cost efficiency or scalability. These additional aspects were beyond the scope of our current study, but we acknowledge that they may be subject to future research in the field of quantum application management.

Overall, these results provide a comprehensive account of the validation process of the proposal and highlight its potential to improve the efficiency and usability of quantum web services.

5 Conclusion

In this research work, we have elaborated a management solution supported by a Task Manager, which integrates a Quantum Load Balancer, designed to adhere to the REST API architectural pattern in cloud environments. This tool exhibits distinct endpoints, each with unique functionalities, aimed at streamlining the execution of quantum tasks across different quantum service providers. Through this framework, our main goal is to simplify and streamline the quantum task execution process.

Nevertheless, it is imperative to recognize that our proposed solution has certain limitations. The main limitation is its dependence on the availability of resources at various service providers, a factor that can introduce variability in the execution of tasks. In addition, obtaining optimal results requires proper configuration of the tool's parameters, which requires attention from developers.

Our research is primarily aimed at simplifying the quantum circuit execution process for developers. We provide a user-friendly tool that transparently selects the best provider, sparing developers from the complexities of interfaces, availability, costs, and other details. This ensures consistently optimal results by abstracting these intricacies. In essence, we allow developers to make the most of quantum resources through intelligent task allocation via load balancing.

Our proposed solution has not only proven its feasibility but also its effectiveness in practice, demonstrating a significant average reduction in response times, with a reduction of 31.6%. The validation was carried out in collaboration with two leading service providers, Amazon Braket and IBM Quantum, confirming the qualitative perspective that our proposal offers concerning available resources. This view allows developers to discern the most appropriate resource for each task, ultimately improving the quality and efficiency of quantum circuit execution. In addition, the load-balancing approach we have adopted promotes superior efficiency when executing quantum tasks across multiple service providers.

Acknowledgements. This work has been partially funded by the European Union "Next GenerationEU /PRTR", by the Ministry of Science, Innovation and Universities (projects PID2021-124045OB-C31, TED2021-130913B-I00, and PDC2022-133465-I00). It is also supported by QSERV: Quantum Service Engineering: Development Quality, Testing and Security of Quantum Microservices project funded by the Spanish Ministry of Science and Innovation and ERDF; by the Regional Ministry of Economy, Science and Digital Agenda of the Regional Government of Extremadura (GR21133); and by European Union under the Agreement - 101083667 of the Project "TECH4E -Tech4effiency EDIH" regarding the Call: DIGITAL-2021-EDIH-01 supported by the European Commission through the Digital Europe Program. It is also supported by grant PRE2022-102070, funded by MCIN/AEI/10.13039/501100011033 and by FSE+.

References

1. Ménard, A., Ostojic, I., Patel, M., Volz, D.: A game plan for quantum computing. McKinsey Q. (2020)
2. Zhao, J.: Quantum software engineering: landscapes and horizons. Arxiv http://arxiv.org/abs/2007.07047 (2020)

3. Romero-Álvarez, J., Alvarado-Valiente, J., Moguel, E., Garcia-Alonso, J.: Quantum web services: development and deployment. In: Garrigos, I., Murillo Rodriguez, J.M., Wimmer, M. (eds.) ICWE 2023, vol. 13893, pp. 421–423. Springer, Heidelberg (2023). https://doi.org/10.1007/978-3-031-34444-2_39
4. Aslam, S., Shah, M.A.: Load balancing algorithms in cloud computing: a survey of modern techniques. In: National Software Engineering Conference (NSEC), pp. 30–35 (2015). https://doi.org/10.1109/NSEC.2015.7396341
5. Leymann, F., Barzen, J., Falkenthal, M., Vietz, D., Weder, B., Wild, K.: Quantum in the cloud: application potentials and research opportunities. In: International Conference on Cloud Computing and Services Science (2020). https://doi.org/10.5220/0009819800090024
6. Serrano, M.A., Cruz-Lemus, J.A., Perez-Castillo, R., Piattini, M.: Quantum software components and platforms: overview and quality assessment. ACM Comput. Surv. **55**(8), 1–31 (2022). https://doi.org/10.1145/3548679
7. Parikh, S.M.: A survey on cloud computing resource allocation techniques. In: 2013 Nirma University International Conference on Engineering (NUiCONE), pp. 1–5. IEEE (2013). https://doi.org/10.1109/NUiCONE.2013.6780076
8. Rahman, M., Iqbal, S., Gao, J.: Load balancer as a service in cloud computing. In: 2014 IEEE 8th International Symposium on Service Oriented System Engineering, pp. 204–211 (2014). https://doi.org/10.1109/SOSE.2014.31
9. Cohen, Y., et al.: Quantum orchestration platform integrated hardware and software for design and execution of complex quantum control protocols. Bull. Am. Phys. Soc. **65** (2020)
10. Singh, J., Duhan, B., Gupta, D., Sharma, N.: Cloud resource management optimization: taxonomy and research challenges. In: 2020 8th International Conference on Reliability, Infocom Technologies and Optimization, pp. 1133–1138. IEEE (2020). https://doi.org/10.1109/ICRITO48877.2020.9197840
11. Wild, K., Breitenbücher, U., Harzenetter, L., Leymann, F., Vietz, D., Zimmermann, M.: TOSCA4QC: two modeling styles for TOSCA to automate the deployment and orchestration of quantum applications. In: 2020 IEEE 24th International Enterprise Distributed Object Computing Conference (EDOC), pp. 125–134. IEEE (2020). https://doi.org/10.1109/EDOC49727.2020.00024
12. Nguyen, H.T., Usman, M., Buyya, R.: QFAAS: a serverless function-as-a-service framework for quantum computing. Fut. Gener. Comput. Syst. **154**, 281–300 (2024). https://doi.org/10.1016/j.future.2024.01.018
13. Sim, S., Cao, Y., Romero, J., Johnson, P., Aspuru-Guzik, A.: A framework for algorithm deployment on cloud-based quantum computers. Quantum Physics (2018). http://arxiv.org/abs/1810.10576
14. Faro, I., Sitdikov, I., Valiñas, D.G., Fernandez, F.J.M., Codella, C., Glick, J.: Middleware for quantum: an orchestration of hybrid quantum-classical systems. In: IEEE International Conference on Quantum Software (QSW), pp. 1–8. IEEE (2023). https://doi.org/10.1109/QSW59989.2023.00011
15. Garcia-Alonso, J., Rojo, J., Valencia, D., Moguel, E., Berrocal, J., Murillo, J.M.: Quantum software as a service through a Quantum API Gateway. IEEE Internet Comput. **26**(1), 34–41 (2022). https://doi.org/10.1109/MIC.2021.3132688
16. Minsky, N.H., Ungureanu, V.: Law-governed interaction: a coordination and control mechanism for heterogeneous distributed systems. ACM Trans. Softw. Eng. Methodol. (2000). https://doi.org/10.1145/352591.352592
17. Zhang, Z., Fan, W.: Web server load balancing: a queueing analysis. Eur. J. Oper. Res. **186**(2), 681–693 (2008). https://doi.org/10.1016/j.ejor.2007.02.011

18. Alvarado-Valiente, J., et al.: Quantum services generation and deployment process: a quality-oriented approach. In: Fernandes, J.M., Travassos, G.H., Lenarduzzi, V., Li, X. (eds.) Quality of Information and Communications Technology, pp. 200–214. Springer, Cham (2023). https://doi.org/10.1007/978-3-031-43703-8_15
19. Aslam, S., Shah, M.A.: Load balancing algorithms in cloud computing: a survey of modern techniques. In: 2015 National software engineering conference (NSEC), pp. 30–35. IEEE (2015). https://doi.org/10.1109/NSEC.2015.7396341
20. Li, L., Chou, W., Zhou, W., Luo, M.: Design patterns and extensibility of REST API for networking applications. IEEE Trans. Netw. Serv. Manag. (2016). https://doi.org/10.1109/TNSM.2016.2516946
21. Romero-Álvarez, J., Alvarado-Valiente, J., Moguel, E., García-Alonso, J., Murillo, J.M.: Enabling continuous deployment techniques for quantum services. Authorea Preprints (2023). https://doi.org/10.22541/au.168998413.35984731/v1
22. Aaronson, S.: Quantum computing, postselection, and probabilistic polynomial-time. Proc. Roy. Soc. A: Math. Phys. Eng. Sci. **461**, 3473–3482 (2005). https://doi.org/10.1098/rspa.2005.1546
23. Simon, D.R.: On the power of quantum computation. SIAM J. Comput. **26**(5), 1474–1483 (1997). https://doi.org/10.1137/S0097539796298637
24. Grover, L.K.: A fast quantum mechanical algorithm for database search. In: Proceedings of the Twenty-Eighth Annual ACM Symposium on Theory of Computing, pp. 212–219 (1996). https://doi.org/10.1145/237814.237866
25. Shor, P.W.: Polynomial-time algorithms for prime factorization and discrete logarithms on a quantum computer. SIAM Rev. **41**(2), 303–332 (1999). https://doi.org/10.1137/S0097539795293172

How Many Web APIs Evolve Following Semantic Versioning?

Souhaila Serbout(✉) and Cesare Pautasso

Software Institute (USI), Lugano, Switzerland
souhaila.serbout@usi.ch, c.pautasso@ieee.org

Abstract. More and more Web APIs use semantic versioning to represent the impact of changes on clients depending on previous versions. Our goal is to provide insights about the extent to which evolving Web APIs align with semantic versioning rules. In this paper we present the results of an empirical study on the descriptions of 3 075 Web APIs, which released at least one new version throughout their history. The APIs descriptions were mined by retrieving 132 909 commits from 2 028 different open source GitHub repositories. We systematically collected and examined 506 273 changes of 195 different types released within 16 053 new API versions. We classified whether each change is likely to break clients or not, and checked whether the corresponding version identifier has been updated following semantic versioning rules. The results indicate that in the best case, only 517 APIs consistently release major upgrades when introducing breaking changes, while 1 970 APIs will not always correctly inform their clients about breaking changes released as part of minor or patch-level upgrades. We also detected 927 APIs which use a backwards-compatible evolution strategy, as they never introduce any breaking change throughout their history.

Keywords: Web APIs · Semantic Versioning · API Evolution · Breaking Changes · OpenAPI

1 Introduction

In the rapidly evolving landscape of software development, Application Programming Interfaces (APIs) stand as critical components [6], facilitating seamless interactions between different software systems and services [15,23]. The management of API evolution through versioning makes it possible to check, ensure or break compatibility and determine how changes will affect API clients [8,10,12]. Semantic Versioning (SemVer) has emerged as a widely adopted set of rules aimed at clarifying how to mint version identifiers to describe the impact of changes on clients depending on previous versions of an API [2]. The adoption and compliance with Semantic Versioning has been empirically studied [4] within repositories of software packages and libraries for different programming languages (e.g., Maven [13,17], npm [16], golang [9]). Despite its prevalence within Web API descriptions [19], there is a lack of empirical studies on the adherence to and the correct usage of semantic versioning [1] in real-world Web APIs.

K. Stefanidis et al. (Eds.): ICWE 2024, LNCS 14629, pp. 344–359, 2024.
https://doi.org/10.1007/978-3-031-62362-2_25

In this paper, we aim at bridging this gap by presenting a method to assess the consistency between changes applied to OpenAPI descriptions and the corresponding version identifier which leads to answering the following:

RQ1) How often APIs introduce breaking vs. non-breaking changes?
RQ2) Are there many Web APIs which consistently follow semantic versioning rules across their entire history?

Given the public nature of Web APIs, the expectation is that their developers carefully assess the impact of every change as they strive to avoid breaking their clients. But if breaking changes are introduced, are semantic versioning rules properly followed? How often can clients rely on semantic versioning identifiers to set their expectations about the impact of new releases they depend on?

In this paper we present a data analysis method to statically classify 195 different types of changes that can be detected by comparing OpenAPI [14] descriptions and predict whether they are likely to break clients with different tolerance levels [3]. We apply the method to a collection of 3 075 API evolution histories mined from open source GitHub repositories. The main findings are that, in the best case, 1) almost one third of APIs in our sample (927) evolves in a backwards compatible way; 2) a minority of APIs (517) which introduce breaking changes does so by consistently adhering to semantic versioning rules.

The rest of this paper is outlined as follows: In Sect. 2, we highlight the principal studies related to our work. Section 3 details the dataset of OpenAPI specifications analyzed in this study. In Sect. 4, we introduce the key definitions utilized throughout the paper. The methodology adopted for our analysis, along with the metrics calculated, are elaborated in Sect. 5, with the findings presented in Sect. 6. Discussions on the implications and the validity threats of these results are found in Sect. 7. Finally, Sect. 8 concludes the paper, outlining our conclusions and directions for future research.

2 Related Work

The consistent adoption of semantic versioning has been studied empirically for software packages released in programming languages like Maven [13,17], npm [16], golang [9]. Analyzing a large dataset from GitHub comprising 124k third-party golang libraries and 532k client programs, the authors of [9] found that 86% of the golang libraries follow semantic versioning but 28.6% of non-major releases introduced breaking changes.

In [17], the authors scrutinize semantic versioning compliance in the Maven repository, analyzing over 10 000 `.jar` files from 22 000 libraries. It uncovers that 33% of releases breach semantic versioning by introducing breaking changes, which deviates from the expected practice of only making breaking changes in major releases. In a more recent replication study [13], the authors analyzed 119 879 Java library upgrades and 293 817 clients revealing that 83.4% of upgrades adhere to semantic versioning.

As public Web APIs are meant to be offered to an unknown set of clients [23] – unlike the previous studies – we do not consider client-side artifacts or usage logs to estimate the impact of changes. Our static analysis therefore produces a conservative assessment on the impact of the detected API changes on clients.

In our previous research on Web API versioning practices [19], we analyzed 7 114 APIs from GitHub, revealing 55 different version formats. We found that 85% of these APIs consistently adopt identifiers syntactically consistent with semantic versioning. In further work [18], we proposed "API Version Clock" a visualization of the evolution of an API over time, emphasizing the relationship between changes of version identifiers and the nature of the changes made (e.g., breaking or non-breaking changes). It employs a sunburst plot to provide a fine-grained, chronological view of API changes, color-coded to distinguish between major, minor, and patch releases. Observing a small gallery of API evolution histories reveals widely different approaches to versioning decisions in response to changes. Building on these preliminary results, in this paper our objective is to systematically and quantitatively assess the consistency between the changes made in Web APIs and whether the corresponding version identifiers have been updated following the actual semantics of semantic versioning [1].

3 Dataset

The OpenAPI Specifications (OAS [14]) analyzed in this study were gathered through the GitHub API [20]. Before filtering, this dataset included 915 885 valid specifications from 270 578 APIs committed to GitHub between 2015 and January 2024. As described in Table 1, our analysis focuses on the evolutionary aspect of APIs. Therefore, we specifically looked at APIs with a history of at least 10 commits, all containing valid OAS documents. Considering the goal of this study, to examine the practical adoption of semantic versioning, we filtered for APIs that consistently use identifiers compatible with semantic versioning throughout their entire history. Additionally, to be able to check the level of compliance with semantic versioning rules, we identified APIs that have released at least one new version during their history that included some modifications impacting the functionalities of the API. As a result, our study includes the history of 3 075 APIs, with a total of 15 856 versions, corresponding to 506 273 changes introduced in their documentation.

Table 1. Data cleaning steps

Filtering Step	# APIs	# Commits
all valid commits	270 578	915 885
at least 10 valid commits	16 401	490 526
always use semantic versioning identifiers	14 489	413 463
have at least one version change	3 075	132 909

4 Definitions

4.1 Semantic Versioning Change Classification

Due to the lack of widely accepted semantics for arbitrary version identifiers, in this paper we focus exclusively on APIs which make consistent use of semantic versioning throughout their evolution history, in both stable and preview releases. More precisely, we analyzed API descriptions versioned with four different schemes: `X` (Major), `X.Y` (Major.Minor), `X.Y.Z` (Major.Minor.Patch), and `X.Y.Z-LABEL` (Major.Minor.Patch-Release Type). Where the release type, if present, labels the maturity of the artifact along the API release lifecycle. The version identifiers have been matched with the following regular expression:
`/^(?i)(v)?\d{1,3}(?:\.\d{1,3})?(?:\.\d{1,3})?(?:-LABEL ))?$/`
Where `LABEL` can be: alpha, beta, dev, snapshot, rc, preview, test, private.

We limit the size of the numbers to three digits because we want to avoid catching identifiers using dates [5], which are often used in versioning but do not provide a clear, incremental progression of versions, reflecting the expected change impact between releases.

Based on the previous regular expression, the parsing operation p transforms a version string into a structured tuple $(X, Y, Z, \mathit{Label})$. E.g,: $p($`v1`$) \rightarrow (1,0,0,\emptyset)$ and $p($`v3.0.1-alpha`$) \rightarrow (3,0,1,\text{alpha})$.

To detect the type of semantic version change, we use a classification function c defined as follows. The function reads the tuples $V_1 = (X_1, Y_1, Z_1, \mathit{Label}_1)$ and $V_2 = (X_2, Y_2, Z_2, \mathit{Label}_2)$ representing two distinct version identifiers. It detects the following version changes:

Major (`X.y.z`): Incremented for incompatible API changes, signaling significant modifications that may require client adjustments.

$$\text{if } X_1 \neq X_2, \text{ then: } \begin{cases} \text{Major Upgrade, if } X_1 < X_2 \\ \text{Major Downgrade, if } X_1 > X_2 \end{cases}$$

Minor (`x.Y.z`): Incremented for adding backward-compatible features, indicating enhancements without breaking existing functionalities.

$$\text{if } X_1 = X_2 \text{ and } Y_1 \neq Y_2, \text{ then: } \begin{cases} \text{Minor Upgrade, if } Y_1 < Y_2 \\ \text{Minor Downgrade, if } Y_1 > Y_2 \end{cases}$$

Patch (`x.y.Z`): Incremented for backward-compatible bug fixes, often associated with routine maintenance updates.

$$\text{if } X_1 = X_2 \text{ and } Y_1 = Y_2 \text{ and } Z_1 \neq Z_2, \text{ then: } \begin{cases} \text{Patch Upgrade, if } Z_1 < Z_2 \\ \text{Patch Downgrade, if } Z_1 > Z_2 \end{cases}$$

Label Change (`x.y.z-LABEL`): Updated to reflect the current (e.g., `alpha`, `beta`, `rc`) pre-release stage, indicating the API is not yet ready for production.

$$\text{if } X_1 = X_2 \text{ and } Y_1 = Y_2 \text{ and } Z_1 = Z_2, \text{ then: } \begin{cases} \text{Label Change, if } Label_1 \neq Label_2 \\ \text{No Change, if } Label_1 = Label_2 \end{cases}$$

4.2 API Changes Classification

Each change that occurs affects different elements of a Web API, such as its endpoints, paths, operations, their request/response body, headers, parameters, media types and schemas. The impact of each change depends on how these elements are modified, added, or removed, and whether these changes maintain backward compatibility with existing client implementations.

For example, within the paths, non-breaking changes include the addition of new paths, whereas breaking changes encompass the removal of paths, with further distinctions based on sunset operations and deprecation notices. Changes on operations follow a similar pattern, with the addition of operations being non-breaking, and their removal, especially without sunset dates or before the sunset date, being breaking.

In this paper, we focus on analyzing API changes through specification commit diffs, excluding from them OpenAPI specific modifications that do not impact the API structure, its data model, and security components. We have identified a total of 195 distinct types of changes (See Tables 3 and 4 for some examples). These changes are categorized into three main types: 96 *Breaking Changes*, 66 *Non-Breaking Changes*, and 33 *Undecidable Changes.*

Breaking Changes (**BC**) can disrupt existing client implementations and require clients to adapt to these changes. These changes include modifying existing properties or types (like changing types to enums), adding properties, request parameters or required elements, deleting paths or properties from response payloads, and changing nullable or optional attributes.

Non-Breaking Changes (**NBC**) do not require existing clients to change their implementations. These are generally additive changes such as adding new properties to response payloads, tags, or media types, and changing types where backward compatibility is maintained (like integer to number).

Undecidable Changes (**UC**) refer to those modifications whose impact on the client varies depending on the client's or backend's tolerance level to dealing with unexpected message payloads [3]. For example, when removing authentication or authorization headers, old clients may not break if the security tokens they still send to a tolerant API are ignored. Likewise, properties that are added to API responses may break strict clients which reject unknown data elements. Undecidable changes, cannot be statically classified into breaking or non-breaking without making further assumptions about the client and the API tolerance level. Given that approx. one third of the changes are undecidable, we take them into account with the following two scenarios:

- Best Case Scenario: We assume that all changes classified as undecidable are treated as non-breaking. This perspective allows us to envision a scenario where the potential for disruption due to those changes is minimized.

- Worst Case Scenario: Conversely, the worst-case analysis adopts a more conservative approach by assuming that all undecidable changes have a breaking impact. This stance takes into account a scenario where the ambiguity surrounding those changes is resolved by erring on the side of caution, thereby assuming the maximum possible disruption and compatibility issues.

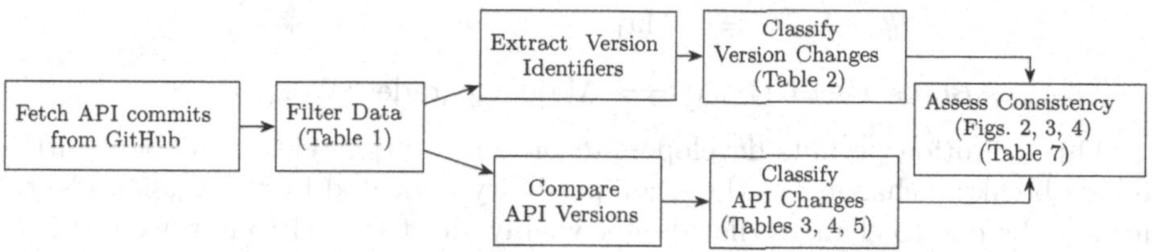

Fig. 1. Data Analytics Pipeline

5 Methodology and Metrics

We implemented a systematic approach to assess consistency between changes detected across API releases (Sect. 4.2) and the corresponding types of semantic version identifier changes (Sect. 4.1). The results of the analysis have been obtained by running a pipeline with the following steps (Fig. 1).

For each API, we retrieve the complete commits history from its respective GitHub repository. We then ensure that the API meets the filtering criteria as detailed in Table 1. Following, we meticulously sift through the commits to isolate the ones where a version identifier change has happened. The detected version change is then classified to distinguish whether developers have made a Major, Minor, Patch-level release or simply changed the release type label. Following this, we extract the differences between the two consecutive versions of the API, we compare their respective specifications using the `oasdiff` library [11]. The extracted changes are then abstracted by matching them against the known list of 195 change types, which have been pre-classified into the Breaking, Non-Breaking, and Undecidable categories.

The outcome of the pipeline is a table listing, for all APIs and all their releases, the API version change classification with the corresponding API changes. To give a quantitative assessment of the consistency between the two according to semantic versioning rules we compute the following metrics:

- Number of version changes (#VC), further subdivided into the number of Major, Minor, Patch and Label changes (#Major, #Minor, #Patch, #LC)
- Number of API changes (#C), comprising the number of breaking changes (#BC), non-breaking Changes (#NBC), undecidable changes (#UC).
- Proportion of Breaking Changes (BC%):

$$BC\% = \frac{\#BC}{\#C} \text{(Best Case)} \qquad BC\% = \frac{\#BC + \#UC}{\#C} \text{(Worst Case)}$$

We assess adherence to semantic versioning by examining if version updates involving at least one breaking change ($\#BC > 0$) or, in the worst-case scenario, at least one undecidable change ($\#UC > 0$), have been accurately categorized as Major. For each API, we define its compliance ratio as $CR = \frac{\#V}{\#VC}$ where $\#V$ is the number of versions which comply with semantic versioning, according to the following rules:

$$\#BC > 0 \implies \text{Major upgrade} \quad \text{(Best Case)}$$

$$\#BC > 0 \vee \#UC > 0 \implies \text{Major upgrade} \quad \text{(Worst Case)}$$

This definition permits developers to produce Major releases without introducing breaking changes, as the incompatibility indicated by the version identifier may be due to changes that do not visibly affect the API interface itself.

6 Results

We present the results of the analysis at two levels of granularity. First we quantitatively study each API release independently by characterizing its type of version identifier change and the types of changes introduced in the API itself, by classifying whether they are expected to break or not break clients. This allows us to determine whether the release complies with semantic versioning. Then we proceed to aggregate each release along the history of the corresponding API. This will make it possible to classify the APIs in the dataset according to various facets: which type of changes they underwent at some release in their history, which type of version identifier change, as well as to which extent the API consistently adhered to semantic versioning throughout its entire history. The raw results are publicly shared in a replication package in GitHub.

6.1 Change-Level Compliance

Types of Version Changes. While the most frequently occurring type of version change (Table 2) is the "Patch Upgrade", "Minor Upgrades" can be found more widely across more than half the APIs in the dataset. Overall, the 14 204 Upgrades outnumber the 1 131 Downgrades. As expected, major releases are the least frequent (both concerning upgrades and downgrades). Among the 3 075 APIs, 2 198 APIs have combined at least two types of version changes during their change history. 764 have only one version change. 133 APIs have more than one version change, but they are all of the same type.

Types of API Changes. In Table 3 we list the most recurrent breaking changes (out of 96). The analysis of breaking change within our dataset prominently highlights "Response property type changed" as the most frequently occurring type of change, followed by the removal of values from enumerated type definitions. The most widespread change affecting 1211 APIs at least once is the removal of paths. Path removal is the complementary change to Path addition, the most prevalent non-breaking change both according to the number of occurrences but also the number (48.14%) of impacted APIs (Table 4).

There is no clear correlation between the presence of specific API changes (e.g., the addition or removal of paths) and the corresponding version identifier changes (listed in the last four columns in the Tables 3 and 4). For example, the removal of paths without deprecation is detected in 246 major releases, which correctly represent the impact of such major change. However, also 629 minor and even 557 patch-level upgrades do include at least one path removal, a clear violation of semantic versioning rules.

Table 2. Classification of version changes (VC) indicating their occurrence (#VC), the total number of breaking, non-breaking and undecidable changes detected in conjunction with each type of version change, as well as their prevalence within all APIs and within how many APIs with breaking changes

	#VC	#UC	#BC	#NBC	#APIs	w/BC	
					Total	Best	Worst
Patch Upgrade	7 108	67 032	63 541	77 490	1 669	1 198	1 498
Minor Upgrade	6 038	87 471	54 443	70 820	1 774	1 240	1 412
Major Upgrade	1 058	7 866	11 920	14 854	808	375	422
Label Change	718	3 085	7 938	6 513	345	85	96
Minor Downgrade	459	2 252	4 508	5 160	265	210	233
Patch Downgrade	434	3 056	6 102	3 519	249	210	231
Major Downgrade	238	2 266	2 877	3 560	163	132	150
Total	16 053	173 028	151 329	181 916	3 075	2 148	2 487

Table 3. Most frequent breaking changes

Breaking Change	Occ.	#APIs	#VC	#Major	#Minor	#Patch	#LC
Response Property Type Changed	23 048	714	872	100	335	406	31
Response Property Enum Value Removed	21 210	319	377	43	182	136	16
Path Removed Without Deprecation	15 877	1 211	1 463	246	629	557	31
Response Required Property Removed	12 587	409	547	68	244	205	30
Request Property Enum Value Removed	9 438	223	252	25	114	107	6
Path Parameter Removed	7 019	678	819	118	330	330	41
Response Media Type Removed	5 744	154	168	27	54	77	10
Response Property Pattern Changed	5 032	96	100	6	34	59	1
Response Property Became Optional	4 341	286	333	41	139	135	18
Response Property All Of Removed	4 261	185	240	27	119	87	7
Response Body Type Changed	3 906	351	380	37	170	163	10
Request Property Type Changed	3 872	448	502	40	188	259	15
Response Property Min Length Decreased	3 758	69	73	1	18	51	3
Request Required Property Added	2 524	339	394	62	169	154	9

Table 4. Most frequent non-breaking changes

Non-Breaking Change	Occ.	#APIs	#VC	#Major	#Minor	#Patch	#LC
Path Added	37 928	2 182	2 881	405	1 201	985	290
Response Optional Property Removed	34 172	826	1 011	117	458	413	23
Request Optional Property Added	19 814	1 019	1 259	105	482	627	45
Response Property Became Required	18 112	507	647	80	280	259	28
Request Property Enum Value Added	15 853	324	399	35	178	174	12
Request Optional Parameter Added	12 794	1 343	1 737	447	775	490	25
Response Media Type Added	10 604	334	360	51	148	149	12
Response Non Success Status Added	8 452	704	790	96	362	317	15
Response Optional Header Removed	2 332	73	79	14	52	11	2
Response Property Pattern Added	2 316	81	88	14	31	41	2
Request Parameter Enum Value Added	2 063	148	171	17	77	74	3
Request Parameter Became Optional	1 523	161	165	14	86	65	0
Request Property Became Nullable	1 493	111	135	8	76	39	12
Request Property Became Optional	1 433	257	293	36	131	112	14
Request Optional Default Parameter Added	1 122	69	75	7	29	38	1
Response Success Status Added	1 052	315	336	53	129	151	3
Response Required Property Became Not Read-Only	925	15	21	0	9	8	4

Table 5. All the non-breaking changes that were associated with a Major version change during which no breaking changes occurred

Non-Breaking Change	Occurrences	#APIs	#VC(=#Major)
Request Optional Parameter Added	917	333	334
Path Added	763	118	141
Response Non Success Status Added	214	20	21
Response Optional Property Removed	10	5	5
Response Success Status Added	6	3	4
Request Parameter Became Optional	6	3	3
Request Optional Default Parameter Added To Existing Path	5	1	1
Response Media Type Added	3	3	3
Request Optional Property Added	2	1	1
Request Property Became Optional	2	1	1
Request Property Enum Value Added	2	1	1
Request Parameter Enum Value Added	1	1	1

Version Changes classification by API Change Type. How many major releases contain at least some breaking changes? According to the aggregated results in Table 2 – listing the total number of breaking, non-breaking and undecidable changes for each type of version change – there are 1 058 major upgrades with 7 866 breaking changes in total. While according to semantic versioning, there should be no breaking changes for patch and minor upgrades, we can read that the highest number of breaking changes (87 471) is actually detected in conjunction with minor upgrades. Notably, label changes, despite their lower frequency, also account for a significant number of breaking changes, indicating that clients can and will be broken as an API `alpha` release is updated to `beta`.

The total number of breaking changes listed in Table 2 is further decomposed in Table 6 with some statistics. It stands out that the worst major release introduced 723 breaking changes. This is a small number, however, if compared to the 2 508 breaking changes applied to one *minor* release. We also spot that the minimum number of breaking changes is 0 across all version change types. This means that there at least some minor releases without breaking changes. How many? Only 32% of the minor releases and 27% of the Patch releases do include exclusively non-breaking changes as we can see from Fig. 2, showing a complete, detailed map of the major, minor and patch version changes classified according to the corresponding mix of API change types. For example, we can see that while 705 major releases of 375 APIs contain at least one breaking change, 75 releases contain *only* breaking changes. In the worst case, 813 major releases of 422 APIs contain both at least one breaking and one undecidable change. There, we also observe that 37% of major releases include only non-breaking changes, all of which are listed in Table 5.

Table 6. Number of breaking changes detected for each type of version change

#BC (Best)	Max		Min		Average		Median		StdDev	
#BC+#UC (Worst)	Worst	Best	Worst	Best	Worst	Best	Worst	Best	Worst	Best
Major Upgrade	723	509	0	0	18.70	11.27	1	0	64.97	42.77
Minor Upgrade	2 508	2 508	0	0	23.50	9.02	2	0	101.37	57.34
Patch Upgrade	2 308	1 692	0	0	18.37	8.94	2	0	94.25	57.29
Major Downgrade	553	518	0	0	21.61	12.09	5	3	50.60	39.11
Minor Downgrade	362	246	0	0	14.73	9.82	4	3	32.27	20.14
Patch Downgrade	559	349	0	0	21.10	14.06	4	3	58.60	43.12
Label Change	2 637	2 596	0	0	15.35	11.06	0	0	110.29	105.17

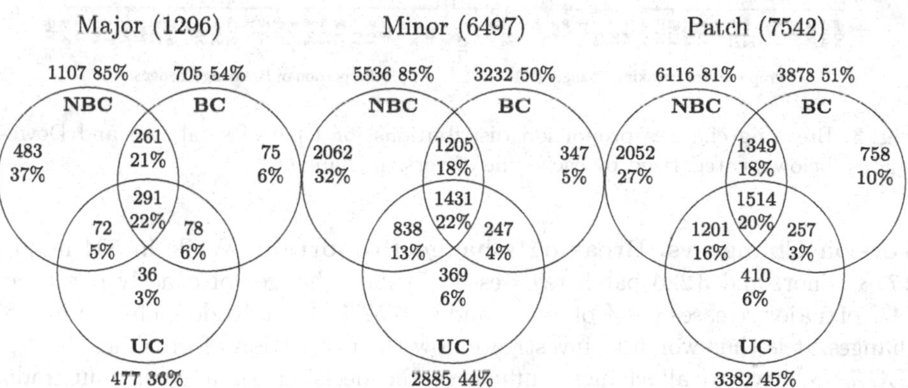

Fig. 2. Classification of the Major, Minor and Patch-level releases according to their mix of breaking (BC), non-breaking (NBC), and undecidable (UC) changes. The values outside the circles refer to the number of version changes with at least one type of API change

Non Breaking Changes in Major Releases. While it is not a violation of semantic versioning to launch a major release that is fully backwards compatible, we observed that there is only a limited number of 12 non-breaking changes when this happens (Table 5). Predominantly, the most frequent changes pertained to modifications in the API structure, such as the inclusion of new paths or the addition of optional request parameters.

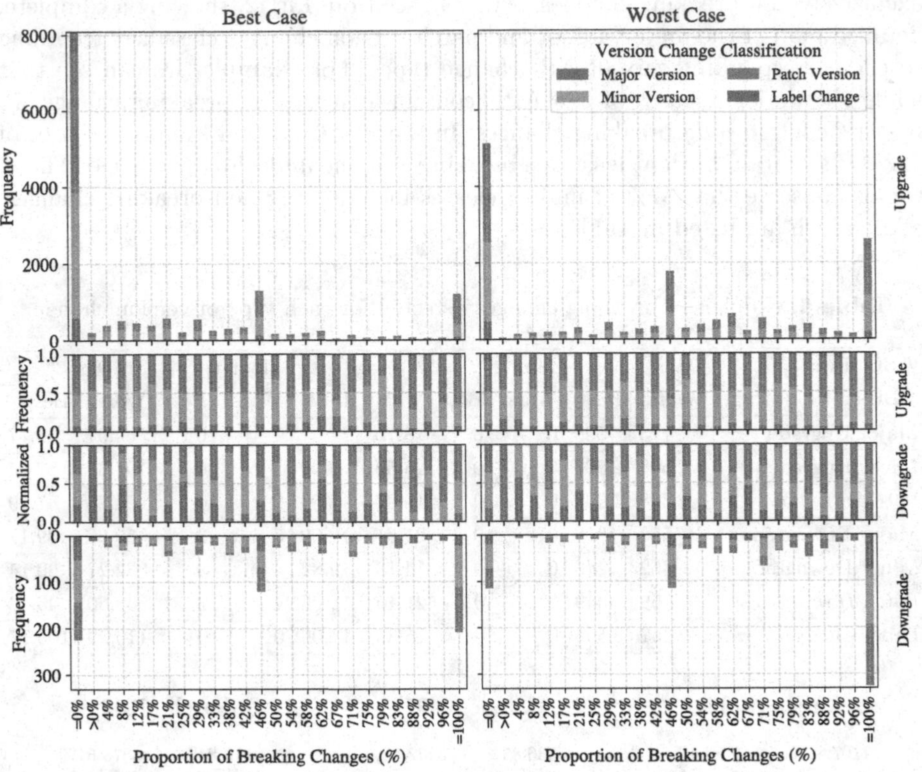

Fig. 3. Breaking changes proportion distributions for Upgrades (above) and Downgrades (below), categorized by each type of version change

Version Change vs. Breaking Change Proportion. While in 594 major, 2 778 minor, and 3 220 patch releases do include changes of exactly one type, 54% of major releases (57% of minor and also 57% of patch) do include a mix of changes. It is thus worth to investigate how the proportion of breaking changes (BC%) relative to all changes influences the decision for a version upgrade. Figure 3 illustrates the BC% distribution both for the best and worst cases, with the APIs segmented according to the type of version change involved (Major, Minor, Patch, Label Change) as well as whether the version was upgraded (top) or downgraded (bottom). The 'Normalized Frequency' plots within the main histograms provide a relative comparison, allowing for the visual assessment of the impact of the proportion of breaking changes on the decision to launch a major or minor release irrespective of the absolute number of version changes.

In both the best and worst-case scenarios, the histograms show that most version changes have a null proportion of breaking changes, as evidenced by the high bars at the left side of the histograms (BC% = 0%). This observation is consistent with the fact that 54.68% of the APIs exclusively undergo non-breaking changes, thus maintaining backward compatibility. The presence of bars across all intervals indicates that breaking changes are spread across the entire spectrum, becoming more and more prevalent, up to thousands of releases which include only breaking changes. The normalized plots reveal that, regardless of whether updates are classified as upgrades or downgrades, the proportion of breaking changes does not significantly affect the assignment of a new version number to the API. This trend persists even in cases where breaking changes constitute 100% of the alterations, indicating scenarios where all the changes were breaking and developers still assigned a non-major version to the release. In the worst-case scenario, we identified that there were 66 distinct types of breaking changes that were applied in the absence of any non-breaking ones.

6.2 API-Level Compliance

APIs that adhere to semantic versioning are those that have consistently maintained backward compatibility or have appropriately notified clients of any compatibility breaks through version identifiers. Within our dataset, under the best case scenario, we identified a total of 962 adhering APIs (out of 3075 that experienced at least one instance of breaking changes (BC), non-breaking changes (NBC), or undecidable changes (UC)). In the worst-case scenario, this number decreases to 588 APIs. When examining the subset of 2487 APIs that introduced breaking changes, we found that 517 APIs in the best case and only 180 in the worst case have adhered to semantic versioning principles (Table 7). These APIs have the highest average number of major releases. The highest average number of releases (#VC) overall, however, is found within the non-compliant APIs. These also underwent a significantly larger number of changes (484 221) than the APIs which adhere to semantic versioning (31 244).

Figure 4 provides a nuanced view of the compliance ratio for both best and worst-case scenarios also distinguishing upgrades from downgrades. It illustrates that only some APIs do consistently adhere to (1 444 in the best case, 768 in the worst) or always deviate (532 in the best case, 766 in the worst) from compliance across all releases. Instead, there is a non-empty subset of 1541 APIs with partial compliance in the worst case. The central peak with 50% compliance ratio accounts for the 582 APIs with two releases, out of which only one is compliant.

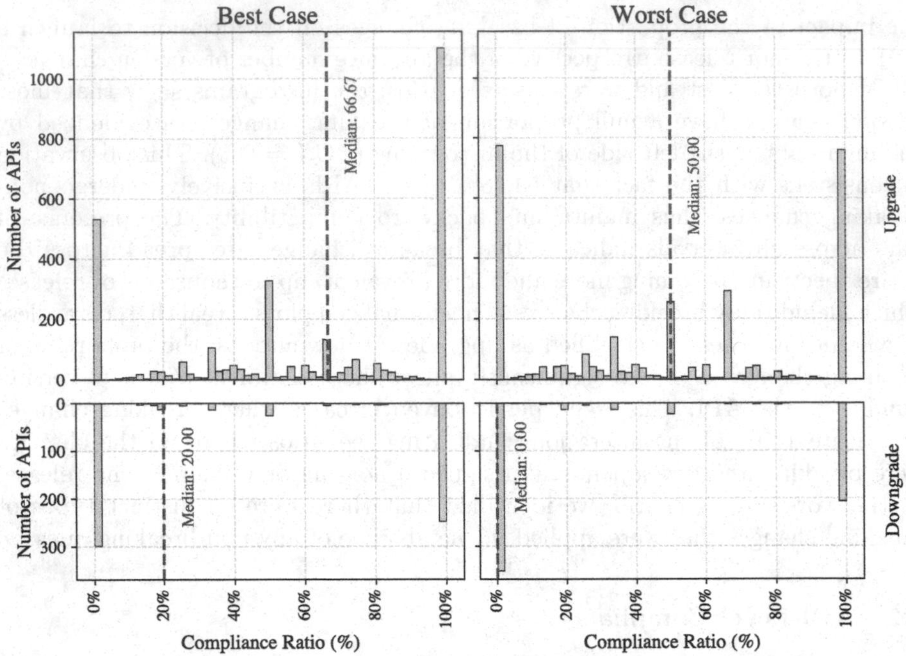

Fig. 4. Compliance Ratio Distribution

Table 7. Metrics comparison for APIs classified according to their compliance

Metric	Adhering to Semantic Versioning				Not Adhering		Total
	BC% = 0		BC% > 0		BC% > 0		
	Best	Worst	Best	Worst	Best	Worst	
#APIs	927	588	517	180	1 970	2 307	3 075
#VC	2 190	1 089	1 527	413	14 423	15 537	16 053
Avg #VC	2.36	1.85	2.95	2.29	7.32	6.73	5.22
Avg #Major	0.17	0.32	0.24	0.86	0.04	0.04	0.08
Avg #Minor	0.27	0.32	0.20	0.10	0.45	0.44	0.42
Avg #Patch	0.33	0.26	0.29	0.04	0.49	0.48	0.46
#BC	0	0	2 723	2 665	148 606	148 664	151 329
#NBC	8 226	4 558	7 584	3 896	169 774	173 462	181 916
#UC	5 523	0	7 188	1 440	165 840	171 588	173 028
Avg BC% (Best)	0.00	0.00	8.81	31.46	24.75	23.00	11.19
Avg BC% (Worst)	12.73	0.00	30.20	42.37	46.38	44.90	29.77

7 Discussion

How often APIs introduce breaking vs. non-breaking changes?
The analysis of histories of 3,075 APIs that experienced changes affecting their functionalities, revealed that 80.87%, included backward incompatible changes. This finding reveals the considerable challenge developers face in maintaining backward compatibility. The prevalence of such changes underlines the critical need for effective versioning strategies and comprehensive documentation to mitigate potential disruptions and ensure a smoother transition for API consumers.

Are there many Web APIs which consistently follow semantic versioning rules across their entire history?
Contrary to theoretical expectations, the study uncovered that only 577 APIs with breaking or potentially breaking changes adequately reflected these alterations by launching a major release, adhering to semantic versioning principles in practice. Moreover, despite SemVer guidelines suggesting that minor versions should only introduce backward-compatible features, 2 282 APIs did release breaking changes as minor or even patch-level updates. This deviation could be due to a misinterpretation of what constitutes a breaking change or a desire to push new features quickly without incrementing the major version.

We also found 910 APIs where Major version updates did not introduce any breaking changes. Interestingly, these non-breaking changes (NBC) were categorized into exactly 12 distinct types. This observation suggests a nuanced approach to versioning, where developers might choose to launch major releases for reasons other than breaking changes, such as significant feature additions or improvements meant to attract new clients without breaking existing ones.

7.1 Threats to Validity

Construct Validity. Not all changes may be documented or detected, especially if they are subtle or indirect, possibly underestimating the true impact of API changes [21]. We rely on a single tool (`oasdiff`) to detect the changes, which may bias the results. The classification of the changes into breaking, non-breaking, and undecidable was manually performed by the authors.

External Validity. A potential threat to the generalizability of the findings arises from the focus on Web APIs specifications hosted on GitHub, raising questions about the applicability of our findings to proprietary or non-GitHub hosted API documentation.

Internal Validity. Establishing a clear causal relationship between the presence of specific types of API changes and the corresponding type of version identifier change remains an open challenge. The decision on which type of major, minor or patch-level release may be influenced by other confounding factors. As most APIs have a only a few releases in their histories, this may produce discretization artifacts in the distributions shown in Figs. 3 and 4.

8 Conclusion

The results of the study presented in this paper underscore a critical need for tools and guidelines tailored specifically for correctly applying semantic versioning to Web APIs. With an empirical analysis tracking the evolution histories of 3 075 Web APIs, we found that in the worst case (assuming clients and backends perform strict checking of message payloads) only 768 (25%) APIs consistently comply with Semantic Versioning by always releasing major upgrades for breaking changes (180), or never breaking their backward compatibility (588). This number grows to 1444 APIs (46%) when assuming clients and backends follow the "tolerant reader" pattern [3].

This finding highlights a discrepancy between the theory [1] and the state of the practice of semantic versioning within the Web APIs described using OpenAPI specifications, tracked using GitHub open source repositories. Based on these results, there is a need for establishing standardized versioning protocols which can be embedded into semantic versioning calculators [7,22] to mitigate the observed inconsistencies, benefiting both Web API developers and consumers by enhancing predictability, reducing potential disruptions, simplifying dependency management, and fostering a more resilient Web API ecosystem.

References

1. Semantic Versioning. https://semver.org/
2. Bogart, C., Kästner, C., Herbsleb, J., Thung, F.: When and how to make breaking changes: policies and practices in 18 open source software ecosystems. ACM TOSEM **30**(4), 1–56 (2021)
3. Daigneau, R.: Service Design Patterns: Fundamental Design Solutions for SOAP/WSDL and Restful Web Services. Addison-Wesley, Boston (2012)
4. Dietrich, J., Pearce, D., Stringer, J., Tahir, A., Blincoe, K.: Dependency versioning in the wild. In: Proceedings of 16th International Conference on Mining Software Repositories (MSR), pp. 349–359 (2019)
5. Giretti, A.: API versioning. In: Beginning gRPC with ASP.NET Core 6, pp. 223–237 (2022)
6. Henning, M.: API design matters. Queue **5**(4), 24–36 (2007)
7. Lam, P., Dietrich, J., Pearce, D.J.: Putting the semantics into semantic versioning. In: Proceedings of the 2020 ACM SIGPLAN International Symposium on New Ideas, New Paradigms, and Reflections on Programming and Software, pp. 157–179 (2020)
8. Lamothe, M., Guéhéneuc, Y.G., Shang, W.: A systematic review of API evolution literature. ACM Comput. Surv. (CSUR) **54**(8), 1–36 (2021)
9. Li, W., Wu, F., Fu, C., Zhou, F.: A large-scale empirical study on semantic versioning in golang ecosystem. In: Proceedings of 38th IEEE/ACM International Conference on Automated Software Engineering (ASE), pp. 1604–1614. IEEE (2023)
10. Medjaoui, M., Wilde, E., Mitra, R., Amundsen, M.: Continuous API Management. O'Reilly, Sebastopol (2021)
11. OASDiff. https://github.com/Tufin/oasdiff

12. Ochoa, L., Degueule, T., Falleri, J.R.: Breakbot: analyzing the impact of breaking changes to assist library evolution. In: Proceedings of 44th International Conference on Software Engineering (ICSE): New Ideas and Emerging Results, pp. 26–30 (2022)
13. Ochoa, L., Degueule, T., Falleri, J.R., Vinju, J.: Breaking bad? Semantic versioning and impact of breaking changes in maven central. Empir. Softw. Eng. **27**(3), 1–42 (2022)
14. OpenAPI Initiative. https://www.openapis.org/
15. Peralta, J.H.: Microservice APIs: Using Python, Flask, FastAPI, OpenAPI and More. Simon and Schuster, New York (2023)
16. Pinckney, D., Cassano, F., Guha, A., Bell, J.: A large scale analysis of semantic versioning in NPM. In: IEEE International Working Conference on Mining Software Repositories (2023)
17. Raemaekers, S., van Deursen, A., Visser, J.: Semantic versioning and impact of breaking changes in the maven repository. J. Syst. Softw. **129**, 140–158 (2017)
18. Serbout, S., Muñoz Hurtado, D.C., Pautasso, C.: Interactively exploring API changes and versioning consistency. In: Proceedings of 11th IEEE Working Conference on Software Visualization (VISSOFT), pp. 28–39 (2023)
19. Serbout, S., Pautasso, C.: An empirical study of web API versioning practices. In: Garrigós, I., Murillo Rodríguez, J.M., Wimmer, M. (eds.) ICWE 2023. LNCS, vol. 13893, pp. 303–318. Springer, Cham (2023). https://doi.org/10.1007/978-3-031-34444-2_22
20. Serbout, S., Pautasso, C.: APIstic: a large collection of OpenAPI metrics. In: Proceedings of 21st IEEE/ACM International Conference on Mining Software Repositories (MSR), Lisbon, Portugal (2024)
21. Stocker, M., Zimmermann, O.: API refactoring to patterns: catalog, template and tools for remote interface evolution. In: Proceedings of 28th European Conference on Pattern Languages of Programs (EuroPLoP). ACM (2023)
22. Zhang, L., et al.: Has my release disobeyed semantic versioning? Static detection based on semantic differencing. In: Proceedings of the 37th IEEE/ACM International Conference on Automated Software Engineering, pp. 1–12 (2022)
23. Zimmermann, O., Stocker, M., Lubke, D., Zdun, U., Pautasso, C.: Patterns for API Design: Simplifying Integration with Loosely Coupled Message Exchanges. Addison-Wesley, Boston (2022)

GitHub-Sourced Web API Evolution: A Large-Scale OpenAPI Dataset

Fabio Di Lauro(✉)

Università della Svizzera Italiana (USI), Lugano, Switzerland
fabio.di.lauro@usi.ch

Abstract. This study presents a dataset curated using a software tool called the crawler, which gathers OpenAPI Specifications (OAS) from GitHub. The crawler efficiently collects versioned OAS files and metadata, reflecting API development evolution. It incorporates functionalities for updating, validating, parsing OAS files, ensuring dataset accuracy and relevance. With over three years of data, including 660,000 artifacts from 2.8 million commits, the dataset offers insights into OpenAPI standards adoption and its impact on API development. This paper discusses the dataset and crawler's application in research and API development, highlighting their role in understanding API practices.

1 Introduction

GitHub, a significant platform for code sharing and collaboration, offers an exceptional resource for mining valuable information, especially OpenAPI (formerly Swagger) artifacts, which are key in defining RESTful APIs [12]. We developed a `crawler` to systematically extract and compile these artifacts into a dataset, initiated in December 2020 and ongoing. This paper aims to share the dataset and the `crawler`'s source code with the scientific community, enhancing understanding of OpenAPI Specifications (OAS) in real-world applications. Our study presents a unique dataset, including OpenAPI specifications from GitHub commits with relevant metadata, facilitating advanced data querying and analysis. This dataset has supported research on Web APIs evolution [5–7], composability and data models [14], and versioning [13], underlining its significance. We aim to contribute to software engineering by offering insights into OpenAPI's impact on software development. The paper is organized as follows: Sect. 2 overviews GitHub and OpenAPI, Sect. 3 reviews related literature, Sect. 4 describes the software architecture, Sect. 5 details the dataset, Sect. 6 discusses findings, Sect. 7 addresses challenges and limitations, and Sect. 8 concludes with future research directions.

2 Background

GitHub's role as a primary hub for software development has catalyzed research into software engineering practices. It offers invaluable data for analyzing

K. Stefanidis et al. (Eds.): ICWE 2024, LNCS 14629, pp. 360–368, 2024.
https://doi.org/10.1007/978-3-031-62362-2_26

development practices, collaboration patterns, and technological trends. Mining GitHub repositories for artifacts like OpenAPI specifications represents a burgeoning field. OpenAPI, backed by the OpenAPI Initiative (OAI), sets a standard for interacting with RESTful APIs that is both human and machine readable, eliminating the need for source code access or network traffic analysis to understand a service's capabilities. While existing research covers code quality, bug detection, and social coding dynamics on GitHub, the focused study on OpenAPI artifact extraction and analysis remains underexplored. This research niche presents a unique opportunity to delve into API development practices and trends. Our work aims to fill this gap by analyzing OpenAPI artifacts in GitHub repositories to offer insights into API specification adoption patterns, design practice variations across domains, and API development evolution [6], enhancing the understanding of current API development landscapes.

3 Related Work

Dabic et al. developed GitHub Search (GHS) [4,10], targeting 25 GitHub attributes across 700,000 repositories, with components for API invocation, web crawling, and mining. Unlike GHS's broader scope, our focus is on OpenAPI Specifications and includes commit data for evolutionary studies. GHTorent [11] collects a comprehensive dataset via GitHub's REST API for diverse research, offering over 900GB of raw data and expanded data collection methods. However, GHTorent's updates ceased in 2020. APIs.guru [3], described as a "Wikipedia for Web APIs," compiles a directory of Web APIs in OpenAPI Specification format. This open-source project encourages community contributions and offers data through an HTTP API, focusing on public APIs. It updates weekly, excludes private APIs, and standardizes formats to OpenAPI 3.0, enhancing data reliability. Our platform extends APIs.guru by incorporating versioning and extracting partial data from OpenAPI files, improving data analysis and enabling tracking of API evolution.

4 System Architecture and Implementation

The `crawler` software, developed in `Python 3`, automates the mining and updating of artifacts, storing them locally and their metadata in a MySQL database. It employs multiprocessing for efficiency, particularly for GitHub interactions (`Path Finder` and `Curiosity`) limited by GitHub token availability, and optimally utilizes CPU cores for other tasks (`Validator`, `Parser`, and `Popularity`) not bound by API rate limits.

4.1 Overview of the Extraction Process

This study uses a mixed-methods approach to systematically identify, extract, and analyze OpenAPI artifacts from GitHub repositories, ensuring comprehensive coverage and focusing on those containing OpenAPI specifications. The

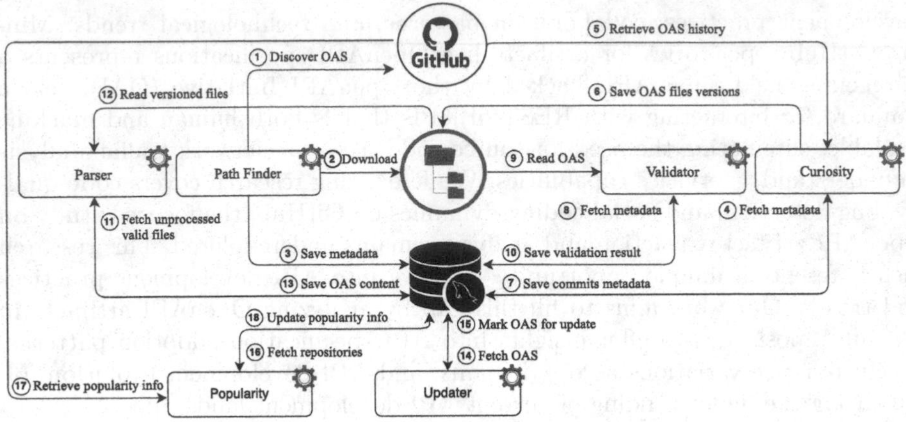

Fig. 1. Macro Components of the Crawler Architecture

architecture overview is shown in Fig. 1, and the extraction process is depicted in BPMN format in Fig. 2. Data collection for OpenAPI artifacts from GitHub involves several steps and components. `Path Finder` queries GitHub using REST API [9] for repositories with OAS files using terms like 'openapi' and 'swagger' ① and it saves this information ②-③. `Curiosity` then fetches metadata ④ and updates histories for these OAS files ⑤, storing versioned files ⑥ and metadata ⑦ locally and in a database. `Validator` checks the compliance of these files with OpenAPI specifications ⑧-⑩, with `Parser` extracting specification details into the database ⑪-⑬. `Updater` reviews ⑭ and flags projects for updates ⑮ if their last processing exceeds 15 days. A manual review of a subset and cross-validation with literature ensure the extraction and analysis accuracy, aiming to reveal API development practices and trends.

4.2 Path Finder

The `Path Finder` component searches GitHub via its API [9] to find repositories ① containing at least one OAS file. These files and their metadata are then downloaded and stored on the server ② and in a MySQL database ③, respectively. Given the widespread adoption of the OpenAPI language, this component discovers a significant number of APIs. To overcome GitHub's API rate limits, a rotation of GitHub tokens and a multi-query mechanism are employed for efficient information retrieval and search across various file formats. Discovered OAS files undergo checks to avoid reprocessing and ensure they're not from excluded projects before being added to a `urls_to_check` database table for further processing. This table centralizes the management of OAS files awaiting validation, parsing, or updates.

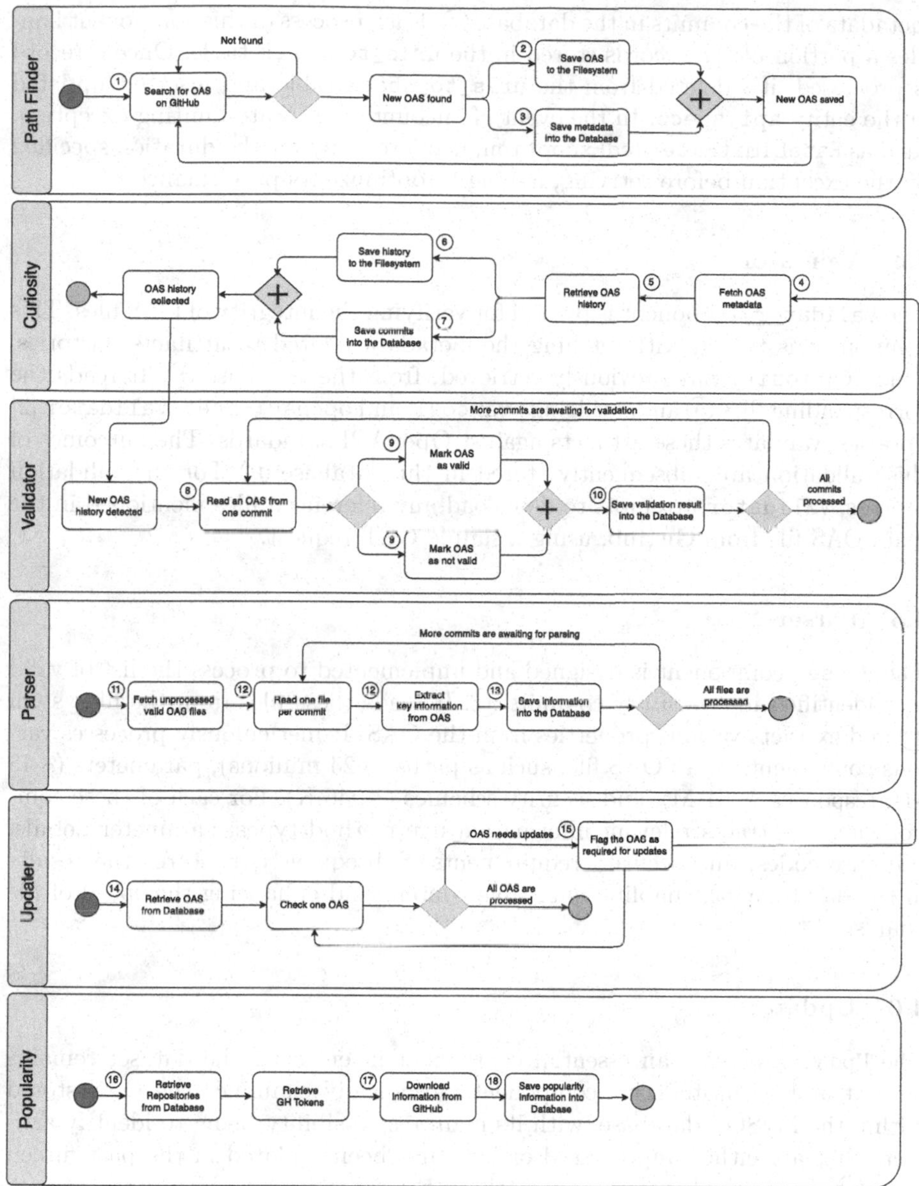

Fig. 2. BPMN Diagram of the Crawler Extraction Process

4.3 Curiosity

`Curiosity` retrieves the metadata identified by `Path Finder` from the database ④, extracts the commits representing the histories of the discovered artifacts ⑤, and subsequently stores these files in the filesystem ⑥ as well as the associated metadata of the commits in the database ⑦. Each process of this component handles a portion of the records stored in the `urls_to_check` table. Once a record is processed, it's deleted from the `urls_to_check` table and inserted/updated in the entity `api_specs`. In the event of encountering a rate-limiting exception, such as `RateLimitExceededException`, it pauses only for the duration specified by the exception before retrying, aiming to optimize its performance.

4.4 Validator

The `Validator` component is pivotal for verifying the integrity of OAS files. This component is tasked with fetching the metadata related to artifacts' histories, which `Curiosity` has previously retrieved, from the database ⑧. It reads the corresponding files ⑨ and, utilizing `prance` [1] and `openapi-spec-validator` [2] libraries, validates these artifacts against OpenAPI standards. The outcomes of this validation are subsequently stored in the database ⑩. For the validation process, `Validator` attempts to download any referenced files mentioned in the main OAS file from GitHub, using a simple GET request.

4.5 Parser

The `Parser` component is designed and implemented to process the list of valid files identified in repository commits ⑪. It reads these files from the filesystem ⑫ and extracts various properties from the OAS. It meticulously processes various components of an OAS file, such as paths (∼24 millions), parameters (∼45 M), responses (∼61 M), and security schemes (∼946 K). For each of these components, it extracts relevant information like method types, parameter details, response codes, and security requirements. Subsequently, it stores the results in the database ⑬, enabling queryable content and enhancing the speed of file analysis.

4.6 Updater

The `Updater` acts as an essential component in ensuring the dataset remains current and accurate. This component periodically examines the OAS stored within the MySQL database, with its main responsibility being to identify artifacts that are either unprocessed or have not been updated in the past fifteen days ⑭. It accomplishes this by fetching the most recent query used for each API from the `api_queries` table. The identified records are subsequently placed in the `crawler` pipeline ⑮ for further processing by the `Curiosity` component.

4.7 Popularity

This component is crucial for understanding the wider impact and usage of APIs in the developer community. The `Popularity` is tasked with gathering popularity metrics from GitHub. This process entails three steps: first, fetching the API repositories already discovered and processed from the database ⑯; second, retrieving data indicative of the repositories' popularity, such as forks, stars, and watchers ⑰; and third, updating a specific table in the database with this information ⑱.

5 Dataset

This section outlines the dataset collected by the `crawler`, focusing on its structure and the database schema. Data from GitHub is retrieved and stored as versioned OAS artifacts in the filesystem and metadata in the MySQL database. Overall, 664,947 artifacts resulting in 2,829,501 commits were crawled, with 386,606 valid OAS files and 1,241,062 commits identified for analysis. Extracted data include 24,095,382 paths, 45,798,272 parameters, 61,602,614 responses, and 946,917 security schemes. Discrepancies in data for 2023 were due to a performance bug, now fixed, with data recovery expected shortly. Figure 3 and Fig. 4 provide visual insights into artifacts, commits, and API evolution. A notable subset includes 21,180 active project APIs with extensive commit histories, offering insights into API development evolution. Future exploration with this subset will delve into API design evolution and trends [5,6], versioning patterns including semantic versioning [13], OAS adoption during a project's lifecycle, the implications of breaking versus non-breaking changes, the quality and timeliness of API documentation updates [7], the effects of API changes on consumers, how APIs integrate within microservices architectures, and the progression of security practices in API development.

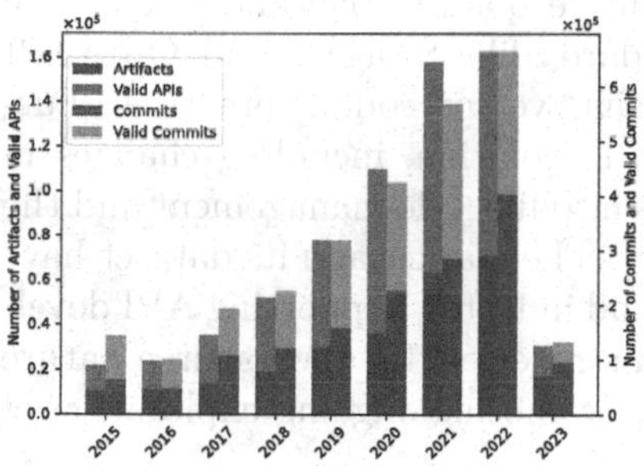

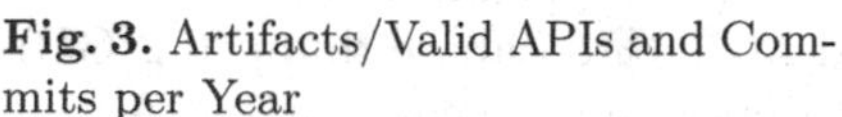

Fig. 3. Artifacts/Valid APIs and Commits per Year

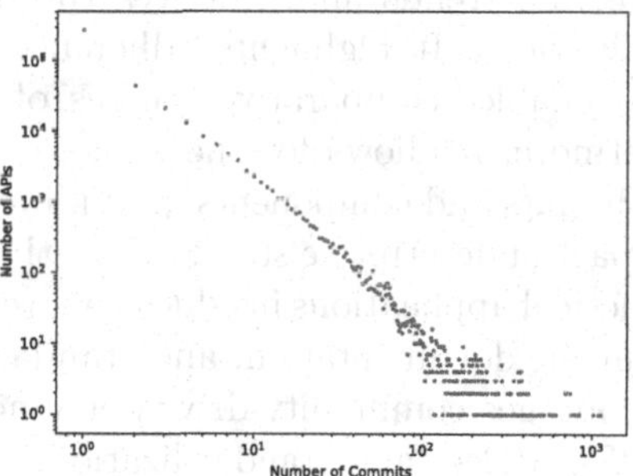

Fig. 4. APIs and their Histories

Filesystem. Each artifact is gathered into the filesystem employing a predefined folder structure that incorporates the use of the owner's name and the name of the repository to which the artifacts belong. Additionally, there is a 'commits' folder (see docs folder in `crawler` GitHub repository [8]) that houses all the versioned iterations of the discovered OAS artifacts. Each folder within the commits directory, referred to as a commit folder, represents a single version and is labeled with the SHA-1 code (or commit hash) assigned by GitHub to the corresponding commit. Inside each commit folder, the OAS file (for example, openapi.json) is stored following its specific folder structure (such as docs/openapi.json). It is important to highlight that the `crawler` does not clone the entire repository for every OAS file it finds. Instead, it merely downloads the specific file discovered, which may have been committed at various times. It's essential to highlight that, given the large volume of files in the archive, using a BTRFS filesystem is necessary to prevent a shortage of inodes.

Database. In the filesystem, the content of each versioned OAS file is preserved, whereas the database stores all related metadata along with a subset of the information extracted from the file. The Entity-Relationship (ER) schema illustrating this arrangement is available in the `crawler` GitHub repository (docs folder) [8] and at the following URL: https://oas-search.inf.usi.ch/img/crawler_ER.pdf. The most connected entities, and the central part of the database, are `api_specs` and `commits` which respectively represent the detected OAS files and their corresponding commits. Another key component of the database is `urls_to_check`, utilized for discovering and updating the OAS artifacts.

6 Discussion

This study introduces a software, the `crawler`, which extracts OAS files from GitHub for a comprehensive dataset. This dataset, beyond being a simple collection, offers a rich basis for both broad and detailed analyses of API development, revealing trends and practices through extensive quantitative and qualitative evaluations. It highlights adherence to standards like Swagger and OpenAPI and enables comparative studies of API design versus coding practices. Furthermore, it allows for the exploration of API evolution, including changes in endpoints and components, providing insights into lifecycle management and the impact of descriptive standards in the industry. The crawler and its dataset have practical applications in education, research, and industry, supporting API development, documentation, and standardization strategies. Its open-source nature encourages community-driven enhancements, promoting ongoing exploration of API practices and standardization.

The software (21 KB) is available on GitHub [8], while a compressed archive of gathered files (62 GB), and a compressed MySQL database dump (12 GB) can be accessed at the following URL: http://web-lab.inf.usi.ch/crawler/. A web interface for querying the dataset is available at the following URL: https://oas-search.inf.usi.ch/.

7 Challenges and Limitations

The `crawler` relies on updated data to track API evolution, constrained by GitHub's API rate limits, thus affecting its throughput. It targets OpenAPI files to focus on API documentation, avoiding full repository downloads. To improve efficiency, it uses multiple, albeit limited, GitHub tokens and can scale up if more tokens become available. Recent updates have addressed issues impacting 2023 data, as shown in Fig. 3. However, it faces limitations, including GitHub API's focus on the default (usually master) branch and a size limit for searchable files up to 384 KB.

8 Conclusion and Future Work

This research concludes with a detailed dataset and the `crawler` software, now open source, facilitating further API development studies. Future enhancements could improve the crawler's efficiency and dataset utility, such as scaling across machines, optimizing GitHub token usage, broadening data collection to include commit messages, and exploring beyond GitHub. Possible expansions like downloading entire repositories and additional repository information could offer deeper API ecosystem insights. These advancements promise to bolster API research, making our tools and dataset vital for ongoing exploration and innovation.

Acknowledgements. We express deep gratitude to Prof. Jordi Cabot and Prof. Antonio Carzaniga for their guidance in drafting and refining this paper, and to Prof. Cesare Pautasso for his contributions to developing the crawler.

References

1. Prance v.0.21.8.0 (2021). https://pypi.org/project/prance/
2. openapi-spec-validator (2024). https://github.com/python-openapi/openapi-spec-validator
3. APIS.guru (2024). https://apis.guru/
4. Dabic, O., Aghajani, E., Bavota, G.: Sampling projects in github for MSR studies. In: 2021 IEEE/ACM 18th International Conference on Mining Software Repositories (MSR), pp. 560–564 (2021)
5. Di Lauro, F., Serbout, S., Pautasso, C.: Towards large-scale empirical assessment of web APIs evolution. In: Brambilla, M., Chbeir, R., Frasincar, F., Manolescu, I. (eds.) ICWE 2021. LNCS, vol. 12706, pp. 124–138. Springer, Cham (2021). https://doi.org/10.1007/978-3-030-74296-6_10
6. Di Lauro, F., Serbout, S., Pautasso, C.: A large-scale empirical assessment of web API size evolution. J. Web Eng. **21**(6), 1937–1979 (2022)
7. Di Lauro, F., Serbout, S., Pautasso, C.: To deprecate or to simply drop operations? An empirical study on the evolution of a large OpenAPI collection. In: Gerostathopoulos, I., Lewis, G., Batista, T., Bureš, T. (eds.) ECSA 2022. LNCS, vol. 13444, pp. 38–46. Springer, Cham (2022). https://doi.org/10.1007/978-3-031-16697-6_3
8. Di Lauro, F.: GitHub OpenAPI Crawler (2024). https://github.com/jindosanda/openapi-crawler
9. GitHub: GitHub REST API Documentation (2022). https://docs.github.com/en/rest?apiVersion=2022-11-28

10. GitHub Search (2021). https://seart-ghs.si.usi.ch
11. Gousios, G.: The ghtorent dataset and tool suite. In: 2013 10th Working Conference on Mining Software Repositories (MSR), pp. 233–236 (2013)
12. OpenAPI Initiative (2022). https://www.openapis.org/
13. Serbout, S., Pautasso, C.: An empirical study of web API versioning practices. In: Garrigós, I., Murillo Rodríguez, J.M., Wimmer, M. (eds.) ICWE 2023. LNCS, vol. 13893, pp. 303–318. Springer, Cham (2023). https://doi.org/10.1007/978-3-031-34444-2_22
14. Serbout, S., Pautasso, C., Zdun, U.: How composable is the web? An empirical study on OpenAPI data model compatibility. In: Proceedings of IEEE World Congress on Services (ICWS Symposium on Services for Machine Learning), Barcelona, Spain. IEEE (2022)

MatchCom: Stable Matching-Based Software Services Composition in Cloud Computing Environments

Satish Kumar[1(✉)], Renyu Yang[2], Rajiv Ranjan Singh[3], Rami Bahsoon[4], Jie Xu[5], and Rajkumar Buyya[6]

[1] School of Built Environment, Engineering and Computing, Leeds Beckett University, Leeds, UK
s.kumar@leedsbeckett.ac.uk

[2] School of Software, Beihang University, Beijing, China
renyu.yang@buaa.edu.cn

[3] Department of Cyber Security and Networks, Glasgow Caledonian University, Glasgow, UK
rajiv.singh@gcu.ac.uk

[4] School of Computer Science, University of Birmingham, Birmingham, UK
r.bahsoon@cs.bham.ac.uk

[5] School of Computing, University of Leeds, Leeds, UK
j.xu@leeds.ac.uk

[6] School of Computing and Information Systems, University of Melbourne, Melbourne, Australia
rbuyya@unimelb.edu.au

Abstract. User preferences on throughput, latency, cost, service location, etc. indicate specific requirements when choosing a web service from the cloud marketplace. Service providers can also adopt preferences to prioritize a set of end-users based on their Service Level Agreement and service usage history. An effective matching between preferences from both parties enables fair service marketing in the cloud marketplace. The existing approaches are insufficient in capturing both parties' preferences in the service composition process. To address this limitation, we propose MatchCom, a novel service composition approach driven by diverse preferences and formulate it as the stable marriage problem. Particularly, we present a novel fair preference ordering mechanism – in the context of a cloud marketplace, for enabling users to specify services provider ranking based on the capability they can provision, and for helping providers select the most suitable users to be served given users' profile. MatchCom extends the Gale-Shapely Algorithm with a service composer algorithm for optimising the stable service composition. We evaluate MatchCom on a service-oriented system with 10 abstract services, each of which has 100 candidate web services. We establish through the experimental results that MatchCom outperforms other baseline approaches and can maximize end-user satisfaction in the composition process.

Keywords: Service Composition · Quality of Services · Stable Matching

1 Introduction

The shift of industrial IT services to cloud-based service models has made service composition a key driving force for building on-demand service-oriented software appli-

K. Stefanidis et al. (Eds.): ICWE 2024, LNCS 14629, pp. 369–377, 2024.
https://doi.org/10.1007/978-3-031-62362-2_27

cations by composing multiple existing web services from the cloud marketplace [1]. However, the emergence of multiple functionally equivalent web services with different Quality of Service (QoS) values in the cloud marketplace can present challenges when selecting an optimal web service for composing software applications [2]. Further, it can be challenging when multiple users express different preferences and constraints to get the same service in the cloud marketplace. On the other hand, cloud service providers aim to maintain a positive service reputation while maximizing service revenue [2,3]. To achieve this, it is important to prioritize users who have long-term business potential based on their Service Level Agreements (SLAs), service usage or other factors. In this context, preferences could be an effective mechanism for creating fair marketing in the cloud marketplace. Users express their preferences on service QoS constraints, service location, service cost, and reputation; and service providers rank the users based on their SLAs and service matches. However, existing research studies [4–6] have the limitation of supporting only end-user preferences, neglecting service provider's preferences when provisioning suitable web services.

To address these challenges, we present a novel Stable Matching Based Service Composition called `MatchCom` that explicitly captures the end user's and service provider's preferences and optimizes the preference stability-aware service composition. We employ Stable Marriage Problem [7] to model our service composition approach. Our key idea is to capture the end-user's preferences from their SLAs. Further, we use these preferences to rank all similar functionally equivalent web services that exhibit different QoS values. Similarly, the service provider ranks end users based on their SLA types. Then, we apply GSA-based `MatchCom` to find the stable service matches to form the composition solutions.

In a nutshell, the major contributions of this paper are ① we formulate the service composition as a stable marriage problem. ② we model a preference generation scheme for both end users and service providers in the global cloud marketplace. This scheme facilitates finding stable service matches driven by the service provider's and end-user's preferences over each other. ③ we tailor a Gale-Shapley Algorithm (GSA) and present a `serviceComposer` algorithm that tends to maximize the end-user's satisfaction in the composition process. ④ we evaluate `MatchCom` on a service composition system with up to 10 abstract services workflow, each of which has 80 to 100 candidate web services, under different QoS values derived from the real-world WS-DREAM dataset [9].

2 Stable Matching Based Service Composition

The stable marriage problem, introduced by Gale and Shapley in 1962 [7], involves matching two sets of agents, such as men and women. A crucial aspect of this problem is the ordering of preferences, where each man and woman rank each other in a strict order of preference and then a Gale and Shapley algorithm exploits these preferences to generate stable matches. We leverage this approach in our research with a particular focus on the diverse preferences-based service compositions in the global cloud marketplace; where QoS constraints, service budget, service region, and SLA types are considered the most preferred parameters for both entities to establish a strict order of preference over each other.

2.1 Preference Order Modelling

Here, we assume that there are x number of users $U_i, i = (1, 2, 3, ...x)$ and each user requests y number of tasks in the composite software application $U_{ij}, j = (1, 2, 3, ...y)$ with z dimension service constraints (e.g., QoS, Cost, service region/location S^{loc}) $U_{ijk}, k = (1, 2, 3, ...z)$ for choosing a web service in the composition. On the other side, based on functional (e.g., task) and QoS requirements, the service providers offer m set of web services $S_p, p = (1, 2, 3, ...m)$ in the global cloud marketplace and each set contains n candidate web services that are functionally equivalent to perform j^{th} task of user U_{ij}, $S_{pq}, q = (1, 2, 3, ...n)$ and each candidate web service has l dimension QoS values $S_{pqr}, r = (1, 2, 3, ...l)$ and SLAs type provisioned by cloud service providers as part of service delivery. Therefore, a matching model is defined $M(U, S)$, where each user U_i needs to rank all candidate web services in a set S_{pq} for a jth task that satisfies the service location constraint $\mathbb{CL}$; otherwise, underlying candidate web service will be discarded from the ranking process using Eq. 1.

$$(S_{pq}) = \begin{cases} 1 \; if \; \mathbb{CL} = S^{loc}_{pq} \\ 0 \; if \text{ otherwise} \end{cases} \tag{1}$$

Similarly, the service provider ranks all users U_i based on their SLAs type and service QoS values S_{pqr} legally provisioned in the SLA [2]. Therefore, the preference of jth task of a user U_i over the qth candidate web service S_{pq} is computed by aggregating the preference of each QoS constraint over QoS value exhibited by the candidate web service or vice-versa [4]. Further, we compute the best-case and worst-case values of each QoS objective (e.g., QoS constraint) imposed by a user or offered by the service providers as part of their service delivery. In the case of positive QoS (e.g., throughput) constraints criteria $\mathbb{CQ}^+$, the best case indicates the expected r^{th} QoS value of a web service must be larger than or equal to the required constraint value of kth objective (constraint weight) of a user U_i, otherwise expected objective value consider as the worst-case value for the kth constraint of a user U_i [6]. However, we calculate the exact values for the best-case and worst-case of each QoS objective required by the users over candidate web services. Further, the best-case and worst-case values are multiplied by $+1$ and -1, respectively, which shows how much the expected value is good or bad for each required objective of the user, as shown in Eq. 2.

$$\mathbb{CQ}^+(S_{pq}) = \begin{cases} \frac{U_{ijk}}{S_{pqr}} \times (-1) \; if S_{pqr} < U_{ijk} \\ \frac{S_{pqr}}{U_{ijk}} \times (+1) \; if S_{pqr} \geq U_{ijk} \end{cases} \tag{2}$$

$$\mathbb{CQ}^-(S_{pq}) = \begin{cases} \frac{S_{pqr}}{U_{ijk}} \times (-1) \; if S_{pqr} > U_{ijk} \\ \frac{U_{ijk}}{S_{pqr}} \times (+1) \; if S_{pqr} \leq U_{ijk} \end{cases} \tag{3}$$

where k indicates the zth constraint weight for the jth task of user U_i.

Similarly, for the negative QoS (e.g., response time) constraints criteria $\mathbb{CQ}^-$, best-case shows the expected objective value should be smaller than the required objective value of a user U_i, other than shows the worst-case value. These values are calculated using Eq. 3.

We generate i^{th} user preference $\mathbb{P}(U_{ij})$ for the jth task over candidate web services by computing the net ranking value using Eq. 4.

$$\mathbb{P}(U_{ijk}) = \Sigma_{r=1}^{l} \mathbb{CQ}^{+}(S_{pqr}) + \Sigma_{r=1}^{l} \mathbb{CQ}^{-}(S_{pqr}) \tag{4}$$

$$\mathbb{P}_{sla}(U_i) = \begin{cases} w_s \; if \; U_i = (sla = Silver) \\ w_g \; if \; U_i = (sla = Gold) \\ w_p \; if \; U_i = (sla = Platinum) \end{cases} \tag{5}$$

Algorithm 1: matchGenerator(U, PU, PS)

Input: The set of users U and service provider's web services S. Users preferences PU ($\forall u_{ij} \in PU$) and candidate web services PS ($\forall s_{pq} \in PS$)
Output: array matrix C
Initialization: $\forall u_{ij} \in PU$ and $\forall s_{pq} \in PS$ to be free, $M \leftarrow \emptyset$
for $\forall u_{ij} \in U$ **do**
    while $s_{pq} \in PS$ *is free and* $PS \neq \emptyset$ **do**
        u_{ij} = j^{th} task of user u_i highest ranked on q^{th} web service of set s_p to whom q^{th} has not proposed yet
        if u_{ij} *is free* **then**
            assign q^{th} web service to j^{th} task of u_i
            $M \leftarrow M \cup (u_{ij}, s_{pq})$
        end
        else if (u_{ij} *prefers* q^{th} *web service over previous assigned* n^{th} *web service of set* s_p) **then**
            assign q^{th} web service to j^{th} task of u_i
            $M \leftarrow$ M (u_{ij}, s_{pq})
            assigned n^{th} web service to be free $M \leftarrow$ M / (u_{ij}, s_{pn})
        end
        else
            j^{th} task of u_{ij} rejects q^{th} web service of set s_{pq} (and q^{th} remain free)
        end
    end
    $C \leftarrow M$
end
serviceComposer(C,U)

$$\mathbb{P}(S_{pqr}) = [\Sigma_{k=1}^{z}\mathbb{CQ}^{+}(U_{ijk}) + \Sigma_{k=1}^{z}\mathbb{CQ}^{-}(U_{ijk})] \times \mathbb{P}_{sla}(U_i) \quad (6)$$

On the other hand, we consider diverse types of SLAs offered by cloud service providers as part of web service delivery in the cloud marketplace. Suppose end-users negotiated different types of SLAs such as silver, gold and platinum with the cloud service providers [11]. In this respect, the cloud service provider gives the highest priority to a user who has platinum SLA rather than gold and silver users SLA, as shown in Eq. 5. For the sake of simplicity, in this work, we give some weight to distinguish each SLA says silver ($w_s = 0.1$), gold ($w_g = 0.3$) and platinum ($w_p = 0.5$). The cloud service provider gives preference over the users U_i based on their SLA types and service QoS provision documented in their SLA. We compute the net ranking over each user service demand using Eq. 6.

2.2 Software Services Composition

After generating the preference matrices PU and PS using Eq. (4) and (6) respectively, Algorithm 1 shows the process of applying the Gale-Shapley Algorithm (GSA) to find the optimal stable match $M(j,q)$ between the jth task of user u_i and q^{th} web service of set s_p. The preference matrices of all users PU and service provider's web services PS are provided as input to the algorithm and initialize all parameters that will be used in the next phase (Lines 5–17). From Lines 5–9, the user u_i selects the most preferred q^{th} web service from the candidate web services set s_p and form the matching $M(u_{ij}, s_{pq})$ if it is not matched with other tasks of user u_i in the PU list. From Lines 10–13, if a jth task of user u_i has already had the match of nth candidate web service in the PS list but j^{th} task prefers to q^{th} web service in the PS list over the current n^{th} web service

Algorithm 2: serviceComposer(C, U)

```
Input: C and U
Output: service composition matrix u_i(cs)
Initialization: u_i(cs) ← ∅, u_d ← ∅
while U ≠ ∅ do
    for ∀u_i ∈ U do
        ℂ_global ← checkQoS(u_i, C_i)
        if (ℂ_global satisfy user u_i constraints) then
            u_i(cs) ← C_i
        else
            u_d ← C_i
        end
    end
    U ← u_d
    matchGenerator(U)
end
return u_i(cs)
```

match. Then, a new optimal match $M(u_{ij}, s_{pq})$ is formed and further, makes the nth web service free in the PS list of candidate web services. However, the jth task of user u_i rejects the qth web service request in the matching process if it already had the higher preference ranking web service match than the preference ranking of qth web service (Lines 14–16). From Lines 5–17, this process is repeated until the first task of all users u_i in PU list assigned the optimal web service from the PS list. After completing the first iteration, the qth web service assigned to the first j^{th} task of all users U are stored in the array matrix C (line 19), and this step is repeated until all users' tasks assigned the set of optimal web services (Lines 4–19).

However, Algorithm 1 produced the sets of concrete web services to form the composition solutions for all the users requesting services in the cloud marketplace. Further, C is provided as input to Algorithm 2 for performing a next-level composition process that guarantees to satisfy all constraints imposed by end-users. In line 6, we calculate the aggregated QoS values and cost of all web services in C_i for the user u_i using QoS aggregation methods [11] and then check whether the global constraints are satisfied or not imposed by i^{th} user u_i (line 7). If true, then form the composite service for the user u_i (line 8), otherwise, user u_i rejects the composition plan and demands a new service composition plan, such user IDs are recorded in array u_d. This process is repeated until all web service sets in C are checked (4–11). In line 13, the current users set U is updated with users set u_d who demand the new service composition plans over the current infeasible plan. Further, Algorithm 1 is invoked with updated user set U to find the optimal set of web services for the users u_d. The whole process is repeated until users set U to get empty and then return the optimal service compositions plans $u_i(cs)$ for all the users u_i.

3 Performance Evaluation

Our experiments aim to answer the research questions – **RQ1:** Is `MatchCom` approach more stable than the baseline approach?; **RQ2:** How `MatchCom` can outperform other baselines including evolutionary algorithm-based approaches?; **RQ3:** What is the running overhead of `MatchCom` compared to other approaches?

3.1 Experiment Setup

For experiment purposes, we employed a service composition system with 10 abstract services, which are sequentially connected to construct a service composition workflow [8]. Further, we deployed 100 candidate web services to perform each abstract service in the composition workflow. However, each candidate web service exhibits different QoS values, which are randomly picked from the real-world WSDream dataset [9]. Further, the service cost value and service region are generated randomly for each candidate web service participating in the composition. Apart from that, we randomly create end-user service requirements (number of tasks in the service, throughput, response time, service cost, and service region), which are generally documented in the end user's SLA.

3.2 Results and Discussion

To answer the above RQs, we examine the performance of MatchCom against Baseline (GSA) [10] and MOEAD [11] based approaches.

RQ1: SLAs Stability of MatchCom Against Baseline: To answer RQ1, we plot the service composition plans optimized by MatchCom and GSA approaches as shown in Fig. 1. In particular, we examine the end-users SLA constraints such as throughput, response time and cost on whether the composed service compositions are satisfied or not. As can be seen from Fig. 1a and 1b, SLA throughput and response time constraints are violated by the composition solutions generated by GSA approach for the end-users u_4, and u_6, whereas, MatchCom satisfies all users SLA constraints. Further, an interesting insight is shown from a cost perspective as shown in Fig. 1c, GSA satisfies the QoS constraints for the end-user u_{10} but fails to meet the service budget requirement. However, MatchCom does not guarantee the higher values of QoS constraints satisfaction but satisfies all constraints under given budget requirements.

RQ2: Performance of MatchCom: To investigate RQ2, we assess the performance of MatchCom by comparing with baseline and evolutionary algorithm (MOEAD) based approaches. We run all approaches 30 times and record the best QoS value of throughput, response time and cost objectives from the optimal set of service composition solutions generated in each run. As shown in the boxplots of Fig. 2a and Fig. 2b, we see that MatchCom achieve much better QoS values for throughput and response time objectives with small variance than GSA and MOEAD approaches. Also, GSA obtains better QoS

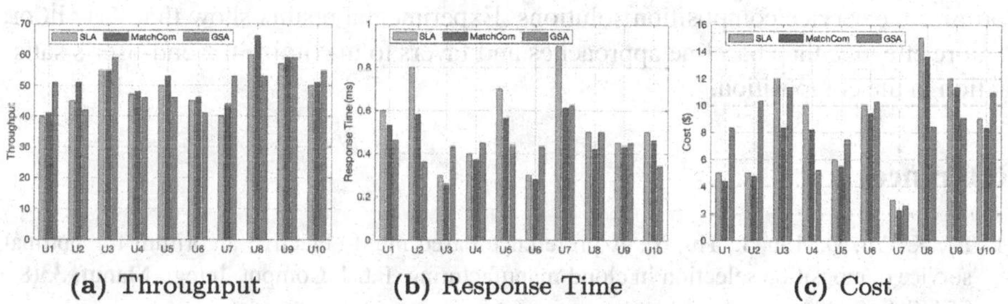

(a) Throughput (b) Response Time (c) Cost

Fig. 1. Users SLA constraints achieved by MatchCom and GSA approaches (users = 10, workflow: number of tasks = 10, number of candidate web service for each task = 100).

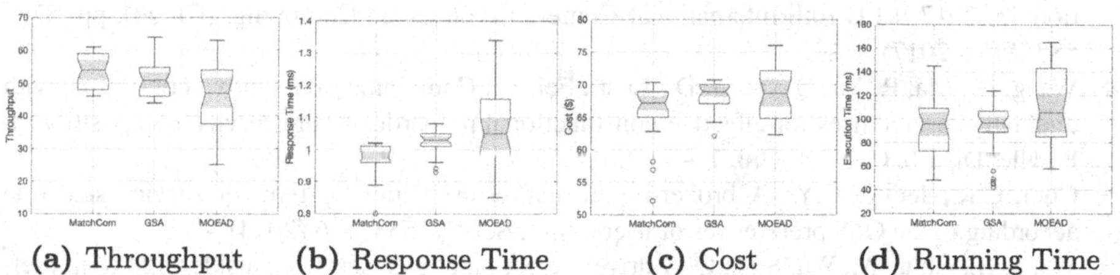

(a) Throughput (b) Response Time (c) Cost (d) Running Time

Fig. 2. Throughput, Response Time, Cost and Running Time yield by MatchCom, GSA and MOEAD approaches.

objectives values than MOEAD. Further, as we can see from Fig. 2c, overall MatchCom achieves better QoS values with less cost than GSA and MOEAD. Overall, MatchCom outperforms other approaches in achieving a better QoS value for each objective in the composition.

RQ3: Running Time of MatchCom: To understand RQ3, we plot the running time of all approaches as shown in Fig. 2d. As we can see MOEAD is the slowest due to exploiting a huge search space of X^N (X denotes an abstract service, and $N = 100$ is the number of candidate services to perform X abstract service). However, GSA and MatchCom take less execution time than MOEAD because they reduce the search space by discarding all candidate web services they are unable to satisfy the service region constraints mentioned in the end-user's preferences (constraints). But, MatchCom is slower than GSA because it favors maximising the end-user satisfaction in the composition process whereas GSA does not care to satisfy all user's constraints, as we have shown in answering RQ1 and RQ2.

4 Conclusions

In this paper, we proposed a stable matching-based service composition approach called MatchCom leveraging stable marriage problem. We introduced a novel bilateral preference model that gives equal ownership to service providers and end users for fairly serving and consuming services in cloud marketplace. MatchCom service composer can generate fair preference ordering for both service providers and end users. The GSA produces stable service matches which the built-in service composer further uses to optimize the service composition solutions. Experimental results show that MatchCom is more effective than baseline approaches and favors to maximize the end-user's satisfaction in the composition.

References

1. Bi, X., Yu, D., Liu, J., Hu, Y.: A preference-based multi-objective algorithm for optimal service composition selection in cloud manufacturing. Int. J. Comput. Integr. Manuf. **33**(8), 751–768 (2020)
2. Kumar, S., Chen, T., Bahsoon, R., Buyya, R.: DebtCom: technical debt-aware service recomposition in SaaS cloud. IEEE Trans. Serv. Comput. **16**(4), 2545–2558 (2023)
3. Pudasaini, D., Ding, C.: Service selection in a cloud marketplace: a multi-perspective solution. In: 2017 IEEE 10th International Conference on Cloud Computing (Cloud), pp. 576–583 IEEE (2017)
4. Wang, H., Ma, P., Yu, Q., Yang, D., Li, J., Fei, H.: Combining quantitative constraints with qualitative preferences for effective non-functional properties-aware service composition. J. Parallel Distrib. Comput. **100**, 71–84 (2017)
5. Choi, C.R., Jeong, H.Y.: A broker-based quality evaluation system for service selection according to the QoS preferences of users. Info. Sci. **77**, 553–566 (2014)
6. Wang, H., Chiu, W., Wu, S.C.: QoS-driven selection of web service considering group preference. Comput. Netw. **99**(1), 111–124 (2015)
7. Gale, D., Shapley, L.S.: College admissions and the stability of marriage. Am. Math. Monthly. **69**(1), 9–15 (1962)

8. Kumar, S., Chen, T., Bahsoon, R., Buyya, R.: DATESSO: self-adapting service composition with debt-aware two levels constraint reasoning. In: 2020 IEEE/ACM 15th International Symposium on Software Engineering for Adaptive and Self-managing Systems, pp. 96–107. IEEE/ACM (2020)
9. Zheng, Z., Zhang, Y., Lyu, M.R.: Investigating QoS of real-world web services. IEEE Trans. Serv. Comput. **7**(1), 32–39 (2012)
10. Li, F., Zhang, L., Liu, Y., Laili, Y.: QoS-aware service composition in cloud manufacturing: a Gale-Shapley algorithm-based approach. IEEE Trans. Syst. Man Cyber. Syst. **50**(7), 2386–2396 (2020)
11. Kumar, S., Chen, T., Bahsoon, R., Buyya, R.: Multi-tenant cloud service composition using evolutionary optimization. In: 2018 IEEE 24th International Conference on Parallel and Distributed Systems (ICPADS), pp. 972–979. IEEE (2020)

Demos and Posters

Demonstrating Liquid Software in IoT Using WebAssembly

Pyry Kotilainen[1(✉)], Viljami Järvinen[1], Teemu Autto[1], Lakshan Rathnayaka[2], and Tommi Mikkonen[1]

[1] Faculty of Information Technology, University of Jyväskylä, Jyväskylä, Finland
{pyry.kotilainen,viljami.a.e.jarvinen,teemu.a.autto, tommi.j.mikkonen}@jyu.fi

[2] Faculty of Computing, Tampere University, Tampere, Finland
lakshan.rathnayaka@tuni.fi

Abstract. In this paper we introduce a demonstration of our prototype orchestration system utilising WebAssembly to achieve isomorphism for a liquid software IoT system. The demonstration hardware consists of two Raspberry Pi IoT devices and a computer acting as the orchestrator. The audience can interact with the orchestrator through a web interface to deploy different software configurations to the devices, and observe the deployment process as well as the deployed application in action.

Keywords: Programmable world · Internet of Things · IoT · Web of Things · WoT · Liquid software

1 Introduction

Liquid Software refers to a programming paradigm where applications can "flow" from one computer to the next [2,7]. Such applications not only can take full advantage of the computing, storage, and communication resources available on all devices owned by the end user but also can seamlessly and dynamically migrate from one device to another continuously following the user's attention and usage context.

In this demo, we aim to demonstrate our orchestration system for IoT devices with an example system of a couple of devices and the orchestrator. The project is available in two GitHub repositories, one for the orchestrator [5] and one for the supervisor [6].

The paper describing the demo is structured as follows. We first discuss our orchestration system in Sect. 2. Then, we outline the demo application in Sect. 3. Finally, we discuss the demo experience in Sect. 4.

2 Demo System Overview

Originally discussed in [3,4], the demonstrated system is shown in Fig. 1. The system consists of an orchestration server or *orchestrator* and a variable number

K. Stefanidis et al. (Eds.): ICWE 2024, LNCS 14629, pp. 381–384, 2024.
https://doi.org/10.1007/978-3-031-62362-2_28

of heterogeneous node devices in the same local area network. An actor (user or another system that interacts with our system) can control the system through the orchestrator.

Aside from communication and application logic, the orchestration server consists of three components:

- *Device database* contains the hardware configurations of the various devices, and it is populated by listening to mDNS messages and requesting information from the associated devices.
- *Deployment registry* contains all executed deployments by the orchestrator, with each deployment listing the devices involved and the services they provide in it.
- *Package manager* maintains a database of all available WebAssembly software modules that can be sent to the devices. It is also capable of resolving dependencies to provide a complete list of required modules for a given module to run.

The system functionality can be split into three phases: device discovery, deployment and execution. Upon first discovery, the orchestrator requests configuration information from the device and adds it to the device database the server maintains. Upon a request for deployment, the orchestration server generates a setup that is a feasible deployment solution and sends out the deployment configuration to involved devices. The devices pull the required microservices and start serving them according to the deployment information.

Device discovery is performed with mDNS which each device uses to advertise their availability to the orchestrator. Each device provides a ReSTful endpoint where capabilities of a discovered device can be queried. ReSTful endpoints are also used for machine-to-machine (M2M) communication between the IoT devices. Finally, all functionality running on the different IoT devices – in particular executing WebAssembly binaries – is controlled by the host process running on the device, which we call *supervisor*. The supervisor is implemented in Python, based on our earlier work, and the WebAssembly runtime for the moving program modules is Wasmtime [1].

3 Demo Application

The aim is to demonstrate the systems ability to perform liquid distributed deployments on IoT devices. The demonstration allows the audience to use the orchestration system to change the software deployment on an example IoT system. The demo system consists of two Raspberry Pi computers acting as IoT devices and an orchestration computer all connected to the same local area network.

The IoT devices can be arranged to do various tasks via the orchestrator, such as sound capture and processing, or image capture, processing and recognition. The orchestrator houses Wasm-software modules for each of these tasks and they

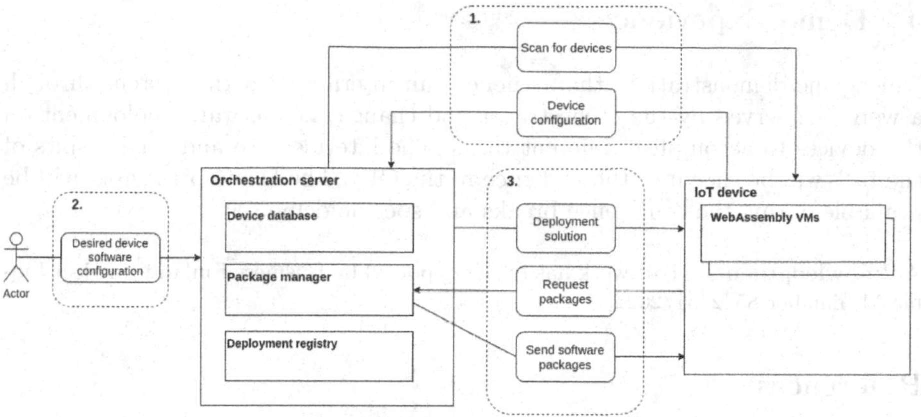

Fig. 1. Demo system.

can be deployed to different devices and piped together to - for example - have one device capture a picture and the other device run image recognition on it.

Orchestrator serves a web GUI through which participants can change deployment on devices and observe the current deployment, changes on it, as well as telemetry from the devices and results of the deployed distributed application. The GUI offers following functionality:

- Configuring a new deployment for the devices.
- Visually follow deployment progress and state.
- Triggering deployed functions if applicable.
- Visual feedback of results of each function.

Figure 2 depicts the orchestration web GUI. Displayed are output windows of both IoT devices, their log outputs, and dropdown menus for selecting applications to deploy. At the bottom are buttons to deploy and run the application. The figure presents the results of a deployment, where device 1 takes a picture and device 2 inverts its colors.

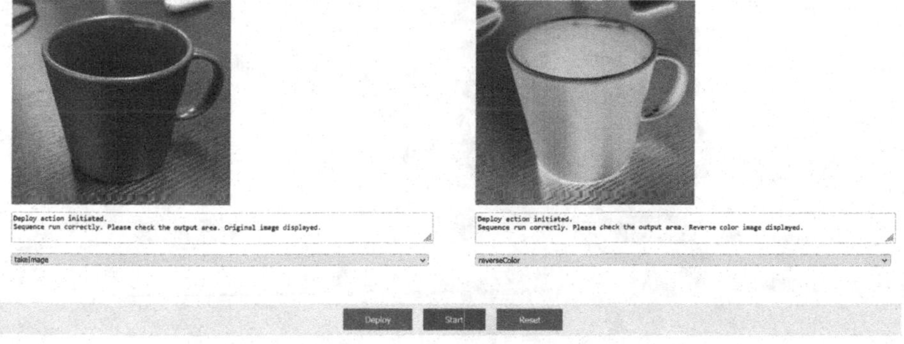

Fig. 2. Web GUI depicting results of a deployment execution.

4 Demo Experience

During the demonstration, the audience can interact with the system through a web GUI served by the orchestrator and change the software deployment on the devices to accomplish different tasks. The intermediate and final results of the task will be shown to the audience in the GUI. The Demo presenters will be available during the conference breaks and specific demo sessions.

Acknowledgments. This work has been supported by Business Finland (project LiquidAI, number 8542/31/2022).

References

1. Bytecode Alliance: Wasmtime. https://wasmtime.dev/. Accessed 13 Mar 2024
2. Hartman, J., Manber, U., Peterson, L., Proebsting, T.: Liquid software: a new paradigm for networked systems. Technical report, Technical Report 96 (1996)
3. Kotilainen, P., et al.: WebAssembly in IoT: beyond toy examples. In: Garrigos, I., Murillo Rodríguez, J.M., Wimmer, M. (eds.) ICWE 2023. LNCS, vol. 13893, pp. 93–100. Springer, Cham (2023). https://doi.org/10.1007/978-3-031-34444-2_7
4. Kotilainen, P., Autto, T., Järvinen, V., Das, T., Tarkkanen, J.: Proposing isomorphic microservices based architecture for heterogeneous IoT environments. In: Taibi, D., Kuhrmann, M., Mikkonen, T., Klünder, J., Abrahamsson, P. (eds.) PROFES 2022. LNCS, vol. 13709, pp. 621–627. Springer, Cham (2022). https://doi.org/10.1007/978-3-031-21388-5_47
5. LiquidAI project: wasmiot-orchestrator. https://github.com/LiquidAI-project/wasmiot-orchestrator. Accessed 28 Mar 2024
6. LiquidAI project: wasmiot-supervisor. https://github.com/LiquidAI-project/wasmiot-supervisor. Accessed 28 Mar 2024
7. Taivalsaari, A., Mikkonen, T., Systä, K.: Liquid software manifesto: the era of multiple device ownership and its implications for software architecture. In: 2014 IEEE 38th Annual Computer Software and Applications Conference, pp. 338–343. IEEE (2014)

KITSPOTLIGHT: A System for Spotlighting Researchers in the Media

Michael Färber(✉), Benjamin Zagoruiko, and Markus Wambach

Karlsruhe Institute of Technology (KIT), Karlsruhe, Germany
michael.faerber@kit.edu,
{benjamin.zagoruiko,markus.wambach}@student.kit.edu

Abstract. Academic institutions, such as universities, heavily rely on public relations and are thus interested in media monitoring. However, tracking mentions of their researchers in news articles presents challenges such as identifying affiliated personnel and their departments, and aggregating the extracted information. In this paper, we introduce KITSPOTLIGHT, a novel system that automatically identifies researchers of the Karlsruhe Institute of Technology (KIT) in newspaper articles, associates these individuals with their departments, and presents this information visually. KITSPOTLIGHT is tailored for both department heads, administrative staff, and individual researchers, focussing on the institution's overall public visibility or individual researcher's public appearance. Analyzing data from 2,280 articles over 12 months, our system offers a model for monitoring academic personnel at any research institution.

Keywords: Media Monitoring · Named Entity Recognition · Information Extraction · Text Mining

1 Motivation

Universities and other academic research institutions face significant challenges in public relations, particularly in tracking mentions of their researchers in news articles. This task has traditionally been complex, typically involving manual processes confined to specific departments within institutions. The manual effort to track relevant news articles demands extensive time and resources. In addition, it risks missing key mentions and delayed data compilation, undermining the completeness of the information. In the context of automated information extraction from journalistic texts, notable progress has been made in leveraging named entity recognition (NER) models to identify individuals [1]. However, a critical gap remains: the absence of a comprehensive system that not only accurately associates identified individuals of specific institutions but also effectively filters and aggregates relevant data and presents it visually.

Recognizing these challenges, we have developed a novel system KITSPOTLIGHT – available online at http://kit-spotlight.de[1] – for spotlighting researchers

[1] The code can be found at https://github.com/michaelfaerber/KITspotlight.

K. Stefanidis et al. (Eds.): ICWE 2024, LNCS 14629, pp. 385–388, 2024.
https://doi.org/10.1007/978-3-031-62362-2_29

of research institutions in the media. It automates the information extraction from newspaper articles, identifies individuals associated with specific organizations, associates these individuals with their departments (at KIT: institutes), and presents this information in a coherent visual format.

Our system is tailored to address two key user groups: (1) heads of institutions and administration focussing on public outreach, and (2) individual researchers. For the first user group, our system provides a detailed analysis of media presence, crucial for evaluating and refining communication strategies. This feature is essential for managing public perception and orchestrating public relations efforts effectively (see strategic controlling). Meanwhile, individual researchers benefit from a user-friendly tool that tracks their media appearances, offering them concise summaries to actively manage and enhance their external visibility, without the need to read manually news articles for their mentioning. Additionally, the system can be used for providing additional impact metrics for researchers beyond traditional metrics such as the citation count of publications.

2 System Design

KITSPOTLIGHT is composed of several components: (1) At its core is a database, created using sqlite3, which functions as the central repository for all data. (2) The Text Analyzing Pipeline processes incoming news articles, performs various analyses, and subsequently stores the resulting data in the database. (3) The frontend, outlined in Sect. 3, is developed with *React* (version 18) and interfaces with the database via a Django API.

Our Text Analyzing Pipeline includes the following data and stages:

Input Data: Our input data consists of PDF files that contain multiple articles in a newspaper-style layout. All articles have been pre-filtered to include mentions of the use case institution *Karlsruhe Institute of Technology (KIT)*. For our demo system, we analyzed 2,280 news articles.

Step 1: Extracting Text. The first step in our pipeline is the conversion of these PDF files into plain text format, using the Python Library `pdftotext`. For extracting metadata like titles, publishers, and dates, we employ rule-based detection techniques based on regular expressions.

Step 2: Extracting Persons. To identify all named entities in the articles, we use a named entity recognition (NER) implementation provided by `spaCy`. The system first determines the article's language using the `langdetect` Python Library. We use the `de_core_news_lg` model from `spaCy` for German articles and the `en_core_web_trf` model for English.

Step 3: Analyzing Individuals. We focus in our analysis on individuals employed by our institution. Thus, the next step is to filter out all other individuals mentioned in articles, for instance authors or interview partners. Furthermore, if an individual is affiliated with our institution, we aim to identify the specific institute they are associated with. We develop three distinct methods to determine whether an individual is employed by the institution of interest: (1) *Google Search:* This method uses a Google search with the individual's

Table 1. Evaluation results.

	Employee Detection			Institute Assignment
	Precision	Recall	F1-Score	Accuracy
Google-Search	0.8166	0.9650	0.8846	58%
SemOpenAlex	1.0000	0.8218	0.9022	0%
Staff-Directory	0.9942	0.9884	0.9913	78%

name in quotes and "kit" to filter for KIT-related webpages. The top search results are then analyzed. (2) *SemOpenAlex Search:* This approach queries SemOpenAlex [2], a large, up-to-date academic knowledge graph. It helps identify researchers but not their specific KIT-institute. (3) *Staff-Directory Search:* This approach accesses KIT's staff directory through POST requests, yielding relevant matches in a JSON array. Privacy settings control the visibility of personal details, with certain information like institute affiliation potentially concealed.

Evaluation. We performed an evaluation based on 174 names selected randomly from news articles, comprising 50 KIT employees and 124 non-KIT employees. The results are given in Table 1. The Staff-Directory method demonstrates the highest F1-score in identifying KIT employment, but privacy settings occasionally obscure institute details, underscoring the relevance of alternate approaches. Both the Google-Search and SemOpenAlex methods showed strong F1-scores. However, SemOpenAlex often lacks institute information. Despite frequently including researchers' ORCID identifiers, the institute data is not always available or differs from the Staff-Directory format. In conclusion, our system starts with a lookup within the Staff-Directory to verify if an individual is working at KIT. Should the result lack institute details, we proceed with an additional Google query to try sourcing the institute from the URL of the researchers' institutional-homepage.

With around 1,600 articles analyzed, we successfully identified 472 mentioned individuals working at KIT, which in total were mentioned 1,979 times. We also achieved to match 78% of the individuals to an institute.

3 User Interaction

Front Page. Figure 1 showcases the main page. A bar chart positioned in the top left tracks the frequency of mentions of KIT employees over time. Adjacent to this, on the right, another chart depicts the proportional occurrence of KIT institutes. In the bottom left, a table lists recent articles with their titles and the KIT employees mentioned therein. In the bottom right corner, a pie chart shows how often different media outlets mention the identified researchers.

Institute-Page. Information of media coverage for specific KIT institutes is given at the respective pages (see Fig. 2), showing, among other things, a time series analysis of the individuals belonging to the institute.

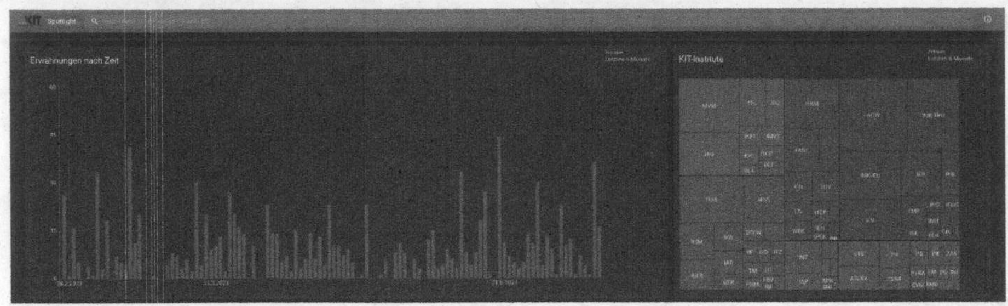

Fig. 1. Part of KIT Spotlight's welcome page with overall statistics

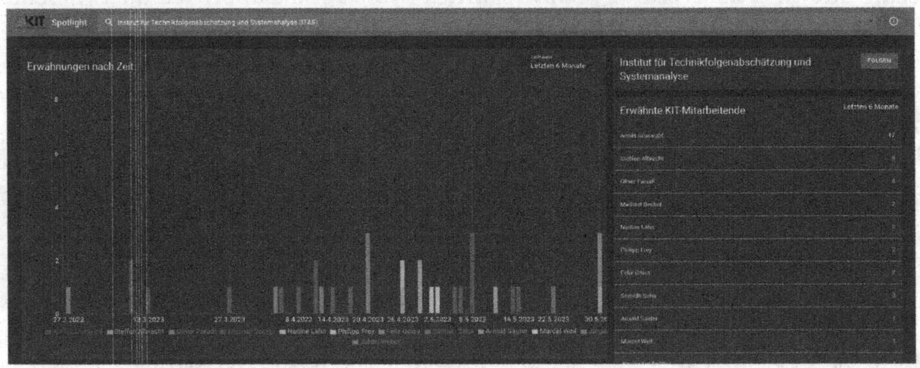

Fig. 2. Page of the KIT Institute for Technology Assessment and Systems Analysis

Person-Page. On the individual's profile page, we include a comprehensive listing of articles in which the person has been mentioned, showing the article titles, the publisher names, and the URLs.

Follow-Function. In addition to viewing and exploring the data on the website, the user has the option to subscribe to an institute or person and get notified via email when a news article mentions the followed entity.

4 Conclusion

In this paper, we developed a system that identifies researchers in news articles, simplifies press monitoring in academia, and serves as a blueprint for global academic media monitoring.

References

1. Buz, C.: Validierung eines NER-Verfahrens zur automatisierten Identifikation von Akteuren in journalistischen Texten (2021). https://doi.org/10.5445/IR/1000131532
2. Färber, M., Lamprecht, D., Krause, J., Aung, L., Haase, P.: SemOpenAlex: the scientific landscape in 26 billion RDF triples. In: Proceedings of ISWC 2023 (2023)

Towards Pricing4SaaS: A Framework for Pricing-Driven Feature Toggling in SaaS

Alejandro García-Fernández(✉), José Antonio Parejo, Pablo Trinidad, and Antonio Ruiz-Cortés

SCORE Lab, I3US Institute, Universidad de Sevilla, Seville, Spain
{agarcia29,japarejo,ptrinidad,aruiz}@us.es

Abstract. In a rapidly evolving digital marketplace, the ability to enable features and services dynamically on SaaS products in alignment with market conditions and pricing strategies is essential for sustaining competitiveness and improving the user experience. This demo paper presents Pricing4SaaS, a reference architecture designed to enhance the integration and management of pricing-driven feature toggles in SaaS systems. It centralizes the configuration of the pricing structure, spreading its changes across the whole application every time it is modified, while securing state synchronization between both the client and server. Additionally, a case study integrating a reference implementation of Pricing4SaaS inside a Spring+React PetClinic project demonstrates how such approach can be leveraged to optimize developer productivity, reducing technical debt, and improving operational efficiency.

Keywords: Web Engineering · Pricing · Software as a Service

1 Introduction

In the evolving world of Software as a Service (SaaS) innovation, the practice of feature toggling stands out as an effective technique for the introduction and management of new features [1], enabling developers to turn functionalities on or off during runtime without the need for deploying fresh code. This method offers a versatile way for conducting A/B tests, performing canary releases, and reducing system downtimes. Moreover, the integration of subscription-based licensing models with various pricing tiers provide SaaS vendors with a steady income flow, while delivering flexibility and scalability to end-users [4].

Within this framework, feature toggling plays a pivotal role in customizing the interface and capabilities of such systems to match the particular subscription of each user. However, its deployment and management can become complex and challenging when the variables and conditions that govern the toggles are influenced by frequent changes. This complexity escalates in environments where features are closely tied to the shifting market dynamics, consumer preferences, or pricing policies. Moreover, when feature toggles are further associated with user subscriptions, the secure transmission and utilization of subscription-related

K. Stefanidis et al. (Eds.): ICWE 2024, LNCS 14629, pp. 389–392, 2024.
https://doi.org/10.1007/978-3-031-62362-2_30

information, along with the control variables for the toggles, become imperative. The crux of the problem lies in the need for a robust system that can manage a multitude of feature toggles and adapt to changes in controlling variables with minimal latency and overhead in distributed environments.

Conventional approaches to feature toggling management, characterized by the manual creation of toggling conditions and hard-coded toggle configurations, often fall short in scenarios where toggles need to react to external influences. Furthermore, they can lead to considerable technical debt, decreased system performance, and a higher risk of errors [5], ultimately affecting the user experience and organizations' ability to respond to market demands swiftly and securely.

This paper introduces a solution that addresses some of the challenges proposed in [3]: Pricing4SaaS. Our approach leverages a centralized pricing configuration to connect every pricing-driven toggle point within the code base, allowing SaaS to rapidly adapt to changes in pricing strategies and market conditions autonomously. By providing a demonstration of Pricing4SaaS' capabilities, we aim to showcase how our solution not only mitigates the complexities associated with pricing-driven feature toggling conditions but also enhances operational efficiency and market responsiveness for teams creating SaaS.

2 Pricing4SaaS Architecture and Features

Pricing4SaaS is presented as a specification of a reference architecture that addresses some of the challenges outlined in [3]. In particular: i) it simplifies the implementation of pricing-driven changes; ii) supports stateful and dynamic pricing-driven feature toggling; and iii) ensures a secure transmission of the subscription status. In short, it elevates pricing plans to a first-class citizen within the architecture of the system, leveraging feature toggles technology to enable dynamic adjustments to the system's functionality without needing to modify the source code, as highlighted by [1].

Figure 1 represents the process of a request within the architecture a system that integrates Pricing4SaaS. The journey begins at the front-end, where users interact with the system's User Interface (UI). Each user's session is associated with a JWT that contains user subscription details, and optionally user permissions. When a client uses a feature F, the front-end can send a request to the back-end, carrying the JWT. In the back-end, a **Feature Checker** middle-ware component intercepts the request, and use the **Pricing Service** to evaluate the user's permissions against a **Yaml4SaaS** specification, a YAML-based syntax that models the rules and conditions of a pricing, providing the information needed to determine which features are available under certain circumstances [2]. If the user can access the feature F, and the token signature is valid, which means it has not suffered any alterations during the transmission over the network, the back-end processes the request and returns the required data back to the Feature Checker which, in the case that the list of allowed features has changed, generates a new JWT containing the authentication information (if provided) and such list. For example, if the usage limit of feature F has been reached after the operation, the user will not be able to use it again.

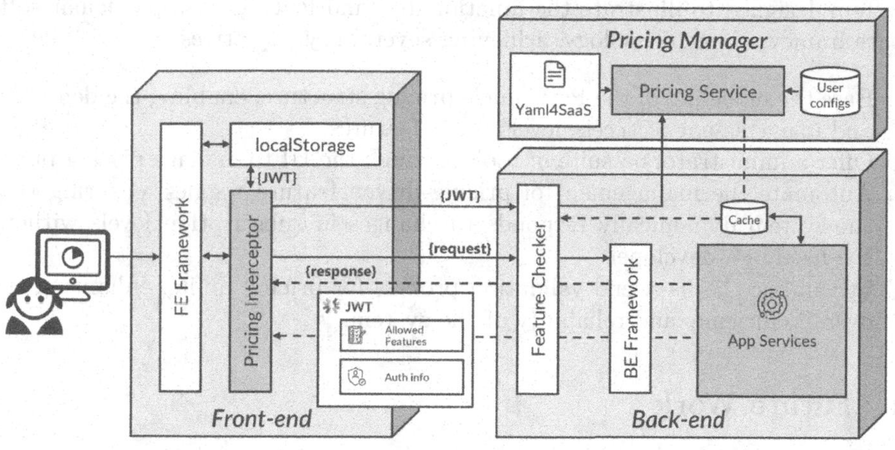

Fig. 1. Architectural design of Pricing4SaaS

Finally, the response is sent back to the front-end, where the new JWT, if present, is processed by the **Pricing Interceptor** and utilized to update the UI according to the new list of allowed features, ensuring a user experience tailored to his subscription. If F is no longer available, the button to invoke it disappears.

In this process, the **Feature Checker** is the cornerstone, since it offers two significant enhancements to streamline the system's responsiveness and security. Firstly, it has the capability to preemptively terminate the invocation of feature F's business logic on the back-end, or even to roll back transactions that involve said logic. This is particularly useful in preventing unnecessary processing if F is not available to the user, thereby optimizing system resources. Secondly, every time an updated JWT is generated and returned to the front-end through standard API response headers, the front-end is immediately aware of any changes, avoiding the need of making specific requests to update such variables, further enhancing system performance and saving resources. Although there is some extra work in transmitting and evaluating the list of allowed features, this is counterbalanced by the reduction of unnecessary requests handled by the server.

These advancements not only ensure that the system adheres to the principles of efficiency but also maintains the access controls imposed by the pricing.

3 Pricing4SaaS Reference Implementation

In order to assure the validity of Pricing4SaaS, we have created a reference implementation of its architecture, consisting of two libraries: Pricing4React for front-end and Pricing4Java for back-end.

These libraries[1] have successfully integrated a pricing into a Spring+React version of PetClinic[2], a sample veterinary clinic management

[1] The documentation of Pricing4SaaS suite can be found here.

[2] The video of the demo can be found at https://youtu.be/uMzywQHCN20.

system designed to illustrate the functionality and features of a particular software framework or technology, achieving several key objectives:

1. Ease the modeling of the PetClinic's pricing structure, enabling the definition and management of access levels to its features.
2. Offer administrators a suite of tools through the UI to manage pricing plans.
3. Automate the management of pricing-driven feature toggles, ensuring that the system dynamically responds to changes in subscription levels without the need of a developer.
4. Streamline the back-end validation process for pricing limits, enhancing the overall efficiency and reliability of the system.

4 Future Work

Several challenges remain for future work, but the main one is to design a built-in UI component for Pricing4React that establish an actual common language between business decision-makers and developers. This will allow non-technical users to apply pricing-driven changes, such as adding a new plan, to the system without modifying the source code. Additionally, we will conduct a more exhaustive comparison of Pricing4SaaS with other existing techniques and architectures that address similar problems. In the long term, we plan to develop equivalent libraries for other technologies, including Angular and Svelte for front-end development, and Django and Flask for back-end systems.

Acknowledgments. Authors are thankful to Pedro Gonzalez Marcos for his collaboration in the development of unit tests for Pricing4Java package. This work has been partially supported by grants PID2021-126227NB-C21, and PID2021-126227NB-C22 funded by MCIN/AEI/10.13039/501100011033/FEDER and European Union "ERDF a way of making Europe"; and TED2021-131023B-C21 and TED2021-131023B-C22 funded by MCIN/AEI/10.13039/501100011033 and European Union "NextGenerationEU"/PRTR. In addition, Fig. 1 was designed using images from Flaticon.com.

References

1. Fowler, M.: Feature toggles (aka feature flags). https://martinfowler.com/articles/feature-toggles.html
2. García-Fernández, A., Parejo, J.A., Ruiz-Cortés, A.: Pricing4SaaS - supplementary material (2023). https://doi.org/10.5281/zenodo.10292553
3. García-Fernández, A., Parejo, J.A., Ruiz-Cortés, A.: Pricing-driven development and operation of SaaS: challenges and opportunities. Accepted in Sistedes JCIS [Preprint] (2024). https://doi.org/10.48550/arXiv.2403.14007
4. Jiang, Z., Sun, W., Tang, K., Snowdon, J., Zhang, X.: A pattern-based design approach for subscription management of software as a service. In: 2009 Congress on Services - I, pp. 678–685 (2009)
5. Tërnava, X., Lesoil, L., Randrianaina, G.A., Khelladi, D.E., Acher, M.: On the interaction of feature toggles. VAMOS (2022). https://doi.org/10.1145/3510466.3510485

Utilizing DNS and VirusTotal for Automated Ad-Malware Detection

Florian Nettersheim[1], Stephan Arlt[1(✉)], and Michael Rademacher[2]

[1] Federal Office for Information Security, Bonn, Germany
{florian.nettersheim,stephan.arlt}@bsi.bund.de
[2] University of Applied Sciences Bonn-Rhein-Sieg, Sankt Augustin, Germany
michael.rademacher@h-brs.de

Abstract. In this paper, we present a novel approach to the automated detection of ad-malware. We efficiently crawl a vast set of websites and extensively fetch all HTTP requests embedded in these websites.Then we query these requests both against filtered DNS resolvers and VirusTotal. The idea is to evaluate, how much content is labeled as a potential threat. The results show that up to 8.8% of the domains found in our approach are labeled as suspicious. Moreover, up to 3.2% of these domains are categorized as ad-malware. However, the overall responses from the used services paint a divergent picture: Both DNS resolvers and VirusTotal have different understandings to the definition of suspicious content.

1 Introduction

Online advertising represents a main instrument for publishers to fund content for their websites. While most advertising is harmless, ad-malware (e.g. cryptojacking, phishing attacks, and drive-by-downloads) represents a growing threat[1]. Studies suggest that the online advertising ecosystem is broken from a security and privacy perspective [1]. Thus, the thorough detection and evaluation of ad-malware campaigns plays a crucial role for the safety of Internet users [2].

The options for protection are limited. On the one hand, the use of ad blockers can prohibit the display of any online advertising. On the other hand, Threat Intelligence (TI) services such as filtered DNS resolvers or crowd-based approaches like VirusTotal (VT) can label suspicious content based on contributions from partners. However, when using these services, the justification whether some content is identified as malicious (or benign) is not transparently discernible. Furthermore, it is open to which extent especially ad-malware is actually taken into account and whether the results differ among these services.

In this paper, we present a novel approach to the automated detection of ad-malware. In a first step, we efficiently crawl a vast set of URLs from the Tranco list [5] and extensively fetch all data transferred on the application layer. This includes in particular all HTTP requests embedded in websites (particularly such that display online advertisements). In a second step, we query all domains

[1] https://www.geoedge.com/q3-2023-ad-quality-report/.

K. Stefanidis et al. (Eds.): ICWE 2024, LNCS 14629, pp. 393–396, 2024.
https://doi.org/10.1007/978-3-031-62362-2_31

extracted from these requests against three filtered DNS resolvers and the TI service VT. All services return information, whether a domain is labeled as a potential threat. In a final step, we evaluate the results coming from these services. The approach is implemented as an extension of our tool KATTI [4].

The results show that up to 8.8% of the domains found using our approach are labeled as suspicious, whereas up to 3.2% of these domains are categorized as ad-malware. However, the overall responses from the used services paint a divergent picture: Both DNS resolvers and VT have different understandings to the definition of suspicious content. Thus, we urge for a discussion within the Web Engineering community, leading to a common understanding of ad-malware.

2 Approach and Demonstration Scenario

This section summarizes the implementation [3] of our approach. We further outline how attendees of the conference can interact with our tool and experience the novelty of our approach. Our focus is to enable a lively discussion within the community towards the judicious detection and evaluation of ad-malware.

Scalability: Our tool KATTI efficiently analyzes a vast set of websites. More precisely, we take a large list of URLs (e.g. from the Tranco list [5]) and pick a specific browser (e.g. Chrome). Note that KATTI employs real web browsers for crawling, which allows us to utilize more browsers such as Firefox (or even TOR). Attendees can individually choose sets of URLs to be crawled and observe the efficiency of crawling in a wide-scale context.

Exhaustiveness: While crawling websites, a person-in-the-middle HTTP proxy records all traffic passing through and stores it in a data storage. We save all URLs visited in the crawling process, in particular the HTTP requests called within websites (e.g. URLs to online advertisements). Attendees are able to interactively select and explore all data that arises during the execution of our tool.

Flexibility: The *Threat Intel Broker* component of KATTI takes all HTTP requests saved in the data storage and performs queries against multiple TI services. The results delivered from these services are stored in a *Threat Intel Repository*. More precisely, for each HTTP request, KATTI stores knowledge whether the corresponding data item is potentially malicious or benign. Attendees can initiate individual analyses for their desired websites through a user interface. In this context, users can "deep dive" into the results obtained from several TI services.

Continuity: The *Ad-Malware Detector* component of KATTI takes as input the TI repository and an *Ad Repository*. This allows us to filter out online advertisements among all content in the TI repository (which may also contain non ad-related content). By combining these information sources from TI repositories and from ad repositories, the ad-malware detector returns a verdict, whether the corresponding HTTP requests is ad-malware. Here, attendees have multiple options for interaction as they can choose and repeat the experiment on arbitrary websites, TI services, and ad repositories (e.g. ad filter lists).

3 Evaluation and Discussion

This section showcases the applicability [3] of our approach. For this purpose, we validated a total of 1,206,803 domains that originate from crawls that have been performed in the second half of 2023. URLs for crawling were based on the Tranco list [5].

RQ1: How many domains are blocked from DNS resolvers?
In this research question, we query all domains extracted from HTTP requests in our data storage against the filtered DNS resolvers of Cisco, Cloudflare, and Quad9. When a DNS request is sent to filtered resolvers, the response indicates whether the domain is blocked or not. Our naive assumption for RQ1 is that all resolvers label (i.e. block) most of the same domains as malicious resulting in a significant intersection.

The results of our analysis indicate that 5,784 domains are labeled as malicious by at least one DNS resolver. Quad9 and Cloudflare have the highest correlation with 230 domains. With only 28 domains, Quad9 and Cisco have the lowest correlation. Interestingly, only 7 domains from more than 1.2 million domains are blocked from all DNS servers. Hence, our above-mentioned assumption is *not* confirmed, such that DNS resolvers actually have different understandings which kind of domains are labeled as malicious.

RQ2: How many of the blocked domains are ad-malware?
In this research question, we take the set of blocked domains from our RQ1 and check it against the advertising filter lists from the Pi-hole project. If a domain has a positive match on one of the filter lists (and is blocked by a DNS resolver), we assume that the domain is connected to ad-malware. Here, our naive assumption is that we obtain a decent number of ad-malware domains, since ad-malware may be a significant number among all malicious domains (e.g. phishing domains).

The results indicate that the set of blocked domains from Cloudflare contains most ad-malware domains (i.e. 3.23%), whereas Cisco considers only 1.48% of the domains. Hence, our above-mentioned assumption is also *not* confirmed as the number of ad-malware domains is surprisingly low.

Discussion of RQ1 and RQ2: In RQ1 we learned that the results are quite divergent. We assume that providers of DNS resolvers may have different policies which domains should be labeled as malicious. However, information on blocking criteria is largely non-transparent. Since DNS represents a fundamental Internet protocol, providers certainly act restrained with blocking of domains to prevent overblocking and even censorship.

RQ3: How many domains are blocked from VT?
In this research question, we query all domains found in our crawling efforts against VT. The result for each domain is a so-called report, which shows, how many VT partners have categorized the domain as malicious.

In our analysis, the number of domains where *at least one partner* flags the domain as a potential threat is 8.8%. Similar to RQ2, we are additionally interested in the share of online advertisements from these potential threats. Here, only 0.71% from the potential threats are identified as ad-malware.

RQ4: How consistent are the results from VT partners?
VT works with a variety of different partners (e.g. "Google Safe Browsing") to provide a differentiated opinion if a certain domain is a potential threat. Similar to RQ1, we are interested if the opinions of the different partners vary. For 141 domains, all partners agree that the domain is a potential threat. For 975,338 domains, all partners agreed that the domain is harmless. In between, for overall 94,521 domains, the opinion differs as partners are divided over the classification of the domains.
Discussion of RQ3 and RQ4: Compared to DNS resolvers, VT flags significantly more domains as a potential threat to users (0.47% vs. 8.8%). In addition, there also exists varying opinions among the different VT partners what is considered a potential threat to users.

4 Conclusion and Future Work

TI services such as filtered DNS resolvers and VT are essential for the detection and evaluation of potentially malicious web resources such as URLs. They make it easy to participate in the knowledge of leading cybersecurity services. The results of our brief evaluation have shown that we need to develop further approaches to the interpretation of the results of such TI services as future work.

An elementary part of ad-malware detection is to identify specific web resources that were involved in the delivery of ad impressions. One promising line of research is to integrate an instrumentation of adblock engines in our current tooling efforts. The varying options of TI services show the need for a more general and transparent definition what is considered as malicious in the WWW.
AI disclosure: We hereby confirm that the creation of this paper did not involve the utilization of artificial intelligence (AI).

References

1. Chua, M.Y.K., Yee, G.O.M., Gu, Y.X., Lung, C.H.: Threats to online advertising and countermeasures: a technical survey. Digit. Threats **1**(2), 1–27 (2020)
2. Li, Z., Zhang, K., Xie, Y., Yu, F., Wang, X.: Knowing your enemy: understanding and detecting malicious web advertising. In: the ACM Conference on Computer and Communications Security, vol. 2012, pp. 674–686. ACM (2012)
3. Nettersheim, F., Arlt, S., Rademacher, M.: Dismantling common internet services for ad-malware detection (2024). https://arxiv.org/abs/2404.14190
4. Nettersheim, F., Arlt, S., Rademacher, M., Dehling, F.: Katti: an extensive and scalable tool for website analyses. In: Companion Proceedings of the ACM Web Conference 2023, WWW 2023, pp. 217–220. ACM (2023)
5. Pochat, V.L., van Goethem, T., Tajalizadehkhoob, S., Korczynski, M., Joosen, W.: Tranco: a research-oriented top sites ranking hardened against manipulation. In: 26th Annual Network and Distributed System Security Symposium, 2019. The Internet Society (2019)

A User Interface Design for Collaborations Between Humans and Intelligent Vehicles

Yong Zhao, Yatai Ji, Sihang Qiu, Zhengqiu Zhu, and Rusheng Ju(✉)

National University of Defense Technology, Changsha, China
{zhaoyong15,jiyatai1209,zhuzhengqiu12}@nudt.edu.cn, sihangq@acm.org, jrscy@sina.com

Abstract. Intelligent vehicles have been widely applied in the industry, academia, and our daily lives, to complete various tasks. However, existing AI that drives intelligent vehicles sometimes falls short as they may not ensure completeness or optimality, leading to issues like local optima or infinite loops. In response to these limitations, we proposed a user interface design for online crowdsourcing tasks, which enables collaborations between crowd workers and intelligent vehicles. This design aims to bolster existing intelligent vehicles' AI with human intelligence as external support, while also leveraging AI predictions to minimize human effort. This research provides significant insights into the design of collaborative systems that effectively integrate human and artificial intelligence.

Keywords: user interface · crowdsourcing · human-AI collaboration · intelligent vehicle

1 Introduction

Research on intelligent vehicles has become an important domain in the fields of AI, robotics, and cybernetics. Researchers and practitioners have used intelligent vehicles in a variety of applications, to complete tasks that humans are not willing to do. Such tasks could be either highly dangerous or repetitive, like searching for the fire source and hazardous gas source. These intelligent vehicles can autonomously move and complete tasks, driven by AI algorithms. However, existing AI algorithms sometimes fall short as they may not ensure completeness or optimality, leading to fatal problems that they cannot handle on their own [6].

Crowd-powered systems and human-AI collaborations [1] provide a new perspective on improving existing AI models and algorithms. These approaches enable humans to participate in processes that would otherwise be fully automated or intelligent. Currently, human-AI collaborations have been applied in various fields and have been shown to be effective in improving AI's effectiveness. Therefore, we are interested in whether human intelligence can improve intelligent vehicles' AI algorithms.

K. Stefanidis et al. (Eds.): ICWE 2024, LNCS 14629, pp. 397–400, 2024.
https://doi.org/10.1007/978-3-031-62362-2_32

In this work, we provided a user interface design to enable human-AI collaborations that could improve the existing intelligent vehicles' AI algorithms. The user interface can be used on a web crowdsourcing platform where online crowd workers are paid to complete microtasks that assist AI in solving specific problems. The user interface is also responsible for explaining the fatal problems detected in AI algorithms, and then giving suggestions to workers. Our work provides a feasible application and valuable insights into leveraging human-AI collaboration to improve current AI algorithms for intelligent vehicles.

2 User Interface Design

In this section, we introduce the design of the human-AI collaborative user interface for intelligent vehicles, and explain how human intelligence can be used through crowdsourcing, to improve the effectiveness and efficiency of AI.

In the initialization step, we define the goal, parameters, and configurations of the vehicle's AI. Then, in the execution step, we enable AI to drive the vehicles, or to solve problems autonomously. During the execution, the fatal problems can be detected (e.g., by setting some heuristic rules). To this end, crowdsourcing tasks can be generated using our designed user interface to enable crowd workers to solve the problem.

On the user interface[1], the explanation of the problem and solution suggestions are given as task instructions. The user interface features a map showing the environment where intelligent vehicles are moving. On the map, the current status (e.g., current moving directions, destinations) is displayed to let crowd workers understand the current situation and understand the problem that intelligent vehicles are encountering. Crowd workers are asked to operate intelligent vehicles through mouse-clicking on the map, in order to change vehicles' status or alter their destinations. Once the problem is solved, crowd workers can submit the task.

Upon task submission, the AI execution resumes. Finally, the execution ends after the stopping criteria are met.

3 Application I: Source Search

A source search problem aims to enable intelligent vehicles to autonomously find and move to the locations of sources (e.g., fire source, gas emission source, etc.) [3]. Since the source environments become increasingly complex, traditional search algorithms can no longer meet the requirements of the existing source search applications. Therefore, various novel heuristic search algorithms combined with human cognition have been proposed [2,5]. However, these search algorithms still have problems in terms of search completeness and optimality. In this application, we study the feasibility of our proposed human-AI collaborative user interface in a source search scenario (where an intelligent vehicle autonomously searches a gas emission source).

[1] The video of the designed interface can be found at https://osf.io/4e8pb/.

We designed a prototype crowdsourcing task interface following the proposed idea. The interface has two control modes: `FULL` control mode and `AIDED` control mode. The former allows users to take over the vehicle and the search process entirely, providing maximum flexibility for problem-solving. The latter enables users to set temporary destinations for the vehicle, aiding the vehicle without fully taking over control.

The source search algorithm used in this system is Infotaxis [4], which is one of the most popular novel source search strategies. The screenshot of the prototype crowdsourcing task is shown in Fig. 1 (a). We asked 10 participants to test the prototype user interface. The outcomes of this study underscore the efficacy, efficiency, and user-centric design of the proposed human-AI collaborative user interface. Independent of the participants' pre-existing knowledge regarding source search challenges, they were able to rapidly acclimate to the interface's operations and complete the tasks. Furthermore, during post-experiment interviews, several participants expressed a desire for more human-computer interaction modalities within our user interface, such as conversational interaction. The details of this study have been published in [6].

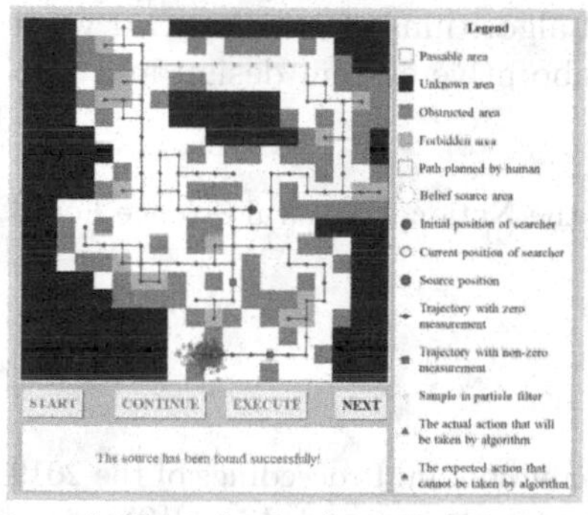

(a) The user interface for source search

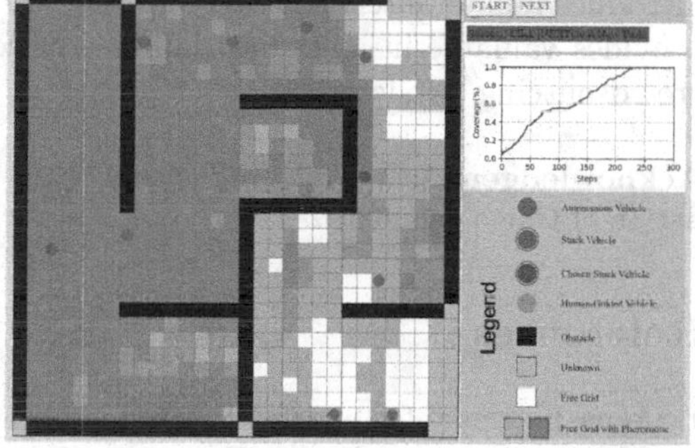

(b) The user interface for collaborative exploration

Fig. 1. Screenshots of web crowdsourcing tasks generated by the prototype system.

4 Application II: Collaborative Exploration

Cooperative exploration is another important research direction in the field of intelligent vehicles, which controls multiple vehicles to explore an unknown environment. This is also important in terms of search and rescue in emergencies. Traditional cooperative exploration methods are proposed based on swarm intelligence algorithms. However, they also have problems with regard to local optima, particularly in complex environments (like source search). In this application, we study the feasibility of our user interface in a collaborative exploration scenario (where multiple intelligent vehicles autonomously explore an indoor environment to achieve maximum coverage).

We designed a prototype crowdsourcing task interface, which also has two control modes for humans, namely the `PRECISE` mode and the `COLLECTIVE` mode. The `PRECISE` mode refers to highly precise means of interaction, which enables workers to directly control the movement of a single vehicle (similar to the FULL control in Application I). The `COLLECTIVE` mode refers to the interaction with the swarm instead of single vehicles, which enables workers to control the overall motion trend of the swarm.

The screenshot of the prototype crowdsourcing task is shown in Fig. 1 (b). We are conducting experiments with both experts and non-experts. We will also investigate the potential benefits of learning from humans, meaning the AI algorithm autonomously evolves by adopting human habits and preferences during operations. However, any bias resulting from human intervention must be approached with caution. Therefore, this study is still in progress.

5 Conclusion

In this work, we proposed a design of a user interface to facilitate human-AI collaborations for intelligent vehicles. Based on crowdsourcing approaches, we introduce human intelligence to improve the AI algorithms of vehicles. Our work provides valuable insights into human-AI collaborative system design and web crowdsourcing applications.

Acknowledgement.. This work is supported by the National Natural Science Foundation of China (no. 62202477).

References

1. Amershi, S., et al.: Guidelines for human-AI interaction. In: Proceedings of the 2019 CHI Conference on Human Factors in Computing Systems, pp. 1–13 (2019)
2. Ji, Y., Zhao, Y., Chen, B., Zhu, Z., Liu, Y., Zhu, H., Qiu, S.: Source searching in unknown obstructed environments through source estimation, target determination, and path planning. Build. Environ. **221**, 109266 (2022)
3. Ristic, B., Skvortsov, A., Gunatilaka, A.: A study of cognitive strategies for an autonomous search. Inf. Fusion **28**, 1–9 (2016)
4. Vergassola, M., Villermaux, E., Shraiman, B.I.: Infotaxis as a strategy for searching without gradients. Nature **445**(7126), 406–409 (2007)
5. Zhao, Y., Chen, B., Zhu, Z., Chen, F., Wang, Y., Ji, Y.: Searching the diffusive source in an unknown obstructed environment by cognitive strategies with forbidden areas. Build. Environ. **186**, 107349 (2020)
6. Zhao, Y., Zhu, Z., Chen, B., Qiu, S.: Leveraging human-AI collaboration in crowd-powered source search: a preliminary study. J. Soc. Comput. **4**(2), 95–111 (2023)

Utilizing a Standards-Based Toolchain to Model and Execute Quantum Workflows

Martin Beisel[1(✉)], Jaime Alvarado-Valiente[2], Johanna Barzen[1], Frank Leymann[1], Javier Romero-Álvarez[2], Lavinia Stiliadou[1], and Benjamin Weder[1]

[1] University of Stuttgart, Institute of Architecture of Application Systems, Stuttgart, Germany
{Beisel,Barzen,Leymann,Stiliadou,Weder}@iaas.uni-stuttgart.de

[2] University of Extremadura, Quercus Software Engineering Group, Badajoz, Spain
{jaimeav,jromero}@unex.es

Abstract. The increasing availability of quantum devices via the cloud led to a multitude of commercial and scientific tools for developing quantum applications. However, since quantum applications are typically hybrid, comprising both quantum and classical parts, these tools are very heterogeneous. Therefore, combining them within a single application is complicated by incompatible programming languages, data formats, and interfaces. Hence, to enable the development of portable and interoperable quantum applications a standards-based toolchain is required. In this demonstration, we present a holistic toolchain for developing quantum applications utilizing well-established standards for defining workflows, deployment topologies, application interfaces, and provenance data. To demonstrate the practical feasibility of our toolchain, we showcase it for two use cases from the cryptography and machine learning domains.

Keywords: Quantum Computing · Quantum Software Engineering · Hybrid Quantum Applications · SoC · Workflow Technology

1 Introduction

With the rapid development of quantum computing, a steadily growing number of commercial and scientific tools are available for developing quantum applications. However, these tools are very heterogeneous: They use different languages, interfaces, and cover different phases of the quantum software development lifecycle [6]. Consequently, combining multiple tools in a single application is a challenging task that is further complicated by the hybridity of quantum applications. Since quantum devices are exclusively used for solving specific problems and the remaining tasks are executed on classical computers, quantum applications always integrate both quantum and classical programs. Thus, quantum application development requires (i) tools covering classical and quantum aspects, (ii) techniques for integrating both parts, and (iii) developers with

K. Stefanidis et al. (Eds.): ICWE 2024, LNCS 14629, pp. 401–405, 2024.
https://doi.org/10.1007/978-3-031-62362-2_33

expertise in both quantum computing and software engineering [4]. To enable the development of portable and interoperable quantum applications, and improve the accessibility of quantum computing, a standards-based toolchain is required.

In this demonstration, we present a holistic toolchain for building quantum applications utilizing the established standards *BPMN*, *OpenAPI*, *PROV*, and the *Topology and Orchestration Specification for Cloud Applications (TOSCA)*. Thereby, the tasks of quantum applications are modularized in a service-oriented architecture [1]. To orchestrate the different services, BPMN workflows are used, as they enable the integration of heterogeneous tasks while providing benefits such as robustness and scalability [3]. The modeling of quantum applications is facilitated by a standard-compliant approach, comprising the *Quantum Modeling Extension (QuantME)* and a transformation into native BPMN workflows [5]. To facilitate the invocation of quantum-related services in workflows OpenAPI is used to generate requests, easing the configuration for the user. Further, the OpenAPI specification was extended to dynamically generate services for executing quantum circuits using different quantum cloud platforms [2]. Since today's applications are typically distributed across different cloud providers, we employ TOSCA as a provider-independent standard for the automated deployment of services. To improve the observability of quantum applications, we collect relevant data utilizing a provenance system implementing the PROV standard.

2 Standards-Based Quantum Application Development

In this section, we describe the system architecture of our standards-based toolchain and showcase it for two typical use cases from the quantum domain.

2.1 System Architecture

The system architecture implementing our toolchain comprises six components, as depicted in Fig. 1. The *QuantME Framework* enables the graphical modeling of quantum workflows using BPMN and QuantME. The *Camunda Workflow Engine* enables the execution and monitoring of BPMN workflows. To generate services for executing quantum circuits on the fly, the OpenAPI-based *Quantum Service Generator* is employed. The quantum provenance system *QProv* stores provenance data about the workflow execution and its execution environment to support observability, reproducibility, and analysis. *Winery* is utilized to model deployment topologies using the TOSCA standard. These topologies are deployed by the provider-independent deployment system *OpenTOSCA Container*.

Modeling quantum workflows is enabled by the *QuantME Modeler & Transformator*, which supports BPMN as well as QuantME-specific modeling constructs. The portability of workflows comprising QuantME constructs is ensured by an automated transformation into native BPMN constructs. Different process views facilitating workflow observability, e.g., a view for quantum experts, are

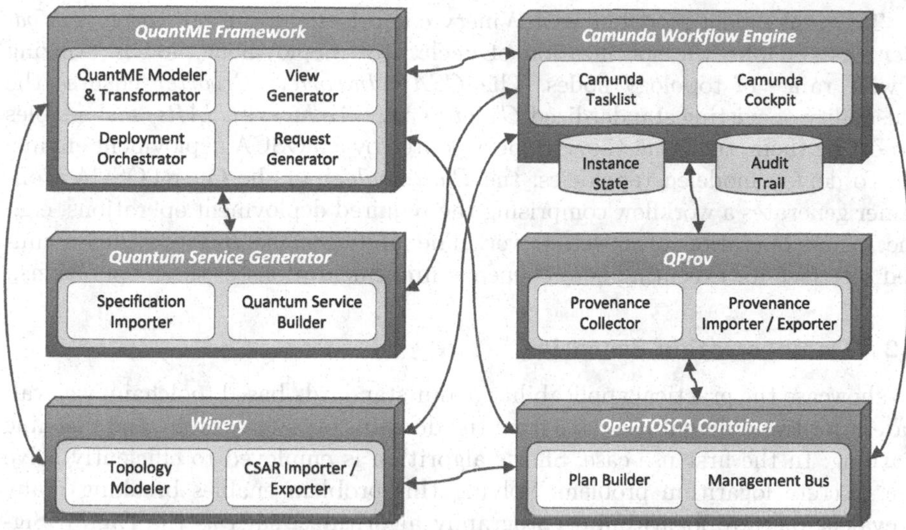

Fig. 1. Overview of the architecture to realize the standards-based toolchain

generated by the *View Generator*. Deployment-related functionalities are handled by the *Deployment Orchestrator*, which uses Winery for storing and retrieving deployment models, the OpenTOSCA Container for deploying services, and the Camunda Workflow Engine for deploying workflows, as well as the generated views. To facilitate the invocation of services in workflows, the *Request Generator* enables the generation of suitable service tasks based on OpenAPI specifications.

The Camunda Workflow Engine enables the instantiation of workflows via the *Camunda Tasklist*. Once a workflow is started, its execution can be observed within the *Camunda Cockpit*. Furthermore, the Camunda Cockpit enables the visualization of the different process views generated by the QuantME Framework. Instance data of the workflow is stored in the *Instance State* database during runtime. Once the workflow execution is finished, the instance data is transferred into the *Audit Trail*. During the execution of the workflow, the workflow engine employs the Quantum Service Generator to generate the necessary quantum services and the OpenTOSCA Container to deploy the required self-hosted services.

The *Specification Importer* of the Quantum Service Generator enables loading any OpenAPI specification supporting the quantum service extension. This specification is used by the *Quantum Service Builder* to compose a new service capable of executing the quantum program referenced in the loaded specification.

The *Provenance Collector* of QProv automatically collects and stores data available via an API, e.g., quantum device characteristics or the status of service deployments. Furthermore, the *Provenance Importer / Exporter* enables storing and retrieving arbitrary provenance data that comply with the PROV standard.

The deployment modeling tool Winery comprises a graphical *Topology Modeler* that enables the specification of declarative deployment models utilizing a wide range of topology nodes. The *CSAR Importer/Exporter* ensures the reusability of existing standardized *Cloud Service Archives (CSARs)* and enables exporting them, such that they can be executed by a TOSCA deployment engine.

To deploy modeled topologies, the *Plan Builder* of the OpenTOSCA Container generates a workflow comprising the required deployment operations, e.g., the install operation of a web server. The *Management Bus* provides a unified interface for executing heterogeneous implementations of these operations.

2.2 Demonstration Scenarios

To showcase the practical applicability of our standards-based toolchain, we evaluate it for two different use cases from the domains of cryptography and machine learning: In the first use case, Shor's algorithm is employed to efficiently solve the discrete logarithm problem. Solving this problem enables breaking many prevalent discrete logarithm cryptography algorithms, such as the Digital Signature Algorithm (DSA), once fault-tolerant quantum devices with a sufficient number of qubits are available. The second use case performs clustering by solving the *Maximum Cut* problem utilizing the *Quantum Approximate Optimization Algorithm (QAOA)*. QAOA is a variational quantum algorithm that already provides meaningful results on today's noisy intermediate-scale quantum devices by alternating between quantum and classical execution blocks. The source code repositories, documentation, and a comprehensive step-by-step tutorial can be found on GitHub: https://github.com/UST-QuAntiL/QuantME-UseCases. The demonstration video showcasing our toolchain and the user-interaction with the different tools is available on YouTube: https://youtu.be/U9kJvRw3WjY.

2.3 Discussion

While many established standards in classical computing can be applied in hybrid applications, there is a lack of standards specifically tailored for the quantum computing domain. For example, the representation of quantum circuits is often provider-specific, reducing portability and interoperability. However, various standards in quantum computing are under development, e.g., OpenQASM. In future work, we plan to extend our toolchain to incorporate these standards.

Acknowledgments.. This work was partially funded by the BMWK projects *EniQmA* (01MQ22007B) and *SeQuenC* (01MQ22009B). It was also partially funded by the Ministry of Science, Innovation, and Universities of Spain (project PID2021-1240454OB-C31) and by the Regional Ministry of Economy, Science and Digital Agenda of the Regional Government of Extremadura (GR21133).

References

1. Beisel, M., et al.: Quokka: a service ecosystem for workflow-based execution of variational quantum algorithms. In: Troya, J., et al. (ed.) Service-Oriented Computing

- ICSOC 2022 Workshops, ICSOC 2022, LNCS, vol. 13821, pp. 369–373. Springer, Cham (2023). https://doi.org/10.1007/978-3-031-26507-5_35

2. Garcia-Alonso, J., et al.: Quantum software as a service through a quantum API gateway. IEEE Internet Comput. **26**(1), 34–41 (2021)
3. Leymann, F., Roller, D.: Production Workflow: Concepts and Techniques. Prentice Hall PTR, Hoboken (2000)
4. Vietz, D., et al.: An exploratory study on the challenges of engineering quantum applications in the cloud. In: Proceedings of the 2nd Quantum Software Engineering and Technology Workshop (Q-SET), pp. 1–12. CEUR Workshop Proceedings (2021)
5. Weder, B., et al.: Integrating quantum computing into workflow modeling and execution. In: Proceedings of the 13th IEEE/ACM International Conference on Utility and Cloud Computing (UCC), pp. 279–291. IEEE (2020)
6. Weder, B., Barzen, J., Leymann, F., Vietz, D.: Quantum software development lifecycle. In: Serrano, M.A., Pérez-Castillo, R., Piattini, M. (eds.) Quantum Software Engineering, pp. 61–83. Springer, Cham (2022). https://doi.org/10.1007/978-3-031-05324-5_4

A Prototype Design of LLM-Based Autonomous Web Crowdsensing

Zhengqiu Zhu, Yatai Ji, Sihang Qiu, Yong Zhao, Kai Xu, Rusheng Ju(✉), and Bin Chen

National University of Defense Technology, Changsha, China
{zhuzhengqiu12,jiyatai_1209,zhaoyong15,xukai09,chenbin06}@nudt.edu.cn, sihangq@acm.org, jrscy@sina.com

Abstract. The expanded demands of complex sensing campaigns involving Cyber-Physical-Social spaces have brought forth a multitude of challenges for web crowdsensing applications, such as substantial human efforts, potential user privacy breaches, and interest diminishes of users. Significant advancements have occurred in the application of Large Language Models (LLMs) for various tasks, such as conversational engagement, social simulation, and decision-making. Despite this, their potential to empower web crowdsensing activities is under-explored. To bridge this gap, we explore the design of a LLM-based autonomous web crowdsensing framework for flood-related data collection to mitigate the workload and professional demands on individuals in this poster.

Keywords: Web Crowdsensing · Cyber-Physical-Social · Large Language Models · Mobile Web Applications

1 Introduction

The rapid development of Web of Things and mobile web technologies has fostered the emergence of a social, open, and large-scale sensing paradigm, namely web crowdsensing (also known as social sensors) [7]. It harnesses the collective intelligence of individuals and organizations to enable efficient collection and sharing of real-time information within web applications like Twitter [5]. However, the expanded demands of complex sensing tasks have brought forth a multitude of challenges and issues for it, such as substantial human efforts, sluggish system response, and personal privacy protection concerns [9]. Consequently, these factors impede the broader adoption of this sensing paradigm.

In this context, a novel generation of web crowdsensing is imperative to enable autonomous, intelligent, dependable, and interactive sensing [11]. Large language models (LLMs), such as GPT-4 [1], have gained significant attention due to their exceptional abilities in natural language processing. Recent studies have extended the capabilities of these LLMs beyond text generation, positioning LLMs as versatile agents capable of conversational reasoning and task

K. Stefanidis et al. (Eds.): ICWE 2024, LNCS 14629, pp. 406–409, 2024.
https://doi.org/10.1007/978-3-031-62362-2_34

completion [8]. By leveraging LLMs, web crowdsensing could enhance intelligence throughout the entire process and facilitate interactions among humans, humans and AI, as well as AI with AI, thereby resulting in more effective task comprehension and completion. However, the potential of LLM-based AI agents in empowering web crowdsensing activities remains untapped.

Therefore, we posit that the integration of LLM-based AI agent technology [4] into web crowdsensing holds promise for uncovering valuable insights pertaining to autonomous sensing and the development of mobile web applications. To that end, we investigate the design of a LLM-based autonomous web crowdsensing framework, featuring a four-component architecture. To answer how this framework works, we conduct a case study on flooding data collection and flooding prediction. Our findings indicate that LLM-based AI Agent technology has the potential to revolutionize web crowdsensing by alleviating human workload and enhancing system response efficiency.

2 LLM-Based Autonomous Web Crowdsensing Framework Design

Existing research has yet to explore the capabilities of LLM-based AI agents for autonomous task planning and execution within the realm of web crowdsensing tasks. In an effort to fill this void, this poster introduces a novel framework based on LLMs, which integrates the construction of prompt templates, the planning and completion of tasks, and the aggregation of results. Illustrated in Fig. 1(a), the framework is structured around four pivotal components:

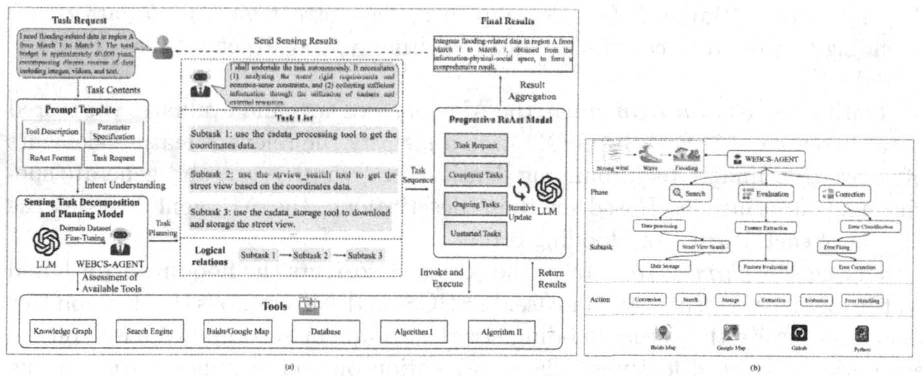

Fig. 1. An overview of the LLM-based autonomous web crowdsensing framework.

Prompt Templates. It acts as the foundational input to the framework, encompassing task requests, tool descriptions, parameter specification, and the Reason+Action (ReAct) [10] format, among others. Historical or application examples can also be applied to facilitate contextual learning by AI agents [3].

Toolset. This component augments the AI agents' capabilities [6], enabling them to access and process information that lies beyond their inherent knowledge base and to facilitate interactions with other systems.

Sensing Task Decomposition and Planning Model. The model is capable of efficiently decomposing sensing task requests into a sequence of subtasks. By fine-tuning an open-source LLM, we derive a sensing task decomposition and planning model, thus birthing a LLM-based AI agent.

Progressive ReAct Model. To address the problems of forgetting and confusion, the model is designated to complete a planned sequence of subtasks; during which, it consistently updates the status of these subtasks and amalgamates historical data to produce the ultimate execution outcomes of the task.

Here we use a case to illustrate how this framework works. In this case, we intend to collect comprehensive flood-related data via web crowdsensing for enhancing depth prediction of flooding. Firstly, we fine-tune the Qwen-7B model[1] and ensure that it is capable of decomposing the complex tasks of web crowdsensing. Additionally, we construct a toolset of web crowdsensing to assist the completion of assigned online subtasks automatically. The Progressive ReAct Model is used to accurately invoke tools to complete sensing-related subtasks. As shown in Fig. 1(b), the AI agent sequentially performs three phases of tasks: ***Search***, ***Evaluation***, and ***Correction***.

During the ***Search*** stage, WEBCS-AGENT searches for relevant data on mobile web applications based on the task objective. In our case, WEBCS-AGENT initially processes the collected dataset, extracting the necessary coordinates and flood depth data for accurate flooding prediction while simultaneously performing essential format conversions. Subsequently, WEBCS-AGENT utilizes API interface of Baidu or Google Map to retrieve street view map data corresponding to the given coordinate location. Finally, the street view map data is stored.

During the ***Evaluation*** stage, the AI agent extracts and evaluates the stored data. In our case, WEBCS-AGENT would identify the relevant feature elements of street view images (e.g., building density, road width, etc.) and generate specific text descriptions. Based on these descriptions, the AI agent assesses the impact of each feature on flooding errors.

During the ***Correction*** stage, the AI agent corrects the flooding error based on the evaluation results. In our case, WEBCS-AGENT employs the decision tree model to classify the actual flooding errors at different coordinates based on the evaluation results of features. The classification outcomes indicate the varying degrees of influence that different features have on flooding errors. WEBCS-AGENT selects the features with high influence to train a support vector regression (SVR) model [2] for predicting flooding errors. Finally, the AI agent utilizes the obtained fitting results from the SVR model to rectify the error outcomes.

Experimental results indicate that the LLM-based AI agent exhibits enhanced accuracy in task decomposition and execution of corresponding web-

[1] https://github.com/QwenLM/Qwen-7B.

based subtasks according to the defined *TCR* (Task Completion Rate) and *TSR* (Task Success Rate) indicators. Since most sensing activities are completed by LLM-based AI agents, thereby greatly reducing human participation as well as facilitating rapid responses and wide application of web crowdsensing systems.

3 Conclusions

In this work, we investigate the design of a LLM-based autonomous web crowdsensing framework. Specifically, we conduct a case study on flooding data collection and flooding prediction to reveal the capability of LLMs empowering the entire life cycle of web-based sensing activities in an autonomous mode with minimal human intervention. The future is expected to witness the emergence of a novel human-oriented web crowdsensing paradigm through multi-agent dialogue.

Acknowledgement. This study is supported by Youth Independent Innovation Foundation of NUDT (ZK-2023-21) and National Natural Science Foundation of China (62202477, 62173337, 21808181, 72071207).

References

1. Achiam, J., et al.: GPT-4 technical report (2023). https://arxiv.org/pdf/2303.08774.pdf
2. Basak, D., Pal, S., Patranabis, D.C., et al.: Support vector regression. Neural Inf. Proc.-Lett. Rev. **11**(10), 203–224 (2007)
3. Dong, Q., et al.: A survey on in-context learning (2022). https://arxiv.org/pdf/2301.00234.pdf
4. OPENPM, T.: WorkGPT (2023). https://github.com/team-openpm/workgpt
5. Sakaki, T., Okazaki, M., Matsuo, Y.: Earthquake shakes twitter users: real-time event detection by social sensors. In: Proceedings of the 19th International Conference on World Wide Web, pp. 851–860 (2010)
6. Schick, T., et al.: Toolformer: language models can teach themselves to use tools. In: Advances in Neural Information Processing Systems, vol. 36, pp. 68539–68551. Curran Associates, Inc. (2023)
7. Vepsäläinen, J., Hellas, A., Vuorimaa, P.: The rise of disappearing frameworks in web development. In: Garrigos, I., Murillo Rodriguez, J.M., Wimmer, M. (eds.) Web Engineering. Lecture Notes in Computer Science, vol. 13893, pp. 319–326. Springer, Cham (2023). https://doi.org/10.1007/978-3-031-34444-2_23
8. Wang, L., et al.: A survey on large language model based autonomous agents (2023). https://arxiv.org/pdf/2308.11432.pdf
9. Wu, W., et al.: Autonomous crowdsensing: operating and organizing crowdsensing for sensing automation. IEEE Trans. Intell. Veh. (2024)
10. Yao, S., et al.: ReAct: synergizing reasoning and acting in language models (2022). https://arxiv.org/pdf/2210.03629.pdf
11. Zhu, Z., et al.: Strategy evaluation and optimization with an artificial society toward a pareto optimum. Innov. **3**(5), 100274 (2022). https://doi.org/10.1016/j.xinn.2022.100274

Web Crowdsourcing for Coastal Flood Prevention and Management

Sihang Qiu, Yatai Ji, Zhengqiu Zhu, Yong Zhao, Rusheng Ju, and Xiaohui Wang(✉)

National University of Defense Technology, Changsha, China
sihangq@acm.org,
{jiyatai1209,zhuzhengqiu12,zhaoyong15,wangxiaohui11}@nudt.edu.cn,
jrscy@sina.com

Abstract. Coastal floods have been causing massive casualties and economic loss to human societies. To better understand and manage coastal floods, existing research has comprehensively studied their physical processes, but we still face the challenges of inaccurate predictions, insufficient information, and imprecise management. Web crowdsourcing has emerged as an effective tool to collect and leverage crowd intelligence. However, there is a research gap in terms of using web crowdsourcing to aid flood disaster prevention and management. Therefore, in this poster, we present a crowdsourcing design that uses various web applications and technologies, to improve flood prediction, collect necessary information, and help in management optimization.

1 Introduction

Coastal disasters, such as floods, storms, and tsunamis, can have extremely negative impacts on human beings living in coastal regions. People suffer from these disasters because we lack an understanding of their consequences. Since we cannot accurately predict their consequences and cannot comprehensively obtain social reactions, it is difficult to make precise management strategies for people in danger in response to the emergency. Therefore, for both research institutes and emergency departments, there is an urgent need for precisely predicting the disaster, collecting social information, and organizing scientific management.

Researchers have proposed plenty of ocean models to predict coastal floods and other ocean disasters [2,5]. However, there are unaddressed challenges in terms of applying such models in supporting effective management during coastal flood disasters. We categorize the challenges into three aspects: 1) Inaccurate predictions. While state-of-the-art ocean models can produce accurate predictions in the ocean, the prediction of how they impact the land, particularly the coastal cities, needs to be corrected. Particularly, environmental factors could be more complex in cities and towns considering human activities. 2) Insufficient information. Even if ocean models can make accurate predictions, it is necessary to collect sufficient information in terms of the reaction of society, people's opinions,

K. Stefanidis et al. (Eds.): ICWE 2024, LNCS 14629, pp. 410–413, 2024.
https://doi.org/10.1007/978-3-031-62362-2_35

and physical/mental wellness. Such subjective data could play a dominant role in decision-making. 3) Imprecise management. Traditional management strategies are not designed specifically for flood disasters. Therefore, they are usually costly and imprecise. A good management strategy should truly satisfy people's needs, and be optimized to reduce the casualty, economic loss, and waste of resources simultaneously.

We noticed that crowdsourcing, featuring high flexibility and scalability, shows great potential in aggregating human intelligence during disasters. To tackle the above-mentioned challenges, in this poster, we propose a crowdsourcing design to achieve three goals: 1) leveraging human intelligence to improve the state-of-the-art coastal flood models, 2) comprehensively collecting subjective information related to disasters, and 3) acquiring people's needs and accordingly optimizing management strategies. We anticipate that web crowdsourcing for coastal flood prevention and management will provide valuable insights in the future.

2 Crowdsourcing Framework Design

To address the challenges with regard to inaccurate predictions, insufficient information, and imprecise management respectively, we propose a framework integrating crowdsourced flood model improvement, social information collection, and management strategy optimization, as shown in Fig. 1.

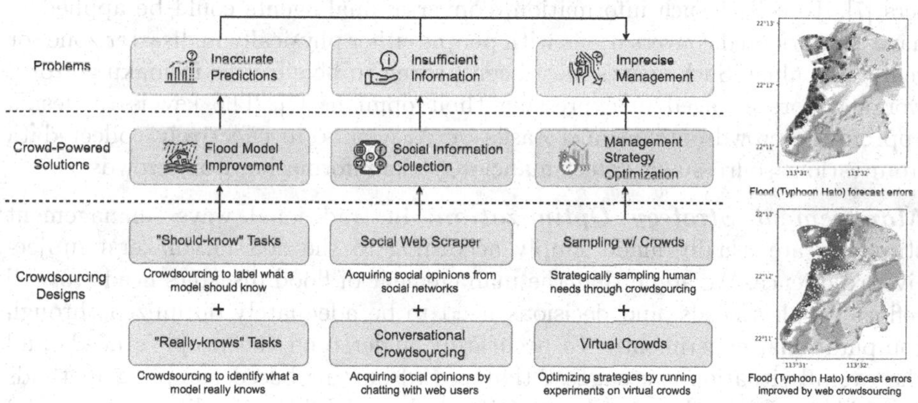

Fig. 1. An overview of the crowdsourcing framework. We also show an example of forecasts of the flood event induced by Typhoon Hato improved by web crowdsourcing [11]

Flood Model Improvement. Inspired by the previous crowdsourcing design [10], the flood model improvement method consists of two crowdsourcing tasks – the "should-know" task and the "really-knows" task. The "should-knows" task requires workers to label important elements that a flood disaster should particularly pay attention to (elements that could lead to bad model performances), on street-level imagery of disaster zones. The "really-knows" task asks workers to make comparisons between model outputs with observational data, to understand what a model really knows and where it makes mistakes. Observational data can be acquired via mobile crowdsensing, which assigns data-collecting tasks to workers via mobile web applications. Furthermore, web-based crowd-mapping is an effective task design to let workers complete tasks remotely (not in the disaster regions) [1,8]. Online workers can use map applications equipped with street-level imagery (e.g., Google Map), to acquire high-quality geographic/environmental information, so as to label important factors that the model should know or really knows. After "should-know" and "really-knows" tasks, we could understand why and where a flood prediction model makes mistakes. For different types of model drawbacks, the model could be improved through while-/gray-/black-box system identification methods, which are well-studied in the field of control science and cybernetics.

Social Information Collection. Social information collection uses crowdsourcing to acquire sufficient information from social media to assist in disaster management. Particularly, subjective social information such as perceived disaster risks, people's opinions, and their wellness could play an important role in disaster management [3]. Information could be collected from posts and comments on existing social applications such as Twitter and TikTok, by publishing crowdsourcing tasks to crowd workers, or by using AI scrapers. Conversational crowdsourcing is a feasible way to directly collect information related to disasters [7]. To collect such information, conversational agents could be applied to have task-oriented conversations with people either physically in disaster zones or remotely online. Such agents have been proven to be effective in making crowd workers more engaged in expressing their opinions [7]. The key is to design appropriate crowdsourcing microtasks or AI agents, to effectively collect data from various sources and detect malicious/fake information from crowds.

Management Strategy Optimization. In traditional ways, management strategies are usually made simply according to the decision-maker's subjective experience. We argue that the management of flood disasters needs to well reflect people's needs, and decisions need to be adequately optimized through computational experiments. To accurately understand the people's needs and the overall situation, we suggest that crowdsourcing-based sampling methods (e.g., Monte Carlo Markov Chain with people and Gibbs sampling with people) need to be carried out [4,9], so as to estimate the risk of different coastal areas and to know the needs of local residents. To optimize management strategies, we highlight the importance of building a crowdsourcing simulation system [6]. Through iterative computational experiments with virtual crowds in a parallel artificial society [6,12], prevention measures and management strategies could be optimized, to achieve minimum casualty and economic loss.

3 Conclusions

In this work, we show how crowdsourcing could assist in coastal flood prevention and management. Specifically, we provide a few web-based crowdsourcing designs with regard to improving flood models, collecting flood-related social information, and optimizing management strategies.

Acknowledgement. This work is supported by the National Natural Science Foundation of China (nos. 42306217 & 62202477).

References

1. van Alphen, G., Qiu, S., Bozzon, A., Houben, G.J.: Analyzing workers performance in online mapping tasks across web, mobile, and virtual reality platforms. In: Proceedings of the AAAI Conference on Human Computation and Crowdsourcing, vol. 8, pp. 141–149 (2020)
2. Dong, W., et al.: Observational and modeling studies of oceanic responses and feedbacks to typhoons Hato and Mangkhut over the northern shelf of the South China sea. Prog. Oceanogr. **191**, 102507 (2021)
3. Gao, H., Barbier, G., Goolsby, R.: Harnessing the crowdsourcing power of social media for disaster relief. IEEE Intell. Syst. **26**(3), 10–14 (2011)
4. Harrison, P., et al.: Gibbs sampling with people. In: Larochelle, H., Ranzato, M., Hadsell, R., Balcan, M., Lin, H. (eds.) Advances in Neural Information Processing Systems, vol. 33, pp. 10659–10671. Curran Associates, Inc. (2020)
5. Luettich, R.A., Westerink, J.J.: Formulation and Numerical Implementation of the 2D/3D ADCIRC Finite Element Model Version 44, vol. 20. R. Luettich Chapel Hill, NC, USA (2004)
6. Qiu, S., Bozzon, A., Houben, G.J.: VirtualCrowd: a simulation platform for microtask crowdsourcing campaigns. In: Companion Proceedings of the Web Conference 2020, WWW'20, pp. 222-225. Association for Computing Machinery, New York (2020). https://doi.org/10.1145/3366424.3383546
7. Qiu, S., Gadiraju, U., Bozzon, A.: Improving worker engagement through conversational microtask crowdsourcing. In: Proceedings of the 2020 CHI Conference on Human Factors in Computing Systems, pp. 1–12 (2020)
8. Qiu, S., Psyllidis, A., Bozzon, A., Houben, G.J.: Crowd-mapping urban objects from street-level imagery. In: The World Wide Web Conference, pp. 1521–1531 (2019)
9. Sanborn, A., Griffiths, T.: Markov chain monte Carlo with people. In: Platt, J., Koller, D., Singer, Y., Roweis, S. (eds.) Advances in Neural Information Processing Systems, vol. 20. Curran Associates, Inc. (2007)
10. Sharifi Noorian, S., Qiu, S., Gadiraju, U., Yang, J., Bozzon, A.: What should you know? A human-in-the-loop approach to unknown unknowns characterization in image recognition. In: Proceedings of the ACM Web Conference 2022, pp. 882–892 (2022)
11. Wang, X., et al.: Crowdsourcing intelligence for improving disaster forecasts. Innovation (2024)
12. Zhu, Z., et al.: Strategy evaluation and optimization with an artificial society toward a pareto optimum. Innovation **3**(5), 100274 (2022). https://doi.org/10.1016/j.xinn.2022.100274

Unveiling Human-AI Interaction and Subjective Perceptions About Artificial Intelligent Agents

Mathyas Giudici(✉), Federica Liguori, Andrea Tocchetti, and Marco Brambilla

Politecnico di Milano, DEIB, 20133 Milano, Italy
{mathyas.giudici,federica.liguori,andrea.tocchetti, marco.brambilla}@polimi.it

Abstract. This work focuses on human-AI interactions, employing a crowd-based methodology to collect and assess the reactions and perceptions of a human audience to a dialogue between a human and an artificial intelligent agent. The study is conducted through a live streaming platform where human streamers broadcast interviews to a custom-made GPT voice interface. The questions extracted from the dialogues were categorized based on emotional and cognitive criteria. Our method covers thematic, emotional, and sentiment analyses of the comments platform users shared during the interview. This work aims to contribute to Human-Computer Interaction (HCI) and Human-Centered AI, emphasizing the need for a paradigm shift in AI research from focusing on technological development to considering its impact on human beings.

Keywords: Artificial Intelligence · Human-AI Interaction · Human-Centered AI · Crowdsourcing · Human-Computer Interaction

1 Introduction

Recent artificial intelligence (AI) developments influence people's work and daily lives. However, the development of AI systems has been predominantly driven by a technology-centered design approach. Recently, AI development has taken a broader perspective on the problem: technological enhancement meets ethical and human factors design. *Human-centered AI* [5] embodies an approach where AI and machine learning systems are designed with a keen awareness that they are part of a broader context, including various stakeholders and focusing on ensuring fairness, maintaining accountability, enhancing interpretability, and upholding transparency. *Human factors design* is crucial in ensuring that AI solutions are explainable, understandable, useful, and usable to humans, also considering Human-Computer Interaction, user perception, and technology acceptance [1]. More recent research has broadened the scope by introducing trust, encompassing *cognitive* and *emotional* (support) aspects, thus enabling broader user engagement analyses [4]. Crowdsourcing approaches have emerged as a valuable tool for gathering human knowledge relevant to technology development in

K. Stefanidis et al. (Eds.): ICWE 2024, LNCS 14629, pp. 414–418, 2024.
https://doi.org/10.1007/978-3-031-62362-2_36

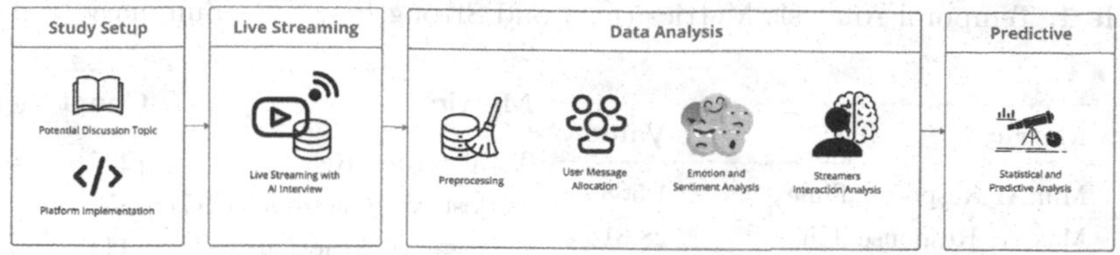

Fig. 1. Experimental Approach

AI interpretability and explainability [2], also using gamification techniques to gain enhanced user participation [6]. This work evaluates AI models from a human-centered perspective, investigating the emotions of humans towards AI as a proxy to emotional trust in AI models [3]. Pursuing such an objective, we developed a new approach using an online streaming platform, where live sessions in an interview style were broadcast by volunteer human streamers who asked questions to an AI generative model (GPT). We analyzed the audience's reaction using a crowdsourcing method to gather data from user comments posted on the platform in real time as responses to the ongoing interviews. The interviews focused on thoughtfully crafted questions derived from the fundamental notion of trust. Our study, therefore, aims to better understand human factors in human-AI interactions by directly observing users in an interactive digital setting.

2 Method

Our research evaluates the user's interaction with responses to the generative AI model OpenAI GPT3.5. Volunteer streamers from a popular streaming platform interviewed the AI model and involved in real time the audience from their community in the interaction. The communication between the streamers and the AI was oral (without any visual clues or avatar representing the AI), using a web application delivering Speech-To-Text and Text-To-Speech services between streamers and the API of the model. At the same time, the audience comments were typed into the chat UI. Our system recorded interview utterances and live-users comments. Figure 1 shows the phases of the approach:

Setup. Streamers were selected, and a set of potential discussion topics was provided to them. The proposed questions were categorized into two groups: (i) *Cognitive* - highlighting the AI's capabilities and skills, the tasks and how well it can perform them; (ii) *Emotional* - stressing ethical issues, abstract reasoning capabilities, or subjects requiring the AI to take a stance.

Preprocessing. All the texts (from streamer-AI interviews and users' live comments) were translated from Italian to English using DeepL APIs and the data was properly formatted.

User Message Allocation. Live sessions were segmented into 15-second slots timeframes to gain a more detailed overview of the temporal distribution of

Table 1. Temporal Analysis Metrics (left) and Strong Reactions Summary (right)

Metric	Value
Min AI Response Time	1.568 s
Max AI Response Time	28.313 s
Avg AI Response Time	12.14 s
Comments before AI Response	10.9%
Comments after AI Response	89.1%

Metric	Count
Total Strong Reactions	1297
> Positive Reactions (PR)	853
> Negative Reactions (NR)	444
PR Unique Comments	459
NR Unique Comments	124
PN- NR Unique Comments	226

the collected messages and then obtain a proper association between the AI's responses and user comments.

Emotion Analysis. Emotion of users' comments was analyzed using a pre-trained model[1] based on the 'roberta-base' model and trained for multi-label classification on 28 emotion labels (along with their score). We selected only the *strong reactions* (i.e., with a minimum score of 0.1), excluding the *neutral* label.

Sentiment Analysis. User sentiment was assessed through the 'twitter-roberta-base-sentiment'[2] model. The output of the model for each user message consisted of *neutral*, *positive*, and *negative* labels and their corresponding scores.

Streamers' Interaction Analysis: A topic analysis on the interviews' content was performed. The first part of the process entailed classifying the interactions into cognitive or emotional categories (as defined above). In the second part, we implemented keyword extraction and clustering methods using BERT embeddings and LDA method (although the latter didn't prove useful) (Table 1).

3 Results and Discussion

User Messages Analysis. The results showed that the majority of comments (57.7%) held a neutral sentiment, followed by positive comments (21.6%), which were slightly more prevalent than negative ones (20.7%). Instead, the emotions extracted were categorized into positive or negative (see Supplementary Material[3]). We observed that the number of positive reactions was almost double that of negative reactions. The predominant positive emotions identified from users' comments were curiosity, approval, and amusement, while the strong negative reactions were predominantly linked to emotions of confusion, disapproval, and annoyance. Such results suggest a positive and curious reaction in the online streaming community when the streamer interacts with AI.

[1] huggingface.co/SamLowe/roberta-base-go_emotions.

[2] huggingface.co/cardiffnlp/twitter-xlm-roberta-base-sentiment.

[3] Supplementary Material: 10.5281/zenodo.10819620.

Streamer Interactions Analysis. This phase involved analyzing the topics touched upon in streamers' interviews. The first part entailed classifying the 311 interactions into cognitive or emotional categories, finally labeling 46.2% of the interactions as Emotional and 53.8% as Cognitive. A comprehensive description of the touched topics is provided in the Supplementary Material (See footnote 3).

Statistical and Predictive Analysis. Statistical metrics show that cognitive ($M = 0.428$, $SD = 0.271$) and emotional ($M = 0.421$, $SD = 0.273$) interactions generated similar emotional intensity in user comments. The number of generated strong reactions was also similar in cognitive ($M=8.05$, $SD=9.51$) and emotional ($M = 7.30$, $SD = 8.34$) interactions, with a slightly higher mean - but not statistically significant difference - in the case of cognitive ones. Such results allow us to speculate that a novel AI model does not generate dominant reactions in the context of a live-streaming community. Finally, we conducted a predictive statistical analysis using linear regression on the number of high reactions for each interaction (80% train - 20% test). The results indicated that the number of comments was the only significant parameter (with a $p\text{-value} < 0.001$) explaining the predicted variable, while the topic discussed in the interview does not influence the prediction of reactions.

4 Conclusion and Future Works

We presented and evaluated a potential method for analyzing user reactions to AI using a crowd-based approach in a live-streaming setting, emphasizing the importance of collecting such reactions in a context as unbiased as possible (thus avoiding explicit requests or polls by researchers). We showed the advantage of using a new practice to grab spontaneous reactions and emotions of human-AI interaction, paving the way for future research in the field. Still, the usage of a live streaming platform allowed a diverse range of users to participate in the study, offering a familiar environment in which users can interact. However, the lack of a large and normalized dataset limited the application of advanced statistical and predictive methods able to elicit complex patterns, which would have been beneficial in understanding more of the ways users perceive and interact with AI. Future work may aim to overcome these limitations by: (1) conducting more live-streaming (or podcast) sessions based on English communities to reach a broader target audience; (2) include users from diverse cultural backgrounds; and (3) testing and comparing the reactions other AI models.

References

1. Davis, F.D.: Perceived usefulness, perceived ease of use, and user acceptance of information technology. MIS Q., 319–340 (1989)
2. Estellés-Arolas, E., González-Ladrón-de Guevara, F.: Towards an integrated crowdsourcing definition. J. Inf. Sci. **38**(2), 189–200 (2012)
3. Glikson, E., Woolley, A.W.: Human trust in artificial intelligence: review of empirical research. Acad. Manag. Ann. **14**(2), 627–660 (2020)
4. McAllister, D.J.: Affect-and cognition-based trust as foundations for interpersonal cooperation in organizations. Acad. Manag. J. **38**(1), 24–59 (1995)
5. Riedl, M.O.: Human-centered artificial intelligence and machine learning. Hum. Behav. Emerg. Technol. **1**(1), 33–36 (2019)
6. Tocchetti, A., Corti, L., Brambilla, M., Celino, I.: EXP-crowd: a gamified crowdsourcing framework for explainability. Front. Artif. Intell. **5**, 826499 (2022)

EMiGRe: Unveiling Why Your Recommendations are Not What You Expect

Herve-Madelein Attolou[1(✉)], Katerina Tzompanaki[1], Kostas Stefanidis[2], and Dimitris Kotzinos[1]

[1] ETIS, CY Cergy Paris University, ENSEA, CNRS UMR8051, Paris, France
herve-madelein.attolou@cyu.fr

[2] Tampere University, Tampere, Finland

Abstract. This demonstration showcases *EMiGRe*, a system tailored for computing explanations for *missing* recommendations in a graph-based recommendation system. The users can interact with the system through our intuitive visualization interface to navigate the graph, select their missing recommendations, choose their preferred explanation mode (add or remove user actions), and finally consume the explanations in textual or graphical form. n. Throughout, they are guided through important steps of *EMiGRe* (The source code for this demonstration is available here https://git.cyu.fr/hattolou/emigre_icwe2024) and useful statistics that clarify the scenario.

Keywords: Explanations · Graph-based Recommendation Systems · Why-Not questions · Explainable AI

1 Introduction

Recommendation Systems (RS) allow users to discover personalized content in vast data collections. Graph recommendation systems modelize entities (users, items, categories, etc.) as nodes and relationships (interactions) as edges. They rely on the number and types of connections among the nodes in order to produce the final recommendation list for a user of the system. In this way, users can more effectively explore the data space and find interesting items. Recommendations are frequently coupled with *explanations* - pieces of information that can justify the recommendations. In our graph-based RS, explanations can be modeled as (existing or absent) user-rooted actions (edges) that are responsible for the recommendation. Depending on whether the final recipient is a final user or a system developer, explanations can enhance the trust of the system, or help them debug it in case of non-desired behavior.

In this demonstration, we demonstrate *EMiGRe* [1], a *Why-Not* explanation system for graph-based recommenders. *Why-Not* explanations answer why the system failed to return an expected item in the recommendation list, and

K. Stefanidis et al. (Eds.): ICWE 2024, LNCS 14629, pp. 419–423, 2024.
https://doi.org/10.1007/978-3-031-62362-2_37

are extremely pertinent during the testing phase of the RS, advertisement campaigns, or fairness assessment.

As a use case, refer to Fig. 1. The example illustrates the case of Paul, who wonders why they are not recommended the book 'Harry Potter'. *EMiGRe* provides an *actionable Why-Not* explanation in the form of a set of edges (user actions) to be removed (Fig. 1(a)) or to be added (Fig. 1(b)) to the graph. More concretely, Fig. 1a provides the Why-Not explanation composed by two *past actions of the user*, and can be read as "Had you not interacted with 'Candide' and 'C', your top recommendation would be 'Harry Potter'.". Alternatively, Fig. 1b provides the Why-Not explanation composed by one *possible, future action* that the user can perform, and can be read as "Had you interacted with 'Lord of the Rings', your top recommendation would be 'Harry Potter'.".

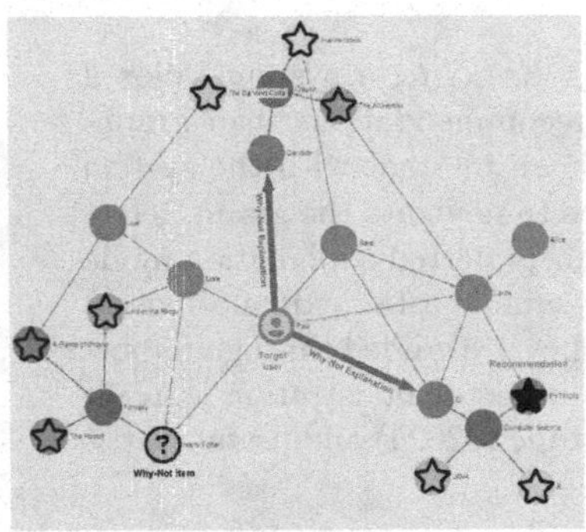

(a) Why-Not explanation (purple edges) in remove mode.

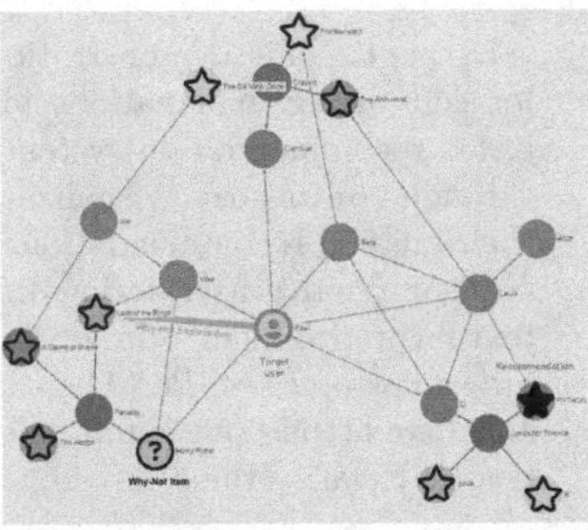

(b) Why-Not explanation (orange edge) in add mode.

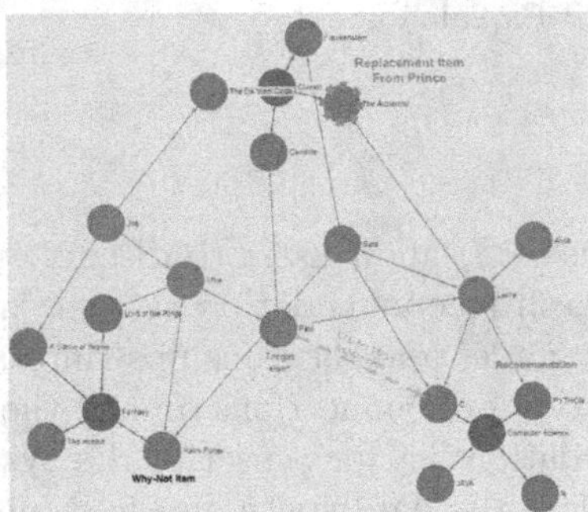

(c) Why-Explanation for Python (yellow edge).

Fig. 1. A graph book recommendation system with users (green), books (red), and book categories (purple). Paul is the target user, and nodes with stars denote the recommendation items, with the full star (*Python*) being the top recommendation. Paul wonders "Why-Not *Harry Potter* (node with a question mark)?". (Color figure online)

Related work (for instance [2]) has addressed mainly the *Why* Explanation problem. However, as we discuss in [1], Why and Why-Not Explanations are not equivalent. In Fig. 1c we can see that the Why explanation for the top-recommendation ('Python') provided by [2] is 'Had you not interacted with 'C', you would have been recommended 'The Alchemist'. It is evident that this is not a correct explanation for not obtaining 'Harry Potter'.

During this demonstration, the participants will have the opportunity to understand the problem of *Why-Not explanations* and how this differs from the *Why* counterpart. They will be guided through the steps of *EMiGRe*, while interacting with the system through an interactive and intuitive interface. Finally, they will be able to appreciate the nature of the 'actionable' explanations, by applying (removing or adding) the proposed actions in the Why-Not explanations. The demonstration is built on real-life and synthetic datasets.

2 System Description

EMiGRe is a Why-Not explanation framework tailored for graph-based recommenders. It uses the popular Personalized Page Rank algorithm [5] but can be adapted to other user-defined functions that compute the importance of a node for another node monotonically in the number of edges that connect the two nodes. In more detail, *EMiGRe* receives in the input the graph-based RS, a user, and an item that is not the top-1 recommendation for the user, to serve as the Why-Not (aka missing) recommendation. *EMiGRe* computes counterfactual-like explanations for the missing recommendation, in two modes. In the *Add* (*Remove*) mode, it proposes the edges to be added (*removed*) so that the missing recommendation appears at the top of the list. As multiple explanations may exist, *EMiGRe* additionally may operate in a computation-time or explanation-size optimization mode, returning either fast or short explanations. More details can be found in the research paper [1].

Implementation-wise, the back-end implements *EMiGRe* in Python[1] and uses Flask for the REST API. The front end is implemented with React and the Sigma.js library to manage and display the graph.

3 Demonstration

Attendees will be exposed to the Why-Not explanation problem in recommendations through predefined use cases designed on two real-world and synthetic datasets. They will also have the possibility to freely interact with the platform, defining their own scenarios.

The first use-case is an 'online' scenario on a small graph inspired by the Goodreads dataset [4]. The second use-case is an 'offline', simulated scenario featuring the Food.com [3] dataset. The selected scenarios showcase the different outcomes of the algorithm in both *Remove* and *Add* modes. We highlight

[1] https://git.cyu.fr/hattolou/why-not-explainable-graph-recommender.

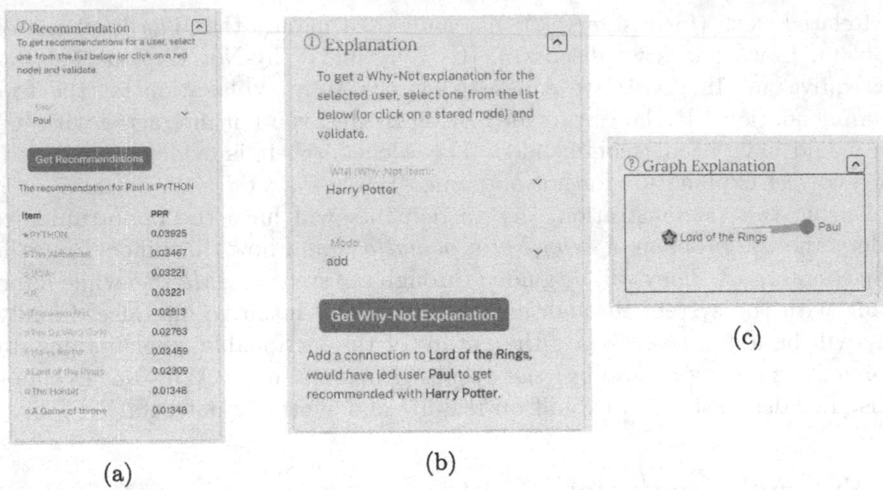

Fig. 2. Different panels of the demonstration interface. (a) Recommendation configuration and results panel. (b) Why-Not configuration and Text Explanation panel. (c) Graph Why-Not Explanation panel.

scenarios where (i) the smallest (one edge) explanation is available, (ii) when a more complex one is needed (multiple changes in the graph), and (iii) when a Why-Not explanation cannot be found.

3.1 Demonstration Scenario Example

First, the attendee is presented with a visualization of the dataset as a labeled graph with edges describing the relationship between items, users, and categories (as Fig. 1, ignoring the explanations). The graph is also going to be used in the later steps to display the follow-up recommendations and explanations graphically, but we exclude it in the figures to enhance the readability of the individual panels. In Fig. 2a, the attendee can select a target user via the recommendations panel (or by double-clicking the node in the original graph). Then, the personalized recommendations are displayed on the graph using the same heat-map color palette as on the result table on the recommendations panel (color corresponding to the Personalized Page Rank score (PPR) of the item). In Fig. 2b, the attendee can select the Why-Not item and the explanation mode (Add or Remove) via the explanations panel, where they also receive a text representation of the produced explanation. Finally, Fig. 2c displays the graph visualization of the explanation.

Acknowledgments. This work is partially supported by the National French Agency, under the EXPIDA - ANR-22-CE23-0017 project.

References

1. Attolou, H.M., Tzompanaki, K., Stefanidis, K., Kotzinos, D.: Why-not explainable graph recommender. In: ICDE (2024)
2. Ghazimatin, A., Balalau, O., Roy, R.S., Weikum, G.: PRINCE: provider-side interpretability with counterfactual explanations in recommender systems. In: WSDM (2020)
3. Li, S.: Food.com recipes and interactions (2019). https://www.kaggle.com/dsv/783630
4. Wan, M., Misra, R., Nakashole, N., McAuley, J.J.: Fine-grained spoiler detection from large-scale review corpora. In: ACL (2019)
5. Zhang, H., Lofgren, P., Goel, A.: Approximate personalized pagerank on dynamic graphs. In: SIGKDD. ACM (2016)

Handling Data Transformations in Virtual Knowledge Graphs with RML View Unfolding

Julián Arenas-Guerrero(✉)

Universidad Politécnica de Madrid, Madrid, Spain
julian.arenas.guerrero@upm.es

Abstract. Although declarative data transformation functions defined in RML-FNML were implemented in KG materialization systems, they have not yet been studied or implemented in virtual knowledge graph systems. In this work we propose to translate RML-FNML mapping to RML Views, which can be transparently used by virtual knowledge graph systems without modifying them. We implemented a research prototype of RML-FNML to RML Views unfolding and applied it to GTFS data to show the feasibility of the approach.

Keywords: RML · RML-FNML · Virtual Knowledge Graphs

1 Introduction

Public and private organizations usually store their data in relational database (RDB) management systems. However, the flexibility of RDBs is limited, and in some cases exploiting this data as knowledge graphs (KGs) can unlock additional value and further use cases. Virtual knowledge graphs [8] (VKGs) are a common approach to exploit relational data as KGs while maintaining the data in the RDB. To access the relational data with SPARQL, the most extended approach is to perform on-the-fly SPARQL-to-SQL query unfolding and delegating computation to the underlying database management system. VKGs are opposed to the materialization [1] approach in which an RDF dump is created from the RDB and then exploited using an RDF graph store. Virtualization presents the advantages of avoiding the costly materialization of RDF dumps, duplication of data (and the need for additional storage), and it also provides fresh results for queries (desirable in scenarios with highly dynamic data).

VKG systems typically use the R2RML [3] and RML [5] declarative mapping languages to describe schema transformations from the RDB to a target ontology. In addition to schema transformations, declarative data transformations [4] might also be needed in scenarios with messy data. RML-FNML [5] is the RML module for declarative data transformations, which has already been implemented in materialization systems by executing the transformations locally. However, query translation VKG systems push down computations to

K. Stefanidis et al. (Eds.): ICWE 2024, LNCS 14629, pp. 424–427, 2024.
https://doi.org/10.1007/978-3-031-62362-2_38

RDBs and avoid local computations as much as possible. To our knowledge, there is no VKG query translation system that supports RML-FNML or any proposal for handling them.

In this work, we address the problem of executing declarative data transformation functions in VKG systems defined with RML-FNML. Our proposal consists in unfolding RML-FNML to RML Views. This approach follows the traditional idea of query translation in which computations are delegated to the underlying RDB.

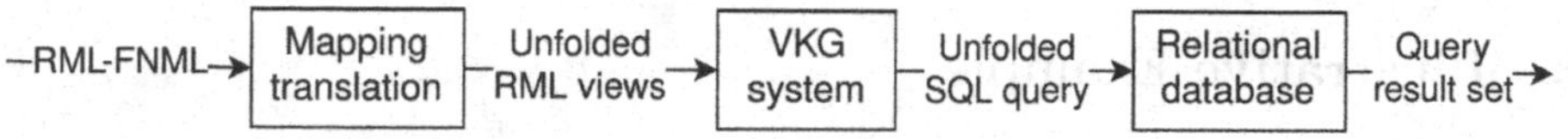

Fig. 1. Overview of the proposal. Data transformations defined in RML-FNML are unfolded to data transformations defined in RML Views. The mappings with RML Views are then used as input for VKG systems which perform SPARQL-to-SQL query translation.

2 RML-FNML to RML View Translation

Data transformations in VKG systems have traditionally been defined in R2RML and RML using views. Indeed, the W3C R2RML Recommendation endorses encoding data transformation as R2RML Views[1]. An [R2]RML view is an SQL query that obtains the input data for a mapping rule. Figure 1 depicts the overview of our proposed solution which consists in unfolding data transformations specified in RML-FNML into RML Views which can then be used by VKG systems. Mapping translation from RML-FNML to RML Views is performed as a preprocessing step in the VKG pipeline. This can be implemented as an auxiliary task in the *starting phase* [7] of VKG systems. The unfolded mappings with RML Views can then be used as input for VKG systems. The approach is transparent for VKG systems, which do not need to interpret RML-FNML. It also presents the advantage of pushing down computations to RDBs, which are widely studied systems likely to efficiently perform the data transformations.

The mapping translation step is similar to the execution of RML-FNML in materialization systems, but instead of transforming the data, the functions transform the effective SQL queries[2] in the mappings. Functions can be divided into two categories: (i) *transformations* (e.g., converting strings to lowercase), and (ii) *filtering*, which correspond to the selection operator (σ) in the relational algebra. In Sect. 3 we show an example of these functions and their unfolding.

It is worth mentioning the FunMap [6] approach for executing data transformation in the materialization approach. FunMap applies the data transformation in the mappings to the heterogeneous data sources and removes the functions in

[1] https://www.w3.org/TR/r2rml/#dfn-r2rml-view.
[2] https://www.w3.org/TR/r2rml/#dfn-effective-sql-query.

the mappings. Function-free mappings and transformed data sources can then be used with an [R2]RML materialization system (which does not need to support RML-FNML) to perform schema transformations. The FunMap approach transforms mappings and data (which may become a bottleneck when processing large volumes of data) before using an [R2]RML materialization system, while ours only translates mappings before using the [R2]RML virtualization system. FunMap is suitable for materialization, but not for virtualization. Our proposal focuses on virtualization (since many materialization systems already support RML-FNML), and can also be applied in materialization.

3 Illustrative Example

```
<#frequencies>
 rml:logicalSource [
  rml:source "FREQUENCIES" ] ;
 rml:subjectMap [ rml:template
   "http://linkeddata.es/madrid/metro/
    frequency/{trip_id}-{start_time}";];
 rml:predicateObjectMap [
  rml:predicate gtfs:exactTimes ;
   rml:objectMap [
    fnml:execution <#frequenciesExe1> ;
    rml:datatype xsd:boolean ] ; ] .

<#frequenciesExe1>
 fnml:function grel:string_replace ;
 fnml:input
   [ fnml:parameter grel:valueParam ;
     fnml:valueMap [
      fnml:execution <#frequenciesExe2>]],
   [ fnml:parameter grel:value_find ;
     fnml:value "1" ] ,
   [ fnml:parameter grel:value_replace ;
     fnml:value "true" ] .

<#frequenciesExe2>
 fnml:function grel:controls_filter ;
 fnml:input
  [ fnml:parameter grel:param_a ;
    fnml:valueMap [
      rml:reference "exact_times" ] ] ,
  [ fnml:parameter grel:uri_value ;
    fnml:value "1" ] .
```

Listing 1: RML-FNML mapping that transforms boolean "*1s*" into the RDF "*true*" form.

```
<#frequencies>
 rml:logicalSource [
  rml:query """
   SELECT trip_id, start_time,
      REPLACE(
        CAST(exact_times AS VARCHAR),
        '1', 'true')
      AS v2d2bb5b65c
   FROM FREQUENCIES
   WHERE exact_times='1'
  """ ] ;
 rml:subjectMap [ rml:template
 "http://linkeddata.es/madrid/metro/
  frequency/{trip_id}-{start_time}";];
 rml:predicateObjectMap [
  rml:predicate gtfs:exactTimes ;
   rml:objectMap [
    rml:reference "v2d2bb5b65c" ;
    rml:datatype xsd:boolean ] ; ] .
```

Listing 2: Translated mapping in Listing 1 with RML Views. It unfolds `grel:string_replace` into the `REPLACE` SQL function and `grel:controls_filter` into the `WHERE` clause in SQL.

We use General Transit Feed Specification (GTFS) [2] data to illustrate our proposal. Boolean values in GTFS are encoded as "*0s*" and "*1s*", which must be transformed into the value space of `xsd:boolean` ("*true*" and "*false*" values). This can be done with data transformations in RML-FNML. Listing 1 depicts an RML-FNML mapping that transforms "*1s*" in the `exact_times` column of the `FREQUENCIES` table to "*true*". To do this, the values in a column are first filtered (with `grel:controls_filter`) to keep only those values equal to "*1*"; then these values are replaced (`grel:string_replace`) with "*true*". Listing 2 shows the unfolded mapping with RML Views. The function `grel:string_replace` is unfolded into the `REPLACE` SQL function and `grel:controls_filter` into the `WHERE` clause in SQL. The translation of "*0s*" to "*false*" can be done in a similar manner.

We implemented a research prototype for translating RML-FNML into RML Views and made it openly available in GitHub[3].

Acknowledgments. This work received partial financial support in the frame of the Euratom Research and Training Programme 2019–2020 under grant agreement No 900018 (ENTENTE project).

References

1. Arenas-Guerrero, J., et al.: Knowledge graph construction with R2RML and RML: an ETL system-based overview. In: Proceedings of the 2nd International Workshop on Knowledge Graph Construction, vol. 2873. CEUR Workshop Proceedings (2021). http://ceur-ws.org/Vol-2873/paper11.pdf
2. Chaves-Fraga, D., Priyatna, F., Cimmino, A., Toledo, J., Ruckhaus, E., Corcho, O.: GTFS-Madrid-bench: a benchmark for virtual knowledge graph access in the transport domain. J. Web Semant. **65**, 100596 (2020). https://doi.org/10.1016/j.websem.2020.100596
3. Das, S., Sundara, S., Cyganiak, R.: R2RML: RDB to RDF Mapping Language. W3C Recommendation, World Wide Web Consortium (W3C) (2012). http://www.w3.org/TR/r2rml/
4. De Meester, B., Seymoens, T., Dimou, A., Verborgh, R.: Implementation-independent function reuse. Futur. Gener. Comput. Syst. **110**, 946–959 (2020). https://doi.org/10.1016/j.future.2019.10.006
5. Iglesias-Molina, A., et al.: The RML ontology: a community-driven modular redesign after a decade of experience in mapping heterogeneous data to RDF. In: Payne, T.R., et al. (eds.) ISWC 2023. LNCS, pp. 152–175. Springer, Cham (2023). https://doi.org/10.1007/978-3-031-47243-5_9
6. Jozashoori, S., Chaves-Fraga, D., Iglesias, E., Vidal, M.-E., Corcho, O.: FunMap: efficient execution of functional mappings for knowledge graph creation. In: Pan, J.Z., et al. (eds.) ISWC 2020. LNCS, vol. 12506, pp. 276–293. Springer, Cham (2020). https://doi.org/10.1007/978-3-030-62419-4_16
7. Lanti, D., Rezk, M., Xiao, G., Calvanese, D.: The NPD benchmark: reality check for OBDA systems. In: Proceedings of the 18th International Conference on Extending Database Technology, pp. 617–628. OpenProceedings.org (2015). https://doi.org/10.5441/002/edbt.2015.62
8. Xiao, G., Ding, L., Cogrel, B., Calvanese, D.: Virtual knowledge graphs: an overview of systems and use cases. Data Intell. **1**(3), 201–223 (2019). https://doi.org/10.1162/dint_a_00011

[3] https://github.com/arenas-guerrero-julian/fnml-translator.

MyLearningTalk: An LLM-Based Intelligent Tutoring System

Ludovica Piro(✉), Tommaso Bianchi, Luca Alessandrelli, Andrea Chizzola, Daniela Casiraghi, Susanna Sancassani, and Nicola Gatti

Dipartimento di Elettronica Informazione e Bioingegneria, Politecnico di Milano, 20133 Milan, Italy
{ludovica.piro,tommaso.bianchi,luca.alessandrelli,daniela.casiraghi, susanna.sancassani,nicola.gatti}@polimi.it,
andrea.chizzola@mail.polimi.it

Abstract. Thanks to recent advancements in natural language interaction, dialogue-based online Intelligent Tutoring Systems (ITS) employing Large Language Models (LLMs) have begun to emerge. However, the effective design of LLM-based ITS interfaces to support learning still requires attention. In this demo, we present the initial implementation of *MyLearningTalk* (MLT), a web-based ITS powered by LLMs. MLT exploits state-of-the-art techniques such as retrieval augmented generation to offer interactive features to provide users with grounded answers and a tailored experience to enhance and facilitate the learning process.

Keywords: Web User Interfaces · Intelligent Tutoring Systems · LLMs

1 Introduction

Intelligent tutoring systems aid students in learning thanks to individually tailored dialogue and learning paths. Research has shown that they have a positive impact on learning thanks to the possibility of customizing instructional activities based on students' characteristics and needs. Artificial Intelligence is widely used in this field, to tailor the experience, deliver feedback, generate personalized quizzes or aid in grading and evaluating students [9].

LLMs based dialogue systems allow users to express their requests without the typical constraints of conversational agents built on defined sets of intents. In the last year, the integration of LLMs into ITSs has gained traction. However, dialogue tutoring systems have remained mostly unaffected by this advancement. By incorporating LLMs, ITSs could benefit from unprecedented adaptive capabilities allowing them to deliver learning experiences customized on individual students' needs, ultimately bettering students' academic performances. However, there are many open questions regarding the design of this kind of systems in terms of interaction design as well as pedagogical strategies [7].

This demo presents MyLearningTalk, a web-based ITS leveraging LLMs to deliver a tailored learning experience to university students. We present its architecture and the interface's design rationale focusing on the pedagogical strategies leveraged to support effective learning.

K. Stefanidis et al. (Eds.): ICWE 2024, LNCS 14629, pp. 428–431, 2024.
https://doi.org/10.1007/978-3-031-62362-2_39

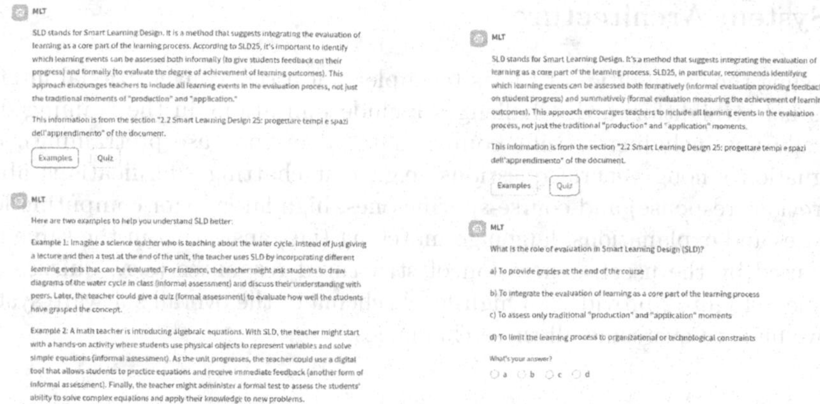

Fig. 1. Screen-capture of MLT demonstrating the Example and Quiz features.

2 Interface Design

MLT follows a conversational paradigm. The conversational interaction with the tutoring agent (shown in Fig. 1) is supported by graphical components, such as the *Example* and *Quiz* buttons to give visibility and on-demand access to specific learning devices, which are included in the system. With dialogue systems, indeed, users have less control over the interaction as well as a more limited understanding of its capabilities. Moreover, while dialogue allows for an engaging and adaptable form of learning, it is not sufficient for effective learning. Thus, it is crucial to include multiple pedagogical strategies to give students different ways to reflect on known information and integrate new knowledge.

To start, users are guided by system prompts suggesting topics of interest and possible starter questions. Once users start chatting, they can engage with the system using natural language, expressing questions and requests in their preferred language. Employing the user's native language, in fact, enhances comprehension and aids information retention. Each system message is paired with the *examples* and *quiz* buttons.

Examples. By using examples, learners can understand difficult concepts by relating them to familiar contexts, making abstract concepts easier to understand [11]. By providing real-world applications of theoretical concepts, examples promote analogical thinking, particularly valuable in complex domains [4], and engagement, increasing students' interest and motivation to learn [3].

Quizzes. The use of quizzes, instead, enhances the understanding of complex concepts through effective feedback, providing guidance on correct answers, clarifying misconceptions, and suggesting sources for further exploration. By requiring students to retrieve information, quizzes also support durable learning [12] and the adaptation of acquired knowledge to new situations.

3 System Architecture

Leveraging the capabilities of LLMs to implement a rich conversational interaction is not straightforward. Challenges include limitations in the training data (typically not including specific course material in the base pretraining), disambiguation among general questions (e.g., chit chatting, clarifications about the previous response) and course-specific ones, high latency for computing long responses and explanations, language matching (i.e., answering in the same language used by the user), generation of structured responses (e.g., quizzes and examples). Figure 2 provides an high-level schema of the overall software system that we built to overcome all these challenges.

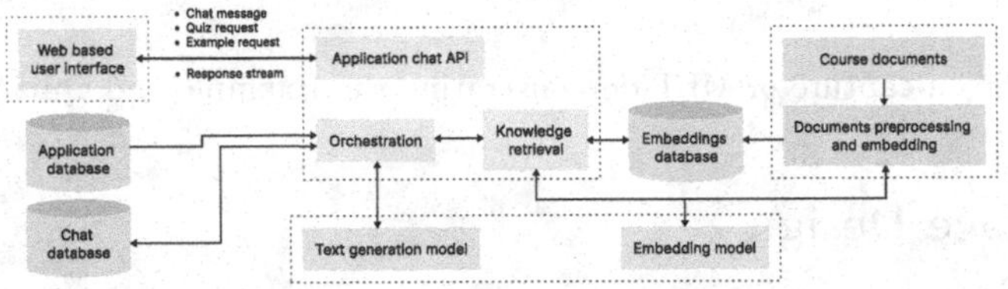

Fig. 2. MLT software architecture.

Document Pre-processing Pipeline. Documents corresponding to course material (i.e., book chapters, lecture notes, video transcriptions) are preprocessed to then be used for enriching the LLM context in order to overcome limitations in training data. The pipeline consists in extrapolating the schematic representations of knowledge within the documents [13], partitioning the documents in chunks and embedding [2,8] such chunks in a vector space for later retrieval. This step – known in the literature as Retrieval Augmented Generation or RAG [6,10] – is crucial to ensure that the system is able to give factual and grounded responses, as well as references to the course material.

Response Orchestration. The access to the underlying foundational AI capabilities is mediated in a significant way by our backend, which coordinates both the retrieval of content from the embeddings database, the reconstruction of the chat history from the chat database (which holds messages exchanged between the students and the assistant indefinitely, unless removal is requested by students), and the implementation of the learning interaction. To ensure low perceived latency in providing answers to user queries, responses are streamed as they are generated. This enables us to deliver results to the user within seconds, even when the whole answer takes a minute or more to be produced.

Deployment Details. The system is designed to leverage two classes of models: text generation models and embedding models, both accessed through APIs. Currently, we use the GPT4 models [1] as text generation models, and the Ada 2 model [5] as embedding model; both are provided by OpenAI in its cloud platform. The demo system's components are all deployed in the cloud, to ensure high performance, high availability and low maintenance costs.

4 Conclusions and Future Work

In this work, we present MyLearningTalk, a web-based ITS employing a LLM within a novel and unified system architecture. We advocate for the importance of going beyond dialogue design as well as focusing on user control and designing appropriate features to support learning and enhance students' understanding of the subject. Future work will focus on consolidating the features already present and expand user control over the course material by introducing navigation mechanisms and content maps to give students proper tools to track their advancements in the learning experience. Finally, we will be conducting a large scale user study to evaluate the tool's design and impact on students' learning.

Acknowledgement. This paper is supported by PNRR-PE-AI FAIR project funded by the NextGeneration EU program.

References

1. Achiam, J., et al.: GPT-4 technical report. arXiv preprint arXiv:2303.08774 (2023)
2. Bengio, Y., Ducharme, R., Vincent, P.: A neural probabilistic language model. In: Advances in Neural Information Processing Systems, vol. 13 (2000)
3. Carroll, W.M.: Using worked examples as an instructional support in the algebra classroom. J. Educ. Psychol. **86**, 360–367 (1994)
4. Gentner, D., Loewenstein, J., Thompson, L.: Learning and transfer: a general role for analogical encoding. J. Educ. Psychol. **95**, 393–408 (2003)
5. Greene, R., Sanders, T., Weng, L., Neelakantan, A.: New and improved embedding model. https://openai.com/blog/new-and-improved-embedding-model/. Accessed 26 Mar 2024
6. Karpukhin, V., et al.: Dense passage retrieval for open-domain question answering. arXiv preprint arXiv:2004.04906 (2020)
7. Macina, J., et al.: Opportunities and challenges in neural dialog tutoring (2023)
8. Mikolov, T., Chen, K., Corrado, G., Dean, J.: Efficient estimation of word representations in vector space. arXiv preprint arXiv:1301.3781 (2013)
9. Paladines, J., Ramirez, J.: A systematic literature review of intelligent tutoring systems with dialogue in natural language. IEEE Access **8**, 164246–164267 (2020)
10. Petroni, F., et al.: How context affects language models' factual predictions. arXiv preprint arXiv:2005.04611 (2020)
11. Renkl, A.: Toward an instructionally oriented theory of example-based learning. Cogn. Sci. **38**(1), 1–37 (2014)
12. Roediger, H.L., III., Agarwal, P.K., McDaniel, M.A., McDermott, K.B.: Test-enhanced learning in the classroom: long-term improvements from quizzing. J. Exp. Psychol. Appl. **17**, 382–395 (2011)
13. Saad-Falcon, J., et al.: PDFTriage: question answering over long, structured documents. arXiv preprint arXiv:2309.08872 (2023)

PhD Symposium

Dynamic Hybrid Recommendation System for E-Commerce: Overcoming Challenges of Sparse Data and Anonymity

Kailash Chowdary Bodduluri[1(✉)], Arianit Kurti[1], Francis Palma[2], Ilir Jusufi[3], and Henrik Löwenadler[4]

[1] Linnaeus University, Universitetsplatsen 1, 35252 Växjö, Sweden
kailashchowdary.bodduluri@lnu.se
[2] SE+AI Lab, Faculty of Computer Science, University of New Brunswick, Fredericton, Canada
[3] Blekinge Institute of Technology, 37179 Karlskrona, Sweden
[4] Enode, 35230 Växjö, Sweden

Abstract. In the evolving landscape of e-commerce, personalizing user experience through recommendation systems has become a way to boost user satisfaction and engagement. However, small-scale e-commerce platforms struggle with significant challenges, including data sparsity and user anonymity. These issues make it hard to effectively implement recommendation systems, resulting in difficulty in recommending the right products to users. This study introduces an innovative Hybrid Recommendation System (HRS) to address challenges in e-commerce personalization caused by data sparsity and user anonymity. By blending multiple dimensions of the data into one unified system for producing recommendations, this system represents a notable advancement in web engineering for achieving personalized user experiences in the context of limited data. This research emphasizes the significance of innovative and tech-driven solutions in transforming small-scale e-commerce platforms, providing direction for future research and development in the field.

Keywords: Hybrid Recommendation System · E-Commerce · Epsilon-Greedy · Sparse Data

1 Introduction

In the current digital age, the widespread presence of the web in our daily lives has become a source of extensive digital traces left by users through their interactions online. These traces, when harnessed effectively, transform into valuable commodities for businesses, offering unprecedented opportunities to understand and cater to individual preferences. This phenomenon has particularly revolutionized the e-commerce sector, where the ability to personalize user experience and optimize product visibility has become crucial. Despite the advancement in web technologies and the proliferation of data analytics, e-commerce platforms face significant challenges in leveraging this wealth of digital traces due to issues such as data sparsity and cold start [5].

K. Stefanidis et al. (Eds.): ICWE 2024, LNCS 14629, pp. 435–440, 2024.
https://doi.org/10.1007/978-3-031-62362-2_40

1.1 Problem Statement

In e-commerce, most recommendation systems rely on user ratings and reviews [1], which poses challenges for small-scale companies. Acquiring sufficient ratings is difficult due to low engagement and user reluctance [5], hindering the implementation of recommendation systems. Additionally, user identification is problematic, with many users avoiding providing personal information, further complicating the issue. The absence of user data not only limits personalized recommendations but also hampers effective recommendation system implementation.

1.2 Research Question

Given these challenges, our study seeks to answer the pivotal question: *How can we develop a recommendation system tailored to address the challenges posed by data sparsity and user anonymity?*

To address this question, we introduced a dynamic and innovative hybrid recommendation system (HRS) that combines three modules into one framework: leveraging image and description similarities, analyzing historical purchase data, and tracking user interactions. Through a weighted hybrid methodology and an epsilon-greedy algorithm, it addresses challenges in sparse data and user anonymity while setting a new benchmark for personalized recommendations.

2 Related Work

The integration of recommendation systems within e-commerce platforms represents a critical intersection of web engineering and data science, aiming to refine user experience and engagement across digital marketplaces [8]. Research emphasizes scalable, efficient systems adaptable to the web's dynamic nature [9], highlighting challenges such as the cold-start problem and robust user identification, especially for small-scale businesses with limited data. Our Hybrid Recommendation System (HRS) addresses these challenges by combining image and description similarities with historical purchase analysis and user behaviour patterns. Key contributions include the unification of image and description-based recommendations, inspired by similar works such as Alamdari et al. [2] and Shrivastava et al. [4], who focused on image and description similarity, respectively. Additionally, our HRS employs Minhash to analyze user behaviour and the epsilon-greedy algorithm to balance recommendation exploration and exploitation. This technique, alongside the incorporation of various methodologies such as those explored by Beleveslis and Dimosthenis [10], allows for a robust and adaptable hybrid system.

3 Proposed Hybrid Recommendation System

This section identifies our research objectives and introduces our proposed hybrid recommendation system.

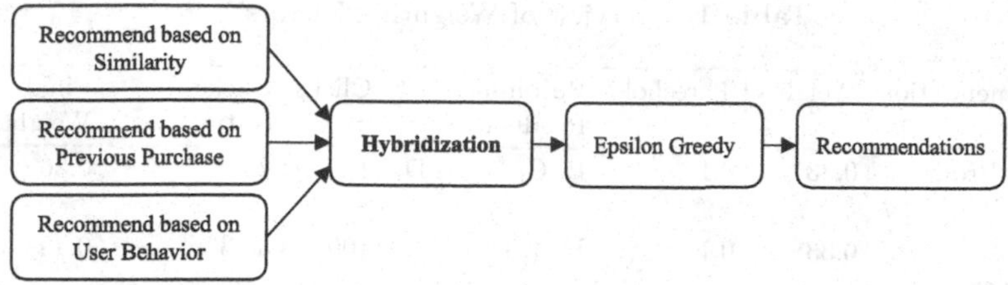

Fig. 1. Architecture of the proposed HRS.

3.1 Aims and Objectives

The primary aim of our proposed HRS is to address the unique challenges faced by e-commerce businesses, specifically in scenarios where data is sparse, and user identification is complex. The objectives include developing an innovative HRS utilizing image and description similarities, historical purchase patterns, and user behaviour analysis. This system aims to harmonize these modules through a weighted hybrid methodology and introduce an epsilon-greedy algorithm for balanced recommendations. Our proposed HRS integrates three distinct modules to generate recommendations as shown in Fig. 1, employing a weighted approach to hybridize these modules. It is important to note that all data sources, such as product images, product descriptions, purchase history, and user interactions, used to build the HRS originate from the same store where the recommendation system is deployed.

3.2 Three Different Recommendation Modules Used

The HRS comprises individual modules that can function as stand-alone approaches. However, the hybrid approach for recommendations has demonstrated itself as the most effective strategy for enhancing the profits of e-commerce owners [6]. We explore the three recommendation modules in the following.

Recommending Products Based on Similarity: The implementation involves a four-level approach: (1) determining similarity using images, (2) identifying similarity based on product descriptions, (3) combining results from image and description similarities, and (4) optimizing through a Click-Through Rate (CTR) optimization algorithm, termed as the Image-Description CTR Combination (IDCC) module.

The image similarity aspect involves converting main images into features using a tuned version of VGG-16, selected based on the study by Alamdari et al. [2] as VGG-16 is capable of accurately predicting similar product images in the context of large-scale data. Principal Component Analysis (PCA) reduces feature size, and Euclidean distance is used to determine similarity between products. The description similarity utilizes a refined BERT called eComBERT which has

Table 1. Overview of Weighting Factors.

Recommendation Module	Weights	Threshold	Recommended Products	Clicks	Clicks Ratio	Final Weights
Similar Products	0.33	0.1	B, C, E, G, D, F	150	25	0.36
Previous Purchases	0.33	0.1	H, J, I	100	33.3	0.49
Personalization	0.33	0.1	L, K, F, T, R	50	10	0.15

the capability to deeply understand the e-commerce domain and place the similar products closer [3]. Additionally, PCA is used for feature size reduction and cosine similarity for assessing similarity. The recommendations from both setups are combined by considering the distances calculated for products. In addition to combining similarity setups, CTR optimization is introduced. CTR, measuring the ratio of users who click on a link to total views, influences the ranking of recommended products [11]. Products with higher CTR values secure top positions in the recommendations list.

Recommending Products Based on Previous Purchases: To identify frequently bought product pairs, a straightforward SQL function was employed. The process involves determining frequently bought products concerning the currently viewed product and obtaining their respective frequency counts. Products exhibiting high-frequency counts are subsequently recommended to users.

Recommending Products Based on User Behaviour: During a user's interaction with the e-commerce webpage, comprehensive sessions are recorded, capturing events such as clicks, purchases, items added to the cart, and more. This data is organized into sessions, each assigned a unique ID to distinguish individual users. To identify users with similar behaviours, we utilize these recorded website sessions. Minhash, a technique employed for estimating similarity between two datasets, is widely applied in recommendation systems to reveal analogous users or content [7].

3.3 Hybridization

Recommendations generated from the three modules are combined using a weighted approach, presenting the most favourable recommendations to the user.

Table 1 shows the recommended products corresponding to A from all three modules while a user is browsing product A. In this hybrid approach, an initial weight of 0.33 is assigned to each module (second column), and a threshold of 0.1 is set to prevent the weight from becoming 0 (third column). The weights are updated based on the click ratio. Each product receives a weight when substituted into Eq. 1; let X be a recommended product.

$$\text{Product X: } \sum_{i=1}^{3}(\text{Weight}_i \times \text{Final Weights}_i) \tag{1}$$

We substitute the weights for product F into Eq. 1 as follows:

$$\text{Product F: } (0.36 \times 1) + (0.49 \times 0) + (0.15 \times 1) = 0.51$$

The substitution process is iteratively applied to all products, prioritizing those with higher weights for user presentation. As shown in Table 1, there are several products recommended by all three modules, each with its own weight assigned based on the click ratio. Initially, each product receives the weight of its respective module, which is then augmented with the weight of other modules if the product is also recommended by them. For instance, product F receives a weight of 0.51 as it is recommended by both the "Similar Products" and "Personalization" modules, which have weights of 0.36 and 0.51, respectively. After substituting all the products from Table 1 into Eq. 1, the recommended ordered list is as follows: F, H, J, I, B, C, E, G, D, L, K, T, R.

3.4 Epsilon Greedy

One major issue in recommendation systems is their tendency to overlook the exploration of new recommendations. To address this concern, we implemented the epsilon-greedy function-a strategy designed to balance exploring new recommendations and exploiting known preferences. This strategy, using a small value called "epsilon," balances between exploring new recommendations and exploiting known preferences. During exploration, a random recommendation is generated with a probability of epsilon, facilitating the discovery of new items aligned with user interests. Conversely, during exploitation, the system leans towards known preferences based on historical data.

4 Current State and Roadmap

This research is part of an industrial doctoral project addressing challenges faced by small-scale e-commerce businesses in implementing recommendation systems due to insufficient data and cold start issues. The project spans five years, and we are currently in the beginning of the third year. Currently, the entire recommendation system has been developed, and discussions are underway with potential clients for applying the HRS and for real-time testing. The next steps involve applying the HRS on a potential e-commerce client, fine-tuning it until satisfactory results are achieved and evaluate the HRS. Following the completion of the evaluation, the focus will shift towards enhancing personalization in recommendation systems, educating e-commerce clients on the significance of user feedback and data quality, and incorporating third-party data for recommendations.

5 Contributions to Web Engineering

Our proposed HRS, developed in response to the challenges faced by e-commerce businesses, contributes significantly to web engineering in the following ways. The system amalgamates three distinct recommendation modules ensuring personalized and context-aware recommendations. By introducing an epsilon-greedy algorithm, the system strikes a balance between exploring novel suggestions and exploiting known user preferences, enhancing adaptability and accuracy. The proposed HRS, prepared for real-time testing, holds the potential to set a new benchmark for recommendation systems in e-commerce environments, offering a roadmap for continual improvement and adaptation to evolving user needs.

References

1. Ko, H., Lee, S., Park, Y., Choi, A.: A survey of recommendation systems: recommendation models, techniques, and application fields. Electronics **11**(1), 141 (2022). https://doi.org/10.3390/electronics11010141
2. Alamdari, P.M., Navimipour, N.J., Hosseinzadeh, M., Safaei, A.A., Darwesh, A.: An image-based product recommendation for E-commerce applications using convolutional neural networks. Acta Informatica Pragensia **11**(1), 15–35 (2022)
3. Tracz, J., Wójcik, P.I., Jasinska-Kobus, K., Belluzzo, R., Mroczkowski, R., Gawlik, I.: BERT-based similarity learning for product matching. In: Proceedings of Workshop on Natural Language Processing in E-Commerce, pp. 66–75 (2020)
4. Rasyid, I., Yudianto, M.R.A., Maimunah, M., Purnomo, T.A.: Electronic Product Recommendation System Using the Cosine Similarity Algorithm and VGG-16. Sinkron (2023). https://api.semanticscholar.org/CorpusID:263615126
5. Yang, Q.: Research on E-commerce Customer Satisfaction Evaluation Method Based on PSO-LSTM and Text Mining. 3C Empresa. Investigación y pensamiento crítico (2023). https://api.semanticscholar.org/CorpusID:258248872
6. Gupta, G., Newase, A.D.: Hybrid recommendation system for better mining rules generation of user and consumer data. BSSS J. Comput. (2020). https://api.semanticscholar.org/CorpusID:234700217
7. Mala, R.: Classifying User Predilections using Naïve Bayes Classifier (NBC) and Jaccard Similarity for Service Recommender System in Big Data Applications (2017). https://api.semanticscholar.org/CorpusID:212562902
8. Silvester, S., Kurian, S.: Recommendation systems: enhancing personalization and customer experience. In: 2023 3rd International Conference on Smart Generation Computing, Communication and Networking (SMART GENCON), Bangalore, India, pp. 1–6 (2023). https://doi.org/10.1109/SMARTGENCON60755.2023.10442402
9. Shahabi, C., Banaei-Kashani, F., Chen, Y.-S., McLeod, D.: Yoda: an accurate and scalable web-based recommendation system. In: Batini, C., Giunchiglia, F., Giorgini, P., Mecella, M. (eds.) CoopIS 2001. LNCS, vol. 2172, pp. 418–432. Springer, Heidelberg (2001). https://doi.org/10.1007/3-540-44751-2_31
10. Beleveslis, D.: Heuristic Approach for Content Based Recommendation System Based on Feature Weighting and LSH (2020)
11. Jeon, M.: A study on CTR (click through ratio) in relation to product involvement for keyword search advertising strategy in E-commerce. Korea Int. Trade Res. Inst. **13**, 543–562 (2017). https://api.semanticscholar.org/CorpusID:168790208

Model-Driven Development of Single Page Applications

Alexander Müller-Lobeck(✉) and Gefei Zhang

Hochschule für Technik und Wirtschaft, Berlin, Germany
{lobeck,gefei.zhang}@htw-berlin.de

Abstract. Prevalent approaches to Model-Driven Web Engineering focus on traditional, hypertext-based web applications, but do not scale well for modern, single page applications (SPAs), where the functionalities are rather reflected by changes of their HTML elements' properties and dependencies between them than hypertext structures and navigation paths. In the realm of SPAs, modeling, formal model validation, and code generation need better support. We propose an approach to the model-driven development of SPAs. We model the behavior of SPAs with UML state machines and translate these to JavaScript as well as a formal specification, which can be formally verified. Our approach thus provides an intuitive and easy-to-use means, which is backed by formal methods, to model-driven development of SPAs.

1 Introduction

Prevalent approaches (see [14,15] for an overview) to Model-Driven Web Engineering (MDWE) focus on traditional, hypertext-based web applications. Consequently, their models mainly address the aspects hyptertext structure and navigation paths of the web application. The presentation aspect, the key aspect of modern, single page applications (SPAs), however, is supported only in a rather abstract manner. While interactive GUI is considered in approaches (see [16]) concerning Rich Internet Applications (RIAs), the modeling support is not fine granular enough to express the different states of HTML widget. Moreover, modeling techniques for interactions between HTML widgets, formal validation of the models, and code generation also need better support.

In the planned PhD research of the first author, we aim to develop a method of model-driven development of SPAs. From a UML state machine model of the application, we generate JavaScript code and a formal model in a formal specification language such as Maude [5], so that desired properties of the SPA can be formally verified. Our approach thus allows us to verify that the SPA "does the right thing".

The basic idea of the approach is illustrated in Fig. 1: The developer models the behavior of the SPA with a UML state machine and verifies that it does have the desired properties with formal methods. They then develop a simple prototype of the application, in which only the layout of the application, but

K. Stefanidis et al. (Eds.): ICWE 2024, LNCS 14629, pp. 441–447, 2024.
https://doi.org/10.1007/978-3-031-62362-2_41

not its behavior is defined. That is, the prototype contains HTML and CSS, and only minimum skeletons for JavaScript functions. These functions will then be generated automatically from the state machine. In Fig. 1, the solid line arrows refer to the automated part of the process that is provided by our method.

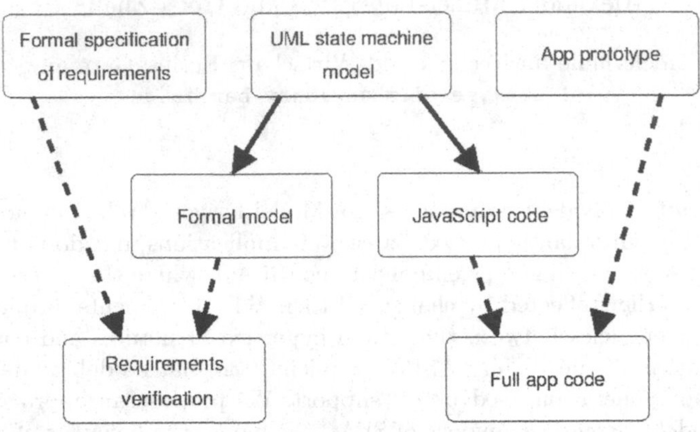

Fig. 1. Overview of the development process

The remainder of this paper is organized as follows: In Sect. 2 we discuss the current state of the art in this area. Then we explain our research proposal in more details and show our preliminary results as well as a tentative plan for the future in Sect. 3. Finally, conclusions are drawn in Sect. 4.

2 Related Work

Model-driven engineering of web applications has a long history (see [14,15]). Established approaches like WebML/IFML [3,12], UWE [9] or WAVE [3] focus mainly on the navigation structure of web applications rather than presentation elements, and, unlike our approach, do not include the attributes of the HTML widgets' visual appearance. These are considered in some RIA-modeling approaches (see [16]), but only rudimentarily. Consequently, model verification (see [8] for an example) and code generation is only provided for the navigation structure, but not for the dynamic properties of the presentation, which, however, is exactly the part of SPAs which realizes their behavior.

UML state machines are very well-suited for modeling reactive systems, and provide an excellent base for both generating application code and formal specifications to undergo model verification. There are a number of approaches for turning UML state machines into code. The target language is C++ in [13] and [1] and Java in [4,6,7,11,17]. Model-checking UML state machines via Promela/SPIN is provided in [7]. None of these is concerned with web applications or has a web application framework, like Vue.js (https://vuejs.org/), as their target.

Formal validation of SPAs is also supported by [18], which uses Temporal Logic of Action (TLA$^+$, [10]) for doing this. In comparison, the planned PhD research also includes Maude [5] to allow for verification by rewriting instead of temporal logic. Also, we extend the approach of [18] by modeling SPAs with UML state machines, as well as algorithms for deriving a formal specification and JavaScript code from the model.

Compared with low-code approaches (see [2]), our approach proposes a more rigorous modeling, uses a standard modeling language (UML), separates the UI design from the program logic, and provides model-to-formal-model translation to enable model verification.

3 Research Proposal and Preliminary Results

The basic idea is to develop an SPA by a template that only implements the UI elements and model their behavior by a UML state machine diagram. From that, we generate the event handler code in JavaScript and a formal model in a formal specification language, which then can be used to verify the model. Thus we make sure that the application will do "the right thing".

We use an example to explain our approach: suppose we want to develop a calculator as an SPA. The calculator should be "smart" in the sense that only those buttons are enabled that may lead to a valid arithmetic expression. For example, in the Screenshot given in Fig. 2, where the user has already input the string `"(1-3"`, the buttons opening parenthesis (() and equals (=) are disabled, because they would not produce any valid expression in the current situation.

As sketched in Sect. 1, the development starts with a prototype to define in an HTML-like syntax the layout of the HTML widgets, and a UML state machine to define the behavior of the widgets. For the running example, the part defining the button 4, which should invoke the JavaScript function **`enabled`** to determine if it is enabled/disabled or not, and the function **`handler('4')`** when the button is clicked, is defined as follows in the prototype:

```
<button :disabled="!enabled('4')"
@click="handler('4')"> 4 </button>
```

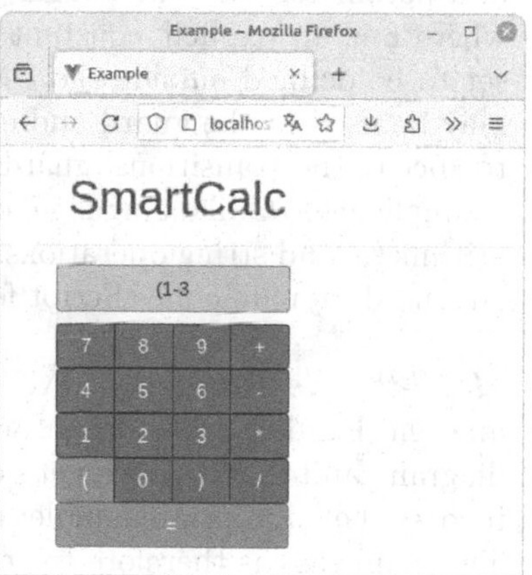

Fig. 2. Screenshot

The UML state machine is shown in Fig. 3, in which we distinguish three states to model the different reactions of the application to user input.

Our approach can then generate a formal model as well as JavaScript code implementing the two functions mentioned above in an automated way. More details will be explained in the following.

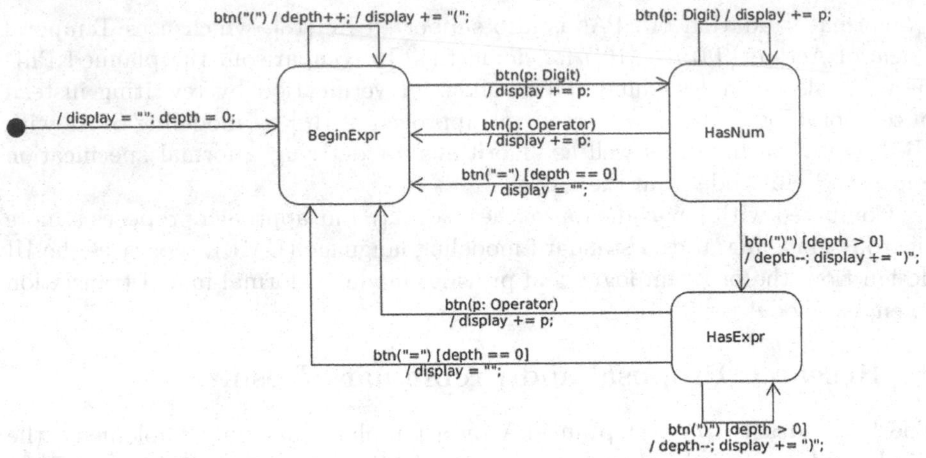

Fig. 3. Example: UML state machine for the smart calculator

UML Statemachines. Currently, our method is limited to flat UML state machines without parallel, orthogonal regions. We plan, however, to extend our method to more general state machines to allow for parallel logical states, e.g. to model different attribute states independently from each other.

We allow the event to be parameterized, and a parameter may be an element of a parameter set. The trigger of an event may thus have either the form `e(c)`, where `c` is an explicit constant parameter, or `e(p: P)`, where `P` is a parameter set to be defined outside the UML diagram and `p` is a parameter variable that may be used in the guard and effect. For the action language, i.e. the language to specify the transitions' guards and effects in the UML state machine, we use a simple Java/C-like language, currently allowing assignments as well as simple arithmetic and string operations. We plan to keep this language simple and make advanced, dynamic JavaScript features as transparent as possible.

Model-to-code Translation. We assume that the application skeleton has defined an event handler method `handler_e` for each event name `e` occurring in the UML diagram, and that each widget's event handler attribute (e.g. `@click` for a button) invokes the appropriate handler method, possibly passing on an event parameter. The main task is therefore to generate the code for the handler methods.

The function `enabled_e` is used to check if a widget should be enabled or not. We generate its code by checking if the state machine is in a state that reacts to event `e`. For the handler method, we construct for each transition an `if` block to check if the precondition of the transition satisfied and, if this is true, to perform the effect and sets the target state to be active. For example, the code generated for our running example includes the following snippet, which checks if any digit button (from `0` to `9`) should be enabled.

```
enabled(p) {
```

```
    if (this.state === "BeginExpr" && this.isDigit(p)
        || this.state === "HasNum" && this.isiDigit(p)) {
      return true;
    }
    // Check if other buttons should be enabled.
    // Details omitted here
    return false;
}
```

Model-to-formal-model Translation and Model Verification. We have experimented with the well-accepted formal specification languages (TLA$^+$ [10]) and Maude. While having very different mathematical foundations, they both provide appropriate constructs—*actions* in TLA$^+$and *rules* in Maude—to express a transition in terms of a precondition and a postcondition. The translation from the action language to the formal language is a little more involved than that to JavaScript, but simple code constructs can still be handled relatively easily. For example, the transition from `HasNum` to `HasExpr` in Fig. 3, if we only consider the event of the user clicking the plus (+) button, can be translated to following the Maude rule:

```
crl [ display: d, depth: i, state: "HasExpr" ] =>
[ display: d + p, depth: i, state: " BeginExpr" ] if "+"
    => p .
```

4 Conclusions

Our proposal is to our knowledge the first approach for modeling SPAs with UML state machines, as well as automated generation of JavaScript code and a corresponding formal specification which can then be formally verified. It provides model-to-code and model-to-formal-model transformation with the ability to verify visual properties of the modeled single page web application.

We plan to implement a practically usable tool for our approach and thus facilitate model-driven development of SPAs. Moreover, we are working on extending our method to more general UML state machines, including composite and orthogonal regions to allow for more general modeling.

References

1. Benowitz, E., Clark, K., Watney, G.: Auto-coding UML statecharts for flight software. In: Proceedings of the 2nd IEEE International Conference on Space Mission Challenges for Information Technology, pp. 413–417. SMC-IT '06, IEEE (2006)
2. Bock, A.C., Frank, U.: Low-code platform. Bus. Inf. Syst. Eng. **63**(6), 733–740 (2021)
3. Brambilla, M., Cabot, J., Moreno, N.: Tool support for model checking of web application designs. In: Baresi, L., Fraternali, P., Houben, G.-J. (eds.) ICWE 2007. LNCS, vol. 4607, pp. 533–538. Springer, Heidelberg (2007). https://doi.org/10.1007/978-3-540-73597-7_50
4. Cariou, E., Brunschwig, L., Goaër, O.L., Barbier, F.: A software development process based on UML state machines. In: 4th International Conference on Advanced Aspects of Software Engineering, ICAASE 2020, Constantine, Algeria, 28–30 November 2020, pp. 1–8. IEEE (2020)
5. Clavel, M., et al.: Maude: specification and programming in rewriting logic. Theor. Comput. Sci. **285**(2), 187–243 (2002)
6. Jakimi, A., Elkoutbi, M.: Automatic code generation from UML statechart. Int. J. Eng. Technol. **1**(2), 1793–8236 (2009)
7. Knapp, A., Merz, S.: Model checking and code generation for UML state machines and collaborations. In: Schellhorn, G., Reif, W. (eds.) FM-TOOLS 2002: 5th Workshop on Tools for System Design and Verification. Report 2002-11, Institut für Informatik, Universität Augsburg, Reisensburg, Germany, July 2002
8. Knapp, A., Zhang, G.: Model transformations for integrating and validating web application models. In: Mayr, H.C., Breu, R. (eds.) Proceedings of the Modellierung 2006 (MOD'06). Lect. Notes Informatics, vol. P-82, pp. 115–128. Gesellschaft für Informatik (2006)
9. Koch, N., Knapp, A., Zhang, G., Baumeister, H.: UML-based web engineering - an approach based on standards. In: Rossi, G., Pastor, O., Schwabe, D., Olsina, L. (eds.) Web Engineering: Modelling and Implementing Web Applications, Human-Computer Interaction Series, LNCS, pp. 157–191. Springer, Berlin, Heidelberg (2008). https://doi.org/10.1007/978-1-84628-923-1_7.
10. Lamport, L.: The TLA+ Language and Tools for Hardware and Software Engineers. Addison-Wesley, Boston (2003)
11. Niaz, I.A., Tanaka, J.: Mapping UML statecharts to java code. In: Hamza, M.H. (ed.) IASTED International Conference on Software Engineering, part of the 22nd Multi-Conference on Applied Informatics, Innsbruck, Austria, 17–19 February 2004, pp. 111–116. IASTED/ACTA Press (2004)
12. Object Management Group: Interaction Flow Modeling Language, Version 1.0. Sepcification, OMG (2014). https://www.omg.org/spec/IFML/1.0/PDF
13. Pham, V.C., Radermacher, A., Gérard, S., Li, S.: Complete code generation from UML state machine. In: Pires, L.F., Hammoudi, S., Selic, B. (eds.) Proceedings of the 5th International Conference on Model-Driven Engineering and Software Development, MODELSWARD 2017, Porto, Portugal, 19–21 February 2017, pp. 208–219. SciTePress (2017)
14. Rossi, G., Urbieta, M., Distante, D., Rivero, J.M., Firmenich, S.: 25 years of model-driven web engineering: what we achieved, what is missing. CLEI Electron. J. **19**(3), 1 (2016)
15. Schwinger, W., et al.: A survey on web modeling approaches for ubiquitous web applications. Int. J. Web Inf. Syst. **4**(3), 234–305 (2008)

16. Toffetti, G., Comai, S., Preciado, J.C., Trigueros, M.L.: State-of-the art and trends in the systematic development of rich internet applications. J. Web Eng. **10**(1), 70–86 (2011)
17. Viswanathan, S.E., Samuel, P.: Automatic code generation from UML state chart diagrams. IEEE Access **7**, 8591–8608 (2019)
18. Zhang, G.: Specifying and model checking workflows of single page applications with TLA+. In: IEEE 20th International Conference on Software Quality, Reliability and Security Companion (QRS-C), pp. 406–410. IEEE (2020)

Sequential Group Recommendations with Responsibility Constraints

Maria Stratigi(✉)

University of Tampere, Tampere, Finland

maria.stratigi@tuni.fi

Abstract. This paper addresses the aspects of fairness and transparency in Group Recommender Systems (GRS), crucial for fostering user trust and system reliability. With Recommender Systems (RS) being pivotal in modern applications, ensuring responsible recommendation techniques is paramount. We focus on two key responsibility constraints: fairness and transparency. Fairness in group recommendations poses challenges, particularly in the context of sequential recommendation rounds. We introduce the concept of sequential group recommendations, emphasizing the need to consider multiple rounds to prevent bias against any group member and ensure overall satisfaction. Additionally, we explore transparency in recommendations, proposing explanations for why certain items are excluded from recommendation lists. Our work enhances the ethical and user-centric aspects of web engineering, which are essential for the success of web applications.

Keywords: Group recommendations · Sequential recommendations · Fairness · Transparency

1 Motivation

In recent years, Recommender Systems (RS) have been one of the most active research areas in computer science. They play a key role in the majority of applications aimed at end-users. At the same time, organizing groups to carry out an activity is also simpler. Consequently, Group Recommender Systems (GRS) is a significant area of study [1].

Furthermore, irresponsible recommendation techniques have been cited as having counter-effects and being untrustworthy. Unfair treatment of different users, non-transparency and extensive personalization based on users' data can reduce users' trust in the system. To encourage users to trust an RS, it must adhere to several responsibility constraints, such as fairness and transparency [13]. Each of these constraints has a wide range of definitions, and they can be implemented in different ways. Generally, fairness corresponds to a lack of bias towards users and data items and transparency enables users to understand the system's inner workings better. Fairness in group recommendations can be vague with multiple interpretations [7,8]. Nonetheless, a general description of a *fair*

K. Stefanidis et al. (Eds.): ICWE 2024, LNCS 14629, pp. 448–452, 2024.
https://doi.org/10.1007/978-3-031-62362-2_42

group recommender system is a system that lacks bias against any group member. Simple solutions will not work for this issue, which demands a complicated solution.

The problem of fair group recommendations is complex enough, but it becomes even more complicated when the system needs to consider multiple recommendation rounds instead of just one. In most cases, a GRS perceives each interaction with the group as a standalone process. However, a group normally uses a GRS multiple times. Thus, a group recommender system should consider a *sequence* of interactions with the group. A *sequential group recommender* should record all recommendations provided to the group, along with group members' satisfaction with them, and consider both when producing suggestions for the next round.

Additionally, we examine *transparency* in recommendations, commonly referred to as explanations in recommendations. Although recommenders try to make relevant suggestions to users based on their preferences, they often cannot find the most relevant data items to offer. This causes the users to lose faith in the system, frequently resulting in them refusing to use it. The most common solution is to provide explanations in conjunction with recommendations so that the user or the person who designed the system can then gain an understanding of the rationale behind a suggestion [20].

Users can be presented with explanations of recommendations automatically or after providing feedback [2]. In the latter case, the feedback often takes the form of a query from the user to the system (e.g., [9]). Such questions can be either positive or negative concerning the existence of a data item in the recommendation list. For example, a question can be either why an item is suggested or why an item was not suggested. Many works explore the first case. However, questions concerning the non-existence of a data item remain unexplored.

2 Related Work

2.1 Fairness in Group Recommendations

Fairness in group recommendations is a widely researched area. However, it is essential to note that group recommendations are challenged when defining fairness. There is no formal definition, and each work presents a new perspective on group fairness.

Among the various methods for assessing fairness, [19] measures the degree of satisfaction, or utility, for each group member with the group recommendation list, based on the relevance of the recommended items for each member, i.e., what is the predicted score of each recommended item in the user's personal recommendation list. In contrast to using group members' utility for group recommendation, [10] uses the position of the items in the group recommendation list. The authors proposed approach for fair group recommendations is based on the concept of Pareto optimality: an item i is Pareto optimal if none of the other items j rank higher than it, i.e., no item j dominates item i. Similar to this, to facilitate the aggregation phase, [6] introduces the concept of rank-sensitive balance. The group's first recommendation should strive to balance all members' interests to the maximum extent possible. In the same way, the first two items must accomplish the same task, etc.

Recent work presented in [12] has offered two definitions of fairness: *fairness proportionality* and *envy-freeness*. In *fairness proportionality*, when the user u likes at least m items in the recommended list, the user considers the list fair for them. In *envy-freeness*, if the recommendation list contains at least m items for which the user does not feel envious, then u will consider the list fair.

2.2 Explanations for Recommendations

According to how explanations are provided, they can also be classified as user-invoked, automatic, or intelligent [2]. User-invoked explanations are explanations that are provided only after the user requests them. Automatic explanations are always produced by the system and cannot be controlled by the user. Finally, intelligent explanations are provided when the system, through some inner process determines that they are required.

[5] examines how different display styles affect the effectiveness of explanations. An explanation can be presented as either an aggregated histogram of the peers' ratings or as a detailed analysis of their ratings. Additionally, [11] suggests that it is also possible to explain recommendations by showing the user that the recommended items are similar to those they have liked. As a result, many of the items rated highly by the user are provided as an explanation.

3 Aims and Objectives

Sequential group recommendations are a relatively new area of research. In our work, we formally define the sequential group recommendation problem and explore how to achieve fair sequential group recommendations. A system should adapt to changes between recommendation rounds and still produce fair recommendations. Finally, the ability to automatically explain why a data item was not displayed as expected is an essential tool for the developer when calibrating their system. This dissertation proposes a formalization of Why-not questions and offers a method to provide their corresponding explanations. Therefore, this work strives to fulfill the following objectives.

1. Define sequential group recommendations and develop fair methods. These methods should ensure relevance to group members in each round and prevent member dissatisfaction over multiple rounds.
2. Design questions and explanations regarding omitted items in recommendation lists. These explanations aim to provide insights into system errors and reasoning, aiding system administrators in calibration and debugging.

4 Research Methodology

In all the works, we used quantitative data analysis on free online datasets commonly used in recommendation system research. However, no such dataset exists for group recommendations, namely already formed groups of users, with their preferences and the group's ultimate suggestion. Thus, we generated our groups based on specific diverse criteria for all different datasets.

[14] first introduces the sequential group recommendation problem and the notion of satisfaction and disagreement. It proposes a new group recommendation method that aims to provide a recommendation list that is both satisfying and fair to all group members. This method was extensively evaluated in a series of experiments using the MovieLens 20M dataset [3]. [15] is an expansion on the previous publication. It further refines the sequential group recommendation problem and proposes two additional group recommendation methods. The evaluation is more extensive by utilizing an additional real-world dataset, GoodReads [18]. In addition, it extends the sequential group recommendation scenario by including ephemeral groups, i.e., groups that change their members between rounds of recommendations. It evaluates the effect such groups have on the proposed sequential group recommendation methods. [16] proposes a sequential group recommendation model based on reinforcement learning. The experimental procedure is further expanded by adding a third real-world dataset, Amazon [4]. [17] contribution is formulating questions to a system about why an item does not appear in an expected position in the recommendation list and providing the corresponding explanation. We propose a structure and properties for these questions to handle complex queries. Additionally, a method is proposed to generate explanations of such questions. A series of evaluations show the effectiveness of the method mentioned above.

5 Future Work

This dissertation may result in several research areas being explored. We consider combining the fairness and transparency constraints in a sequential group recommender system, where the system would also provide the group with an explanation of why a suggestion was made. This has the potential to be complex since the system considers multiple recommendation rounds, and such explanations can be very cumbersome for an average user to understand. So, a degree of generality should be considered in the explanation details.

6 Contributions to Web Engineering

By their nature, recommender systems are an integral part of any web application that offers a service to end-users. RS help users navigate the vast amount of information such applications offer and generate. They help to enhance the user's experience, and by extension, they are a major reason for the success of a web application.

References

1. Amer-Yahia, S., Roy, S.B., Chawlat, A., Das, G., Yu, C.: Group recommendation: semantics and efficiency. PVLDB **2**(1), 754–765 (2009)
2. Gönül, M.S., Önkal, D., Lawrence, M.: The effects of structural characteristics of explanations on use of a DSS. Decis. Support Syst. **42**(3), 1481–1493 (2006)
3. Harper, F.M., Konstan, J.A.: The movielens datasets: history and context. ACM Trans. Interact. Intell. Syst. **5**(4), 19:1–19:19 (2015)
4. He, R., McAuley, J.: Ups and downs: modeling the visual evolution of fashion trends with one-class collaborative filtering. In: WWW (2016)
5. Herlocker, J.L., Konstan, J.A., Riedl, J.: Explaining collaborative filtering recommendations. In: CSCW (2000)
6. Kaya, M., Bridge, D., Tintarev, N.: Ensuring fairness in group recommendations by rank-sensitive balancing of relevance. In: RecSys (2020)
7. Pitoura, E., Stefanidis, K., Koutrika, G.: Fairness in rankings and recommenders: models, methods and research directions. In: 37th IEEE International Conference on Data Engineering, ICDE 2021, Chania, Greece, April 19-22, 2021, pp. 2358–2361. IEEE (2021)
8. Pitoura, E., Stefanidis, K., Koutrika, G.: Fairness in rankings and recommendations: an overview. VLDB J. **31**(3), 431–458 (2022)
9. Resnick, P., Iacovou, N., Suchak, M., Bergstrom, P., Riedl, J.: Grouplens: an open architecture for collaborative filtering of netnews. In: CSCW (1994)
10. Sacharidis, D.: Top-n group recommendations with fairness. In: SAC (2019)
11. Sarwar, B.M., Karypis, G., Konstan, J.A., Riedl, J.: Item-based collaborative filtering recommendation algorithms. In: WWW (2001)
12. Serbos, D., Qi, S., Mamoulis, N., Pitoura, E., Tsaparas, P.: Fairness in package-to-group recommendations. In: WWW (2017)
13. Stoyanovich, J., Abiteboul, S., Miklau, G.: Data, responsibly: fairness, neutrality and transparency in data analysis. In: International Conference on Extending Database Technology (2016). https://hal.inria.fr/hal-01290695
14. Stratigi, M., Nummenmaa, J., Pitoura, E., Stefanidis, K.: Fair sequential group recommendations. In: ACM SAC (2020)
15. Stratigi, M., Pitoura, E., Nummenmaa, J., Stefanidis, K.: Sequential group recommendations based on satisfaction and disagreement scores. J. Intell. Inf. Syst. (2021)
16. Stratigi, M., Pitoura, E., Stefanidis, K.: Squirrel: a framework for sequential group recommendations through reinforcement learning. Inf. Syst. **112**, 102128 (2023)
17. Stratigi, M., Tzompanaki, K., Stefanidis, K.: Why-not questions & explanations for collaborative filtering. In: Huang, Z., Beek, W., Wang, H., Zhou, R., Zhang, Y. (eds.) Web Information Systems Engineering - WISE 2020. LNCS, pp. 301–315. Springer, Cham (2020). https://doi.org/10.1007/978-3-030-62008-0_21
18. Wan, M., Misra, R., Nakashole, N., McAuley, J.: Fine-grained spoiler detection from large-scale review corpora (2019)
19. Xiao, L., Min, Z., Yongfeng, Z., Zhaoquan, G., Yiqun, L., Shaoping, M.: Fairness-aware group recommendation with pareto-efficiency. In: RecSys (2017)
20. Yu, C., Lakshmanan, L.V.S., Amer-Yahia, S.: Recommendation diversification using explanations. In: ICDE (2009)

Overview of Serendipity in Recommender Systems

Denis Kotkov(✉)

Department of Computer Science, University of Helsinki, Yliopistonkatu 4, 00100 Helsinki, Finland
kotkov.denis.ig@gmail.com

Abstract. Has it ever happened to you that services like Spotify, Netflix or YouTube showed you recommendations on the same topic over and over again? This might be caused by the lack of serendipity in recommender systems of these services. Recommender systems are software tools that suggest items, such as audio recordings or videos, of interest to users. Meanwhile, serendipity is the property of these systems, which indicates the degree, to which they suggest items that pleasantly surprise users. In this talk, I will provide an overview of serendipity in recommender systems. In particular, I will talk about how the concept of serendipity has been defined and measured in recommender systems, and what experiments have been conducted to investigate this concept. I will also touch on recommendation algorithms designed to suggest serendipitous items and discuss future directions of the topic.

Keywords: serendipity · recommender systems · overview

1 Introduction

Recommender systems are software tools that suggest items, such as movies or articles, to users [15]. To optimize for items that users would enjoy, recommender systems tend to generate recommendations that are similar to what users would usually consume and, therefore, could potentially be found without the aid of a recommender system. To overcome this problem, system designers take serendipity into account during system optimization [7]. In this talk, I will provide an overview of this topic and discuss definitions of serendipity in recommender systems, user studies conducted to investigate it, datasets containing serendipity labels, serendipity-oriented recommendation algorithms and future directions.

2 Definitions

According to the recent study [7], there are three definitions of serendipity that can be applied to recommender systems: generalized serendipity, RecSys serendipity and user serendipity. **Generalized serendipity** is based on how

K. Stefanidis et al. (Eds.): ICWE 2024, LNCS 14629, pp. 453–457, 2024.
https://doi.org/10.1007/978-3-031-62362-2_43

the term is defined in social sciences, which corresponds closely with the dictionary definition[1]: "*luck that takes the form of finding valuable or pleasant things that are not looked for*". **RecSys serendipity** is based on how the term has been defined historically in the recommender systems literature, which differs from the definition in social sciences. There is no consensus on the definition of serendipity in recommender systems [5,7]. However, according to most authors, an item needs to correspond to one or more of the following components to be serendipitous [5]: relevance, novelty and unexpectedness. Relevance indicates that the item is beneficial to the user, while novelty that the user has limited level of familiarity with the item [5,16]. The unexpectedness component has a number of definitions. For example, according to one of the definitions, an item is unexpected to the user if the user does not think that they would have come across this item by themselves [5,13]. Lastly, **user serendipity** is based on each user's personal understanding of serendipity and, therefore, can cover a broad range of meanings.

3 Datasets

The following three publicly available datasets contain serendipity labels, i.e. information on whether a particular item is considered serendipitous by the user: Serendipity 2018, Taobao Serendipity and SerenLens datasets. **The Serendipity 2018 dataset** was collected in the movie recommender system MovieLens[2] [5]. The dataset contains 10 million relevance ratings, 2,150 RecSys serendipity labels on movies and movie metadata. The serendipity ratings include user ratings of statements regarding relevance, two variations of novelty and four variations of unexpectedness.

The Taobao Serendipity dataset was collected in Taobao, a popular Chinese mobile e-commerce application [1,20]. The dataset contains 11,383 RecSys serendipity ratings on products. The authors used the following statement to measure serendipity: "*The item recommended to me is a pleasant surprise*" [1]. The dataset also contains extensive information on users, such as age, gender and previous purchases.

The SerenLens dataset is based on user reviews [4]. To generate the dataset, the authors selected a set of reviews and recruited Amazon Mechanical Turk workers to annotate them. The workers needed to specify whether the review indicated that the item was serendipitous to the review author. Overall, the SerenLens dataset contains 265,037 serendipity labels on books and 74,967 labels on movies.

4 User Studies

A few studies investigated serendipity in recommender systems with real users. For example, Kotkov et al. conducted a user study in MovieLens, where users

[1] https://www.britannica.com/dictionary/serendipity.
[2] https://movielens.org/.

retrospectively indicated if particular movies were RecSys serendipitous to them [5]. The authors investigated associations between different variations of RecSys serendipity and user behavior. The results suggested that most variations of RecSys serendipity are positively associated with preference broadening. The authors also found that ratings predicted by MovieLens, popularity, content-based and collaborative similarity to a user profile are effective predictors of whether an item is considered RecSys serendipitous by the user.

Chen et al. conducted a user study where they collected user responses to survey questions regarding RecSys serendipity in the e-commerce domain [1]. According to the results of the study, RecSys serendipity is positively associated with user satisfaction, purchase intention and timeliness.

Smets et al. carried out a survey on venues in an urban recommender system [16]. In the survey, the authors included questions regarding relevance, novelty, diversity, RecSys serendipity, satisfaction and conversion. The authors found that the more often the users visit venues, the higher the rate of them finding RecSys serendipitous venues.

Kotkov et al. ran a field study in Soulie[3], a recommender system that suggests articles to users [10]. In the study, the users were interacting with the articles and were prompted to reply to surveys. Based on user replies, the authors labeled articles RecSys, generalized and user serendipitous. The authors found that RecSys serendipity misses items that should be considered serendipitous according to generalized and user serendipity. Similarly, the authors found that user understanding of serendipity differs from generalized and RecSys serendipity. Finally, the authors discovered that different types of serendipity are associated with different patterns of user behavior.

5 Algorithms

There have been various algorithms designed to recommend serendipitous items. To achieve this goal, serendipity-oriented algorithms often rerank the output of accuracy-oriented algorithms. For example, the serendipity-oriented greedy algorithm improves serendipity of accuracy-oriented algorithms through diversification [11]. Another strategy to improve serendipity is to modify an accuracy-oriented algorithm. For example, Zheng et al. modified the objective function of PureSVD [2] to improve serendipity [21].

Due to the limited number of serendipity labels in datasets, there have been efforts to utilize transfer learning for serendipity improvement. For example, Pandey et al. trained a deep learning recommendation algorithm based on relevance ratings and tuned it based on serendipity labels to mitigate data sparsity [14].

[3] https://www.soulie.io/.

6 Future Directions

Future directions of serendipity in recommender systems include several key areas: contextual factors, user and item characteristics, the impact of user interfaces, and cross-domain recommendations. **Context factors,** such as time of day or weather, have demonstrated a significant influence on recommendation accuracy, implying their potential to affect serendipitous discoveries [17]. Similarly, **user and item characteristics,** such as user age or item popularity, have been linked to serendipity in recommender systems, suggesting their importance for other serendipity types [19].

User interfaces play a pivotal role in shaping user perceptions of recommendations, and therefore can have an impact on serendipity. For instance, recommendation explanations can affect user interest in suggested items [8]. Another example is MovieTuner, the system that allows users to fine-tune their recommendation preferences, such as adjusting the intensity of certain features, e.g. "more comedy" or "less mafia" [18]. To design MovieTuner, the authors used the tag genome dataset, which indicates the degree to which a particular tag applies to an item [6,18]. Tag genome potentially enables the creation of user interfaces tailored to enhance serendipity in a single- or cross-domain settings [9].

Cross-domain recommender systems leverage data from various domains to mitigate the data sparsity problem [3]. This problem is particularly pertinent to serendipity due to the difficulty in labeling serendipitous encounters. Cross-domain approaches offer promising solutions for recommending serendipitous items by capitalizing on multiple data sources [12].

References

1. Chen, L., Yang, Y., Wang, N., Yang, K., Yuan, Q.: How serendipity improves user satisfaction with recommendations? a large-scale user evaluation. In: The World Wide Web Conference, pp. 240–250 (2019)
2. Cremonesi, P., Koren, Y., Turrin, R.: Performance of recommender algorithms on top-n recommendation tasks. In: Proceedings of RecSys 2010, pp. 39–46. ACM, New York, NY, USA (2010). https://doi.org/10.1145/1864708.1864721
3. Fu, Z., Niu, X., Maher, M.L.: Deep learning models for serendipity recommendations: a survey and new perspectives. ACM Comput. Surv. **56**(1), 1–26 (2023)
4. Fu, Z., Niu, X., Yu, L.: Wisdom of crowds and fine-grained learning for serendipity recommendations. In: Proceedings of the 46th International ACM SIGIR Conference on Research and Development in Information Retrieval, pp. 739–748 (2023)
5. Kotkov, D., Konstan, J.A., Zhao, Q., Veijalainen, J.: Investigating serendipity in recommender systems based on real user feedback. In: Proceedings of the 33rd Annual ACM Symposium on Applied Computing, pp. 1341–1350 (2018)
6. Kotkov, D., Maslov, A., Neovius, M.: Revisiting the tag relevance prediction problem. In: Proceedings of the 44th International ACM SIGIR Conference on Research and Development in Information Retrieval, pp. 1768–1772. SIGIR 2021, Association for Computing Machinery, New York, NY, USA (2021). https://doi.org/10.1145/3404835.3463019

7. Kotkov, D., Medlar, A., Glowacka, D.: Rethinking serendipity in recommender systems. In: ACM SIGIR Conference on Human Information Interaction and Retrieval. CHIIR 2023, Association for Computing Machinery, New York, NY, USA (2023)
8. Kotkov, D., Medlar, A., Liu, Y., Glowacka, D.: On the negative perception of cross-domain recommendations and explanations. In: Proceedings of the 47th International ACM SIGIR Conference on Research and Development in Information Retrieval. SIGIR 2024. Association for Computing Machinery, New York, USA (2024). https://doi.org/10.1145/3626772.3657735
9. Kotkov, D., Medlar, A., Maslov, A., Satyal, U.R., Neovius, M., Glowacka, D.: The tag genome dataset for books. In: ACM SIGIR Conference on Human Information Interaction and Retrieval, pp. 353–357. CHIIR 2022, Association for Computing Machinery, New York, NY, USA (2022). https://doi.org/10.1145/3498366.3505833
10. Kotkov, D., Medlar, A., Triin, K., Glowacka, D.: The dark matter of serendipity in recommender systems. In: Proceedings of the 2024 ACM SIGIR Conference on Human Information Interaction and Retrieval. CHIIR 2024, Association for Computing Machinery, New York, NY, USA (2024). https://doi.org/10.1145/3627508.3638342
11. Kotkov, D., Veijalainen, J., Wang, S.: A serendipity-oriented greedy algorithm for recommendations. In: Proceedings of the 13th International Conference on Web Information systems and Technologies. SCITEPRESS (2017)
12. Kotkov, D., Wang, S., Veijalainen, J.: Improving serendipity and accuracy in cross-domain recommender systems. In: Monfort, V., Krempels, K.-H., Majchrzak, T.A., Traverso, P. (eds.) WEBIST 2016. LNBIP, vol. 292, pp. 105–119. Springer, Cham (2017). https://doi.org/10.1007/978-3-319-66468-2_6
13. Kotkov, D., Zhao, Q., Launis, K., Neovius, M.: Clusterexplorer: enable user control over related recommendations via collaborative filtering and clustering. In: Proceedings of the 2020 ACM conference on Recommender systems (2020)
14. Pandey, G., Kotkov, D., Semenov, A.: Recommending serendipitous items using transfer learning. In: Proceedings of the 27th ACM International Conference on Information and Knowledge Management, pp. 1771–1774 (2018)
15. Ricci, F., Rokach, L., Shapira, B.: Recommender Systems Handbook, chap. Introduction to Recommender Systems Handbook, pp. 1–35. Springer US (2011)
16. Smets, A., Vannieuwenhuyze, J., Ballon, P.: Serendipity in the city: user evaluations of urban recommender systems. J. Am. Soc. Inf. Sci. **73**(1), 19–30 (2022)
17. Trattner, C., Oberegger, A., Marinho, L., Parra, D.: Investigating the utility of the weather context for point of interest recommendations. Inf. Technol. Tourism **19**, 117–150 (2018)
18. Vig, J., Sen, S., Riedl, J.: The tag genome: encoding community knowledge to support novel interaction. ACM Trans. Interact. Intell. Syst. **2**(3), 13:1–13:44 (2012). https://doi.org/10.1145/2362394.2362395
19. Wang, N., Chen, L.: How do item features and user characteristics affect users' perceptions of recommendation serendipity? A cross-domain analysis. User Model. User-Adap. Interact. **33**, 1–39 (2022)
20. Wang, N., Chen, L., Yang, Y.: The impacts of item features and user characteristics on users' perceived serendipity of recommendations. In: Proceedings of the 28th ACM Conference on User Modeling, Adaptation and Personalization, pp. 266–274 (2020)
21. Zheng, Q., Chan, C.-K., Ip, H.H.S.: An unexpectedness-augmented utility model for making serendipitous recommendation. In: Perner, P. (ed.) ICDM 2015. LNCS (LNAI), vol. 9165, pp. 216–230. Springer, Cham (2015). https://doi.org/10.1007/978-3-319-20910-4_16

Tutorials

Vanilla JS - Design and Implementation of a Progressive Web Application from Scratch

Tobias Münch(✉)

Münch Ges. für IT Solutions mbH, Gewerbering 1, 49393 Lohne, Germany
to.muench@muench-its.de
http://www.muench-its.de

Abstract. Nowadays, web applications are developed using different kind of web frameworks. The usage of them is always a trade-off between comfort, resource efficiency, and long-term dependency. This dependency can have a negative effect on maintainability. The Vanilla JS approach avoids the use of frameworks and consequently relies on the strict use of W3C standards. In this tutorial, an offline-ready progressive web application (PWA) build, according to the frameworkless approach without increasing the development effort compared to development with respective frameworks. To solve this complex tasks, components of the web standard "Web Components" are introduced and used. Additionally, patterns for state management and offline capability as well as routing between different pages are discussed. Finally, the sample application is extended by a responsive design. The sample application is build in an iterative way, so the participants will learn theoretical concepts as well as practical implementation.

Keywords: Developer Experience · Web Components · frameworkless · Progressive Web App

1 Introduction

The public discussion about carbon footprint reduction has reached web applications [1,2]. It has been widely discussed, that Vanilla JS has the superior resource efficiency in comparison to popular frameworks like React or Angular based on package size, execution speed, development and client-side resources [3]. Therefore, we can see a renaissance of web standards. The so called Frameworkless movement describes different approaches of building a web application [4]. However, due to the lack of experience of many developers, the vanilla JS approach has not yet become widely accepted. For this reason, this tutorial, will develop an offline-capable PWA from scratch to show that the effort for the developer is comparable to that of the framework-based approach.

1.1 Objectives

This tutorial has the primary objective to achieve a deeper understanding of the current web standards and transfer the knowledge for practical implemen-

K. Stefanidis et al. (Eds.): ICWE 2024, LNCS 14629, pp. 461–464, 2024.
https://doi.org/10.1007/978-3-031-62362-2_44

tation. This supports the overarching objective to build more sustainable and maintainable web applications.

1.2 Requirements

The tutorial requires previous knowledge of the topics HTML, CSS and JavaScript/Typescript or another object oriented programming language. Each attendee needs a notebook with nodeJS, Visual Studio Code and GIT.

2 Basics

2.1 Web Components

Web Components are a composite standard from the W3C, WHATWG and ECMA. They are highly reuseable in web applications. They are defined by the following parts [5,6]: 1) Custom Elements enable the creation of maintainable, reusable, encapsulated HTML elements better known as Web Components. 2) Shadow DOM provides encapsulation for elements, shielding component styles and structure from external influence. 3) ES Modules allow developers to create self-contained, reusable modules to enhance modularity, reusability, and dependency management. 4) HTML Templates define reusable HTML fragments, enabling dynamic, data-driven web applications without excessive DOM manipulation, crucial for rendering content within web components.

2.2 Atomic Design

Brad Forst developed the Atomic design [7]. It is a method for creating design systems by deconstructing complex interfaces into fundamental components [7]. Applied to web components, this approach fosters the development of modular, reusable elements, ensuring consistency and scalability [7]. This leads to more efficient development and easier maintenance [8] and should therefore be used as the development approach in this tutorial.

2.3 Persistence Concepts

To make an PWA offline capable, it needs to know its state and have the possibility of local data storage. For this purpose, different browser-based peristence concepts like local and session storage, as well as the indexedDB approach are presented

3 Tutorial Structure

The tutorial is designed to last six hours. It consists out of seven different chapters which sequentially transfer knowledge. The introducing and the closing chapter are 30 min long. Each other chapter is build equally in the three Sects. 1) knowledge transfer (15 min), 2) knowledge application and implementation (40 min) and 3) retrospective (5 min).

3.1 Workspace, Typescript and RollupJS

At first, the tools for the development will be presented in this session and set up by all attendees. For this purpose, an appropriately prepared GitHub-project will be cloned. The session describes the basics of the used build-chain with Typescript and the javascript module-bundler RollupJS. The outcome of this first step is that all attendees have the same development environment and have understood the basics of typescript and its transpile and deployment tools.

3.2 Web Component from Scratch

After these preparation steps, the attendees will learn the W3C standards associatedwith web components. This includes predefined interfaces, lifecycle management, shadow elements, template management and events. In order to practice this new knowledge, a simple welcome component with a custom template will be build. Afterwards, there will be a discussion on what are the common problems with developer experience. After this session, the attendees know how to build a web component from scratch and what problems come along with them.

3.3 Boost the Developer Experience

Based on the discussion from the previous session, the developer experience get's increased to be comparable to frameworks like React. Therefore, Typescript decorators get introduced and explained how they can be used for classes, properties and methods. By means of them, we can then outsource extensive parts of development to a small library of self build decorators, which can than be used with any web component. After this session, the attendees know how decorators are working and how to extend web components practically.

3.4 Connecting Web Components to a Page

After mastering a single web component, the communication between web components will be explained in detail. To do this in a structured way, the Atomic Design approach, developed by Brad Frost is briefly introduced. This has, the goal, that the participants know the structure of larger web applications. The outcome is the understanding of event and shared state management within a single page with multiple components.

3.5 Offline-Ready Progressive Web App

This session has the goal to build a PWA from the previous implemented page. The web app manifest, Service-Workers and experimental background synchronization are theoretically explained. For the Service-Workers, the tool WorkBoxJS is used to build a strategic for external APIs. At the end of the session, the attendees will have an installable PWA which is offline-ready.

3.6 Routing and Storing Data

The PWA implemented so far is then extended to a multi-page application. This extension allows to understand routing and the different browser based persistence comcepts. In detail, it is about URL parameters, Local-Storage, Session-Storage and IndexedDB. After this session, the attendees have implemented a multipage PWA with routing and data stored in the browser for offline usage.

3.7 Evaluation and Reflection

In the last section, a summarization and reflection of the tutorial takes place. Each attendee has the option to discuss the lessons learned and describe their personal outcomes. In addition, future topics are presented for a further guide.

4 Outcome

After this tutorial the attendees have a deeper understanding of web components, PWAs, the standards and current problems. They know how to build a PWA with a comparable developer experience, event management and complex pages based on atomic design. This tutorial helps to build more sustainable web apps.

References

1. Mageswari, S.D.U., Suganthi, P., Meena, M.: Carbon footprint of information and communication technologies. In: 2022 International Conference on Edge Computing and Applications (ICECAA). IEEE (2022)
2. Wholegrain Digital: Website Carbon Calculator. https://www.websitecarbon.com/how-does-it-work/. Accessed 15 Oct 2023
3. Persson, M.: JavaScript DOM manipulation performance: comparing vanilla JavaScript and leading JavaScript front-end frameworks (2020)
4. Strazzullo, F.: Frameworkless front-end development - do you control your dependencies or are they controlling you?. Apress (2019)
5. WHATWG: HTML Living Standard - Last Updated 12 October 2023. https://html.spec.whatwg.org/multipage/. Accessed 14 Oct 2023
6. ECMAScript 2024 Language Specification. https://tc39.es/ecma262. Accessed 14 Oct 2023
7. Frost, B.: Atomic Design Methodology. https://atomicdesign.bradfrost.com/chapter-2/. Accessed 14 Oct 2023
8. Augusdi, R.F., et al.: Development of sandbox english conversation training applications with atomic design. In: 2021 International Electronics Symposium (IES). IEEE (2021)

Quantum Service-Oriented Computing: A Practical Introduction to Quantum Web Services and Quantum Workflows

Martin Beisel[1(✉)], Jose Garcia-Alonso[2], Juan M. Murillo[2], and Benjamin Weder[1]

[1] Institute of Architecture of Application Systems, University of Stuttgart, Stuttgart, Germany
{beisel,weder}@iaas.uni-stuttgart.de

[2] Quercus Software Engineering Group, University of Extremadura, Badajoz, Spain
{jgaralo,juanmamu}@unex.es

Abstract. Quantum applications are hybrid and require quantum and classical programs. Similar to classical applications, they can benefit from modularity, maintainability, and reusability. This can be achieved by implementing the different functionalities of quantum applications as independent web services. In this tutorial, we provide an overview of concepts to develop and execute quantum applications based on the paradigm of service-oriented computing. This includes the development of quantum web services and corresponding OpenAPI specifications. Further, these services are orchestrated using quantum workflows to achieve robustness, scalability, and reliability. Thereby, concepts and tools for their modeling, execution, and monitoring are introduced and practically applied.

Keywords: Quantum Computing · Quantum Software Engineering · Hybrid Quantum Applications · SoC · Workflow Technology

1 Introduction

Quantum computers provide a computational advantage over classical computers by exploiting quantum mechanical phenomena, such as entanglement and superposition [4]. However, quantum computers won't replace classical computers but rather serve as co-processors for specific problems, as they are not suitable for many traditional tasks, such as data persistence [5]. Hence, hybrid quantum applications require the integration of classical and quantum programs. These applications can benefit from classical software engineering principles, such as modularization and separation of concerns [1]. In particular, service-based access of quantum computers is suitable, as they are typically provided via the cloud [3]. However, the development of quantum web services requires expert knowledge of quantum programming and hardware. To tackle this issue, an approach for the automated generation of quantum web services using OpenAPI

K. Stefanidis et al. (Eds.): ICWE 2024, LNCS 14629, pp. 465–468, 2024.
https://doi.org/10.1007/978-3-031-62362-2_45

specifications, as well as their automated deployment, has been presented [2]. Since hybrid quantum applications typically comprise many of these services, they must be orchestrated, i.e., the control and data flow between them must be defined [6]. Due to advantages, such as transaction processing, reliability, and robustness, workflows are a suitable technology for this orchestration.

2 Tutorial Overview

In the following, we provide the tutorial's structure, intended audience, and technical requirements, as well as the learning goals of the tutorial.

2.1 Intended Audience

Attendees of this tutorial do not require any previous knowledge of quantum computing or quantum software engineering. The tutorial provides basic knowledge about designing, developing, deploying, and executing hybrid quantum applications. Therefore, it teaches attendees to develop and deploy quantum web services, as well as how to orchestrate them utilizing quantum workflows.

2.2 Tutorial Structure

The tutorial is designed for half a conference day (three hours) including lectures, demonstrations, and practical activities. It comprises the following five parts:

- First, basic concepts of quantum software engineering are introduced.
- The second part of the tutorial presents a concept and a corresponding toolchain to convert quantum algorithms into quantum web services. Thereby, OpenAPI is employed to standardize the development and deployment process of web services. This toolchain will be used in a practical session, in which attendees deploy a web service based on the Qiskit SDK.
- Third, an approach for orchestrating hybrid quantum applications utilizing workflows is presented, facilitating the integration of classical and quantum programs. Further, a concept using process views is demonstrated that enables their unified observability in heterogeneous execution environments.
- Next, a holistic approach for the automated deployment of quantum workflows and the corresponding web services using TOSCA is presented.
- Finally, a practical session is planned in which attendees can model and execute two different quantum workflows, orchestrating state-of-the-art quantum algorithms. The required web services will be provided and attendees will focus on orchestrating them to build the quantum application.

2.3 Technical Requirements

The practical part of the tutorial requires a laptop with Docker and Docker-Compose installed. Further, to employ state-of-the-art quantum computers for executing the modeled hybrid quantum applications, an IBMQ account is needed, which can be created free of charge. Alternatively, a local simulator can be used for executing the quantum circuits, as described in the tutorial materials.

2.4 Learning Goals

Attendees will have obtained knowledge on:

- Fundamentals about quantum computing and quantum software engineering.
- How to develop quantum web services utilizing OpenAPI specifications.
- Modular development of hybrid quantum applications, their orchestration using workflows, and automatic deployment using TOSCA.
- How to observe and analyze quantum workflows using process views in a unified and user-specific manner.

2.5 Tutorial Material

The tutorial material consists of slides, a detailed description of how to conduct the practical parts of the tutorial, as well as pointers to corresponding papers and tools. It is available at https://ust-quantil.github.io/icwe-tutorial-2024/.

2.6 Previous Related Tutorials

In last year's edition of the ICWE, the authors provided two distinct tutorials about quantum services and quantum workflows. As the topics are highly related, we want to provide a joint tutorial connecting both topics and highlighting how the corresponding tools can be combined to develop hybrid quantum applications. Furthermore, we added new concepts developed since last year's tutorials.

Acknowledgments. This work was partially funded by the BMWK projects *EniQmA* (01MQ22007B) and *SeQuenC* (01MQ22009B). It was also partially funded by the Ministry of Science, Innovation and Universities of Spain (project PID2021-124045OB-C31) and by the Regional Ministry of Economy, Science and Digital Agenda of the Regional Government of Extremadura (GR21133).

References

1. Beisel, M., Barzen, J., Garhofer, S., Leymann, F., Truger, F., Weder, B., Yussupov, V.: Quokka: A Service Ecosystem for Workflow-Based Execution of Variational Quantum Algorithms. In: Service-Oriented Computing – ICSOC 2022 Workshops. Springer (2023)
2. Garcia-Alonso, J., Rojo, J., Valencia, D., Moguel, E., Berrocal, J., Murillo, J.M.: Quantum Software as a Service Through a Quantum API Gateway. IEEE Internet Comput. **26**(1), 34–41 (2021)
3. Moguel, E., Rojo, J., Valencia, D., Berrocal, J., Garcia-Alonso, J., Murillo, J.M.: Quantum service-oriented computing: current landscape and challenges. Software Qual. J. **30**(4), 983–1002 (2022)

4. Nielsen, M.A., Chuang, I.: Quantum Computation and Quantum Information. AAPT (2010)
5. Weder, B., Barzen, J., Leymann, F., Vietz, D.: Quantum Software Development Lifecycle, pp. 61–83. Springer (2022)
6. Weder, B., Breitenbücher, U., Leymann, F., Wild, K.: Integrating Quantum Computing into Workflow Modeling and Execution. In: Proceedings of the 13th IEEE/ACM International Conference on Utility and Cloud Computing (UCC). pp. 279–291. IEEE (2020)

The Five Generations of Entity Resolution on Web Data

Konstantinos Nikoletos[1(✉)], Ekaterini Ioannou[2], and George Papadakis[1]

[1] University of Athens, Athens, Greece
{k.nikoletos,gpapadis}@di.uoa.gr
[2] Tilburg University, Tilburg, The Netherlands
Ekaterini.Ioannou@uvt.nl

Abstract. Entity Resolution constitutes a core data integration task that has attracted a bulk of works on improving its effectiveness and time efficiency. This tutorial provides a comprehensive overview of the field, distinguishing relevant methods into five main generations. The first one targets Veracity in the context of structured data with a clean schema. The second generation extends its focus to cover Volume, as well, leveraging multi-core or massive parallelization to process large-scale datasets. The third generation addresses the additional challenge of Variety, targeting voluminous, noisy, semi-structured, and highly heterogeneous data from the Semantic Web. The fourth generation also tackles Velocity so as to process data collections of a continuously increasing volume. The latest works, though, belong to the fifth generation, involving pre-trained (large) language models which heavily rely on external knowledge to address all four Vs with high effectiveness.

Keywords: Entity Resolution · Data Integration · LLMs

1 Content and Goals

The process of linking instances describing identical real-world objects and deduplication is known as *Entity Resolution (ER)* [19]. This is a particularly important task for Web Data. Knowledge graphs, ontologies, structured, and semi-structured data are only a few examples of the Web's data volume and complexity that ER must deal with. To establish links between these entities, numerous techniques have been developed, centered around four key aspects: Veracity, Volume, Variety, and Velocity. In this tutorial, we will explain that ER has evolved through five generations, each with a distinct focus on various aspects.

The **1st ER generation** focused on tackling Veracity, through end-to-end pipelines involving three consecutive steps: *Schema Matching*, *Blocking*, and *Entity Matching*. Each of these steps has a separate role. First, Schema Matching tries to match the relevant attributes across two structured datasets with different schemata [2,15]. After inter-linking the different schemata, another problem arose. Performing comparisons between every entity and all others would lead

K. Stefanidis et al. (Eds.): ICWE 2024, LNCS 14629, pp. 469–473, 2024.
https://doi.org/10.1007/978-3-031-62362-2_46

to a quadratic time complexity of $O(n^2)$ [4]. Therefore, algorithms and techniques have been designed to mitigate this complexity, aiming to decrease the number of comparisons and similarity calculations. To address this requirement, a technique known as *Blocking* is introduced. Blocking aims to limit the computational cost by focusing on comparing only the most similar entity profiles. This is achieved by using signatures composed of combinations of parts of values corresponding to the most informative attribute names. Finally, a method for similarity checking between each pair of entities fall in the same block, were added in the ER pipeline. Named *Entity Matching*, this step provides the information if two entities are a match, non-match or uncertain [4]. However, as the needs for ER emerged, more and bigger datasets needed to be evaluated, posing a problem of bringing ER to Big Data challenges.

The **2nd ER generation** tackled Volume and Veracity. It follows the same principles with the 1st generation plus challenges related to Big data. In order to provide ER solutions, with sufficient performance and scalability, several techniques were tested. Firstly, many ER procedures were parallelized and techniques such as Map/Reduce [5] were utilized. Blocks after the Blocking phase could now be handled in parallel, and reduce time complexity drastically [11]. The same parallelization approach can be applied to Entity Matching [3]. However, this raises the issue of Load Balancing between the computational resources [12].

After optimizing the time complexity due to the larger data volumes, highly heterogeneous and noisy data with unclear semantic and contextual information, needed to be processed. For tackling this need, a new generation emerged, the **3rd ER Generation**, tackling Variety, Volume and Veracity. *Variety*, is now the key-point of this era. At this point, schemas should be categorized regardless of their semantics but given the values of each attribute [7]. This method is known as *Schema Clustering*. Schema Clustering was set as the first step of the ER pipeline, and worked in combination with *Blocking* in each of the clusters formed, resulting in increase of the precision without counteracting with recall. In this era, where a schema-agnostic approach is needed, another step, the Block Building, takes all entity profile information and builds blocks without the need of schema alignment and human intervention. In order to optimize the selection of blocks, the next step is to process them. So, a new workflow step was introduced, the Block Processing, which removes insufficient blocks and isolates blocks containing valuable information. As in the previous eras, Entity Matching is again applied to the candidate pairs in each of the blocks generated from the previous steps. A similarity graph is the result of Entity Matching [13,14,20], where each node is an entity and each edge the similarity between them. Having this graph, multiple optimization techniques could be added to the ER pipeline, introducing the Entity Clustering step [9].

A new challenge, witch will mark the next generation is the speed and cost of performing ER in various datasets, introducing the **4th ER Generation**, tackling Velocity, Variety, Volume and Veracity. Datasets became more dynamic and as the Web was evolving and more apps and systems were deployed, data became bigger and with a more incoming/streaming nature. For this reason, the number of comparisons and/or resources needed should be in many cases restricted. Adding the sense of *budget*, Progressive ER provides practitioners with a pay-as-gou-go ability, by prioritizing the most valuable comparisons between the data sources. Another approach that emerged in this generation is the Incremental ER [8], that minimizes the cost of updates when a streaming use-case, like a web REST-API, provides a streaming input on the data. Finally, Query-driven ER [1] was defined as a process that systematically resolves entities returned as results to incoming queries over time [10].

After exploring the foundational stages of ER, our tutorial will delve into the latest advancements in methods and algorithms, corresponding to the **5th ER Generation**. We will examine Deep Learning and the impact of Language Models (LMs), particularly pre-trained ones. These models enable the transformation of entity profiles into a vector space, merging textual data with semantic and contextual information extracted from the underlying LMs knowledge base [21]. Finally, we will discuss the current evolution of Language Models, specifically Large LMs (LLMs), which further enhance ER pipelines. LLMs can contribute significantly to both the Block Building and Entity Matching steps. In Block Building, they facilitate the creation of embeddings rich in information, while in Entity Matching, a prompting mechanism to an LLM can yield matching or non-matching predictions.

A hands-on tutorial will also be presented, using pyJedAI [16]. pyJedAI is an open-source Python package implementing most of the pipelines described above. From Blocking to LMs, a developer becomes an architect of the pipelines, as all methods are implemented. Attendees will gain the know-how of tackling in a starting and novice way ER problems, while at the same time will get familiar with a framework that can be used in challenging ER tasks, both in academia and industry as it is available under the Apache License 2.0. Finally, we will present the future of this area and will delve into the challenges and the problems that are still open for work until now, like the auto-configuration of end-to-end ER pipelines [6].

2 Sessions and Target Audience

This tutorial will provide a holistic view over the research status in the area of Entity Resolution, spanning from the first approaches, but emphasizing the latest state-of-the-art research developments. The five ER generations will be presented in chronological time, leading to the following structure:

(i) introduction and motivation, including ER preliminaries, fundamental assumptions, principles, and overview of the generations;

(ii) 1st generation, focusing on Veracity, with schema matching, blocking, entity matching, and methods using external Knowledge;

(iii) 2nd generation tackling Volume and Veracity, including parallel blocking, parallel entity matching, and load balancing;

(iv) 3rd generation tackling Variety, Volume and Veracity with techniques including schema clustering, block building, block processing, entity matching, entity clustering;

(v) 4th generation tackling Velocity, Variety, Volume and Veracity with progressive and incremental ER, as well as query-driven resolution;

(vi) 5th generation, leveraging external knowledge with pre-trained LLMs pipelines, and crowdsourcing, LLMs;

(vii) hands-on session with pyJedAI; an open-source Python package with which we will build demos from scratch over real data; and lastly

(viii) challenges and final remarks, including automatic parameter configuration and future research directions.

The overall duration of this tutorial is 1 h, with 15 min kept for audience questions and brief discussion. There will be an additional hands-on session, lasting 15 min, in which we will present applications and demos in ER tasks using pyJedAI.

Target Audience and Learning Outcome. Our tutorial is focusing on providing examples and use-cases on ER for Web data. Novice audience, with a fundamental knowledge on data management and Web engineering, can attend this tutorial. Also, researchers and developers familiar with these ER, will be interested in all the latest advancements about the use of (large) language models, which is the focus of this tutorial. As a result, our tutorial targets a broad audience, including conference attendees with diverse knowledge backgrounds. Additionally, the hands-on session, demonstrating pyJedAI, offers the attendees of this tutorial a starting know-how of addressing an ER problem.

3 Related Material and Presenters

Tutorial Information. A website[1] dedicated to our tutorial will be made available few weeks before the tutorial. This will provide the tutorial slides a week prior the presentation date and keep them online afterwards. In addition, the website will provide guidance for using the Entity Resolution toolbox during the hands-on session. The necessary code will be made available under the Apache License 2.0, which allows for both academic and commercial usage.

Related Material. Part of the tutorial is related to a book [18] and a past tutorial [17]. The present tutorial, though, focuses on the fifth generation of ER solutions, emphasizing the use of pre-trained language models as well as of large language models (LLMs) in ER solutions. Note of these very works has been considered in [17,18].

Acknowledgement. This work was supported by the Horizon Europe project STELAR (Grant No. 101070122).

[1] https://pyjedai.readthedocs.io/en/latest/pages/icwe2024.html.

References

1. Altwaijry, H., et al.: Query: a framework for integrating entity resolution with query processing. PVLDB **9**, 120–131 (2015)
2. Bernstein, P.A., Madhavan, J., Rahm, E.: Generic schema matching, ten years later. PVLDB **4**(11), 695–701 (2011)
3. Böhm, C., et al.: LINDA: distributed web-of-data-scale entity matching. In: CIKM, pp. 2104–2108 (2012)
4. Christen, P.: Data Matching. Springer, Heidelberg (2012). https://doi.org/10.1007/978-3-642-31164-2
5. Dean, J., Ghemawat, S.: Mapreduce: simplified data processing on large clusters. Commun. ACM **51**(1), 107–113 (2008)
6. Efthymiou, V., et al.: Self-configured entity resolution with pyJedAI. In: IEEE Big Data (2023)
7. Golshan, B., Halevy, A., Mihaila, G., Tan, W.: Data integration: after the teenage years. In: PODS, pp. 101–106 (2017)
8. Gruenheid, A., Dong, X.L., Srivastava, D.: Incremental record linkage. PVLDB **7**(9), 697–708 (2014)
9. Hassanzadeh, O., et al.: Framework for evaluating clustering algorithms in duplicate detection. PVLDB **2**(1), 1282–1293 (2009)
10. Ioannou, E., Garofalakis, M.: Query analytics over probabilistic databases with unmerged duplicates. TKDE **27**, 2245–2260 (2015)
11. Kolb, L., Thor, A., Rahm, E.: Dedoop: efficient deduplication with hadoop. PVLDB **5**(12), 1878–1881 (2012)
12. Kolb, L., Thor, A., Rahm, E.: Load balancing for mapreduce-based entity resolution. In: ICDE, pp. 618–629 (2012)
13. Lacoste-Julien, S., et al.: Sigma: simple greedy matching for aligning large knowledge bases. In: KDD, pp. 572–580 (2013)
14. Li, J., et al.: Rimom: a dynamic multistrategy ontology alignment framework. TKDE **21**(8), 1218–1232 (2009)
15. Madhavan, J., Bernstein, P.A., Rahm, E.: Generic schema matching with cupid. In: VLDB, pp. 49–58 (2001)
16. Nikoletos, K., Papadakis, G., Koubarakis, M.: pyJedAI: a lightsaber for Link Discovery. In: ISWC (2022)
17. Papadakis, G., Ioannou, E., Palpanas, T.: Entity resolution: past, present and yet-to-come. In: EDBT, pp. 647–650 (2020)
18. Papadakis, G., Ioannou, E., Thanos, E., Palpanas, T.: The Four Generations of Entity Resolution. Synthesis Lectures on Data Management, Morgan & Claypool Publishers, San Rafael (2021)
19. Stefanidis, K., Efthymiou, V., Herschel, M., Christophides, V.: Entity resolution in the web of data. In: WWW (2014)
20. Suchanek, F.M., et al.: PARIS: probabilistic alignment of relations, instances, and schema. PVLDB **5**(3), 157–168 (2011)
21. Zeakis, A., Papadakis, G., Skoutas, D., Koubarakis, M.: Pre-trained embeddings for entity resolution: an experimental analysis. In: VLDB (2023)

Author Index

K. Stefanidis et al. (Eds.): ICWE 2024, LNCS 14629, pp. 475–477, 2024.
https://doi.org/10.1007/978-3-031-62362-2

Printed in the United States
by Baker & Taylor Publisher Services